Forced Migration in/to Canada

MCGILL-QUEEN'S REFUGEE AND FORCED MIGRATION STUDIES

Series editors: Megan Bradley and James Milner

Forced migration is a local, national, regional, and global challenge with profound political and social implications. Understanding the causes and consequences of, and possible responses to, forced migration requires careful analysis from a range of disciplinary perspectives, as well as interdisciplinary dialogue.

The purpose of the McGill-Queen's Refugee and Forced Migration Studies series is to advance in-depth examination of diverse forms, dimensions, and experiences of displacement, including in the context of conflict and violence, repression and persecution, and disasters and environmental change. The series will explore responses to refugees, internal displacement, and other forms of forced migration to illuminate the dynamics surrounding forced migration in global, national, and local contexts, including Canada, the perspectives of displaced individuals and communities, and the connections to broader patterns of human mobility. Featuring research from fields including politics, international relations, law, anthropology, sociology, geography, and history, the series highlights new and critical areas of enquiry within the field, especially conversations across disciplines and from the perspective of researchers in the global South, where the majority of forced migration unfolds. The series benefits from an international advisory board made up of leading scholars in refugee and forced migration studies.

11 Kingdom of Barracks
Polish Displaced Persons in Allied-Occupied Germany and Austria
Katarzyna Nowak

12 Urban Refugees and Digital Technology
Reshaping Social, Political, and Economic Networks
Charles Martin-Shields

13 Migration Governance in North America
Policy, Politics, and Community
Edited by Kiran Banerjee and Craig Damian Smith

14 Write to Return
Huguenot Refugees on the Frontiers of the French Enlightenment
Bryan A. Banks

15 The Politics of Refugee Policy in the Global South
Ola G. El-Taliawi

16 Forced Migration in/to Canada
From Colonization to Refugee Resettlement
Edited by Christina R. Clark-Kazak

FORCED MIGRATION IN/TO CANADA

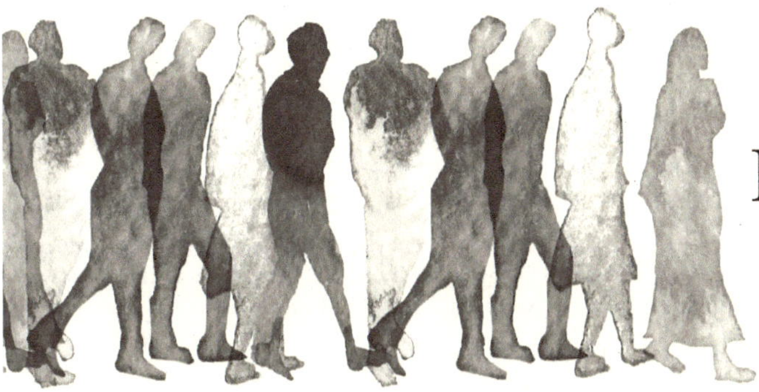

From Colonization to Refugee Resettlement

Edited by
Christina R. Clark-Kazak

McGill-Queen's University Press
Montreal & Kingston • London • Chicago

ISBN 978-0-2280-2217-6 (paper)
ISBN 978-0-2280-2218-3 (ePDF)
ISBN 978-0-2280-2219-0 (ePUB)
ISBN 978-0-2280-2350-0 (open access)

Legal deposit fourth quarter 2024
Bibliothèque nationale du Québec

Printed in Canada on acid-free paper that is 100% ancient forest free (100% post-consumer recycled), processed chlorine free

This book has been published with the help of a grant from the Federation for the Humanities and Social Sciences, through the Awards to Scholarly Publications Program, using funds provided by the Social Sciences and Humanities Research Council of Canada.

Additional funding provided by the University of Ottawa.

Funded by the Government of Canada | Financé par le gouvernement du Canada | Canada

Canada Council for the Arts | Conseil des arts du Canada

We acknowledge the support of the Canada Council for the Arts.
Nous remercions le Conseil des arts du Canada de son soutien.

McGill-Queen's University Press in Montreal is on land which long served as a site of meeting and exchange amongst Indigenous Peoples, including the Haudenosaunee and Anishinabeg nations. In Kingston it is situated on the territory of the Haudenosaunee and Anishinaabek. We acknowledge and thank the diverse Indigenous Peoples whose footsteps have marked these territories on which peoples of the world now gather.

Library and Archives Canada Cataloguing in Publication

Title: Forced migration in/to Canada : from colonization to refugee resettlement / edited by Christina R. Clark-Kazak.
Names: Clark-Kazak, Christina R., 1975– editor.
Series: McGill-Queen's refugee and forced migration studies ; 16.
Description: Series statement: McGill-Queen's refugee and forced migration studies ; 16 | Includes bibliographical references and index.
Identifiers: Canadiana (print) 20240391764 | Canadiana (ebook) 20240391772 | ISBN 9780228022176 (paper) | ISBN 9780228022190 (ePUB) | ISBN 9780228023500 (OA) | ISBN 9780228022183 (ePDF)
Subjects: LCSH: Forced migration—Canada. | LCSH: Refugees—Canada. | LCSH: Canada Emigration and immigration.
Classification: LCC JV7225.2.F67 2024 | DDC 325.71—dc23

This book was typeset in 10/13 Sabon by Sayre Street Books.
Copyediting by Paula Sarson.

For Jennifer Hyndman and Susan McGrath, who have shaped the field of forced migration studies in Canada and globally, through their extraordinary leadership, mentorship, and care.

Contents

Tables and Figures

TABLES

FIGURES

Abbreviations

2SLGBTQI+	Two-Spirit, lesbian, gay, bisexual, transgender, queer and/or questioning, intersex, with the "+" added to recognize and affirm the range of identities
AEHO	Alliance to End Homelessness Ottawa
ATD	alternatives to detention
AWO	Afghan Women's Organization
BVOR	Blended Visa Office-Referred program
CAD	Canadian currency
CBC	Canadian Broadcasting Corporation
CBSA	Canada Border Services Agency
CCC	Canadian Council of Churches
CCCRR	Canadian Christian Council for the Resettlement of Refugees
CCR	Canadian Council for Refugees
CCS	Catholic Crosscultural Services
CESCR	(United Nations) Committee on Economic, Social and Cultural Rights
CIC	Citizenship and Immigration Canada; renamed to Immigration, Refugees and Citizenship Canada (IRCC)
CICIC	Canadian Information Centre for International Credentials
CISSA-ACSEI	Canadian Immigrant Settlement Sector Alliance–Alliance canadienne du secteur de l'établissement des immigrants
CJC	Canadian Jewish Congress
CMHC	Canada Mortgage and Housing Corporation
COA	Canadian Orientation Abroad
COVID-19	coronavirus disease
CRC	(United Nations) Convention on the Rights of the Child
CRPD	(United Nations) Convention on the Rights of Persons with Disabilities

CRS	Centre for Refugee Studies
CSS	Client Support Services
CUAET	Canada-Ukraine Authorization for Emergency Travel
DFN	Designated Foreign National
DSBs	district school boards
EMPP	Economic Mobility Pathways Pilot
EU	European Union
FCJ	Faithful Companions of Jesus Refugee Centre
FRFCA	Faster Removal of Foreign Criminals Act
G5	Group of Five
GAC	Global Affairs Canada
GAR	Government-Assisted Refugee program
GCENR	Global Campaign for Equal Nationality Rights
GCR	(United Nations) Global Compact on Refugees
GRSI	Global Refugee Sponsorship Initiative
H&C	Humanitarian and Compassionate Grounds
IASFM	International Association for the Study of Forced Migration
ICCPR	International Covenant on Civil and Political Rights
ICE	Immigration and Customs Enforcement
ICESCR	International Covenants on Economic, Social and Cultural Rights
IDMC	International Displacement Monitoring Centre
IDP	internally displaced person
IFA	internal flight alternative
IFHP	Interim Federal Health Program
IHC	immigration holding centres
IMDB	Longitudinal Immigration Database
IOM	International Organization for Migration
IPCC	Intergovernmental Panel on Climate Change
IRB	Immigration and Refugee Board (of Canada)
IRCA	Immigration Reform and Control Act
IRCC	Immigration, Refugees and Citizenship Canada
IRPA	Immigration and Refugee Protection Act
IRPR	Immigration and Refugee Protection Regulations
IRS	Indian Residential School system
JAS	Joint Assistance Sponsorship
JIAS	Jewish Immigrant Aid Services
MCCC	Mennonite Central Committee Canada
MIRPS	Comprehensive Regional Protection and Solutions Framework
NATO	North Atlantic Treaty Organization
NGO	non-governmental organization
NHS	National Housing Strategy

NIDF	National Immigration Detention Framework
OCASI	Ontario Council of Agencies Serving Immigrants
OHIP	Ontario Health Insurance Plan
PA	principal applicant
PRRA	pre-removal risk assessment
PSR	Private Sponsorship of Refugees
RAN	Canada Refugee Advisory Network of Canada
RAP	Resettlement Assistance Program
RCMP	Royal Canadian Mounted Police
REB	research ethics board
RPD	Refugee Protection Division
RSD	refugee status determination
RSTP	Refugee Sponsorship Training Program
SAH	Sponsorship Agreement Holder
SC	Statutes of Canada
SCC	Supreme Court of Canada
SOGIE	Sexual Orientation, Gender Identity and Expression
SOGIESC	Sexual Orientation, Gender Identity and Expression, and Sex Characteristics
SSHRC	Social Sciences and Humanities Research Council
STCA	(Canada–United States) Safe Third Country Agreement
TCPS 2	*Tri-Council Policy Statement: Ethical Conduct for Research Involving Humans*
TCRI	Table de concertation des organismes au service des personnes réfugiées et immigrantes
TIP	trafficking in persons
TRC	Truth and Reconciliation Commission
UDHR	Universal Declaration of Human Rights
UN TIP	Protocol to Prevent, Suppress and Punish Trafficking in Persons, especially Women and Children
UNDRIP	United Nation Declaration on the Rights of Indigenous People
UNHCR	United Nations High Commissioner for Refugees, also known as "the UN Refugee Agency"
UNODC	United Nations Office on Drugs and Crime
VR	voice reporting
WCC	World Council of Churches
WUSC	World University Service of Canada

Acknowledgments

A book of this size and complexity is the culmination of the time, talents, and knowledge of many people. *Forced Migration in/to Canada: From Colonization to Refugee Resettlement* would not have been possible without the enthusiastic commitment of the thirty-eight contributors who prioritized writing, editing, and discussing their chapters in the midst of busy professional and personal lives. I am grateful for the creativity, dedication, and patience of each author as we generated this book together. While each chapter stands on its own as an important contribution to a particular issue or theme, collectively, the book also represents a pan-Canadian conversation about how forced migration has shaped individual lives, policies, and national identity. By centring lived experiences of displacement – including Indigenous displacement and slavery – our chapters have required us to reflexively question the narratives we tell to ourselves and the outside world about the country we now call Canada. We hope this is the beginning of ongoing discussions, reflections, and analysis of the role of forced migration studies within Canadian academic, public, and policy spaces.

Two reviewers gave in-depth, constructive feedback that helped us improve the manuscript immeasurably. Reviewing is a thankless job at the best of times. To have agreed to review such a long and diverse manuscript, and to have done so with such thoroughness and thoughtfulness, is true public service. I hope the reviewers can recognize their impact on *Forced Migration in/to Canada* as they read the final version.

Martha Vargas Aguirre provided invaluable research assistance at the beginning of this project and then agreed to write the chapter on trafficking. Sarah Dubuc coordinated the submission of the manuscript, as well as the adaptation of the book into French. I am grateful for her careful work, attention to detail, and patience with the many moving parts of such an epic project. Students in my FSS 4550 *Recherche dirigée* course in winter 2023 engaged with the book material and helped identify resources for the French language adaptation.

Emily Andrew at McGill-Queen's University Press has been our fiercest advocate and our most constructive critic. She championed this book at all levels, despite its length and unique format. I am grateful for her wise counsel, calm competence, kindness, and humanity. Jacqueline Mason, Jonathan Crago, Megan Bradley, and James Milner enthusiastically embraced this project from its earliest stages. I am particularly thankful for MQUP's commitment to publishing *Forced Migration in/to Canada* in open access format and consenting to a discrete French translation and adaptation. In the context of shrinking non-profit press budgets, this commitment is remarkable and appreciated.

A Connection Grant from the Social Sciences and Humanities Research Council and additional funding support from the University of Ottawa have allowed us to translate the text into French and publish both versions in open access format. Given the relevance of the issues for the general public, I am particularly grateful that SSHRC and uOttawa have expanded the book's impact through open access and bilingualism.

My approach to forced migration – and the subsequent commissioning of chapters for this book and its unique format – were inspired by mentorship from Susan McGrath and Jennifer Hyndman, to whom this book is dedicated. I am grateful for their leadership of York University's Centre for Refugee Studies early in my academic career, as well as their ongoing support and care for this and many other projects. The majority of the contributors to *Forced Migration in/to Canada* have interacted with Susan and Jennifer in some capacity. This book, and the field of forced migration studies in Canada, have been directly and indirectly shaped by their extraordinary intelligence, passion, care, and dedication to teaching and mentoring.

Books have a way of permeating the lives of their creators. This one is no exception. I am grateful to my husband and partner of more than twenty years, Sam, and our children, Anahita and Rustom, for living beside this book over the course of many months and for taking up the slack on the home front when the demands of shepherding this through the publication process spilled over into our family time. They brought me tea and food, forced me to take breaks, and reminded me that life exists beyond work.

I hope readers of *Forced migration in/to Canada* will remember that all of us – authors, editors, and people with lived experiences of forced migration – are human beings with human rights, including the right to live with dignity. We also all make mistakes. As editor, I accept fully any shortcomings, errors, and omissions in this book. As an academic, I have the privilege of being able to learn continuously and hope that any such mistakes will generate important conversations and learnings.

Foreword

Jennifer Hyndman

Research by scholars analyzing refugee and other expressions of forced migration in Canada is distinct from elsewhere in the world. While national and international contexts cannot be neatly separated on the subject of displacement (see Demoz, chapter 7), the amount of research with, for, on, and by people from forced migration backgrounds flourishes here like nowhere else. This book stands out among peers in at least three ways: (1) it focuses on Canada as a place of reception for diasporas from other parts of the world and their uneven inclusion in its polity as well as the global constellations of geopolitics, law, intergovernmental organizations, and humanitarianism that make this possible; (2) it centres "the lived experiences of people through testimonies, case studies, and materials produced by people who have experienced forced migration" (Clark-Kazak, introduction); and (3) it addresses the intersection of these constellations of forced migration with racial justice, colonial violence and Indigenous displacement, and global issues such as climate change and COVID-19.

With the number of displaced persons worldwide now exceeding one hundred million and of these more than 32 per cent outside their country of origin, providing sustained protection and new places to call home is as important as ever. At the time of writing, Canada ranks first in the world in terms of the number of resettled refugees accepted, even if these numbers are modest. In relation to other states on the asylum front, it ranks much lower and does much less of the heavy lifting given its geographical isolation, cold oceans, and long border with the USA, fortified by the Safe Third Country Agreement (STCA). This collection is novel and important because its thirty-eight authors squarely address these processes, politics, and practices of forced migration of people *to* and *within* Canada.

Research with former refugees living in Canada has become a major focus in forced migration studies, with recent books about Canada's Operation Syrian Refugees (Hamilton, Veronis, and Walton-Roberts 2020; Hynie et al. 2019), the private sponsorship of refugees (Labman and Cameron 2020; see also

Labman, chapter 18), and even the legal frameworks of refugee resettlement (Labman 2019). In chapter 17, Idil Atak deftly juxtaposes resettlement, based on humanitarian priorities and selection from abroad, with asylum processes in Canada; each protection stream is so distinct that it almost defies direct comparison with the other. Negotiating citizenship and securing permanent status (see Moffette, chapter 19) for those whose refugee claims are rejected or those who toggle between temporary status and a path to permanence are struggles that can last for years.

The lively scholarship featured here on refugee inclusion and integration is critical to exposing the shortcomings and changes needed in Canadian institutions – schools, health-care services, and the labour force to name a few (see Hynie, chapter 23). Hynie's holistic integration model interrogates how well Canadian communities, cities, and levels of government engage and include these newcomers and, in turn, how these newcomers are faring in their new Canadian homes (see also Chen, chapter 24; Ogoe and Wilkinson, chapter 25).

In this collection, *settlement* – a fraught term that could be the focus of another entire book – does not efface the violence and displacement that Indigenous persons in Canada have faced. Veldon Coburn in chapter 1 and Christina R. Clark-Kazak in chapters 13 and 28 engage squarely with the cultural genocide and displacements caused by settler colonialism in Canada. A thoughtful and deliberate commissioning on slavery in the Canadian context by Natasha Henry-Dixon in chapter 2 also draws out the racialized dispersion of African peoples from their original homes and their resistance to it.

Scholars of forced migration have at times essentialized "the refugee" as a figure who can never shed their designation as a displaced person, a positionality that Martha Kwee Kumsa (2006) struggled with from her vantage point as a Canadian professor conducting research with refugees. She writes about her work with refugees of Oromo background after they have arrived in Toronto and illustrates how they no longer self-identify as refugees once in Canada. She reveals how from the point of view of these Oromo youth, refugees are the people living in camps back in East Africa from which they came. The differentiated and racialized inclusion and exclusion of people from forced migration backgrounds are incisively elaborated upon (see Mahrouse and El Omari, chapter 15).

Intersectionality points to the numerous axes of difference that generate a range of identities across the conventional categories of the 1951 Convention definition of refugee – people persecuted because of their nationality, race, religion, membership of a social group or political opinion. But the concept of "refugeehood" also includes many more identities than those covered by the 1951 Convention and the 1967 Protocol, which extended the temporal and geographical reach of the convention definition to the rest of the world. The definition of refugee nonetheless remained Eurocentric and specific to the civil and political rights violation of World War II. This volume systematically addresses other dimensions of difference and possible persecution that have received far less attention. For example, in chapter 12 Aberman shows how gender and sexual identities constitute membership in a social group to meet the refugee definition. Clark-Kazak's highly original research in chapter 13 shows how social age can differ dramatically from chronological age. For example, the meaning of what it is to be a child varies tremendously across time and space. Disability is another fascinating entry point into forced migration studies as a criterion of "vulnerability" for selecting refugees at the UN High Commissioner for Refugees (UNHCR) for referral to Canada (see McNally, chapter 14). The strategies of refugee newcomer households supporting family members with disabilities are poorly understood; they face distinct challenges related to supporting the differently abled family member in a new country.

Diaspora subjects who are scholars in Canada may analyze the political dynamics of forced displacement in the ethnonational communities of which they are part (Amarasingam 2015; Demoz, chapter 7; Yousuf and Hyndman 2023). Or they may use their social locations and geographically diverse networks to examine, for example, gendered strategies of seeking protection through marriage (Taha 2021).

Refugee and forced migration studies have "always been critical" (Biorklund and Hyndman 2023), stemming from people-centred humanitarian and human rights approaches to geopolitical displacement caused by the Cold War. The epistemology and positionality of researchers in forced migration studies, however, have not always been as inclusive of lived experience as they could be. Critical refugee studies in the US and Canada have emphasized the importance of diaspora subjectivities, knowledge production, and self-representation in settler states where these have historically been effaced (Nguyen and Phu 2021). Scholarship flourishes by Canadian researchers who embody a wide range of subject positions that include forced migration backgrounds (Amarasingam 2015; Taha 2021; Demoz, chapter 7), and this book includes the most extensive range of scholars and subject positions, curated deliberately and thoughtfully.

The dominance of scholars located in the Global North who are studying the displacement of people located in the Global South and related research partnerships that reflect this same power dynamic, often means that Global South scholars and institutions collect data for those with more access to funds, without fully getting credit for co-producing knowledge stemming from these data (Chimni 1998, 2009; Landau 2012; Hyndman 2023). This book tackles these disparate power relations in many of the chapters.

Equally, not all war zones and displaced persons garner the same attention. I recently wrote about "humanitarian nationalism" in relation to Canada's unwavering military and humanitarian support for Ukraine in defending itself again the Russian invasion and for its open-door protection policy for all Ukrainians to come to Canada on a temporary visitor visa (Hyndman 2023). Humanitarian nationalism refers to a consensus across governments and civil society that Canada must thwart Russian aggression and assist Ukrainians affected and those who have fled. As Canadian military aid for Ukraine tops CAD$1.5 billion just twenty months after the Russian invasion began, more than one million Ukrainians have applied for temporary visitor status in Canada. The comprehensive scope of this humanitarian gesture is laudable, but Canada has not done so much so quickly for any other group of refugees coming to Canada in recent history. Should this level of support become the "new normal" for all displaced persons in humanitarian emergencies? Canada has harmonized its offer of temporary protection with EU provisions under the Temporary Protection Directive but in so doing raised expectations for all refugee resettlement to Canada.

By focusing on Canada in global and local contexts, this collection provides a comprehensive portrait of migration under involuntary conditions. The book exposes where and how Canadian society and institutions fall short (and where they succeed) in their inclusion of and engagement with newcomers from forced migration backgrounds, constituting an effective "report card" on what is not working, what is, and how the former could be done differently.

Forced Migration in/to Canada

INTRODUCTION

In/to Canada

Christina R. Clark-Kazak

KEY TERMS

- Asylum seeker
- Externalization
- Forced migration
- Internal displacement
- Refugee claimant
- Resettlement
- Undocumented
- Voluntary migration

INTRODUCTION

This book aims to provide a comprehensive state-of-the-art analysis of key issues relating to the forced migration of people to and within Canada. Forced migration has shaped the creation of what we now know as the federal state of Canada and is arguably one of the defining features of the twenty-first century – nationally and globally. Migration is politically and socially significant and is subject to widespread misinformation, politicization, and criminalization. This book provides an entry point into current research on a variety of topics, and offers reputable sources of additional information. It presents some of the key critical analysis tools to ask questions that will help evaluate information in the news and from government officials, colleagues, family members, and non-governmental organizations (NGOs). The book also highlights controversies, gaps, and questions that persist. In this way, it is intended as a reference point in the vast and varied landscape of forced migration but not a final destination. We hope that it gives a sense of key issues on forced migration in Canada – both historically and contemporarily – and also opens up new areas for enquiry, discussion, research, advocacy, and action.

WHY CARE ABOUT FORCED MIGRATION?

In 2022 the UN Refugee Agency (UNHCR) estimated that almost one hundred million people are forcibly displaced globally – both within and outside their countries of origin. As discussed in the next section, forcible displacement encompasses a wide range of reasons for migration and legal statuses. The number of people in forced migration contexts is likely to continue to increase due to ongoing violence, global inequities, human rights abuses, and vulnerabilities associated with climate change. The right to asylum is a well-established international norm, codified in international law, domestic legislation, cultural practices, and most religious traditions. However, many countries, including Canada, have explicit and implicit laws and policies that try to keep people from making a refugee claim. As discussed further on in chapters 3, 5, and 17, governments are intent on managing all forms of migration. It is important to understand rights and responsibilities in relation to migration and refuge but also the reality of lived experiences that falls short of these ideals.

Forced migration intersects with key global issues, including pandemics like COVID-19 and other health issues, climate change, racial justice, and Indigenous reconciliation. This book situates displacement within these related phenomena and takes an explicitly people-centred and intersectional approach. We aim to foreground migration as a human phenomenon involving lived experiences. After all, forced migration is ultimately about human beings: people who, individually and collectively, leave their homes because of persecution, violence, human rights abuses, and/or threats to their livelihoods and ways of life.

Once in Canada, people rebuild their lives and contribute to the economy, communities, and religious, social, and political life (see Hynie, chapter 23). They send remittances back to relatives left behind (Elcioglu and Shams 2023) and maintain transnational political, social, religious, and cultural ties. While newcomers are technically protected by Canadian law and the Charter of Rights and Freedoms, they may face racism (see Mahrouse and El Omari, chapter 15); ageism (see Clark-Kazak, chapter 13); ableism (see McNally, chapter 14); gendered violence (see Aberman, chapter 12); Islamophobia (see Cameron, chapter 26); and barriers to accessing employment (see Hari and Quintero, chapter 16; Ogoe and Wilkinson, chapter 25), health care (see Chen, chapter 29), housing (Clark-Kazak, chapter 28), and education (see Obradović-Ratković, Longboat, and Burgess, chapter 27).

WHAT IS FORCED MIGRATION?

This book focuses on forced migration in/to Canada. What does this mean? Several chapters address the multiple facets and faces of migration as well as debates over definitions, conceptualizations, and labelling. For the purposes of this introduction, I outline some overarching categories of terms, which are discussed in more detail throughout the chapters. The glossary at the end of this book lists definitions of key terms that appear at each chapter's opening.

Migration, broadly speaking, is the movement of people. Individuals and groups have moved in search of livelihoods and safety since the beginning of time. In the context of the contemporary system of sovereign states, there are currently legal and policy distinctions between voluntary and forced migration.

Voluntary migration generally entails people choosing to move in order to work or set up businesses (labour migration), study (educational migration), join other family members (family reunification and marriage migration), or visit other countries temporarily (tourism). While there are obviously structural constraints that limit people's choices about where, when, and how to move, voluntary migration is usually planned.

Forced migration, on the other hand, involves limited choices by people who are forced to move through colonization (see Coburn, chapter 1), slavery (see Henry-Dixon, chapter 2), human trafficking (see Vargas Aguirre, chapter 11), or to flee due to conflict, human rights abuses, persecution, or environmental degradation (see Minville and Su, chapter 22). There are different legal categories depending on the sources of forced migration and whether one crosses an international border or stays within the boundaries of a state (internal displacement). Some people also fall between categories as they navigate complex legal and administrative processes, resulting in precariousness or undocumented situations. These distinctions are discussed further in chapters 3, 8, and 17. For present purposes, it is important to note that the legal term "refugee" only applies to people who fulfill certain criteria under Canadian and international law.

The key international reference point is the UN Refugee Convention, which came into force in 1951 following mass displacement due to World War II. In the 1951 Convention and subsequent 1967 Protocol, which expanded the geographic and temporal application of the convention, a refugee is defined in article 1 as: "any person who … owing to a well-founded fear of being persecuted for reasons of race, religion, nationality, membership of a particular social group or political opinion, is outside the country of his nationality and is unable or, owing to such fear, is unwilling to avail himself of the protection of that country; or who, not having a nationality and being outside the country of his former habitual residence as a result of such events, is unable or, owing to such fear, is unwilling to return to it."

This definition has three important aspects. First, the person must have crossed an international border. If they have not, they are considered internally displaced persons (IDPs; see Young, chapter 3). Second, the person must fear persecution for one of the reasons listed. Note, for example, that environmental displacement is not enumerated as a reason for refugee status (see Minville and Su, chapter 22). Third, the definition is primarily individualistic, with a refugee claim based on "well-founded fear of persecution." Given the reality of mass displacement due to collective events – like war or generalized violence – the African Union has an expanded definition to include these large-scale sources of forced migration. Similarly, the Cartagena Declaration, adopted by the Colloquium on the International Protection of Refugees in Central America, Mexico, and Panama in 1984, while not legally binding, also includes an expansive definition of refugees that recognizes generalized violence, conflict, and mass human rights violations. However, the refugee definition in international law remains narrowly focused, causing some to question its continued relevance.

In Canada, as is discussed further in chapters 8 and 17, the legal definition of "refugee" is broader than the UN Refugee Convention but narrower than the African Convention. Canada's Immigration and Refugee Protection Act (IRPA) extends refugee protection to include those who are at risk of torture and cruel and inhumane treatment if deported. The Canadian asylum system has also broadened the interpretation of "social group" to include gender, gender identity, and sexual orientation (see Aberman, chapter 12).

People who are seeking asylum but do not yet have refugee status are called "refugee claimants" (the preferred term in Canada) or "asylum seekers" (more common in the US and other countries). Those who do not fall under the UN Refugee Convention are usually included in the broader term "migrant." These labels can be dehumanizing, stigmatizing, and politicized. So, in this book, we prefer to describe the situations in which people move and live and try to minimize the use of problematic labels (Hamlin 2021; Zetter 1991, 2007; see also Goheen Glanville and Arbel, chapter 4).

While voluntary and forced migration are different categories under law and policy, in reality, there is in many contexts mixed migration – that is, people move for a combination of different reasons. It is important to note that even forced migration involves decision-making and agency, where different people assess risks and decide whether, when, and where to flee (Cameron 2018). Similarly, even "voluntary" migration involves constraints, and not all family members have equal access to decision-making power about collective migration.

Moreover, people may move in and out of different migration categories, especially as governments change policies, laws, and programs, and migration processes have become more complex over time. For example, an international student may not be able to return to their home country because war has broken out there. They may be forced to overstay their student visa, or they may make a refugee claim. In some cases, this results in them becoming undocumented. Goldring and Landolt (2013) discuss the "chutes and ladders" of people's lives that result in precarious legal status in Canada. Indeed, in some cases, policies contribute to the institutionalization of precarity (Goldring, Berinstein, and Bernhard 2009).

While labels and categories have legal, political, and practical significance, we should not lose sight of the fact that migration involves human beings. In this book, we aim to centre the lived experiences of people through testimonies, case studies, and materials produced by people who have experienced forced migration, including some of the authors in this book. This is a deliberate attempt to counteract dehumanizing tendencies behind labels, statistics, and discourses (see Goheen Glanville and Arbel, chapter 4).

Finally, while much of forced migration research is focused on movement, we also acknowledge long periods of forced immobility (Brun 2015). People are trapped in detention centres (see Silverman, chapter 21), refugee and displacement camps, and prolonged irregular and precarious status (see Moffette, chapter 19; Cowper-Smith and Kane, chapter 20). Indeed, protracted displacement is a defining feature of the contemporary forced migration regime, where the three durable solutions identified by the UN Refugee Agency – that is, repatriation, local integration, or resettlement (see Atak, chapter 17; Labman, chapter 18) – are available to a small minority of refugees (Hyndman and Giles 2017; see also Demoz, chapter 7). As a result, the norm is for long-term displacement, with some refugees living in camps or with precarious immigration status for generations (Hyndman and Giles 2011). There are also significant barriers to freedom of movement, including militarized borders, immigration detention (see Silverman, chapter 21), and externalization policies (Young, chapter 3).

Given these definitional realities, but also the conceptual debates, we have chosen to interpret "forced migration" broadly within this book. We are interested in moving beyond legal, administrative, and policy categories to understand people's experiences in migration contexts. For this reason, the book's focus is on structures, processes, and relationships, rather than categories. The chapters are organized into themes that explain the legal, social, economic, and political contexts in which forced migration occurs. Therefore, we do not limit ourselves to "refugees," but rather think of forced migration as a manifestation of the abuse of power across time, space, and place – from the forcible displacement of Indigenous Peoples and slavery through to the contemporary contexts of political violence, human rights abuses, environmental degradation, and global inequalities that uproot people from their homes. We define forced migration broadly to include these contexts of forced movement but also to cover forced immobility behind closed borders, in displacement encampments, immigration detention, and protracted legal precarity.

THE IMPORTANCE OF FORCED MIGRATION IN AND TO CANADA

The book focuses particularly on forced migration in and to Canada. The creation of what is now Canada involved the forcible displacement of Indigenous Peoples from their lands, communities, culture, and families (see Coburn, chapter 1). While forced migration studies in Canada have mostly focused on people arriving in Canada as refugee claimants or resettled refugees, we instead choose to foreground our analysis in the history, legacy, and contemporary realities of colonization in Canada. We contend that understandings of forced migration cannot be separated from Indigenous world views, epistemologies, and lived experiences. Indigenous displacement was not only a deliberate strategy of colonization and state building, but also it is intertwined with the settlement experiences of newcomers.

Similarly, Canada was both a terminus of the Underground Railroad of escaped slaves from the US and a source of institutionalized slavery and racism (see Henry-Dixon, chapter 2; Mahrouse and El Omari, chapter 15). Racialized injustice permeates the origins of Canada, our immigration policies and practices, and the lives of racialized newcomers and Canadians (D. Thompson 2022).

Due to ongoing environmental degradation and climate change, communities across Canada experience environmental displacement (see Minville and Su, chapter 22). Trafficking in Canada is primarily a domestic phenomenon, with Indigenous and newcomer women, girls and 2SLGBTQI+ people disproportionately forced within and across provinces and territories (see Vargas Aguirre, chapter 11). Despite our isolated geography and externalization policies, Canada regularly receives tens of thousands of asylum claims per year (see Young, chapter 3; Atak, chapter 17). The presence of refugee claimants crossing the US-Canada border has often been used to politicize and polarize public opinion (A. Gagnon and Larios 2021). Forced migration is thus a pressing domestic policy issue.

It is also a significant foreign policy issue. Canada has led global refugee resettlement efforts since 2018 (UNHCR 2021a). Resettlement involves refugees relocating from one country of asylum to another country of more permanent protection (see Atak, chapter 17; Labman, chapter 18). The Private Sponsorship of Refugees (PSR) program (see Labman, chapter 18) is an innovative approach to resettlement and has contributed to these resettlement efforts for over forty years. It is cited globally as a promising practice of expanding protection spaces, leading to Canadian efforts to "export" it elsewhere. Those who come to Canada under resettlement programs land in Canada as permanent residents, facilitating access to social services. However, it is important to note that resettlement involves less than 0.5 per cent of refugees globally, and there is a growing resettlement gap between the number of people in need of resettlement and resettlement spaces (UNHCR 2021a).

Canada has also been a moderately important player in the development of international refugee policy (Milner 2021a; see also Demoz, chapter 7). The Canadian government has been a regular financial contributor to UNHCR, the UN Refugee Agency (Grayson and Audet 2017), and periodically chairs its Executive Committee. In this capacity, it played an important diplomatic role in supporting UNHCR's drafting and coordination of the Global Compact on Refugees. As Demoz demonstrates in chapter 7, Canada has also shown international leadership in facilitating refugee participation in policy-making (Milner, Alio, and Gardi 2022).

Given the context specificity of Indigenous displacement (Coburn, chapter 1) and slavery (Henry-Dixon, chapter 2) in Canada, federal-provincial jurisdictions (see Garnier, chapter 10) and localized laws, policies, and integration issues such as health (Chen, chapter 24), the book specifically focuses on forced migration in and to Canada. However, we situate our Canadian focus within the broader international trends, norms, and structures of forced migration (see, for example, K. Banerjee, chapter 5; Demoz, chapter 7).

CURRENT ISSUES AND TRENDS

Indeed, while this book is explicitly focused on the Canadian context, it is important to note that Canada is a relatively small player in the broader context of forced migration globally. Most forced migration takes place in the Global South, where low- and middle-income countries host large numbers of internally displaced people and refugees. Generally speaking, people stay close to home when they flee, resulting in countries both producing and hosting large numbers of people in situations of forced migration. Table 0.1 shows top host and source countries in 2021 for people fleeing across international borders.

These global inequalities in providing refuge have resulted in a growing political consensus on the need for stronger international co-operation on forced migration. In 2016 then US president Obama hosted an international summit that led to the New York Declaration for Refugees and Migrants. Out of this meeting came two parallel processes leading to the 2018 Global Compact for Migration and the Global Compact on Refugees. Adopted by the UN General Assembly, these compacts represent a political commitment to international co-operation to address migration. However, they are not legally binding. Moreover, while they were intended to redress some of the inequalities in hosting, and providing protection for, people in contexts of migration globally, the compacts have been critiqued for reproducing global inequalities (Hyndman and Reynolds 2020).

Forced migration is increasing in scale, duration, and complexity. While people forcibly displaced due to environmental degradation and climate change are not considered refugees under the UN Refugee Convention, their numbers are projected to increase over the coming decade. This means that the total sum of those forcibly displaced worldwide is likely to continue to increase, especially in the context of little progress on international co-operation for long-term durable solutions (see Demoz, chapter 7).

Indeed, recent years have witnessed the rise of temporary protection and solutions. For example, in response to Ukrainian displacement, most countries,

Table 0.1 | Top host and source countries of refugees and people of concern under UNHCR and UNRWA mandates

Host countries	Source countries
Turkey – 3.7 million	Ukraine – 7.8 million
Jordan – 2.4 million	Syria – 6.7 million
Colombia – 1.7 million	Palestine – 6.4 million
Poland – 1.4 million	Venezuela – 4 million
Pakistan – 1.4 million	Afghanistan – 2.6 million
Uganda – 1.4 million	South Sudan – 2.2 million
Germany – 1.2 million	Myanmar – 1.1 million

Note: Not all have refugee status.
Sources: Data compiled by Christina R. Clark-Kazak from UNHCR 2022a; UNHCR 2022d; and UNRWA 2021.

including Canada and neighbouring states in Europe, granted temporary protection rather than permanent refugee status. While in the Canadian context this facilitated a rapid response with no caps on admissions (see Demoz, chapter 7; Mahrouse and El Omari, chapter 15), it also created gaps in terms of longer-term settlement services and legal protection (see Atak, chapter 17). Similarly, in the context of creating complementary pathways to resettlement to increase opportunities for displaced people to come to safety, many of these employment and study opportunities are temporary and precarious.

Precarity is also related to another trend in forced migration: criminalization of migration (Atak and Simeon 2018a; Moffette and Aksin 2018) and solidarity. As rich countries like Canada enact externalization policies, such as visas, carrier sanctions, and border enforcement and third country agreements, this increases the likelihood of irregular crossings, the use of smugglers, and trafficking (see Young, chapter 3; Vargas Aguirre, chapter 11). Solidarity is also increasingly criminalized, with high-profile cases of rescuers charged with colluding with smugglers (Mainwaring and DeBono 2021).

A more positive trend is the growing recognition of the need to include people with lived experiences of forced migration in research, policy-making, and programming. As outlined in chapters 7 and 9, we are still far from the ideal of "nothing about us without us" (Alio and Gardi 2021). However, there is movement in the right direction. In this book, we intentionally foreground these lived experiences in each chapter through a variety of media.

FORCED MIGRATION STUDIES IN CANADA

In the current context of increased scale of and attention to forced migration, there have been a growing number of professional development and academic courses, training, and programs available in Canada and internationally. Canada has historically been at the forefront of forced migration studies internationally. For example, what is now the Centre for Refugee Studies (CRS), established in 1981 at York University, is one of the longest-standing and important refugee studies centres globally. It is the secretariat of the International Association for the Study of Forced Migration (IASFM), for which Canada-based researchers have sat on the Executive Committee since its inception. Under the leadership of Susan McGrath, CRS also led the Refugee Research Network, connecting major refugee studies centres from around the world. Similarly, *Refuge: Canada's Journal on Refugees* was one of the first peer-reviewed journals in the field and remains the only bilingual (French-English), open access, academic journal in forced migration.

Canada-based researchers have also led critical examinations of the power relations in the production of knowledge about and with refugees. For example, the Critical Refugee and Migration Studies Network (Canada) "take up issues of forced migration by foregrounding a refugee-based perspective and by developing theoretically grounded methods for analysis" (Nguyen and Phu 2021, 8). Drawing on international networks of critical migration researchers, this work centres lived experiences and counteracts a problematic deficit approach common in too much research on displacement (Espiritu and Duong 2018; Chatzipanagiotidou and Murphy 2022).

STRUCTURE OF THE BOOK: KEY THEMES

This book is intended as an entry point to current research and resources for students, researchers, educators, and people working with and for people in situations of forced migration in Canada. We have consciously negotiated open access to allow for a diverse readership regardless of income or library access. We have also opted for a non-academic and jargon-free style to ensure that we are communicating the information to a broad audience. We have included a comprehensive list of common acronyms and a glossary of key terms to provide common points of reference across chapters. Recognizing the hegemony of English and the reality of francophone minorities in Canada (see Garnier, chapter 10), we have also negotiated a French language version of this book.

While there are linkages and cross-referencing across the collection, each chapter can be read alone to provide an overview of a specific topic. We recognize some duplication across chapters arises due to our vision of a collection that can also be read in stand-alone sections and chapters. We hope that the echoing of central principles and ideas is generative rather than distracting.

Authors have identified key take-away points, further reading and resources, and a forward-looking conclusion for each chapter. This large volume covering diverse topics is intended to be comprehensive, but is not exhaustive. We have aimed to help orient the reader by breaking the text into sections.

Section one, "Situating Forced Migration in Canada," provides the historical context, framing, as well as the contemporary legal and policy issues. We purposefully chose to begin the book with chapters on the forced displacement of Indigenous Peoples (Coburn, chapter 1) and slavery in Canada (Henry-Dixon, chapter 2). Although Canada likes to project itself as a safe haven and refuge, the reality is that the creation of a settler state was built on forced migration, forced labour, and racism (see also Mahrouse and El Omari, chapter 15). As Hyndman (2023) has argued, the myth of humanitarian nationalism obscures the limits of Canadian hospitality and generosity and also glosses over the ongoing violence of settler colonialism. Indigenous experiences are woven throughout the book. It was important to us, as primarily settler writers, to acknowledge Indigenous displacement not only historically but also in contemporary forced migration through trafficking (see Vargas Aguirre, chapter 11) and child separation (see Clark-Kazak, chapter 13), for example. We also wanted to foreground and honour Indigenous perspectives and ways of knowing on issues as diverse as gender (Aberman, chapter 12), environment (Minville and Su, chapter 22), and disability (McNally, chapter 14). Our intent is a first step toward rethinking the field of forced migration studies in Canada to point to the ways that Indigenous perspectives illustrate the nature and logic of forced displacement policies.

In this way, our book is a critical analysis of historical and contemporary forced migration in and to Canada. We do not shy away from holding the government and Canadians to account for historical and contemporary violation of rights (Fynn Bruey and Fantauzzi, chapter 8), including the right to asylum (see Young, chapter 3; Atak, chapter 17). But we also point to promising practices and recommendations to improve policy, practice, and programming. For example, Granados and Klassen (chapter 6) suggest ethical ways of engaging in research and practice, while K. Banerjee (chapter 5) reminds readers of the normative underpinnings of protection. We hope that this book can be a source of both learning and unlearning.

We also acknowledge the diversity of Canada, especially in the context of a federal state where jurisdiction and service delivery are shared with provinces, territories, and municipalities (Garnier, chapter 10). Policy-making at national and subnational levels must also be contextualized within international trends (Demoz, chapter 7), law (Young, chapter 3; Fynn Bruey and Fantauzzi, chapter 8), and norms (K. Banerjee, chapter 5). "Canada" is neither a monolithic nor an independent actor but rather a network of institutions and individuals with different mandates, perspectives, and roles (Araya, chapter 9).

By foregrounding human experiences of displacement, in section two, "Intersectionalities of Forced Migration Experiences," we pay particular attention to intersectionalities of power relations. Intersectionality, developed by Black American feminist Crenshaw (1989), refers to how structural opportunities and constraints frame differential experiences. We have devoted specific chapters to gender and sexual orientation (Aberman, chapter 12), disability (McNally, chapter 14), racialization (Mahrouse and El Omari, chapter 15), religion (Cameron, chapter 26), age (Clark-Kazak, chapter 13), and class (Hari and Quintero, chapter 16). In these chapters, contributors critically unpack the conceptual and analytical underpinnings of exclusionary experiences of forced migration, globally and in Canada. They also offer equity perspectives to transform the ways academics, policy-makers, and practitioners engage with migration beyond static categories to think about the complexities of intersecting human relationships.

These experiences are not limited to a specific chapter of people's lives. Rather, intersecting power relations are embedded in structures and relationships. Therefore, in other chapters and sections, contributors have made a conscious decision to foreground these intersecting lived experiences. Our intention is to counteract homogenizing and essentializing tendencies in forced migration policy, practice, and research by highlighting a diversity of experiences of forced migration throughout the book. We also use multiple media and methods – stories, poems, art, videos, and storytelling (Obradović-Ratković, Longboat, and Burgess, chapter 27). While each chapter is intentionally written to ensure the same key elements recur throughout the book, the form and tone of the chapters also intentionally vary. We acknowledge that our readers will engage with different ways of knowing and learning in varying ways, and we want to provide different reading experiences, just as we acknowledge the diversity of forced migration experiences.

As mentioned previously in this introduction, refugee is a legal category, a problematic label and discourse, and also an identity that some embrace (see Young, chapter 3; Goheen Glanville and Arbel, chapter 4). Section three of the book, "'Becoming' and Un-becoming a Refugee in Canada," critically analyzes the legal processes by which people access refugee protection (see Atak, chapter 17; Labman, chapter 18) and citizenship (Moffette, chapter 19) in Canada, as well as the structural shortcomings that render people stateless (Cowper-Smith and Kane, chapter 20), detained indefinitely (Silverman, chapter 21), and precarious (Moffette, chapter 19; Silverman, chapter 21; Young, chapter 3). This section also addresses the growing phenomenon of environmental displacement in Canada and the need to address internal displacement within our borders (Minville and Su, chapter 22).

This third section highlights a key theme that recurs throughout the book: the widening gap between the right to asylum and the "right to have rights"

(Arendt 2004) on the one hand (see K. Banerjee, chapter 5; Granados and Klassen, chapter 6), and the elusiveness and precarity of the realization of these rights for the vast majority of displaced people globally, on the other hand. As chapters in this section and throughout the book demonstrate, access to protection in Canada is constrained and precarious.

The final section of the book, "Making Home and Place," shows how people make Canada home. While the notion of "integration" is complex and contested, as Hynie's chapter 23 demonstrates, we have identified key ways in which people settle and resettle once they arrive in Canada. Chapters analyze the opportunities and challenges of accessing quality health care (Chen, chapter 24), employment (Ogoe and Wilkinson, chapter 25), faith communities (Cameron, chapter 26), education (Obradović-Ratković, Longboat, and Burgess, chapter 27), and housing (Clark-Kazak, chapter 28). Woven through these chapters are practical examples of the different ways in which structural barriers manifest depending on people's positionalities within social hierarchies based on immigration status, race, gender, sexual orientation, ability, class, and age.

But, if integration is a multidirectional process, as Hynie explains in chapter 23, then the (re)settlement of newcomers also transforms social, political, and economic relationships in Canada. In this section and throughout the book, we attempt to address the multifaceted ways that migration shapes Canada as a settler state but also as a social imaginary that manifests in people's daily interactions. It is our contention that migration is everybody's business. While we propose specific policy and programming recommendations to attempt to address structural inequalities, our purpose in writing this book is also to raise awareness among ordinary people who are – individually and collectively – reproducing or contesting these structures by everyday encounters. Living and working on Indigenous land and interacting with newcomers, we all have a responsibility to learn about forced migration in/to what is now Canada.

CONCLUSION

This book draws on the knowledge and experience of thirty-eight contributors from across Canada. We have explicitly sought out diverse perspectives, with particular attention to Indigenous knowledge, lived experience of forced migration, stage of career, socio-linguistic background, discipline, practical experience, and institutional affiliation. We acknowledge that forced migration studies in Canada and globally have been dominated by academics racialized as White with no lived experience of forced migration, including the editor of this volume. This is neither to belittle the importance of scholarly curiosity nor to essentialize researchers' identities (Biorklund and Hyndman 2022) but rather to intentionally reflect on power inequities in the production of knowledge. Therefore, this book consciously amplifies the important work of many other colleagues whose perspectives enrich and challenge dominant discourses on displacement and Canada's role within forced migration – domestically and internationally. Collectively and individually, contributors to this book critically analyze the state of forced migration in Canada and dare to imagine an "otherwise" (Povinelli 2012). We believe that the Canadian government and those who live and work on the territories of Indigenous people can – and must – do better to promote and protect the rights, livelihoods, and knowledge of people in varied situations of displacement. We hope that this book provides a starting point for these conversations and actions.

SECTION ONE

Situating Forced Migration in Canada

1

Migrants in Their Own Territory: Indigenous Displacement and Settler Colonialism in Canada

Veldon Coburn

KEY TAKEAWAYS

- Immigration is central to the settler colonial logics of Indigenous elimination.
- Official Canadian nationalism has been successful in producing a Canadian ethnic identity and cultivating patriotism with immigrants.
- The Canadian settler state continues to eliminate Indigenous identities through a biopolitical project that controls the production and reproduction of the Indigenous population.

KEY TERMS

- Indigenous
- Settler colonialism
- Sovereignty
- *Terra nullius*

INTRODUCTION

1.1 Forced relocation of Mi'kmaq People: https://www.aptnnews.ca/national-news/uprooted-the-little-known-story-about-mikmaw-history-of-forced-relocation.

In *Delgamuukw v. British Columbia*, Chief Justice Antonio Lamer of the Supreme Court of Canada (SCC) closed out the conclusion of the court by remarking, "Let us face it, we are all here to stay" (SCC para. 186). The 1997 case was a landmark decision in the emerging jurisprudence concerning the constitutionality of Indigenous territorial title and rights where Indigenous nations maintained both prior and exclusive occupancy, preceding assertions of colonial sovereignty. But Lamer's comment – the final sentence of an 186-paragraph decision – registers the wider colonial consciousness: the Canadian colonial project will continue unabated, despite the priority of Indigenous nations and their population on their territories. Lamer's successor, Chief Justice Beverley McLachlin, would similarly muse about the fact of colonialism, interpolating Indigenous people into the colonial vision of an unfinished national project. Reflecting on Canada's defining constitutional moments in 2014, McLachlin asserted that "reconciliation recognizes the reality that Canada is made up of people of Aboriginal descent but also people who are descended, not just from different European forbears, but from people from all parts of the globe. Whatever our views about that, it is a reality and we must accept it" (McLachlin 2014). Unmoved by the colonial position, many Indigenous Peoples are not resigned to accept this as their reality.

Immigration has been fundamental to the Canadian settler colonial project and critical to its maintenance. Many Canadians share McLachlin's view of reality, embracing – even romanticizing – the foundational narrative of Canada's birth as a "nation of immigrants" (C. Anderson 2001). From an Indigenous perspective, however, the Canadian state remains an illegitimate apparatus of settler colonialism where immigration is instrumental to this political project. Outwardly, Canada's polished international reputation – as well as that of other settler states, such as the US, Australia, and New Zealand – as a champion for human rights and an advanced economy discourages any questions of its legitimacy (Kymlicka 2004). Colonialism and its injustices, culminating in genocide, are framed as artifacts of historical societies – primitive Indigenous collectives and early settlers – that bear no resemblance to the liberal democracy of the present day (A. Turner 2016; Waldron 1992). Yet for Indigenous nations and their people, the Canadian state has not merely inherited a legacy from its European forebears, but also it continues to coordinate mass relocation and settlement on their territories

(Shipley 2020; Thobani 2007). Just as in previous eras, migrants arriving to settle in Canada find space on the territories of dispossessed Indigenous nations and displaced Indigenous Peoples.

Canadian immigration policy and programming have continued in the tradition of settler colonial geopolitics, but contemporary Canadian statecraft and nation building have adopted modern technologies of governing populations. From the stance of Indigenous nations and their people, colonial immigration programs have always been concerned with territorial dispossession. That is, Indigenous sovereignties have been subjugated to colonial authorities violently seizing and redistributing Indigenous territorial holdings in accordance with colonial prerogatives and impulses (Coulthard 2014; Moreton-Robinson 2015). But, in tandem with the sovereign powers of state coercion and its monopoly on violence, the Canadian state not only governs the territory seized from Indigenous Peoples, but it is also guided by a rationality of population management. As Patrick Wolfe observes, settler colonialism is underwritten by a "logic of elimination" of Indigenous Peoples: "Negatively, it strives for the dissolution of native societies. Positively, it erects a new colonial society on the expropriated land base" (2006, 388). In the analysis that follows, I draw on Michel Foucault's insights on biopower and population management to illustrate the role of immigration in service of present-day settler colonialism in Canada (Foucault 2003, 2004a, 2004b; Hammerstadt 2014; Morgensen 2011).

A "NATION OF IMMIGRANTS": CANADIAN NATIONALISM AND INDIGENOUS ERASURE

In a statement to observe Canadian Multiculturalism Day in 2006, then prime minister Stephen Harper recited the familiar nationalist refrain that "Canada is a nation of immigrants." Harper gave some history of Canadian settlement and reflected on the symbiosis between immigration and the birth of the nation: "For more than 400 years, men and women have come to these shores in search of new opportunities and a better life for themselves and their families. These newcomers have brought with them valuable skills, a commitment to hard work and a strong desire to succeed. They have added immeasurably to every community in which they have settled" (2006). There is nothing particularly distinctive in Harper's remarks; the views expressed enjoy widespread popularity both inside and outside Canada. But the predominant view of Canada as both a "nation of immigrants" and an attractive destination for new migrants – a status cultivated internally among its citizenry as much as it is projected on the international stage – is troubled by the continued presence of Indigenous Peoples and the ongoing violence of settler colonialism against Indigenous nations. In other words, the construction and promotion of Canada is an act of Indigenous erasure.

Canada's emergence as a nation is a relatively new occurrence in geopolitical history. This is not surprising; present-day Western nations and nationalism are distinctly modern phenomena. Prominent theorists, such as Ernest Gellner and Anthony Giddens, situate the appearance of what we recognize as "nations" as the product of recent centuries (Gellner 1983; Giddens 1987). It is not exceptional then, that the cultural fragments of Britain and France, combined with the territorialization of state structures in the "new world," would synthesize a new national consciousness at this historical juncture. Unlike much of the current global community of nations that consolidated out of ancient societies and collectivities, Canada was manufactured out of the remnants of European colonies. Constructivist theories help explain the genesis of Canadian settler colonial nationalism. B. Anderson (1983) tells us that modern nations are "imagined communities"; E. Hobsbawm (2012) points to the "invented traditions" at the core of modern nationalism; and C. Taylor observes that the background of community consciousness is the "social imaginary" built on "images, stories and legends" (2004, 23). The production of Canadian national consciousness is a discursive effect; in other words, this identity emerges out of various discourses that animate conceptions of Canadianness.

Nationalist discourses – the various blend of imaginations and inventions – are both organic and contrived, and Canadian nationalism is no exception. The colonial nationalism that would give birth to Canada was, and continues to be, an elite discourse. As B. Anderson has observed, "It is generally recognized that the intelligentsias were central to the rise of nationalism in the colonial territories" (1983, 116). In Canada, the colonial intellectual elites deliberately devised a program for the nation and its nationals. Official nationalism in Canada was propelled as the colonial state began to consolidate and centralize functions for the administration of the colony and settlers. Robust nationalist ideology – the elite discourses of Canada as a nation of immigrants, a place not only welcoming to immigrants but also continuously reliant upon new immigration – was circulated through state administration, education systems, and the mass media (B. Anderson 1983, 114). Like other modern nation-states, Canadian colonial nationalism enjoys considerable help from official state policy and programming.

Colonial narrative construction and the manufacture of Canadian national consciousness is a dual process with both positive and negative mechanisms, operating in similar fashion to Wolfe's "logic of elimination." Positively, official nationalism is productive – it produces the Canadian social imaginary. Negatively, colonial nationalism destroys competing conceptions of Indigenous existence. For Euro-descended settlers and new immigrants from elsewhere, the state cultivates national identity through the administration of formal education as well as other modes of civic instruction, such as citizenship training programs (Gellner 1983). But for Indigenous Peoples, the colonial state has a long history of violent inculcation of Canadianness and the eradication of

Indigenous national consciousness. In studying his own nation and people, Innu sociologist and theorist Pierrot Ross-Tremblay has examined colonial memory and "mnemohistory" – not an account of the past but rather how the past is remembered. As Ross-Tremblay observes, "Colonisation comes with a myth-making process and the reshaping of memory, through the colonisers' production of 'myths' and their strained absorption by the dominated groups" (2019, 29).

Indeed, colonial efforts have taken a much more forceful and coercive tack in the uptake of Canadian nationalism by Indigenous Peoples. The Indian Residential School (IRS) system specifically targeted Indigenous Peoples in a violent program to destroy Indigenous national memory and, instead, install a Canadian consciousness (Spencer and Sinclair 2019). On 11 June 2008, the Government of Canada issued a national apology to former students of IRS as part of a class action legal settlement. Delivering the apology in Parliament, then prime minister Harper acknowledged the violence of the IRS system and its colonial-nationalist purposes:

> Two primary objectives of the Residential Schools system were to remove and isolate children from the influence of their homes, families, traditions and cultures, and to assimilate them into the dominant culture. These objectives were based on the assumption Aboriginal cultures and spiritual beliefs were inferior and unequal. Indeed, some sought, as it was infamously said, "*to kill the Indian in the child.*" (Government of Canada 2008, n.p.; emphasis added)

Despite the apology and the solemnity of the occasion, the production of Canadianness and the propagation of its image entails deliberate forgetting, disregarding its settler colonial foundations and the erasure of Indigenous Peoples. The next year, in 2009, Harper surprised many observers of Indigenous politics and history in Canada when he told an international audience at the G20 meeting that Canada has "no history of colonialism." Similarly, Jean Chrétien, Canada's prime minister from 1993 to 2003 and minister of Indian Affairs from 1968 until 1974, denied knowledge of the rampant abuses and violence throughout the extensive network of federally operated Indian Residential Schools. When asked about abuses in 2021, Chrétien stated, "This problem was never mentioned when I was minister. Never."

There have been noticeable efforts by colonial state and settler civil institutions to acknowledge Indigenous Peoples. However, the inclusion strikes many as either tokenistic or whitewashing both the colonial past and present. As Tricia Logan tells us, the contemporary nation building "narrative in Canada has often come to the conclusion that the nation was built in amiable partnership with First Peoples rather than their eliminationist removal" (Logan 2014a, 155). Nowhere is this more evident than in the current official study guide for the Canadian citizenship test, *Discover Canada: The Rights and Responsibilities of Citizenship* – official nationalism produced by the federal department of Immigration, Refugees and Citizenship Canada (IRCC). Today, the colonial state discourse portrays Indigenous Peoples as equals in the founding of Canada. Privileging the country's European heritage, the guide states: "To understand what it means to be Canadian, it is important to know about our three founding peoples – Aboriginal, French and British" (Government of Canada 2015a). The guide takes significant liberty in representing the position of Indigenous people – many do not identify with the colonial state or its settler nation. The guide collapses Indigenous nations into the nebulous category of "Aboriginal" – a colonial term deployed by the settler state with juridico-legal context (Younging 2018). This discursive move homogenizes otherwise discrete political nationalities, erasing the political identities of nearly eighty Indigenous nations that pre-existed European contact. For the uninitiated, Indigenous Peoples are merely another cultural tile in Canada's multicultural mosaic (McCormack 2020).

Despite recent moves to recognize Indigenous Peoples and their prior occupation in Canada, official Canadian nationalism has recuperated the "nation of immigrants" trope at the heart of Canada's origin story. The Canadian state and its officials now frame Indigenous people as Canada's "first immigrants." In 2017 Governor General David Johnston remarked, "We're a country based on immigration going right back to quote indigenous peoples unquote who were immigrants as well, going back 10, 12, 14,000 years ago" (cited in Tasker 2017, n.p.). Johnston would later apologize, following adverse reaction from Indigenous Peoples, and clarify in a statement on social media that "Indigenous peoples are immigrants" and that "[t]hey are the original peoples of this land." The Canadian state continues to suggest that Indigenous Peoples are immigrants to Canada. The citizenship study guide, *Discover Canada*, tells the prospective Canadian citizen that, "ancestors of Aboriginal peoples are *believed* to have migrated from Asia many thousands of years ago" (Government of Canada 2015a; emphasis added). From the perspective of many Indigenous people, the normative significance of prior occupation outweighs what is "believed" by settler society. The fact remains that organized Indigenous governments established their polities long before European contact – there was no Canada in existence as a destination for Indigenous Peoples even in the event that they did migrate from elsewhere.

INDIGENOUS DISPOSSESSION AND DISPLACEMENT

As a project of settler colonialism, Canadian nation building has entailed the dual strategy of removing Indigenous people from their territory and re-peopling the region with surplus populations from elsewhere. Unlike other modes of colonialism where Indigenous populations were subjugated and exploited by the colonial authorities, settler colonialism makes little or no use of the original inhabitants. Much of the colonial experience of elimination of Indigenous Peoples from territory set aside for immigrant settlement has entailed a combination of coerced relocation and induced migration (Veracini 2023). In other instances, the colonial state has availed itself of lethal force, resulting in mass casualties and the physical destruction of Indigenous people. Indeed, the largely untold history of the Canadian nation is teeming with instances of colonial barbarity visited upon Indigenous people, forcing them to leave their homes and settlements in order to open up space for the construction of new communities constituted by strangers arriving from distant places.

The settler state was explicit that territorial dispossession was to serve its immigrant settlement program. All the Numbered Treaties – eleven post-Confederation treaties executed between 1871 and 1921 – expressly indicated that Indigenous territory was sought because it was the Crown's "desire to open for settlement and immigration" (this phrase varied slightly among the text of the treaties). At the same time as the colonial state was securing Indigenous territory and displacing Indigenous Peoples, it undertook an aggressive colonial development and immigrant settlement program. The Dominion Lands Act, a Canadian law enacted in 1872, introduced the Land Grants policy for the purposes of settling Western Canada with immigrants. Under the policy, Indigenous territory was liberally distributed to immigrant homesteaders and organizations, such as the Hudson's Bay Company, which voraciously consolidated its hold over Indigenous lands (Warnock 2007). Immigrants were lured to settle Western Canada by the promises of a significant land grant under the policy: 160 acres of land, as a starting point, for a ten-dollar registration fee (Phillips, Girard, and Brown 2022).

While the colonial authorities were generously awarding Indigenous lands to European newcomers as part of imperial expansion (and explicitly withholding the same from Asian immigrants), Indigenous Peoples were forcibly removed from the same territory and relocated to the least desirable parcels of land (Backhouse 1999; Mosher 1998). Colonial settlement programs have long-entailed the stringent spatial regulation of Indigenous Peoples; in most cases, this has been achieved through the coercive mechanisms of the settler state with very rare instances of voluntary migration (which were nonetheless coercively enforced). As displaced migrants – mostly within their own territory – Indigenous Peoples watched colonial authorities destroy both the physical and social infrastructure of their societies as they were uprooted to the least desirable regions. This colonial violence continued well beyond Canada's founding in 1867, moving from one Indigenous nation to the next into the late twentieth century. Throughout the 1950s and 1960s, for example, the Government of Canada forcibly removed the people of the Sayisi Dene First Nation from their homes and communities. Beginning in 1956, the state undertook several relocation exercises, collecting the Sayisi Dene people and relocating them multiple times with dire, often fatal, consequences (Government of Canada 2016). The Dene were transported by the Government of Canada from their homeland to distant places, leaving them in unfamiliar terrain without the infrastructure or implements necessary to preserve life. By the early 1970s, 117 of approximately 300 Sayisi Dene that had been forcibly relocated had perished, largely as a result of the gross deprivation and social anomie that ensued from the violent disruption of their lives (Basso, Ciaschi, and Akesson 2020).

Canadian national narratives deliberately overlook the extensive colonial undertakings that entailed the removal of Indigenous Peoples from their lands and the enclosure of Indigenous commons (Thomas and Coburn 2022). The vast majority of colonial dispossession and eradication of Indigenous Peoples from their territories was completed by the end of the twentieth century. Traces of Indigenous territorial dispossession and displacement are still evident in the Indian Reserve system. Although reserves predate Canadian Confederation in 1867, the system underwent extensive organization and formalization soon thereafter. It was under the Constitution Act of 1867 that the colonial state gave itself exclusive jurisdiction over "Indians, and Lands reserved for the Indians." In the decades that followed, the Canadian state undertook a program of voracious expansion through Indigenous nations, claiming sovereignty over their territory and forcibly removing them to the reserves. The Innu, for example, have occupied the territory of what is now known as Labrador and Quebec for over eight thousand years (Ross-Tremblay 2019). In the middle of the twentieth century, the colonial government removed the Innu from their lands and relocated them to Indian Reserves (Samson 2008).

The colonial state's initiation of immigrants to Canada glosses over the horrors and violence of Indigenous displacement and the ongoing human rights abuses endured by Indigenous Peoples. For the new immigrant to Canada seeking citizenship, the study guide provides some brief mention: "Today, about half of First Nations people live on reserve land in about six hundred communities" (Government of Canada 2021b, 10). The guide gives no indication to the prospective Canadian of the violent history of the Indian Reserve system and the magnitude of territorial dispossession. For Indigenous nations that occupied and exercised jurisdiction over approximately ten million square kilometres claimed by the Canadian state, a mere 0.2 per cent of that land mass, about twenty-six thousand square kilometres, is set aside for over one million First Nations people (Government of Canada 2010; Statistics Canada 2022a). For the untrained immigrant receiving this new information, there is no suggestion of the cruelty that Indigenous people endured at the hands of colonial authorities as they were forcibly removed to small parcels of land, often the least desirable region of the territory. The contemporary existence of First Nations living on Indian reserves is passed over with little attention to the hardship of current conditions. As Pierrot Ross-Tremblay notes of the experience of his own people, the confinement to the reserve introduced a "colonial terror" to the collective and individual Innu consciousness – an internalized, neurotic "fear factor" (2019, 64).

For settler society, Indigenous Peoples remain largely "out of sight, out of mind," and this view is constantly reproduced for new Canadians, both immigrant and natural-born citizens alike. The motif of *terra nullius* – the Latin maxim for "nobody's land" – lies at the heart of this Canadian colonial narrative. The view that Canada was merely empty land for settlement is deeply seated in the settler colonial consciousness, shoring up attitudes of White sovereignty over Indigenous Peoples and territories (Moreton-Robinson 2015). As an invention of the settler imaginary, the predominance of this imagining relies upon a vast archive of Canadian cultural production. Much of the settler colonial arts, especially celebrated literary and visual icons such as the Group of Seven, depict a pristine region of the world outside European homelands, untainted by Indigenous presence (Furniss 1999). The idea of barren wilderness erases not only prior Indigenous occupancy but also whitewashes the colonial barbarity of dispossession and displacement (Logan 2014b, 112). An entire oeuvre of frontier survival has emerged in Canadian lore, providing comforting narratives for the settler and immigrant alike. As Rebecca Hall explains: "In the frontier account, white settler labour carved a resource economy out of wild and rough terrain. The colonial violence that exploited peoples and resources has been reframed as perseverance and in a hostile environment, while subsistence socio-economies are trapped outside history, in anachronistic space" (R. Hall 2022, 4).

In perhaps the most callous exercise of settler colonial violence, the colonial Crown transformed Indigenous Peoples into objects of colonial imperialism, using them as "human flagpoles" but denying their humanity at the same time. In addition to inventing legal fictions for its claim to sovereignty, such as *terra nullius* and the Doctrine of Discovery, the colonial Crown made Indigenous people instruments of its claims to territorial sovereignty. The Inuit High Arctic relocation is illustrative of both the low value settler society placed on the moral worth of Indigenous life itself and also the Crown's callous brutality (Loo 2019). Between 1939 and 1963 the colonial state sought to assert sovereignty in the highest reaches of the Arctic (Tester and Kulchyski 1994). Not content with mere bald assertion, the colonial Crown physically relocated southern Inuit to the very Far North where these individuals would serve as "human flagpoles": indicators of Canadian occupation in the High Arctic in the face of competing claims by Russia (S. Wright 2014). This program was nothing short of inhumane and cruel. Relocated over two thousand kilometres from southern sub-Arctic Inukjuak to Grise Fiord and Resolute Bay, the Inuit inhabitants were not accustomed to the High Arctic, nor did the colonial authorities furnish them with the appropriate accoutrements for survival in the unfamiliar climate. Reckoning with this colonial brutality, the Government of Canada issued an apology in 2010.

BIOPOLITICS OF CANADIAN SETTLER COLONIALISM

Colonialism in Canada is much more than seizing territory in the name of the sovereign. Although territorial dispossession is at the core of colonialism, settler colonialism – as a distinguishable form of colonialism – takes up the attendant concern of people and population (Wolfe 2006; Veracini 2010). As Gregory Smithers notes, "Settler colonialism is a specific form of colonialism characterized by the 'mass transfer' of people to lands they intend to 'conquer' and permanently settle ... settlers work to establish 'perfect settler sovereignty,' removing any remaining Indigenous challenges to the settler state's sovereignty and redefining themselves as the 'native' inhabitants" (2022). And, in this respect, immigration is critical to settler "self-Indigenization"; far-off places provide the pool of "new Canadians," those who would take up political claims to sovereignty over Indigenous lands, dispossessing and displacing Indigenous people – and, sometimes, altogether eradicating the Indigenous population (S. Pearson 2013; TallBear 2019; Leroux 2019).

Canadian immigration policy has always been imbricated in the colonization of Indigenous Peoples and nations. In 1917 the Government of Canada laid any doubt to rest when it created the first federal immigration ministry that was expressly styled the "Office of Immigration and Colonization." With its own federal department, Canadian immigration policy and programming are concerned with producing a particular mode of colonial citizen and colonial social subjectivities. As Lorenzo Veracini has observed, settler colonies strive to construct homogeneity: "Under settler colonialism, homogeneity is a byproduct of the destruction of Indigenous lifeworlds and autonomy. Homogeneity must be created by way of reducing Indigenous difference" (2023, 76). The Canadian colonial drive to ethnic and racial homogeneity is borne out in the demographics. According to the United Nations International Organization for Migration (IOM), Canada was the eighth most prominent destination country for international immigrants in 2020 (McAuliffe, Lee, and Abel 2020). And reporting on the 2021 Canadian Census tells us that almost one in four Canadians – approximately 23 per cent or eight million three hundred thousand – were born outside Canada; in contrast, the same census enumerated one million eight hundred thousand individuals that identified as Indigenous, amounting to 5 per cent of the Canadian population (Statistics Canada 2022a, 2022b).

The Canadian colonial state has assembled an entire edifice that serves settler imperatives to regulate the racial composition of the nation and its population. The Canadian state, like other settler states in modernity, goes beyond the mere assertion of sovereignty; this state is guided by governmental rationalities that surpass questions of territory and, instead, adopt modern technologies of governing a population (Foucault 2004a, 2004b; Goldberg 2002). Technologies of population control extend security to Canadian society while regulating Indigenous existence – immigrants are instrumental in the production and reproduction of settler society (Zylinska 2004). Foucault's studies of modernity and modern forms of government are instructive in the understanding of the Canadian settler colonial project. In *The History of Sexuality, vol. 1*, Foucault observes this new art of government: "the administration of bodies and the calculated management of life" (1990, 140).

In his 1977–78 lecture series at the Collège de France titled Security, Territory, Population, Foucault explained that the state, in modernity, takes up the problem of the biological processes of life, concerning itself with "the security (*sécurité*) of the population and, consequently, of those who govern it" (2004a, 65). For Foucault, the nexus of biology and politics entailed the mechanism of biopower, a modern politics that seizes the functions of the biological and takes the potential of life as its target. Modern biopower operates according to the maxim, "to make live and let die" (Foucault 1990, 136). In terms of Canadian biopolitics, immigration policy sought to generate a thriving colonial populace that would replace the Indigenous Peoples, nations that were marked out for liquidation.

Evidence of the biopolitical objective of Canadian colonialism – the replacement of Indigenous Peoples with a new settler society – is noticeable in recent trends around national identification. As a corollary of this nascent country, there is a similarly embryonic conception of national subjects – Canadians. Despite the symbolic significance of the founding nationalities – Great Britain and France – in the national consciousness, the early aspirations of elites such as the Fathers of Confederation for a distinct "Canadian ethnicity" have materialized in contemporary society (Howard-Hassmann 1999; Paragg 2015; Thomas 2005). Census respondents have begun to identify "Canadian" as their ethnic identity in the last decades (Boyd 1999). Census reporting in recent times has shown an increasing trend in respondents identifying their ethnicity as "Canadian"; analysis shows that this growth has been drawn from and displaced previous ethnicity identification with both British and French (S. Lee and Edmonston 2009). In the 2016 census, approximately nineteen million seven hundred thousand Canadians, more than 57 per cent of the population, identify as ethnically European. However, as a testament to its conceptual ascendancy as a promising ethnicity, eleven million one hundred thousand individuals, approximately one-third of the population, reported their ethnicity to be "Canadian."

Discourses of European superiority and the predominance of White racial supremacy have long underwritten the ideal of Canadian citizenship. For much of Canada's history, immigration policy has favoured migrants originating in White-dominant regions, such as Northwestern Europe (Akbari and MacDonald 2014; see also Fynn Bruey and Fantauzzi, chapter 8; Mahrouse and El Omari, chapter 15). In more recent times, tensions emerging out of Quebecois nationalism and resistance to English/British subjugation have introduced new colonial strata (Giroux 2023). Anti-Indigenous political rhetoric has maintained a cultural hegemony in Canada to this day; the social sensibilities that indemnified colonial dominance over Indigenous Peoples at the dawn of Confederation – namely the view that Indigenous people were racially and culturally inferior to White Europeans – are woven into contemporary Canadian culture (Warry 2007). Some of the most pernicious stigma remains popular in the Canadian consciousness, a fixture of the settler imaginary that owes its longevity to mainstream media. A number of familiar racist stereotypes and tropes that characterize Indigenous people as lazy, drunk, degenerate, bawdy, incompetent, infantile, dependent on government aid, and so forth is regular news fodder (Burns and Shor 2021).

The political purchase of these racist discourses is evident in the colonial management of the Indigenous population. In contrast to the intense focus of the colonial state to secure the vitality of the settler population, the lives of Indigenous Peoples are regulated by a vast bureaucratic apparatus. The federal Indian Act, first enacted by the colonial state in 1876 and still in force today, established a biologized adversary to settler society. In *Accounting for Genocide*, Neu and Therrien examine how the colonial state organized a biopolitical regime that adopted technocratic mechanisms in efforts to manage Indigenous biological life processes. As Neu and Therrien observe, the colonial genocide of Indigenous Peoples in Canada was a calculated undertaking, an actuarial campaign to administer the elimination of Indigenous existence. To manipulate the life of an Indigenous multiplicity, the state adopted quantitative methods such as accounting to coordinate and control the accumulations and flows of the necessities of life and other resources (Neu and Therrien 2003). This biological management is reflected in the considerable divergence in life expectancy figures – on average, the lifespan of Indigenous Peoples is fifteen years shorter than non-Indigenous peoples (Canadian Press 2018; see also Park 2021).

To this day, the colonial state administers the stock of the First Nation population, tracking births and other vital statistics and overseeing the issuance of Indian status, the legal registration of a biologically recognized "Indian." Under the Indian Act, the Canadian state introduced a racial regime that, as Pamela Palmater notes, incorporates blood quantum calculus to determine when an "Indian bloodline" has become extinct (2011). After two generations of miscegenation – known more colloquially among First Nations as the second-generation cut-off – the colonial state deems the Indian lineage defunct, accomplishing the impulses of settler colonialism for the elimination of the "Native."

CONCLUSION

Official Canadian nationalism has propagated a narrative of a "new" country, emerging out of the settlement of British and French subjects on nobody's land. Generations of immigrants, mostly from Europe until recent times, assimilated these origin stories, shoring up nascent conceptions of Canadianness and emerging as a new Canadian ethnicity. But this prominent account tells only part of the story and relies upon a number of misrepresentations. Canada is a settler colonial project and, it is true, that it is a nation of migrants; however, this sketch erases the history and presence of Indigenous nations and peoples. Canada is built on violent dispossession of Indigenous Peoples and their forcible relocation, which opened space for immigrant settlement. At the same time as the colonial state dispossesses Indigenous people, it aims to destroy their nations and replace them with new societies. To achieve these ends, Canadian settler colonialism has relied upon immigration policy and programming to effect the mass transfer and settlement of foreign populations on Indigenous lands.

FURTHER READING AND RESOURCES

Abbott, Louise, dir. 2020. *The Ahiarmiut: Out-of-the-Way Dwellers | Tell Our Stories*. Friends of Canada. YouTube video, 5:00. https://www.youtube.com/watch?v=7zZKKS_ByBo.

Belanger, Yale D., and P. Whitney Lackenbauer. 2014. *Blockades or Breakthroughs? Aboriginal Peoples Confront the Canadian State*. Montreal and Kingston: McGill-Queen's University Press.

Duncan, John. 2010. "Apology for the Inuit High Arctic Relocation: Speaking Notes for the Honourable John Duncan." Government of Canada, 18 August 2010. https://www.rcaanc-cirnac.gc.ca/eng/1100100016115/1534786491628.

Obomsawin, Alanis, dir. 2014. "Trick or Treaty?" National Film Board of Canada, 84:00. https://www.nfb.ca/film/trick_or_treaty.

Smith, Keith D. 2014. *Strange Visitors: Documents in Indigenous-Settler Relations in Canada from 1876*. Toronto: University of Toronto Press.

Truth and Reconciliation Commission (TRC). 2015. *Honouring the Truth, Reconciling for the Future*. https://nctr.ca/records/reports.

2

"Sold for a Slave for Life": Black Enslavement in Colonial Canada

Natasha Henry-Dixon

KEY TAKEAWAYS

- The forced migration of African captives and the subsequent waves of African diasporic peoples were fuelled by the emergence of global racial capitalism and growth of European imperial powers connected to the Black presence in the colonies that became Canada.
- Racial chattel slavery does not receive adequate discussion in Canadian historiography.
- Although lay historians in late nineteenth-century historical accounts and in twentieth-century academia have written about Black enslavement in Canada, how the subject has been taken up has shifted: Canadian slavery is becoming a stand-alone subfield of historiography.

KEY TERMS

- Chattel slavery
- Enslavement
- Freedom seekers
- Race
- Racialization

INTRODUCTION

How did race influence the forced migration of African peoples during the transatlantic slave trade from the sixteenth to the early nineteenth centuries? How is the territory now called Canada connected to this global system? How did this forced migration shape the African diaspora into Canada from the nineteenth century to today? This chapter addresses these central questions to inform understandings of forced migration in the creation of what is now known as Canada.

The transatlantic slave trade was the largest forced migration in world history (Eltis et al. 2011, 27). Led by the Portuguese, British, Spanish, French, Dutch, and Danish empires, the four-hundred-year human trafficking phenomenon displaced twelve million African people, forcibly relocating them to European colonies in the Americas. During the seventeenth century, trafficking in African people extended to New France.[1] The first recorded enslaved Black person was a young African boy sold in Quebec City in 1628. He was given the name Olivier LeJeune by his enslavers. Captive Black people were taken involuntarily to the French and later British colonies that became British North America[2] through secondary and tertiary forced migration from the Caribbean and the Thirteen Colonies that formed the United States after the American Revolution.

Upwards of 4,500 Black persons were held in hereditary bondage throughout French and British colonization. In New France, Indigenous Peoples comprised two-thirds of the enslaved population and one-third were African people. Slavery among Indigenous people was also practised since before European contact. This form of slavery differed from chattel slavery.[3] After the 1760 British defeat of the French during the Seven Years War, most of the people enslaved in the colonies of British North America were of African descent, and the racial designation of "negro" or "Black" came to define enslavement. The migration of United Empire Loyalist refugees into these colonies after the British loss of the American Revolution (1775–83) resulted in a significant increase in the number of enslaved Black people in Canada. As a British colony, British North America (Canada) was also very much entangled in the transatlantic slave trade in other ways. Salted cod and timber were exported from Canada to the Caribbean. Nineteen slave ships were constructed in the Maritime colonies for British merchants who traded in African captives (Slave Voyages Database 2021) As part of the interconnected colonial economic system, goods produced in the slave economies of the Caribbean – rum, molasses, tobacco, cotton, and sugar – were imported to Canada for consumption.

This chapter examines the history of the enslavement of Black people in the territory now called Canada and highlights how forced migration and its various historical contexts related to the regimes of imperialism and colonization influenced the movement of people of African descent into and out of Canada and explores the trends and patterns that have emerged in Canadian slavery historiography.

2.1 Between April and November of 1783, over 3,000 free and 333 enslaved Black men, women, and children sailed or were forcibly transported from New York to Nova Scotia (which included New Brunswick at that time). They were taken by British officials to British North America at the end of the American Revolutionary War) and each individual was recorded in the military ledger called the "Book of Negroes." The book is a register of Black Loyalists, formerly enslaved by Patriots, who obtained their freedom after they escaped to British military lines during the American Revolution. They responded to the call for enslaved people to serve in exchange for freedom. To gain their liberty and to live in freedom, they were relocated to the British colony of Nova Scotia to live in freedom. The "Book of Negroes" also included the names of enslaved Black people who were held in bondage by White Loyalists in the Thirteen Colonies or were recently acquired by them prior to their expulsion. White Loyalists, some of them enslavers, were also on the passenger list. At the same time, hundreds of White Loyalists, many enslaved Black people, and a small number of Black Loyalists entered Upper Canada. Following the relocation of White Loyalist refugees to British North America, the population of enslaved Black people exploded and led to a demographic shift in the population of the enslaved. For some Black Loyalists, freedom was tenuous and short lived; they were re-enslaved or forced into indenture. The complexities of enslavement and precarities of freedom for people of African descent British North America, and the Americas more broadly, were shaped by forced migration. (Carleton 1783)

KEY CONCEPTS

Before analyzing the history of slavery in Canada and its present-day legacy, it is important to understand key concepts. This section defines these terms that will be used in this chapter and throughout the book.

Race and Racialization

"Race" is a socially constructed colonial concept (see also Mahrouse and El Omari, chapter 15). The ideas of race and racial classification are based on presumed inherent differences in phenotype (e.g., skin colour, hair texture), culture, and behaviour between groups. The modern meaning of race, as Barrington Walker summarizes, has "emerged as a concept in Europe during the Enlightenment, classifying and hierarchizing human beings into essential types based primarily on phenotypic criteria. These hierarchies, in turn, were used to justify slavery and colonization, laying the foundation for racial states in various white settler colonies" (2017, 203).

Transatlantic ventures, including the transatlantic slave trade and the establishment of the institution of slavery, formed and consolidated modern ideas of race and racial difference and informed the processes of racialization. "Racialization" is "the complex set of historical and sociopolitical processes of attributing superior or inferior status based on the presumption of biological difference" (Pierre 2020, 220).

The colonial social construction of race in British North America replicated ideas of race and racial difference in other colonized places in the New World where White superiority was reinforced and exploited to justify the subordination of people of African descent. Early ideas of racial formation represented a White-Black binary. But far from being a binary, this paradigm also included Indigenous Peoples as part of the racialization process (see Coburn, chapter 1). The proliferation and evolution of racial categories and their meanings happened within the myriad of interactions among actors of the various groups, including through the entrenchment of chattel slavery.

Racial Slavery

"Chattel slavery" was the enslaving and owning of humans and their offspring as legal, disposable property. Colonial laws, practices, and customs enabled the system where people racially categorized as Black were bought, sold, and forced to work without wages, distinct from other systems of forced, unpaid, or low-wage labour that have been deemed slavery. Enslaved people were considered the property of their enslaver and legally not persons. The laws of chattel slavery were strengthened by the doctrine of *partus sequitur ventrem* ("That which is born follows the womb"), making enslavement permanent and hereditary through enslaved women.

Racial chattel slavery, the subjugation of Indigenous Americans and Indigenous African peoples, was a feature of White settler colonialism in colonial Canada. The ideological justification for the trafficking of African people in the Atlantic world was rooted in European notions of White supremacy and Black inferiority based on scientific racism. These beliefs also resulted in the shift from enslaving Indigenous Americans to trafficking and enslaving Indigenous Africans. Europeans expanded the trafficking of Africans because they believed that "Indians," or Indigenous Americans, could not handle the physically demanding labour of plantation systems in the Americas and that they were more susceptible to European diseases, but that Indigenous African people were biologically built to withstand hard labour and were more resistant to European diseases. The system of slavery during the eighteenth century became more entrenched in colonial Canada, similar to other jurisdictions in the Atlantic world, reinforcing beliefs and attitudes about Whiteness and Blackness.

Chattel slavery in Canada was legally institutionalized and religiously sanctioned. The enslavement of humans was legal through property and contract laws and was confirmed in legislation in some colonies. For instance, in 1781, the legislature of the colony of St John's Island (today Prince Edward Island) passed An Act, declaring that Baptism of SLAVES shall not exempt them from BONDAGE (or, An Act Respecting the Baptism of Slaves). This law declared:

> 1) Be it therefore enacted by the Governor, Council and Assembly, That all Slaves, whether Negroes or Mulattoes, residing at present on this Island, or that may hereafter be imported or brought therein, shall be deemed Slaves, notwithstanding his, her or their Conversion to Christianity; nor shall the Act of Baptism performed on any such Negro or Mulatto alter his, her or their Condition ...
> 3) And be it further enacted by the Authority aforesaid, That all Children born of Women Slaves shall belong to and be the property of the Masters or Mistresses of such Slaves. (Riddell 1921, 308)

The 1793 act to prevent the further introduction of slaves and to limit the Term of Contracts for Servitude within the province in Upper Canada (known as the 1793 Act to Limit Slavery), recognized enslavement as a legally and socially accepted institution. The second clause stated:

> nothing herein contained shall extend, or be construed to extend to liberate any Negro, or other person subjected to such service as aforesaid, or to discharge them or any of them from the possession of the owner thereof, his or her executors, administrators or assigns, who shall have come or been brought into the Province, in conformity to the conditions prescribed by any authority for that purpose exercised, ... or shall have otherwise come into the possession of any person, by gift, bequest or *bona fide* purchase before the passing of this Act, whose property therein is hereby confirmed ... (Upper Canada 1975)

Catholic and Protestant churches that were key colonial institutions performed some baptisms, marriages, and burials of enslaved people. During the more than two-hundred-year practice of racial chattel enslavement in the colonies that became Canada, from the seventeenth to the early nineteenth centuries, no denomination called for the abolition of slavery; in fact, several clergy members enslaved Indigenous and Black people.

The slave labour regime introduced by European colonists was a specific and unique form of racial slavery. It established a cheap, controllable labour force that was shaped by the creation of social categories based on racial and physical differences. These differences were systematized and legalized to solidify White dominance through the implementation and adoption of hereditary racial chattel servitude. The institutionalization of slavery was an explicit colonial policy to build a White settler state. It is important to underscore the interconnectedness of the dispossession of Indigenous Peoples from their lands in North America and the trafficking of African people to the Americas as captive labourers in the processes of Spanish, French, and British imperialism and colonization from the seventeenth century to the nineteenth century. Lands were acquired from Indigenous Peoples through conquest and involuntary assimilation informed by the Doctrine of Discovery that led to forcible removal, land theft, and uneven treaty agreements. These two processes of displacement are inextricably linked. The act of making someone a slave through subjugation and commodification is enslavement. This term separates a person's identity from their forced condition (Collins Dictionary 2023).

Freedom Seekers

"Freedom seeker" describes an enslaved person who acted to obtain freedom from slavery. They laid claim to their right to be free persons by fleeing. The terms "fugitive slaves" and "runaway slaves" were constructs of White slaveholding society and condescending abolitionists. The construction and use of these terms illustrates how the US viewed the efforts of African Americans to secure individual and collective freedom by employing the legal system in another effort to deprive them of their individual agency. The term "fugitive" is connected to the two Fugitive Slave Acts (1793, 1850) passed by the US Congress. Both versions emphasized that the "fugitive" was acting criminally against their enslaver and the government in escaping from bondage (Foner 2015, 39).

Forced Movement, Forced Labour

Slavery as a forced labour system was instituted to facilitate the sustainability of local and household economies and by extension stretched into the sustaining of colonial economies. White men, women, and children and a small number of Indigenous men and women held property in enslaved Black people and utilized their coerced labour for personal gain. Enslaved Black women, men, and children performed all kinds of labour, including agricultural, domestic, and trade. Enslaved men cleared land, chopped wood, and built structures like homes and barns on their enslaver's property. Many helped establish and operate family farms. Enslaved men also worked in a wide range of occupations as hunters, voyageurs, sailors, miners, fishermen, and dock workers.

Newspaper advertisements of enslaved people for sale show the range of feminized duties that enslaved women performed – cooking, churning butter, washing laundry, hairdressing, making candles and soap, milking cows, making preserves, and chicken tending. They also fetched water, gathered firewood, sewed, knitted, carded wool, served families and guests, washed dishes, and completed a litany of household chores. They provided personal care services like bathing and dressing. Enslaved women often had the role of taking care of their enslaver's children. Additionally, the reproductive labour of enslaved women – the natural increase of enslaved women bearing children – added property value to their enslavers' assets and enhanced the enslavers' wealth and status.

2.2 I also bequeath to my said son James the following six negro slaves or such of them as may be living at the time of my death, viz: Jim or James, Hannah, Joe, Jack, Betsy and Tom, and also the children which may hereafter be born of the said Hannah and Betsy. And to my daughter I bequeath my negro wench called Sall, and also a negro woman called Nancy with her five children, which said Nancy was the property of the mother of my said children and intended by her for my said daughter and also the children who may hereafter be born of their bodies or the bodies of their children respectively. (Will of James Girty 1817)

Enslaved women, men, and young people laboured on farms. They prepared fields for planting and helped produce staple crops – wheat, oats, barley, and other grains, vegetables and fruits like potatoes, melons, cauliflower, cabbage, parsnips, carrots, beets, spinach, raspberries, and orchard fruits. They harvested crops and tended to livestock such as horses, cows, sheep, and pigs. Women often tended to smaller kitchen gardens. Many enslaved women and men laboured alongside their enslavers in the businesses the latter operated, including skilled trades shops (coopers, blacksmiths, carpenters, wheelwrights, etc.), merchant stores, mills, inns, and taverns. Enslavers were also enriched by the wages they received for the labour of the those they enslaved when they hired them out. As French and British settlers engaged in a range of economic activities and worked to establish their families and settle the colony, many used slave labour to help in these economic activities and to increase their wealth and profitability – a driving force in raising global capitalism.

The settler households that enslaved Black and Indigenous people cultivated more land and produced more yield than the non-slaveholding counterparts (Rushforth 2012, 276). Hence, the coerced labour of enslaved Black people contributed to the development of early Canada.

CANADIAN SLAVERY HISTORIOGRAPHY

How has the field of Canadian history taken up the matter of slavery? The history of the enslavement of Black people in Canada has been explored by academic scholars and lay historians to some degree since the late nineteenth century. In general, the earlier slavery historiography in Canada written by White anglophone and some francophone men simultaneously illuminated, obscured, and marginalized Canada's slave history. The majority of the early written sources that discuss Black enslavement provided a rudimentary discussion on slavery and those who were held in forced servitude. Although there were some texts that focused on slavery (T. Smith 1899; Jack 1898; Nielson 1906), the majority of texts that mention slavery discussed it as an addendum to the main focus of their work, which tended to be the lives of other White settler men (see Pringle 1890).

From the mid to late nineteenth century to the twentieth century, many Canadian historians did not believe that slavery in Canada merited any serious independent scholarly study. Of those who did discuss slavery, many perpetuated racist views of Black people, and through their imperialist stances, the enslaved Black people they discussed were treated as commodities. They did not critique or challenge the structures of slavery. Many of these writers followed the common Western practice of examining Black life primarily in response to White subjugation. Their texts rendered a paternalistic interpretation of slavery and defended slavery. Numerous authors framed hereditary bondage as a fact of life and portrayed enslavement as benign (Canniff 1869, 1872; Riddell 1919, 1920a, 1920b, 1921, 1923, 1924, 1929, 1932). Additionally, some writers posited that slavery was essentially an American and Caribbean condition and that the chattel slavery practised in Canada was somehow more benign (Winks 1997). There was a pattern of minimizing Canada's own history of enslavement and promoting Canada as a "haven" for African American freedom seekers. Even in attempts to be sympathetic, some White scholars propagated racist tropes such as Black people being naturally inferior, enslaved Black people being content with their condition, being childlike and incapable of sustaining themselves without benevolent White authority, and being overly devoted to the families that enslaved them.

Some publications by academics and community historians in the post–World War II period that discussed slavery tended to position Black Canadians as "clients" or "recipients" of White benevolence (Walker 1997). The brutal violence of slavery was not acknowledged and the subjecthood of the enslaved was not explored (Fleming 1953). In the 1950s, Marcel Trudel, a White francophone Canadian historian, began an extensive quantitative demographic study of slavery in Quebec. He published a dictionary of slavery in 1963 and a revised version in 1990 (Trudel 1963, 1990). Trudel dissects the two-hundred-year history of slavery in New France. He argues that slavery was an accepted social reality in French colonial society and continued after the British conquest of 1760. His work challenges the broader refusal of Quebec and Canadian societies in general to acknowledge the history of slavery in colonial Canada.

Since the late twentieth century, several scholars comprised of an increasing number of Black academics and some community members, have led a shift in the subfield of Canadian slavery historiography. Through their research, which draws on various analytical and interpretive methods, new themes have emerged that demonstrate there is much to explore and unearth about the enslavement of Black people in colonial Canada. Their work endeavours to critically deconstruct the institution of slavery, acknowledge the subjugation and oppression of the system of chattel enslavement (Sweeney 1994; Hamilton 1994; Cooper 2007b; Donovan 2014; Walker 2017), and investigate slavery as a labour regime. The concepts of race, patriarchy, class, social status, imperialism, and colonization inform their analysis. Many of these scholars also examine resistance (Cooper 2007b; Whitfield 2005, 2006, 2007, 2009, 2010, 2016a, 2016b), the gendered experiences of enslaved women (Cooper 2007b; Nelson 2016; Donovan 2014), power dynamics, and social relations.

This recent research aims to recover the hidden histories of Canadian slavery, centre the enslaved as historical actors, and counter the silencing of enslavement's realities from the dominant Eurocentric narrative of Canadian history. Additionally, this work places the Canadian experience of slavery in the wider transnational context, raising pertinent questions about racial chattel slavery and its legacies across the globe. Contemporary research has disrupted the commonly held view that reliance on enslaved labour in British North America was less significant in comparison to the southern United States and the Caribbean. Enslavers in British North America transplanted and adapted slavery to suit their localized physical, economic, and political landscapes because they relied on the coerced labour of enslaved people to the same extent as White settlers in the northern United States, and slavery took shape based on several regional factors, including legislation, custom, and geography. The system of slavery played an integral role in the expansion of colonization and was foundational to the economic and social systems of British North American colonies.

THE VESTIGES OF SLAVERY

Enslavement was abolished in most British colonies in 1834, including British North America, ending the two-hundred-plus-year institution. However, the racial hierarchies and anti-Black logics born out of imperialism and the transatlantic slave trade persist to this day. The "afterlife of slavery," as Saidiya Hartman names it, refers to the enduring modern-day, virulent forms of structural racial injustice and the different forms of structural inequalities that African-descended people in Canada and in other parts of the world continue to experience.

2.3 In 1999 the United Nations declared the transatlantic slave trade and slavery to be a crime against humanity:

> We acknowledge that slavery and the slave trade, including the transatlantic slave trade, were appalling tragedies in the history of humanity not only because of their abhorrent barbarism but also in terms of their magnitude, organized nature and especially their negation of the essence of the victims, and further acknowledge that slavery and the slave trade are a crime against humanity and should always have been so, especially the transatlantic slave trade and are among the major sources and manifestations of racism, racial discrimination, xenophobia and related intolerance, and that Africans and people of African descent, Asians and people of Asian descent and indigenous peoples were victims of these acts and continue to be victims of their consequences. ("Declaration of the World Conference Against Racism …" 2001, para. 13)

The 2017 United Nations *Working Group of Experts on People of African Descent* report explicitly outlines environmental racism, over-surveillance, racially disproportionate outcomes in the education system, chronic underemployment, and the generational wealth gap that Canada's Black communities have endured for nearly two centuries. The group argues that current social conditions and outcomes of Black life today are the legacies of enslavement, a past that Canada has yet to reckon with.

CONCLUSION

Enslaved Black people were forced to migrate to the French and British colonies that formed the nation-state of Canada. They did not choose to live in colonial Canada under indefinite captivity or to have their labour exploited. On the contrary, these individuals were coerced and violently displaced. It is important to connect the lived experiences of Black people who were held in racial chattel slavery to transnational and regional trajectories of forced migration and White settler colonialism that depended on forced migration, coerced and exploited labour, and structural racism.

Research on slavery in Canada has grown and evolved. Scholars specializing in the enslavement of Black people have reinterpreted, reoriented, and reimagined the subject. They centre the enslaved as historical subjects and are asking different questions, including interrogating the interconnectedness of race and gender in the experiences of the enslaved and the relations of power. Their work fosters a more critical understanding of race, racism, and racialization in the Canadian context. These scholars are rewriting the history of slavery in Canada in a way that contextualizes the lives and experiences of enslaved Black women, men, and children in British North America and locates racial chattel slavery in British North America within the transnational system of African enslavement. Additionally, these works position enslavement squarely within the collective Canadian memory, unsettling the dominant narrative and persistent myth that slavery was inconsequential in Canadian history.

NOTES

"Sold for a Slave for Life": Joe Gutches Complaint, August 1787, Civil and Provincial Secretary Lower Canada "S series," RG 4, A1, vol. 33, 10753–4.

1 New France was the geographical area colonized by France in North America beginning in 1535. It began from the Gulf of St Lawrence and covered a vast area including Newfoundland, Quebec, and Acadia (Nova Scotia), most of the Great Lakes region, and southward to Louisiana and the Mississippi Valley.

2 British North America refers to the geographical area under Britain's control north of the United States from 1783 until Confederation in 1867. It included Nova Scotia, New Brunswick, Cape Breton Island, Prince Edward Island, Lower Canada, and Upper Canada.

3 See Rushforth 2012.

FURTHER READING AND RESOURCES

Cooper, Afua. 2022. *The Enslavement of Africans in Canada.* Immigration and Ethnicity in Canada Series, booklet no. 39. Ottawa: Canadian Historical Association and Department of Canadian Heritage, Government of Canada.

Henry, Natasha. 2020a. "Apology, Truth, and Reparations: The Overdue Reckoning with Canada's Slave Past." *Spacing Toronto*, 23 July 2020. https://spacing.ca/toronto/2020/07/23/apology-truth-and-reparations-the-overdue-reckoning-with-canadas-slave-past.

– 2020b. "If Black Lives Truly Matter in Canada, an Apology for Slavery Is Only a First Step." *Spacing Toronto*, 9 June 2020. https://spacing.ca/toronto/2020/06/09/if-black-lives-truly-matter-in-canada-an-apology-for-slavery-is-only-a-first-step.

– 2022. “Black Enslavement in Canada.” *The Canadian Encyclopedia*. Historica Canada, article published 13 June 2016; last edited 9 February 2022. https://www.thecanadianencyclopedia.ca/en/article/black-enslavement.

– n.d. “Brought in Bondage: Downtown Walking Tour.” Myseum. https://www.myseumoftoronto.com/collection/brought-in-bondage-black-enslavement-in-upper-canada.

House of Bâby. n.d. “House of Bâby.” Camal & Camille. https://www.camalandcamille.com/house-of-baby.

Nova Scotia Archives. 2020. “African Nova Scotians in the Age of Slavery and Abolition.” 20 April 2020.

One Too Many: Enslaved Africans in Early Ontario, 1760–1834. n.d. http://enslavedafricansinearlyontario.ca/home.

Ontario Ministry of Public and Business Service Delivery. n.d. “Enslaved Africans in Upper Canada.” https://www.archives.gov.on.ca/en/explore/online/slavery/index.aspx.

Pirbhai, Camal, and Camille Turner. n.d. “Wanted.” Art Gallery of Ontario. https://ago.ca/RewardWanted.

Shaw, Melissa N. 2022. “Historical Legacies, Black Canadian Slavery, and Institutional Histories.” *Black Perspectives*, 22 September 2022. https://www.aaihs.org/historical-legacies-black-canadian-slavery-institutional-histories.

3

Selectivity, Crisis, and "Loopholes": A Critical Geography of Canada's Bordering of Refuge

Julie E.E. Young

KEY TAKEAWAYS

- Borders are enforced and negotiated at a range of sites beyond physical territorial boundaries.
- Borders are fundamental to the UN Refugee Convention definition that frames how refuge is determined and, by extension, how refugees are received and/or refused.
- Externalization practices contradict the commitments states have made to refugee protection.
- Canada maintains a great degree of control and selectivity over who can arrive in the country as a refugee, including through policies such as the Canada–United States Safe Third Country Agreement (STCA).

KEY TERMS

- Bordering
- Canada–United States Safe Third Country Agreement (STCA)
- Externalization
- Interdiction
- Non-penalization
- Non-refoulement
- Sovereignty

INTRODUCTION

> 3.1 Javier's Story of Refuge, Sanctuary, and Solidarity
> Javier lived in Guatemala during the civil war (1960-96) and helped organize a union of electrical workers. He decided to leave the country when it became clear state actors were following him and he feared for his life. His journey to safety included traversing Mexico by freight train and then connecting with members of the Sanctuary Movement who facilitated his crossing of the US-Mexico border, after which he spent time in sanctuary in Indiana, USA, before arriving in Ontario, Canada, in 1991. His story is captured in the Remembering Refuge: Between Sanctuary and Solidarity counter-archive. In this excerpt, Javier describes how he and his daughter crossed the US-Mexico border as they sought refuge: https://www.rememberingrefuge.com/oral-histories/audio-history/javier.

What are the relationships between borders and refuge? This chapter considers the policies, practices, and politics that define who is recognized as a refugee. I also discuss how nation-state borders have been increasingly mobilized to control and prevent migration. Javier's story reveals the differing forms that contestations of bordering practices can take, from the organized work of the Sanctuary Movement that assisted Central American refugees in the 1980s to the more mundane ways that people navigate borders to seek safety and security.

The situation of Canada – bordering only the US and surrounded by oceans – means Canadian officials can exercise considerable selectivity over who is able to arrive at the country's borders to have their refugee claims considered, as well as who is resettled from situations of displacement abroad. Although Canada has been a global leader in refugee resettlement (see Atak, chapter 17; Labman chapter 18), it has also enacted a range of policies that undermine the country's commitment to refugee protection because they prevent people from arriving safely at the country's border to seek refuge (see Atak, chapter 17 for a discussion of inland claims versus resettlement).

One of these key policies is the STCA. Under the STCA, individuals must make their claim in the first "safe country" in which they arrive – in this case, the agreement designates the US as a safe country for refugees. First written into Canadian law in the late 1980s, when Central American asylum seekers arrived at the Canada-US border in significant numbers, the safe third country provisions did not come into force because no countries were listed at the time. Once implemented at the end of 2004, the STCA reshaped the geography of asylum in Canada.

WHAT ARE THE RELATIONSHIPS BETWEEN BORDERS AND REFUGE?

Borders are often understood as absolutes – clear lines that mark the edges of state territories and demarcate inside from outside. Critical border studies, however, start from a recognition that borders are more complex than this depiction would suggest. Borders are understood as a set of practices to get at the active, dynamic ways in which they work: in this sense, bordering – that is, the enactment and maintenance of borders – is an ongoing process carried out by a range of actors across different spaces and relationships. It is important to consider these multiple spaces of the border and examine how bordering practices contribute to marginalization and inequality as well as contestation and resistance.

In forced migration studies, acknowledging this active, dynamic character of borders helps make sense of some of the politics underlying how the international refugee regime functions as well as how individual countries respond to situations of displacement. The international refugee regime is built around the right to asylum, which was enshrined in the Universal Declaration of Human Rights (UDHR) in 1948. Importantly, however, the UDHR enshrined the right to *seek* asylum but not the related right to *find* it. In other words, it left the granting of asylum – or not – to the discretion of individual governments. When the right to asylum was formalized in the UN Convention relating to the Status of Refugees in the aftermath of World War II, it reinforced the sovereignty of nation-states over decisions on the right to asylum, that is, it affirmed the authority of individual countries to decide what happens within the boundaries of their territories (Arendt [1951] 2004).

Even more importantly, the UN Refugee Convention made crossing a border a vital component of the refugee definition that underpins the international refugee regime. A closer look at the wording of the convention definition will help us better understand how borders became central to the politics of refuge.

3.2 Borders in/and the Convention Refugee Definition

"The term 'refugee' shall apply to any person who: owing to well-founded fear of being persecuted for reasons of race, religion, nationality, membership of a particular social group or political opinion, is outside the country of his nationality and is unable or, owing to such fear, is unwilling to avail himself of the protection of that country; or who, not having a nationality and being outside the country of his former habitual residence as a result of such events, is unable or, owing to such fear, is unwilling to return to it" (UN Convention Relating to the Status of Refugees 1951, art. 1A(2), amended as per UN Protocol).

Later chapters in this volume address different components of this definition. The key phrase here is, "the term 'refugee' shall apply to any person who ... is *outside the country of his nationality*" (emphasis added). The 1951 Convention definition underpinning the international refugee regime is premised on individuals crossing borders to seek asylum. This means that one gains access to the possibility of asylum by crossing a border and making a claim on another state for protection and security. In this sense, the geography of the nation-state - and its grounding in sovereign borders - is a critical component of how refuge was institutionalized under the international refugee regime. This relationship between borders and refuge lies at the foundation of how the asylum process would be organized as individual countries wrote the 1951 Convention definition and the right to asylum into their domestic laws. This foundation informs how states respond to situations of people who are displaced and who is recognized as a refugee.

The 1951 Convention definition, then, sets up a tension between the individual right to asylum and the sovereign authority of individual nation-states to decide the terms of entry and membership within their territories. As Dauvergne (2008) notes, one of the most important ways countries express sovereignty is through migration laws and policies that determine who is permitted to enter and/or remain on their territory. For this reason, Mountz refers to the design and application of migration policies as "daily nation-building exercises" (2003, 626) because they shape who can become a member of a given country and set the terms of that membership. As Glanville and Arbel's chapter 4 explores in greater depth, bordering practices are central to processes of categorization through which people crossing – or attempting to cross – borders are labelled, which, in turn, influences how they are treated (see also Goldring and Landolt 2013; Hamlin 2021; Menjívar 2014). This power to control borders and determine the boundaries of membership is central to how countries stake and maintain their claims to sovereign territory (Arendt [1951] 2004; Nyers 2006; Walia 2021).

Of course, such claims exist in tension with ongoing and unsettled Indigenous claims to territories, which is especially relevant in the context of Canada, and raises questions about how borders are managed and who claims sovereignty (Bhatia 2013; Nguyen and Phu 2021; Simpson 2014; Walia 2021). Coburn's chapter 1 examines the imposition of borders over Indigenous people through colonization. It is important to understand that contestation and transgression are also part of how borders work. For example, borders imposed over communities are regularly refused by Indigenous and migration activists (Cisneros 2014; Fortier 2013; Simpson 2014).

These contestations are also relevant to understanding the negotiations involved in seeking asylum. Indeed, the framing of the UN Refugee Convention acknowledged that people may need to cross borders without authorization as they flee and seek refuge. Known as the non-penalization principle, art. 31.1 of the Convention asserts that states should not penalize refugees who "enter or are present in their territory without authorization, provided they present themselves without delay to the authorities and show good cause for their illegal entry or presence." This principle recognizes "that seeking asylum can require refugees to breach immigration rules" (Muiznieks 2016). For example, if you are fleeing persecution at the hands of your government, you are unlikely to report to authorities to secure the requisite travel documents (passports, visas, etc.) and may instead travel with false documents. You may feel compelled to employ the services of a human smuggler to get you out of that country and/or into another.

Despite the principle of non-penalization, the use of detention has become a widespread response to the arrival of asylum seekers on many countries' territories, as Silverman discusses in chapter 21. Detention is part of a suite of measures that states implement with the aim of deterring people from arriving on their territories and being able to make a claim for asylum. At the same time that nation-states have been investing in the security of their territories' borders, they are becoming increasingly creative in their border control efforts and have invested in a range of externalization policies and practices: border control measures applied outside their territorial boundaries that in effect prevent asylum seekers from arriving on official state territory. An example of this is the imposition of visa requirements, which means that people encounter the Canadian border in an embassy or consulate in Guatemala City, Beirut, or Nairobi and can be denied entry – by being denied a visa – without ever setting foot on Canadian territory. Several authors have referred to these practices as "remote control" of borders (FitzGerald 2020; Guild and Bigo 2010; Guiraudon 2003).

In this sense, borders increasingly rely on what Stockdale (2016) has referred to as the "politics of anticipatory governance." Part of how states govern is by anticipating unwanted outcomes and implementing policies to prevent them from happening – and vice versa. For migration policies, states put their borders on the move through space and time, including implementing policies and practices that aim to pre-empt and deter potential border crossings. Many of these policies are aimed at interdiction: preventing migration either before it begins or while it is in process. Borders have become mobile not only in their effects but also in their locations (Hyndman and Mountz 2007; Isin and Rygiel 2007; Menjívar 2014). Border control policies affect people who live elsewhere (e.g., by separating families). Increasingly, countries like Canada have also implemented their borders outside their national territories. Bordering takes place at a range of sites beyond the physical boundary line. See, for example,

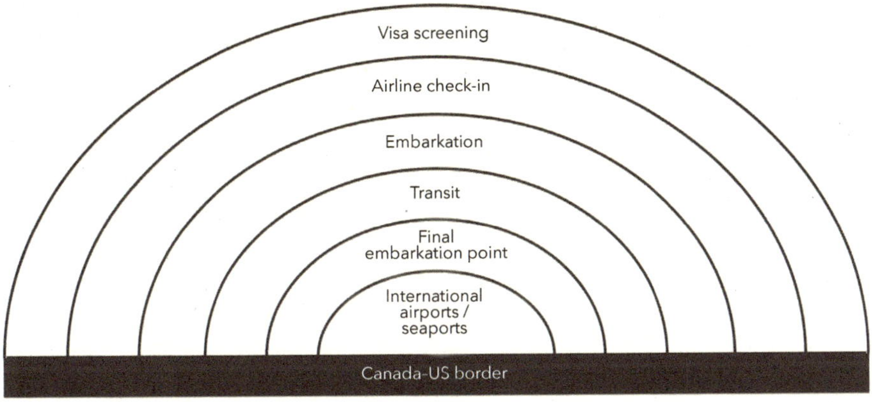

Figure 3.1 Canada's multiple borders strategy.

figure 3.1, which depicts the Canadian government's approach to border control. Referred to as the Multiple Borders Strategy, it reconceptualizes the border "not as a geo-political line but rather a continuum of checkpoints along a route of travel from the country of origin to Canada or the United States" (IRCC 2003).

When considering the impacts of externalization practices, Gibney characterizes the response of states in the Global North to refugee claimants as a "kind of 'organized hypocrisy'" (2004, 229) meaning that "great importance is attached to the principle of asylum but enormous efforts are made to ensure that refugees ... never reach the territory of the state where they could receive its protection" (2). Kernerman (2008, 230) refers to "the interdiction contradiction" because measures run counter to the principles underlying the UN Refugee Convention. While states have ratified this convention, they have implemented increasingly creative ways to prevent people from arriving on their territory so they do not have to honour their commitments to refugee protection.

Hyndman and Mountz (2007) have coined the term "neo-refoulement," referencing how externalization practices undermine another principle that underpins the UN Refugee Convention: non-refoulement. Article 33 affirms that states cannot "expel or return (*refouler*) a refugee in any manner whatsoever to the frontiers of territories where [their] life or freedom would be threatened." Moreover, the convention makes clear that the principle of non-refoulement is so fundamental that it is one of the articles on which states cannot place reservations (Goodwin-Gill 2008, 6). However, externalization practices that prevent people from arriving on a state's territory amount to indirect deportation because such policies and practices effectively expel asylum seekers before they can arrive on state territory (Hyndman and Mountz 2007).

SELECTIVITY AND CRISIS: BORDERING REFUGE IN CANADA

In light of these broader geopolitical and legal contexts, this section focuses on how the Canadian border has operated in response to forced migration. As noted in the introduction to this chapter, Canada is essentially "protected" by its geography from confronting large-scale movements of refugees and is therefore able to be highly selective about who can enter the country as a refugee. It is difficult and often costly to arrive on the physical territory of Canada to make a refugee claim. Indeed, the few boats carrying refugees that have managed to arrive on Canadian shores have seen an outsized and crisis-oriented response from officials and in media coverage, likely because of this concern with selectivity and control (Bradimore and Bauder 2012; Hier and Greenberg 2002; Mountz 2003, 2011). Despite this geographical reality, Canadian policies and practices actively contribute to the externalization of asylum – whether by preventing movement toward the country altogether (e.g., through the imposition of visa requirements) or by directing people back to the US to make their refugee claims if they do succeed in reaching the territorial boundary line (in the case of the STCA).

To understand the contemporary context, it is necessary to consider a key historical turning point for the bordering of refuge in Canada. The 1980s saw negotiations of the parameters of both the international refugee regime and Canada's place within it. A crucial aspect of the late 1980s context was the shift in the spaces of asylum, where asylum seekers began to arrive in significant numbers at the threshold of Canadian territory to make claims for refugee status. Although refugees were permitted to make claims at a Canadian port of entry, this provision was seldom used until the late 1980s. Until this period, most of Canada's efforts with refugees had involved a high degree of control and pre-selection from refugee camps and through embassies and consulates abroad. Indeed, Nolin notes that this was "the first time in which the Canada-USA border became a contested zone of refuge" (2006, 107). Although Canadian law provided for it, the practice of arriving at a land border port of entry and claiming asylum had been used infrequently.

Central American refugees comprised a significant contingent of the people arriving in Canada to claim refuge in the 1980s. Fleeing conflicts in their countries of origin, refugees from El Salvador and Guatemala sought safety in Mexico and the US. The refuge that was possible in the latter was constrained by the fact that US foreign, economic, and military policies played an outsized role in the conflicts that had led to large-scale displacement of people from rural Indigenous communities in the case of Guatemala and urban student and labour movements in the case of El Salvador (García 2006). While initially Canada was much more likely to accept refugee claims by people from these two countries of origin – a factor which influenced the emergence of the

Sanctuary Movement – a US policy shift in late 1986 influenced the scale and geography of refugee arrivals to Canada and altered the Canadian response (Young 2018).

> 3.3 The 1980s Sanctuary Movement
> https://www.youtube.com/watch?v=wMSKqyn7fG8
> Featuring: Dr Enrique Ochoa, professor of Latin American studies and history at Cal State Los Angeles
> Produced by: UCLA History-Geography Project, co-produced by UCLA Center
> Executive Producers: California History Project
> Filmed, directed, and edited by: GotChaDigi/Gary Clarke, https://gotchadigi.com
> Duration: 38:53

The 1986 US Immigration Reform and Control Act (IRCA) offered amnesty to those who had been in the US without legal status prior to 1982 but threatened to deport people who had entered after that year. Figures from the 1985 US Census estimated there were two hundred eighty thousand Salvadorans (eighty thousand with legal status) and two hundred fifty thousand Guatemalans (seventy thousand with legal status) living in the country at that time. Elbow noted these were "conservative estimates; independent sources place the numbers of Salvadoran nationals living in the United States at two to three times the official estimates" (1992, 58), while census estimates for Guatemalans were thought to be more accurate. More than half of the Salvadorans in the US at the time of IRCA did not qualify for amnesty as they had not arrived before 1982 (Menjívar 2000, 82). Making use of Canada's interpretation of refugee law and a network of advocates that facilitated the journey, refugees from El Salvador and Guatemala living precariously in the US made their way to the border to submit refugee claims.

In the weeks immediately following the implementation of IRCA in November 1986, increased numbers of Central Americans sought refuge at border crossings from the US into Canada. Crittenden writes: "Voting with their feet on [the] prospect [of being deported], more than 6,000 'bus people,' most of them Salvadorans, flocked to the Canadian border in the first weeks following the passage of the immigration bill" (1988, 348). Between December 1986 and February 1987, ten thousand refugees arrived in Canada, most of whom were from Central America (Lemco 1991). These arrivals were represented as an exceptional occurrence and constructed as a moment of crisis in which the integrity of the refugee determination system and control over Canada's borders were threatened (Young 2018).

In response, Canadian officials introduced a suite of measures: they imposed a visa requirement on nationals of El Salvador and Guatemala, removed both countries from the moratorium on deportations list, and instituted a direct-back policy to the US while individuals awaited their hearings in Canada (Canadian Press 1987). The provisions preventing deportations to El Salvador and Guatemala had been in effect since 1983 and 1984, respectively. At the same time, the B-1 list of countries that had been established in May 1986 was abolished; prior to this, citizens of listed countries who were arriving in Canada "could not be sent back to their native countries against their will" (Lemco 1991, 156). People arriving at the border from B-1 listed countries would no longer be automatically granted entry to the country on special minister's visas to await their refugee hearings. Instead, they would be directed back to the US until the date of their hearing.

On the surface, the direct-back policy was contradictory in that Canada temporarily refused entry to individuals whose cases it planned to examine; these people would later be admitted to Canada to attend their refugee hearings. This was not simply about the cost of assisting refugee claimants while they awaited their hearings – this action contributed to reframing the narrative of refugee claimants as suspect, while also making it much more challenging for people to seek safety in Canada. The irony is that Canadian officials acknowledged that Central Americans were likely to be recognized as refugees. In this sense, the shift in approach to refugees from these countries – who just weeks earlier Canada had recognized as "legitimate refugees" – made it easier to dismiss subsequent claimants arriving at Canada's borders as undeserving of protection (Young 2018).

There are three critical legacies of this period: (1) a new geography of asylum; (2) transnational advocacy work and collaboration; and (3) the introduction of the safe third country concept into Canadian legislation. The first impact was the emergence of a new geography of asylum in Canada. Refugees arriving at the border reconfigured and proclaimed Canada as a "country of first asylum" (Dirks 1995, 51), whereas Canadian officials had presumed that geography would protect the country from such a position or at least from refugees being able to arrive at the border to assert their legal right to claim asylum. As Nolin asserts, the arrival of Central Americans at the border in the late 1980s shifted the geography of refuge in Canada "from asylum control in the embassies and consulates abroad to asylum demand at the border" (2020, 106). Refugee claimants continue to comprise a considerable proportion of the people who enter the country via the humanitarian immigration stream each year. Unfortunately, the discourses of abuse of the system by "bogus" refugees that emerged continue to characterize those who seek asylum at the border in the contemporary context.

A second development from the 1980s context that persists is a strong refugee advocacy network. The US-based Sanctuary Movement emerged in the

1970s and strengthened across the 1980s into the 1990s (Crittenden 1988; Cunningham 1998; Ridgley 2011). This included a Canadian end of the movement that saw organizations form in border cities like Buffalo-Fort Erie, Plattsburgh-Lacolle, and Detroit-Windsor to support the work of the Sanctuary Movement as US policy decisions meant that people would not be recognized as refugees and would need to secure other routes to safety (Rosinbum 2015; Young 2018). Some of these organizations like Freedom House in Detroit and Vive la Casa in Buffalo persist. What was noteworthy about the advocacy networks that emerged in the 1980s is that they were transborder in orientation, seeing the boundary line as a resource to be mobilized to secure refuge and legal status (Young 2018). The transboundary nature of solidarity and advocacy work ebbed and flowed over subsequent decades but re-emerged around the crisis of irregular migration at Roxham Road from 2017 to 2020 and the border closures that were a crucial aspect of state responses to the global COVID-19 pandemic in 2020–21.

A final and critical legacy of this period was the introduction of the safe third country concept into Canadian legislation. In May 1987, a bill to amend the Immigration Act was introduced in Parliament. Titled Bill C-55 (the Refugee Reform Bill), it established the Immigration and Refugee Board (IRB), the independent tribunal that adjudicates inland refugee claims to this day (see Fynn Bruey and Fantauzzi, chapter 8; Atak, chapter 17; Araya, chapter 9). The bill was passed in June 1988 and came into effect in January 1989. Bill C-55 also included a provision that made people who had arrived in Canada via a "prescribed safe third country" ineligible to make a refugee claim. When the legislation was implemented in 1989, its regulations did not list any "safe countries," which rendered the provision inoperable. This was most likely due to the US conundrum in relation to this provision: that is, there would be repercussions whether or not the US was listed as a safe country for refugees (Dirks 1995). Nevertheless, this policy discussion opened a debate that would lead to the decision fifteen years later to implement the STCA that came into effect in December 2004.

THE CANADA–UNITED STATES SAFE THIRD COUNTRY AGREEMENT AND "DISCURSIVE DISAPPEARANCE OF THE REFUGEE" (MACKLIN 2005)

Despite the publicity connected to the 1987 Central American crisis at Canada's border with the US, borders are often enforced in mundane, routine, and invisible ways. This is not incidental but rather strategic and deliberate. Carens argues the invisibility of interdiction practices helps avoid discussion of the contradiction between principle and practice around asylum: such measures can be "presented as a neutral and normal operation of government" (1997, 33). In other words, the perceived ease of acquiring travel visas and identity documents hides the active ways in which these practices of states in the Global North produce mobilities and identities as either authorized or unauthorized. To Carens, "[u]nlike open interdiction, the force that lies behind a refusal to grant someone a document or to permit someone to board an airplane is so much a part of everyday life that it is largely invisible and difficult to communicate effectively" (1997, 33). States establish borders in other places, away from the physical boundary line, because they are less visible; these routine practices of border control remove people – and the reality of their exclusion – from sight.

Macklin argues that "refugees are vanishing from the territory of wealthy industrialized nations ... [referring] not to the legal and material reality of refugees, but rather to the erosion of the idea that people who seek asylum may actually be refugees" (2005, 365). Macklin terms this "the discursive disappearance of the refugee" (365) and underscores that policies and practices of Global North states contribute to this process. Bureaucratic requirements that control access to state territory function by drawing a distinction between the idealized refugee contained in a refugee camp overseas and the asylum seeker at the border who is seen as undeserving of refuge: "The deserving refugee is always already 'over there.' If [they] managed to get here [they] must, by definition, be an illegal. And like magic, the refugee is disappeared ... displaced by the pariah illegal" (369). This equation drawn between refugee claimants arriving at the border and assumptions of illegality reinforces laws and practices that limit access to asylum (see also Labman and Liew 2019).

In the Canadian context, one such policy is the 2004 STCA. As noted earlier in the chapter, the STCA requires individuals to make their claim in the first "safe country" in which they arrive – in this case, the agreement designates the US as a safe country for refugees. By signing onto the agreement, Canada outsourced part of its refugee determination process to US officials and became reliant on the US interpretation of the UN Refugee Convention definition. Importantly, there are several ways in which Canadian and US applications of the refugee definition differ. For example, individuals making claims of persecution based on gender identity or sexual orientation are much more likely to be accepted through the Canadian system (CCR 2005; Hyndman and Mountz 2007; Macklin 2003; see also Aberman, chapter 12). Moreover, since 1996, the US has followed a policy of expedited removal of individuals who arrive on its territory with inadequate documentation and/or who are suspected of fraud or misrepresentation. Although refugee claimants are supposed to be exempt from this procedure due to the principle of non-penalization examined earlier, this is not consistently followed, and asylum seekers can be removed before having their claim considered (Harvard Law School 2006; Macklin 2003). In 2003 the US implemented a policy of mandatory detention for individuals from designated countries; asylum seekers from such countries would be detained for the duration of their determination process, which could take months or years (CCR 2005; Harvard Law School 2006; Macklin 2003).

It is important to note that the STCA does not apply universally; there are several exceptions, including people who would be required to have a visa to enter the US but not Canada, people who have a family member in Canada, and unaccompanied or separated minors (Clark-Kazak, chapter 13 for more on the impacts of these last two exceptions). Another critical aspect to understand about the STCA is its unusual geography: for the first two decades it was in place, the policy only applied to people making a claim at an official land border crossing or arriving by train (IRCC 2020a). Refugee advocates highlighted this as an issue prior to the passage of the STCA into law, arguing that it would push refugee claimants into the hands of human smugglers who might help them find other routes and modes of crossing the border (Macklin 2003; Matas 2003). A report released on the tenth anniversary of the entry into force of the STCA confirmed this trend (Arbel and Brenner 2013). The policy encouraged people to pursue unofficial entries to the country at more remote and potentially dangerous crossings. While data show that interceptions at unofficial sectors increased after the implementation of the agreement, it was policy changes introduced soon after the inauguration of President Donald Trump in the US that led to a new period of crisis at the Canada-US border, turning Roxham Road, a quiet street in rural Quebec/New York, into a busy but unofficial entry point, as reported in the resource linked in box 3.4.

3.4 Asylum Seekers Return to Northern Border
Mountain Lake Journal. PBS. 14 January 2022. https://www.youtube.com/watch?v=9Xh-s8pXLUg.

CONCLUSION

The space created around the Canada-US border by the STCA is important. Roxham Road was simultaneously a formalized but unofficial entry point to Canada, which politicians, policy-makers, and media referred to as a "loophole" in the law around the border (Mercier and Rehaag 2021). In fact, it was a space where the state was highly present in the way it structured and policed movement, entry, and rejection, but it was also a space where the state was "strategically absent" in terms of human rights obligations and refugee protection concerns (E. Gilbert 2019; Hyndman and Mountz 2007). Hyndman and Mountz argue that through externalization practices states are "rewriting the geography of their relationships with potential refugees in daily practice and underscoring these geographical moves with legal weight" (2007, 86). States restrict access to asylum by producing and maintaining "zones of uncertainty and legal ambiguity" (Gill 2010, 636–7). Indeed, Gill argues that the "deployment of stealth, confusion, change, mismanagement and legal/jurisdictional ambiguity all facilitate these strategies" (639). In the case of the STCA, the policy uses geography to deter, pre-empt, and redirect the arrival of asylum seekers – "exploit[ing] Canada's geography to lessen the perceived burden of receiving refugees" (Hyndman and Mountz 2007, 82), while also making the border less safe for those seeking protection and security.

The STCA not only redefined the Canada-US border for the purposes of refuge, but it also redefined the concept of "safety" in this context. Canada's official declaration of the US as a "safe country" changed the politics and logistics of asylum by foreclosing options for refugees. The existence and force of the agreement limit the ability of advocates to contest its terms because it has harmonized refugee policy at the boundary line. This redefinition of space has an impact on the relationships that are possible around the border and the advocacy work that can happen. Moreover, it has affected the representation and reception of refugee claimants arriving at the Canadian border via the US as irregular, illegal, and/or threatening (Labman and Liew 2019; Watson 2007).

In early 2020, another crisis emerged to reframe bordering practices globally: the response to the declaration of the COVID-19 pandemic was the closure of most borders to all but "essential" movement. Crucially, refugee protection was not considered essential (Chaulagain, Nasser, and Young 2022; Macklin 2020b; Mercier and Rehaag 2020). The land border between Canada and the US remained closed to asylum seekers from March 2020 through November 2021. During this period, people arriving at official and unofficial crossings to make refugee claims were directed back to the US without assurance that they would not be deported in the interim (Chaulagain, Nasser, and Young 2022). Advocates wondered whether the pandemic border closures were a dress rehearsal for further restriction of access to asylum. In March 2023, during an official visit by US president Joe Biden to Canada, the two countries announced an additional protocol to the STCA that expanded its application to the entire border, rather than limiting it to official ports of entry. This despite the fact that the STCA was facing a legal challenge before the Supreme Court of Canada (SSC) that questioned its constitutionality (Bellavance 2022). In June 2023, the court issued a ruling that left the STCA in place while acknowledging that the US may not be a safe country for all people seeking asylum and sending the case back to the federal court to examine concerns related to gender-based persecution (Amnesty International Canada 2023). Advocates working on both sides of the border continue to insist on the need to abolish the STCA in order to protect people seeking protection. Unauthorized pathways and smuggling operations that have become even more viable as a consequence of the STCA's implementation in 2004 continue to present opportunities to people seeking safety and security for themselves and their families, despite Canada's attempts to prevent their movements toward and across the border.

FURTHER READING AND RESOURCES

Akwesasne TV, dir. 2020. "Akwesasne History Project: Border Crossing." YouTube video, 5:33. https://www.youtube.com/watch?v=4_aDqHCYwxc.

Arbel, Efrat. 2014. "The Shifting Landscape of the Canadian Border and the Politics of Refugee Exclusion." *Border Criminologies*, 27 January 2014. https://blogs.law.ox.ac.uk/research-subject-groups/centre-criminology/centre-border-criminologies/blog/2014/01/shifting.

CBC Radio. 2018. "The Border Next Door." *The Doc Project*. https://www.cbc.ca/radio/docproject/the-border-next-door-1.4595074.

Ellis, Claire, Idil Atak, and Zainab Abu Elrob. 2021. "Expanding Canada's Borders." *Forced Migration Review* 68 (November). https://www.fmreview.org/externalisation/ellis-atak-abualrob.

Remembering Refuge: Between Sanctuary and Solidarity. https://www.rememberingrefuge.com.

4

Labels, Discourse, and Meaning-Making

Erin Goheen Glanville and Efrat Arbel

KEY TAKEAWAYS

- Forced migration categories that determine the legal significance of one's situation in purportedly universal ways are shaped by history, politics, and culture, and their meaning is defined by their contextual applications.
- Forced migration categories often function as labels, accruing extralegal meaning that relates to peoples' identities.
- Foregrounding lived experience is a way to understand the cultural production of labels.
- Labels determine how a person is treated under Canadian law.
- Labels are shaped not just by law but also discourse. The label "refugee" is an example of how categories can acquire diverse but related meanings culturally, legally, and personally.
- Canada's Designated Foreign National regime provides a case study in refugee label making, demonstrating the legal, cultural, and discursive operation of the "refugee" label.

KEY TERMS

- Cultural figure of the refugee
- Cultural production
- Discourse
- Displacement
- Label

INTRODUCTION

"Forced Migration" is a broad term, which includes a wide variety of migratory circumstances, legal categories, and disciplinary approaches. Under this umbrella we find terms such as "internally displaced person" (IDP), "Convention refugee," "asylum seeker," "environmental migrant," "irregular migrant," and "trafficked person," each of which signifies differently across different legal and national contexts. What these terms hold in common is that they reference human movement initiated by circumstances that are, in one way or another, outside a person's control. While there is often a degree of human agency involved, this kind of migration is a choice that has been forced in some sense.

Legal definitions – and the legal documents, regimes, and policies by which they are enacted – have understandably dominated academic conversations about the meaning of labels such as refugee, asylum seeker, or migrant. Consider the habitual use of the United Nations High Commissioner for Refugees (UNHCR) definition of a "Convention refugee" at the start of many studies and reports. In this simple way, researchers contribute to the broader process whereby legal definitions are embedded in discourse – and sometimes determine discourse. What is less often explored is how these legal definitions are constructed, enacted, revised, and interpreted via obliquely defined cultural narratives and histories. In other words, beyond the enforced clarity of definitions and status, what and how do labels mean?

The authors of this chapter see labels as embedded in discourse – or a shared set of normatively determined terms – and so we employ both "labels" and "discourse" to unpack how communities make meaning from legal frameworks and policies. This chapter engages in dynamic process of meaning-making. First, we critically examine the process by which labels derive meaning. Second, we reflect on the broader process of labelling and meaning-making through a case study focused on Canada's Designated Foreign National regime. Co-writing as researchers in culture and law, respectively, we bring together the pragmatics of legal necessities and the complexities of lived culture. As such, our goal is not to collapse the tensions that arise in the interplay of law and culture but rather, we view the codependencies of refugee law, Canadian settler cultures, and refugee cultures as a mix of limitations and possibilities. In the back and forth of these systemic and human relationships, the meaning of migration labels is negotiated, defined, and redefined. With a particular focus on the legal category of the "refugee," this chapter explores that process and what we can learn from it. Throughout the chapter, numbered boxes contain storied or poetic excerpts related to the theme of a section. Rather than advancing our argument, they are meant to sidestep away from argument toward experience in order to expand our themes in a different epistemological plane. For instance, box 4.1 opens up the theme of categories in relation to Vinh Nguyen's experience of refugee stigma.

> 4.1 I was once a refugee, although no one would mistake me for being a refugee now. Because of this, I insist on being called a refugee, since the temptation to pretend that I am not a refugee is strong. It would be so much easier to call myself an immigrant, to pass myself off as belonging to a category of migratory humanity that is less controversial, less demanding, and less threatening than the refugee. I was born a citizen and a human being. At four years of age I became something less than human, at least in the eyes of those who do not think of refugees as human.
> (Nguyen et al. 2018, 11)

Another umbrella term that researchers use is "displacement," or in certain contexts, "forced displacement." Displacement is a helpful concept to describe those who "have been unwillingly uprooted" because they "have been seen as standing 'in the way of development'" (Coleman 2012, xiv). Among the values researchers see in using the term displacement is that it can bring forced migration studies into conversation with Indigenous studies by focusing on broader displacement phenomena like colonization and gentrification – challenges to sovereignty and xenophobia. This can open up questions about how resource extraction and land ownership factor into our study of both local and global movement (see Coburn, chapter 1).

In Roger Zetter's seminal 1991 article, "Labelling Refugees: Forming and Reforming a Bureaucratic Identity," he analyzes the concept of labels as a way of exploring refugee identities. His analysis is situated at the intersection of lived realities and the legal and institutional policies and practices that manage and define those realities. Zetter argues that humanitarian management is a well-meaning but disempowering mismatch with the lived realities of those impacted by such policies. The term "label," Zetter argues, is conceptually useful in contrast to a word like "definition" because it is capacious enough to encompass an individual's process of identity formation – both the claiming of a label and the revision of a label's meaning – in relationship with the realities of legal categorization. As Zetter writes in a follow-up article, the refugee label has "tangible and real world meaning, but is also metaphorical and symbolic" and can result in the "fractioning" of refugee identity in a more complex global refugee regime (2007, 173).

B.S. Chimni similarly engages with the concept of labels, arguing that "legal categories are not merely devices for inclusion but also of exclusion" (2008, 12). Chimni's aim is to defend the interdisciplinary field of forced migration and demonstrate the importance of expanding the understanding of refugee realities beyond the law and legal studies. Heaven Crawley and Dimitris Skleparis comparably seek to expand the understanding of refugee realities, arguing that dominant existing categories "do not simply exist but rather are made.

Choosing to label – or equally not label – someone as a 'refugee' is a powerful, and deeply political, process, as lawyers, advocates and academics push at the boundaries of international law (Gauci, Giuffre, and Tsourdi 2015)" (2018, 51). One alternative possibility is attunement to refugee voices already present within "powerful discursive fields" such as asylum courts (Sigona 2014). In Georgia Cole's work, the capacity of language itself (i.e., semiotics) integrates law and culture: words can both create shared understanding and remain polyvalent (2018). Cole conceptualizes "the word 'refugee' as just that: as a word that at times functions as a label" (18).

Labels are sticky. They can outlast their legal significance, whether because of a person's choice to hold onto and redefine any given label or because of some external social or cultural pressure. For example, when people migrate to Canada through refugee resettlement programs, they arrive as permanent residents, having already received refugee status overseas and having been offered permanent residence in Canada. Still, their landing is celebrated in news media and in support communities as the "arrival of refugees." People often wear labels long after the legal category to which the label relates has become irrelevant, and even beyond the period within which the label is empowering to the individual or community. People who are displaced may claim or reject labels for a variety of reasons, be it legal purchase, rehabilitating the term's popular use, or rejecting it for legal accuracy or due to stigma.

THE ROLE OF CULTURE IN MEANING-MAKING

A cultural studies approach to forced migration research – that is, studying cultural artifacts (policy documents, movies, advertisements, etc.) in context – is one place where labels and the process of meaning-making have been deeply explored. Our use of illustrative texts in boxes throughout this chapter exemplifies a cultural approach. This kind of research helps us understand how publics make meaning out of labels and how that meaning-making relates to popular discourses and legal categories. For example, research on news media about refugees has established the popularity of metaphors about rising pressure, water, and natural disasters (such as waves or floods) to describe human migration (Abid, Manan, and Rahman 2017). This raises a myriad of questions around meaning-making. What is the impact of repeated natural disaster metaphors in news media on popular perceptions of refugees? Does this popular symbol resemble the international definition in any way? What else does the popular symbol influence, and how does it impact the lives of displaced people? How do refugees and refugee communities appropriate and revise these symbols in their own work? A cultural approach examines the role of culture production both in popularizing labels (e.g., "illegal migrant") and in determining the meaning and applications of these labels under different legal regimes.

> 4.2 We representing peeps, they don't play us on the FM
> We talkin' in our sleep, they still listen on a system
> We sittin' on a stoop
> Where we get a scoop
> This is how we keep it cool
> This is how we do
> (M.I.A., Lennox, Patel 2015)

The term "cultural production" comes from French sociologist Pierre Bourdieu (1993). It encompasses the processes of generation, circulation, and reception of all cultural artifacts, but especially in the cultural industries. In cultural studies, cultural production includes all the forms of communication (not only textual or involving language) that we encounter in our daily lives: online communications, newspapers, policy briefs, advertising, fiction, music, games, political speeches, et cetera. In these cultural artifacts, we find patterns – repeated symbols, practices, genres, objects – that shape a particular understanding of forced migration labels. By studying these patterns within the contexts of their production, circulation, and reception, researchers can understand who and what dominate the meaning-making process, what labels mean, and how the labels are leveraged in popular culture.

> 4.3 My mom gave birth to me in a refugee camp because she wanted me ... I wanted to be a writer even though I grew up in a home without books ... One of the lovely things about fiction is that it can get to the truth a lot clearer than the truth itself ... In fiction ... [you] have the freedom to create, to not need someone else to lean on to make your narrative, to tell your truth. So I really love that quality of fiction ... to have that agency ... I do see a lot in the news and in literature ... that whenever we encounter narratives of refugees, they tend to be incredibly sad and tragic. And that's very true; that's very real. But also, in my experience of my own family life, we're also incredibly hilarious and fun and ferocious and ungrateful ... And when I was writing my own stories I wanted to bring out these other aspects of refugee life. (Thammavongsa 2020)

DISCOURSE

In the mid-1990s Liisa Malkki's research on the refugee as an object of knowledge in anthropology articulated the "discursive fields" used to produce knowledge about the refugee label (1995). Malkki's early survey included international relations, the international refugee regime, development, refugee studies, and literary conversations about exile. As globalization increases the complexity of migration so too have refugee discourses become intertwined with other cultural issues, such as terrorism, xenophobia, racism, and national identity. More recently researchers have explored the discourses of emergency (Nyers 2006), pathology (Pupavac 2008), multiculturalism (Nguyen 2013), humanitarianism (Madokoro 2016), victimization (Kim 2022), and securitization (Dauvergne 2008). And each label under the forced migration studies umbrella engenders its own set of relevant discourses.

Discourse does not mean simply communication or language. To speak about a particular discourse is to reference a set of related terms that are associated with a specific domain of intellectual or social activity. These terms produce a set of themes, concepts, and values that indicate the normative direction of that domain of knowledge. For instance, we might group the terms "human," "help," "empathy," "apolitical," "impartiality," "suffering," and "aid" as part of humanitarian discourse. This discourse emerges from the domain of humanitarian institutions and activity, but it also sets a normative direction for that activity. To test this, consider adding the term "resistance" or "agency" to that list. Does it fit? If so, what does it mean, now that it is in relation to those other terms?

In the present age of global mass migration and mass media, the discourses within which migration terms are embedded can go unnoticed – that is, they can be assumed to be neutral descriptive language. Consider our previous example of the discourse of humanitarian emergency, which is so commonly used in refugee discourse that it has become almost synonymous with the cultural understanding of refugee protection. Yet to speak about refugee displacement as an emergency is to predetermine the range of actions as well as the kinds of actors that can be imagined in response to that displacement. The language of humanitarian emergency or crisis calls for urgent, sympathetic action. An emergency does not call for slowing down to reflect on how our systems are creating the emergencies. Cast as an emergency, displacement does not call for revising definitions to more accurately reflect peoples' complex realities. This, in turn, operates as one of the roadblocks to providing material solutions for the problem: the discourse within which a term is embedded produces extralegal meaning that shapes public conversations about refugee cultures in predictive ways.

4.4 Ever since I was forced to leave Syria five years ago, I have been sharing my personal story in the hope of raising awareness about the human rights violations in my home country. My experience of storytelling has been both positive and disappointing ...

Last year, I was approached by a prominent TV news network to discuss US airstrikes in Syria. I saw the invitation as an opportunity to share my academic perspective as the topic was closely related to what I was researching as part of my doctoral degree at the time. The interview proceeded with personal questions focused on my life in Syria. As I was not being asked about the airstrikes, I requested to share my view and they agreed.

A few days later, the reporter emailed with me the news clip of their coverage of the strikes. The clip started with a brief summary of what happened. I was then featured for a few seconds, half in tears and conspicuously traumatised while mentioning the loss of my brother and father. The clip then continued with a white Australian observer who gave his "objective" and scholarly analysis of the situation. While the journalist apologised for the "heavy editing," this humiliating experience taught me that despite my background as a citizen journalist and an academic, for some I will forever be a traumatised Syrian refugee whose primary role is to evoke sympathy and tears. (Tammas 2019)

LIVED EXPERIENCES

The relationships among law, politics, and culture are complex. In the interdisciplinary field of forced migration studies, to study "culture" in the tradition of cultural studies is to examine the ordinary and "everyday life that people engage in" and "the complex ways their activities and practices shape a public culture" (Coleman 2012). The focus on that which is "ordinary" is also key for a field in which subjects (i.e., refugees) have been narrated as extraordinary survivors (Nguyen and Phu 2021).

A cultural studies approach to forced migration aims to unpack everyday – or ordinary – cultures, and does so largely by foregrounding the cultural production emerging from communities and individuals with lived experience of forced migration. Knowledge that is offered through personal memoirs, community memorial events, political actions, and storytelling produces an essential layer to ubiquitous legal discourse. Cultural production can "story" labels with a proliferation of meaning. Researchers across the disciplines value cultural production pedagogically because it provides a culturally and experientially grounded narration of global realities that can help critics see dead angles and structural exclusions more clearly. Galvanizing critics to consider not only what is but also what could be imaginative cultural production produced by displaced communities shapes our imaginations about global futures and forced migration. A cultural studies research approach prioritizes the insights of ordinary lived expertise, from people whose experiences at times challenge and at times rely on the rigidity of traditional labels. You will find examples of lived experiences throughout this chapter and this book.

4.5 "And Amin?" he says.
Jeremy Windhook hesitates. Then: "Amin was refused."
"Refused?"
"They've classified him an economic refugee."
"No entiendo." Joaquin thinks: Are you less a refugee, Jeremy Windhook, if you are in danger of dying from hunger rather than a bullet?
"He doesn't qualify under the UN definition. He'll be deported tomorrow."
"To his country?"
"To Germany."
"Germany? Why Germany?"
"Because he made his way here from there."
"But if they say he is in no danger in his own country, why do they not send him back there?"
"Because –" He shakes his head. "Because it's the rule." (Bisoondath 1991, 25)

In an age of mass migration and mass media, as the means of cultural production proliferate and as cultures split, hyphenate, fuse, and renew, so do the processes of meaning-making multiply and increase in complexity. If meaning-making around forced migration cultures becomes rigid or enforced, as it often does in polarized public discourse, migrants are at risk of being disempowered from acting and speaking in ways that might challenge the predominant meanings. Daniel and Knudsen (1995) argue that nurturing trust is essential for "the survival of the cultural process" and ultimately for a sense of meaningfulness. Articulated prescriptively, "The refugee needs to be a full participant in the formulation and reformulation of culture" (Daniel and Knudsen 1995, 4–5). In line with this, researchers are increasingly prioritizing the participation of refugees in making meaning out of the "data" that is their lives. Community engagement or participatory art-based methodologies have been two common ways of experimenting with research that values shared meaning-making processes, autoethnography is another. Collaborative or participatory research acknowledges refugee communities as knowledge holders and co-producers of knowledge. But this kind of work requires a genuine and persistent development of trusting relationships.

4.6 I think the first step that we need to take, and the main step that we need to take, is passing the mic. I don't think the conversations that are happening at the moment ... are happening between people who have

> the actual experience of being refugees. Those are conversations that are happening with people who are sitting in their offices, who never had that experience of being refugees before … I think that the best way to deal [with] refugees is to actually ask them. Just sit down with them and ask them, as you're doing right now, I guess … And give them a space to actually make decisions, not just to give feedback. You know what I mean? Put them in a place where they're not just saying what they want and then waiting for years and years until that thing happens. But instead, put them in charge of actually making this thing happen. (Ahmed Danny Ramadan cited in Glanville 2018, n.p.)

THE REFUGEE LABEL

In legal terms, a refugee is someone who satisfies art. 1(A)(2) of the 1951 Refugee Convention, which defines a refugee as: "a person who owing to well-founded fear of being persecuted for reasons of race, religion, nationality, membership of a particular social group or political opinion, is outside the country of his nationality and is unable or, owing to such fear, is unwilling to avail himself of the protection of that country; or who, not having a nationality and being outside the country of his former habitual residence as a result of such events, is unable or, owing to such fear, is unwilling to return to it." Other regional definitions exist, but the UN Convention guides the determination of refugee status under Canadian law and is incorporated almost verbatim into section 96 of the Immigration and Refugee Protection Act (IRPA) RSC 2001, c. 27.

Outside these legal documents, the label refugee has been embedded in popular discourses and is associated with various cultural symbols. In her teaching, Erin Goheen Glanville describes the refugee label as containing at least three layers:

1. *Refugee as a legal category.* This is the layer most relevant to the determination of refugee status under Canadian law. When a person arrives in Canada to seek refuge, they must appear before the Immigration and Refugee Board (IRB) – an adjudicative body tasked, in part, with the determination of refugee status – and demonstrate that they satisfy the terms of the definition (see Atak, chapter 17). Researchers who study "refugee" as a legal category might ask how decision-makers interpret the refugee definition. What kinds of experiences and subject positions does the legal definition embrace, and what does it ignore or exclude?
2. *Refugee as a human person* who experiences displacement and then claims this label for a time and for specific reasons. In other words, refugee refers to a person, which may seem obvious but is not always acknowledged.

A refugee is a person who has had this label superimposed onto their lives, migration paths, and often family or community. It may be forcibly imposed, it may be chosen, but it is an identity layer, removed from the actual person who is a brother, a mother, an engineer, a runner, et cetera. Those who study this layer might ask, what is the human experience of forced migration?

3 *Refugee as a cultural figure.* The cultural figure refers to the gathered popular significance of the label that exceeds or goes beyond the legal category (Espiritu 2006). Citizens can share a "social imaginary" of what it means to be a refugee (C. Taylor 2004) that fits as an exception to the "imagined national community" (B. Anderson 2016). When we begin to imagine communities or collectives, telling stories about ourselves and our origins, the question of who belongs where (and who might not) is quick to follow. So how we imagine and speak about our nations, our cities, our neighbourhoods has a formative role to play in determining who belongs on the inside, who belongs on the outside, and who is the exception to that rule and why. By studying patterns in cultural production, researchers unpack the extralegal meaning that has accrued to this label.

Several terms have been coined to describe different aspects of the cultural figure of the refugee. "Refugeeness" is Peter Nyers's term to describe "the various qualities and characteristics that are regularly associated with and assigned to refugee identity" (2006, xv). It refers to the "politics of being a refugee [which] has as much to do with the cultural expectation of certain qualities and behaviors that are demonstrative of 'authentic' refugeeness (e.g., silence, passivity, victimhood) as it does with legal definitions and regulations" (xv; see also Arbel 2013). Nyers's articulation of refugeeness traces silence and fear as central identity markers.

Vinh Nguyen's term "refugeetude" offers an apt point of reflection for this chapter (2019, 110–11). In using the suffix "-tude" Nguyen aims to initiate a "critical reorientation" for the contemporary use of the refugee label that aligns more closely with the psychic experience of displacement" (110). In this reorientation, the "negative experiences" so often associated with refugee lives are not a problem but are rather characterized by "enduring creative force" (110). Refugeetude is "a means by which refugee subjects – people who have been touched by the processes of violent displacement and border control – come to understand, articulate, and resist their conditions" (111). The term constitutes a challenge to "conventional understandings that confine refugee to a legal definition, short time frame, and pitiful existence" (111). Conceived in this way, refugee lives can be more readily seen not through the legal category but rather as "an experiential resource for developing significant and durable ways of being in and moving through the world" (111).

4.7 "We're talking about people who were living their own lives, building their own hopes and dreams, having their own culture ... then being forced out from their own countries by multiple causes that are outside their ability to control ... Then they ended up on the other side of the world ... reborn in a new country that is completely different than anything they've experienced. And then they were resilient to all that and they made something out of themselves. And that's beautiful ... That's a person I would like to learn from." (Danny Ramadan cited in Glanville 2020, n.p.)

In thinking through the application of these various approaches – and to invite reflection on the legal, cultural, and discursive operation of the refugee as label – consider a case study in refugee label making, focused on Canada's Designated Foreign National (DFN) regime. The DFN regime empowers the minister of public safety to label groups of migrants who cross the border together as "irregular" based on vague and discretionary criteria set out in IRPA, s. 20.1(1)) (Public Safety Canada 2012b). The label irregular is applied to the group but determines the legal status of the individuals within that group. Once they are so labelled, the regime requires that Canada automatically detain and arrest designated persons according to IRPA, ss. 55(3.1) and 57.1. The regime requires that all designated persons be detained for a minimum period of two weeks but empowers the minister to extend detention orders by six-month increments in accordance with IRPA, s. 57.1(2). Since Canadian law does not impose clear time limits on detention orders, designated persons may in theory be detained indefinitely according to IRPA, s. 56(2) (see also Silverman, chapter 21). While the regime applies broadly to all migrants, since its implementation in 2012, the Canadian government has directed its application only toward eighty-five refugees (CBSA 2014; T. Cohen 2012).

The regime is enacted through immigration law, not criminal law, yet it does not require proof that a designated person engaged in any criminal wrongdoing. In this way, in "both legal approaches and public imagination" (Dauvergne 2004, 601), the regime depicts designated persons as dangerous subjects to be feared and contained (Arbel 2015). Analyzing the DFN regime at the intersection of law and cultural studies directs attention to the myriad of ways in which it is embedded in cultural representations of danger and crime control. When the DFN regime was first introduced in 2012, for example, what was then Citizenship and Immigration Canada explained on its website that the regime is targeted at "possible human smugglers and traffickers, terrorists, or individuals who have committed crimes against humanity," without mentioning its application to refugee claimants (CIC 2012, n.p.). Blurring lines between labels like "smuggler," "smuggled," "trafficker," and "terrorist," the website cast designated persons as criminal wrongdoers determined to "abuse our generosity and take advantage of our country" (CIC 2012, n.p.). Deploying the rhetoric of threat and risk, the website further explained that releasing designated persons into Canadian communities would pose an "unacceptable risk" to the public (CIC 2012).

On the day in which the first designation was made, several news sources issued stories bearing the headline "Hunt is on for Romanians Believed to be Part of Human Smuggling Ring" (Levitz 2012). The language of catch and capture here becomes material to our understanding of how patterns of cultural productions emerge. The extralegal meaning that accrues to the DFN label constitutes designated persons as dangerous. By raising the spectre of threat, such depictions engender popular hostility toward designated persons and, by deliberate association, toward refugees.

This analysis of the DFN regime reveals the broader discursive effects of its operation. Here we observe how labels can prove sticky, and we reflect on the coercive effects of deploying "irregularity" as a label in Canadian law. This labelling process is not only enabled by but also creates discourse. Underpinning it is a fundamental discursive – and in some contexts, material – violence whereby certain individuals are deemed transgressors, and whereby the "refugee" label is associated with crime, risk, and threat. Notwithstanding that some individuals who were designated under this law did indeed prove their compliance with the refugee definition and were granted refugee status, by application of the irregular label, all eighty-five individuals were cast as lawbreakers whose arrival, in the words of government, threatened the "security and safety of Canadians" (Public Safety Canada 2012b). They were labelled by Canadian law and discourse not as refugees but as dangerous subjects to be captured and contained. Such depictions entrench the line between "us" and "them" – and associated discourses of outsiders, insiders, and belonging – into cultural knowledge and maintain that line in ways that drive the normative direction of discourse.

4.8 I am a refugee and
I am a prisoner in your country,
I am a student,
I am political,
I am opposed to any military dictatorship,
I am the grandfather of two girls,
I am the father of four children - one girl and three boys,
I am a Muslim,
I am very happy with my teacher,
I am friendly, honest, and serious.
(Mohamed Ali Aissaoui cited in Nyers 2006, 63)

CONCLUSIONS AND WAYS FORWARD

To analyze the DFN regime from the perspective of law directs attention toward the coercive legal ramifications of deeming a person as irregular. A legal analysis, for example, reveals the fundamental material harm caused by subjecting a person to mandatory arrest and detention without any due process (see also Silverman, chapter 21). To analyze the DFN regime from the perspective of culture also underscores the tensions that arise in the interplay between law and culture – to the violence caused by the uncritical imposition of labels on human bodies. From the perspective of culture, we may focus on the lived experience of being deemed irregular – the material harms of being designated as such and the possibilities for reclamation of the label.

To analyze the DFN regime through a methodology that recognizes the codependencies of refugee law and Canadian settler cultures illuminates the broader political implications caused by the Canadian state's decision to deprive people of liberty because of how they crossed a border and invites critical reflection on the violence of colonialism and the artifice of a singular authoritative Canadian sovereignty. In the interplay of these analyses, we witness the label "irregular" shift in meaning. Scrutinizing the broader process by which such meanings are formed further illuminates not only the normative direction set by this process but also sets a normative direction for that activity. In moving forward, this approach compels us to think carefully and critically about how that process may be reconstituted, how labels may be reconstrued to lessen harm and minimize violence, and how these subtle but important shifts in method, process, and thought can work to usher in change, thus unsticking what too often remains stuck.

NOTE

We are deeply grateful to Atreyi Bhattacharjee for her invaluable research and editorial assistance.

FURTHER READING AND RESOURCES

Bhatia, Amar. 2013. "We Are All Here to Stay? Indigeneity, Migration, and 'Decolonizing' the Treaty Right to be Here." *Windsor Journal of Access to Justice* 13 (2): 39–64.

Coombes, Thomas. 2022. "How Talking about 'Humanity' and not 'Crisis' Can Aid all Refugees Right Now." *New Humanitarian*, 29 March 2022. https://www.thenewhumanitarian.org/opinion/2022/03/29/humanity-not-crisis-aid-refugees#.

Covering Migration. n.d. "5.3 Terminology Matters: From 'Economic Migrants' to Refugees." https://coveringmigration.com/learning_pages/terminology-matters-from-economic-migrants-to-refugees/#.

Hamlin, Rebecca. 2022. "'Migrants'? 'Refugees'? Terminology is Contested, Powerful, and Evolving." *Migration Policy Institute*, 24 March 2022.

5

Theorizing Forced Migration and the Purpose of International Protection

Kiran Banerjee

KEY TAKEAWAYS

- Theoretical reflection and normative analysis are crucial complements to explanatory and policy-oriented approaches to forced migration.
- Refugee protection can be framed in "political" terms by focusing specifically on the political nature of state-based persecution and the subsequent provision of asylum.
- The "human rights" perspective understands the duty to provide international protection to forced migrants as premised on the failure of effective domestic protection of basic rights in the state of origin.
- A "humanitarian" approach to protection takes a broad perspective on the harms displaced persons potentially face that justifies offering refuge but also privileges the prerogative of states to balance these considerations against their national interests.

KEY TERMS

- Global refugee regime
- International protection
- Normativity
- "Right to have rights"

INTRODUCTION

> 5.1 We must not accept the denial of access to territory for those seeking asylum, often through violent pushbacks; we must not normalize attempts to outsource asylum responsibilities. Legally; morally; and practically I oppose efforts to evade a State's responsibility by externalizing its asylum obligations, and I hope that those thinking of those approaches will reconsider carefully. (Grandi 2022b)

How and why should states respond to the protection needs of refugees and other forced migrants? What considerations should inform the duty of countries like Canada to provide access to asylum or resettlement to displaced persons? Are there ethical standards that should inform state practices toward displaced persons, and how should these standards be defined? These questions are inherently normative – and frequently underlie discussions of refugee policy in broader public debates. Pragmatic and legal reasons for states to offer refugee protection are often entwined with more fundamental considerations that both justify states' responsibilities and determine the scope of legitimate responses. In this chapter, I engage with forced migration from an explicitly conceptual perspective by focusing on the justificatory basis of international protection.[1] I analyze how researchers have grappled with the underlying normative grounds – the ethical and moral reasons – that should shape state responses to displacement in both law and policy. My engagement is intentionally narrow: I confine my analysis to liberal democratic states, such as Canada, where the dual imperatives of the rule of law and accountability to voting publics make such questions of justification and legitimacy unavoidable.[2]

In the first section, I frame the context in which international protection has emerged as both a widely accepted – and simultaneously contested – foundational concept for the refugee regime, that is, the "rules, norms, principles, and decision-making procedures" governing states' responses to refugees (Betts 2015). To do so I begin by examining forced migration from a critically informed historical and normative perspective. In section two, I briefly reconstruct three normative paradigms for thinking about the institution of refugeehood and fundamental purposes of international protection: political, human rights, and humanitarian conceptions. Section three addresses how these different conceptualizations are mirrored in different historical moments and institutional contexts in Canada. I do not claim a causal relationship between theory and policy but rather emphasize how conceptual analysis can illuminate the normative stakes – and ethical trade-offs – inherent in different approaches to international protection. The last section argues for the enduring importance of normative analysis for research on forced migration.

THEORIZING FORCED MIGRATION FROM A HISTORICAL AND NORMATIVE PERSPECTIVE

> 5.2 Something much more fundamental than freedom and justice, which are rights of citizens, is at stake when belonging to a community into which one is born is no longer a matter of course and not belonging no longer a matter of choice ... We become aware of the existence of a right to have rights (and that means to live in a framework where one is judged by one's actions and opinions) and a right to belong to some kind of organized community, only when millions of people emerge who had lost and could not regain these rights because of the new global political situation. (Arendt [1951] 1973, 177)

As the political theorist Hannah Arendt noted over half a century ago, forced displacement fundamentally complicates conventional understandings of such basic concepts as citizenship, rights, freedom, and justice. Forced migration challenges dominate normative frameworks in law and politics because these are overwhelmingly rooted in the background assumption of membership in a political community. For Arendt, whose reflections were informed by her experience as a stateless refugee, these tensions were not merely abstract considerations. Rather, grappling with them was integral to understanding the situation of displaced persons and the broader nature of forced migration. Accordingly, in this section I begin by taking up key features of Arendt's account. I address why traditional theories of migration are of limited use in displacement contexts and underscore the enduring value of continued theoretical engagement by those working on forced migration. I then turn to the role normative analysis can play in the work of researchers and why it is useful to make this explicit when assessing contemporary practices of international protection.

Engaging with Arendt is a helpful starting point for theorizing forced migration because her work provides an important touchstone for normative approaches. Arendt has argued that the central harm refugees face was the denial of the "right to have rights," which arose from their de facto loss of citizenship status. While Arendt has acknowledged refugees' material deprivations and lack of legal status, she argued that, above all, the absence of political status rendered their position precarious ([1951] 1973, 296). This loss of citizenship foreclosed the context in which particular rights could have any substantive meaning. While refugees might contingently be granted the "right" of freedom of movement or freedom of opinion, they could still remain fundamentally rightless according to Arendt. Ironically, it was only with the emergence of displacement on a global scale that the underlying significance of the "right to have rights" – understood as a right to membership in a particular community – became fully apparent.

Arendt's account also explicitly historicizes forced migration. As a corollary to her analysis of the loss of membership, she has suggested that the emergence and persistence of mass displacement was the result of relatively recent transformations in the nature of the state system (Arendt [1951] 1973, 297). The dilemmas confronting refugees were the direct product of a global context in which nation-states were rapidly becoming the only legitimate form of political community (also see Zolberg 1983). At the same time, the emerging order of a world of states was defined by a nearly absolute prerogative on sovereign control of entrance and membership. Although such norms are now viewed as timeless components of statehood, backed by the discourse of contemporary international law, these "essential" features of state practice are relatively novel. Indeed, it was only at the cusp of the twentieth century that states began to engage in the regulation of cross-border movement, which soon thereafter became an accepted feature of the broader international system (Sahlins 2003, 151; Torpey 1999, 9). Of course, these developments significantly impacted state responses to forced migration, essentially constituting the contemporary refugee as a category in international society (Malkki 1995, 498; also see Haddad 2008).[3] This underscores how displacement is not merely produced by the actions of particular states but is conditioned by the broader international state system.

A third insight of Arendt's analysis is that realizing claims to membership in a world of states would prove an enduring challenge. Her account of forced displacement preceded the formation of today's global refugee regime and the development of international protection (see also Demoz, chapter 7). The subsequent creation of the 1951 Refugee Convention would codify a schedule of rights for those forced to flee their homes into a multilateral framework that today is nearly global in scope. In doing so, the convention identified refugees as an exception to the norms of migration control in the international system and formalized state obligations to provide protection. However, Arendt anticipated enduring tensions in this architecture and the difficulties of ensuring access to protection in an international order where states remain the central actors. Although representing a significant advancement in state practice, the convention was notably silent in articulating a right to asylum and implicitly devolved control over refugee status determination (RSD) to states (see Young, chapter 3; Atak, chapter 17). The parallel absence of a right to naturalization further confirmed Arendt's concerns that securing full membership would remain a matter of state discretion, presaging the persistent difficulties in finding durable solutions to displacement. Perhaps most striking, the convention also provides no definition of the term "protection," despite its ubiquitous role in the contemporary refugee regime.[4]

Arendt's account is primarily diagnostic rather than prescriptive, confronting the nature of displacement as a global phenomenon without offering clear solutions.[5] At the same time, her analysis highlights the enduring importance of normative theorizing – and theory more broadly – for work on forced migration. To borrow a phrase from her later work, such efforts remain crucial to enable us to "think what we are doing" in a context where presupposed assumptions and intuitions should be questioned. Arendt's injunction converges with the subsequent interventions of researchers – that this section now turns to – who have expressed concern that a narrow emphasis on policy relevance can entail a lack of theoretical rigour or critical engagement. Policy-driven approaches often assume rather than question what Malkki has called the "national order of things" thereby eliding the role of the state system in conditioning both displacement and the state-centric nature of refugee law (1995, 516; see Aleinikoff 1992 on the latter).

In a similar vein, Chimni (1998) has drawn attention to the broader role of global power dynamics in shaping the study of displacement. His intervention highlights the degree to which "the geopolitics of knowledge production" have informed refugee studies, arguing that the policy priorities of Global North states often overdetermine research imperatives within the field, at the expense of perspectives from the Global South, or refugees themselves (Chimni 1998, 351). Chimni's observations regarding the implication of research on forced migration with relations of power in the international system underscore the need for a critical orientation toward how the development and deployment of categories and distinctions within the field are often linked to the imperatives of dominant state actors. As R. Black has noted, refugee studies has grown dramatically as an area of research; however, the dependence of the field "on policy definitions and concerns might be seen to be one of its principal weaknesses" (2001, 58). While the study of displacement is rightly entwined with policy considerations, this should not "obviate the need for critical theoretical reflection" on the basic assumptions that inform contemporary approaches (R. Black 2001, 71). From a complementary perspective, Bakewell (2008) has highlighted a problematic blurring by researchers in forced migration studies of categories of policy and analysis. Bakewell notes that the tendency of the former to overdetermine the latter can lead to research that largely endorses the status quo of the politics of the refugee regime rather than creating opportunities to challenge practices that favour the interests of institutional actors over those of the forcibly displaced (Bakewell 2008).

These critical perspectives on the study of displacement highlight how reliance on categories and distinctions derived from policy discourse masks ways that key concepts within the field are far from neutral or given (see also Goheen Glanville and Arbel, chapter 4). Indeed, they foreground the contested nature of terms such as "refugee," "irregular migration," "burden sharing," and "international protection." Drawing on the work of political theorists, we might cast these as "essentially contested concepts" in the sense of being inherently normative, insofar as they are bound up with evaluative and appraisive judgments (Gallie 1955; Connolly 1993; also K. Banerjee 2010). Such concepts are often treated as fixed or certain, especially when operationalized for policy purposes.[6] However, this obscures the competing framings or "conceptions" that have marked the deployment of these concepts throughout the history of the refugee regime and which continue to shape state responses to forced migration today.

Engaging with these insights also underscores the importance of not simply applying conceptual frameworks from international migration more broadly. For example, "functionalist" neoclassical theories attempt to explain trends in cross-border mobility in terms of economic differentials between states of origin and destination. While these models often underlie both popular and policy-based perspectives on migration as a whole, such approaches largely miss the underlying factors that shape the experiences and decisions of forced migrants. Other theoretical frameworks, such as historical-structural approaches and world system theory, provide similarly limited analytic resources for explaining forced displacement (for an overview of theories of migration *writ large*, see Haas, Castles, and Miller 2020; Massey et al. 1993). For example, these frameworks fail to identify precipitating factors for flight or explain why some flee and others do not. At the same time, these models are ill-suited to illuminating the purposes of international protection, which cannot be divorced from the normative considerations that inform the rationale of the refugee regime. While state actors have mostly continued to guard their authority over immigration, providing protection for refugees and other forced migrants is widely recognized as a fundamentally international duty (Kneebone 2003). However, like other key concepts within the field of forced migration, international protection is often taken as self-evident rather than variable and contested, despite the significant role that different conceptions play in informing state practices. This in turn requires analyzing the conceptual basis of state responsibilities toward those in need of protection.

THREE NORMATIVE MODELS OF INTERNATIONAL PROTECTION: POLITICAL, HUMAN RIGHTS, AND HUMANITARIAN

In this section I draw on and reconstruct three conceptual perspectives that offer importantly divergent accounts of the underlying logic of, and entitlement to, international protection. My engagement here is meant to be illustrative rather than exhaustive. I neither claim to encompass the state of the art nor to fully unpack the wider theoretical implications of these accounts for key concepts such as citizenship, refugeehood, and international responsibility sharing between states.[7] Rather, in this section I focus on how these frameworks inform differing models for understanding and justifying state-based responses to displacement.

The "Political Conception"

A distinct and influential strand in normative work on forced migration approaches the purpose of international protection by emphasizing the unique role played by asylum in the context of state responses to refugees. In this vein Matthew Price (2004, 2009) has identified what he views as the "political" core inherent in the practice of asylum as it has been subsequently institutionalized in the context of the postwar refugee regime. There are three key elements: the provision of refugee protection responds to a fundamentally political harm; the granting of asylum is an inherently political and expressive act; and state policies ought to be informed by underlying political considerations necessary to sustain public support for refugee assistance.

D.A. Martin (1991) and M. Lister (2013) have similarly insisted that contemporary notions of international protection should focus on state-based persecution when assessing claims to refugee status. They argue that persecution represents a special harm because of its targeted and political nature, one that uniquely grounds the justificatory basis of asylum and refugee status (see Cherem 2016 for a similar view). A commitment to an appropriately "narrow political standard" entails resisting the urge to widen the "radius of the definitional circle" of those entitled to refugee protection for both principled and pragmatic reasons (D.A. Martin 1991, 35). This in turn requires a strict construal of what they see as the underlying "persecution requirement" that defines those eligible for protection under the 1951 Convention.

Following the logic of this conception, international protection should only be offered to persons with a well-founded fear of state-based persecution on the basis of their race, religion, political opinion, nationality, or social group. Further, asylum should be delimited for those able to prove the role of state culpability in persecution in order to secure a pathway to durable legal status and membership in their host state. To be clear, defenders of the primacy of the political basis of asylum are not indifferent to displaced persons who might fall outside a narrow application of the five enumerated 1951 Convention grounds. However, this perspective entails a decidedly constrained application of asylum norms, even relative to existing state practice in countries such as Canada and the US, as well as within the European Union, and diverges strongly from the more expansive approaches articulated in regional instruments that have been developed beyond the Global North.

This perspective not only highlights the implication of persecutory states in justifying the grounds for claiming refugee status, but also stresses the politically expressive nature of granting asylum. Price emphasizes that providing protection should not be understood in merely humanitarian terms but as delivering a critical judgment of recalcitrant governments. As he notes, "[a]sylum not only provides refugees with protection, but also has an expressive dimension:

it directs condemnation toward other states for having egregiously mistreated the refugees it protects" (Price 2009, 70). This implied foreign policy role of international protection leads Price to emphasize the instrumental dimension of asylum in potentially addressing the domestic policies of persecutory regimes and to offer a qualified defence of state practices that favour asylum seekers from specific countries (2009, 85–90). D.A. Martin suggests a more controversial linkage with foreign policy, namely that an excessively liberal approach may diminish domestic sources of opposition necessary to effect substantive changes within an oppressive state (1991, 44–5).

Finally, there is a realist edge to the "political conception" that underscores how asylum has increasingly become a limited resource with its own "special fragility" (D.A. Martin 1991, 34). Continued support among domestic audiences for such policies may be undermined by a more expansive approach to those entitled to international protection. The source of this tension can in part be identified in the underlying logic of the international system noted above, which assumes a broader prerogative of states to control entrance and membership. Beyond providing a pretext for political leaders to invest increasing resources in interdiction policies, public anxieties grounded in perceptions of a loss of control over borders may precipitate backlashes not only in the immigration context but also in responses to forced migrants. From this perspective, policies that unduly expand access to asylum run the risk of undermining domestic support for refugee assistance, both in the context of asylum access and more generally.

The "Human Rights Conception"

The "human rights" approach is perhaps the most influential framing of international protection within contemporary refugee law and policy in Canada and internationally. This conception, which is most closely associated with the work of James Hathaway, advances a systematic interpretation of the rationale and purpose of the global refugee regime as providing a form of "surrogate" human rights protection (Hathaway 1991a, 1991b; also Hathaway and Foster 2014). An underlying motivation for this interpretation is the fact that the Refugee Convention does not explicitly articulate the meaning of persecution, with international human rights standards providing a potential foundation for specifying the basis of claims to protection. Key elements of this perspective therefore include: reading the meaning of persecution in the Refugee Convention through a broad "human rights" lens, understanding the duty to provide international protection as premised on failures of effective domestic protection in the state of origin, and adopting a flexible orientation to the traditional convention grounds for evaluating claims to refugee status.

The core of this approach lies in arguing for the interrelation (and explicit imbrication) of global human rights with international protection. This in turn requires interpreting persecution as the basis for claims to protection in terms that extend beyond the narrow framing adopted by the "political conception" of the Refugee Convention. In Hathaway's original formulation he argued that the definition of persecution that underlies claims to refugee status should instead be understood as the "sustained or systematic violation of basic human rights demonstrative of a failure of state protection" (1991a, 104–5). This perspective diverges sharply from the "political conception" by more broadly connecting the grounds of international protection with standards from human rights law. The "human rights conception" also decentres the role of direct governmental culpability in defining persecution. Rather, the focus is on whether individuals can secure their human rights domestically or if they require recourse to protection offered by the international community under the refugee regime.

A key implication of the human rights approach is that the underlying justification for countries such as Canada to provide protection to refugees and other forced migrants is premised on the lack of effective protection within an individual's state of origin. The focus for this perspective is largely on whether individuals are unable to avail themselves of their human rights domestically. International protection is therefore explicitly conceptualized as a form of "surrogate" or substitute protection, undertaken in response to the failure or absence of the state of origin's otherwise presumptive role in securing fundamental rights. As Hathaway has argued, the duty of states to "provide surrogate protection arises only in relation to persons who are either unable to benefit from the protection of their own state, or who are unwilling to accept that state's protection because of a well-founded fear of persecution" (1999, 134). Within this framework, breakdowns in national protection do not require the culpability of governmental officials or state institutions in perpetrating targeted forms of persecution. Rather, Hathaway (1991, 124–34) explicitly contemplates the possibility of claims to protection arising from threats posed by non-state actors giving greater recognition to their potential role in causing forced displacement.

Directly building on these elements, this perspective informs a potentially more dynamic view of the relevant grounds for claims to international protection. For C. Foster, such an approach is "central to the ability of the Refugee Convention to be applied in a progressive manner in order to encompass claims involving, for example, gender-based persecution" (2007, 27). In this sense, the human rights perspective advances an understanding of international protection that demands we treat the traditional convention grounds as evolving standards reflective of contemporary causes of forced migration. Hathaway and Foster support an "approach to 'being persecuted' that is flexible" but also capable of providing objective and principled guidance through appealing to globally recognized human rights standards (2014, 183). In this framework, the surrogate protection entailed by refugee status should be entitled to persons confronting serious human rights violations that cannot be remedied in their state of origin. While some may argue that the Refugee Convention is not in principle a human rights treaty, the "human rights conception" asserts that contemporary responses to displacement are rightly informed by the subsequent human rights agreements states have undertaken, and these agreements should guide their approach to international protection.

The "Humanitarian Conception"

The humanitarian paradigm perhaps comes closest to the understanding of refugee protection in contemporary popular sentiment – in Canada and many other Global North states. On one level, it presents something of a concatenation of the "political" and "human rights" approaches with regard to the grounds for claims to protection by displaced persons, but with an important shift in how responsibility for international protection should be understood. Michael Walzer (1983) is perhaps best known for offering an initial philosophical articulation of this perspective on the special claims of "necessitous strangers" such as refugees. However, David Miller has provided the most systematic treatment of how states should respond to forced displacement in a world where they are otherwise justified in exercising full discretion over immigration. Miller's account combines a potentially expansive approach to those who might be recognized as needing international protection, with an emphasis on states' entitlement to discretion on admissions criteria and the scope of their responsibilities in responding to global displacement.

Within this conception there is recognition that both political persecution and threats to basic human rights are equally valid grounds for offering international protection. Indeed, according to Miller there is a "good case for broadening the definition" to include persons endangered by generalized violence as well as those "deprived of rights to subsistence, basic health care" or other sources of harm (Miller 2005, 202; 2007, 225). In later work, he explicitly includes threats "either from natural calamities or from private acts of violence" (Miller 2016, 83). The humanitarian perspective's emphasis on harm *tout court* in approaching international protection supports a more inclusive definition of refugeehood than that offered by the 1951 Convention, one that sees little need to either carefully replicate or alternatively reinterpret the traditional persecution-based grounds. Miller does not attach great significance to the distinction between indirect applications for resettlement and "spontaneous" asylum claims made by individuals who present themselves at the border of a particular state (for differences in asylum versus resettlement, see Atak, chapter 17). Given the overall emphasis of this perspective on international protection as a response to harm, the criteria imposed by the convention grounds as well as the distinction between asylum reception and resettlement are viewed as somewhat morally irrelevant.

In contrast to its broad reading of the grounds for international protection, this perspective adopts a narrow view of binding obligations and entitlements. The "humanitarian conception" is thus in some senses the most state-centric of the three paradigms insofar as it privileges the prerogative of states to balance these considerations against the interests of nationals. As Miller suggests, even an avowedly liberal state may unilaterally limit itself to "discharge its fair share of the burden" of refugees as decided by that state; this is warranted even if it means that the "net effect, nonetheless, may be that there are some refugees for whom no state is willing to take responsibility" (2016, 93; 2005, 203). A corollary of this is effectively consigning these individuals to Arendt's predicament. In this sense, the "humanitarian conception" frames the normative demands of international protection in a manner analogous to moral claims to charity, giving significant scope to state discretion in line with national interests. For the humanitarian perspective, under the decentralized refugee system that currently exists at the global level, responsibility for international protection is limited to what states are willing to accept based on the judgments of national governments responding to the preferences of domestic constituencies.

A final corollary of the "humanitarian conception" is a further emphasis on an expansive state prerogative in determining the contours of their assistance to forced migrants. In addition to deciding the scope of what it means to discharge its fair share, states are permitted to apply a significant amount of discretion in the provision of international protection. In Miller's earlier work, this entails recognizing a considerable degree of autonomy by states to weigh overall application numbers in relation to "the demands that temporary or longer-term accommodation of refugees will place on existing citizens, and whether there exists any special link between the refugee and the host community – for instance, similarities of language or culture, or a sense of historical responsibility on the part of the receiving state" because they are implicated in the causes of displacement (2007, 226–7). As he puts it, "judgement must rest with the members of the receiving state" with regard to deciding whether and how they have contributed sufficiently to international protection (227). This in turn extends to determining on what terms they wish to do so with regard to adjudicating claims by asylum seekers or engaging in third country resettlement. Consequently, this position diminishes the import of the state-endorsed norms on these issues articulated in the Refugee Convention.

PARADIGMS IN PRACTICE? JUSTIFICATION'S ROLE IN CANADIAN RESPONSES TO FORCED MIGRATION

The three approaches unpacked above offer distinct conceptualizations of state responses to forced migration. Not only do the political, human rights, and humanitarian perspectives offer competing accounts of the justification for providing international protection, but also they lead to differing views of the considerations that should inform state practice. Analyzing them provides a helpful lens for drawing attention to the normative logics that underlie different moments in Canada's approach to international protection and how these resonate with practices across other liberal democratic states.

Elements of the "political conception" are reflected in the refugee policies enacted by Canada and other "Western" countries (see Mahrouse and El Omari, chapter 15 for a critique of this terminology) in the immediate wake of World War II. This is most conspicuous in Canada's embrace of an overtly political definition of refugees up to the end of 1969. The Canadian approach, paralleling that of the US, defined refugees in starkly Cold War terms, identifying those in need of protection as "people fleeing the domination of the Soviet Union" (Molloy et al. 2017, 18; also Vineberg 2018, 3). Arguably, the broader Cold War ideological context did much to encourage "Western" states to strengthen the refugee regime and support resettlement policy within UNHCR. Indeed, during this period support across governments – as well as their voting publics – was strongly in favour of offering sanctuary to those framed as political refugees in flight from communist oppression. In this sense, however, Western support for refugee and asylum policies might be read in expressive terms as part of a broader political project to undermine the legitimacy of their Soviet adversaries, especially with regard to providing refuge to individuals wishing to flee the confines of the Iron Curtain or other communist regimes.

Following the passage of the Immigration Act of 1976, Canada formally moved to a more explicitly "apolitical" definition of those in need of international protection – one that cohered with Canadian accession to the 1951 Refugee Convention and its 1967 Protocol. Canada's approach toward adjudicating asylum claims also gradually shifted from focusing on state-based persecution to encompass persons threatened by non-state actors or endangered by generalized violence. These trends can also be observed in other Global North states, as well as many states in the Global South, which have been responsible for formalizing a more expansive approach through regional instruments and declarations.[8]

The imprint of the human rights perspective has perhaps been most pervasive in Canada's impact on contemporary refugee policy and jurisprudence. This is especially evident given the integral role apparently played by the "human rights conception" of international protection in the landmark 1993 *Ward* decision of the Supreme Court of Canada (SCC). Among a number of developments that have decisively influenced Canada's approach to refugee status claims, the SCC's ruling was crucial in realigning Canadian refugee law to accept that individual claims to protection could be justified on the basis of a state's failure to secure basic human rights and in no longer requiring state complicity as an integral element of persecution. This represented a significant evolution in the principles guiding state practice: recognizing the protection needs of persons facing "sustained or systemic violation of basic human rights" regardless of whether their reasons for flight fell within the nexus of the traditional convention grounds (Hathaway 1991b, quoted in *Canada v. Ward* 1993). In this context, the SCC was equally explicit in invoking the framing of international protection that informs the human rights perspective, noting that the "rationale underlying international refugee protection is to serve as 'surrogate' shelter coming into play *only* upon failure of national support" (*Canada v. Ward* 1993; emphasis added).

This juridical reconceptualization of the basis of international protection in Canada has been widely emulated by other liberal democracies. As M. Foster notes, this reframing has been most apparent in the context of common law states, such as the UK and Australia, but it is debatably the predominant perspective across a broader array of legal jurisdictions (2007, 29–31). However, the uptake of the human rights approach has arguably proved deeply ambivalent in the context of state approaches to international protection. While M. Foster and Hathaway have emphasized how linking refugee law to the values and standards articulated in human rights law has enabled flexibility and space for progressive development, other researchers have highlighted the potentially restrictive and regressive implications of states embracing the model of surrogate protection that forms the flip side of this approach.[9]

The humanitarian framing of international protection forefronts a particular balancing of the claims of forced migrants alongside the demands of state interests. In doing so, it combines a potentially broader view of the grounds for protection claims, while according space for significant discretion in the context of both asylum reception and resettlement. This approach widely maps onto contemporary state practices across much of the Global North. The humanitarian conception widens potential grounds for protection, like the human rights perspective. Indeed, it moves beyond a focus on persecution and recasts international protection as a response to harm more broadly. Importantly, it also reflects the contemporary adoption by many states of various temporary and subsidiary protection frameworks to address individuals' claims that explicitly fall outside the 1951 Refugee Convention though they face fundamental threats to their well-being, such as interstate conflict, domestic political turmoil, or natural disasters.[10] At the same time, the humanitarian conception mirrors the continued priority that countries such as Canada place on exercising significant control over the scope of their engagement in international protection, at the cost of effacing the fundamentally global nature of this responsibility as articulated in the opening of the Refugee Convention. This is evident in the context of refugee resettlement, which is widely treated as entirely a matter of state discretion (see Atak, chapter 17; Labman, chapter 18). For example, although Canada currently emphasizes its role as the global leader in resettlement, Canadian commitments have varied quite significantly over the past decade, ranging from 9,653 in 2012 to a high point of 46,705 in 2016.[11]

The weight of state interests relative to international protection is often more implicit than explicit in the context of adjudicating RSD. This is perhaps in part because countries such as Canada are in principle expected to be relatively uniform in honouring their formal legal obligations under the Refugee Convention.[12] However, elements of the humanitarian perspective can be found in the SCC's *Febles* decision, which significantly redefined Canada's application of its obligations toward those seeking international protection. As the court's judgment stated, the "Convention has twin purposes: it aims to strike a balance between helping victims of oppression by allowing them to start new lives in other countries, while also protecting the interests of receiving countries, which they did not renounce simply by negotiating specific provisions to aid victims of oppression" (*Febles v. Canada* 2014). Here the SCC rejected arguments by UNHCR advocating for a less restrictive approach (UNHCR 2014), despite the organization's otherwise widely recognized expert authority in providing guidance on international refugee law (Barnett 2011). This reflects the reality that in Canada, as well as other Global North states, the provision of protection remains bound up in considerations of domestic interests even in the context of asylum reception.

CONCLUSION

This chapter has explored forced migration and international protection from a theoretical perspective to shed light on how normative analysis and critique can inform understandings of displacement. While the ongoing policy import of research on forced migration is undeniable, an emphasis on policy relevance should not obscure the enduring value of critical reflection. Theoretical perspectives are integral to interrogating the underlying assumptions that strictly policy-driven research programs may take for granted. By directing attention to the implication of the modern state system in conditioning processes of displacement, critical approaches illuminate the role of power relations in the refugee regime and enable reflection on the impact of such dynamics on the production of both knowledge and policy. Engaging with normative approaches helps foreground the often implicit ethical and moral justifications that inform both public debates and governments' responses to protection needs. The conceptual frameworks surveyed in this chapter present distinct visions of the logics of justification that underlie international refugee protection. By juxtaposing these reconstructions of the purposes of protection and placing them in dialogue with different instances of state practice, this chapter has highlighted how conceptual analysis can contribute to the broader study of forced migration. The salience of this, of course, extends beyond scholarly analysis given that research on displacement not only shapes the contours of what is defined as relevant in the context of policy-making but also helps inform and articulate ongoing public discourse in liberal democratic states on the contours of our responsibilities toward refugees and other displaced persons.

NOTES

The author thanks Christina R. Clark-Kazak, Anthony Mohen, and Anne Staver for their comments on this chapter.

1 The term "international protection" is commonly used as shorthand for the aspects of refugee law that provide for the protection of individuals outside their country of origin as a result of feared harm. Such claims to protection are widely accepted to apply to those recognized under the Refugee Convention but have also been applied more broadly to those in flight from other serious threats (see UNHCR 2018b). The legitimate scope of international protection – who it applies to and why – is a central question that researchers have increasingly sought to address. However, a number of scholars have also highlighted the continued "definitional uncertainty" surrounding the meaning of "protection" (Stevens 2013, 234; Storey 2016) despite its centrality to refugee policy.

2 Many of these states, including Canada, were directly involved in the postwar development of the refugee regime and have continued to exercise significant power and institutional influence within the regime for much of its existence.

3 As Sassen argues, it was the "coupling of state sovereignty and nationalism with border control" within interwar Europe that gave states "the power and the institutional legitimacy to exclude refugees from civil society" (2000, 78).

4 See Storey (2016, 4). As Stevens notes, "[e]very student of refugee law knows that, notwithstanding many references to the term 'protection,' the Refugee Convention provides no definition" (2013, 235). A similar lacuna is found in UNHCR's statute, where the "actual nature of protection is not articulated; rather, the Statute seeks to assist the establishment of a framework that will facilitate protection" (239).

5 Given the imbrication of the international system in generating forced migration, Arendt has lamented that fully resolving tensions between norms of state sovereignty and the securing of the "right to have rights" for all persons would prove impossible.

6 This is perhaps most obvious for the concept of refugeehood. Although seemingly formalized by the 1951 Convention, the meaning of "refugee" has received considerable interpretive variation in the context of state practices, as well as sustained analytic engagement by scholars. Arguably, the meaning of international protection is even less defined both in policy and research. As Storey notes, one "searches in vain for any clear definition of 'protection.' What one finds instead is frequent reliance on vague or circular definitions. It is as if we all assume everyone knows what it means whereas in truth no one is sure" (2016, 2). While some researchers, particularly scholars of refugee law, may be concerned with my emphasis on the contested nature of key concepts, I should stress that I am not denying better or worse interpretations of obligations entailed by the convention;

rather, this analytic lens helps us grapple with variations in state practices by making explicit the underlying conceptions that frame and justify these practices.

7 For broader surveys of these issues, see Carens 1991, Gibney 2014.

8 However, remnants of linkages between foreign policy and international protection can be found in relatively recent state practice: for example, the US only formally ended preferential treatment of Cuban asylum seekers in 2017.

9 As Schultz argues, the spread of the surrogacy framing has led to the normalization of problematic state practices, such as incorporating an "Internal Flight Alternative" (IFA) as a basis for denying protection claims (2018; also 2019). IFA – also referred to as "Internal Protection Alternative" – assumes states can justifiably refuse protection to individuals who, hypothetically, could mitigate their need for protection domestically by relocating within their state of origin. Another corollary of the surrogacy model, noted by Cantor, is to obscure how international protection is meant to address the impact of the loss of effective nationality that leaves refugees and other forced migrants unable to avail themselves of the assistance of their country of origin (2016, 359).

10 Although Canada has been something of an outlier relative to the EU and US in not formalizing such policies, recent developments in Canada's response to the war in Ukraine arguably represent an important movement in this direction.

11 Indeed, Canada's ongoing commitments to formal resettlement have subsequently declined despite an overall rise in global displacement since 2016.

12 Researchers have drawn attention to significant variability in refugee recognition rates across Global North states: these studies highlight marked historical shifts *within* particular countries, as well as contemporary divergences *between* states in assessing RSD. While liberal democracies in the Global North are uniform in implementing their own domestic asylum systems, the idea that RSD should remain a national competency is not given. This is not required by the Refugee Convention, and as others have noted the delegation of this role to UNHCR is prevalent in many contexts across the Global South (Abdelaaty 2021). Notably, the domain of discretion is not limited to the individual level of refugee status claims but informs approaches to the broader exclusion criteria for accessing protection.

FURTHER READING AND RESOURCES

Ansari, Sadiya. 2019. "What Do Borders Really Do?" *University of Toronto Magazine*, 2 October 2019. https://magazine.utoronto.ca/research-ideas/culture-society/what-do-borders-really-do-immigration-ethics.

Betts, Alexander. 2015. "The Normative Terrain of the Global Refugee Regime." *Ethics and International Affairs* 29 (4). https://www.ethicsandinternationalaffairs.org/2015/the-normative-terrain-of-the-global-refugee-regime.

CBC News. 2015. "Ideas from the Trenches – Refuge." CBC/Radio-Canada,

26 November 2015. https://www.cbc.ca/radio/ideas/ideas-from-the-trenches-refuge-1.3336921.

Gibney, Matthew J. 2014. "Political Theory, Ethics, and Forced Migration." In *The Oxford Handbook of Refugee and Forced Migration Studies*, edited by Elena Fiddian-Qasmiyeh, Gil Loescher, Katy Long, and Nando Sigona, 48–59. Oxford: Oxford University Press.

Parekh, Serena. 2016. *Refugees and the Ethics of Forced Displacement*. New York: Routledge. https://doi.org/10.4324/9781315883854.

6

Reflecting on Ethics in Forced Migration Art and Research

Francisco-Fernando Granados and Lois Klassen

KEY TAKEAWAYS

- Ethics is understood through relationships. To work ethically in forced migration, critical awareness is needed of the "positionalities" of everyone involved in the research or art project.
- Critical reflection ("reflexivity") about power dynamics affecting the project's relationships and context is needed to work ethically and with cultural safety.
- Research-creation and art in forced migration contexts offer valuable methodological alternatives, as well as ethical challenges.
- Forced migration studies present specific challenges in terms of the ethical principles of "respect for persons" (autonomy and consent), "concern for welfare" ("do no harm"), and "justice" (cultural safety, fairness, equity, diversity, competence, and partnership).

KEY TERMS

- Ethics
- Relational ethics
- Positionality
- Reflexivity

INTRODUCTION

Co-writing a reflective summary of ethics in art and research has been an opportunity to reconnect. The use of first-person point of view signals the authors' focus on "relational ethics," which we understand to be part of the everyday decisions facing artists and researchers in forced migration settings. Our friendship started in the early 2000s, when I (Francisco-Fernando) was a young refugee claimant working as a peer facilitator and advocate with other newcomer teenagers. Some of those opportunities were associated with advocacy and research projects by both academics and non-profit organizations. Participating in these community projects, most of which offered immigrant and refugee youth creative outlets, gave me a sense of belonging, even while my refugee status was not ensured. Participating was essential for my mental well-being. At the same time, the need to be involved was driven by an urgent need to prove that I could "do well" in Canada. I needed to show that I could integrate and be useful and that my family was worthy of asylum in the face of a refugee determination process, which I knew had in many instances rejected and deported people from my community, including close friends. So, I felt compelled to participate. I agreed enthusiastically, perhaps even compulsively, to help ensure my family had a chance of staying in the country, to be a part of a variety of projects researching the lives of young refugees living under the larger threat of being deemed inadmissible by the Immigration and Refugee Board (IRB). When we first met, I (Lois) was also an emerging artist, but even so I was able to provide you (Francisco-Fernando) with an opportunity to present your work outside of service and advocacy settings, in one of Canada's publicly funded artist-run venues. This shift from the mostly instrumental use of a young person's refugee story of asylum to a context in which my (Francisco-Fernando's) work could be acknowledged for its cultural contributions became key in eventually allowing me to imagine myself as an artist, researcher, and citizen.

This chapter represents our combined capacity, twenty years later, to reflect on the ethical complexity that produced that moment of creativity and optimism. It leads us to ask, for instance, how can consent to participate be obtained in the face of desperate migration experiences? All the creative projects that were embedded inside the service sector involving me (Francisco-Fernando) and my peers used our lived experience inside Canada's refugee settlement system to benefit their organizations – maybe even more than we benefited. In the best scenarios, these opportunities benefited me by giving the sense that I could claim agency over how my story was being told, as was my experience with the project "Redefining Canadian" (Lui 2005). At worst, projects in the immigrant and refugee service sector tokenized my presence and manipulated my story for purposes that were never made fully clear to me. In one instance, I was taken

Figure 6.1 | Francisco-Fernando Granados, *refugees run the seas ...*, 2014–16.

to a public consultation by a non-profit manager without being told what the meeting was about, only to be introduced as a "representative" of newcomer youth communities. In another case, my name and details of my story, which I had shared with a journalist, were published verbatim without my consent in an English language textbook.

When we use the term "ethics" in this chapter, we are describing how principles of respect, concern for welfare, and justice are applied when artists and researchers form and maintain relationships in their forced migration work. In other words, our reflections concern applied ethics in art and research. In institutions like universities and other research organizations, research ethics boards (REBs) are required to provide formal approvals for projects that involve human participants. Other service and professional organizations, including some non-governmental organizations (NGOs), also adopt codes of ethics or conduct. While official standards aim to ensure ethical treatment of people, their implementation is sometimes criticized for being overly procedural and preoccupied with reducing risks rather than applying ethical principles in everyday work with underserved or vulnerable people (Guillemin and Gillam 2004; Lenette 2019). In the tension between procedural ethics and everyday ethics, we emphasize relationships. This chapter considers all the relationships in art or research projects, including with participants who have lived experience (maybe the artists and researchers share these experiences), with collaborators or partner groups, and later with audiences and publics. Some of the relationships involve written consent, media release documents, or partnership agreements. Beyond official agreements, though, ethical relationships in art and research depend on critical awareness, beginning with the artists' and researchers' positionality. In our writing, together we aim to model ways of articulating positionality and critical reflexivity as ethical and decolonial processes. Our chapter ends with case studies that apply ethical principles to forced migration work.

6.1 Positionality

I (Lois) am a settler artist-researcher, working as a research ethics coordinator on unceded traditional territories of the xʷməθkwəy̓əm (Musqueam), Skwxwú7mesh (Squamish), and Səlílwətaɬ (Tsleil-Waututh) Nations. My home is in the southeast part of the City of Vancouver, not too far from c̓əʔsnaʔəm, the Musqueam "city before the city." Over many years, c̓əʔsnaʔəm was the site of looting and desecration in the name of research (Museum of Vancouver n.d.). Unethical research practices at this site and elsewhere have produced lasting distrust and anger that continue to impact relationships between Indigenous people and non-Indigenous researchers (Leona Sparrow quoted in Roy 2016, 22). In research ethics work I bring information to researchers about the importance of protocols and self-determined regulations by First Nations, Inuit, and Métis people. In co-authoring this chapter, I also acknowledge that I am a Postdoctoral Fellow at Critical Media Art Studio at Simon Fraser University, with funding from the Government of Canada's Social Sciences and Humanities Research Council (SSHRC). My ongoing art project, *Reading the Migration Library*, combines migration studies and participatory art.

This chapter's opening partially reveals how we both bring prior art practices to our research. That I (Francisco-Fernando) encountered art as part of research projects about refugee youth, and that I (Lois) had opportunities to integrate my art practice into cultural studies about migration demonstrate how commonly creative disciplines are included in forced migration services and research (noted also in, for instance, Clark-Kazak and Grabska 2022, 4; Martiniello 2022; Lenette 2019; and others). Because Canada offers no forms of official recognition for people fleeing that are not mediated by colonial laws (see Coburn, chapter 1; Fynn Bruey and Fantauzzi, chapter 8), art can function as an alternative framework of recognition that opens up the possibility of a decolonizing conscience for refugees. Of relevance to forced migration contexts is the way art can occupy an interface between justice and the law (Korsten 2021). I (Francisco-Fernando) have on a few occasions (including at an in-person event on art and displacement) heard Gayatri Chakravorty Spivak publicly declare that "[i]t is just that there be law, but law is not justice!" Spivak was commenting on the human rights abuses Rohinga refugees faced (Spivak 2017).

With the capacity to make perceptible those injustices that are otherwise invisible, unspeakable, and illogical, art's disruptions can help us imagine alternatives (Korsten 2021, 13). But art projects in forced migration fields also pose unique ethical dilemmas. Unlike research, standards of practice in art are variable and ill defined. In Canada the term "research-creation" is used to describe the integration of arts-based methods into other research disciplines, or the integration of research methods into artists' projects. Whereas creative methods may lessen barriers caused by language difference or experiences with trauma, contemporary artworks may also be associated with barriers related to culture and translation. Although many artists bring expertise in the politics of representation to forced migration settings, misrecognition in art can reinforce damaging stereotypes and leave participants feeling exploited. For art's possibilities and failings, in this chapter we urge artists and other creative practitioners to join researchers in applying the examples and resources described in this chapter.

6.2 Positionality

I (Francisco-Fernando) was born in Guatemala and live in Toronto, the traditional territory of the Mississaugas of the Credit, the Anishnabeg, the Chippewa, the Haudenosaunee, and the Wendat peoples covered by the Dish With One Spoon Wampum Belt Covenant. Since 2005, my practice as an artist has traced my movement from Convention refugee to critical citizen, using abstraction performatively, site specifically, and relationally, to create projects that challenge the stability of practices of recognition. My work has developed from the intersection of formal artistic training, working in performance through artist-run spaces, studying queer and feminist theory, and early activism as a peer support worker with newcomer communities. My artistic practice has received grants from the Canada Council for the Arts, Ontario Arts Council, and Toronto Arts Council, as well as through commissions from public galleries. My academic research has been supported through SSHRC, Ontario Graduate Scholarship Program, and a non-profit organization serving immigrant and refugee communities. I am in the PhD program in Media & Design Innovation at Toronto Metropolitan University.

POSITIONALITY AND CRITICAL REFLEXIVITY IN RESEARCH

Ethics in art and research requires awareness of one's relationship to land and territory, the artist's or researcher's role (or multiple roles) in the art or research project, and what the artist or researcher brings to the work. The sidebars titled "6.1 Positionality" and "6.2 Positionality" offer examples of how we position ourselves in the work of co-writing this chapter. Our positionality statements begin by describing our relationship to local Indigenous territories in respect for Indigenous protocols and laws. The land acknowledgments also represent a gesture to build trust that has been severely damaged by research violations. My (Lois) positionality statement touches on a history of research violations affecting Musqueam peoples, for instance. We also make declarations in our statements of professional affiliations and funding. This situates us as employees and professionals, with policies and procedures guiding funding, research ethics, and other areas of conduct. Declarations such as these can be found alongside publications or presentations, especially in settings where researchers may be affiliated with

6.3 Reflexivity
I (Lois) am a second-generation Canadian of White settler descent, born on Treaty Two Territory. Treaty Two took effect in 1872 and enabled a large migration of agricultural settlers to Manitoba that extended to include my grandparents' arrival from Russian-occupied Ukraine in the 1920s. Though their stories of fleeing under threat included the fear and desperation similar to the experiences of other refugees and asylum seekers, I need to acknowledge that my ancestors' citizenships and integration into Canadian culture were made easier owing to Government of Canada programs to build the agricultural sector. If I used the experience of my ancestors as an example of what current immigrants could expect in Canada I would be reinforcing colonialism and systemic racism. It could undermine the cultural safety in my relationships with those who have experienced racism and colonial attitudes, as Indigenous people or as immigrants.

for-profit companies. Arguably, even an affiliation with a university or a non-profit organization could produce a bias in analysis. For this reason it is ethical to disclose institutional affiliations when presenting to researchers and communities involved in your research.

Positionality is inextricably linked to the concept of "relational ethics." Our emphasis on the relationships in forced migration art and research follows other writers (Bilotta 2019, 2020, 2021; Klassen 2020; Hugman, Bartolomei, and Pittaway 2011a; Hugman, Pittaway, and Bartolomei 2011b; Vervliet et al. 2015). Locating our accountability in relationships also echoes Eve Tuck and Monique Guishard's decolonial approaches. They write, "'Relationality' is an alchemy of trust, representation, and reciprocity … A trustworthy researcher does not attempt to downplay or diminish the significance of authorship in her own life, but fully discloses the expectations, benefits, and politics of publication" (Tuck and Guishard 2013, 21–2). For Linda Tuhiwai Smith some questions decolonial relationality poses include: "Whose research is it? Who owns it? Whose interests does it serve? Who will benefit from it? Who has designed its questions and framed its scope? Who will carry it out? Who will write it up? How will its results be disseminated?" (Tuhiwai Smith 2021, 10). Decolonial approaches to ethics emphasize the accountability of the researcher to the communities whose lives may be the subject of the art or research. Eve Tuck writes that ethical Indigenous research needs to reflect desires for strong communities, rather than perpetuate "damage-centred" content (2009, 414). In a forced migration context, Yến Lê Espiritu and Lan Duong describe, with artwork examples, how their "feminist refugee epistemology" can reorient research toward seeing the refugee as a "site of social and political critiques of militarized empires" rather than objects to be rescued (Espiritu and Duong 2018, 588). When I (Lois) read these decolonial approaches I am reminded of the way your (Francisco-Fernando's) artwork, *refugees run the seas …* turns a popular song lyric ("refugees run the seas, 'cause we own our own boats" by Shakira) into an assertion that refugees vote, at least through their presence in public ("refugees run the seas cause we own our own votes," in the artwork as shown in fig. 6.1).

Alongside positionality, a process of critical reflexivity is necessary to address social and historical specificity impacting the relationships and research overall. It is also required to ensure cultural safety when artists and researchers work across cultures in participatory art and research projects. Caroline Lenette insists on the following:

> 1 Stating your positionality alone does not equate to being an ethical researcher if you do not have the capacity to be reflexive.
> 2 No research method, participatory or not, is culturally safe in and of itself.
> 3 We all have the potential to use methods in culturally unsafe ways because of our privileges and a lack of reflexivity. So good intentions alone don't equate to good processes or good practices. Without an explicit commitment to identifying how our identities and privileges shape our research, our choice of methodology, and who we collaborate with, we risk reinforcing rather than challenging colonial-infused research methodologies in migration studies. (2021, n.p.)

6.4 Reflexivity
I (Francisco-Fernando) came with my family to unceded Coast Salish territories, asking Canada for refuge before the STCA first took effect in 2004. We would not have been able to make our claim for asylum in Canada after that date. We went through a three-year process with the IRB and were eventually granted Convention refugee status; I acknowledge the privileges of this path. This form of civic recognition from Canada enfolds me in the settler colonial state. I also recognize that my refugee experience is often rendered invisible due to my appearance as a light-skinned and thus ambiguously racialized, able-bodied Latinx man. It is a privilege not everybody in my family has. The ambiguity of my body spares me many experiences of racism, even as it denies a recognition of a deeply formative experience. (My queerness, however, is far more perceptible!)

Our "reflexivity" statements (sidebars 6.3 and 6.4) describe our awareness of how our work could be culturally unsafe at times. Stating our awareness does not ensure cultural safety, but it indicates commitment to continually critique the impact of our positionality in our work.

GENERAL AND SPECIFIC: ETHICAL PRINCIPLES IN FORCED MIGRATION ART AND RESEARCH

Harm caused by research or art projects can have long-lasting consequences. The *Tri-Council Policy Statement: Ethical Conduct for Research Involving Humans* (TCPS 2), which guides funded academic research in Canada, puts it this way, "Given the fundamental importance of research and of human participation in research, we must do all that we can as a society to ensure that research is conducted in an ethical manner so as to build public confidence and trust" (CIHR, NSERC, and SSHRC 2018, 5). Codes of ethics and research ethics guidelines offer principles and procedures for anticipating benefits and risks of harm, in general. This section reviews specific ethical considerations in forced migration through general principles adopted by researchers in Canada. Creative practices in Canada that involve participants are exempt from research ethics review (TCPS 2 2018, 20). There are situations where the distinction between art and research activities involving participants are not easily distinguished, such as research involving refugee youth, as our story at the beginning of this chapter illustrates. Artists and those using research-creation are urged to be aware of other ethical tools where they exist. For instance, the organization RISE, which describes itself as the "first eX-detainee, Refugee and Asylum seeker organisation in Australia" has published a list of ethical standards for artists by Tania Canas. (See "Further Reading and Resources" at the chapter's end.)

For publicly funded research in Canada, the core ethical principles that guide the work of research ethics boards are, "respect for persons," "concern for welfare," and "justice" (TCPS 2 2018, 6). A Canadian guideline statement entitled "Ethical Considerations: Research with People in Situations of Forced Migration" was drafted in 2017 and was followed by "Code of Ethics: Critical Reflections on Research Ethics in Situations of Forced Migration" by the International Association for the Study of Forced Migration (IASFM) in 2018. These statements deal with specific approaches to ethics in forced migration and were developed through workshops and consultations with communities of researchers and service providers. The IASFM Code of Ethics (listed in Further Reading and Resources) can be used as a topic for team discussions at an early stage of art and research project planning, even before a research ethics application is made.

Unanticipated "microethics" that researchers face in everyday settings demand "ethics in practice" according to Guillemin and Gillam (2004, 263, 265). Skills for ethics in practice are developed through experience and reference to experiences of others that are increasingly documented in research publications. For example, in Lea Müller-Funk's description of qualitative research involving Syrian refugees, everyday ethical decisions relied on principles beyond the IASFM Code of Ethics. Müller-Funk's practice required attention to relationality in order "to balance power inequalities, build trust among participants, discuss the relevance and appropriateness of research and interview questions, and include feedback mechanisms for data analysis and writing" (Müller-Funk 2021, 2309). The following descriptions of three ethical principles and their related case studies demonstrate how conditions of forced migration require specific consideration by artists and researchers.

Respect for Persons

Codes of research ethics since the mid-twentieth century, including the IASFM's, begin with a statement about how autonomy of individual persons must be respected in research and realized through a process of informed consent, which documents the independent decision of individuals to participate in data collection, interviews, recordings, creative, or other activities. "The voluntary consent of the human subject is absolutely essential," is the first principle of the Nuremberg Code, an outcome of the trials of Nazi doctors charged with war crimes for subjecting prison camp residents to egregiously harmful research. The primacy of research participants' right to choose or refuse to participate in research is a lasting legacy of the Nuremberg trials (Shuster 1997, 1439). But in forced migration studies, as in other areas, the ideal of autonomous consent is often compromised. It is challenged when there is unequal access to citizenship and basic resources, as we demonstrated in our chapter's opening story. Long and legalistic consent forms are inappropriate when individuals have trouble understanding the contents, are wary of legalistic paperwork, or may be at risk of leaving a record of their participation or location. Richard Hugman, Eileen Pittaway, and Linda Bartolomei, in a review of ethical responsibilities for social work researchers in refugee contexts, describe how their project took a more relational approach to consent: "consent is given through a process that involves groups meeting and discussing all the implications of the research and, should they agree to participate, continuing to think about their involvement in such a way that either individuals may withdraw or even a whole group can decide to end their involvement" (2011a, 1280). In this model, respect for persons is realized when researchers engage participants in ongoing and responsive consent processes.

Field Example: "Respect for Persons" in Participatory Photography

Participatory photography projects taking place in the informal encampments at the UK/France border in Calais can face challenges in terms of respect, autonomy, and consent. For researchers Marie Godin and Giorgia Donà (2022) their citizen photography project *Displaces* was just one of many research, art, and activism projects that sought to actively involve camp residents in photographically documenting their travels through Europe and their time at the camp. The projects they described ranged from photojournalism, art photography, *photo voce* [photo voice], to NGO-initiated fundraising. Recognizing the inherent difficulties of circulating identifiable images of participants with limited legal status, *Displaces* addressed "respect for autonomy" in deliberate ways. Godin and Donà describe how issues of consent grew well beyond a one-time agreement to participate in this university-aligned project. It required training for the participants in photography and editing, as well as access to equipment during the participants' varied times in the camp. Over time, participants came to decisions on the use of their own photos (including copyright), the possession and storage of the cameras (which they could keep or sell), and on the level of engagement they wanted to maintain with the project and its archive.

Informed consent was not given just once. Instead, it consisted of a set of renewals, applicable each time the researchers wished to make use of the participants' photographic material, either in presentations or publications. *Displaces* not only honoured copyrights but also worked to provide the resources needed to adequately exercise copyrights.

Concern for Welfare

In guidelines used by research ethics boards in Canada, "concern for welfare" is explained as an expectation for researchers to ensure that the welfare of participants' "physical, mental and spiritual health, as well as their physical, economic and social circumstances" are not hampered by the research (TCPS 2 2018, 7). The guidelines further describe how economic and social circumstances may include "housing, employment, security, family life, community membership and social participation, among other aspects of life." They elaborate how concern for welfare should extend to groups since, "[g]roups may benefit from the knowledge gained from the research, but they may also suffer from stigmatization, discrimination or damage to reputation" (TCPS 2 2018, 7). Concern for the welfare of groups is considered when researchers "commit themselves to be open and accountable to participants, other researchers and to the wider community," according to Hugman, Pittaway, and Bartolomei (2011b, 669). This responsibility is shared by assessors of research proposals, research ethics boards, funders, peer reviewers of publications, or partners who draft research agreements. The IASFM code of ethics includes the directive to "do no harm," especially in forced migration fields where trauma experiences and insecure legal status are prevalent conditions for participants. An abbreviated version of what is commonly attributed to the ancient Hippocratic Oath, "First, do no harm" (*primum non nocere*) sets a minimum standard of conduct. As a directive it could be interpreted as patronizing toward the participants since it assigns the power of assessing harm to the practitioner (or doctor, in medical settings). Researchers in forced migration studies have insisted that "do no harm" is a limited ethical principle in a field where research needs to be fully accountable to those needing the research, including providing direct benefits to improve the welfare of those affected by or impacted by the research and its outcomes (Hugman, Pittaway, and Bartolomei 2011b).

Field Example: "Concern for Welfare" of Peer Researchers

In a study of Syrian refugees who have resettled in Canada, researchers hired community members as peer researchers who shared some of the community's characteristics (language, in this case) to conduct interviews and surveys (Oda et al. 2022). Concern for the welfare of the Syrian immigrants was a priority, and that was reflected in the researchers' choice of a community-based research methodology. But this approach also presented ethical challenges. Peer researchers Anna Oda, Adnan Al Mhamied, Riham Al-Saadi, Neil Arya, Mona Awwad, Oula Hajjar, Jill Hanley, Michaela Hynie, Nicole Ives, Rabih Jamil, Mahi Khalaf, Rim Khyar, Ben C.H. Kuo, May Massijeh, Rana Mohammad, and Kathy Sherrell critically reflected on these challenges in a text about the impact of the research on their own well-being (Oda et al. 2022). They describe the project's regular debriefing sessions, sometimes including creative and expressive activities, during which they could reflect on challenges they had experienced with positionality and identity. This included their professional role conflicts, compassion fatigue and burnout, as well as more generalized distress and secondary trauma (Oda et al. 2022, 51). Along with debriefing, there were sessions about self-care and ethical issues around conducting interviews with vulnerable groups. The peer researchers concluded that this reflexive practice continually addressed the concern for welfare of the research team itself and contributed valuable insights for the larger project (Oda et al. 2022, 52).

Justice

This term is a core ethical principle that is meant to encompass fairness and equity, as well as issues of unequal power relationships and vulnerabilities associated with art or research projects. The IASFM code of ethics separates out several components of this principle to emphasize how ensuring justice in forced migration studies is particularly challenging. It highlights equity, diversity, competence, and partnership. Equity reflects the expectation that the benefits of research are fairly distributed, even in circumstances of extreme disparity. People who have the greatest need for research are often in situations that make research difficult to carry out. It is a matter of justice to prioritize the needs of "under researched" groups over those who are already "over researched." Diversity is an ethical consideration in the criteria and selection of research participants, as well as in composition of project teams. Further, project teams are advised to take the lead from team members and community partners who bring lived experience in forced migration. The initiative Share the Platform has listed ways to bring the voices of refugees to the centre when developing and implementing such things as "policy, programs, and practice" affecting refugees. These include co-authorship, professional networking, and seeing those with lived experience as possessing expertise rather than vulnerabilities. To develop competence, highlighted in the IASFM code, those new to forced migration are advised to take advantage of training opportunities in cultural safety, justice, equity, diversity, decolonization, and inclusion. Partnership, the final IASFM principle, and close supervision are necessary especially for first-time artists and researchers in encampments or

Figure 6.2 | Francisco-Fernando Granados, *spatial profiling* ...

sites of detention, or with people who are otherwise at risk of being made vulnerable by the art or research activities as described by Goeff Gilbert and others (see Atak et al. 2020).

Field Example: Seeking "Justice" in Centring Refugee Spaces

This chapter began with my (Francisco-Fernando) recounting the ways art offered me a sense of belonging, even before my refugee determination process was completed. We end with field experience from a later art project in which I approached the ethical principle of justice through a commission to install artwork in a building providing services for refugees. The project involved consultation with and involvement of the newcomer community at the YMCA Newcomer Connections Centre in Saint John, New Brunswick. The resulting exhibition, *1. Make a line*, presented artworks that coexisted with and enhanced the centre's educational and recreational activities, through processes of ongoing permissions and consent (see figs 6.1 and 6.2). As an artist from another part of Canada invited to create an exhibition for the community members, my interactions were mediated by workers with lived experience. I was pleased to read later in an art review how a worker at the centre described what it was like to encounter the exhibition inside the space. The review starts by quoting a community engagement officer: "The big thing for us was, after ... talking to [Francisco-Fernando Granados] about his journey and how that influenced his work ... that really helped to explain, 'Why?' That's the main question that comes up ... because that really puts the heart to it." The review goes on: "After performing *spatial profiling* ... in which he continuously traces the outline of his profile while moving along the wall, Granados invited audience members to do the same. Mattie [quoted above] watched as he disappeared into the small crowd. 'You couldn't tell who was the artist, anymore,' she says" (K. Wallace 2016). This partnership developed through a relational process that invited equitable participation by building trust and reciprocity over time.

CONCLUSION

In reflecting on ethics in forced migration art and research, we have focused on the way relationships form the applied ethics of forced migration projects. Beyond good intentions, ethical practices grow from managing everyday ethics, and from hearing the perspectives of others in the field. We urge artists and researchers to prepare by taking advantage of ethics training, by working with NGOs in non-research or non-art contexts, and by seeking out existing ethical guidelines, protocols, or other cultural mores that exist in the location of the research. Take an active approach to ethics by engaging in discussions about issues raised in art or research, including in languages other than English (Clark-Kazak 2021). Also, be active in your projects' research ethics reviews by supplying resources listed in this chapter or names of experts from your field to assist with the review, if your REB is not already familiar with forced migration work. Share the document "Your Rights in Research" with participants (available in multiple languages and included as a resource, below) (Clark-Kazak 2018). Recognize the authorship and ownership of your participants' contributions. In a recent presentation, Caroline Lenette asked those in attendance to post in the meeting's chat box a citation of "reflexive writing that you are most proud of in terms of articulating ethical issues and dilemmas, and clearly outlining your positionality" (Lenette 2021). We encourage readers and learners to take Lenette's challenge and reflect critically on your positionality and ethics in projects as they take place, and later in a public venue. Finally, we urge artists and researchers to learn and share decolonial methods, as we have aimed to do in the collaborative writing of this chapter.

FURTHER READING AND RESOURCES

Canas, Tania. 2015. "10 Things You Need to Consider If You Are an Artist – Not of the Refugee and Asylum Seeker Community – Looking to Work with Our Community." *RISE. Refugees, Survivors and eX-Detainees*. https://aktiontanz.de/wp-content/uploads/2017/03/RISE-statement-on-working-with-the-refugee-community.pdf.

Clark-Kazak, Christina R. 2018. "Your Rights in Research." CARFMS. https://carfms.org/your-rights-in-research.

– 2021. "Ethics in Forced Migration Research: Taking Stock and Potential Ways Forward." *Journal on Migration and Human Security* 9 (3): 125–38. https://doi.org/10.1177/23315024211034401.

IASFM. 2018. "International Association for the Study of Forced Migration Studies (IASFM) Code of Ethics: Critical Reflections on Research Ethics in Situations of Forced Migration." 30 November 2018. http://iasfm.org/blog/2018/11/30/adoption-of-iasfm-research-code-of-ethics.

Share the Platform. n.d. "Centering the Expertise of Refugees to Improve Policy, Programs, and Practice." https://www.sharetheplatform.org.

Downloadable texts on decolonial "ethics of research" are available on Eve Tuck's website (http://www.evetuck.com/writing), including:

Tuck, Eve. 2009. "Suspending Damage: A Letter to Communities." *Harvard Educational Review* 79, no. 3 (Fall).

Tuck, Eve, and Monique Guishard. 2013. "Uncollapsing Ethics: Racialized Sciencism, Settler Coloniality, and an Ethical Framework of Decolonial Participatory Action Research." In *Challenging Status Quo Retrenchment: New Directions in Critical Research*, edited by Tricia M. Kress, Curry Malott, and Bradley J. Porfilio. Critical Constructions: Studies on Education and Society. Charlotte: Information Age Publishing.

7

Forced Migration into Canada from a Global Perspective

Dawit Demoz

KEY TAKEAWAYS

- Canada is a leader in refugee resettlement, but only a small percentage of refugees globally are resettled. National security, economic and humanitarian considerations drive priorities for resettlement to Canada.
- Canada has played an important role in developing and promoting international refugee policy. In addition, the Canadian government should acknowledge the inherent and inextricable link between foreign policy and refugee policy.
- Canada's promotion of refugee participation and inclusion has recently focused on involving refugee delegates at diplomatic events and offering limited funding. More could be done at all levels of government to support refugee-led initiatives and increase employment of people with lived experiences of displacement.

KEY TERMS

- Refugee participation
- Resettlement
- Durable solutions

INTRODUCTION

For the last several decades, the United Nations High Commissioner for Refugees (UNHCR) and the international community have applied the traditional framework of durable solutions aimed at "solving" forced migration and the refugee crisis. These solutions include local integration, repatriation, and resettlement (Long 2010; R. Black and Koser 1999). While the durable solutions framework has the objective of ending the suffering of refugees globally, in practice it has very little effect. For example, in 2021, about 429,300 refugees repatriated to their countries of origin and some 57,500 were resettled (UNHCR 2022b). Although data on how many refugees were locally integrated into their host countries are lacking, with 100 million displaced persons globally at the time of writing, it is safe to conclude that the durable solutions framework has been far from successful in providing a comprehensive solution to forced migration.

Against this backdrop, Canada has taken an ever-growing role both at home and abroad to address forced migration and assist those who have been forced to flee. This chapter aims to assess Canada's policies and practices with respect to global forced migration.

HISTORICAL REVIEW OF CANADA'S IMMIGRATION POLICIES

Since the European colonial conquest of Indigenous Peoples and territories, Canada has had a history of immigration policies influenced by economic, national security, and discriminatory factors. From the late 1800s to the mid-1900s, Canada favoured "White" European immigrants while imposing restrictions on non-White immigrants, rooted in the perception of Europeans as industrious and adaptable (García 2006). National security concerns also shaped immigration policies, as seen during World War I, when immigration from enemy states was suspended (Boyd and Vickers 2000). Canada's immigration policies have been marred by racism and xenophobia, with restrictions heavily impacting individuals of Asian, Jewish, and African origins (Abella and Troper 2012; Konadu-Agyemang 1999). Examples such as the return of Jewish refugees fleeing Europe and the exclusion of Chinese immigrants exemplify the discriminatory nature of the Canadian immigration system. The 1952 amendment to the Immigration Act codified discriminatory measures that allowed for the refusal of entry to immigrants based on nationality, ethnic group, geographical origin, customs, habits, ability to assimilate, and other factors. It codified discriminatory practices that heavily restricted the immigration of individuals based on race and ethnicity (Abella and Troper 2012).

However, there were instances where Canada welcomed immigrants from specific countries to further foreign policy goals, like admitting Hungarian refugees in response to the 1956 Hungarian Uprising (Dench 1999). It was only in 1960 that Canada began actively resettling Asian refugees (Madokoro 2016). The shift in policy in 1960 marked a turning point in Canada's approach to welcoming and resettling refugees from Asian countries. Notably, from 1979 to 1980, Canada resettled a significant number of refugees from Southeast Asia in response to Cold War conflicts, which was considered a success (Dench 1999; Hou 2021). Such success, according to Reynolds and Hyndman, was due to the "serendipitous alignment of government policy, public opinion, and citizens action" (2021, 28). The 1952 amendment to the Immigration Act in Canada was eventually repealed and replaced by a subsequent amendment in 1976. However, significant revisions to the immigration system occurred with the passing of the Immigration and Refugee Protection Act (IRPA) in 2001, which entered into force in 2002 (García 2006). IRPA introduced a new framework for immigration, emphasizing humanitarian principles, fairness, and non-discrimination (Government of Canada 2017b). This legislation aimed to address some of the discriminatory practices of the past and create a more inclusive and equitable immigration system.

While positive public opinion on immigration continues to influence government policies in addressing global refugee issues mostly since 2015 (Su and Clark-Kazak 2022), the chapter aims to critically examine whether Canada has fully moved beyond its problematic history. It assesses Canada's resettlement priorities from an international perspective, its role in developing and promoting international refugee policy, and its advocacy for refugee participation and inclusion.

CANADA'S REFUGEE RESETTLEMENT

7.1 "Why Do Some [Refugees] Make It into the West Quickly – While Others Have to Wait More than a Decade?"

"After my uncle spent 15 years in the Shimelba [refugee] camp in Ethiopia's Tigray region, we lost all contact with him for two years until 2021, when he was found homeless on the streets of Addis Ababa … Canada moving at a breakneck speed to implement targeted supports for Ukrainian asylum seekers was a reminder that our refugee policies are not race-blind commitments to humanitarianism" (Kuluberhan 2022, para. 5 and 7).

Canada prides itself on its liberal and innovative immigration policies. For example, in the 2015 federal election, Trudeau's Liberal Party promised to resettle twenty-five thousand Syrians to Canada by the end of 2015 and pledged CAD$200 million to the issue, with half directed to increase refugee services in Canada and the other half to support relief activities in the Middle East (Milner 2021a). The Liberals lived up to this promise; since 2015, more than seventy-three thousand Syrians have resettled to Canada (Martani 2021). Since 2018, unlike the years before that, it was Canada, and not the United States, that resettled more refugees than any other country in the world (Radford and Connor 2019). This shift in refugee resettlement can be attributed to the unique circumstances surrounding the Trump administration in the United States.

When those numbers are evaluated in isolation and in comparison to Canada's overall population, they are quite high. However, Canada's commitment to refugee resettlement is less generous relative to the number of refugees hosted by countries in the global south and countries bordering conflicts (see table 0.1 in the introduction). Countries like Uganda, Turkey, and Poland, for example, host the largest number of refugees escaping persecution and war in their home countries (UNHCR 2022c).

Currently, refugees abroad can be resettled to Canada through the Government-Assisted Resettlement program, the Private Sponsorship of Refugees (PSR) program, and other hybrid programs where private citizens and the government share the responsibility (for more details see Atak, chapter 17; Labman, chapter 18). Part of what makes the PSR program so unique and sustainable is the fact that ordinary Canadians are involved – from identifying the refugees they would like to sponsor to providing financial and settlement support. While other, mostly Western, countries have government-assisted resettlement programs, Canada remains one of just a few countries in the world that has a private, or community, sponsorship program, and the only country so far where private citizens can name the refugees they want to sponsor.

Inspired by those positive experiences at home, Canada has attempted to "export" the PSR model to other countries through bilateral negotiations and at multilateral meetings. Canada's objectives are to encourage other countries to increase and improve refugee resettlement by engaging private citizens, communities, and businesses in resettlement, to strengthen local host communities to welcome newcomers, and to encourage a broader narrative that supports refugee protection (Government of Canada 2021c). For example, in December 2016, representatives from the governments of Argentina, Australia, Brazil, Chile, Germany, New Zealand, the UK, and the US participated in a three-day conference in Canada to discuss how their countries could adopt tailored versions of Canada's PSR program. And as of 2021, Australia, Argentina, the UK, Ireland, and New Zealand have all committed to developing private or community sponsorship programs because of Canada's advocacy (Mismash 2021).

Although the unique model of the PSR program represents a welcome opportunity for refugees to move to Canada, critics argue that it shifts the responsibility for refugee resettlement away from the government and toward private citizens and communities (Hyndman et al. 2021). Between 2010 and 2020, for example, according to Hyndman and colleagues, while the quota for privately sponsored refugees increased by 400 per cent, the number of GARs increased by 25 per cent during the same time period. An increase in private sponsorship should never correlate to a decrease in government-assisted resettlement. After all, its principle of additionality is one of the key factors that make the PSR program unique.

In addition to the regular resettlement programs, Canada has also occasionally created special programs by which nationals from specific countries may resettle to Canada. In August 2021 Canada committed to welcoming at least forty thousand Afghans. Specifically, the government created a special program for Afghans who assisted the Government of Canada, and it established a humanitarian program that created additional resettlement allocations for other Afghan nationals (Government of Canada 2022e).

In March 2022 Canada introduced a new immigration pathway for Ukrainians fleeing the war with Russia. Canada launched the Canada-Ukraine Authorization for Emergency Travel program, which allows Ukrainians to enter Canada on an expedited basis, without undergoing the normal visa requirements, and obtain open work permits upon arrival. Between 17 March and 27 July 2022, Canadian immigration authorities approved 238,409 applications for emergency travel under this program and 82,704 had arrived by land and air by the first week of September 2022 (Government of Canada 2022b).

Although Canada's responses to the situations in Ukraine and Afghanistan are commendable, critics have pointed out that those emergency measures are discriminatory and are implemented at the expense of other populations (House of Commons 2022; Kuluberhan 2022; Simardone and Khaki 2022). For example, people fleeing other just as acute situations – like the active conflicts and human-made famine in Tigray, Ethiopia, and Yemen – may face similarly dire conditions as those fleeing Afghanistan or Ukraine, but they are not being considered for such emergency assistance. Those contradictions were recognized by the multi-party Standing Committee on Immigration, Citizenship and Refugees of the House of Commons, which called on the minister of Immigration, Refugees and Citizenship to extend the special immigration measures adopted for Ukrainian nationals to individuals escaping conflict in other countries (House of Commons 2022). In addition, Canadian refugee law practitioners raised the same concerns and criticized Canada's double standards in hopes of extending such assistance to all refugees (Simardone and Khaki 2022). To date, their recommendation has not been adopted.

Moreover, the use of formal and informal quotas and the discrepancies in processing times over the past several years reflect bias in resettlement. As Reynolds and Hyndman (2021) point out, under the Harper government (2006–15), visa posts that served sub-Saharan African refugee applicants had smaller PSR quotas than visa posts serving applicants from the Middle East. This meant that the application processing time for sub-Saharan African applicants was significantly longer than for those from other countries.

Table 7.1 | Processing times from different visa offices

Country	Processing times (in months)
Ethiopia	33
Kenya	30
Pakistan	21
Sudan	32
Tajikistan	21
Turkey	26

Note: The processing times do not reflect the delays caused by countries of residence after the visa is approved.
Source: Dawit Demoz from Government of Canada (2018).

Those same issues persist today and have been exacerbated by COVID-19. The pandemic has led to long backlogs across the board, further preventing the Canadian government from expediting African refugee applications to make up for prior processing time discrepancies. Additionally, the current emphasis on bringing Ukrainian and Afghan applicants has redirected human resources that could have otherwise ensured equity in the PSR program. Indeed, it could reinforce prior bias by further exacerbating the discrepancies in processing times for refugee applicants from certain regions.

Using the IRCC online platform, I verified the current processing times for refugees coming from six countries in the Middle East and East Africa. Once sponsorship applications are submitted to IRCC, there are two stages of assessment: the assessment of the sponsorship application and the refugee application. The assessment for the sponsorship application is done within Canada, and the processing time is somewhat the same. The processing times in table 7.1 reflect the processing of the refugee application, which is done at the visa offices abroad.

As table 7.1 reflects, mostly Black refugees coming from sub-Saharan Africa (like Ethiopia, Kenya, and Sudan), wait between four and twelve months longer than refugees coming from other regions (like Pakistan, Tajikistan, and Turkey). More must be done to eliminate and correct these disparities. For a deeper exploration of the issues related to temporality, waiting times, and disparities in processing durations, readers are encouraged to consult the following sources: Fee 2022; Hyndman and Giles 2016; Mountz 2011.

CANADA'S INTERNATIONAL POLICY AND FORCED MIGRATION

> 7.2 "Nevsun in Eritrea: Dealing with a Dictator - *The Fifth Estate*"
> "More than half of the world's mining companies are Canadian. But do they promote Canadian values when they do business abroad?"
> (CBC News 2016)

In recent years, Canada has been active in forced migration issues on the world stage. Although Canada's leadership is commendable, the government has failed to fully appreciate the overlap between foreign policy and forced migration policy. In a similar vein, Canada's focus has been on assisting refugees but not on addressing the root causes of displacement.

In terms of refugee assistance, Canada is a major funder of UNHCR. Canada's financial contributions to UNHCR more than doubled from 2006 to 2013, from CAD$37.3 million to CAD$84.9 million (Grayson and Audet 2017). In 2021 Canada was the eleventh largest funder of UNHCR, contributing more funds than both the UK and Australia (UNHCR 2022b).

Canada's pre-eminent role on refugee issues globally is also evident through its leadership on the UN Global Compact on Refugees (GCR), which was affirmed by the UN General Assembly in December 2018 (Milner 2021a). The Canadian Government was a perceived moral and expert authority in these negotiations, deriving from its resettlement of refugees and its financial contributions to the international refugee regime, as well as its sustained political and diplomatic engagement with the international community (Milner 2021a).

During the consultations related to drafting the agreement, Canada was one of the first countries to offer concrete suggestions about what issues the GCR should highlight and address. Those issues included "increas[ing] accountability, includ[ing] complementary pathways for refugees to be resettled, main-streaming a gender-sensitive approach throughout the GCR, and the development of clear mechanisms to ensure effective implementation" (Milner 2021a, 56). Canada, which chaired the UNHCR Executive Committee during the development of the GCR, successfully gained support for most of its positions, as the final text of the GCR reflects (Milner 2021a).

Canada also plays a productive role in regional support platforms. Canada is a member of the Comprehensive Regional Protection and Solutions Framework (MIRPS) support platform, a mechanism for forced migration in Central America and Mexico that aims to promote "regional cooperation among countries of origin, transit and destination for a greater responsibility sharing in matters of prevention, protection and durable solutions" (MIRPS n.d.). Canada chaired MIRPS in 2022 and hosted a signature event that assembled a diverse group of stakeholders, including state representatives, UN agencies, international financial institutions, the private sector, civil society, and refugee-led organizations to promote best practices of responsibility sharing and protecting forcibly displaced persons in the region (Government of Canada 2022a). Canada also hosted the International Donors' Conference in Solidarity with Venezuelan Refugees and Migrants in June 2021.

Despite this leadership, the Canadian government has failed to fully appreciate the overlap between foreign policy and forced migration policy. Individuals would not be forced to flee their home countries if the root causes of migration were addressed. Additionally, the durable solution of "repatriation," in which a refugee returns home because the conditions which caused him or her to flee no longer exist, is dependent upon changes for the better in countries of origin. But just as with resettlement bias, Canada's appreciation of the intersection of foreign policy with forced migration is subject to racialized discrepancies (see also Mahrouse and El Omari, chapter 15). For example, the close nexus between Canada's policies toward those fleeing the conflict in Ukraine and its foreign policy objectives in that region is demonstrated by the tweet from Prime Minister Trudeau:

> The atrocities committed by Russian forces in Ukraine are appalling – and we, the G7 leaders, are united in condemning them. I want to be very clear: Those responsible for recently-revealed war crimes and atrocities will be held accountable. We stand with Ukraine. (Trudeau 2022a)

At the same time that Canada has a unique program to offer protection in Canada for those fleeing Ukraine, the Canadian government, as the tweet indicates, has taken a hardline stance against Russia and is actively working to bring an end to the underlying conflict that caused the forced migration in the first place.

However, Canada does not take the same approach with respect to other conflicts globally. For example, Eritreans and Ethiopians comprise a significant portion of the refugee applicants who seek protection in Canada. Yet Canada's involvement in ending the war and human-made famine in Tigray, Ethiopia is lukewarm at best. That approach is encapsulated in a tweet by Trudeau, published less than twenty-four hours before his quoted tweet about Ukraine:

> I spoke with Prime Minister @AbiyAhmedAli today about the conflict in Ethiopia, and the humanitarian truce. I called for further steps to make sure those affected can get the humanitarian assistance they need, and I reiterated Canada's support for a peaceful resolution. (Trudeau 2022b)

Instead of calling out Prime Minister Abiy Ahmed for UN reported war crimes (Keaten 2022), Trudeau used muted language and called for amorphous "further steps" to be taken toward resolving the conflict. As UN and human rights groups have recognized, the government of Eritrea conscripts much of its adult population under the auspices of indefinite national service (Amnesty International 2020; Human Rights Watch 2019; UN 2016). Conscripts are forced to work on projects deemed in the national interest. Many Eritreans flee to escape the harsh treatment imposed as part of the conscription (Amnesty International 2019; Human Rights Watch 2019).

According to Donna Gabaccia (2017), diasporic politics exert a significant influence on foreign policy and refugee policy. Diaspora communities in the US often possess a strong sense of affiliation and attachment to their countries of origin, prompting active engagement in advocating for the interests of their fellow compatriots. This engagement can pressure host governments, influencing policy priorities and decision-making (Gabaccia 2017). In the Canadian context, the presence of a large Ukrainian diaspora may have influenced the higher admission of Ukrainian refugees to Canada. This demonstrates the complex interplay between diasporic politics, foreign policy formulation, and refugee admission policies, highlighting the need for policy-makers to navigate diverse interests and considerations in a balanced and equitable manner.

Additionally, Canada's economic foreign policy often exacerbates the root causes of forced migration. For example, Canada fails to hold accountable Canadian mining companies that contribute to human rights violations and conflict. A notorious example is Nevsun Resources Ltd, a Canadian mining company that had been active at the Bisha Mine in Eritrea, where slave labour and torture were alleged (Brend 2020). The Canadian government did not hold hearings or utilize regulatory enforcement to end such practices and hold the company accountable. Rather, a group of Eritrean refugees living in Canada, who had fled those mines, retained counsel and managed to secure a legal victory against the company (Amnesty International 2020; Beedell and Tamrat 2020). Amnesty International Canada has stated that "[t]his settlement speaks to the incredible courage of the mine workers who came forward with their horrific experiences of torture, slavery, and forced labour while working at the mine ... This case underscores the urgent need for legislation requiring Canadian companies to conduct human right due diligence throughout global operations" (Amnesty International 2020, para. 3 and 5).

The Nevsun case is not an isolated example. The Canadian Council for Refugees (CCR) called for Canadian companies to be held accountable for contributing to forced displacement worldwide. Then CCR president Claire Roque said, "[I]n Canada and around the world, mining activities often contribute to forced migration. It is increasingly clear that better accountability structures are needed for the Canadian resource extraction industry" (CCR 2019, para.

2). Despite the ongoing atrocities in the Tigray region of Ethiopia, Canadian mining companies have been lobbying the perpetrators of those atrocities for licences to mine gold in the region (York and Zelalem 2021). At the same time that Canada receives refugee claims, its companies are exploiting – and in some cases exacerbating – the atrocities that cause those to flee in the first place. In sum, while being a leader on refugee resettlement efforts is an admirable achievement, there is much more Canada can do to ensure that its foreign policy and economic objectives align with its humanitarian ideals.

MEANINGFUL REFUGEE PARTICIPATION AND INCLUSION

> 7.3 End the Tokenism. Give Refugees a Voice about Our Own Futures
> "Refugee participation can help transform the global refugee system to be more equitable, effective, responsive, and legitimate. Together, we need to reimagine a system where refugees have a seat at the table and can add our expertise and lived experience to a system we depend on for protection and that we know inside and out"
> (Alio and Gardi 2021, n.p.).

Governments, donors, and aid agencies have traditionally dominated the debate over refugee policy without showing "much interest in how affected people see these things" (Praag 2022, 8). Refugees' views and expertise have for the most part been ignored in the design and implementation of refugee policies and humanitarian aid programs (see also Araya, chapter 9). Refugees are "expected to abide by the decisions of the refugee regime, despite their inability to have access to the process that creates these policies and decisions" (Milner 2021b, 7). Imperialism and colonial attitudes underlie the tendency to ignore affected peoples in the development of policies and programs aimed to assist them (Alio and Gardi 2021; Harley and Hobbs 2020; Milner 2021b).

Recently, the Canadian government has attempted to respond through limited initiatives on refugee participation. Since 2019 Canada has led advocacy on refugee participation in meetings of the global refugee regime (Milner, Alio, and Gardi 2022). Bob Rae, while serving as Canada's special envoy on humanitarian and refugee issues, argued that Canada has "led the way in refugee inclusion with policies, recommendations, and decision-making as well as in Canadian delegations to international conferences" (2020, para. 14). At the 2019 Global Refugee Forum, Canada included a refugee adviser in its delegation for the first time and committed to including refugee advisers in future delegations.

Encouraged by these developments, the Refugee Advisory Network of Canada (RAN Canada) was established in September 2020. Run by a group of diverse former refugees, RAN Canada aims "to promote the meaningful participation of refugees in Canada's engagement with the international refugee system. RAN Canada advocates for, and strives to achieve, the meaningful inclusion of the perspectives, skills and knowledge of refugees in global policy and decision-making processes that affect the lives of refugees. RAN Canada works to bring the perspectives, skills and knowledge of refugees into public discourse, policy discussions, and wider discussions on refugees" (RAN Canada n.d.)

The government has worked with RAN Canada since its establishment to select refugees to join its delegations to international meetings. Additionally, Canada has encouraged other countries to follow its lead and include refugees in its delegations. For example, Germany and the United States followed Canada's example and included refugees in their delegations to the 2021 UNHCR High-Level Officials Meeting (Milner, Alio, and Gardi 2022). The network selected me, an advising member of RAN Canada, to join the Canadian delegation for the UNHCR High-Level Officials Meeting conducted virtually in December 2021.

Canada has also shown some commitment to funding refugee-led organizations. For example, following the 2021 UNHCR Executive Committee meeting, Canada pledged to fund "Together for Learning," a refugee education initiative led by refugees. Additionally, Canada agreed to fund eight research chairs on the issue of forced migration based in four regions of the Global South in an effort to create a localized knowledge base. To institutionalize such support, the government created its first-ever dedicated fund to support refugee-led organizations. The fund was started with CAD$40 million (Government of Canada 2021c).

Although Canada is at the forefront of refugee participation and inclusion, there remains considerable room for improvement. When it comes to funding refugee-led organizations and aid efforts, the Canadian government – as well as other governments, UNHCR, and international aid agencies – must recognize the most effective assistance comes from the community itself. Well before a refugee interacts with UNHCR or another externally funded organization, they sought and received assistance from their community (Getachew et al. 2022; see also Araya, chapter 9).

That baseline understanding – that assistance directed by affected communities is most effective (Pincock, Betts, and Easton-Calabria 2021) – should drive Canada's funding of humanitarian programs. In 2021 Canada committed CAD$40 million to support initiatives, especially refugee-led initiatives, on education in sub-Saharan Africa over the next five years (Government of Canada 2021c). While that commitment is commendable, there is no reason it should be limited to educational initiatives in one region when affected communities engage in all kinds of assistance efforts globally. Moreover, only organizations registered in Canada are eligible to apply for the funding. Refugee-led assistance is effective because it is localized; requiring Canadian registration eliminates a key component of what drives the success of such work. Additionally, the CAD$40 million represents a small investment compared to Canada's overall aid budget. Were the Canadian government to truly adopt the understanding that programs driven by affected communities are most effective, then the proportion of funding going to such initiatives would far outweigh funding going to external or international bodies that are not led by the communities impacted by such funding.

To enhance support for refugees, Canada should consider providing direct funding to refugee-led organizations in the Global South. By channelling resources directly to these organizations, Canada can empower and amplify refugees' voices, enabling them to address their own unique challenges and shape local solutions. However, "in many refugee host contexts, humanitarian and social services are either not readily available, or the host state makes them legally unavailable to refugees" (Motalebi and Martin-Shields 2023, 2). Canada should actively encourage UNHCR to establish funding mechanisms and meaningful partnerships with refugee-led organizations. This collaborative approach recognizes the valuable expertise and perspectives refugees offer and ensures their active involvement in decision-making processes and program implementation. While UNHCR carries out its own programs, like refugee status determination (RSD) and resettlement, it also is a major funder of what it calls "implementing partners," which are local organizations that provide direct assistance to refugees (UNHCR n.d.b). In many places, implementing partners are not refugee-led organizations but rather international aid groups or organizations comprised of nationals of the host country.

In addition to funding refugee-led organizations, Canada can do more to promote refugee inclusion in international and domestic policy-making. Canada's insistence that governmental delegations attend international conferences and other diplomatic events on forced migration issues is laudable. Alongside such efforts, the Canadian government should work to ensure that refugees are represented at all levels of government and on the staff of key partners working across the globe. If refugees were truly represented as employees across all levels of government, the need to incorporate refugee viewpoints would be more organic.

Similarly, Canada should urge its international partners to employ refugees on staff in leadership positions. Although many organizations employ refugees in outreach positions, such as resettlement workers, cultural mediators, or interpreters, that remains insufficient. International aid groups that work on refugee issues should value lived experience and expertise in all hiring, including at the top of the organizational structure. By employing refugees in top positions, powerful organizations can eliminate tokenization and ensure that those who best understand forced migration drive the work on the ground.

Last, Canada's recent efforts to include refugee delegates as advisers on forced migration issues should be extended to include foreign policy issues. Diaspora communities have an outsized understanding of the dynamics at home, which can be shared with key stakeholders in the government. Moreover, diaspora communities play a significant role in changing conditions in their country of origin, including through remittances, advocacy, and envisioning new forms of governance. By including and consulting refugees as delegates in international meetings on their countries of origin, the Canadian government could more explicitly recognize the robust link between refugee policy and foreign policy.

CONCLUSION

To address the issues discussed in this chapter, the government of Canada should consider taking actions in the areas of refugee resettlement, international policy, and meaningful refugee participation and inclusion. Canada must first ensure that objective criteria, and not national security or economic considerations, drive who can access the resettlement programs. With respect to international policy, Canada should recognize the inherent and inextricable link between foreign policy and refugee policy, ensure an even-handed approach in foreign policy objectives and positions with respect to conflicts that contribute to forced migration, and hold Canadian companies and other entities accountable for actions abroad that violate human rights standards and contribute to forced migration.

Concerning refugee participation and inclusion, the government of Canada should recognize that refugee-led programs are the most effective, realign funding priorities to reflect that baseline understanding, and make funding for refugee-led organizations and initiatives more accessible by eliminating requirements that recipient organizations be registered in Canada. Additionally, Canada should require that Canadian funding to UNHCR go toward implementing refugee-led partners. And Canada should employ refugees at all levels of government, advocate for the employment of refugees in leadership positions at UNHCR as well as other international partners, consult with refugees in foreign policy development, and include refugees in delegations to diplomatic meetings on issues relating to their countries of origin. For a more comprehensive understanding of the definition of refugee, "the end of the refugee cycle," and refugee-led organizations, further sources are recommended (R. Black and Koser 1999; Motalebi and Martin-Shields 2023; UNHCR 2023a).

FURTHER READING AND RESOURCES

Alio, Mustafa, and Rez Gardi. 2021. "End the Tokenism: Give Refugees a Voice on Our Own Futures." *New Humanitarian*, 15 December 2021. https://www.thenewhumanitarian.org/opinion/2021/12/15/give-refugees-a-voice-on-our-own-futures.

Canadian Council for Refugees. 2019. "Canadian Companies Must be Held Accountable for Contributing to Forced Displacement." CCR media release. https://www.ccrweb.ca/en/media/canadian-companies-accountability-forced-displacement.

House of Commons. 2022. "Extending Special Immigration Measures to Regions Faced with Humanitarian Crises," CIMM Committee news release, Our Commons, 6 April 2022. https://www.ourcommons.ca/DocumentViewer/en/44-1/CIMM/news-release/11693680.

8

Canada's Legal and Policy Framework for Migration

Veronica Fynn Bruey and Robert Fantauzzi

KEY TAKEAWAYS

- Canada's colonial origins shape its legal and policy framework for migration.
- Indigenous Peoples have been excluded from participating in decisions related to forced migration law and policy in Canada.
- Although human rights are not limited to citizens, there are barriers to non-citizens exercising their rights, including migration-specific rights.
- The *Singh* decision by the Supreme Court of Canada (SCC) in 1985 established that every person physically present in Canada – including non-citizens – is protected by the Charter of Rights and Freedoms.

KEY TERMS

- Chinese head tax
- Immigration and Refugee Protection Act (IRPA)
- *Singh* decision (1985)

INTRODUCTION: A BRIEF HISTORICAL BACKGROUND IN (IM)MIGRATION LAW AND POLITICS IN CANADA

8.1 Perspectives on Indigenous Laws by Professor John Borrows, Chippewas of the Nawash, Anishinabek Nation, Law Foundation Chair in Aboriginal Justice and Governance, Faculty of Law, University of Victoria

> For thousands of years there was no such thing as an Indian Act. As First Nations we lived free from its constraints. We observed laws that encouraged us to be wise, humble, respectful, truthful, brave, loving, and honest in our dealings with others. Other people did not define our citizenship. We held our land in accordance with our own traditions. Children and grandchildren lived with parents and great-grandparents throughout the generations without being removed through other's rules. If people from other nations wanted to share with us, we worked something out through mutual customs or agreement. If someone from another nation wanted to live amongst us, we adopted or hospitably welcomed them unless they meant harm. When someone died, we memorialized and buried them in accordance with our own laws and spiritual beliefs. Their possessions would be dealt with through long-established practice. When it came time to choose political leaders we did so on our terms. We controlled our own laws. Most other areas of our lives were more firmly within our control. Consistent with our own aspirations and ideas we exercised power over commerce, punishment, enforcement, dispute resolution, education and numerous other matters. (Borrows 2008, 1)

8.2 Lived Experience of Migration
Veronica Fynn Bruey, an Indigenous Liberian migrant, came to Canada in 2001 after surviving three years of the Liberian civil war and nearly a decade of refugeehood in Ghana. Colonial laws and policies in and out of Canada entrench European settlers' citizenship (called British subjects prior to 1947) irrespective of systemic violence they committed against the First Peoples of Turtle Island. Incongruent to the rule of law principles (Bingham 2011, 55–9), the same cannot be said for Fynn Bruey and many other forced migrants to Canada, whose citizenships could be revoked.

The perpetuity of Canadian citizenships for colonizers and their progenies are guaranteed, while the same settler law denies similar rights to children of Fynn Bruey's son, who is a Canadian, born outside of Canada pursuant to section 5, Citizenship Act, 1985 (see also Moffette, chapter 19; Cowper-Smith and Kane, chapter 20). As a born and bred Liberian woman, Fynn Bruey could not pass on Liberian citizenship to her son until quite recently. On 25 July 2022, the Legislature of Liberia enacted an amendment to the Aliens and Nationality Law 1973 section 20(1) by replacing a provision that allows only men to pass on their Liberian citizenship to their children and repealing the ban on dual citizenship. Formerly enslaved settlers, whose immigration and creation of the Liberian State were supported by the American Colonization Society are the drafters of the Aliens and Nationality Law.

More complexity arises in the immigration mix of Fynn Bruey as an "alien" spouse of an American. According to the Immigration and Nationality Act, 1952, Fynn Bruey must maintain continuous residence in the US as a lawful green card holder. To be clear, in order to be a lawful permanent resident in the US, she cannot stay outside the US for an extended period (usually more than 180 days), otherwise she could lose residence status and potentially risk access to her only child according to the Immigration and Nationality Act, section 216. Fynn Bruey's lived experience situates, anchors, and shapes the perspectives of the chapter beyond political and legal frameworks, starting with an examination of the history of Indigenous and settler (im)migration by acknowledging but also separating the two migration processes (Pellerin 2019, 3-4).

The roots of legal and policy frameworks for contemporary migration in Canada can be traced to a wave of European immigrants dominated by French and English settlers in Canada to the complete exclusion of Indigenous Peoples (Bauder and Breen 2023; Reid and Peace 2016). From the arrival of a few "explorers" in the 1400s–1500s to 1763, Canada/New France's population rose to between 70,000 and 78,880, mostly male immigrants who needed *filles du roi* [king's daughters] – whose immigration was financed by the king – to help increase the settlement's numbers naturally (Charbonneau et al. 2000, 131; Statistics Canada 2015). A series of historical legal documents harnessed the political rhetoric needed to construct a containment system of Indigenous Peoples while keeping non-European immigrants out. First, the Royal Proclamation, 1763 monopolized England's stronghold over Indigenous lands, granting exclusive jurisdiction to the confederation of Canada/England to extinguish Indigenous rights and title via treaty (Bartlett 1977, 581). Second, the Constitutional Act, 1791 – an act of the British Parliament – separated Lower Canada (French-Catholic Quebec) from Upper Canada (Protestant English-speaking Loyalists).

Third, after subjecting their legal status to the Queen of England, the colonies of Canada, (i.e., Nova Scotia and New Brunswick) were united under the Constitution Act, 1867 (formerly the British North America Act, 1867). Increasing numbers was critical to subjugating colonized bodies, hence the rationale for the fourth measure, enactment of the Dominion Lands Act, 1872. This law, sometimes referred to as the Homestead Act, limited land inheritance to a few privileged European settlers and their posterity in western Canada by "grant[ing] a quarter section of free land [160 acres or 64.7 hectares] to any settler 21 years of age or older who paid a ten-dollar registration fee, lived on his quarter section for three years, cultivated 30 acres [12.1 hectares] and built a permanent dwelling." Finally, the Indian Act, 1876 attempted to infantilize Indigenous Peoples, allocated Indigenous lands to the British Crown, confined First Nations to reserve lands, and instituted the notorious Indian Residential School (IRS) system (Bartlett 1977, 582; Borrows 2008, 2; Leslie 2002, 24; Hurley 2009, 1).

Together, these oppressive laws, which form part of the *rule of law* in Canada, continue to prevent Indigenous Peoples from having equal access to economic wealth and political participation, while regulating who is permitted to enter/stay in Canada, access economic resources, or participate in politico-legal governance of the country (Pellerin 2019, 6). The philosophy behind the Eurocentric Westphalian modern state is divisive in that it imposes and legitimizes colonial forms of universal governance by separating "us" (White settlers) from "them" (the rest) (Nicol 2017, 796). Politically, Canada is still a constitutional monarchy with King Charles III of Great Britain as the head of state represented by the Governor General.

Since the creation of the Dominion of Canada in 1867, all twenty-three prime ministers have been of White, European ancestral background with Canada's first two prime ministers born in Scotland. While the research on the racial identity of parliament is scarce, in 2015 and 2019, White men making up 36 per cent of Canada's population accounted for 65 per cent of all incumbent members of parliament (Ouellet, Shiab, and Gilchrist 2021). The House of Commons 2015 report show that visible groups represented 18.2 per cent of all candidates for the six major parties (1,653) with fifty-three (15.7 per cent) being elected in 2021 compared to fifty (14.8 per cent) in 2019 (J. Black 2020, 17–23; J. Black and Griffith 2022). These statistics demonstrate that research on racial inequity in the heart of law-making and political governance in Canada is long overdue (Tolley 2016). As stated by Prime Minister Justin Trudeau, "[w]e need to acknowledge that our history includes darker moments: the Chinese head tax, the internment of Ukrainian, Japanese, and Italian Canadians during World War I and II, our turning away boats of Jewish or Punjabi refugees, our own history of slavery" (2015).

It is against this backdrop that this chapter aims to analyze trends in Canadian immigration law and policy. Parallel to the "land of immigrants" and "multicultural" myths is a derogatory and explicitly racist immigration system (Fynn Bruey 2021, 31–2; see also Mahrouse and El Omari, chapter 15). This chapter discusses Canada's commitments and its shortcomings in relation to protecting immigrants under international law and national statutes/acts, regulations, and policies.

CONTEXT FOR CURRENT LEGISLATIVE IMMIGRATION FRAMEWORK

The Constitution Act, 1867, which began the constitutional process of nation building in Canada, was a White supremacy document designed to systematically disenfranchise Indigenous, Black, and Asian Peoples (Manuel and Derrickson 2017). The British North America Act was an act of the UK Parliament. However ceremonious, the king of England is still the head of Canada. Up until 1978, despite regulatory reforms in 1962 and 1967, immigration acts in Canada granted cabinet the power to prohibit immigrants of any race from entering the country.

Since 1869 colonial settler law and policy has regulated who is allowed into Canada and who is not. Immigration Acts of 1869, 1906, and 1910 respectively included conditions of entry and expanded a long list of deporting unwanted and undesirable migrants from Canada. Immediately after the railway was built, the Chinese Immigration Act (or the Chinese Exclusion Act), 1885 imposed a $50 fee (federal head tax) on each Chinese person entering Canada to isolate and discriminate one specific group of people based solely on their race (Cho 2018, 381; McRae 2022). The federal head tax, which was increased to $100 in 1901 and $500 in 1903 until 1947, did not deter more than ninety-seven thousand Chinese from immigrating to Canada between 1885 and 1923.

The majority of migrants seeking asylum and protection stay close to countries neighbouring their own (see also Clark-Kazak, introduction). However, Canada, along with other rich countries, continues to stoke anti-immigrant sentiment and limit access to asylum by: (1) externalization policies that extend Canada's border beyond its physical boundaries for the purpose of controlling migration flow (see also Young, chapter 3); and (2) securitization of borders requiring protection from "terrorists" to ensure national security (Menjívar 2014, 354–7; Bigo 2014, 211; Salter and Piché 2011, 929–33; Crépeau 2010, 4). Border externalization is a unilateral, bilateral, or multilateral action taken by states to enforce extraterritorial control in preventing (im)migrants entering the jurisdiction of destination countries or making them inadmissible, contrary to the non-penalization principle in the 1951 Refugee Convention (Frelick, Kysel, and Podkul 2016, 193; Everett 2019, 12–33).

Border securitization is an iterative legal/policy process that departs from human rights-based and humanitarian protection toward criminalizing and prosecuting migrants as terrorists, smugglers, and human traffickers (Grondin and de Larrinaga 2009, 667; Frelick, Kysel, and Podkul 2016, 210; James and Paquin 2014, 65, 155, 175). For instance, border securitization was accelerated under former prime minister Stephen Harper's regime backing a media and government rhetoric around "bogus refugees" and "queue jumpers" (e.g., Tamils arriving by boat; see Fynn Bruey 2021, 107), wherein refugees and asylum seekers are broadly conceived of "as dangerous, deceitful, or otherwise threatening, all for the purposes of rationalizing economically beneficial social and territorial exclusion" (Atak, Hudson, and Nakache 2018, 4–8). The attacks on 11 September 2001 in the US led to the introduction of security certificates, which permit the states to remove permanent residents and foreign nationals on security grounds. These certificates, relics of anti-Soviet Cold War doctrine, also allow for pre-emptive detention of individuals targeted and allow for denial of critical evidence and information to defence council on grounds of national security (see *Suresh v. Canada [Minister of Citizenship and Immigration]* 2002, 1 SCR 3; *Mostafa Dadar v. Canada* 2005, 1 CAT 2005).

LAW, STATUTE, REGULATION, AND POLICY: (IM)MIGRANTS, REFUGEES, RESIDENTS, AND CITIZENS

The legal framework for migration in Canada should have been fundamentally informed by the First Peoples in Canada. Upon initial arrival, settler colonists signed various treaties intended to respect First Peoples' prior and informed consent for the purpose of regulating and governing immigration flow in Canada. For example, the Royal Proclamation, 1763 "forbade settlers from claiming lands from Indigenous occupants, unless it has been first bought by the Crown and then sold to settlers" (First Nations and Indigenous Studies 2009).

The Comprehensive Land Claims Policy, following *Calder et al. v. Attorney-General of British Columbia* 1973, demonstrates Indigenous Peoples' persistent challenge with ensuring that the Crown (i.e., the settler colonial Government of Canada) validates and honours their treaty rights (Aboriginal Affairs and Northern Development Canada, 2014). Rather than entrenching the legal and political frameworks for coexisting and sharing Indigenous lands, settler colonists continue to dishonour these treaties and exclude Indigenous perspectives on who is allowed (or not) to migrate to Canada. Notably, the existing treaty rights of Indigenous Peoples are affirmed in section 35 of the Constitution Act, 1982 and are also integral to the United Nations Declaration on the Rights of Indigenous Peoples (UDRIP) 2007.

Canada is signatory to major international human rights instruments providing for the protection of (im)migrants and migration; yet guaranteeing such protection for migrants is far from reality. The Universal Declaration of Human Rights (UDHR) 1948 was drafted by Canada's own John Peters Humphrey, who said, "[i]f there is to be perpetual peace in a world of nation states, the individuals who live in them must be free, their human rights must be respected" (Canadian Museum of Human Rights 2022). The UDHR safeguards fundamental human rights for *all*, not just citizens, and also has specific provisions to protect (im)migrants. Article 13 protects freedom of movement and states, "[e]veryone has the right to leave any country, including his own, and to return to his country." Article 14 of the UDHR grants the right to seek asylum. Under customary international law, Canada agrees to respect the rights protected in the UDHR as one of the original fifty founding countries admitted to the United Nations on 26 June 1945 as well as one of the first forty-eight countries to vote for the UDHR on 10 December 1948. While the UDHR is not legally binding, many of the rights are reiterated in the International Covenant on Civil and Political Rights (ICCPR) and the International Covenant on Economic, Social and Cultural Rights (ICESCR), which Canada has ratified. For example, the right to freedom of movement is codified in the ICCPR.

Canada is also a party to the 1951 Refugee Convention and its 1967 Protocol. These legally binding treaties commit Canada to respect refugee-specific rights, including the right to asylum and the right to freedom of movement. In addition, the principle of non-refoulement is central to the refugee regime (see Young, chapter 3; K. Banerjee, chapter 5; Atak, chapter 17) and prohibits deportation to a country where a person's life or freedom is at risk because of "race, religion, nationality, membership in a particular social group or political opinion." Even if a person enters a country irregularly, they cannot be deported until their refugee claim is heard.

At the regional level, the Canada–United States Safe Third Country Agreement (STCA) 2004 (see also Young, chapter 3) is an integral part of the Canada-US Smart Border Action Plan (SBAP). Signed in December 2001, the SBAP is a thirty-point declaration to enhance security while facilitating the legitimate flow of people and goods between the two countries (Bureau of Public Affairs Department of State 2002), requiring refugee claimants to request protection in the first safe country they arrive in, unless they qualify for an STCA agreement exception. Since the US is currently the only safe third country designated by Canada, the STCA applies to refugee claimants seeking entry at the Canada-US land border and at irregular land and water crossings. The only exception to the above rule considers family unity, the best interests of children, and the public interest. A safe third country is one where an individual, passing through that country, could have made a claim for refugee protection (see subsection 102(2) of IRPA 2001). Although the STCA was subject to a legal challenge and saw an injunction issued against it in July 2020, the Trudeau regime has successfully appealed the ruling, meaning the STCA remains in effect as of the time of this writing (see *Canada (Citizenship and Immigration) v. Canadian Council for Refugees* 2021, 72 FCA).

Domestically, several (im)migration statuses and policies are in place to regulate migrant flow in and out of Canada. Jurisdiction over (im)migration is a shared responsibility between the provincial and federal governments (see also Garnier, chapter 10). Of specific relevance to this chapter are IRPA and the Criminal Code, 1985. One of the main objectives of IRPA is "to promote international justice and security by fostering respect for human rights and by denying access to Canadian territory to persons who are criminals or security risks" (2001, subsection 3(1)(i)). Similarly, with respect to refugees, two objectives, *inter alia*, are to "recognize that the refugee program is in the first instance about saving lives and offering protection to the displaced and persecuted" (IRPA 2001, subsection 2(a)) and "promote international justice and security by denying access to Canadian territory to persons, including refugee claimants, who are security risks or serious criminals" (IRPA 2001, subsection 2(h)).

The above objectives not only clearly affirm concerns of prioritizing border securitization over human rights protections but also constrict the diverse category of (im)migrants (except for trafficked persons, see IRPA 2001, sections 117 and 118; Fynn Bruey 2021, 114) needing legal protection by streamlining their entry in Canada toward criminalization, illegality, and national security. With less emphasis on survivors' protection and safety, sections 279.01 and 279.011 of the Canadian Criminal Code 1985 criminalize human trafficking with penalties of four to fourteen years imprisonment for trafficking adults and five to fourteen years imprisonment for trafficking children. Section 118 of IRPA 2001 prohibits coming into Canada by means of abduction, fraud, deception, or use of threat of force or coercion with penalties of up to $1 million, life imprisonment, or both (Fynn Bruey 2021, 114–15).

CONTEMPORARY POLITICS AND LAW OF FORCED MIGRATION IN CANADA: PERSONS IN NEED OF PROTECTION

Since its colonial establishment in 1867, Canada has preferred immigration from White Western European countries (C. Foster 2005, 15). Unlike the seemingly open-arms embrace European immigrants receive upon entry to settler colonial Canada, non-Europeans usually arrived desperately fleeing dehumanizing and violent situations. As Henry-Dixon discusses in chapter 2, the first recorded history of refugees in Canada occurred between 1782 and 1807, when hundreds of Loyalists with their families, servants, and slaves left New York to make their new home in Africville, Nova Scotia (a Black settlement community nearly destroyed) (Library and Archives Canada 2013). Further, Upper Canada's legislation of the Act to Prevent the further Introduction of Slaves and to limit the Term of Contracts for Servitude (the Act to Limit Slavery) in 1793 drove thousands of Black slaves via the Underground Railroad to Canada in the 1800s, never mind that many Black migrants were domestic servants and labourers prior to enactment of the law (Cooper 2007a, 5; Riddell 1919, 375; Wigmore 2011, 439–41; Reese 2011, 209). The Act to Limit Slavery "did not free a single slave, but prevented their importation and freed the future children of slaves at age twenty-five. Faced with growing opposition in the colonies, slavery declined. The *Imperial Act of 1833* finally abolished slavery in the British territories in 1834" (Government of Canada 2022h).

With an immigration and citizenship policy first favouring White British subjects – and later widening to include other nationalities across Europe – when between the 1700s and 1952 hundreds of thousands of refugees from Scotland, Poland, Italy, Ukraine, and displaced peoples/persecuted Jews come to Canada (C. Foster 2005, 125–6; Kaprielian-Churchill 1994, 1–2). However, Jews seeking entry into Canada during this period continued to face widespread prejudice and restrictions on entry, culminating in the MS *St Louis* tragedy in which Canada – among other nations – refused entry to all the roughly nine hundred passengers aboard (Anctil and Comeau 2021). While some European states did eventually offer asylum to Jewish passengers, many of these nations would soon fall to the Reich's advance, with the result that many of the MS *St Louis*'s passengers met their end in the fires of the Holocaust (Anctil and Comeau 2021). It was not until the 1950s when Canada admitted the first Palestinians who became displaced due to the Israel-Arab war of 1948.

In 1985 the Supreme Court's *Singh v. Minister of Employment and Immigration* case definitively decided the question of whether each and every refugee claimant has the right to an oral hearing before having their application in the affirmative, offering further procedural protections to those claiming asylum in Canada (Grey 1986, 12; Atak, chapter 17). The *Singh* case was also important because it reaffirmed that the legal guarantees in the Canadian Charter of Rights and Freedoms 1982 apply to "everyone" who is physically present on Canadian territory, not just Canadian citizens. This ruling upholds the notion of the universality of human rights, which apply to everyone, everywhere.

In 2022 as a short-term response to the Russian invasion of Ukraine, the Canadian government implemented a new temporary status program for Ukrainians fleeing the conflict. The Canada-Ukraine Authorization for Emergency Travel (CUAET) offered Ukrainians and their family members temporary residence in Canada to work and study. While this program is an example of discretionary policy-making in the face of changing geopolitical events in the world, offering a possible precedent for the development of future temporary programs, there are several factors worth noting.

First, it has been suggested that CUAET's aim was not so much humanitarianism as a means to address the current worker shortage in Canada (Bejan et al. 2023). Second, the cost of air travel meant that only the more affluent Ukrainians were able to apply and make the journey to Canada, effectively allowing Canada to select from an "elite" class of Ukrainians, while those lacking the requisite resources sought protection in countries neighbouring the conflict (Bejan et al 2023). Finally, while those fleeing the fighting in Ukraine certainly deserve – like *all* peoples – a safe place to find shelter and support, it is evident that Canada has not responded to similar conflicts across the world by offering such robust and welcoming programs, exposing a troubling disconnect in both governmental policy and public opinion around questions of what peoples(s) are deemed "worthy" of admittance and support upon arrival, and what people(s) are to be cast as "queue jumpers" and "bogus" refugees (Falconer 2022). The unflattering test of the broader applicability of programs like CUAET will be if and how they are utilized for peoples of non-European ancestry fleeing similar conflict and violence. For example, as this book is going to press, much less generous responses have been offered to people fleeing violence in Gaza, Sudan, and South Sudan.

CONCLUSION

This chapter offers an overview of the political and legal factors that have helped shape Canada's (im)migration system over the past four hundred years. Acknowledging Indigenous Peoples as the original inhabitants of what is now Canada, the chapter reveals that White European settlers implemented racist laws and policies that are the foundation of the contemporary system. Systemic, structural, and institutional racism strongly maintains this discrimination, which has been intensified by laws and policies on deskilling, border securitization, and national security following the 9/11 attacks. These restrictive instruments continue to hamper the necessity for reforming an inclusive law and policy that will protect both citizens and (im)migrants equally, thus honouring Canada's obligation under international law. We propose three recommendations to ensure that Canada's political and legal framework for (im)migration is inclusive, fair, compassionate, and equal. First, Indigenous Peoples should have greater decision-making power in Canada's immigration law and policy. Second, the Canada–United States Safe Third Country Agreement (STCA) should be abolished to prevent violation of international human rights law. Third, more research is needed on diversity and representation of people with lived experiences of forced migration in policy- and law-making.

FURTHER READING AND RESOURCES

Canadian Council for Refugees (CCR). 2016. Resolutions on Indigenous Rights. https://ccrweb.ca/en/resolutions-subject/indigenous-peoples.

Clark-Kazak, Christina R. 2023. "Refuge Rights ... and Realities in Canada." Collabzium video, 6:41. https://collabzium.com/en/articles/introduction-to-forced-migration-by-christina-clark-kazak-part-6-migrants-rights.

Dennler, Katherine Tomko, and Brianna Garneau. 2022. "How the Canada

Border Services Agency Tolerates and Even Encourages Refugee Mistreatment." *The Conversation*, 27 November 2022. https://theconversation.com/how-the-canada-border-services-agency-tolerates-and-even-encourages-refugee-mistreatment-193881.

Foot, Richard. 2006. "Singh Case." *The Canadian Encyclopedia*. Historica Canada, article published 7 February 2006, last edited 26 May 2021. https://www.thecanadianencyclopedia.ca/en/article/singh-case.

Van Dyk, Lindsay. n.d. "What Do Immigration Rules Tell Us About Canada?" *Canadian Museum of Immigration at Pier 21*. https://pier21.ca/research/immigration-history/canadian-immigration-acts-and-legislation.

9

Key Actors in Forced Migration Management and Response in Canada

Yosief Araya

KEY TAKEAWAYS

- Government departments, intergovernmental organizations, civil society organizations, and people with lived experience of forced migration contribute to the Canadian response to global refugee movements.
- Although different actors have very different mandates and approaches, they often work together to provide refugee resettlement and protection. For example, the Government of Canada relies on partnerships with intergovernmental and civil society organizations to implement essential programs and services.
- Forced migration is a human phenomenon – behind each actor there are people making decisions.
- While people with lived experiences of forced migration have historically been marginalized from policy-making, they are key actors in refugee protection, sponsorship and (re)settlement.

KEY TERMS

- Canada Border Services Agency (CBSA)
- Canadian Council for Refugees (CCR)
- Global Affairs Canada (GAC)
- Immigration Refugees and Citizenship Canada (IRCC)
- Immigration and Refugee Board (IRB)
- Sanctuary cities

INTRODUCTION

This chapter introduces the histories, functions, and roles of key actors participating in Canadian management and response to forced migration situations. Many institutions and individuals are involved directly or indirectly in Canadian management and response to forced migration situations. This chapter, however, is limited to some actors playing important and influential roles over an extended period in formulating, impacting, or implementing public policies related to forced migration. While the discussion recognizes the idiosyncratic traits of each actor, the differing opinions, and sometimes tension or power dynamics among the various players, the chapter does not provide an in-depth analysis of each actor or their interrelationships. Rather, the chapter is intended primarily as a descriptive overview of the different actors to raise awareness of the many different groups and institutions involved in refugee protection, sponsorship, resettlement, and settlement in Canada.

These key actors can be broadly grouped into four categories:

- Government (including a quasi-government agency).
- Intergovernmental agencies.
- Civil society.
- Refugees and other forcibly displaced persons.

GOVERNMENT AGENCIES

Perhaps the most obvious actor in Canada's response to forced migration is the Canadian government. Analysis reveals a mixed record of protection as well as a complex constellation of government agencies performing complementary and, at times, contradictory or overlapping roles. As the CCR notes, "there has been good and bad in Canadian responses to refugees, both before and after signing the Refugee Convention" (n.d., para. 3).

The International Organization for Migration (IOM 2019, 13) asserts that Canada has "a well-developed migration program" with dedicated federal government departments that formulate and implement migration policies. As a federal state, the federal, provincial, and territorial governments share responsibility for migration-related issues (IOM 2019, 14; see also Garnier, chapter 10). Municipal governments are also involved in local settlement services, and some have declared themselves "sanctuary cities" (Moffette and Ridgley 2018). However, refugee protection and resettlement are mainly the federal government's jurisdiction. The Immigration and Refugee Protection Act (IRPA), enacted by the federal government in 2001, stipulates the objectives of the law related to refugees (IRPA 2001, s. 9) and the government agencies responsible for their implementation (IRPA 2001, s. 4).

IRCC is the federal government department primarily responsible for managing the selection, settlement, and integration of newcomers, including refugees and other forcibly displaced persons. IRCC is expected to uphold Canada's human rights obligations under international and domestic law. IRCC conducts security and health screening of people who are considered for permanent resident status through Canadian resettlement programs. IRCC is also responsible for issuing Canadian travel documents to facilitate the travel of refugees and other protected persons recognized by Canada. The department seeks to facilitate settlement and integration (Government of Canada 2022f; see also Hynie, chapter 23). IRCC carries out its mandate via programs implemented directly by the department or indirectly through contracted third parties, including UN agencies (see next section), non-profit organizations (see below), or other government agencies (Government of Canada 2022f).

The CBSA is tasked with providing integrated border services that assist national security and public safety priorities and enable the free movement of people, including forcefully displaced people meeting legal requirements (CBSA Act 2005). The Department of Public Safety and Emergency Preparedness is responsible for the administration and enforcement of Canadian laws governing the admissibility of people (IRPA 2001, s. 4, para. 2), and it has subsequently authorized CBSA to implement them. CBSA detains those deemed to pose a threat to Canada (see Silverman, chapter 21), bars them from entering, or removes people who are inadmissible to Canada, including by reason of posing a security threat to Canada, involvement in organized crime, or violating human rights (IRPA, s. 4, para. 2. c); CBSA Act 2005, s. 5, para. 1).

The Immigration Refugee Board (IRB) is the largest Canadian independent, quasi-judicial decision-making administrative tribunal entrusted with the mandate to hear and determine refugee claims (IRB 2021a). Although this body reports to Parliament through the minister of immigration, the IRB remains independent. Created in 1989, following the landmark decision of the Supreme Court of Canada in the *Singh* case that granted refugee claimants a right to a fair hearing (*Singh v. Canada (Minister of Employment and Immigration)* 1985), the IRB is mandated to make "well-reasoned decisions on immigration and refugee matters, efficiently, fairly and in accordance with the law" (IRB 2021b). Bonisteel states that Canadian law provides the IRB with "a full and unqualified decision-making authority" to hear and determine a refugee claim (2011, 104). Moreover, it hears and determines refugee claims made inside Canada (see Atak, chapter 17).

The IRB has four divisions, and each one plays important roles relevant to forced migration response and management. The Refugee Protection Division hears and determines refugee claims made in Canada. The Refugee Appeal Division deals with appeals of negative decisions rendered by the Refugee Protection Division. The Immigration Division conducts admissibility hearings for those considered inadmissible or facing removal from Canada. The Immigration Appeal Division decides on appeals of removal orders (IRB 2021b). Another essential organ of the IRB is its national research and documentation centre. The centre produces country condition information, including national country packages, responses to inquiries, and other reports that assist IRB decision-makers, lawyers, immigration officials, refugee claimants, and the public with credible and reliable information. The centre was established on the assumption that comprehensive knowledge of a refugee claimant's country conditions aids in rendering a fair decision (IRB 2021b; Rusu 1989, 322).

As Demoz notes in chapter 7, GAC is involved in international migration policy and development and humanitarian assistance for refugees overseas and in countries hosting refugees. GAC also oversees Canada's relationship with UNHCR headquarters, including Canada's role on the UNHCR Executive Committee. Migration officers who make decisions on refugee resettlement cases operate in the network of Canadian offices located in Canadian embassies (IOM 2019, 14). The COVID-19 pandemic has also highlighted the roles of the federal and provincial public health agencies concerning international travel of forcibly displaced persons and the protection of public health. (Government of Canada 2022e).

INTERGOVERNMENTAL AGENCIES

The United Nations High Commissioner for Refugees (UNHCR) and International Organization for Migration (IOM) are two intergovernmental organizations that play essential roles in Canada's response and management of forced migration situations.

The office of UNHCR was created in 1950, following World War II, to help millions of people displaced in Europe. The 1950 UNHCR Statute, the 1951 Convention Relating to the Status of Refugees, and the 1967 Protocol Relating to the Status of Refugees stipulate UNHCR's roles and scope of activities. The UNHCR was established to promote international protection and interstate co-operation in finding durable solutions for refugees (Milner 2021a, 44). The organization is regarded as a guardian of the international refugee norms, including the 1951 Refugee Convention because of its mandate of monitoring the implementation of its provisions (Loescher and Milner 2011, 189).

Since the inception of UNHCR, Canada has not only worked closely with it but has also served as a major donor. UNHCR Canada monitors whether Canada follows its international obligations stipulated in local and international refugee laws. It also works with local non-governmental organizations (NGOs) to "promote the highest standards of refugee protection and find an alternative to detentions of refugee claimants" (UNHCR Canada n.d.). The UN Refugee Agency supports Canada's response to forced migration by referring refugees who need resettlement. UNHCR officers identify, select, and refer refugees resettled under the Government-Assisted Refugees (GARs) and Blended Visa Office-Referred (BVOR) programs annually (UNHCR 2018d, 3; see also Atak, chapter 17).

The IOM, established in 1951, is an intergovernmental agency, which recently joined the UN. From the outset, IOM has worked closely with the Canadian government. The Government of Canada contracts IOM as an essential service delivery agent for many migration-focused projects (Government of Canada 2015b, 3). Canada uses panel physicians designated by IOM to conduct health examinations of refugees who are being resettled. IOM also assists Canada with transportation logistics, including booking flights, securing exit visas from refugee-hosting countries, and arranging medical escorts for sick or disabled refugees (Government of Canada 2015b). For example, at the end of 2015, the Government of Canada requested that IOM support the large-scale resettlement of Syrian refugees. IOM mobilized its resources and completed this operation in three months by arranging ninety-seven charter flights and assisting in the resettlement of more than twenty-six thousand Syrian refugees (IOM n.d.). In addition, IOM delivers the Canadian Orientation Abroad (COA) program, which provides pre-departure information and prepares refugees for life in Canada (IOM 2019).

CIVIL SOCIETY

In a global refugee context, civil society is described as constituting various organizations, institutions, and groups that strive to protect, help, and find durable solutions for refugees (Milner and Klassen 2020, 8). Similarly, civil society actors play critical and diverse roles in Canada's response to forced migration. These include: refugee sponsoring organizations or groups, agencies providing settlement services, refugee houses, and refugee advocacy organizations.

Although Indigenous organizations and people have been the traditional guardians of Turtle Island, they have been historically neglected in Canada's migration narration and response to forced migration situations (Pellerin 2019, 3). Canada's response to the refugee crisis has been part of Canada's settler colonial tradition. However, since the Truth and Reconciliation Commission (TRC) recommended raising the newcomer communities' awareness about Indigenous Peoples' history (TRC 2015, 10), there is more recognition of common issues and tensions affecting Indigenous Peoples and refugees serving organizations and of the need to reflect critically, take settler responsibilities, and renew relationships with the land (Nobe-Ghelani and Lumor 2022, 121).

Refugee Sponsoring Organizations/Groups

Refugee sponsoring organizations or groups are significant players in the Canadian response to global displacement. Canadians have been sponsoring refugees for more than forty years under the Private Sponsorship of Refugees

(PSR) program (see Labman, chapter 18), resettling over 327,000 persons since the beginning of the PSR program up to 2020 (Government of Canada 2020a). The three main groups are Sponsorship Agreement Holders (SAHs), community sponsors, and Groups of Five (G5). SAHs are incorporated organizations that have signed a sponsorship agreement with the Canadian government to sponsor refugees. Community sponsors are organizations, associations, or corporations that sponsor refugees without signing formal sponsorship agreements with the Government of Canada. As their name indicates, G5s are five or more Canadian citizens or permanent residents who make arrangements to sponsor refugees (Government of Canada 2019c). Similarly, groups of two to five and registered charities can sponsor refugees under the Quebec program (Government of Quebec 2022).

The Refugee Sponsorship Training Program (RSTP) is a national program that trains and supports groups and individuals that sponsor refugees across Canada, except in Quebec. Created in 1998, funded by the federal government, and administered by Catholic Crosscultural Services (CCS), the RSTP program organizes training workshops and conferences, offers online courses, and produces training materials to equip Canadians with knowledge and skills to sponsor and help settle refugees in Canada. The program also promotes and matches refugees resettled in Canada through a BVOR program (RSTP 2022; see also Labman, chapter 18; Atak, chapter 17).

Settlement Service-Providing Organizations (SPOs)

Settlement service-providing organizations (SPOs) provide "specialized services geared to facilitate the full and equitable participation of all newcomers in Canadian society" (CCR 1998). The federal government funds about five hundred SPOs (Government of Canada 2022g). Their service includes settlement needs assessment, referrals, information and orientation, language training, skills development, employment services, community connections, and other help to support newcomers. Some agencies provide specialized services to refugees dealing with mental health issues or survivors of torture and trauma. For instance, the Canadian Centre for Victims of Torture assists refugees who are survivors of torture in recovering and building their lives by creating strong social connections in Canada and helping them move from "victims to active community members" (Kidd, McKenzie, and Abai 2014, 160).

Umbrella organizations of agencies that provide settlement and integration services support their members to improve their capacities to settle and integrate forcibly displaced people through research, communication, information sharing, advocacy, networking, capacity building, and collaboration. They also act as a collective and unified voice, represent their members, and advance their interests in their engagements with government officials. For example, the Canadian Immigrant Settlement Sector Alliance comprises six provincial/regional umbrella groups of service-providing organizations (CISSA-ACSEI 2021). The Ontario Council Agencies Serving Immigrants (OCASI) was formed in 1978 "to champion equity and human rights for immigrants and refugees through advocacy, collective action, collaborative planning, research, capacity-building, and information and knowledge transfer" (OCASI n.d.). The Table de concertation des organismes au service des personnes réfugiées et immigrantes (TCRI), established in 1979, comprises agencies that defend the rights of refugees and other vulnerable groups and settles them in Quebec. The organization promotes collaboration among its members, engages in consultations with Quebec government officials, and raises public awareness (TCRI 2022).

Refugee Advocacy Organizations

At a national level, CCR is a network of more than two hundred organizations across Canada working in the protection of refugees inside Canada, resettlement of refugees, and settlement of refugees and immigrants. It advocates for the rights and protections of refugees and other vulnerable people in and outside Canada and the settlement of refugees and immigrants in Canada. CCR offers networking and information-exchange opportunities and advocates on behalf of its membership. The Canadian Refugee Sponsorship Agreement Holders Association is a national association of SAHs, established in May 2011 to enhance the unity of its members and develop a common perspective. The association is led by elected SAH council members, who represent the member associations in the quarterly meetings of the non-governmental organization (NGO)/Government Committee on the Private Sponsorship of Refugees and engage in discourse and advocacy aimed at improving the PSR program (Canadian Refugee Sponsorship Agreement Holders Association 2022).

Refugee Reception Centres and Shelters

Refugee reception centres and shelters are critical to receiving refugees and offering accommodations, especially given limited housing options (see Clark-Kazak, chapter 28). The federal government funds refugee reception centres that provide temporary housing and support to Government-Assisted Refugees (GARs). There are thirty-nine centres in communities across Canada (Government of Canada n.d.), with additional shelters in Quebec. They offer a port of entry and reception services, transitional housing between four and six weeks (depending on housing availability), support for finding permanent accommodation, settlement needs assessment and referral to other settlement services, information and orientation, life skill training, and linkage to government programs. (Government of Canada 2019e).

Other refugee shelters run by NGOs offer temporary housing to refugee claimants. Although services provided by these shelters depend on the size, staffing, financial, and other resources, most provide forcibly displaced persons with a roof and bed, a cupboard, food, clothing, and other necessities. For instance, the list of shelters based in Ontario and the accompanying website show shared services and other organizational differences (FCJ Refugee Centre 2020). They also help refugee claimants process their claims, which can include assisting them with filing applications, finding lawyers, applying for legal aid, escorting them to medical screening, preparing them for refugee hearings, and finding interpreters and translators. Some also support refugees whose claims have been rejected in an appeal of negative decisions or to seek other remedies (FCJ Refugee Centre 2012).

Educational Institutions

Academic and other educational institutions and their members have played various essential roles in Canada's response to global forced migration. Canada's higher education institutions contribute to education, research, writing, or publications addressing forced migration issues. The Centre for Refugee Studies (CRS) at York University and the Canadian Association for Refugee and Forced Migration Studies (CARFMS) are notable academic entities. Established in 1998, CRS is an internationally recognized centre with diverse researchers who produce, mobilize, and share information dedicated to advancing the welling of refugees and other displaced persons (York University n.d.). Similarly, the Canadian Association for Refugee and Forced Migration Studies, created in 2008, is mandated to promote and disseminate research on Canadian refugee and forced migration issues and promote partnership and collaboration among Canadian scholars by creating networking opportunities, such as conferences and workshops (CARFMS 2020).

Currently, many Canadian universities and colleges offer courses on forced migration or displacement studies in undergraduate degree studies, the graduate level, or professional. Even if their desired impact on policy-making is questioned (R. Black 2001, 68), research and knowledge produced by higher educational institutions (including Canadian institutions) at least inform public discourses and debates on refugee protection, resettlement, settlement, and integration of forcibly displaced people.

Canadian higher education institutions also offer training programs, scholarships, and initiatives specifically for displaced students and researchers. The World University Services of Canada Student Refugee Program sponsors refugees at over one hundred campuses across Canada through youth-led local committees. The Scholars at Risk program has operated in Canada since 2012 to bring researchers and graduate students whose research puts them at risk to Canadian universities and colleges. York University has a specific program for students with precarious migration status. The International Students Overcoming War program at Wilfrid Laurier University brings students from conflict areas to study in Canada. Many tertiary education institutions offer scholarships for refugees and other displaced students. While these are all promising practices, more could be done to institutionalize access to research and learning opportunities in Canadian universities and colleges (Azari and Clark-Kazak 2022).

REFUGEES AND OTHER FORCIBLY DISPLACED PERSONS

9.1 Afghan Women's Organization (AWO): Refugee and Immigrant Services
Founded in 1990 by Adeena Niazi and other refugee women from Afghanistan, AWO is a Sponsorship Agreement Holder (SAH) and a settlement service providing agency based in Toronto. Over the years, it has sponsored and successfully settled thousands of refugees and provided services to more than nineteen thousand clients (AWO 2022).

9.2 Eritrean Canadian Community Association of Calgary
Former refugees from Eritrea established the Eritrean Canadian Community Association of Calgary in 1983. The organization has sponsored refugees for many years, first under other SAHs and later by becoming an SAH. According to a conversation with former staff in 2022, the organization sponsored between two and four hundred refugees annually in the last five years, which is more than the number of refugees resettled by ten resettlement countries in 2021 (UNHCR 2021b).

9.3 The Faithful Companions of Jesus (FCJ) Refugee Centre
The FCJ Centre is one of Canada's most prominent refugee centres. The late Francisco Rio Martinez and his wife, Loly Rico Martinez, renowned refugee advocates who also came to Canada fleeing persecution in El Salvador, founded the centre in 1991 with the help of Catholic Sisters. The centre offers shelter for vulnerable women and children refugee claimants and provides information, training, and legal support to refugee claimants and other uprooted people (Boudreau 2016; FCJ Refugee Centre 2012).

Refugees and other forcibly displaced persons are important actors in managing and responding to forced migration situations, but they are often overlooked. In the last few years, there has been more recognition of refugees' knowledge, skills, and meaningful participation in the global management and response to refugee crises. For instance, enhancing the self-reliance of refugees is one of the pillar objectives of the Global Compact on Refugees, which was confirmed by the UN General Assembly in September 2018 (UN 2018, 4). The Global Compact calls on states to enable refugees to use their skills and abilities and to invest in building refugees' human capital, self-reliance, and transferable skills (UN 2018, 50).

The meaningful participation of refugees in global refugee management and response is an emerging norm (Milner, Alio, Gardi 2022, 27) that will assist in addressing questions of "legitimacy, efficacy and accountability" (Milner 2021, 18). The establishment of the Refugee Advisory Network of Canada (RAN Canada), which is working to secure "a meaningful inclusion of the perspectives, skills and knowledge of refugees in global policy and decision-making processes that affect the lives of refugees" (RAN Canada n.d.) and participation of refugee leaders in high-level global consultations on refugee resettlement, are steps in the right direction (see also Demoz, chapter 7).

In Canada, diaspora communities, especially those from countries experiencing forced migration, have been actively responding to displacement issues and sponsoring refugees. As noted in the box examples 9.1–3, many refugee-led organizations provide important settlement services and undertake advocacy. Further, many diaspora communities are SAHs – 30 per cent, according to Government of Canada data (2022g). Others partner with sponsoring organizations as co-sponsors or constituent groups and/or raise funds and organize to resettle and support refugees. Even though sponsorship is a demanding endeavour, former refugees living in Canada are motivated by their commitment to "help family members, or ethnonational friends and activists still living as refugees in precarious conditions" (Hyndman et al. 2021, 10).

CONCLUSION

The key actors in forced migration management and response include government agencies, intergovernment organizations, civil society, refugees, and other displaced persons. Even though their functions or standings differ, they collectively play significant roles in either formulating, impacting, or implementing Canada's response to forced migration situations. In the context of refugee sponsorship, the diaspora communities, including former refugees, are sponsoring, financing, and settling large numbers of refugees. There is an emerging norm regarding the meaningful involvement of refugees in efforts to address their plights. The nature, scope, extent, and impacts of these engagements require further observation.

FURTHER READING AND RESOURCES

Liew, Jamie. 2020. "The Global Organization: Introducing the UNHCR." *Migration Conversations* podcast, episode 11, 34:02. https://migration-conversations.simplecast.com/episodes/the-global-organization-introducing-the-unhcr.

– 2022. "Immigration Bureaucracy & Postwar Policymaking." *Migration Conversations* podcast, episode 37, 56:46. https://migration-conversations.simplecast.com/episodes/immigration-bureaucracy-postwar-policymaking.

UNHCR. 2022. "Nothing About Us, Without Us: 7 Ways You Can Promote Refugee Leadership." Global Compact on Refugees, 2 March 2022. https://globalcompactrefugees.org/news-stories/nothing-about-us-without-us-7-ways-you-can-promote-refugee-leadership.

10

Federal-Provincial Relations and Refugee Policy in Canada

Adèle Garnier

KEY TAKEAWAYS

- In accordance with Canada's constitution, immigration is a shared responsibility of the federal and provincial jurisdictions.
- The provincial roles in refugee settlement services vary across provinces and have varied over time.
- In Quebec, the provincial government is responsible for the admission of resettled refugees, while the federal government is responsible for the admission of landed refugees. Quebec has more autonomy than other provinces in the management of its integration budget and policies.
- The management of asylum claims at the US-Canada border has been a central federal-provincial issue in recent years.
- The role of municipalities is an emerging issue for the future of federal-provincial relations in refugee policy.

KEY TERMS

- Federalism
- Intergovernmental relations
- Asymmetrical federalism
- Canada-Quebec Accord

INTRODUCTION

Canada is a federal state. This means that law- and policy-making is shared between government levels: the federal level, and the provinces and territories. A significant body of research has developed on federalism in Canada's immigration policy (e.g., Leo and August 2009; Banting 2010; Paquet 2019; Paquet and Larios 2018). This includes comparisons with other federal states (Schmidt 2007; Baglay and Nakache 2014; Ianni Segatto 2019; Paquet 2020), between Canadian provinces (McGrath and McGrath 2013; Jeram and Nicolaides 2019; Paquet and Xhardez 2020), and between Canadian provinces and other subnational entities (Xhardez 2019). Yet research specifically addressing federal-provincial relations in refugee policy remains scant. Existing studies mostly focus on relations between the federal government and the province of Quebec, which has far more autonomy over immigration and refugee policy than other provinces (Paquet and Schertzer 2020; Garnier 2016; 2018; Labman and Garnier, forthcoming). The fact that Quebec stands out in its autonomy means that Canada is an example of asymmetrical federalism, in which the autonomy and prerogatives of subnational units vary. Federal-provincial relations are the most important in intergovernmental relations regarding immigration policy: municipalities have limited fiscal capacity and almost no power over policy design, even though their role in welcoming newcomers is critical (Tolley and Young 2011; Fourot 2013; 2015).

This chapter first provides an overview of federal-provincial relations in Canada's refugee policy. The unique situation of Quebec is then discussed, because Quebec's control over refugee policy, just as with control over the province's immigration policy, is much greater than that of other provinces. The following section focuses on a significant issue of the last few years: the management of asylum claims at the US-Canada border, which has been called a "complex intergovernmental problem" (Paquet and Schertzer 2020). Last, the role of municipalities within federal-provincial relations is discussed as an emerging issue.

OVERVIEW OF FEDERAL-PROVINCIAL RELATIONS IN CANADA'S REFUGEE POLICY

Federal forms of governance have existed on what is now Canadian territory before settler colonialism (Abu-Laban 2020 a). However, Indigenous nations were excluded from the establishment of the settler colonial federal political system (see also Coburn, chapter 1). The only minority rights to be addressed at Confederation were those of French Canadians and Catholics. Indigenous rights have not fared better in the historically francophone, Catholic province of Quebec. "Settler colonial society" is a label that has often been refused in a Province that has frequently presented itself as colonized by English Canadian society (Binette 2022). In addition, Paquet (2021) notes that population and immigrant distribution in Canada, is highly unequal. Regional disparities can weigh on provincial demands. Abu-Laban (2020a) argues that federalism can be understood as more or less exclusive, with pluralist federalism encompassing the role of community organizations. This chapter only focuses on federal-provincial relations; however, it acknowledges the critical role of municipal government and civil society in federal governance.

In accordance with section 95 of the Constitution Act, 1867 immigration is a concurrent jurisdiction of federal and provincial governments, although in cases of disputes, federal jurisdictions prevail. Excluded from immigration is the "naturalisation and aliens," that is, the provision of citizenship and the enforcement of immigration regulations, which are exclusive federal prerogatives (see Constitution Act 1867, s. 91(25)). Historically, the federal government has played the greatest role in Canada's refugee policy. Concurrent jurisdiction over immigration was only reflected in immigration legislation in the Immigration Act of 1976 (Vineberg 2014, 29). Section 109 of the 1976 act required that the federal government "enter into an agreement with any province or group of provinces for the purpose of facilitating the formulation, coordination and implementation of immigration policies and programs." Section 109(1) required that the "Minister shall consult with the provinces respecting the measures to be undertaken to facilitate the adaptation of permanent residents to Canadian society and the pattern of immigrant settlement in Canada in relation to regional demographic requirements." The Immigration and Refugee Protection Act (IRPA, 2001) that entered into force in 2002 entails similar provisions (ss. 8(1) and 10(2)), after clarifying in s. 4(1) that "[e]xcept as otherwise provided in this section, the Minister of Citizenship and Immigration is responsible for the administration of this Act."

All Canadian provinces and territories (except Nunavut) have entered bilateral agreements on immigration with the federal government. Except for agreements between the federal government and the province of Quebec (see below), however, bilateral immigration agreements barely address refugee policy and mostly focus on economic immigration, notably the Provincial Nominee Program (Paquet and Xhardez 2020; for an overview of existing provincial-federal agreements, see Government of Canada 2002). Contrary to provincial pressure to gain more control over economic immigration (see Paquet 2020), outside Quebec there are no provincial demands to increase provincial power over refugee admission policy.

By contrast, the role of provinces in refugee settlement has increased over time. It is important to note that actual settlement services delivery in Canada largely devolves to third sector, NGOs (Praznik and Shields 2018), but here we are concerned with control over settlement delivery. Vineberg (2014) argues that such increased control is not primarily due to provincial demands but rather to financial pressure on the federal government. Jeram and Nicolaides

(2019) state the federal government was also keen to ensure that Quebec was not the only province to have a large degree of control over immigration policy (see below). In the mid-1990s, all federal departments were required to identify services that could be transferred to provinces to limit federal spending. The federal immigration department, then Citizenship and Immigration Canada, identified the delivery of immigrant and refugee settlement services. Several provinces entered into negotiations with the federal government; yet only British Columbia and Manitoba agreed to take control over the administration of settlement. Because of provincial capacity issues, or because they feared the federal government would not transfer enough financial resources, other provinces entered varied forms of co-operation with the federal immigration department, including federal leadership, provincial leadership, and co-management (Vineberg 2014).

However, the Conservative Harper government (2006–15), pursuing a broader agenda of "national identity" and increased executive control that proved increasingly hostile to refugees, unilaterally recentralized the administration of immigrant settlement in British Columbia and Manitoba in 2012 (Vineberg 2014; Jeram and Nicolaides 2019). The Harper government did not work collaboratively with provinces as it reduced asylum seekers' access to health services (see Chen, chapter 24) and streamlined the asylum appeals process (Paquet and Schertzer 2020). Paquet and Larios (2018) argue the Harper government was pursuing a venue shopping strategy regarding immigration. If some provincial governments lost settlement prerogatives, other actors such as employers were granted more power over the selection of immigrants. The Harper government also fostered the establishment of Local Immigration Partnerships to facilitate local collaboration on immigrant and refugee settlement.

Importantly, provinces are mostly responsible for non-specialized, mainstream welfare services (including welfare services to refugees), encompassing the provision of health, education, housing, and employment support (Praznik and Shields 2018; Garnier 2018; 2022). However, the federal government is responsible for health-care provision to asylum seekers and refugees who are yet to be covered by provincial health coverage through the Interim Federal Health Program (IFHP) (Paquet and Schertzer 2020; see also Chen, chapter 24). IFHP health coverage was restricted under the Harper government (2012–16), which led provinces to fill the gaps, with Manitoba acting faster than other provinces (Harris and Zuberi 2015). In 2016 the Trudeau government restored the IFHP as it was prior to the 2012 reform (Mursal and Dong 2022).

In sum, outside the province of Quebec, the federal government remains in control of refugee admission. Contrary to economic migration, again outside Quebec there is no provincial pressure for more provincial control over refugee admission. Overall, federal-provincial relations relating to refugee settlement have become more heterogeneous as various models of settlement delivery have been created, with variable implication of non-governmental and municipal actors in policy design. As we will see below, provincial-federal relations regarding the admission of refugee claimants are contentious and have been tense on the issue of federal interim health coverage for refugee claimants and refugees excluded from provincial health coverage. Regarding other aspects of Canada's refugee policy, federal-provincial relations are barely visible.

THE PROVINCE OF QUEBEC: ASYMMETRICAL FEDERALISM AND REFUGEE POLICY

The francophone province of Quebec established an immigration service in 1965 and was the first to demand a say in immigrant admission in order to keep its distinctive character in Canada's federation (Vineberg 2014, 30ff). A series of agreements followed, which many argued were borne out of the threat of Quebec's independence from Canada. The Cullen-Couture Agreement of 1978 granted Quebec the power to select its own economic immigrants. The 1991 Canada-Quebec Accord relating to Immigration and Temporary Admission of Aliens is the most comprehensive bilateral agreement over immigration and refugee policy in Canada. Hence, Quebec is a stark illustration of asymmetrical federalism. Quebec can set its own immigration levels with an objective to receive the proportion of its demographic weight in permanent immigrants. The accord allows this target to exceed by 5 per cent. This target includes humanitarian immigration. In accordance with section 8 of the accord: "In order to assume its full responsibility for the reception of immigrants based on humanitarian considerations, Quebec undertakes to receive, out of the total number of refugees and persons in similar situations received by Canada, a percentage at least equal to the percentage of immigrants that it undertakes to accept" (Government of Canada 1991).

Because Quebec has the power to select its permanent immigrants, the province manages its own refugee resettlement program. It is distinct from the federal resettlement program insofar as it includes government-assisted and privately sponsored resettlement, yet neither engages with joint assistance sponsorship nor with blended visa office-referred resettlement (Labman and Garnier forthcoming; see also Labman, chapter 18). In French, Government-Assisted Refugees (GARs) are referred to as "*réfugiés publics*" (public refugees) or "*réfugiés pris en charge par le gouvernement*" (refugees under government care) and "*réfugiés parrainés par le secteur privé*" (privately sponsored refugees) even though private sponsorship is referred to as "*parrainage collectif*" (collective sponsorship) (Guyon 2011; Blain et al. 2019). Resettled GARs are sent to thirteen municipalities across the province (Arsenault 2021).

Quebec's immigration regulations mirror federal admission criteria as cited in the Immigration and Refugee Protection Regulations (IRPR). In selecting refugees for resettlement, the province prioritizes protection needs, but integration prospects and retention potential also matter. The higher the need for protection, the lower the latter criteria play a role (Labman and Garnier, forthcoming). As mentioned, Quebec plays no role in refugee status determination (RSD), which is solely a federal prerogative, but the federal government commits to swiftly inform the province in case "the file of a person claiming refugee status is being considered by a Canadian immigration centre located in Quebec" (Canada-Quebec Accord, Annex A s. 8(f)). In cases where refugees are in transit between provinces, Quebec commits to provide services for refugees bound to other provinces, and the federal government commits to provide services to Quebec-bound refugees (Canada-Quebec Accord, Annex B, s. 6).

Chapter 3 of the Canada-Quebec Accord addresses immigrants' and refugees' "reception and integration." According to sections 25 and 26 of the accord, the federal government withdraws from the provision of "reception, linguistic and cultural integration." The federal government also withdraws from the provision of "specialised economic services" to permanent residents (thus including refugees) and commits to provide a "reasonable compensation" to the province for the provision of these services. Annex B entails the formula used to calculate this compensation. The federal and provincial governments agreed to consult each other regularly on the modalities and implementation of the accord, for instance regarding planned immigration levels and immigrant and refugee selection criteria (Annex A, ss. 11 and 12).

We now turn to the implementation of the accord, first with a focus on Quebec's refugee admission. If Quebec is allowed a proportion of Canada's refugees that is "at least equal to the percentage of immigrants that it undertakes to accept," in practice the proportion of refugees admitted by Quebec has declined over time, particularly in the case of GARs (Labman and Garnier, forthcoming). In recent years, Quebec has also altered procedures for private refugee sponsorship by imposing quotas on distinct sponsor regions, and some regional sponsors have struggled to fill their quotas, yet sponsorship slots could not be transferred to other regions. The provincial government has also imposed verification procedures as some sponsors were accused of lacking accountability. Many provincial sponsors and refugee advocacy groups have welcomed the focus on accountability but deplored how the process unfolded in practice (Garnier and Labman 2020; Parent-Chartier, Santamaria, and van Haren 2023).

Regarding the federal transfer of compensation to fund Quebec's immigrant and refugee settlement services, the grant has steadily increased over time, from $75 million in 1991–92 (Government of Canada 1991) to $697 million in 2021–22 (Bellavance 2022). The umbrella organization representing refugee and immigrant settlement services in the province, Table de concertation des organismes au service des personnes réfugiées et immigrantes (TCRI), has long criticized the province's lack of accountability in spending the federal settlement grant (see Garnier 2016, box 10.1).

10.1 Quebec Accused of Using a Fraction of Federal Funding to Support Immigrants' and Refugees' French Language Classes

In 2021–22 the federal government transferred the record amount of $697 million to the provincial government to fund its settlement services according to the 1991 Canada-Quebec Accord. However, Quebec's provincial department of immigration, the Ministère de l'Immigration, de la Francisation et de l'Intégration (Ministry of Immigration, Francisation and Integration) allegedly spent only 25 per cent of the budget on French language classes for newcomers.

A ministry spokesperson mentions that her department has massively invested in training and financial incentives for newcomers learning French. Other sources within the ministry mention that overall, it spent $295 millions on settlement services in 2021–22, and that other departments, namely health, education and work, are also funded through the federal transfer to provide support services to immigrants and refugees (Bellavance, 2022).

MANAGEMENT OF ASYLUM CLAIMS AT THE US-CANADA BORDER: A COMPLEX INTERGOVERNMENTAL PROBLEM

Relations between levels of governments are not well-codified on asylum matters. Existing intergovernmental fora on immigration matters focus primarily on economic migration, and government agencies that play a role in asylum processes do not belong to these fora. Municipalities are also not part of immigration-focused intergovernmental fora. Yet if processing asylum claims and provision of health coverage through IFHP, are federal prerogatives, provinces are responsible for other service provision such as housing and education, and municipalities play a key role in delivering services. Hence the admission and settlement of refugee claimants is a salient federal-provincial issue, and this came to a head with the increase of claimants at irregular border crossings between 2017 and 2023. Paquet and Schertzer (2020) labelled the situation a complex intergovernmental problem.

Since the Canada–United States Safe Third Country Agreement (STCA) entered into force in 2004, it is impossible for asylum claimants who first arrive in either the US or Canada to make a refugee claim in the STCA country at official border posts (see Young, chapter 3 for a detailed discussion of the STCA). In March 2023 the STCA was expanded to the entire Canada-US border (Raycraft 2023), and the Supreme Court upheld the agreement in June 2023 (Tasker 2023). Before March 2023 the STCA did not apply outside these official border posts, so that it was possible to claim asylum in either country following an irregular border crossing. Such crossings increased from 2016, and 95 per cent of the crossings occurred in the province of Quebec through Roxham Road, between the town of Champlain in the state of New York and Saint-Bernard-de-Lacolle in the Montérégie region (Paquet and Schertzer 2020; Boyd and Ly 2021).

When irregular border crossing first spiked in 2017, the federal government was slow to respond and had not anticipated an increase of border crossings, even though some officials argued that this increase had been predictable, given changing US politics and a slower increase of claims in months preceding the 2017 spike (Paquet and Schertzer 2020, 22). In political discourse, both Prime Minister Trudeau and then Montreal mayor Denis Coderre appeared to welcome forced migrants entering Canada via Roxham Road (Trudeau 2017; Coderre 2017). Quebec's provincial government played a critical role in providing services to those who arrived, such as transportation and housing. The federal government's involvement increased following the opening of temporary shelters at the Montreal Olympic Stadium in August 2017. The Ad Hoc Intergovernmental Task Force on Irregular Migration was established in mid-August 2017 (Paquet and Schertzer 2020, 23). The task force included immigration ministers from Quebec and Ontario and representatives from various federal departments, including Immigration, Refugees and Citizenship Canada (IRCC), public safety, and national defence. The forum first focused on data-sharing and shelter and later on delays in processing asylum claims. Overall, the task force met twelve times in 2017–18. It developed a shared understanding of problems among federal and provincial officials and clarified roles and responsibilities.

Dynamics changed with Quebec's 2018 provincial election campaign, as the Coalition Avenir Quebec party politicized the issue and blamed the federal government, requesting a reform of the STCA to prevent all asylum claims along the US-Canada border (Xhardez and Paquet 2021). The Coalition Avenir Quebec won the 2018 and the 2022 provincial elections respectively. The politicization of border crossings diminished during the pandemic because of the US-Canada border closure. It became a contentious issue in Quebec once again from the re-opening of the US-Canada border in November 2021, as border crossings at Roxham Road increased (Serebrin 2022). The Quebec government requested the transfer of Roxham Road refugee claimants to other provinces. Interprovincial transfer started in June 2022 and Premier Legault became increasingly vocal about the need to "close Roxham Road." He referred to the expansion of the STCA as "a very happy victory" while insisting on Quebec' commitment to its "humanitarian duty" (Angers 2023).

10.2 Transferring Roxham Road Refugee Claimants from Quebec to Ontario: Lived Experience

Between June and October 2022 more than 2,000 refugee claimants who arrived in Canada via Roxham Road in Quebec were transferred by the federal government to Ontario. According to IRCC data, 1,178 refugee claimants were sent to Niagara Falls, 720 to Cornwall and 293 to Ottawa. According to IRCC, the cost of these transfers is $10,770,000, or $4,900 per person. The Quebec government requested these transfers as it considered the province overwhelmed with the number of refugee claimants.

IRCC argues that transfers occur on a voluntary basis and that claimants can return to Quebec as soon as housing is available. Yet community organizations and refugee claimants report that transfers are not always voluntary.

For instance, Juan, his wife, and two children were quarantining in a Montreal hotel after having arrived in Quebec via Roxham Road. One day, a manager came into their bedroom and asked Juan's wife to pack and leave, either for a transfer to Ontario or to a more permanent housing in Montreal they had to find themselves. Juan's wife called him in distress as she spoke neither French no English. At the time, Juan was meeting a social worker, who was able to find housing for the family in an accommodation for asylum seekers. The family was subsequently able to find an apartment in Montreal, start French language classes, and send their children to school (Rességuier 2022).

EMERGING ISSUE: MUNICIPALITIES AND FEDERAL-PROVINCIAL RELATIONS IN CANADA'S REFUGEE POLICY

In accordance with the Canadian constitution, municipalities do not play a role in refugee policy. However, municipalities are critical to federal and provincial policy implementation. Increasingly, especially large cities in Canada demand to be included in policy formulation (Gunn 2012). Regarding refugee policy, these demands have been most visible in the case of sanctuary cities (Bauder 2017; Atak and Hudson 2022; Paquet and Joy 2022).

The meaning of "sanctuary city" varies across contexts (Bauder 2017). In Canada, "sanctuary city" refers to cities developing practices to protect migrants with no legal status, which include individuals fleeing persecution who have been denied refugee status. Sanctuary city policies include providing municipal services to non-status migrants, such as access to health care, schools, and parks (Access without Fear policies). Such municipal interventions go against federal (and in Quebec, provincial) legal categorizations dividing individuals by status.

In addition to such inclusive elements, sanctuary city policies also prohibit municipal staff from co-operating with authorities aiming to deport non-status migrants ("don't ask, don't tell" policies). Lack of co-operation can lead to tensions with national and subnational enforcement bodies (Paquet and Joy 2022).

In Canada, urban sanctuary policies were first demanded by Chilean refugee advocates in Toronto in the 1980s. Following strong community support for municipal "don't ask, don't tell" policies, such policies were incrementally developed from 2004, even though many municipal officials did not implement them. In 2013 Toronto City Council adopted sanctuary city bylaws (Bauder 2017). Since then, six other Canadian cities have followed (see policy overview in Paquet and Joy 2022, 636). One could argue that successful bottom-up pressure for the adoption of sanctuary policies indicates a mode of governance that is more inclusive than traditional federal and provincial regulations (Abu-Laban 2020a).

Yet Paquet and Joy (2022) consider that the development of sanctuary city policies in Canada is surprising. First, the size of the undocumented population in Canadian cities is comparatively smaller than in US and European cities, so that the issue is not politically salient. Hence, there is no widespread demand for such policies. Second, municipalities' lack of jurisdiction over enforcement and immigration means that sanctuary policies' implementation is bound to be limited. Paquet and Joy argue that sanctuary city policies in Canada "aim at information provision and at easing access to existing municipal services, while presenting the city as an inclusive and progressive place" (2022, 631).

In practice however, municipal sanctuary city policies have so far yielded limited results. Activists in Vancouver noted in 2018 that municipal staff still mostly required identification documents to provide services, while Toronto's sanctuary city policies were supported by committed individual municipal staff and networks rather than by the city council at large (Paquet and Joy 2022, 632). Montreal, which labelled itself a sanctuary city in 2017 under the municipal administration of then mayor Denis Coderre, withdrew from this label in 2018 under the administration of the city's next mayor Valérie Plante. Plante argued that the label made "false promises." Plante faced increasing pressure from the provincially regulated municipal police service, which is known to co-operate with federal authorities on immigration enforcement. Montreal still endorses Access without Fear measures but now uses the label "inclusive city" (Atak and Hudson 2022). As part of these measures, it has developed a municipal ID card, drawing on examples of municipal ID cards in US cities, especially New York (Atak and Hudson 2022; see de Graauw and Vermeulen 2016).

10.3 Montreal Renews Program of Municipal IDs for Undocumented Migrants

In February 2022, Montreal City Council unanimously voted to renew the municipal program offering identification cards to non-status migrants until at least the end of 2023. It allows non-status migrants and migrants with precarious status to "use services such as food banks, pools, libraries and day camps ... [and] to sign a lease, get vaccinated, and register their children for school" (McKenna 2022, n.p.). About five hundred municipal IDs have been handed out since 2019, when the program was started. The program is facilitated by the non-governmental organization Doctors of the World. According to Doctors of the World national director Pénélope Boudreault, there are about fifty thousand undocumented people in Montreal. According to Josefina Blanco, Montreal executive committee member responsible for diversity, Montreal's police force SPVM does not recognize the ID, although the city is working to change the situation (McKenna 2022).

CONCLUSION

Federal-provincial relations are key to our understanding of Canada's refugee policy. The federal government is exclusively responsible for the determination of refugee claims and for the enforcement of immigration control. The federal government also controls the admission of refugees through refugee resettlement, except in the province of Quebec. The role of the federal government in refugee settlement has fluctuated. From the 1990s financial pressure led to the devolution of immigrant and refugee settlement services to the provincial level in several provinces. However, devolved settlement services were unilaterally recentralized under the Harper government, which sought partnerships with other actors. Provinces are responsible for mainstream social and welfare services available to all residents, including refugees. Provincial responsibilities include housing, education, social assistance, and health care, except for asylum seekers' health care, which is controlled by the federal government.

Quebec has far more autonomy over immigration and refugee policy than other provinces and as such is a stark illustration of asymmetrical federalism. Quebec manages its own version of refugee resettlement, which includes government-assisted and privately sponsored resettlement, but excludes joint-assisted sponsorship and blended visa office-referred resettlement. As per the 1991 Canada-Quebec Accord, Quebec receives a federal settlement grant to fund the province's refugee and immigrant services. The Canada-Quebec Accord allows Quebec to resettle far more refugees than it has in recent years.

Managing the increase of asylum claims made by individuals crossing the US-Canada border outside official border posts has been described as a complex intergovernmental problem and became a highly politicized issue between the province of Quebec – where most of the crossings occur – and the federal government. It remains to be seen whether the issue will remain as politicized now that the STCA has been expanded to the entire US-Canada land border. An emerging issue in federal-provincial relations in refugee policy is the increasing visibility of cities. The development of municipal policies that are broadening access to municipal services to migrants with precarious status can create tensions with federal and provincial authorities emphasizing immigration enforcement.

FURTHER READING AND RESOURCES

Bureau, Brigitte. 2022. "Manitoba Becomes 4th Province to Say it Will Stop Imprisoning Migrants." CBC News, 24 October 2022. https://www.cbc.ca/news/canada/manitoba/manitoba-migrant-prison-stop-1.6625106.

CBC Radio. 2019. "Quebec's New Immigration Law Could be an Attempt to Win More Power from Ottawa." *The Current*, 18 June 2019. https://www.cbc.ca/radio/thecurrent/the-current-for-june-18-2019-1.5178745/quebec-s-new-immigration-law-could-be-attempt-to-win-more-powers-from-ottawa-expert-1.5178750.

Elrick, Jennifer, and Daniel Béland. 2023. "Managing Asylum Claims in a Federal System with Lessons from Germany." IRPP *Policy Options*, 14 March 2023. https://policyoptions.irpp.org/magazines/march-2023/managing-asylum-claims.

Mercer, Juanita. 2023 "Aging Newfoundland and Labrador is Facing a Bleak Long-Term 'Population Crisis' and while Immigration is Crucial, it's not the 'Solution to Everything.'" SaltWire, 30 January 2023. https://www.saltwire.com/cape-breton/news/aging-newfoundland-and-labrador-is-facing-a-bleak-long-term-population-crisis-and-while-immigration-is-crucial-its-not-the-solution-to-everything-100819145.

11

Human Trafficking in Canada: An Overview of an Invisible Crime

Martha Vargas Aguirre

KEY TAKEAWAYS

- Human trafficking involves the recruitment, transportation, or harbouring of persons for the purpose of exploitation.
- Human trafficking can take many forms and frequently intertwines with other actions, making it difficult to define and easy to conflate with other activities like migrant smuggling.
- In Canada, human trafficking is largely a domestic and gender-related phenomenon. Most victims/survivors[1] are Canadian-born women, with Indigenous women disproportionately affected, followed by 2SLGBTQI+ people, racialized minorities, and migrants.
- Canada has developed a legislative and public policy framework to combat this crime. However, it focuses on enforcing the criminal justice system and border control measures, which effectively marginalize responses addressing the multifactorial nature of human trafficking.

KEY TERMS

- Trafficking (also called trafficking in persons, TIP)
- Smuggling

INTRODUCTION

> 11.1 "Vulnerable Victims, Strong Survivors"
> Covenant House Toronto, dir. n.d. *Stop Sex Trafficking in Ontario,* YouTube video, 4:07.

Every day, thousands of people are stripped of their humanity and turned into commodities to be trafficked. The exact impact and scope of human trafficking, also known as trafficking in persons (TIP), are unknown. However, a rough estimate suggests that six to eight hundred thousand people are trafficked worldwide every year (Samarasinghe and Burton 2007, 52). In Canada between 2010 and 2020, the police reported 2,977 cases of trafficking (Conroy and Sutton 2020, 5).

These figures underestimate the magnitude of TIP, which affects almost all states in all regions of the world[2] (UNODC 2020) but is an "invisible crime." Although efforts to collect data, produce statistics, and develop research on the subject have expanded in recent decades, knowledge about TIP remains limited. Its clandestine nature, underreporting, and difficulties in identifying victims/survivors and traffickers are a few of the complex factors that hinder compilation of data and understanding (Farrell et al. 2015).

This chapter exposes key aspects of TIP and provides a succinct introduction to a complex phenomenon not yet fully understood. It also gives an overview of the key elements of this issue in the Canadian context. The first section covers the main generalities of the phenomenon such as its definition, the international framework that encompasses it, the issues surrounding this aspect, as well as its differences from migrant smuggling, which is commonly confused with TIP. The second section of this chapter explores human trafficking in Canada. It exposes how this phenomenon is most prevalent in the Canadian context among populations affected by multiple intersecting forms of oppression. Subsequently, it describes the Canadian responses to TIP, as well as the main criticisms levied against these measures.

INTERNATIONAL LEGAL FRAMEWORK

In general terms, TIP involves the recruitment, transportation, or harbouring of persons for exploitation. Beyond a criminal activity, it is one of the most serious human rights violations. Therefore, TIP is a focus of intergovernmental organizations for priority intervention, particularly in recent decades.

The first historical antecedent of international character related to the prevention and eradication of trafficking dates from the eighteenth century, with the first conventions aimed at eliminating slavery in Europe. Subsequent conventions in the nineteenth and early twentieth centuries focused on preventing and combating trafficking of European White women, known as the "white slave trade" (Lammasniemi 2019).

After World War II, the scope of protection broadened. The Universal Declaration of Human Rights (UDHR)[3] became the basis for the subsequent development of international instruments in this area. In 1949 the UN General Assembly developed the Convention for the Suppression of the Traffic in Persons and of the Exploitation of the Prostitution of Others, which is the "first legally binding international instrument on TIP" (Bruey 2021, 111). Later, in 1979, the Convention on the Elimination of All Forms of Discrimination Against Women was enacted, and subsequently, international instruments regarding child protection also started addressing this phenomenon.

During the 1990s, the steep rise of human trafficking, its identification as a transnational practice linked to international organizations, and the limitations of the existing international instruments led the United Nations to create an ad hoc committee focused on preventing and repressing these acts.[4] This initiative eventually culminated on 15 December 2000, with adoption by the UN General Assembly of the Protocol to Prevent, Suppress and Punish Trafficking in Persons, especially Women and Children (UN TIP Protocol), which is currently the main international instrument for the fight against TIP. It was created within the framework of the development of the UN Convention against Transnational Organized Crime.[5]

DEFINING HUMAN TRAFFICKING: A COMPLEX TASK

TIP is a phenomenon that can take many forms, and it frequently intertwines with other activities, making it difficult to define (Dandurand and Jahn 2020). Consequently, reaching a consensus about what constitutes TIP has remained an almost impossible task, and there is no uniformity in how the phenomenon is defined in the literature.[6] Notwithstanding, the legal realm, as well as the academic sphere, have reached a certain level of consensus over the years on the conceptual understanding of this issue. However, TIP is still considered a "slippery concept that is hard to pin down" (Gould 2006, 19).

Despite the "never-ending" discussion (Di Nicola 2007) about the limits of this concept, the debates at the level of international law came to a relative end at the turn of the twenty-first century, when the UN TIP Protocol came into force. Article 3 of this international instrument contains the first definition of human trafficking accepted worldwide.[7]

Although the definition of the protocol is considered the main conceptual understanding of this phenomenon, the challenges in establishing clear boundaries of what constitutes TIP have not been overcome. However, there is relative agreement on three central, basic elements of trafficking, which are set out in the protocol definition:

- An act: the recruitment, transportation, transfer, harbouring, or taking receipt of persons.
- The use of certain means: threat, force, any form of coercion, abduction, fraud, deception, abuse of power or a position of vulnerability, or giving or receiving payments or benefits.
- The purpose of the act: exploitation, which can take different forms.

The definition in the international UN TIP Protocol is the basis for most national legislation criminalizing this conduct. Since article 3 of this international instrument establishes minimum standards of protection, it is left to the discretion of its signatory states to define the specificities of the crime as well as the responding mechanisms of repression and prevention. This margin of discretion available to the states means there are as many definitions as there are related state acts of legislation.

Within this framework, states may extend the limits of the protocol's definition according to what they consider are the practices constituting the crime (Mattar 2020). For instance, Canadian law goes beyond the scope of what is defined in the UN TIP Protocol. While the protocol establishes exploitation as an essential element of the crime, the Criminal Code of Canada does not require the objectively established act of exploitation to be a mandatory element of the offence; it is only necessary for the victim to have a "reasonable belief that failure to comply with the demands of the trafficker would have jeopardized their safety" (Roots 2013, 30). Countries not only broaden their definitions but can also omit certain elements, and the most common omission relates to the elements of the means. In countries like Canada, Colombia, Luxembourg, Panama, and Switzerland, the means are only considered an aggravating factor of the crime and not a constituent one (Silver 2021).

The definitional inconsistencies of TIP can affect data collection, in turn impacting research findings and, subsequently, the development or improvements of measures aimed at fighting this crime (Winkler 2021). This problem is particularly evident at the level of national legislation, where definitional ambiguity can result in dissimilar judicial or legislative interpretations. For instance, some countries (e.g., Australia, Panama, South Korea, etc.) consider movement a basic element of this behaviour (Silver 2021). In these cases, the use of the term "trafficking" involves geographical displacement or transit of some kind from one place to another. Even though some activities described in the UN TIP Protocol do involve movement (transportation and transfer), others, like harbouring and recruitment, are not defined by this limitation (Weitzer 2015). Therefore, acts that could be considered human trafficking under the UN TIP Protocol are judged as different offences in different states.

TRAFFICKING VERSUS MIGRANT SMUGGLING

Difficulties in defining TIP and the erroneous idea that it always involves movement, particularly at a cross-border level, also cause frequent confusion with migrant smuggling. TIP and migrant smuggling are clearly differentiated in international instruments and criminal legislation. Notwithstanding, there is a misconception about the two acts, and they are often used interchangeably (Szablewska 2022), not only in everyday language but also in the press, political discourse (Dandurand and Jahn 2020; Lockhart and Boland 2021; Perry 2018), and even in information campaigns for their prevention (Nieuwenhuys and Pécoud 2007).

Like TIP, migrant smuggling requires certain constituent elements that differentiate the former from the latter. In migrant smuggling, smugglers serve as intermediaries or facilitators for the transnational movement of people through irregularized routes. Therefore, this practice always presupposes cross-border mobility. In this framework, there is the express consent of the smuggled person, which entails an exchange (mostly economic) for the benefit of the smuggler, and which is agreed upon before the journey (Campana 2020).

Unlike trafficking, the profit from smuggling is obtained from the facilitation of the movement of people and not from their subsequent exploitation. Hence, in principle, migrant smuggling terminates with arrival at the agreed destination, so prolonged or temporary exploitation is not a fundamental part of the crime as in the case of TIP. However, there are situations where trafficking and smuggling may be intertwined, a fact that helps fuel the conflation of terms. In many cases, migrants and displaced people decide to put themselves in the hands of smugglers to leave their country of residence, and then through subsequent coercion or deception, are subjected to trafficking (Baird and van Liempt 2016).

The confusion between TIP and migrant smuggling fuels and reinforces the construction of migrants and forced migrants as an issue related to security and control (Farrell and Fahy 2009; Geddes 2005; Lobasz 2009). Although at the normative and public policy levels the definitions of the two concepts are clear, these terms are usually juxtaposed when it comes to developing prevention and repression directives. Hence, human trafficking is framed as a problem directly linked to "risky" migratory movements. This approach substantiates the idea that the border crossing of certain populations constitutes a threat to the security of states.

Anti-trafficking policies are used to control and restrict the migratory movement of certain groups (Bernstein 2012; Chapkis 2003; Pickering 2004; Sharma 2005), which encourage processes where these populations are irregularized, deepening their state of vulnerability (Chacon 2010). The reinforcement of migratory restrictions is legitimized as a strategy conceived to defend

TIP victims, conflating the protection of human rights with surveillance and control practices (David, Bryant, and Joudo Larsen 2019; Gallagher 2002; Uhl 2010).

HUMAN TRAFFICKING IN CANADA

TIP is commonly regarded as a phenomenon specific to low- or middle-income countries known to be key centres for sex tourism. However, this heinous practice is enmeshed in the Canadian social fabric. Its true scope and impact remain unclear not only for mainstream society but also for governmental authorities (Public Safety Canada 2019). One of the biggest challenges for the Canadian government is the collection of data on TIP (Housefather 2018). There is no nationally held database that accurately depicts the prevalence of this crime. This is not only due to the underground nature of the problem but also to methodological shortcomings in defining, measuring, and reporting this phenomenon (Millar, O'Doherty, and Roots 2017).

Although the existing information is inaccurate and shows only a superficial overview of the problem, it is nonetheless alarming: TIP cases in Canada are increasing (Conroy and Sutton 2020; D. Ibrahim 2019). TIP is a crime committed in the most varied contexts of Canadian society, occurring in big urban centres like Montreal, Toronto, and Calgary, as well as in small cities and rural communities (Public Safety Canada 2012a). TIP affects almost every province of the country (Statistics Canada 2022e), with Ontario and Nova Scotia having the highest incidence of this crime (Conroy and Sutton 2020).

TIP is rooted in people's vulnerability. The economic, social, political, cultural, environmental, and psychological fragility of victims/survivors facilitates the actions of traffickers. In Canada, individuals who are more likely to experience various forms of oppression are the main targets. Therefore, populations like children and young people (Baird, McDonald, and Connolly 2020), Indigenous people, women in general, 2SLGBTQI+ people, and newcomers are particularly vulnerable to perpetrators of this crime (Public Safety Canada 2019).

DOMESTIC HUMAN TRAFFICKING IN CANADA: GENDER AND COLONIALISM

TIP is an issue that is commonly, but erroneously, linked to the international migratory movements of non-citizens. Thus, until the early 2000s, the policy debate around TIP in Canada focused on the cross-border trafficking of non-citizen women coming to the country as exotic dancers or sex workers (Durisin and van der Meulen 2021; J. Kaye 2017). Similarly, most research focused on international trafficking, leaving a significant gap in the understanding of domestic trafficking in Canada (Roots 2018).

Later, with the development of public policy and the increase of studies in the field, this phenomenon started to be understood as a significantly domestic and gender-based issue. Between 2019 and 2020 the Canadian Human Trafficking Hotline indicated that 90 per cent of reported cases involved female victims (Canadian Centre to End Human Trafficking 2019). The last report of the Canadian government establishes that in 96 per cent of the TIP cases reported, women and girls were the victims/survivors (Conroy and Sutton 2020). Most TIP cases in this country involve the sex trafficking of Canadian-born women.

11.2 A TIP victim/survivor recounts, "As I got older that effect of colonialism that legacy was handed down to me by you know the whole meaning of what a squad is or a dirty Indian, um I was almost ashamed of being native, it damaged me ... I was lured into prostitution ... every one of those men that bought me felt entitled to me ... I flew Canadian airlines and no one ever stopped me and said little girl where are you going, like, nobody asked" (Victim Services 2021, 0:59).

All women are vulnerable to being trafficked. However, in Canada, TIP disproportionately affects Indigenous people. It is estimated that 50 per cent of the victims of this crime are Indigenous women and girls (Conroy and Sutton 2020). The legacy of colonization and the pervasiveness of settler colonialism underpin the vulnerability of this group to TIP (Bourgeois 2015; Hunt 2015). Enduring colonial tropes reproduce sexist and racist stereotypes that hypersexualize Indigenous women, framing their bodies as "expendable and inherently violable" (A. Smith 2015, 201). These stereotypes perpetrate dynamics of violence,[8] fuelling social causes of their sexual exploitation (Hunt 2015; A. Smith and Ross 2004). Thus, structural challenges such as poverty, isolation, substance abuse, lack of adequate services, and different forms of discrimination, are among the various complex and interrelated aspects that make these women highly vulnerable to being trapped in trafficking activities (Sethi 2007).

The true impact of the phenomenon on Indigenous people is still very unclear (Hodgins et al. 2022). However, research in this area is more developed in comparison to studies focused on other vulnerable groups, particularly 2SLGBTQI+ people. This remains an alarmingly understudied field not only in Canada but also worldwide (Wills 2022). Nevertheless, existing research demonstrates that as a product of settler colonialism, sexual violence disproportionately also affects 2SLGBTQI+ (Lezard et al. 2021; Roudometkina and Wakeford 2018). This situation is exacerbated by other serious problems, similar to those endured by Indigenous women, such as lack of adequate health services, isolation, and inadequate housing, also making this population highly vulnerable to sexual exploitation and trafficking in Canada (Roudometkina and Wakeford 2018).

TRAFFICKING NON-CITIZENS IN CANADA

> 11.3 A TIP victim/survivor recalls, "I came to Canada to work. However, I soon found out I was deceived and was actually sold to a family here in order to work without pay. I was held against my will, and although I managed to escape, my life was threatened. I testified against those who were involved in buying and selling people from Europe for forced labour, as well as those who utilized their labour within Canada" (Government of British Columbia 2014).

Although TIP in Canada is more prevalent among Canadian-born individuals, every year hundreds of non-citizens are trafficked into this country (Perrin 2011). The exact numbers are unknown, but 30 per cent of the cases reported to the police between 2010 and 2020 involved newcomers (Statistics Canada 2022c). In Canada, newcomers and foreign workers are predominately vulnerable to being trafficked for sexual and labour exploitation. Irregularized young females are the main target for the former (Pashang 2019) and temporary foreign workers for the latter (Beatson, Hanley, and Ricard-Guay 2017). Such factors as isolation, language barriers, limited access to services, as well as the regulations that protect them facilitate the exploitation of these individuals (Public Safety Canada 2019).

While irregularized immigrants are more likely to be trafficked, many people who enter Canada on visas granted by the country's immigration authorities are also victims/survivors of this crime.[9] Precarious immigration status is a key factor for their vulnerability. The threat of deportation and detention for non-compliance with immigration regulations are tools traffickers use to maintain power over these people and avoid being reported to the police (Matte Guilmain and Hanley 2021).

CANADIAN RESPONSES TO HUMAN TRAFFICKING

In 2002 Canada ratified the UN TIP Protocol and, to comply with its international commitment, issued domestic legislation aimed at combating TIP. In 2002, for the first time, Canada criminalized TIP through the Immigration and Refugee Protection Act (IRPA). Subsection 118(1) focuses on cross-border trafficking committed by individuals or criminal organizations.[10] Later, in

November 2005, Canada enacted the first criminal code legislation addressing TIP through Bill C-49, which amended the Criminal Code of Canada to include sections 279.01–279.04 that focus on this crime.[11]

IRPA and the Criminal Code of Canada are the key legal instruments to combat TIP at the federal level. Within this framework, the provinces can take legislative measures to address the crime. However, only two provinces have legal instruments in this area. Manitoba was the first province to take action. In 2012 it passed the Child Sexual Exploitation and Human Trafficking Act. Eight years later, Alberta joined the fight against TIP at the legal level and enacted the Protecting Survivors of Human Trafficking Act.

In the public policy arena, in 2012 the Canadian government issued the National Action Plan to Combat Human Trafficking. This policy instrument outlines programmatic guidelines at the federal level for the prevention of TIP, the protection of victims, and the prosecution of traffickers (Public Safety Canada 2019). The implementation of the national action plan led to the creation of the Human Trafficking Task Force, a division that works under the leadership of Public Safety Canada and is composed of different federal agencies and departments considered key in the fight against this offence. The objective of this task force was to have a body in charge of overseeing the implementation of the action plan (Housefather 2018).

To complement the action arising from the national action plan, in 2019 Public Safety Canada issued the National Strategy to Combat Human Trafficking 2019–24. It seeks to focus on victim identification and empowerment, with an emphasis on respecting and addressing the vulnerability of certain groups such as Indigenous communities and the 2SLGBTQI+ population. This approach led to the implementation of the Canadian Human Trafficking Hotline, which supports victims/survivors of TIP and connects them to different social and law enforcement agencies.

The initiatives developed by the Canadian government to address TIP are important but insufficient to tackle a problem fuelled by a confluence of complex and wide-ranging factors. One of the main criticisms is the heavy and exclusive reliance on the use of the criminal justice system as the key tool to combat TIP, rendering invisible the underlying factors that perpetuate victims' experiences of vulnerability and make them easy targets for exploitation. Although the latest development in public policy focuses more on the experiences of the affected populations, governmental measures are still mainly focused on advancing and strengthening law enforcement measures (Olson-Pitawanakwat and Baskin 2021; Dyment 2021; J. Kaye, Winterdyk, and Quarterman 2014; Kaye 2017; J. Kaye, Millar, and O'Doherty 2020; Simunic 2021). In addition, the Canadian government's responses to TIP have focused on the area of sexual exploitation, marginalizing other variants of this phenomenon, such as labour trafficking and organ trafficking (Beatson, Hanley, and Ricard-Guay 2017).

This focus not only marginalizes non-sex trafficking victims but also reproduces stereotypes that reinforce the criminalization of sex work by framing sex workers in general as victims of exploitation without agency (Kempadoo et al. 2017; Lam and Lepp 2019).

Canadian authorities also address TIP as an issue linked to irregular migration and cross-border mobility. Therefore, Canada Border Services Agency (CBSA) along with the Royal Canadian Mounted Police (RCMP) take leading roles, with the reinforcement of border control and immigration measures framed as ideal prevention strategies. Border points are portrayed as the best place to identify and combat TIP. However, research has shown these assertions lack empirical evidence[12] (Miller and Baumeister 2013), and they simply reinforce the scrutiny of certain individuals because of their gender, sexual orientation, or origin (Roots and De Shalit 2015; J. Kaye 2017).

Likewise, scholars claim that the underpinnings of Canadian anti-trafficking measures are embedded in colonial violence (Millar and O'Doherty 2020; Pabla 2021). In this sense, the governmental response is described as perpetuating social inequalities by naturalizing assumptions that marginalize, disempower, or reinforce the need for over-surveillance of certain groups. In this framework and through a feminist and anti-colonialist study, J. Kaye (2017) claims that the Canadian government reproduces the colonialist legacies that subjugate Indigenous people through its anti-trafficking efforts, which are focused on Indigenous women. These anti-trafficking measures portray the state as the developed and benevolent protector that aims to "save" racialized victims, thereby reinforcing and creating "particular national, racial, and sexual notions of what it means to be Canadian" (33).

To counter this limitation Indigenous organizations have sought to promote responses that break with the colonialist dynamics of violence and oppression identified as the basis of Canada's anti-trafficking policy. Thus, Indigenous activism has developed initiatives based on the sovereignty and self-determination of Indigenous Peoples; these programs focus on the inclusion of their cultures and the centrality of survivors as a foundation of their development. For example, the Ontario Native Women's Association has two programs focused on survivors of TIP: the Indigenous Anti-Human Trafficking Liaison, which focuses on prevention and awareness, and the Aakwa'ode'ewin (Courage for Change) program, where through culture-based practices it supports survivors of sexual exploitation.

While such initiatives promote the development of more appropriate responses, the prevention and combating of TIP remains a highly complex task. One of the elements that fuels this complexity is limited access to information. For instance, access to data concerning prosecutions and legal proceedings remains limited. Hence, a comprehensive and accurate evaluation of government actions to combat TIP is a complicated task. The highly politicized nature of the problem, the high costs of accessing information, and recent delays caused by the COVID-19 pandemic are important limitations in research and evaluation (Bruey 2021; Millar, O'Doherty, and Roots 2017). Millar, O'Doherty, and Roots (2017) find that governments, including Canada, measure the success of anti-trafficking legislation in terms of the number of investigations and charges related to this crime. These types of evaluations are limited because they lack the depth of analysis that such a complex phenomenon as TIP requires through all stages of the criminal process.

CONCLUSION

As mentioned, TIP is particularly complex in nature. National and international responses conceived to address this activity remain limited. Responses focused on criminal law enforcement measures fail to highlight how trafficking is closely linked to dynamics of oppression, where intersectional discrimination shapes the experiences of survivors in an asymmetrical manner. TIP demands an institutional response centring on the homogeneously integrated life experiences of its victims/survivors as a mechanism to avoid reinforcing violent power dynamics legitimized as protection. The multiple factors that perpetuate and facilitate this practice arise from historical and deeply embedded structural inequalities. Therefore, anti-trafficking measures must be multisectoral, animated by a multidisciplinary dialogu, and centred on the life experiences of the affected populations. Although the place of the victims/survivors has gained wider recognition over the decades, this should not be relegated to a supporting aspect in the development of anti-trafficking policy and legislation; instead, it must become the guiding light of such legislation.

NOTES

1 There is a debate about whether to refer to those who survive human trafficking as victims or survivors.

2 According to the UN Office on Drugs and Crime (UNODC) report, more than 120 countries reported various cases of human trafficking. The victims came from 140 different countries.

3 Article 4 of the UDHR states: "No one shall be held in slavery or servitude; slavery and the slave trade shall be prohibited in all their forms."

4 Other international organizations such as the International Organization for Migration and the International Labour Organization have also adopted provisions to address this crime.

5 Besides the UN TIP Protocol, the UNTOC is supported by two additional supplementary protocols: the *Protocol against the Smuggling of Migrants by Land, Sea, and Air* and the *Protocol against the Illicit Manufacturing and Trafficking in Firearms.*

6 The research by Laczko, Thompson, and Salt (2000) is proof of this issue. In their research, these authors identified more than twenty different definitions of human trafficking.

7 The protocol defines TIP as:

> (a) "Trafficking in persons" shall mean the recruitment, transportation, transfer, harbouring or receipt of persons, by means of the threat or use of force or other forms of coercion, of abduction, of fraud, of deception, of the abuse of power or of a position of vulnerability or of the giving or receiving of payments or benefits to achieve the consent of a person having control over another person, for the purpose of exploitation. Exploitation shall include, at a minimum, the exploitation of the prostitution of others or other forms of sexual exploitation, forced labour or services, slavery or practices similar to slavery, servitude or the removal of organs; (b) The consent of a victim of trafficking in persons to the intended exploitation set forth in subparagraph (a) of this article shall be irrelevant where any of the means set forth in subparagraph (a) have been used; (c) The recruitment, transportation, transfer, harbouring or receipt of a child for the purpose of exploitation shall be considered "trafficking in persons" even if this does not involve any of the means set forth in subparagraph (a) of this article; (d) "Child" shall mean any person under eighteen years of age. (UN TIP Protocol 2000)

8 Studies indicate that Indigenous women and girls suffer a high percentage of family and sexual violence. It is estimated that six out of ten Indigenous women have been victims of physical abuse and 46 per cent of them were sexually abused (Heidinger 2022). In addition, compared to other groups of women, they are twelve times more likely to disappear or be murdered (Buller et al. 2019).

9 Some immigration programs promoted by the Canadian government make certain individuals more vulnerable to exploitation, as was the case of the Live-in Care Giver Program (Oxman-Martinez, Martinez, and Hanley 2001), which ended in 2014 and was replaced by the Caring for Children and for People with High Medical Needs program that closed to new applications in 2014 (IRCC 2019).

10 It establishes: "No person shall knowingly organize the coming into Canada of one or more persons by means of abduction, fraud, deception, or use or threat of force or coercion" (IRPA 2001).

11 Section 279.01 describes the offence: "Every person who recruits, transports, transfers, receives, holds, conceals, or harbours a person, or exercises control, direction, or influence over the movements of a person, for the purpose of exploiting them or facilitating their exploitation is guilty of an indictable offense."

12 For instance, border control can be ineffective in detecting cases of TIP because traffickers usually provide their victims with sophisticated forged documents that are unidentifiable to Canadian authorities (Perry 2018).

FURTHER READING AND RESOURCES

Canadian Centre to End Human Trafficking. 2020. "About Human Trafficking." https://www.canadiancentretoendhumantrafficking.ca/about-human-trafficking.

CBC News. 2017. "Canada a Target for Human Traffickers." *The National.* YouTube video, 19:13. https://www.youtube.com/watch?v=L-1rrIr6SKQ.

Government of British Columbia. n.d. "What Is Human Trafficking?" Province of British Columbia. https://www2.gov.bc.ca/gov/content/justice/criminal-justice/victims-of-crime/human-trafficking/what-is-it.

SECTION TWO

Intersectionalities of Forced Migration Experiences

12

(Re)Conceptualizing Gender and Sexuality: Current Understandings and Debates in Forced Migration Research and Policy in Canada

Tanya Aberman

KEY TAKEAWAYS

- The gender binary is a colonial social construct.
- Sexual orientation and gender identity exist on a broad spectrum and can be fluid and context specific.
- Gender identity and sexual orientation intersect with race, class, age, ability, and religion in shaping life experiences in forced migration contexts.
- Gender guidelines and Sexual Orientation, Gender Identity and Expression, and Sex Characteristics (SOGIESC) guidelines have been developed within the Canadian refugee determination system to better recognize diverse experiences of persecution and forced migration. These guidelines have noted limitations.
- Gender and sexuality constructs and realities impact forced migrants navigating refugee and humanitarian processes.

KEY TERMS

- Gender: Gender binary, cis/trans gender, gender expression, patriarchy
- Sexual identity: 2SLGBTQI+ (Two-Spirit, Lesbian, Gay, Bisexual, Transgender, Queer and/or Questioning, Intersex, +), heteronormativity, SOGIESC
- Intersectionality

INTRODUCTION

How do gender and sexuality affect experiences of forced migration and refugee processes and procedures? In what ways does the Canadian state respond to the diverse expression of gender and sexual identity in forced migration contexts? This chapter begins to answer these questions by first deconstructing binary ideas of gender and sexual orientation to highlight diverse and complicated experiences of forced migration. I use an intersectional framework to explore how gender identity and sexual orientation necessarily intersect with other identities including race, class, religion, and ability.

Canada has often been praised as a safe haven for women and 2SLGBTQI+ forced migrants. However, this chapter juxtaposes that image with the challenges people have faced in seeking protection and establishing themselves in Canada. By exploring Canada's humanitarian immigration processes, including the refugee determination process and the gender and SOGIESC guidelines, the discussion highlights limitations of Canada's "welcome."

GENDER IDENTITY AND EXPRESSION

In this chapter, gender is understood as a non-binary and relational social construct, which is *not biological* but rather variable, fluid, and learned. Binary cis-gender understandings of gender posit that the assignation of male and female usually happens at birth or during gestation by assessing a baby's genitals. This fails to consider the extremely diverse combinations of reproductive organs, chromosomes, gametes, hormones, secondary sex characteristics, and genital configurations that exist across human beings. People are then gendered and socialized in accordance with their sex assigned at birth, effectively prescribing how people should look and behave based solely on the characteristics of their sexual organs. These cis-normative understandings are based in colonial, Eurocentric ideas that demand certain appearances and behaviours and create hierarchies around identity. Value is in turn assigned to gender by patriarchal power relations to privilege certain expressions of male identity. Feminine identities, and the associated social roles, are largely devalued both economically and socially. People whose gender identity and expression do not fit within the binary and transgender individuals whose gender identity does not align with physical sex assigned at birth are further devalued within patriarchal hierarchies. These hierarchies are constituted and regulated through specific regimes of colonial power that privilege certain identities and experiences, while oppressing and negating others (Carastathis et al. 2018; E. Lee 2018). As Martin-Hill (2003) argues, colonial beliefs around gender and power erase the diverse roles held by women and gender non-conforming community members in different societies, devaluing their existence or eliminating them altogether (see Coburn, chapter 1).

Therefore, it has been argued that upholding the binary gender categories maintains and reproduces colonial state logic (Carastathis et al. 2018).

Binary understandings of gender identity and gendered roles have been complicated and challenged, with gender being conceptualized as fluid and evolving (Ristock et al. 2019), and as a "performance" (Butler 1999). Analyzing and deconstructing hierarchical gender constructs and their impacts allow for conceptualizations of and contestations against patriarchal inequalities and oppressions. This understanding of gender has significant implications in the field of forced migration studies.

SEXUAL ORIENTATION

Interconnected, yet distinct from gender, are social constructs related to sexuality. Much like gender, these constructs are historically – and contextually – specific and produce identity categories to define what sexual and romantic desires, behaviours, and actions are considered "acceptable." Heteronormativity is the hegemonic belief that heterosexuality is the "norm" by valorizing reproductive sexuality between cis-gender women and men, and marginalizing other forms of sexuality as "deviant" (Luibhéid 2008). It also imposes a binary logic between heterosexuality and homosexuality, disavowing and devaluing the diverse spectrum of sexualities, sexual desires, and behaviours.

Additionally, heteronormativity produces a hierarchy based on particular heterosexual expectations, relationships, and life goals, which can be reproduced at both ends of the constructed binary. As Manalansan argues, "sexuality is disciplined by social institutions and practices that normalize and naturalize heterosexuality and [certain] homosexual practices including marriage, family, and biological reproduction by marginalizing persons, institutions, or practices that deviate from these norms" (2006, 225). Therefore, relationships that are not heterosexual can be understood as socially acceptable in certain contexts, as long as they ascribe to monogamous heterosexual expectations, parameters, and trajectories. This disciplining defines where the "acceptable" boundaries are to exclude those considered too subversive (Rinaldi and Fernando 2019). These constructs are again based in Eurocentric colonial ideals, as colonial powers defined and controlled sexual relations through education, imposed moral norms, health care, and constructed family structures (E. Lee 2018). They are fundamentally rooted in binary gender constructs linked to the prescription of appropriate romantic and/or sexual attraction and desire.

Non-heterosexual sexual identity is often divided into categories, including the commonly used acronym, 2SLGBTQI+ (Two-Spirit, Lesbian, Gay, Bisexual, Transgender, Queer and/or Questioning, Intersex), with the "+" added to recognize and affirm the range of identities or experiences with which people may identify. Moreover, sexual identity can be understood as fluid over lifespans, as well as context specific, which can have particularly important implications within forced migration contexts.

12.1 Amina grew up in Afghanistan. Her gender expression never conformed to her society's expectation, as she always preferred to dress in boys' clothes and play with male friends. Amina was harassed for her clothing choices and expelled from school for not adhering to the dress code. Amina's parents were also targeted as a result. Due to the exclusions she faced, Amina struggled with her mental health and became suicidal as a teenager, but her parents continued to show her unconditional love and support, which helped her get through. As Amina got older, she was able to go to university and connect with 2SLGBTQI+ groups on campus. Amina identified as a lesbian and was able to build a strong network and become a leader within the 2SLGBTQI+ community at her university. When the Taliban took power, Amina was persecuted due to her gender expression, her sexuality, and her leadership within the university community. She was forced to leave Afghanistan and apply for refugee protection in the UK (Rainbow Railroad 2021).

INTERSECTIONALITY

Experiences of gender and sexuality are inherently shaped by their intersection with other social identities, including but not limited to race (see Mahrouse and El Omari, chapter 15), class (see Hari and Quintero, chapter 16), ability (see McNally, chapter 14), religion (see Cameron, chapter 26), and age (see Clark-Kazak, chapter 13). Kimberlé Crenshaw (1989) coined the term "intersectionality," an approach that recognizes the importance of conceptualizing how different identities intersect to create and/or impact people's experiences. Every person experiences a multiplicity of identities, which interact with one another; an intersectional framework is critical to a nuanced analysis, and necessarily problematizes dichotomies, divisions, and compartmentalizations.

An intersectional analysis of the experiences of forced migrants provides a framework for understanding the ways different identities shift, coalesce, or compete at different moments. Different aspects of people's identities may take prominence during certain events or interactions, but it is the interconnectedness of all their identities that shape their overall experiences and social positionings. For example, intersecting identities are interpreted and understood by immigration and border officials in different ways, and particular understandings of gender, sexuality, racialization, class, and ability are used to target certain people for inclusion and others for exclusion. Luibhéid (2002) argues that gender and sexuality become points of exclusion as they intersect with racialization, ethnicity, and class. She highlights how certain cis-gender women have historically been targeted for exclusion, for example: (1) Chinese women who were suspected of being sex workers simply by virtue of race and gender stereotypes; (2) Japanese "picture brides" whose heteronormative sexuality was considered threatening; (3) lesbians, whose sexuality, if determined, could cause exclusion and deportation; and (4) female refugee claimants, whose encounters with border officials often hinged on recounting experiences of heterosexual violence. Dua (2007) further explores these intersectionalities, highlighting debates that occurred in Canada in the late nineteenth century regarding the exclusion of Asian women. The dominant arguments centred on ensuring that Asian male migrants, needed for their labour, would only remain temporary residents if their families were not permitted to migrate with them. However, other arguments focused on Asian women's inclusion in order to avoid interracial heterosexual relationships between Asian men and White women. All these examples demonstrate government and immigration officials' history of relying on racist ideologies intersecting with gender identity and sexuality constructs in making policy and border enforcement decisions.

THE GENDERED UNDERSTANDING OF FORCED MIGRATION: EVOLUTION OF THE GENDERED REFUGEE

Migration research has historically failed to adequately consider the intersecting identities of people in contexts of migration. The "typical migrant" was implicitly assumed to be a cis-gender heterosexual male, and to either be a rationale actor migrating for economic reasons or a political dissident seeking asylum. Multidisciplinary critical scholars have long advocated for intersectional approaches to conceptualize migration experiences. It is important to note that the dichotomy between voluntary and forced migration, upheld in mainstream discourse around migration, has also been consistently critiqued (see also Goheen Glanville and Arbel, chapter 4).

In the context of forced migration studies in particular, the construct of "the refugee" has changed significantly due to major geopolitical events. The end of the Cold War in the early 1990s shifted the ideas of refugees from active political dissidents (primarily cis-gender males) to passive and vulnerable victims (based on constructs related to gender, ethnicity, religion, etc.). The events of 11 September 2001 further concretized this shift, as political actors resisting their governments were frequently categorized as potential terrorists (Yuval-Davis 2011). As "refugeeness" became increasingly depoliticized, it also became feminized. This feminization of the "appropriate refugee victim" was based in notions of vulnerability, weakness, and passivity. It was also inherently connected to heteronormative motherhood, as "refugee" became a "women-and-children" construct (Bhabha 2004; Judge 2010). As such, cis-gender men often found themselves unable to conform to the ideas of who was deemed an appropriate victim and thereby worthy of protection (Judge 2010). These changes were also necessarily intersectional, as the shifting conceptualizations of the gendered refugee were also connected to sexuality, race, and religion. States therefore largely remained hostile to the arrival of refugees and the adjudication of their claims, as Espiritu et.al. argue: "states invariably interpret international refugee laws according to their perceived national security, economic, and cultural interests, denying many displaced people inclusion ..." (2022, 55).

While cis-gender women may have been perceived as the more "deserving" victims, their need for protection was expected to correspond with particular racialized tropes that constructed their societies and cultures as inherently violent. Reifying these tropes induced the need for protection from states in the Global North, as "bad patriarchies" were cast as necessarily happening in the Global South and onto racialized female bodies (Mulinari 2007; Hajdukowski-Ahmed 2008). This not only criminalized racialized men but also invisibilized the global patriarchal power structures that make women susceptible to violence everywhere. These constructs were further nuanced by incorporating particular sexual and religious identities. In recent years 2SLGBTQI+ refugees have also been prioritized by certain states, including Canada, which then constructs other societies as inherently homophobic and violent and valorizes the receiving state as a welcoming safe haven.

GENDER, REFUGEE DETERMINATION, AND SETTLEMENT IN CANADA

In 1993 Canada became the first country to implement guidelines at the IRB for the adjudication of refugee claims based on gender-related persecution. These guidelines focused on persecution experienced by cis-gender women, with broader understandings of gender and gender expression being implemented only in the SOGIESC guidelines in 2017. While the 1951 Refugee Convention did not include gendered persecution as a legitimate ground for refugee protection, the pervasiveness of gender-based violence and lack of state protection in different contexts was finally recognized as a significant cause of forced migration (and often a reality while in transit or during settlement). The "Chairperson's Guideline 4: Women Refugee Claimants Fearing Gender-Related Persecution," importantly encouraged board members to consider the connections between gender, the fear of persecution, and the evidence that should be examined (IRB 2008). The guidelines articulate recognition of the patriarchal power relations that create vulnerabilities and incite violence against women in different contexts, including persecution related to kinship, gender discrimination, and violence for which the state is unable or unwilling to provide protection or discrimination or violence based on perceived transgression of the expected ways female gender should be expressed or enacted (Boyd 2006).

However, the guidelines remain unevenly applied, because board members' subjective biases based on the intersections of gender with race, class, sexuality, age, and ability may affect their understanding of gender-related persecution (Aberman 2014; Tastsoglou and Nourpanah 2019). Women who do not share the experiences of expected persecution based on the region, ethnicity, or religion they come from may be more likely to be refused. As such, experiences of trauma are linked to particular locations and cultures, while disavowing violence in other locations. The lack of trauma-informed approaches also demands linear and chronological accounts of gender-based violence, leading to credibility concerns when experiences are not recounted as expected. Moreover, women who present themselves as, or are perceived to be, "strong" may have their claims refused because they are expected to be able to protect themselves or seek local protection (Murdocca and Razack 2008). These constructs of strength are intersectional, as they are frequently based in colonial constructions of race, class, and ability. Consequently, these expectations, may lead refugee women to apply the victim constructs to themselves as a strategy to have their claim recognizable and acceptable to decision-makers (Hajdukowski-Ahmed 2008).

The Canadian government has also deemed certain experiences of gender-based violence as undeserving of protection. These political biases influence board members' decision-making processes, despite their supposed arm's length structure. For example, when the number of refugee claimants arriving in Canada from Mexico in the mid-2000s increased substantially, policy-makers attempted to find ways to exclude them. One approach was to designate Mexico a "safe country," thereby discrediting refugee claims from Mexican nationals, including those based on intimate partner violence. As such, despite the gender guidelines, the specific risks Mexican women faced were largely overlooked, with "little attention [paid] to the context of impunity for violent crimes against women in Mexico" (Bhuyan, Vargas, and Píntín-Perez 2016).

Although the guidelines were implemented nearly two decades ago, gender-based violence can still be misinterpreted or overlooked within the discretionary decision-making at the IRB. One particularly egregious case is outlined in box 12.2.

12.2 In April 2019, a female refugee claimant shared her experiences of abuse during her refugee hearing. She explained to the board member that for many years she had endured physical and sexual violence inflicted by her husband. She was unable to escape him, despite leaving the relationship, and could not access state protection.

However, instead of considering the board's gender guidelines, the adjudicator chose not to believe her, and inappropriately challenged her claim by asking, "Why wouldn't he just kill you then? Why spend all these years, just, like, harassing you?"

The blatant disregard for her experience and her claim directly contradicted considerations outlined in the guidelines. While this egregious case was brought to light by the media, and the adjucator faced a review of his decision, this example demonstrates that the guidelines do not resolve all misogynistic misunderstandings of gender-based violence (Hill and Mauracher 2019).

When the 2010 Balanced Refugee Reform Act, and the subsequent 2012 Protecting Canada's Immigration System Act, were passed by the Conservative federal government, they drastically redesigned the refugee determination process, as well as other immigration pathways in Canada. These significant changes had multi-layered impacts based on an applicant's gender and sexual identities, some of which are still part of immigration law and are discussed later. This overhaul of the refugee and immigration system was conducted against a backdrop which also created a binary between "good refugees" in refugee camps waiting to be sponsored by the Canadian government, and "bogus refugees" who spontaneously and autonomously arrive in Canada seeking protection (Hyndman and Giles 2011; Labman 2020; Molnar Diop 2014). This division is inherently understood in gendered ways, as Hyndman and Giles argue, since "those who stay still are viewed as genuine, immobile, depoliticized, feminized, while those on the move are potential liabilities at best, and security threats at worst" (2011, 363). At the same time as this divisive discourse was circulating, the Conservative government maintained low resettlement targets for all sponsored refugees but used their plight to delegitimize the refugee claims of others. When these small numbers were critiqued in light of the Syrian "refugee crisis," the government agreed to increase their numbers slightly but stated that they would prioritize only Christian refugees and other religious minorities.

The so-called refugee crisis ultimately became an election issue in 2016, with the Liberal campaign committing to resettling twenty-five thousand refugees, more than doubling the Conservative targets. When Justin Trudeau's Liberals won the election, the plan for Syrian refugee resettlement was devised to only include (1) complete families, (2) single women considered at risk, and (3) members of 2SLGBTQI+ communities. Single men would only be considered if their sexual orientation or gender identity or expression put them at risk, or if they were accompanying their parents. This exclusion of single heterosexual cis-gender men reified the gendered understandings of appropriate victims, while relying on the intersections of gender, race, and religion to mark all single heterosexual Syrian men as potentially dangerous and/or terrorists.

Although receiving protected person/Convention refugee status (see Atak, chapter 17) or being resettled through the government or private sponsorship programs is a crucial step to seeking stability and permanence in Canada, the settlement and integration experiences that follow are frequently accented by gendered realities. At that stage, some commonalities have been noted among cis-gender immigrant and refugee women, whether they arrive in Canada with permanent resident status or acquire it after arrival. It has been documented that gendered expectations, and women's relationships to those expectations, frequently change during migration and resettlement. Gender constructs may be challenged after arriving in Canada, which can lead to individual and family/community conflicts as roles, responsibilities, and behaviours shift and change. Moreover, Bhuyan and Schmidt have found that newcomer women (including immigrant, refugee and precarious status women) "are more vulnerable to systemic challenges including poverty, social isolation, and poor health" (2019, vi). This is a result of challenges in accessing health care, including maternal care and mental health support, due to various systemic barriers, lack of familiarity with the health-care system, and language barriers. Bhuyan and Schmidt (2019) also found that newcomer women struggled to find work commensurate with their experience and often ended up in low-paid, exploitative jobs. Challenges in accessing reliable and affordable childcare augment these barriers. Furthermore, throughout these experiences, gender intersects with race, class, ability, and religion as women experience racism and discrimination interwoven within all these systems. Settlement organizations have increased their programming and support for newcomer women over the last several years to begin to address some of these inequities; yet the patriarchal, racist, classist, and ablest structures that persist continue to maintain oppressive inequities.

GETTING TO THE SOGIESC GUIDELINES

While the recognition of refugee claims based on sexual orientation started in Canada in the early 1990s, these claims were often heavily scrutinized by IRB board members. In order to be recognized as a person needing protection, claimants needed to prove belonging to a social group (2SLGBTQI+) and that their identity put them at risk due to systemic and institutionalized homophobia and/or transphobia in their country of origin. Early claims frequently faced difficulty proving persecution because individual evidence and reports of persecution were often unavailable. While board members may have believed that claimants would be discriminated against due to their sexual orientation or gender expression, they often challenged whether that discrimination could amount to persecution. Discrimination was recognizable since transgressing socially constructed patriarchal gender norms regarding appropriate behaviour, appearance, and sexuality was unacceptable in many contexts; however, persecution was held to a higher standard (LaViolette 2014).

As reports of state criminalization of 2SLGBTQI+ communities and societal violence became increasingly available, documenting proof of persecution continued to be a challenge for many 2SLGBTQI+ claimants. Rainbow Railroad (2021) reported that family-based rejection and violence were the foremost safety concerns for many 2SLGBTQI+ forced migrants – something no less dangerous and yet significantly more difficult to prove. Currently, at least sixty-nine countries have laws that criminalize same-sex sexual relations, and thirty-seven countries have laws criminalizing transgender identity and gender expression that subverts binary socially constructed expectations (Rainbow Railroad 2021).

Proof of persecution was not the only barrier facing 2SLGBTQI+ claimants. They also had to find ways to prove their sexual orientation and gender identities to IRB members. Murray (2014) argues that the construct of the "real" 2SLGBTQI+ refugee, which would be recognizable to adjudicators, relied on a particular historical, gendered, raced, classed, and ablest idea of how sexuality was experienced and expressed. For example, claimants whose gender presentation conformed too closely with binary and patriarchal societal expectations had their sexual orientation questioned. Board members were less likely to believe women who presented as too feminine or men who were viewed as conventionally masculine as 2SLGBTQI+ members and therefore had their experiences challenged more often (Rinaldi and Fernando 2019). Board members often had difficulty distinguishing between gender identity and expression and sexual orientation and were deeply influenced by Eurocentric conceptualizations of gender and sexuality. This, in turn, further marginalized transgender claimants, whose claims were often categorized as sexual orientation cases, thereby eclipsing significant aspects of the persecution they faced (LaViolette 2014).

In order to "prove" their identities, forced migrants were expected to participate in 2SLGBTQI+ communities in Canada (e.g., attending pride events or frequenting queer bars and other social spaces). These select activities upheld specific classist, racialized, and ablest expectations of 2SLGBTQI+ experience, which may not be comfortable for racialized claimants, who may experience racism in particular spaces, and may be inaccessible to poor claimants or those living with disabilities (Murray 2014; Rehaag 2008). Forced migrants were also often asked offensive and inappropriate questions about their relationships and sexual encounters. Many described the complexity associated with the transition from having to hide sexual orientation and gender identity for safety reasons back home, and then having to prove identities to authority figures by being as "out" as possible. Changes to immigration and refugee policy in 2012 exacerbated these challenges, as claimants had less time to prepare themselves to discuss their claims and also had less time to join community and show 2SLGBTQI+ connections in Canada (Rinaldi and Fernando 2019).

Rehaag (2008) further demonstrated that claims based on bisexuality were less successful than other sexual orientation-based claims due to rigid binary ideas about sexuality, which overlooked understandings of sexual and gender identity as fluid, expansive, and evolving over a person's lifetime. Bisexuality was often disbelieved or challenged by decision-makers, leading to problematic determinations that bisexual people would not experience persecution if they prioritized their heterosexual-presenting attractions and hid other aspects of their sexuality. This determination was not limited to bisexual claimants, as others seeking protection based on sexual or gender identity or expression were also refused, based on the presumption that they could be safe in their country of origin if they hid their identity and lived discreetly. Board members also invoked internal flight alternatives (IFAs), based on the belief that forced migrants may experience persecution in parts of their country of origin, but they could move to other areas, where different laws may apply, or to larger cities, where they may be perceived as safer than in rural areas (LaViolette 2014).

Although these limitations and challenges persisted in refugee determination, the prioritizing of certain 2SLGBTQI+ constructs allowed the Canadian state to present itself as a welcoming safe haven for 2SLGBTQI+ refugees, while excluding anyone who did not fit, anyone whose identities and identity expression were disavowed. This colonial approach also allowed the Canadian state, and by extension its citizens, to "save" 2SLGBTQI+ refugees from their violent, regressive, homophobic societies (Kinsman 2018; E. Lee 2018; Murray 2020), much like the expectations in the gender guidelines.

The UNHCR released guidelines on Sexual Orientation, Gender Identity and Expression (SOGIE) in 2012 (LaViolette 2014). Lagging behind the UNHCR, and after considerable advocacy from 2SLGBTQI+ activists, lawyers, academics, and forced migrants, the IRB implemented guidelines on claims related to Sexual Orientation, Gender Identity and Expression, and Sex Characteristics (SOGIESC) in 2017, revising the guidelines in 2021 (IRB 2021b). The guidelines provide detailed explanations for terminology related to SOGIESC realities and experiences, recognizing that identities may be fluid, intersectional, and that terminology cannot be exhaustive. The guidelines also provide approaches for board members to follow in adjudicating SOGIESC claims, including avoiding stereotyping, using appropriate language, safeguarding sensitive information, allowing for alternative ways of assessing credibility, and proceeding in a sensitive and non-confrontational manner. The guidelines also importantly outline reasons why there may be inconsistencies, omissions, and lack of evidence in SOGIESC cases. Board members are asked to proceed with understandings of how intersecting identities and interrelated forms of persecution may compound impacts on forced migrants and the reasons they may be reluctant to discuss their experiences. They are also directed to avoid determining that SOGIESC claimants would not face persecution if they hid parts of their identities. The guidelines must factor into decision-making regarding SOGIESC.

The SOGIESC guidelines are an important amendment to the Canadian refugee determination system and offer a significant improvement upon previous practice; yet important gaps and limitations remain (Rinaldi and Fernando 2019). As Mulé (2020) argues, the need to prove SOGIESC was maintained when developing the guidelines, which may uphold Eurocentric constructs of SOGIESC and may continue to demand particular forms of evidence. Moreover, these improvements to the refugee determination process obfuscate the continued policies that prevent 2SLGBTQI+ forced migrants from reaching Canada to seek refugee protection, including visa obligations and border restrictions (E. Lee 2018; see also Young, chapter 3).

Many of the same limitations and stereotypes have been encountered when 2SLGBTQI+ refugees are sponsored to come to Canada. A program for groups to privately sponsor 2SLGBTQI+ refugees was introduced in 2011 by the Conservative government, which allowed government officials to claim they were prioritizing these claims, while keeping actual resettlement numbers very low (Kinsman 2018). Organizations and groups working with and advocating for 2SLGBTQI+ forced migrants have continuously worked to increase the numbers sponsored and to raise awareness of the persecution and violence experienced based on SOGIESC.

Additionally, after 2SLGBTQI+ people arrive in Canada through sponsorship or as refugee claimants, the settlement and integration process may still be underpinned with homophobic and transphobic exclusion. As Alessi (2016) points out, while others may be able to seek support and information from their diasporic communities, this may not be possible for 2SLGBTQI+ forced migrants. Settlement organizations often do not have the awareness or understanding to offer safe spaces and specific services for 2SLGBTQI+ newcomers (OCASI 2009). Through research done by the Ontario Council of Agencies Serving Immigrants (OCASI), 2SLGBTQI+ newcomers shared feelings of isolation, sentiments of both shame and pride for their 2SLGBTQI+ identities, the importance of peer support, the complexities of being "out," experiences of racism and violence, the challenges of finding good legal support, issues with identification documents when transitioning, language barriers, and the need for safe spaces (OCASI 2009). Nonetheless, several settlement agencies, community organizations, and informal groups have offered support in meeting the multifaceted needs of 2SLGBTQI+ newcomers in safe and inclusive ways. Alessi (2016) also notes that inclusive religious institutions played a significant role in overcoming the challenges of settlement for 2SLGBTQI+ newcomers.

12.3 Arsham Parsi is a gay man from Iran, where being gay can be punishable by death. When his work within the LGBTQI+ community was discovered by the authorities, he was forced to flee to Turkey and was eventually resettled in Canada. He recounts his experience:

> LGBTQ refugees face serious obstacles such as limited access to employment, housing, and particularly mental health services when they arrive in Canada. Many of us have experienced trauma during our years of waiting and are in need of counselling. But there's a long wait list for psychotherapists and Farsi interpreters. Finding a real friend to talk to is so hard that many LGBTQ refugee newcomers become suicidal.
>
> Even living in a safe country like Canada, most LGBTQ refugees are not fully "out and proud." Many of us continue to be in the closet when we interact with the Iranian community here because we cannot afford to lose the emotional support of our families in Iran if they were to find out about our sexual orientation. (Parsi n.d.)

OTHER HUMANITARIAN PROCESSES

As mentioned, many of the changes to immigration policy implemented during the Conservative period (2006–15) still underpin current immigration processes. For example, the 2012 reform made it impossible for forced migrants to make refugee claims and Humanitarian and Compassionate Grounds (H&C) applications at the same time; if a refugee claim was made and refused, forced migrants would then have to wait twelve months from the last negative decision to make an H&C application (with exemptions for minors, families with minor children, and people with serious health conditions). Forced migrants were and are still also barred from making a pre-removal risk assessment (PRRA) application for one year after a refugee claim is refused. These imposed timelines, which are still maintained, have significant impacts, as forced migrants often cannot have compelling factors considered outside their refugee claims. For forced migrants applying on SOGIESC grounds, the stereotypes and constructs outlined may prevent a thorough assessment of their risk of persecution, which could have been remedied by a PRRA, yet the one-year bar can mean that forced migrants may face deportation before they are eligible. Moreover, country conditions that had changed since the refugee claim was denied, or new threats that had been made in their country of origin cannot be assessed. In cases of heterosexual couples, the man is often the principal applicant (PA), which means that the woman's experience may not be fully considered (CCR 2016b). Furthermore, women who may be experiencing intimate partner violence during the time of the refugee claim may not be able to fully disclose the risk they face. Access to the PRRA provided a new space for violence and risk to be revealed (CCR 2016b).

H&C applications also provide new platforms where violence, discrimination, and exclusion (though not risk) can be assessed. An H&C application considers additional factors for granting status in Canada, with supposedly fewer rigid restrictions. Community and family connections, establishment and integration, best interest of children, and experiences of discrimination and violence can be considered in these discretionary applications. Presenting this constellation of factors can offer opportunities to express diverse experiences of forced migration. Restricting these applications particularly impact 2SLGBTQI+ and cis-gender female forced migrants.

CONCLUSION

This chapter explores forced migration and settlement in Canada from an intersectional framework that challenges and deconstructs gender and sexual orientation binaries. While the Canadian state has often been praised for welcoming forced migrants, specifically "vulnerable" women and 2SLGBTQI+ refugees, colonial Eurocentric constructs around gender identity and sexuality, as well as suspicion and hostility in the adjudication process, continue to exclude and marginalize many. In order to address these gaps, Canadian adjudicators and decision-makers should further their training to nuance and complicate their understandings of gender identity and sexual orientation to avoid decisions made based on Eurocentric tropes, stereotypes, and misunderstandings. Moreover, research on forced migration should further incorporate intersectional and non-binary frameworks to better capture the tensions and complexities within diverse experiences of forced migration.

FURTHER READING AND RESOURCES

Carastathis, Anna, Natalie Kouri-Towe, Gada Mahrouse, Leila Whitley, Johanna Reynolds, and Dianna Shandy, eds. 2018. "Special Issue: Intersectional Feminist Interventions in the 'Refugee Crisis.'" *Refuge: Canada's Journal on Refugees* 34 (1). https://refuge.journals.yorku.ca/index.php/refuge/issue/view/2318.

Envisioning Global LGBT Human Rights. n.d. "Introduction to the Website." http://envisioninglgbt.blogspot.com.

Mattoo, Deepa. 2017. "Race, Gendered Violence, and the Rights of Women with Precarious Immigration Status." Community Leadership in Justice Fellowship of Law Foundation of Ontario, November 2017. https://schliferclinic.com/wp-content/uploads/2018/03/Race-Gendered-Violence-and-the-Rights-of-Women-with-Precarious-Immgration-Status.pdf.

Ontario Council of Agencies Serving Immigrants (OCASI). n.d. "Positive Spaces Initiative (PSI)." https://ocasi.org/positive-spaces-initiative-psi.

13

Forced Migration across the Life Course: Social Age, Chronological Age, and Family Status

Christina R. Clark-Kazak

KEY TAKEAWAYS

- While migration law and policy in Canada are primarily focused on chronological age, people's experiences of forced migration are also shaped by social age and family status.
- Aging is a biological process of human development, which is also socially constructed.
- Social age refers to socially constructed meanings of different age categories, as well as intra- and intergenerational relationships.
- Age-sensitive approaches to forced migration acknowledge how migration experiences differ based on social age and family status, which intersect with gender, (dis)ability, class, religion, education, and other factors.

KEY TERMS

- Age
  - » Chronological age
  - » Social age
  - » Age discrimination
- Bureaucratic birthdates
- Externalization
- Separated children
- Stateless

INTRODUCTION

How do chronological age, social age, and family status intersect with other social positions to affect people's experiences of forced migration in and to Canada? This chapter conceptualizes aging as both a biological and socially constructed process and then analyzes age- and family-related considerations of forced migration experiences. In Canada, there are specific protections and programs for refugee children under the age of eighteen. For example, Canada has guidelines and programming for separated children and unaccompanied minors. In contrast, very little information and programming is available for older people who are displaced. Experiences of forced migration also depend on family status and roles. While Canadian law and policy conceptualize family narrowly, people are part of wider, in some cases transnational, family and kin networks. These family relationships determine access to Canadian immigration processes and services, as well as the caregiving and reproductive labour that impact people's migration, settlement, and integration experiences.

WHAT IS AGE? CONCEPTUAL, DEFINITIONAL, AND POLICY DEBATES

13.1 The *Globe and Mail* reported:

> In 2000, Bara-a Mubarak Salim, then just four years old, travelled with her Darfuri family from Sudan, where life was difficult and dangerous, to Egypt, where it wasn't much better. Her family did not have access to their birth certificates, so the UNHCR registered them all – with the exception of her father – with 1 January birthdates. The error, compounded by incorrect birth years, followed them to Canada after they arrived in Vancouver as refugees in 2004.
>
> They were eventually reunited with their Sudanese birth certificates, but countless attempts to work with settlement agencies and government caseworkers to get their real identities recognized on their new documents hit roadblock after roadblock.
>
> "Sometimes even people when they see my ID they're, like, 'What?!' I have to explain it to everybody all the time – even at school, even to my teachers," she said. "I couldn't go with something that wasn't right."
>
> Her year of birth is also off by two years on her ID, so Ms. Salim had to bring her birth certificate to school so she would be allowed to graduate. (Bascaramurty 2016)

Aging is a biological process of human development that impacts all aspects of our life, including in contexts of forced migration. Every human being experiences physical, cognitive, social, and emotional development over their life course. However, this aging process is also socially constructed. This means that experiences of aging depend on the context in which one lives, the social norms and structures in that context, and other personal characteristics, such as gender, sexual orientation, (dis)ability, religion, class, race, and ethnicity. Social age (Clark-Kazak 2009b) is a concept that helps consider how different societies make meaning of the aging process and different age categories, such as childhood or old age. It also takes into account power relations within and between generations, especially as they intersect with other social hierarchies and norms.

In forced migration law and policy in Canada, chronological age is the most widely used measurement of aging. It is often assumed to be a "neutral" or objective way to determine biological development and age categories, such as who is a child. In Canadian immigration law, a child is generally considered to be under the age of eighteen, with some variations. However, chronological age is insufficient as a measurement of age for several reasons. First, as illustrated in box 13.1, newcomers to Canada may not necessarily know their chronological age or may not have documents to prove it (Silverman 2016). Indeed, there is a widespread problem of "bureaucratic birthdates" (Seibel 2016): arbitrary dates, usually 1 January and an estimated year that UNHCR assigns based on people's memories of historic or natural events, like an earthquake, war, or election. In some cases, these estimates can be off by several years, causing problems for access to services based on chronological age, such as education or old age pensions (Nibbs 2014).

Second, chronological age is ethnocentric, centring White settler Canadian preoccupations with chronometric time. However, many other cultures use different markers of aging, including rites of passage, social relationships like marriage or parenthood, or physical changes like puberty. For example, some Indigenous Peoples in Canada perform rites of passage that coincide with puberty to initiate young people into adulthood (Wabie 2019; Mellor 2020). As Markstrom (2008, 1) argues: "Coming-of-age practices are embedded in broader belief systems of cosmological constructions, which include origin stories, explanations for the cyclical nature of creation and patterns of life, and the complex relationships between humans and the spiritual realm." Similarly, newcomers may come from other social, cultural, and religious contexts that use initiation ceremonies or other social markers to signify the end of childhood.

Third, chronological age categories are arbitrary. In Canada, when a young person is permitted to drive, work, marry, and engage in consensual sex varies across provinces and territories. Even within the same law or policy, there can be differences in chronological age. For example, in Canada's Immigration and Refugee Protection Act (IRPA, 2001), there is no explicit definition of "the child," but different chronological ages are specified in relation to particular activities or eligibility. In the case of minor applicants, the age of fourteen is given as a cut-off for signatory powers. For permanent residency, applicants aged fourteen years or older but less than eighteen must co-sign their application along with one of their parents or a person legally responsible for them, whereas those under the age of fourteen have the form signed on their behalf by a parent or adult responsible for them. Similarly, people aged fourteen years or older may sign their own permanent residency card, while those under fourteen must have it signed by one of their parents or a person legally responsible for them. In contrast, for detention, a minor child is defined more broadly as anyone under the age of eighteen (see below and Silverman, chapter 21).

Fourth, while intended to be an objective measurement of physical, cognitive and emotional development, strict chronological age categories overlook large variations in individual development due to genetics and environmental factors, including displacement. Indeed, these variations complicate biomedical chronological age assessments. For example, forensic dental investigations show a standard deviation of +/– three years (Nuzzolese and Di Vella 2008), which is significant when considering the eighteen-year cut-off point for determining who is a child.

Finally, chronological age is individualistic, but people grow up in relationships, families, and communities. Experiences of childhood, for example, will be affected not only by chronological age but also gender, birth order, family context, and social norms about children's labour and place in the world. These family contexts are explored further below.

In this chapter, I therefore take a more holistic approach to thinking about how age impacts on differential migration experiences. A social age approach does not deny the reality that much of Canada's law and policy, as well as social services, are framed in terms of chronological age. Moreover, chronological age-disaggregated statistics do give an important overall demographic portrait of a context. However, in this chapter, I will also consider social constructions of aging and family relationships, as well as the intersectionality of age with other power relations. Similarly, at an international level, UNHCR (2018c, 5) has a policy on age, gender, and diversity to take into account "the impact of intersecting personal characteristics on people's experiences of forced displacement." While some analyses show that this policy does not go far enough in implementing real change (Clark-Kazak 2009a), it is an important framework to highlight age in relation to other social relationships.

SEPARATED AND UNACCOMPANIED CHILDREN: HISTORICAL AND CONTEMPORARY CONTEXTS

13.2 CBC Report on Matthew House for Unaccompanied Minors
CBC News. 2019. "Shelter Aims to help Growing Number of Refugees Arriving as Unaccompanied Minors." CBC videos, 4:10. https://www.cbc.ca/player/play/1423113795652.

As Coburn in chapter 1 and Young in chapter 3 discuss, the creation of Canada as a settler state was part of a colonial project that systematically displaced Indigenous Peoples from their lands, language, culture, communities, and social relationships. This "logic of elimination" (Wolfe 2006) included specific actions against children and young people, including child abduction, forcible religious conversion, and "resocialization" through a "network of government-funded and church-run residential schools that separated some one hundred fifty thousand Indigenous children from their families and communities between the late nineteenth and late twentieth centuries" (Alexander 2016, 397). Forced separation continues today, indicated by the disproportionate number of Indigenous babies, children, and young people in foster families and institutional care (Mellor 2020).

The involuntary displacement of immigrant children to Canada was also integral to the colonial project. One of the most infamous examples involved over one hundred thousand "British Home Children," who were poor and/or orphaned children sent from the UK to work as labourers in Canada between 1869 and the late 1930s. Many were placed with families in rural Canada and never saw their own families or friends again.

Other children have come to Canada alone as part of global refugee movements. Under international policy and practice, there is a distinction between separated children and unaccompanied minors. Separated children migrate without their parents, a guardian, or caregiver but are accompanied by an adult who is responsible – formally or informally – for their care. In contrast, unaccompanied minor is a more specialized category of children under the age of eighteen who are "separated from both parents and other relatives and are not being cared for by an adult who, by law or custom, is responsible for doing so" (ICRC 2004, n.p.). Some researchers prefer the term "independent child migration" to reinforce the agency of children and young people migrating alone and also to convey the idea that, in some cases, family separation is part of a deliberate individual or collective strategy to escape intergenerational violence, or to manage risks across household and family members (Orgocka and Clark-Kazak 2012).

Because of Canada's relative geographic isolation and our externalization policies (see also Young, chapter 3; Atak, chapter 17), fewer separated and unaccompanied children arrive in Canada than in other displacement contexts. However, an exception to the Safe Third Country Agreement (STCA) exists for unaccompanied minors with no parent or legal guardian in either Canada or the US. Prior to the COVID-19 pandemic, as many as three thousand unaccompanied children arrived in Canada each year (Sadoway 2018, 299). Separated children are normally considered dependents under the accompanying adult's refugee claim. Some advocates believe this disadvantages these separated children because the individual merits of their respective cases are not considered and because they do not have access to child-specific services (Sadoway 2018). Unaccompanied minors are appointed a designated representative in their refugee hearings (IRB n.d.). However, research indicates varying levels of quality representation and suspicion (Denov and Bryan 2014; Bryan and Denov 2011), as well as differential access to social services depending on province (CCR 2000; Sadoway 2018).

CHILD PROTECTION RIGHTS UNDER INTERNATIONAL AND CANADIAN LAW

13.3 A report on children in immigration detention in Canada profiles a four-month-old whose mother was detained at the Toronto detention facility. The mother was detained because CBSA suspected that she was a flight risk, and the baby accompanied her as a "guest" of the facility.

According to the mother, she constantly felt pressured by CBSA to part with her infant son. "But I'm his mom, I'm his caregiver, he's breastfeeding, how can he leave?" she said. After three months in detention, the mother was diagnosed with Major Depressive Episode and Complex Post-Traumatic Stress Disorder. "I think they robbed a lot from me and my baby" (University of Toronto 2017).

All children and young people under the age of eighteen – whether they migrate alone or with their parents or guardians – have specific rights and protections under international and Canadian law. The Convention on the Rights of the Child (CRC) is the most widely ratified human rights treaty in the world and provides specific protections for children generally, as well as for refugee children specifically. Under article 22 of the CRC, refugee children are entitled to the same rights as nationals, including the right to education, health, birth registration, and nationality. For all children, the CRC promotes the best interests of the child principle (article 3), which means that decisions should always be taken with a view to what is best for the child(ren) involved. Article 12 also requires adults to seek children's participation in decisions that affect them.

However, just because all children in Canada, including non-citizens in situations of forced migration, have rights does not mean that these rights are always respected. For example, the UN Committee on the Rights of the Child has repeatedly raised concerns about the presence of children in immigration detention (see box 13.3; Silverman, chapter 21). Under IRPA and international law, detention of children should only be used as a last resort, once alternatives are exhausted and taking into account the best interests principle. Children should also never be detained in adult correctional facilities. However, children, including Canadian citizens whose parents do not have citizenship, are regularly held in immigration detention (Gros and Song 2016). Research shows that detention has disproportionately negative effects on children's physical, emotional, cognitive, and mental health and development (Kronick, Rousseau, and Cleveland 2011; Kronick and Rousseau 2015).

The UN Committee on the Rights of the Child and other child rights advocates have also expressed concern with Canada's citizenship law and policies, which could leave some children stateless (see also Cowper-Smith and Kane, chapter 20). A person is considered stateless when no country recognizes them as a citizen. Under changes to Canada's Citizenship Act, which came into effect in 2009, a Canadian citizen born outside Canada who acquired citizenship through descent cannot pass on citizenship to their children born outside Canada. If the latter cannot acquire citizenship through the other parent or from the country of birth, they will be stateless.

INVISIBILITY OF OLDER REFUGEES IN POLICY AND PROGRAMMING

13.4 Mercedes is an eighty-four year old mother and grandmother from Colombia. She was raised by her paternal grandmother and worked for approximately thirty years as a nurse in hospitals, clinics, and nursing homes in Colombia. Balancing the demands of her career and motherhood became challenging after the birth of her daughter in 1963. In response, she worked night shifts and drew on the support of family and friends to help her raise her daughter. It was only after the birth of her first grandchild that Mercedes decided to retire from her nursing career, which she finally did in 1987. Mercedes came to Canada in 2002 as a refugee. Her son-in-law applied for his family to immigrate due to security and violence that were on the rise in Colombia. Mercedes' family first settled in a small town in Quebec where they received a warm welcome. In an effort to find work, the family later moved to the suburbs of Montreal.

Mercedes describes family unity as being the most important value both for her and within Colombian culture. Today, she lives with her daughter, son-in-law, and grandchildren, where she finds happiness in being with her family. Notably, she feels a deep emotional connection between herself and the female members of her family, finding solidarity and connection in their bond. She used to be active in the local community, but now, with age, Mercedes spends more time at home gardening and watching Catholic mass on Colombian television. Mercedes has a strong sense of spirituality. She also enjoys going for walks outdoors, especially in the summer months, and writes in her notebook daily to study French. (Brotman, Koehn, and Ferrer 2017, 28)

In many cultures, older adults, particularly those who have status as elders, are respected and venerated for their knowledge and experience. For example, Indigenous elders play important roles in health and wellness (Viscogliosi et al. 2020), justice (Shelly Johnson 2014), environmental stewardship (Berkes 2009), livelihood skills (Ohmagari and Berkes 1997), education and socialization (Pace and Grenier 2016; Kinzel 2020), spirituality, and language. In contrast, within much of Canada's forced migration policy and programming, older people are either invisibilized or constructed as burdens. For example, in IRPA, elderly people are only referenced five times – in relation to the Old Age Security Act and senior home care. In some cases, older people are less likely to flee because of physical disabilities (see also McNally, chapter 14), attachment to home or place, or logistical inability to move. Those who do leave may face loss of social status as their knowledge, language (Boutmira 2021), and ways of being may be perceived as less relevant in the new context.

Many receiving states and communities perceive older people as burdens, particularly on health care. Because unremunerated caregiving and reproductive roles are not "counted" in formal economic measures like taxes and GNP, the important work that older people do is often not valued in Canada. Due to shifting power relations in migration contexts, they may also experience loss of social status and "subordinate integration" (Kahil, Iqbal, and Maghbouleh 2022). Research indicates that elders, particularly those who do not learn English or French (Boutmira 2021), experience high levels of social isolation and loneliness in Canada (Koehn, Ferrer, and Brotman 2020; Shanthi Johnson et al. 2019).

FAMILY STATUS AND REUNIFICATION

13.5 "Nowhere in the whole world should parents and children be separated for such a long time. The children I carried are not with me. What I feel inside me every day, the emotional pain, prevents me from being the person I can be. My children are at risk and I live in fear and desperation" (cited in CCR, n.d.).

Family status has an important impact on people's differential immigration experiences. In Canadian law and policy, there is a narrow interpretation of parent-child relationships and conjugality (Gaucher 2018), based on ethnocentric nuclear-family norms. Researchers and advocates have critiqued the discrimination inherent in the biological and legal definitions of "the child" in IRPA (Baldassi 2007); ethical issues related to DNA testing (Joly et al. 2017); and the problematic emphasis on Western "nuclear" families, to the exclusion of more extended understandings of family (Lippert and Pyykkönen 2012; Gaucher 2018).

Indeed, different notions of family exist within Indigenous and immigrant communities. Because of the relational ontology of many Indigenous Peoples, family is not just a biological relationship; kinship is also an important source of knowledge and culture. As a result, many Indigenous groups include extended family and kinship relationships and Indigenous children may have "multiple caregivers, familial and non-familial" from multiple generations across extended family members (Tam, Findlay, and Kohen 2017, 244; see also Downe 2021). Similarly, many newcomers in Canada have different perceptions of kinship and family (Bragg and Wong 2016) and rely on social networks and extended family support (Ansion and Merali 2018).

In this context, Canada's restrictive laws and policies can cause family separation and delays in reunification. For example, IRPA has a lifelong ban on sponsoring any family member who is not included in the initial immigration application. Children who are admitted to Canada as unaccompanied minors cannot sponsor family members until they are eighteen, and then must prove financial capacity to support family members, which is often not possible until they secure full-time employment (Sadoway 2018). Historically (Madokoro 2012) and contemporarily (Clark-Kazak forthcoming), the Canadian government has had different chronological and social age markers to determine who qualifies as a "dependent child" for immigration purposes. Sponsorship of parents and grandparents is extremely difficult, with only a few thousand applications accepted each year (IRCC n.d.a), partially due to under-valuing contributions of older migrants (VanderPlaat, Ramos, and Yoshida 2013) and privileging the nuclear family over extended family networks.

CHANGING INTERGENERATIONAL RELATIONSHIPS DUE TO FORCED MIGRATION

13.6 I was thinking that my mom, my dad, they are not speaking English, right? And I am only the one who is looking after them and my brother was in this condition, right? And it's really, really hard for me and then, I just think about that, I, I didn't, I don't know like what I'm going to do, like, you know. I was already nineteen at that time, and

> then I know that I, I'm not getting chance to go high school and then how I'm gonna get high school and then how does it takes to complete the high school ... and then how I'm going to earn, and what I'm gonna work, you know. Yeah, I don't know like that ... when I came first I was really frustrated like you know, I have to deal with everything right. Yeah and then we don't have any relatives. (Cited in Maine 2015)

Differential experiences of forced migration across the life course also impact changing intergenerational relationships within families. Children and young people who go to school in Canada may learn French or English more quickly than their older relatives. They also are socialized into Canadian systems and ways of doing and knowing. As a result, they often serve as interpreters and translators – not just linguistically, but also socially and culturally, becoming "resettlement champions" for their families, households, and communities (Shakya et al. 2014; Hynie, Guruge, and Shakya 2013).

Adults may feel disempowered by young people's new-found leadership roles, especially in age-based social hierarchies (Clark-Kazak 2011). Social age and gender intersect to occasion different intergenerational perspectives on family relationships and attitudes toward sexuality and marriage (Wong et al. 2017).

Older people may take on more caregiving roles in migration contexts (VanderPlaat 2009). Some report coming out of retirement to work in family businesses or undertake care and reproductive work to free up younger adults to enter the labour force (VanderPlaat, Ramos, and Yoshida 2013). As mentioned above, others may lose social status through migration (Kahil, Iqbal, and Maghbouleh 2022).

CONCLUSION: PROSPECTS, RECOMMENDATIONS, AND FUTURE WORK

This chapter highlights some of the key issues related to age, social age, and family status in relation to forced migration in and to Canada. A social age approach acknowledges the shortcomings of the overreliance on chronological age, as well as the importance of family and intergenerational relationships. Current and emerging research and programming, partially referenced in this chapter, is moving in the direction of a more holistic approach to age across the life course and intersecting with gender, sexual orientation, disability, race, religion, and other areas covered in section two. However, Canada's law and policy lag behind. Therefore, looking forward, this chapter concludes with two key recommendations.

First, drawing on progressive approaches to gender identity (see Aberman, chapter 12), the Government of Canada, in collaboration with provincial and territorial governments, should adopt an equity approach to age and family in forced migration. An equity approach moves away from the problematic focus on chronological-age and nuclear-family based categories to address structural barriers that inhibit the full realization of human rights for people in situations of forced migration. For example, currently, IRCC identifies as "examples of persons who may be identified as vulnerable" specific age categories including "elderly, pregnant women, unaccompanied minor children" (IRCC n.d.b). This essentializes particular categories of people as inherently vulnerable. In contrast, an equity approach seeks to address the social age, gender, and other power relations that lead to direct and indirect discrimination and abuse.

Second, researchers and practitioners should adopt an age-sensitive approach in *all* work, not just in programming specifically intended for children, young people, or elders. This means taking into account the differential experiences of migration due to social age and family status, discussed in this chapter, and thinking about how the information we collect and the programs we deliver can be more inclusive across the life cycle.

FURTHER READING AND RESOURCES

CBC Radio. 2022. "Re-building the Child Welfare System through 'Heart Work' and Home Fires." *Unreserved*, 1 March 2022. Video, 50:07. https://www.cbc.ca/radio/unreserved/how-indigenous-people-are-rebuilding-child-welfare-to-lift-up-the-whole-family-1.6364460.

Bowen, Leah-Simone, and Falen Johnson. 2020. "S3: Crash Course on British Home Children." *The Secret Life of Canada* podcast, 16:02. https://radiopublic.com/the-secret-life-of-canada-WwoQnZ/s1!85705

Employment and Social Development Canada. 2018. "Social Isolation of Seniors: A Focus on New Immigrant and Refugee Seniors in Canada." Government of Canada. https://www.canada.ca/en/employment-social-development/corporate/seniors/forum/social-isolation-immigrant-refugee.html.

Rabiah-Mohammed, Fawziah, and Abe Oudshoorn. 2021. "An Exploration of Integration Journeys, Identity and Well-Being with Syrian Refugee Youth." Child and Youth Refugee Research Coalition (CYRRC). https://dalspace.library.dal.ca//handle/10222/80896.

14

(Dis)Ability and Medical Conditions in Canadian Refugee Resettlement

Rachel McNally

KEY TAKEAWAYS

- There is limited knowledge about the experiences of refugees with disabilities in Canada and about how Canadian refugee policy affects refugees with disabilities.
- Disability is not just about individual abilities or impairments but also environmental barriers and discriminatory attitudes.
- Understandings of disability vary widely across different communities and cultures.
- Refugees with disabilities may be referred for resettlement to Canada for a variety of reasons and may come through any of Canada's resettlement programs.
- Resettlement to Canada may offer access to medical care, disability services, and inclusive education opportunities that are not available in the country of asylum.
- After arrival in Canada, refugees with disabilities often struggle to access services and supports specific to their needs because of various barriers.

KEY TERMS

- Ableism
- Disability
- Resettlement
- Social determinants of health

INTRODUCTION

14.1 CBC reports that "[m]any Syrian refugees arrive in Canada with chronic conditions and disabilities that have gone untreated for years" (E. Smith 2018). For five of the members of the Harb family, they suffered from pain and limited mobility in a Jordanian refugee camp but did not receive a diagnosis of muscular dystrophy until after their arrival in Canada. The diagnosis allowed family members to get much-needed medical care and new motorized wheelchairs. In Maher Harb's silent play about his transition to life in Canada, he represents his new life in Canada by pushing away his old manual wheelchair and climbing into his new motorized one. Although the family is happy to be in Canada, they are struggling to find affordable housing appropriate for a family of ten, including three wheelchair users. Their current accommodations are not accessible, so the family members in wheelchairs cannot leave their apartment building without assistance opening doors (E. Smith 2018).

It is estimated that at least twelve million people with disabilities are forcibly displaced globally, some within and others outside their own countries (UNHCR 2021a). Understandings of disability vary greatly across different cultures and communities, as well as over time. According to the United Nations Convention on the Rights of Persons with Disabilities (CRPD): "Persons with disabilities include those who have long-term physical, mental, intellectual or sensory impairments which in interaction with various barriers may hinder their full and effective participation in society on an equal basis with others" (2006, article 1). A key aspect of this definition is that disability is not just about the individual but also "attitudinal and environmental barriers" (preamble (e)) like inaccessible buildings or an unwillingness to hire people with disabilities. This definition reflects a "social model" of disability, a concept that was introduced by Oliver (1983; 2013) to emphasize disabling social barriers. The social model of disability was a reaction to the medical model, which only considered individual impairments and individual supports and not societal barriers or societal changes (Oliver 1983; 2013). The term "ableism" is one way to talk about discrimination on the basis of disability and the way systems, policies, and the physical environment are designed for able-bodied people.

In the Canadian context, there is limited knowledge about how Canadian refugee policy affects refugees with disabilities and about the experiences of refugees with disabilities who have come to Canada. Most research about disability and migration in Canada combines immigrants and refugees together instead of considering refugees separately (Korntheuer et al.

2021, 5; El-Lahib 2016; Kusari, El-Lahib, and Spagnuolo 2019). This chapter describes the pathways for refugees with disabilities to come to Canada, some of the challenges they face following arrival, and certain problematic narratives that reinforce barriers. It concludes by calling for more research about disability and refugees in Canada and beyond. Although refugee claimants who come to Canada and claim refugee status may also live with disability, this chapter primarily focuses on refugees who are selected by Canada overseas, either following a referral from UNHCR or an application by a private sponsor, and who arrive through one of Canada's resettlement programs (see Atak, chapter 17; Labman, chapter 18).

Refugees with disabilities have been called "forgotten refugees" because they are often overlooked in situations of displacement and in academic work (Crock et al. 2017). There are many connections between disability and forced migration, but "disability and forced migration are rarely put together, in policy, research and practice" (Pisani, Grech, and Mostafa 2016, 422). Disability may be caused by the same events that cause displacement (such as injury caused by war) or by dangerous circumstances along journeys to safety (Pisani, Grech, and Mostafa 2016, 428). Aadditionally, both before and after arrival in Canada, refugees face challenges related to the social determinants of health (see also Chen, chapter 24), including stress, trauma, poverty, food insecurity, difficulties in accessing quality affordable housing, transportation barriers, and social isolation (Beer 2018, 5), putting refugees at higher risk of developing chronic diseases and mental health conditions. The challenges displaced people face are exacerbated for those living with a disability (Pisani, Grech, and Mostafa 2016, 428). Sometimes people with disabilities are unable to evacuate or leave conflict zones, so they may be left behind instead of leaving their countries (UNHCR 2021c). For example, many Ukrainians with disabilities have been excluded from evacuations and have faced difficulties in accessing essential information in formats they can understand, like Ukrainian braille (Mao 2022).

In addition to refugee-specific international law and general human rights law, the rights of refugees with disabilities are covered under the UN CRPD. One of the most recent international human rights instruments, the CRPD was adopted in 2006 to "promote, protect and ensure the full and equal enjoyment of all human rights and fundamental freedoms by all persons with disabilities, and to promote respect for their inherent dignity" (CRPD, art. 1). The CRPD also recognizes "the difficult conditions faced by persons with disabilities who are subject to multiple or aggravated forms of discrimination on the basis of race, colour, sex, language, religion, political or other opinion, national, ethnic, indigenous or social origin, property, birth, age or other status" (CRPD, s. preamble (p)). In Canada, refugees with disabilities often face intersecting challenges and discrimination related to disability and refugee background, as well as ethnic, religious, and linguistic differences.

Canadian representatives were involved in developing the CRPD (Mason, Munn-Rivard, and Walker 2021). Canada signed the convention in 2007 and ratified it in 2010 (Mason, Munn-Rivard, and Walker 2021). In the last few decades, the Canadian federal government and several provincial governments have also passed accessibility laws that outline rights for people with disabilities and what organizations and employers need to do to make their buildings, services, and employment accessible. However, in a 2019 visit to Canada, the UN Special Rapporteur on the rights of persons with disabilities concluded: "As a highly-developed nation, Canada still lags behind in the implementation of its obligations under the Convention on the Rights of Persons with Disabilities. There are significant shortcomings in the way the federal, provincial, and territorial governments of Canada respect, protect and fulfill the rights of persons with disabilities" (Devandas-Aguilar 2019, n.p.).

UNDERSTANDING DISABILITY IN DIFFERENT CULTURES AND COMMUNITIES

Different communities and cultures understand disability in varying ways. For disability and settlement service providers, it is important to be sensitive to different cultural understandings of disability (Dew et al. 2020). In some refugee communities, there is significant stigma associated with disability. For example, family members of Syrian and Iraqi refugees with disabilities resettled to Australia reported significant disability-related stigma in their communities and countries of origin, especially for those born with disabilities and those living with mental illnesses (Dew et al. 2020). Overall, family members and service providers shared that within Syrian and Iraqi communities, "disability is often associated with a sense of shame, pity, and seclusion from public" (Dew et al. 2020, 16). Families, especially mothers, are often seen as responsible for their children's disabilities (Dew et al. 2020, 16). For these families, resettlement to Australia offered better access to disability-related services and in general, to a more inclusive and accepting environment (Dew et al. 2020, 16). In addition to cultural differences around disability, because of global inequality, refugee countries of origin and host countries often have few resources to provide basic services for their populations. As a result, capacity is limited to provide disability-specific services and supports. This is another reason why resettlement may offer better access to specialized medical care, inclusive education, assistive devices, and disability supports (see boxes 14.1 and 14.2).

In other communities and cultures, disability is perceived as a part of identity. For example, members of the deaf community generally do not identify as living with a disability or having a medical deficiency that needs to be corrected but rather self-identify as members of a minority cultural group with its own sign languages (such as American Sign Language) and distinct cultures (M. McKee, Schlehofer, and Thew 2013). Many Indigenous Nations understand the concept of disability as a colonial construct that does not align with Indigenous understandings of human difference (Ineese-Nash 2020, 28). For example, in Anishinaabe teaching, children are understood as a gift to the community, and "[i]f a child presents as disabled, there is an understanding that there is something to be learned from that experience to strengthen the community as a whole" (Ineese-Nash 2020, 40). The focus is on the gifts and strengths of the child, rather than on their limitations or impairments.

It is also clear that how people understand disability in Canada and globally has changed over time, like the transition from a "medical model" to a "social model" of disability as described in the introduction. In the past, UNHCR had "a broad and contextualized understanding of disability that is not necessarily exclusively linked to bodily impairment but can also arise from external socio-economic factors" (Flegar 2019, 175). Consequently, UNHCR categorized several groups of people as socially disabled that we would likely not categorize as disabled today, including unmarried mothers, large families who did not have enough income to be self-sufficient, and people with alcohol addictions related to living in a refugee camp (Flegar 2019, 168). Overall, it is important to recognize that understandings of disability and of who counts as disabled can be specific to one time, place, and cultural group.

HOW ARE REFUGEES WITH DISABILITIES SELECTED FOR RESETTLEMENT IN CANADA?

There is a long history of discrimination against people with disabilities within Canadian immigration policy. Many scholars have criticized Canada's long history of excluding potential immigrants on the basis of disability and medical conditions (e.g., Hanes 2009; Capurri 2020; Bisaillon 2022). Historically, some programs made exceptions to the rules in place at the time to admit to Canada small numbers of refugees with disabilities or medical conditions, such as a program for refugees with tuberculosis for World Refugee Year in 1959–60 (Raska 2019). Since the 2001 Immigration and Refugee Protection Act (IRPA), refugees have been exempted from the provisions about medical inadmissibility that deny some potential immigrants from entering Canada if the cost of treatment is estimated to be above a certain cost threshold (IRCC 2018). Refugees are also exempted from some requirements that may pose barriers for other immigrants with disabilities, such as standardized language tests. Overall, there are far fewer barriers in being admitted to Canada for refugees with disabilities than for potential economic immigrants with disabilities. However, refugees can still be rejected or required to complete treatment before they are admitted to Canada if they have a medical condition that the Canadian government considers "likely to be a danger to public health or safety" such as active tuberculosis (Government of Canada 2022g, 9).

With the exception of Canada's Private Sponsorship of Refugees (PSR) program (in which refugees are chosen by sponsors; see Labman, chapter 18), UNHCR refers all refugees resettling to Canada. UNHCR makes these referrals to resettlement countries based on seven categories: Legal and/or Physical Protection Needs; Women and Girls at Risk; Children and Adolescents at Risk; Survivors of Violence and/or Torture; Medical Needs; Restoring Family Unity; and Lack of Foreseeable Alternative Durable Solutions (UNHCR 2023c). The main reason for resettlement may apply to any member of an immediate family, not necessarily the refugee(s) living with disability. UNHCR (2023c) considers age, gender, diversity (including disability status), and family unity as important principles in guiding resettlement referrals.

Some refugees with disabilities may qualify for a referral under the "Medical Needs" category. However, the criteria for this category are very restrictive, as the focus is on refugees with life-threatening medical conditions who could benefit from treatment in a resettlement country (UNHCR 2023c): "Most refugees with medical needs, for example, those relating to old age, disability or mental health, are unlikely to meet the high threshold to qualify for resettlement under this submission category" (UNHCR 2023c, n.p.). This narrow focus on medical need has led one researcher to call for UNHCR to introduce a separate resettlement referral category focused on disability to increase access to resettlement opportunities for refugees with disabilities (Duell-Piening 2018). From UNHCR's perspective, "Opportunities for resettlement based on medical needs are extremely limited, and it is important to identify and prioritize the most serious and compelling cases" (2023c, n.p.). However, UNHCR recognizes that disability or health reasons may relate to other resettlement submission categories. For example, if refugees "are exposed to protection risks on account of their health condition," they may qualify under the Legal and/or Physical Protection Needs category (UNHCR 2023c).

Canada does not place limits on specific UNHCR referral categories. Up until 2023, the Canadian government told UNHCR that less than 5 per cent of the cases it referred to Canada to consider for resettlement should have high medical needs (Government of Canada 2022g). In the latest revision of Canada's country chapter in the "UNHCR Resettlement Handbook," there is no longer the 5 per cent limit on medical cases (Government of Canada 2022g). Instead, the chapter explains:

> Some health conditions may require frequent or costly medical treatment. Depending on the circumstances of the case, refugees with medical conditions may need to be destined to particular areas where the required medical services are available. As a result, processing times for such cases may be lengthy … when recommending refugee cases with medical conditions it is worth considering the suitability and safety of travel to Canada and the presence of accompanying or other family in Canada able to assist the

> refugee. It is recommended that the UNHCR consult with the responsible Canadian migration office if there are questions regarding the referral of a specific case, especially if the referral has been assessed with medical needs. (Government of Canada 2022g, 5)

This new policy is vague. It is unclear whether in practice, moving to a system of case-by-case consultation will allow more refugees with medical needs to settle in Canada.

> 14.2 A family who resettled to Canada as part of the Syrian refugee resettlement initiative can now meet the medical needs of their three disabled children, something that was not possible as refugees living in Lebanon. The mother, Shamsa, shared with UNHCR through an interpreter: "I am so grateful for the opportunity to come to Canada. Having two of my children going to school and the smiles I now see on the faces of my other three disabled children is a dream come true. Back home, they would have been made fun of or ignored but here, everyone wants to help out. I am so touched by this and can't wait to also give back to the community." UNHCR explained the importance of resettlement for this family because "UNHCR and its partners do not receive any funding to provide such special medical care or specific diet that the children's conditions require." (Cabrera 2017, n.p.)

Today, there is no specific resettlement program in Canada for refugees with disabilities, so they may arrive under any of Canada's general resettlement programs (see Atak, chapter 17; Labman, chapter 18). Most UNHCR-referred refugees will arrive as government-assisted refugees (GARs) and receive financial support from the Canadian government and settlement support from government-funded settlement agencies. Alternatively, they may be matched with a sponsorship group through the Blended Visa Office-Referred (BVOR) program, in which the sponsors provide most of the settlement support and share the cost of financial support with the government. Some refugees with disabilities may be referred to the Joint Assistance Sponsorship (JAS) program (either before or after arrival in Canada) to be matched with a sponsor to receive additional support on top of what they receive from settlement agencies (McNally 2023). The JAS program is for refugees who have "special needs," which can include "emotional problems resulting from the refugee experience which could include incidents of trauma or torture" or a "physical or mental disability which could require treatment in Canada" (IRCC 2017, n.p.). In this program, sponsors "provide orientation, significant settlement assistance and emotional support" for two years (IRCC 2017, n.p.).

Apart from UNHCR-referred refugees, private sponsorship groups may also choose to nominate refugees with disabilities for sponsorship under the PSR program. Since most privately sponsored refugees are family members or friends of people in Canada, it is more likely that refugees are chosen because of their connections to people in Canada, rather than for a reason specifically linked to disability. Because refugees with disabilities are referred to Canada under different UNHCR referral categories and arrive under different resettlement programs, it is difficult to track how many refugees with disabilities are arriving or which disabilities and health conditions are represented among resettled refugees. There are no public statistics about resettled refugees with disabilities.

EXPERIENCES AFTER ARRIVAL IN CANADA: SUPPORTS AND BARRIERS

Since resettled refugees arrive in Canada as permanent residents, they are generally entitled to the same health and disability-related federal, provincial, and municipal government supports as Canadians. For the first year, they are also eligible for funding for prescription medications, assistive devices, and some other supports through the Interim Federal Health Program, similar to what is covered for Canadian residents who receive social assistance (see Chen, chapter 24). However, refugees with disabilities face various barriers in accessing both settlement services and disability-related services. For all refugees, the Canadian health system can be difficult to understand and access because it is complex and unfamiliar, and because there are language and cultural barriers (Beer 2018). This is a particular challenge for refugees with disabilities or complex health issues who may need specialized care.

Another challenge is that settlement support systems for refugees in Canada are not well-connected to support systems for people with disabilities (Korntheuer et al. 2021, 8; Kusari, El-Lahib, and Spagnuolo 2019). The federal government oversees refugee resettlement programs and settlement services, whereas provincial and territorial governments are responsible for disability-related services and other programs that are important for people with disabilities, including health care, social services, and education. Settlement service providers are typically not well equipped to serve refugees and immigrants with disabilities, while disability-related agencies rarely offer programming targeted to refugees or immigrants (Kusari, El-Lahib, and Spagnuolo 2019).

In practice, "one is treated either as an immigrant or as someone with disabilities, but never as an individual who exists at the intersection of these and many other identity and social categories" (Kusari, El-Lahib, and Spagnuolo 2019, 111). While refugees have many different identities – such as (dis)ability, ethnicity, age – bureaucratic categories often miss these intersections, and services are often designed to respond to only one identity, like person with a disability, newcomer to Canada, or child (see also Clark-Kazak, chapter 13). For example, translators and interpreters are available to access settlement services but not always in the health and education systems. Although the Canadian school system offers opportunities for refugee children with disabilities, interpretation may not be provided for meetings between schools and parents, which makes it difficult for parents to participate in making education plans for their children (Raymond et al. 2022).

Although refugees with disabilities face many of the same challenges as other refugees coming to Canada, some of these challenges are greater because of their disabilities. For instance, in one study involving four refugee women with disabilities in Saskatoon, language learning was more difficult for the women because of their disabilities and because language classes were not always tailored to their needs (Osei Poku 2018, 73–7). One woman was unable to attend English classes because her disabilities and health issues made it difficult for her to leave her home. For one blind refugee, participation in English classes was limited because the classes relied on visual images and written texts. One deaf refugee only spoke in Arabic sign language upon arrival. Although she was happy to have access to American Sign Language classes, it was difficult to learn to sign in a new language. She also relied extensively on her daughter as an interpreter, given that there was only one interpreter in the area who knew Arabic sign language. Because it took these women longer to learn English, they were dependent on the help of settlement organizations for a longer period of time, and they did not feel one year was enough time for them to become "self-sufficient" as the settlement organizations expected (Osei Poku 2018, 84). For refugee parents who have caregiving responsibilities for children with disabilities, it can be challenging to access childcare adapted to their children's needs, which is necessary for the parents to attend language classes (Raymond et al. 2022).

STIGMA AND PROBLEMATIC NARRATIVES ABOUT REFUGEES WITH DISABILITIES IN CANADA

Although Canada has welcomed refugees with disabilities and may offer a more inclusive environment than other countries of asylum or countries of origin, stigma, discrimination, and ableist narratives remain widespread in Canada. There are also some similarities between the difficult past experiences of refugees and of others with disabilities in Canada. Many people with intellectual disabilities in Canada have been forcibly and traumatically displaced from their homes then confined to live in institutions, with little choice about where they live (Spagnuolo and El-Lahib 2020). Korntheuer et al. (2021) identify similarities between harmful societal discourses that present both refugees and persons with disabilities as a "burden" on society. Refugees with disabilities in Canada experience stigma and discrimination because of both their refugee background and disability (Korntheuer et al. 2021). It is also problematic that "integration" is often understood narrowly in terms of individual adaptation and economic success, rather than looking at the need to change institutions and conditions in Canada to make them more accessible, inclusive, and responsive to the needs of refugees with disabilities (Korntheuer et al. 2021, 12). Returning to the social model of disability and the CRPD mentioned at the beginning of this chapter, there needs to be more of a focus on changing the disabling conditions in the broader society, from inaccessible systems to discriminatory attitudes.

Another common but problematic narrative in Canada is what Mahrouse (2021) calls the "inspirational refugee narrative." Mahrouse draws on critical disability studies, critical refugee studies, and critical race theory to analyze the "inspirational refugee narrative" and how it constructs the figure of what she calls "the super-refugee" (2021, 173–4). Like inspirational stories of people with disabilities who have achieved exceptional success, stories of able-bodied and disabled "super-refugees" focus on the accomplishments of refugees, individual talent, hard work, and positive attitudes in response to difficult circumstances (Mahrouse 2021). Although those promoting these narratives often have good intentions, Mahrouse argues that these super-refugee narratives can be problematic for several reasons. They are not representative of the experiences of most refugees. They place unrealistically high and ableist expectations on individuals. They pressure refugees to show gratitude and to overachieve to meet these expectations. They also downplay systemic challenges and barriers that make it difficult for others to achieve similar successes. Rather than talking about integration as a societal responsibility, they construct successful integration as an individual responsibility. With their focus on what refugees contribute, these narratives frame accepting refugees in terms of economic gains rather than political or legal duties. Finally, they reinforce a national myth about Canada as a welcoming country.

Similarly, El-Lahib (2015; 2016) has critiqued Canadian immigration policy more broadly, questioning narratives that present Canada as a welcoming "land of opportunity" for immigrants. El-Lahib has written about how disabled newcomers to Canada experience ableism, racism, and colonialism during their settlement journeys. In addition, El-Lahib argues that Canadian immigration policies reinforce ableism, racism, and neo-colonialism, instead of challenging these dynamics.

CONCLUSION

This chapter presents an overview of how refugees with disabilities come to Canada and some of the challenges they face upon arrival. The way disability is defined within the social model of disability and within the CRPD emphasizes that disability is not just about individual abilities or impairments but also environmental barriers and discriminatory attitudes. How people understand disability has changed over the years and can vary widely in different communities and cultures, including among Indigenous communities and various refugee communities.

The UNHCR may refer refugees for resettlement to Canada because of serious medical issues, though in the past Canada has limited the number it accepted of refugees with serious medical needs. Refugees with disabilities may also be referred for resettlement for other reasons. After referral by UNHCR or selection by a private sponsor, refugees with disabilities may come through any of Canada's resettlement programs. Resettlement to Canada may offer access to specialized medical care, disability services, assistive devices, and inclusive education opportunities that are unavailable in the country of asylum. However, there barriers persist to access settlement services and disability-related services, such as language barriers, disconnected services, and services that are not adapted to different needs. There are also ongoing issues with stigma, discrimination, and ableist practices and narratives.

Going forward, more research is necessary about the impacts of Canadian refugee policy for refugees with disabilities and the experiences of refugees with disabilities in Canada and beyond. Researchers have called for "methodologically sound and ethical research on the intersection of forced migration and disability that can draw from the strengths and knowledge of critical scholarship in both fields" (Korntheuer et al. 2021, 2). To build capacity to serve refugees and immigrants with disabilities and reduce the disconnect between the settlement service and disability sectors, both settlement and disability service providers would benefit from further training (Kusari, El-Lahib, and Spagnuolo 2019, 114).

There is also potential for greater involvement of Canadian disability organizations and health charities in supporting refugees with disabilities and chronic diseases. A forum hosted by HealthPartners Canada and UNHCR on refugees and chronic disease recommended that health charities expand their programming to include and focus on refugees (Beer 2018, 7). It also suggested taking advantage of the possibility in the PSR program for sponsors to name or select refugees who are part of a group with a connection to the sponsor: "Canadian sponsors should be encouraged to sponsor refugees with whom they share a medical condition, thereby addressing the needs of the most vulnerable," and "given their insights into available treatments and how to address the challenges they may face" (Beer 2018, 3–4). Finally, it is important for refugees with disabilities to have opportunities to tell their own stories (Beer 2018, 8) and to be involved in shaping services and supports. In both the refugee participation movement and disability activism, the popular slogan "Nothing About Us Without Us" reflects the need to meaningfully include refugees and people with disabilities in making decisions and in designing policies and programs that affect their lives.

FURTHER READING AND RESOURCES

Couldrey, Marion, and Maurice Herson, eds. 2010. "Disability and Displacement." *Forced Migration Review* 35 (July). https://www.fmreview.org/disability/contents.

Dada, Suskaina. 2021. "Supporting Intersectional Needs of Refugees with Disabilities and their Families." Ontario Council of Agencies Serving Immigrants. YouTube video, 1:32:01. https://www.youtube.com/watch?v=A2DTTdHuKNs.

Disabilities Research Group, Carleton University, and Beth Robertson. 2016. "Envisioning Technologies: Historical Insights into Educational Technologies for People Who Are Blind or Partially Sighted in Canada, 1820–Present." https://doi.org/10.11574/DRG-1000.

Immigration and Refugee Board of Canada. n.d. "IRB Accessibility Plan for 2023 to 2025." https://irb-cisr.gc.ca/en/transparency/accessibility/Pages/2023-2025-accessibility-plan.aspx.

Joseph, Ameil, and Briarpatch Staff. 2022. "Migration Has Always been a Disability Justice Issue." *Briarpatch*, 7 September 2022. https://briarpatchmagazine.com/articles/view/migration-has-always-been-a-disability-justice-issue.

United Nations. n.d. "Refugees and Migrants with Disabilities." Department of Economic and Social Affairs. https://www.un.org/development/desa/disabilities/refugees_migrants_with_disabilities.html.

15

Making Race Central in Forced Migration Studies

Gada Mahrouse and Zeina El Omari

KEY TAKEAWAYS

- Despite Canada's image as a welcoming and humanitarian country, racism is commonly experienced at individual (i.e., attitudes, beliefs, and opinions) and structural (i.e., institutional or governmental policies, practices, and procedures) levels.
- Refugee advocates perceive the 2022 government programs that were swiftly implemented to welcome those fleeing war in Ukraine as a stark reminder of the racialized double standards in refugee and asylum regimes.
- Although race structures refugee and asylum regimes, it tends to be omitted or inadequately addressed in migration studies.
- Researchers and practitioners need to expand knowledge on race and forced migration by engaging with Black and Indigenous knowledges.
- In recent years organizations serving refugees, such as UNHCR, have explicitly committed to anti-racism by identifying and opposing racism.
- By making evident that race is an essential starting point for understanding refugees and forced migration, critical refugee studies scholars offer paradigm-changing, anti-racist methodological and theoretical frameworks.

KEY TERMS

- Race
- Racism
- Global North/South
- Western

INTRODUCTION

Race is directly implicated in forced migration in several ways. The most explicit link is that racial persecution is the reason why many people flee their countries and a legal basis for asylum claims. Race is also at the core of refugees' experiences because of their portrayal as unwelcome intruders, threats, or economic burdens. Most significantly, forced migration is managed through an inherently racially determined international order that continues to privilege Whiteness (Achiume 2022). Despite its significance to forced migration, race is still largely overlooked and inadequately addressed.

In this chapter, we argue for the necessity of making race a central analytic in forced migration work. Defining race as "a technology for the management of human difference" (Lentin 2020, 5) that serves to maintain White supremacy through exclusion and subordination and as a system of power that interlocks with class, gender, sexuality, ability (Hill Collins and Bilge 2020), state, and nation (Anthias and Yuval-Davis 1996), we make our argument in four parts. First, we discuss the example of Western governments' generous responses to those fleeing Ukraine as indicative of a "glaring double standard" (McCloskey 2022) within "a two-tiered protection scheme that shields Western states from most Third world asylum seekers" (Achiume 2021, 12) while enabling the entry of mostly White populations. Second, we identify gaps in research on forced migration vis-à-vis race and summarize the inextricable link between race and the historical origins of borders through European colonialism. Third, we show how racialized imagery and discourses in Western media contribute to public understandings and influence policy. Fourth, we demonstrate that despite Canada's international reputation as a humanitarian beacon of multicultural acceptance, refugees, migrants, and newcomers are consistently besieged by individual and structural forms of racism. We conclude by calling for the expansion of knowledge on race and forced migration by engaging Indigenous and Black knowledges. We also identify promising anti-racist commitments in organizations working with refugees and in paradigm-changing methodological and theoretical frameworks that centre refugee perspectives.

Our use of the term "refugee" throughout this chapter is purposeful insofar as we intend it to summon the central "figure" of forced migration and not to suggest legal accuracy (see also Goheen Glanville and Arbel, chapter 4). This way of operationalizing the term is meant to draw attention to how representations of *refugee-ness* conjure images of racialized images of foreigners (Espiritu 2014) and as "a category that has been invented and naturalized as being a 'problem' for the international system of states" (Nyers 1999, 4). That stated, it is important to recognize that the "refugee" label is a supranational category and an example of what De Genova refers to as "governmental contrivances" (cited in Carastathis et al. 2018, 4). As Triandafyllidou's (2022) work has shown, these categories and labels are especially murky when it comes to precarious, temporary, and fluid statuses. In other words, despite our caveats, in using "refugee" we nevertheless risk perpetuating the terminology that naturalizes distinctions on people crossing borders who are always imagined as perpetually out of place (in Carastathis et al. 2018, 6).

RACE, BORDERS, AND HOW INTERNATIONAL REFUGEE PROTECTION *SHOULD* WORK

In mid-May 2022, soon after the start of the Russian attack on Ukraine, the Canadian government announced a "special measure" allowing an unlimited number of Ukrainians to settle in Canada for up to three years (IRCC 2022a). The Canada-Ukraine Authorization for Emergency Travel (CUAET) recognized the urgency of the situation and was designed to fast-track Ukrainian admissions to Canada. The Canadian government committed to processing most visa applications in fourteen days, waived some requirements (including fees, language assessments and biometrics for some), exempted Ukrainians from COVID vaccination and overseas medical exam requirements, and facilitated free applications for an open work permit.

These swift measures were both praised and criticized. On the one hand, these immediate interventions made evident that, with political will, governments *can* respond to crises quickly and effectively, with generosity, compassion, flexibility, and leniency. Refugee advocates tirelessly call for these kinds of efficient interventions and seeing this special program unfold gave many hope for a rights-based refugee and asylum regime. As the United Nations' Office for the Coordination of Humanitarian Affairs declared: "This is how the international refugee protection regime *should work*, especially in times of crisis" (McCloskey 2022, 141). On the other hand, many felt dismayed that such special measures have not been used for people fleeing from other countries. Some also drew attention to the fact that the CUAET does not apply to non-Ukrainian nationals attempting to flee Ukraine, many of whom are international students and racialized migrant labourers (see box 15.1).

Canada's rapid measures emulated those of many European countries who also promptly opened their borders to welcome over three million five hundred thousand Ukrainian refugees (Rathe 2022). Referring to "selective solidarity," Paré (2022) points out that European state leaders who were previously known for their anti-immigration stances suddenly allowed thousands of Ukrainian migrants to enter their countries without travel or identification documents. For example, a refugee advocate in Denmark observed that the Danish government had prided itself on strict entry rules and a "zero" asylum seeker policy, then suddenly reversed its rules, and in just three weeks managed to pass a "special law" to accept Ukrainians in a flexible, fast, and efficient way (M. Galloway 2022). A human rights lawyer in Warsaw made a parallel observation that Polish authorities who had harassed and intimidated refugees from the Middle East are "welcoming refugees fleeing Ukraine with open arms and providing them with assistance" (as cited in McCloskey 2022, 141).

Canada's unusually accommodating and immediate response to the Ukraine crisis was explained in various ways. Perhaps anticipating accusations of special treatment, Immigration, Refugees and Citizenship Canada (IRCC) officials immediately clarified that unlike people from Syria or Afghanistan, Ukrainians who arrived through the program would be entering as "temporary residents" and not as refugees, based on the assumption that they would want to go home after the war ends. However, these distinctions and assumptions were confusing to those who work with racialized communities because many fleeing from Global South countries would also want temporary residency with the hope of returning when it is safe (H. Ibrahim 2022). The special CUAET program was also described as one that took into consideration "Canada's unique relationship with Ukraine, extensive diaspora and family links and supports that are already in Canada" (IRCC 2022a).

For critical race scholars in Canada, these explanations hearken back to earlier governmental tactics that refuted preferential treatment, while still ensuring that the rules functioned in favour of Whiteness (Mongia 2003). Similar denials of racism have been observed in the European context where, as De Genova points out, dominant discourses of migration in Europe systematically disavow and dissimulate race in ways that refortify European-ness as a racial formation of Whiteness (2017, 21). The most rigorous explanation of the discrepant ways the crises in Ukraine was managed can be found in research on the history and development of the international refugee regime. Recent laws and policies are an extension of older legal structures that have always excluded others on a discriminatory basis, according to the interests of powerful nations, dating back to the time of the negotiation and adoption of the UN Refugee Convention (Achiume 2021, 12–13; see also Fynn Bruey and Fantauzzi, chapter 8).

The consistent response to Ukraine by Canada and many European countries confirmed what many academics and advocates have been claiming for years: differential responses are entrenched in long-standing racist and colonial structures. Indeed, the welcoming response to Ukrainians underscored the Orientalist and racist logics that deem certain groups of people less deserving of humanitarian aid and refuge (McCloskey 2022). As noted above, evidence of racial distinctions in refugee and asylum regimes became even more apparent when, unlike White Ukrainians, racialized students in Ukraine who also tried to flee at the time of the Russian invasion were flagrantly targeted with "racist treatment, obstruction, and violence" (McCloskey 2022, 142; Riley-Guiu 2022). Some referred to this as a system of "racial tiering," whereby race determines who is allowed to leave (Jackson Sow 2022). Jackson Sow points out this type of tiering is "not merely an unfortunate byproduct of nations' humanitarian policies, but rather that international refugee and human rights law are tools that states use to renegotiate and reinforce White supremacy and racist national and global geopolitical hegemonies" (2022, 705).

> 15.1 "Osarumen, a father-of-three and a Nigerian national who has lived in Ukraine since 2009, said he, his family members and other refugees were told to disembark a bus about to cross the border on Saturday and told, 'No Blacks' ... 'This isn't just happening to Black people – even Indians, Arabs and Syrians,' he added, 'and that shouldn't be the case.'" (White 2022, n.p.)

THE UBIQUITOUS ABSENCES OF RACE AND COLONIALISM IN FORCED MIGRATION STUDIES

Research on the founding of the 1951 Refugee Convention (Abuya, Krause, and Mayblin 2021) shows that the refugee rights regime favoured Europeans from the start. According to Mayblin, the contemporary exclusionary politics of racialized people that obstruct access to the right of asylum can be traced to the origins of the convention where "the British government was hostile to non-European refugees, particularly those from the colonies" (2014, 424). Despite its centrality, race is either omitted or inadequately addressed in migration studies. Writing about the field of international relations, L. Turner notes that despite its importance and centrality, the topic of race is typically absent, which he explains as a type of "racial aphasia" or "calculated forgetting" (2020, 140). Whitley (2017) similarly shows that critical border studies does not articulate a theory of racism or work from a history of racism.

This omission is also evident in the seven-hundred-page *Oxford Handbook of Refugee and Forced Migration Studies* (Fiddian-Qasmiyeh et al., 2014). Its unquestionable importance to the field notwithstanding, it does not have the word "race" nor any of its derivatives ("racism," "racialization," or "racial") in any of the fifty-three chapter titles or in the subject index. That is not to say that none of the contributors address race. Several do, at least tangentially. Rather, the invisibility of race in the titles and subject index suggests that it is not a central analytic or prominent framework for the field. Furthermore, while studies on refugees' *experiences* with racism exist (cited later in this chapter), fewer tackle the notion of race as a structure. The tendency has been to perceive it as a "discreet variable" (Kyriakides et al. 2019) or "an identity attribute of individuals and groups" in ways that ignore how "race operates as a structure of power according to which privileges and rights are allocated" (Achiume 2021, 2).

Work on forced migration also tends to gloss over the ongoing influence of colonialism and imperialism. This omission is especially relevant considering "the rising numbers of people forced out from their homes by civil wars, particularly in the Middle East and in Africa, is a result of the instabilities put in place by their former colonial masters" (Evans and Bauman 2016). Contemporary formations of transnational migration are "inseparable from the histories of European and Euro-American colonization" (De Genova 2013, 1191–2), and legacies of empire continue to shape contemporary refugee discourse and practice (Mayblin 2017; Walia 2013). Indeed, through a lens that privileges race and colonialism, one can ascertain that historical and contemporary borders and migration governance historically served the "specific function of designating and securing the beneficiaries of colonial exploitation on a racial basis, ultimately to privilege whiteness over nonwhiteness" (Achiume 2021, 29).

Writing about what he refers to as the "amnesia that inflects migration studies when it comes to the colonial," Walters (2015, 11) asks, "what is the genesis of the mechanisms that make up migration policy?" To answer this question with the case of the White settler state of Canada is to acknowledge that its borders and migration were entirely established through colonial violence (see Coburn, chapter 1). Yet Canada's international reputation as a generous humanitarian possibility for refugees belies its historical and ongoing colonial and racist violence toward Indigenous populations (Monture-Angus 1995; Simpson 2014). Studying the structural processes of migration in Canada therefore requires contending with the White settler innocence that normalizes Indigenous dispossession (Razack 2002; Thobani 2007).

Achiume (2021) argues for the necessity of tracing the historical origins of racial borders through a genealogy of border and migration governance that reveals how racialized exclusion and exploitation were pursued in the service of European colonialism. A cursory genealogy of Canada's immigration governance as a settler state reveals several blatant examples. With the instance of the head tax on Chinese immigrants, K. Taylor reminds us that from 1885 until the 1970s the law "was explicitly racist in wording and intent: non-White, non-European immigration was openly discouraged and/or prohibited" (1991, 2). In an example of deceptive exclusionary governance in Canada, scholars have shown that although it never explicitly referred to race, the "continuous passage" rule was designed to restrict or curtail the migration of British subjects from India and Sri Lanka (Matas 1985; Mongia 2003). Moreover, during and after World War II, "regulations passed under the authority of the War Measures Act did not merely restrict entry of Japanese from abroad, they provided for the deportation of Canadian citizens of Japanese descent who had been born in Canada" (Mattas 1985, 9). In addition, we see historical examples where Whiteness is conflated with Christianity. As Matas points out, although there were no laws prohibiting the immigration of Jews, "discrimination was incontestable" (1985, 9), enabling Canadian immigration authorities to refuse entry of Jewish people who were fleeing Nazi persecution, the Holocaust, and the aftermath of the Holocaust (Abella and Troper 2012).

In Canada, discriminatory regulations did not just occur in the past. Focusing on contemporary labour migration, Akbar (2022) shows that since the late 2000s, Canada has increased the admission of temporary migrant workers to meet labour shortages and growing labour demands, but this too operates according to a two-tiered racist logic. Akbar argues that "working-class–racialised migrants are deemed undesirable while global elites are seen as preferred and attractive permanent residents and future citizens" (2022, 3943). Similarly, according to Chartrand and Vosko, contemporary Canadian temporary migrant worker programs reveal "continuous patterns of exploitation ... [in ways that] continue to reflect legacies of colonialism and racialization" (2021, 104; see Moffette, chapter 19; Ogoe and Wilkinson, chapter 25).

RACIALIZED DISCOURSES, LABELS, AND MEDIA REPRESENTATIONS

As several chapters in this book show, the categories and labels used to describe people who are displaced through forced migration are inconsistent and have particular implied meanings (see Young, chapter 3; Goheen Glanville and Arbel, chapter 4). For example, as Nguyen and Phu note, "Refugees are, at times, understood as migrants. At highly politicized moments, however, refugees are considered distinct from migrants. The relationship between the two categories is contentious" (2021, 7). Others have argued that a type of "symbolic bordering" linguistic practice occurs which, like the actual geographic borders, determines whether refugees are humanized or vilified (Chouliaraki and Zaborowski 2017; see also R. Kaye 1998; M. Berry, Garcia-Blanco, and Moore 2015). The different usages of the terms are significant because "refugees" and "asylum seekers" are legally protected under international agreements, whereas "migrants" are not. Moreover, because "migrant" is associated with "economic migrants" who travel by choice (Alia and Bull 2012), its use is more likely to provoke public concerns about how their presence reduces the financial resources of host countries.

Studies on the representations of refugees and migrants make evident the ways in which certain groups are attributed or associated with violence, barbarity, and disorder through several familiar and commonly circulating racialized "figures" (R. Kaye 1998), who tend to be represented through negative or positive frames (M. Berry, Garcia-Blanco, and Moore 2015) or archetypes of good or bad that are made recognizable through gender and race (Szczepanik 2016). For example, in Zygmunt Bauman's seminal book *Strangers at Our Door* (2016), he largely attributes the paradoxical yet now commonly accepted Western perspective on refugees as threats in news media. He points out that instead of refugees being defined and treated as a vulnerable members of humanity who are merely searching to restore basic rights of which they have been violently robbed, they have come to be seen as threats to national security.

15.2 In a public education booklet they produced in 2020, Amnesty International Canada's francophone division tackles widely circulating myths about the dangers or threats posed by refugees from certain backgrounds and reminds us that the protection of refugees is not an act of generosity, it is a legal obligation (Amnistie Internationale Canada Francophone 2020, 2). The booklet also offers factual evidence that clarifies these characteristics attributed to refugees are simply not true (i.e., no terrorist act in Canada has ever been committed by a refugee, yet the idea that refugees are terrorists persists).

Examining Canadian news media, Tyyskä et al. argue that coverage of the Syrian refugee crisis "endorse(s) neo-colonial, orientalist, neoliberal, anti-Islamic and patriarchal perspectives" (2021, 162). Studies by Bradimore and Bauder (2012); Medianu, Sutter, and Esses (2015); Tyyskä et al. (2017); R. Wallace (2018); and Mustafa, Pilus, and Mohammad Lotfie (2021) similarly emphasize the role that the Canadian news media plays in shaping public opinion and perpetuating a cycle of "othering."

Whereas "bad" refugees are depicted as invaders, fraudulent opportunists, or threats to national security, the "good" are typically women and children who are seen as vulnerable victims in need of assistance or rescue (see also Aberman, chapter 12). In one striking example of depictions of good deserving victims, Troeung (2022) documents how her family's arrival to Canada as refugees from Cambodia in 1980 became a front-page news story with a staged photograph of her as an eleven-month-old baby waving a Canadian flag as the then Canadian minister of citizenship and immigration welcomed them. For Troeung, this representation of a welcoming reception belied the racism and pressure to assimilate that they subsequently faced. Interestingly, the photo-op Troeung describes has remarkable similarities with Prime Minister Justin Trudeau's widely circulated photograph of greeting a Syrian refugee child at the airport in 2015 (Nguyen and Phu 2021, 3), showing the representational trope of Canada's liberal multiculturalism persists.

Discourses and media representations influence and help create public opinion about refugees. As Reynolds and Hyndman note, public discourse about refugees "shapes the conditions of possibility for policy making and legislation by governments" (2021, 23). In Canada, an Angus Reid poll comparing

Canadians' support of Ukrainian refugees in 2022 with that for twenty-five thousand Syrian refugees in 2015, found the support for welcoming an unlimited number of Ukrainians more than doubled (Renfrew 2022).

REFUGEE, MIGRANT, AND/OR NEWCOMER EXPERIENCES OF RACISM

Part of the Canadian national identity is the well-established imagining of Canada as an exceptionally generous, welcoming multicultural humanitarian country (Nguyen and Phu 2021; Henry and Tator 2006). In contrast, research consistently reveals otherwise. Whether the focus is on children and youth (Khan et al. 2018; Hilario et al. 2015; Rossiter et al. 2015; Walker and Zuberi 2020; M. George and Bassani 2018), women (Sutherland 2017; Baiden et al. 2021), men (Hilario et al. 2018; Wilson-Forsberg et al. 2020), or members of the 2SLGBTQI+ communities (Logie et al. 2016; E. Lee 2018), studies show experiences of refugees, migrants, and/or newcomers in Canada are largely shaped by racism. Similar findings emerge from research that focuses on those from specific geopolitical or linguistic origins. For instance, studies on newcomers who are African (Woodgate and Busolo 2018; Okeke-Ihejirika et al. 2020), Syrian (Drolet and Moorthi 2018), Arab-speaking (Elshahat and Moffat 2022), or visible minority (Agyekum, Siakwah, and Boateng 2021; G. George, Selimos, and Ku 2017; Thomson et al. 2015; Tuyisenge and Goldenberg 2021) all revealed experiences of individual and structural racism.

In the context of individual racism, occurrences include offensive comments on an inability to speak the dominant language (Sutherland 2017) or visible appearance and clothing (Khan et al. 2018) and treatment as outsiders and reminders of minority status (M. George and Bassani 2018; Drolet and Moorthi 2018, 115).

> 15.3 "One of my kids woke up one day for school and told me he really doesn't want to go because whenever he gets into an argument with his friends at school they yell at him 'go back to your country.'" (Government-assisted refugee woman quoted in Drolet and Moorthi 2018, 115)

Studies on Arab-speaking immigrants and refugees revealed that the level of discrimination and stigmatization they encounter has not abated since the 11 September 2001 terrorist attacks (Awad and Amayreh 2016; Elshahat and Moffat 2022) as they continue to be targeted with micro and macro aggressions ranging from a general attitude of exclusion from mainstream society to hate crimes (Elshahat and Moffat 2022; Kira et al. 2006). Likewise, research on gender non-conforming asylum seekers found that Muslim men overtly experienced multiple and overlapping racisms and microaggressions from "the dominant heteronormative community, the heteronormative co-ethnic community, and the dominant homonormative culture" (Kahn 2015, 74). More recently, a researcher found that "many migrants have encountered marginalizing and xenophobic attitudes related to the spread of COVID-19" (Barker 2021, 37). Those of Chinese and other Asian backgrounds have been especially scapegoated as having caused the virus and as a result faced increased racism (Liu, Jurkova, and Morales, as cited in Barker 2021).

Research also unequivocally shows that in Canada racism continues to manifest through structures, institutions, policies, and practices. For example, visible minority migrants, newcomers, and refugees state that they are treated less fairly by teachers, health service providers, border officials, police, and at government offices (M. George and Bassani 2018; Khan et al. 2018; Baiden and Evans 2021; Wilson-Forsberg et al. 2020).

> 15.4 A refugee claimant and former immigration detainee, held in the Laval immigration holding centre in 2020, recounted: "One of the [police] officers said to me: 'Canada is a free country for Canadians, not for foreigners.' He seemed very happy to tell me: 'You're going to sleep in jail tonight.' The other officers were laughing about this …" (Quoted in Stauffer 2021, n.p.)

In schools, children, adolescents, and their families experience institutional racism via social segregation, curriculum content, pedagogical approaches, and discipline procedures (Benner and Graham 2013; Seaton and Yip 2009; Nichols, Ha, and Tyyskä 2019; L. Guo-Brennan and M. Guo-Brennan 2019; Gillborn 2004).

Anti-Black racism in Canada is also well documented.

> 15.5 "I can go to Parliament Hill today and hold my head high and work seamlessly among my colleagues, shake hands with world leaders, but to this day still worry about getting pulled over by police …" (Hussen 2017, n.p.)

A study of Black African newcomer women indicates that they experienced particular forms of racism from health service providers (Baiden and Evans 2021).

> 15.6 "We face a lot of discrimination over here. Sometimes, it might not come out of their mouths, but it says it all on their faces, from their reactions ... some of the nurses look down on you because you're a black woman." (Black African newcomer woman quoted in Baiden and Evans 2020, 205)

Others have argued that structural racism manifests in ways that include severe gaps in health-care access among racialized migrants, such as limited health insurance eligibility, concerns about negative immigration consequences (i.e., medical repatriation, requirement to present proof of status at point of care), and scarce culturally and linguistically appropriate care (M. Abbas et al. 2018). One study found that because of the limited access to resources, newcomer women and children with uncertain or precarious status are "vulnerable to sustained experiences of homelessness and its deleterious effects," leading the researchers to conclude the problem "originates in federal policy, indicating that structural violence and discrimination are embedded in Canadian immigration law, perpetuating [newcomers'] reliance on and subsequent exclusion from the public systems" (Milaney et al. 2020, 13).

In sum, one of the salient reasons for making race a central analytic tool is to uncover the racism refugees encounter. This approach is particularly needed in Canada where refugee experiences with racism tend to be overshadowed by discourses of benevolence and generosity.

ANTI-RACIST FUTURES IN STUDIES ON REFUGEES AND FORCED MIGRATION IN SETTLER COLONIALISM

An understanding of race in forced migration must begin with considering how colonialism and legacies of empire shape contemporary refugee discourse and practice. For example, by employing a mobility justice framework, some have drawn attention to the colonial governance of Indigenous mobilities enacted through the Indian Act, 1876, which was intended to inhibit the mobilities of "dangerous" First Nations community members through formal strict regulations (Sodero and Scott 2016; Morton 2016; see also Coburn, chapter 1). Bauder and Breen's (2023) research on Indigenous perspectives of immigration policies in Canada importantly reveals that for some an "open-borders" policy is inadequate because it reaffirms international colonial borders and laws on state sovereignty. Their research calls instead for a "no-borders" approach. We are also inspired by those making compelling links between forced migration and settler colonialism. For instance, Abu-Laban argues "the fundamental and enduring foundation of settler-colonies on Indigenous lands, coupled with the mythology of the frontier, creates a different historical legacy that remains relevant now, even in the face of elements of convergence in relation to immigration policy and practice in Western states" (2020b, 14). According to Abu-Laban, when settler colonies and migration studies are explicitly linked, not only do important considerations emerge, but also creative possibilities for resistance to colonial borders and racism become possible. Equally significant is Arat-Koc's call for decolonizing refugee studies. She argues that Indigenous knowledge could inform "a place-based episteme to inspire political visions of a world beyond colonialism, imperialism, interventionism, war, capitalist expansion, and environmental degradation" (2021, 373).

Echoing Arat-Koc, we propose that more Indigenous theorizing on borders and mobility would greatly enrich the field in Canada (Simpson 2014; Coburn, chapter 1; Adese and Phung 2021; Young, chapter 3). When Indigenous knowledge and perspectives are addressed, the enduring impacts and processes of colonization become key deliberations, allowing us to grapple with the implications of being in a country that "hosts" refugees on stolen land where Indigenous people continue to be displaced.

Similarly, incorporation of Black epistemologies and knowledges could facilitate more in-depth and nuanced understandings on Black geographies, mobilities, and anti-Black racism in refugee regimes and experiences "from past to present and back" (Hudson, McKittrick, Caribbean Philosophical Association 2014, 239; see also: Henry-Dixon, chapter 2). For example, as Maynard reminds us, "long before the tens of thousands of irregular Black border crossings in recent years, the US-Canada border has been an important site of struggle for Black folks seeking freedom on either side" (2019, 139; see also Henry-Dixon, chapter 2). Maynard therefore insists that studies of migration recognize that "borders and border-enforcement regimes continue to relegate the lives of Black and other poor racialized persons into economic exploitation and precarity, and captivity" (2019, 143). Following these and other contributions (McKittrick and Woods 2007; Trotz 2011; Calliste 1994), we underscore the necessity of privileging critical Black thought to show processes of racialization in relation to geopolitical spaces within historical global relations. By drawing on Black thinkers "that provide deliberate commentary on the ways in which blackness works against the violence that defines it," we might avoid repeating anti-Black epistemic violence (McKittrick quoted in Hudson, McKittrick, and Caribbean Philosophical Association 2014, 240).

We also want to recognize substantial and hopeful anti-racist interventions in forced migration, especially those emerging in critical refugee studies. Race is a foundational rubric used to challenge the objectification of refugees and the idea that refugees are victims or problems to be solved. In response to the lack of depth and complexity in what has been described as the archive of "loss and trauma or success and gratitude" narratives about refugees (V. Nguyen 2013), the critical refugee studies approach interrogates the very category of "refugee" through social and political critiques of colonization, war, human rights, and displacement (Vang 2021; Espiritu 2014). In developing new methods to combat exploitative effects of conventional research, proponents of critical refugee studies emphasize the importance of self-representation and use creative approaches to rethink and reimagine how refugees portray themselves (Espiritu 2014; Troeung 2022; Phu 2011). V. Nguyen (2015) coined the term "Me-Search," to speak of the necessity of making refugees' "selves" the guiding compass for research. Some of the reductive and racialized understandings of refugees can be attributed to conventional research methods that fail to depict refugees as complex historical actors. As some have argued, "methods matter considerably where refugee studies are concerned" (Achiume 2021, 15).

Clark-Kazak (2017a) and others have drawn attention to ethical considerations in studies with refugees because of the research participants' precarious legal statuses, feelings of indebtedness, and/or the power imbalances (see also Granados and Klassen, chapter 6). Another hopeful anti-racist trend in research methods and approaches has been increasing calls for community-driven research. By prioritizing refugee/migrant perspectives as well as employing an anticolonial and intersectionality lens (critical disability, queer, and feminist frameworks) researchers are developing praxis-centred approaches that bridge academic research with knowledge from "on-the-ground" community initiatives (Caron, Lee, and Pullen Sansfaçon 2020; Clark 2018). Together, these methods, approaches, and paradigm shifts have the potential to fundamentally transform understandings and practices and to forge new knowledge, all of which brings the field of forced migration closer to anti-racist goals.

Some promising anti-racist commitments have also emerged from organizations working with refugees. For example, Amnesty International proposed "stopping racism" as one of the solutions for tackling what they refer to as the refugee "crisis": "Governments also need to stop blaming refugees and migrants for economic and social problems, and instead combat all kinds of xenophobia and racial discrimination. Doing otherwise is deeply unfair, stirs up tensions and fear of foreigners, and sometimes leads to violence – even death" (2015, n.p.). It is encouraging to observe that refugee advocate organizations are increasingly attempting link the issues of displacement common to both Indigenous communities and refugees (CCR 2016c). Perhaps the most momentous example is a 2020 UNHCR comprehensive report entitled *Guidance on Racism and Xenophobia: How UNHCR Can Address and Respond to Situations of Racism and Xenophobia Affecting Persons Under Its Mandate*. The report's introduction states that although talk of "cultural diversity" and "inclusion" are important, "there is also a pressing need in many societies for conversations and action to address racism, racial discrimination, xenophobia and related intolerance" (UNHCR 2020, 6). This is significant not only because the UNHCR is arguably the largest and most powerful global organization dedicated to protecting the rights of refugees, but also because the declaration explicitly specifically designates "racism," and not euphemisms like "diversity" that it has used in the past, as its central concern. Framing the issue in terms of racism implies a commitment to systemic change in power relations.

This commitment was underscored on 21 March 2022, on the International Day for the Elimination of Racial Discrimination, when Filippo Grandi, the UN High Commissioner for Refugees, made a public commitment to making the organization anti-racist (Grandi 2022a). This declaration was prompted by the blatantly unequal accommodations made by governments in Global North for those fleeing the war in Ukraine.

15.7 Grandi on the 2022 International Day for the Elimination of Racism
"While millions around the world were rightly moved by the extreme plight of the Ukrainian people, the same hardships – the same pain and sorrow; the same loss and anguish; the same relief at finding safety and trepidation of an uncertain future – are experienced by refugees around the world who also and equally deserve our compassion, our empathy, and our support" (Grandi 2022a, n.p.).

As Grandi's powerful statement makes clear, racialized discrepancies persist in the international refugee protection regime, and we therefore "need to ensure that global responsibility sharing is strengthened for all refugees, no matter where they come" (Grandi 2022a).

CONCLUSION

Racism does not merely occur in forced migration; it structures the very foundations of refugee and asylum regimes. From the granting or denying of entry, to resettlement challenges, race circumscribes every aspect of the refugee encounter. Moreover, refugee and asylum regimes, by default, determine who is to be excluded and included in racially disparate ways that benefit the First World (Achiume 2022). To reveal everyday experiences with racism and the large-scale racialized power structures that systematically construct the conditions between refugees and host states in the Global North, a critical race and intersectional lens is necessary. By setting race as a primary concern, migration studies scholars will be better equipped to identify anti-racist strategies for creating social justice. Indeed, making race a central analytic better equips us to produce knowledge that can determine how deeply rooted structures might be dismantled to enhance our collective moral and legal duty to protect.

FURTHER READING AND RESOURCES

CBC News. 2017. "Questioning Canada's Immigration Model." *The National*. YouTube video, 18:43. https://www.youtube.com/watch?v=N7_2ru-u5RA.

Critical Refugee and the Migration Studies Canada Network. n.d. https://www.criticalrefugeemigrationstudies.ca.

Critical Refugee Studies Collective. n.d. "Refugee Archives." https://criticalrefugeestudies.com.

CTV News. 2023. "Racism at Ukraine Border." CTV News Video Network, 2:16. https://www.ctvnews.ca/video?clipId=2394402.

Kyriakides, Christopher, Dina Taha, Carlo Handy Charles, and Rodolfo D. Torres. 2019. "Special Issue: Racialized Refugee." *Refuge: Canada's Journal on Refugees* 35, no. 1. https://refuge.journals.yorku.ca/index.php/refuge/article/view/40675.

Nguyen, Vinh, and Thy Phu, eds. 2021. *Refugee States: Critical Refugee Studies in Canada*. Cultural Spaces. Toronto: University of Toronto Press.

UNHCR. 2020. *Guidance on Racism and Xenophobia*. https://www.unhcr.org/5f7c860f4.pdf.

UNSW Kaldor Centre for International Refugee Law. 2020. "On Racism and Refugees: In Conversation with E Tendayi Achiume and Nyadol Nyuon." YouTube videos, 1:03:08. https://www.youtube.com/watch?v=xSU_kobHDHE&t=42s.

16

Class Identity, Performance, and Practices in Refugee Selection and Integration in Canada

Amrita Hari and Romeo Joe Quintero

KEY TAKEAWAYS

- Refugee journeys are inevitably classed experiences; however, very little attention has been paid to class as a topic in forced migration studies.
- Class-based integration of refugees is not a uniform experience and is shaped by other social identities, revealing inherently unequal and unruly patterns of mobility and access to membership.
- Two new pathways apply a classed distinction to refugee selection in Canada: Economic Mobility Pathways Pilot (EMPP) and Health-care workers permanent resident pathway.
- Private sponsors draw on their class identities – level of education, language ability, and social networks – to demonstrate their capacity to resettle refugees.
- The positioning of refugees as lacking agency can push claimants and refugees to project poverty and perform vulnerability and victimhood to improve their chances of success in refugee admission pathways.
- Class-based integration challenges have increased, and existing social inequities have deepened for refugees and other migrants during the ongoing COVID-19 pandemic.

KEY TERMS

- Agency
- Class
- Human capital identity
- Intersectionality
- Integration
- Skills

INTRODUCTION

As a concept, class describes systems of stratification within social relations. While a range of class definitions exists, the term commonly refers to descriptive gradations of income, status, and education. Beyond this grouping, class also includes processes of producing, appropriating, and distributing social capital and labour. As Gibson-Graham notes, there are various concepts of class that exist "often within the writings of the same person" (1996, 49). At an abstract level, Marxist political economists identify two class structures: capitalists, who are fewer in number and control the means of production, and workers, who constitute the majority. Some distinguish a middle class who appropriate surplus capital without owning the means of production (E. Wright 1993, 1998).

Many feminist scholars have argued that class does not operate in isolation from other dimensions of power and social division. Intersectionality (as discussed in Aberman, chapter 12) explains how persons identify as, and are ascribed membership in, multiple social categories (e.g., gender, ethnicity, religion, sexual orientation) (Crenshaw 1991; Davis 2008). Their experiences may vary and are influenced by the degrees of oppression and privilege associated with their specific social location. Although there is some recognition that different groups of migrants occupy different social positions in the host country (Levitt and Schiller 2004), very little attention has been paid to class in forced migration studies (Şimşek 2020) or to documenting how refugee journeys are classed experiences.

In this chapter, we bring together some of the disparate directions class analysis has taken in refugee selection, sponsorship applications, adjudication, and integration in Canada and forced migration studies broadly. Our coverage of the ways class is understood and invoked is neither exhaustive nor comprehensive. We conclude with some recommendations for incorporating class as a more relevant and visible category of analysis in forced migration studies.

A CLASSED PERSPECTIVE ON (FORCED) MIGRATION STUDIES

Generally, individuals evaluate their access to financial and social resources when choosing to migrate since moving usually comes with a cost (Adhikari 2013; Schon 2019; Steele 2009; Vignal 2021; World Bank 2017). Within migration studies, immigrants are perceived as strategic actors who carefully weigh their options when choosing to migrate, although often for selfless reasons, such as to improve the living conditions of their families (Hari 2017; Kanal and Rottmann 2021; Paret and Gleeson 2016). In contrast, forced migrants are portrayed as victims with limited agency because of the coerced and involuntary impetus for their migration.

Forcibly displaced individuals – refugees, asylum seekers, and internally displaced persons (IDPs) – are perceived to occupy a specific category that is outside the norm of the territorially bounded citizens (Saunders 2016, 79). As anomalies, they distort the order of things and must be regulated and reproduced as "voiceless, apolitical, [and] victim" without legitimate choice and agency (Saunders 2016, 80). Such notions of victimhood emerge since forced migrants typically have limited access to financial and social resources. Consequently, they may find themselves travelling a shorter distance or remain in "longer periods of waiting, being stuck, and of being in limbo" (Hunkler et al. 2022, 4830). This should not imply complete immobility.

Displaced individuals learn to adapt and develop strategies to plot their trajectories of forced displacement however confined they may be (Vigh 2009). Moreover, people with access to financial, social, and political assets may choose to stay in conflict zones because of perceived economic opportunities to expand their livelihood options (Korf 2004). Drawing on Pierre Bourdieu's theorizations of capital, Van Hear claims that access to different forms of capital – economic, social, and cultural – can shape "the routes and channels migrants can follow, the destination they can reach, and their life chances after migration" (2014, 100). For many people in the Global South, their homes and lands are their main sources of capital (Wigle 2008), which is why some are willing to tolerate armed violence to protect their material and financial assets (e.g., income, employment), while others have the means to stay as they can "bribe combatants on both sides of a conflict" (Van Hear 2014, 113). Before making a refugee claim, asylum seekers might engage in dangerous and informal transactions, such as paying "smugglers, traffickers, guides, drivers, ship captains, kidnappers, lawyers, doctors, and profiteers" with money or sometimes with their bodies, along their journey in search of protection (Holmes 2020, xiii). This complicates what we think we may already know about the experiences of displaced individuals and their migration journeys.

Generally, the depictions of forcibly displaced individuals, described above, are restrictive and essentialist, and they reinforce victim discourse (see also Goheen Glanville and Arbel, chapter 4). Forced migrants can therefore be constrained by the labels ascribed to them by national refugee regimes and international systems of refugee determination and protection (Saunders 2016, 109). Moreover, this distinct social positioning of refugees is often uncritically extrapolated to be a lack of decision-making power in all situations that follow their displacement (Moore and Shellman 2006). Although forced migrants do not necessarily agree with this portrayal, challenging their victimhood in policy, media, activist, and academic discourses could heavily influence how their claims for protection are treated (Mainwaring 2016, 290; Oskay 2016, 25). What is most important is that refugee journeys are classed and do not imply uniform experiences. Our brief discussion illustrates the need for a more nuanced understanding using a classed perspective to consider how social identities shape inherently unequal and unruly patterns of mobility.

16.1 Displacement, Asylum, and Flight: A Classed Journey

On a global scale, millions of people are forced to cross international borders and leave their home countries because of war, violence, or political persecution; many do not survive the passage to reach their intended destination. There are many contemporary examples of search and rescue operations for refugees who are missing because their vessels capsized and sank along the voyage (Al Jazeera 2022). One grievous case is that of a drowned toddler, Alan Kurdi, who was travelling from Turkey to Greece with his family. Investigation into the incident revealed that his family "had previously been refused resettlement to Canada" under the Private Sponsorship of Refugees (PSR) program due to admissibility (Bélanger McMurdo 2016, 82). This revelation generated an outpouring of support for Syrian refugees, prompting the Canadian government to respond "to public opinion in favour of increased resettlement" (Bélanger McMurdo 2016, 82).

In some ways, Alan Kurdi's story illustrates how class shapes trajectories of forced displacement. Since the Kurdi family could not travel to Canada through other immigration streams, they paid smugglers to take them through Turkey to reach Greece, where they planned on seeking asylum and eventually resettling in another European country. A family member shared that their hope was "to have a better life ... possibly [in] Germany or Sweden" (quoted in Crawford 2015, para. 21). The story of Alan Kurdi reflects the experiences of many would-be asylum seekers and refugees who are crossing restrictive international borders, risking death to reach a more desirable destination where they can start anew. There are some who can only go as far as their money will take them (Van Hear 2014, 101).

Upon arrival in a new social environment, refugees face many integration challenges. Despite the lack of consensus on the definition of "integration" (Castles, Vasta, and Vertovec 2002; see also Hynie, chapter 23), there is agreement that the concept varies by motivations, conditions, legal status, and categories of migration (Şimşek 2020). More generally, integration includes functional dimensions (status, safety, and stability) based on access to education, health care, housing, and labour markets (Ager and Strang 2008). Integration is inevitably shaped by immigrants' social class as they move from one social environment (education, income, networks, and resources) to another (Gullestad 2002) and attempt to recreate their previous social status. In Bonjour and Chauvin's (2018) study in the Netherlands, the poor socio-economic prospect of refugees upon arrival is tied to their national origin and religion. In addition, low educational attainment is perceived to indicate "poor work ethics and oppressive gender and family norms" (Bonjour and Chauvin 2018, 7).

Integration is a complex process, influenced not only by the intersectional identities and social positionings of refugees but also multiple contextual factors such as limited access to formal employment (see Ogoe and Wilkinson, chapter 25), integration assistance, and adequate housing (see Clark-Kazak, chapter 28). Refugees commonly experience downward class mobility. More concerning is that it is also possible for refugees to remain unintegrated (Franz 2003). Regardless of their integration challenges, many refugees adapt strategies to circumvent their experience of unemployment by networking within and outside their own diasporic communities. Social networks also play an integral role in determining access to rights and resources.

For example, displaced Bosnian women who arrived in Austria in 1992 secured menial work as housekeepers or babysitters "through word of mouth" from Yugoslavian guest workers who experienced similar social and economic marginalization and from middle-class Austrian citizens (Franz 2003, 141). Many Bosnian refugees in Austria formed meaningful relationships with other racial and ethnic groups that frequently resulted in substantive material support during their integration in the new social and economic environment. This is contrary to the integration experience of Bosnian refugee women in New York City, as "the booming US economy in the late 1990s ... isolated many Bosnians in their socioeconomic struggles from the majority society" (Franz 2003, 154–5). Refugees who struggle in this class journey can become active in ethnic and transnational activities (political, social, and cultural). Holm Pedersen (2012), in a study of Iraqi families living in Denmark, found that well-educated Iraqi women could mobilize their middle-class identities (as event organizers, performers and knowledgeable members of the Iraqi diaspora) to recreate their previous social statuses, despite still occupying a lower-class position in Denmark. Şimşek (2020), in a later case study of Syrian refugees in Turkey, found that class (e.g., skills and financial resources) can help Syrians reach stability and security while they still lack full rights.

Some evidence suggests that government authorities can create obstacles for refugee livelihoods (K. Jacobsen 1996), sometimes compounding the identity and contextual factors discussed above. Some researchers have noted how camps often constitute the worst treatment of refugees by a state legitimated by fear of criminality and security threats, in addition to the fear of displacing workers, increasing worker precarity, and lowering wages (L. Turner 2015). Encampment is an effective policy to control labour market competition and further segregate refugees based on socio-economic classes. In a study of Syrian refugees in Lebanon and Jordan, Lewis Turner (2015) found that encampment of refugee populations contributes to class-based segregation and denial of opportunities essential to integration. Outside camps, refugee newcomers often live in low-income and racialized neighbourhoods with inadequate access to transportation and health-care facilities (Clarke et al. 2021). Others have argued that refugees attempt to overcome segregation and dependence to live complex economic lives – "refugee economies" (Betts et al. 2017).

The intersection between refugees' social class and integration can also contribute to a hierarchy of "class-based integration" (Ager and Strang 2008) favouring refugees with higher investments and skills. Şimşek, based on the experiences of Syrian refugees in Turkey, defines "class-based integration" as the "allocation of rights based on refugees' economic resources" (2020, 541), including labour market and citizenship rights. Refugees' economic resources also aid in creating effective and strong social bridges with members in the new society to overcome legal barriers to integration. The lack of such resources results in struggles to access the labour market, education, housing, and a sense of belonging.

16.2 Economic Contributions and Potential of Refugees

Jumpstart Refugee Talent, a refugee-led non-profit organization based in Toronto, focuses on facilitating economic empowerment for refugee newcomers in Canada by connecting skilled and talented refugees with investors who can support their economic integration (CBC News 2022c). In partnership with Angel Investors Ontario, an organization of investors who can provide capital and membership to start-ups across the province, the two organizations launched a program on World Refugee Day called, REinvest. REinvest aims to provide refugee entrepreneurs with basic funding assistance in industries such as e-commerce, textiles, food and beverage services, among others. This program addresses some of the integration challenges faced by refugee newcomers we have discussed in this chapter; namely, deskilling and underemployment, and inadequate access to education, health care, and housing.

One successful contestant was Amer Maamari, whose construction company, Done Right Inc., wants to address "the shortage of construction workers by offering a service that helps people who have recently come to Canada understand how the Canadian construction industry works" (CBC News 2022c, para. 12). In his pitch, Maamari shared his plan of expanding his business to "include an academy that would provide newcomers who are interested in construction with industry-specific English classes, onsite and online job training ..." equipping them with knowledge and language they need to enter the workforce (CBC News 2022c, para. 13). Amer Maamari shares the vision of many refugee newcomers in Canada who are immensely skillful and talented with creative ideas on how to strengthen the Canadian economy but integration is hindered due to systemic barriers.

THE ROLE OF CLASS IN REFUGEE ADMISSION TO CANADA

Since the early 2000s, traditional immigrant-receiving countries have been manipulating and managing migration movements (Delgado Wise and Marquez 2007; Skeldon 2008) with the aim of capitalist development. Governments in these countries view migration as a key policy tool to enhance global economic competitiveness and smooth the process of accumulating capital and commodity production for market exchange. Bonjour and Chauvin (2018) explain that immigration policies are avenues where interlocking systemic oppressions are upheld. Immigration and refugee admission policies function like filters, keeping unwanted migrants – voluntary or otherwise – away from borders and consequently from attaining legal status.

Immigrants are a vital source of labour to facilitate economic objectives, thereby commodifying labour through migration. This is further entrenched with a shift toward private interests to drive migration flows (Bhuyan et al. 2017; Z. Li and Lowe 2016), particularly the greater reliance on employers to identify future citizens. The global rise in neo-liberalism entrenches a global race for talent (Shachar 2006), often reducing migrants to economic terms of trade, negotiated to gain a comparative advantage in a global economy. In Canada, economic immigration is privileged in constant reference to total human capital gains (Reitz 2001). Human capital has long been regarded as one of the most decisive indicators of immigration candidates' long-standing ability of successful integration (Chiswick 1986; 2000; Dustmann and Fabbri 2003; Friedberg 2000). Overall, migration management favours those whose contributions to the economy outweigh their costs of settlement (Cossman and Fudge 2002; McLaughlin 2010; Sharma 2006).

The primary mechanism for governments to analyze the cost-benefit of potential applicants is a determination of human capital, which relies on a general assessment of skills. In the context of immigration, it would appear that "skill" is definable and distinguishable and presents a win-win for host countries and immigrants (Boucher 2020, 2533). While immigration selection may be based on skills and labour shortages, it is also "shaped by conception of national identity, race and postcolonial relations," as well as gender and sexuality (Bonjour and Chauvin 2018, 6). Research shows how skilled migration can function as discriminatory selection, regardless of whether this is an explicit policy goal, based on race/ethnicity (Shi 2004), class (Tannock 2011), and gender (Boucher 2016).

In the Canadian context, skill is evaluated using the National Occupational Classification, a standard taxonomy and framework to categorize occupational information using skill type (type of work performed with respect to education and field of study) and skill level (education and level of training). The logic of distinguishing among skills continues to shape Canada's immigration, and as we illustrate, increasingly the refugee regime. Two newer pathways apply a classed distinction to refugee selection in Canada: EMPP and Health-care workers permanent resident pathway. In both cases, skills become a proxy measure for class, distinguishing applicants by their means of production and contribution to the Canadian economy and society.

These new pathways must also be understood in the context of the ongoing COVID-19 pandemic. During emergency legislations, such as social distancing, lockdown, travel restrictions, and border closures to mitigate the spread of COVID-19 (Firang 2020), there was a 64 per cent decline in admissions under all immigration categories. The most notable changes were in family sponsorship and refugee intakes. Nonetheless, Canada was one of the few countries that continued to resettle refugees under emergency cases (Levitz 2020). Despite this, Canada did not fulfill the thirty thousand target by the end of 2020 (Levitz 2020) and only resettled over nine thousand refugees. As part of Canada's COVID-19 economic recovery, Immigration, Refugees and Citizenship Canada (IRCC) aims to admit more highly skilled immigrants in the health-care and technology sectors. These new pathways demonstrate how "class serves as an analytical connector" (Bonjour and Chauven 2018, 7) in the assessment of merit in refugee selection.

The EMPP was launched in April 2018 and identified ten to fifteen skilled refugees in the Middle East and East Africa to refer to provincial nominee programs (IRCC 2020b). Employers can also hire skilled refugees who meet the requirements of Canada's economic immigration programs, in partnership with refugee-serving partner organizations, and process permanent residency applications within six months (a much faster processing time). A second phase, started in December 2021, aimed to admit five hundred skilled refugees and their families. The current pandemic exposed extensive and troubling shortages in Canada's health-care sector, and the second EMPP pathway expedites refugee claims for persons who, in addition to meeting all other eligibility criteria, have worked a minimum number of hours in Canada's health-care sector during the pandemic and provided direct patient care as part of their job. The small numbers arriving under these new pathways signal that these are not intended to overtake the national and international humanitarian impetus driving refugee admissions. Nonetheless, the evolution of these pathways should warn us against wider shifts toward the commodification of refugees and Canada's efforts to combine "refugee resettlement and economic immigration" (IRCC 2020b), thereby emphasizing private interests (of employers).

UNDERSTANDING AND INVOKING CLASS IN REFUGEE SPONSORSHIP APPLICATIONS AND ADJUDICATION

In the previous section, we identified some recent examples of applying classed distinction to refugee selection in Canada. These newer pathways to permanent resident status for refugees reify class-based selection by choosing refugees based on skills and potential to serve private interests (employers). In this section, we identify the ways in which refugees' and claimants' class identities, performances, and practices are invoked in the claims and adjudication processes, with specific references to the use of Group of Five (G5) private sponsorship and stereotyping by the Immigration and Refugee Board (IRB).

As explored in greater detail in Labman, chapter 18, claimants with proof of refugee status determination (RSD) issued by the UNHCR or government of the country in which the refugee is residing (Elgersma 2015), can be named by private sponsors in Canada as privately sponsored refugees (PSRs) to qualify for resettlement and arrive with permanent residence status. Generally, PSRs are regarded as favourable, partially due to their stronger employment outcome (Edmonds and Flahault 2021). The class-based argument previously made for integration, whereby refugees with higher skills, investments, resources, and networks are favoured (Ager and Strang 2008; Franz 2003; Holm Pedersen 2012; Şimşek 2020), can be extended to private sponsors since they must demonstrate that they possess the skills and capital to settle refugees. For our examples in this section, we focus on G5 sponsors, who are a self-selected group required to have the necessary skills, resources, and supports (e.g., language ability, family size, levels of education, as well as family and social network connections) to qualify to sponsor a refugee. These criteria however can also be applied to Sponsorship Agreement Holders (SAHs) and community sponsors.

As discussed in Atak, chapter 17 and Labman, chapter 18, an important requirement for any PSR application is the ability of sponsors to support the settlement needs of the principal applicant (PA) and their dependents for at least one year upon arrival in Canada. For G5 sponsors this requirement involves detailing in the Sponsorship Undertaking and Settlement Plan (IMM 5670 form) how they plan to secure housing and support the medical, counselling, and/or special needs of refugees. In addition, G5 sponsors need to identify which group member(s) is responsible for meeting the settlement checklist in the IMM 5670 form, such as finding employment, arranging childcare, enrolling children in school, and connecting refugees with community activities and groups, among other things (Government of Canada 2019d).

When reviewing PSR applications, program officers are most concerned with the sponsors' capacity to provide income support to refugee(s). G5 members are expected to commit to at least $16,500 in income support and start-up costs to sponsor a refugee, which increases depending on the family size of the refugee(s) they want to help settle. While not all G5 members are expected to contribute their personal income to the cost of the sponsorship, those who agree must complete the Financial Profile (IMM 5373B form). This allows program officers to assess sponsors' financial capacity by reviewing their family size, employment history, and notice of assessment issued by the Canada Revenue Agency (Government of Canada 2019d). Based on the requirements outlined in the IMM 5670 and IMM 5373B forms, G5 sponsors must invoke their class privileges to show how they can meet the extensive settlement needs of sponsored refugee(s). Beyond income support, G5 sponsors must also draw on their social and cultural capital to exemplify their capacity to settle refugees, as the class identities of private sponsors – language fluency and level of education – and breadth of social networks can shape the integration outcomes for refugees (Hynie et al. 2019).

Applications for asylum claims are reviewed and adjudicated by the IRB (see Atak, chapter 17). A key part of the adjudication process is the hearing dedicated to critically evaluate "the credibility of the claimant as a member of a particular social group who has faced persecution in their country of origin" (Murray 2013, 128). Refugee claimants must learn quickly how to demonstrate a well-founded fear of persecution when making their claim; however, this is a subjective process. Claimants are positioned so that they seek to intentionally present themselves as the "depoliticized suffering subject incapable of action and necessitating rescue" (Mainwaring 2016, 290). Otherwise, they risk having their claims scrutinized and, at worst, being depicted as suspicious, resulting in rejection of their claims. Understanding how these assumptions operate is important, especially for racialized asylum seekers who face constrained choices when invoking their classed identities in specific ways to facilitate a successful outcome.

Throughout the IRB hearing procedure, asylum seekers are repeatedly reminded by lawyers and support workers that board members take a range of approaches to determine the authenticity of their personal narratives to adjudicate their claims (Holland 2018; Murray 2013). Due to colonial stereotypes that mark black and brown bodies in Western culture as poor and dangerous, racialized asylum seekers are sometimes read as suspicious, especially those coming from Arab nations (Gray and Franck 2019). Thus, to soften how black and brown bodies are read as criminals and potential terrorists in the political climate of "War on Terror," they might feel compelled to perform or project their poverty, vulnerability, and victimhood to be perceived as deserving migrants (M.-S. Abbas 2019; Mainwaring 2016; Wroe 2018). In other words, asylum seekers sometimes must conceal their class identities and privileges to circumvent suspicion and attain refugee status.

Ironically, even though asylum seekers are encouraged to tell their stories "in [their] own voice" (Murray 2013, 131), and in an unrestricted manner (Holland 2018), many claimants have expressed difficulty in sharing their narratives. The RSD process in Canada requires asylum seekers to follow a framework that "fits the parameters of a courtroom in which facts are elicited and tested" (Murray 2013, 131). These parameters include applicants' written statements. Some compare the process of completing the application forms and adjudication procedures to "studying for exams" (Murray 2013, 132).

It is important to note that refugees and asylum seekers are diverse individuals with unique circumstances and experiences of forced migration. While some may intentionally present themselves as poor, vulnerable, and victims of violence, it does not minimize their agency. Intentionally performing labels with vestiges of colonialism that are ascribed to refugees and asylum seekers demonstrates their awareness and capacity to negotiate borders and migration controls. Refugees and asylum seekers deploy various approaches, depending on their access to resources (e.g., financial, social, and cultural) and the information and opportunities presented to them. Choosing among "undesirable options under negative conditions does not negate the autonomy of the actors in making those decisions" (Showden 2011, 45). As Showden (2011) explains, the manifestations of agency are shaped by which aspect of one's positionality – class, gender, race/ethnicity, religion, sexual orientation – is made most salient in specific times and places.

CLASS-BASED INTEGRATION CHALLENGES FOR REFUGEES IN CANADA

So far, we have examined the class-inflected admission of refugees and adjudication of refugee claims. In this section, we explore some of the integration challenges refugees in Canada experience. DeVoretz, Pivnenko, and Beiser (2004) examine post-arrival economic outcomes of refugees and find that although the group sees a rapid increase in earnings over time, it is conditional on their region of origin. The most successful are from Europe in contrast to the lower economic outcomes of refugees from Africa and Southeast Asia. Incomes also vary by stream of refugees whereby PSRs have a 5 per cent increase in earnings as compared to a 20 per cent decline for in-Canada claimants and a 12 per cent decline for Government-Assisted Refugees (GARs) (DeVoretz, Pivnenko, and Beiser 2004, 14). Although PSRs have better employment outcomes (Edmonds and Flahault 2021) in contrast to GARs and Blended Visa Office-Referred refugees (BVORs), many of them are employed in precarious industries as essential or frontline workers. Refugees use employment insurance to a greater degree than economic migrants and their dependents (Edmonds and Flahault 2021). The complex and uneven nature of economic outcomes means that all refugees, regardless of stream of arrival, experience varied socio-economic inequalities, which have only been intensified by the COVID-19 pandemic.

During the pandemic, refugees awaiting resettlement or families anticipating reunification had to postpone their travel plans until Canada fully reopened its borders for "non-essential travellers." Some refugees who were outside Canada or those awaiting permanent resettlement in Canada were excluded from the benefits extended to citizens of their host countries. These benefits include access to health-care and social services, as well as education and employment opportunities that are crucial for human development (Lupieri 2021). The limited economic opportunities available to refugees who landed in Canada were often in industries such as manufacturing, where following health and safety measures is difficult (Clarke et al. 2021).

The need to continue to work because of economic circumstances put refugees at greater risk of exposure to COVID-19; however, due to this risk in combination with fear, stigma, and discrimination, they were less likely to "seek care for suspected COVID-19 symptoms" (Clarke et al. 2021, 185). The closure of community and religious centres, which provide newcomers with tools to integrate into Canadian society, also negatively impacted refugees' ability to connect with their local communities (Edmonds and Flahault 2021). Notably, GARs were severely affected because they lack the social support networks that can connect them to people, jobs, and resources (Hyndman and McLean 2006; Edmonds and Flahault 2021).

CONCLUSION

Despite the definitional dilemmas, class plays an integral role in shaping the social identities and positions of different groups of migrants. There is, however, limited understanding of classed identities and its implications in forced migration. This chapter is an exploration of how class is understood and invoked in refugee selection, adjudication, integration, and settlement, with specific examples from the Canadian context. Skills used as a proxy for class are becoming increasingly important in refugee selection, including new pathways created during the ongoing COVID-19 pandemic to select refugees based on their anticipated contributions to the Canadian economy and society. Additionally, class is invoked in complex ways in private sponsorship applications and hearings with the IRB. Class can be a privilege or obscured intentionally during IRB hearings to improve chances of success. Finally, class plays a vital role in shaping refugees' integration in the host country, including experiences of downward class mobility, enhancing access to rights and entitlements through improved employment outcomes and social networks. The importance of class was further entrenched during the recent pandemic with the increase in precarious work, exposure to COVID-19, and closure of community supports.

There is still much to learn about the significance of class in forced migration studies and the lived experiences of refugees and claimants. It is important to track the application success, integration, settlement, and outcomes for different groups of refugees. Refugee integration is a class journey, which should be understood in relation to their complex social identities, including gender, sexuality, race/ethnicity, disability, age, among other aspects. Given the dominance of capitalist-driven migration management, particularly the increasing role of private actors (employers, recruiters, agents, etc.), it will be important to account for the roles and impacts of various governmental and non-governmental actors in refugee selection and settlement. Moreover, there is a growing need to complement anecdotal and community-based evidence of biased IRB adjudication with further systematic analysis of decision-making. Cross-sectoral and multidisciplinary approaches will assist in better understanding refugee experiences that can be used toward evidence-based policy-making.

Finally, scholars and policy-makers should think deeply about the implications of class invocations in the refugee journey. Based on our limited discussion, an important caution is the increased relevance of class for refugee admissions and whether this signals a move away from humanitarianism – the original impetus of refugee systems nationally and internationally. Alternatively, such varied priorities and perspectives could be understood as a necessary alignment of the understanding of refugees and refugee regimes in the Global North and Global South. Forced migration studies based in the Global South encourages a deeper engagement with the precarity and fluidity of migration categories (P. Banerjee and Samaddar 2019). Improved understanding of the implications of class in the refugee journey might encourage a reimagining of the bifurcation of the Global North and Global South in forced migration studies more generally. Overall, we hope that this chapter argues convincingly for the need to pay more attention to class analyses in forced migration studies.

NOTE

We acknowledge that the lands on which we gather, think, and write, are the traditional and unceded territories of the Algonquin Nation (Amrita Hari), and the area known as Tkaronto (Romeo Joe Quintero) is the traditional territory of many nations including the Mississaugas of the Credit, the Anishnabeg, the Chippewa, the Haudenosaunee, and the Wendat peoples and is now home to many diverse First Nations, Inuit, and Métis peoples. We express gratitude to those whose lands we occupy and a continuous commitment to recognize the complex colonial relations we are embroiled in as immigrants in a settler colonial state and as scholars of migration, citizenship, and diaspora. We recognize that ways in which our presence on these lands upholds settler colonialism and reproduces dispossession and violence for Indigenous people. Through our work, we seek to reveal and better understand the relationship between (im)migration, Indigenous sovereignty, and settler colonialism.

FURTHER READING AND RESOURCES

De Volkskrant. 2012. *Refugee Republic*. Interactive transmedia documentary of Domiz Camp, a Syrian refugee camp in northern Iraq, intended to enrich understandings of everyday life in refugee camps. https://refugeerepublic.submarinechannel.com.

Nichles, Leah, and Sayre Nyce. 2018. "Towards Greater Visibility and Recruitment of Skilled Refugees." *Forced Migration Review* 58 (June). https://www.fmreview.org/economies/nichles-nyce.

Vico, Sanja. 2017. "Class Pervades the Way Migrants are Viewed in Britain." *The Conversation*, 28 March 2017. https://theconversation.com/class-pervades-the-way-migrants-are-viewed-in-britain-70174.

SECTION THREE

“Becoming” and Un-becoming a Refugee in Canada

17

Refugee Protection in Canada: A Comparison of Resettlement and Inland Asylum Systems

Idil Atak

KEY TAKEAWAYS

- Inland asylum has been developed as part of a legally binding framework as opposed to the humanitarian and voluntary nature of resettlement.
- Inland asylum and resettlement are governed by distinct sets of policy rules and processes. Inland asylum represents Canada's legal commitment to fulfilling its international legal obligations under the 1951 Convention Relating to the Status of Refugees. Resettlement is considered an instrument of "burden sharing" with countries hosting the majority of refugees.
- Inland and resettlement regimes share a function of migration management and population control.
- Refugee admission regimes are determined by geopolitical considerations and national and foreign policy interests as much as – if not more than – by humanitarianism and international legal obligations.

KEY TERMS

- Convention refugees
- Government-Assisted Refugees (GARs)
- Humanitarianism
- Inland asylum
- Private Sponsorship of Refugees (PSR)
- Resettlement
- Securitization

INTRODUCTION

Canada has a well-regarded and sophisticated refugee protection system. Inland asylum and resettlement are the two main avenues for refugee admission. Inland asylum involves claims for refugee protection made by foreign nationals, either at a port of entry when they arrive in Canada or at an inland office. The Immigration and Refugee Board of Canada (IRB), Canada's largest administrative tribunal, determines refugee status for inland asylum seekers. Resettlement can be defined as the "selection and transfer of refugees from a State in which they have sought protection to a third State which has agreed to admit them – as refugees – with permanent residence status" (UNHCR 1976, para. 3). Through resettlement, refugee claims are processed overseas. Not only the federal government but also private individuals, groups, and organizations can sponsor refugees. Resettlement programs are administered by the state's executive branch, namely by Immigration, Refugees and Citizenship Canada (IRCC).

This chapter adopts a comparative perspective to explore the nature and the implementation of Canada's refugee admission regimes. It discusses how refugee policy is often shaped by factors unrelated to international protection or humanitarianism, such as, geopolitical conjecture and domestic and foreign policy considerations. This process has deleterious implications for refugees' rights.

RESETTLEMENT

In the last decades, Canada has consistently been among the top resettlement countries in the world and globally known for its PSR program. In 1986 the people of Canada were awarded the Nansen medal by United Nations High Commissioner for Refugees (UNHCR) in recognition of "their major and sustained contribution" to the resettlement of some seventy thousand refugees from Vietnam, Laos, and Cambodia between 1975 and 1980 (CCR n.d.). As a response to the Syrian refugee emergency, Canada resettled more than forty thousand Syrians between 2015 and 2017 (Government of Canada 2020c). More recently, the Government of Canada (2021c) committed to resettle at least forty thousand Afghan refugees in Canada through several special programs and measures.

The Immigration and Refugee Protection Act (IRPA), entered into force in 2002, provides for three types of refugee sponsorship arrangements: government, private, and joint government/private sponsorship (IRPA 2001, s. 13(1), c. 27; see also, Immigration Act 1976–77, c. 52). These arrangements allow community and state resources to be matched to the needs of the sponsored refugees (Baglay and Jones 2017, 189).

GARs are selected by the federal government, usually on the basis of referrals from UNHCR. Resettlement in Canada is open to Convention refugees[1] who fall within the "Convention Refugees Abroad Class" (IRPR, 2002, s. 138) and to people who are outside their countries of nationality and habitual residence and in refugee-like situations, that is, those who are seriously and personally affected by civil war, armed conflict, or massive violation of human rights (IRPR 2002, s. 147). In addition, the federal government sponsors refugees under public policy considerations (Government of Canada 2023). To illustrate, about eight hundred of the Afghan interpreters for Canadian troops in Afghanistan, and their families, were resettled in Canada between 2009 and 2011 (G. Galloway 2018). In 2020 Canada included two hundred fifty refugee spaces to the GAR program to accommodate the creation of a new stream for human rights defenders (IRCC 2021c).

Through the RAP, GARs receive income support, and their basic needs (e.g., food, clothing, and shelter) are covered for typically up to twelve months. Assistance may be extended for an additional twelve months for special needs cases (Government of Canada 2022g, 19).

PSR (see also Labman, chapter 18) involves three types of groups: (i) Groups of Five (G5) or more Canadian citizens or permanent residents; (ii) Sponsorship Agreement Holders (SAH) are most commonly religious or ethnocultural organizations or other humanitarian agencies that have formal agreements with the federal government; and (iii) a constituent group is based in the sponsored refugee's expected community of settlement and works with an SAH (IRPA 2001, s. 13(1); IRPR 2002, s. 53(1)a). The majority of PSRs are supported by SAHs or by constituent groups (Hyndman, Payne, and Jimenez 2017). Sponsors can either "name" the individuals they wish to sponsor or accept a referral from a visa officer of an individual requiring sponsorship (Labman 2016, 69). Sponsors commit to providing the refugee with financial, emotional, social, and integration support and assistance for one year from the refugee's date of arrival in Canada (Government of Canada 2022g, 8). "Complementarity" and "additionality" are key concepts for private sponsorship. PSR is expected to expand refugee protection spaces available in Canada. As such, it complements the government's efforts toward refugee resettlement. Additionality refers to the supplemental nature of private sponsorship, which is not a replacement for publicly funded resettlement (Macklin and Blum 2021, 22).

Launched in 2013, the Blended Visa Office-Referred (BVOR) program allows UNHCR-referred refugees to be matched with a private sponsor. The BVOR program aims to accelerate the resettlement of referred refugees within one to four months. The federal government provides up to six months of income support, and private sponsors step in for another six months (Government of Canada 2022g, 13).

Canada also partners with organizations to resettle refugees with special needs via the Joint Assistance Sponsorship (JAS) program. This program supports those who have greater need of settlement assistance than other applicants owing to personal circumstances, including trauma from violence or torture and medical disabilities (IRPR 2002, s. 157(2)). Under JAS, the government and a private sponsor support refugees for up to twenty-four months, depending on the case, instead of twelve months. Finally, since 1978, students at universities across Canada have privately sponsored refugee students to attend Canadian universities through World University Service of Canada (WUSC).

Immigration, Refugees and Citizenship Canada (IRCC) administers Canada's resettlement program, based on an annual resettlement range established following consultations with provincial governments.[2] The decision to approve or reject a refugee applicant is made by a Canadian migration officer, who, after an interview in the applicant's country of residence, will determine whether the applicant meets Canadian eligibility and admissibility criteria. A medical examination and criminality and security screening must be carried out prior to issuance of an immigrant visa. An interpreter is provided by the Canadian government, if needed. However, refugee applicants are not eligible for state-funded legal aid and, as Pierre-André Thériault (2020, 229) notes, very few can afford or coordinate legal representation. An applicant who is refused abroad can seek leave for judicial review of the decision before the Federal Court of Canada. Refugees processed overseas are granted permanent resident status upon arrival in Canada. All resettled refugees, like other permanent residents, have the right to work and can benefit from settlement and integration services in the province or territory in which they reside.

INLAND ASYLUM

The inland asylum system was established to implement Canada's international legal obligations under the 1951 Convention Relating to the Status of Refugees (the Refugee Convention), which provides a status to persons who are outside their country because they have a well-founded fear of persecution on account of race, religion, nationality, membership of a particular social group, or political opinion (see also Young, chapter 3; Fynn Bruey and Fantauzzi, chapter 8). The Refugee Convention protects refugees' rights and sets forth the principles of non-penalization of refugees for irregular arrival (art. 31) and of non-refoulement, which prohibits deportation of individuals to places where they may face persecution or the substantial risk of torture or similar abuse (Refugee Convention 1951, art. 33(1); IRPA 2001, s. 115).

Canada ratified the Refugee Convention in 1969 and incorporated it into domestic law in 1973. Yet, until the 1980s, resettlement remained the main avenue for refugee admission into Canada (Baglay and Jones 2017, 11). According to Hathaway, in the early 1980s, the total inland intake of Convention refugees averaged well below one thousand persons per year (1988, 703). The inland asylum system was designed to handle only a small number of claims and did not provide due process to claimants. In fact, prior to 1989, the initial determination of whether an individual was a Convention refugee was conducted by public servants at the ministry of employment and immigration and did not include a hearing (C. Anderson 2010, 946–7).

As the number of refugees under UNHCR's mandate increased from nearly three million in 1974 to twelve million in 2001 and to twenty-one million three hundred thousand in 2021 (UNHCR n.d.c), more individuals sought international protection at Canadian borders or within Canada. This development has been accompanied with significant changes in the inland asylum system. The Canadian Charter of Rights and Freedoms (the charter), entered into force in 1982, has been instrumental in advancing constitutional protections for refugees, including procedural fairness. In *Singh v. Canada (Minister of Employment and Immigration)* (1985, 1 SCR 177), the Supreme Court of Canada (SCC) determined that the refugee determination process contravened claimants' right to life, liberty, and security of the persons, protected by section 7 of the charter. The SCC held that asylum seekers who are physically present in Canada are entitled to an opportunity to state their case in an oral hearing, and to know the case they have to meet where credibility is at issue. The *Singh* decision played an important role in the establishment, in 1989, of the IRB, where refugee claimants are entitled to a quasi-judicial oral hearing of their claims. The IRB is responsible for making well-reasoned decisions on immigration and refugee matters. It enjoys institutional and adjudicative independence.

As mentioned, refugee protection claims can be made either at a port of entry or at an inland office. At a port of entry, a Canada Border Services Agency (CBSA) officer decides whether the claim is eligible for referral to the IRB. At an inland office, it can be either a CBSA or an IRCC officer who decides on the claim's eligibility. Eligible claims are referred to the Refugee Protection Division (RPD) of the IRB for RSD (IRPA 2001, ss. 99–100). The RPD process revolves around assessing the credibility of oral testimonies and of documentary evidence submitted by the asylum seeker.

The CBSA investigates issues of admissibility to ensure that individuals who might pose a risk to Canada would not be granted protection. IRCC or the ministry of public safety have the right to intervene in any claim before the RPD to contest some aspect of the claimant's submissions (IRPA 2001, s. 170).

If the refugee claim is accepted by the RPD, the individual can remain in Canada as a refugee and apply for permanent residence six months after receiving refugee status. If the claim is rejected, or if the individual withdrew or abandoned the claim, the individual must leave Canada; otherwise, the CBSA will enforce the removal. Refused claimants can appeal the RPD decision to the Refugee Appeal Division (RAD) of the IRB (IRPA 2001, s. 110(1), s. 159.91). Furthermore, claimants who receive a negative decision from the RAD and those who do not have access to the RAD can file an application for leave and for judicial review of the RAD or RPD decision with the federal court (Atak et al. 2018). Asylum seekers are generally eligible for legal aid, although access to legal aid varies from province to province. They also benefit from other procedural rights, such as the right to an interpreter.

In addition to the establishment of the IRB in 1989, the enactment of IRPA in 2001 and the implementation of the RAD in 2012 are key milestones in RSD. Prior to IRPA, the only category of persons entitled to protection included those who fell under the definition of "Convention refugee." IRPA expanded the categories of persons entitled to refugee protection to include persons at risk of torture as defined in Article 1 of the UN Convention Against Torture and persons at risk of cruel and inhumane treatment upon deportation to their country of nationality or former habitual residence (IRPA 2001, s. 97(1)). To further reinforce the principle of non-refoulement, IRPA introduced the pre-removal risk assessment (PRRA), which allows any person in Canada to apply to an officer for assessment as to whether they would be at risk of persecution, torture, or other forms of cruel and inhumane treatment (Waldman 2021, 17–18).

Since 1989 significant changes have also been made to improve the IRB's decision-making, including members' appointment criteria and training. The IRB's work has been under scrutiny by refugee advocates, researchers, and practitioners. The IRB decision-making process is subject to quality assessments by independent experts. IRB members are assisted by a number of chairperson's guidelines that set out principles for adjudicating and managing cases. Litigation and advocacy in immigration and refugee matters have been part of the efforts to ensure better compliance from Canada with its international obligations (see for instance *De Guzman v. Canada (Minister of Citizenship and Immigration* 2005, FCJ no. 2219). In addition, as Zinn and Perryman argue, the charter had a positive impact on the refugee determination process (2013, 137). These factors led to the development of a sophisticated case law on matters such as refugeehood, exclusion, and the human rights of asylum seekers.

REFUGEE ADMISSION: A TOOL FOR MIGRATION MANAGEMENT

Although they pursue the same overarching objective, that is, offering protection to forced migrants, inland asylum and resettlement are governed by distinct sets of policy rules and processes. Inland asylum has been developed as part of a legally binding framework in which the IRB, a quasi-judicial independent administrative tribunal, plays a central role, whereas resettlement has been promoted as a way of showing solidarity with refugee-hosting countries and an instrument of international "burden sharing" (Milner 2021, 47). Resettlement is presented as a soft-law humanitarian instrument whereby the government's commitments to refugee protection are discretionary and voluntary. As Hashimoto notes, states have no legal obligation to resettle refugees, nor can a refugee claim a "right" to be resettled (2018, 165). By contrast, inland asylum flows from a state's international legal obligations under the 1951 Refugee Convention and its 1967 Protocol. Consequently, the rights afforded to refugees differ as well as popular and political support for the two regimes.

However, both regimes share a migration management function. Refugees are unique compared to other categories of migrants, since refugee protection is premised on forced rather than voluntary movement (see also Clark-Kazak, introduction to this volume). As well, from an ethical perspective, refugees have a stronger moral claim for admission than economic migrants (Carens 2013, 195–6). Nevertheless, although states are constrained by international refugee law, they continue to maintain sovereign power in deciding who can enter and stay in their territory and who should leave (see also Young, chapter 3). Refugee admission, like other migration policies, is considered to shape the boundaries of national membership and a process of social ordering. It fulfills several goals, such as maintaining the integrity of the refugee protection system, protecting national security and the health and safety of citizens, as well as promoting international justice and security (see for instance IRPA 2001, s. 3(2)).

Against this background, it should come as no surprise that Canada has used refugee admission selectively to balance these goals and, ultimately, as a way to manage migration and national membership. Both inland asylum and resettlement policies are determined by ideological orientations of the ruling political party, geopolitical considerations, and national and foreign policy interests as much as – if not more than – by humanitarianism and international legal obligations. Pratt highlights the importance of factors such as ideologies, economic and electoral imperatives, or the changing dynamics of international migration in the implementation of Canada's refugee system (2005, 148–9; see also Falconer 2019, 5). Similarly, Hathaway argues that "the Canadian policy of 'compassion with realism' toward refugees impliedly accepts the promotion of the Canadian national interest – domestic economic development – as the primary determinant of its refugee policy and strives to accommodate other concerns to the extent that they are not incompatible with that dominant focus" (1988, 683).

Relatedly, a defining feature of the refugee admission framework has been its inherently political nature. Dauvergne discusses how refugee law is "highly malleable and closely tied to shifting political winds. It has the appearance of law, but is changed so rapidly (either through amendment or policy shift) that its adherence to rule of law principles has been easily suspect" (2007, 541). In the remainder of the chapter, we further explore these characteristics of the inland asylum and resettlement regimes and how they have been used to exclude unwanted non-citizens.

A Highly Discretionary and Increasingly Privatized Resettlement Process

Resettlement remains relatively popular with the Canadian authorities and public (Hyndman, Payne, and Jimenez 2017), mainly because selection of refugees from overseas is perceived as a controlled and orderly process with states holding broad discretion to choose refugees who fit their interests (Bradley and Duin 2020, 76). Additionally, resettlement saves states from conducting individual RSD procedures upon arrival, which can be costly in financial and political terms (Hashimoto 2018, 182). Bradley and Duin (2020) contend that the rhetoric around refugee resettlement serves Canada to assert its identity and leadership in the international community. For example, they emphasize how the government's discourse on the resettlement of Syrian refugees in 2015–16 was characterized by affirmations of Canadian identity as compassionate and pro-diversity (2020, 84). According to Milner, similar reasons led Canada to commit "exporting" its private sponsorship program and offer other states technical expertise through the Global Refugee Sponsorship Initiative launched in December 2016 (2021, 43). Milner further notes that these initiatives were understood to be part of "Canada's re-engagement with multilateralism and the UN System under the Trudeau government, and an opportunity to enhance Canada's global reputation – both among refugee-hosting states in the global South and with other donor and resettlement countries in the global North" (2021, 54).

Despite this positive narrative, resettlement has a distinctly selective nature (Macklin and Blum 2021, 22; Kneebone and Macklin, 2021, 1080; Labman 2019, 4). It has been criticized for unfolding away from public and judicial scrutiny. Kneebone and Macklin note that the conceptualization of resettlement as a "demonstration of generosity" to the refugee and an "expression of solidarity" with other states contributes to the lack of transparency and external accountability for the resettlement process (2021, 1092). P.-A. Thériault's research exposes the opaqueness of resettlement decisions and the issues of procedural fairness. He observes that not only is visa officers' training in refugee law insufficient and inconsistent but also the decisions they render are often neither well reasoned nor publicly available (P.-A. Thériault 2021, 241). Moreover, unlike most inland refugee claimants, refused resettlement applicants do not have access to an appeal on the merits. Thériault finds that requests for reconsideration made directly to the visa office are unreliable. And refused applicants often lack the means to pursue judicial review before the Federal Court of Canada since they are not guaranteed access to legal aid or counsel (P.-A. Thériault 2021, 231).

These issues in resettlement process contradict the administrative law principles. As underlined by the SCC, "all decision-making powers have legal limits, derived from the enabling statute itself, the common or civil law or the Constitution"

(*Dunsmuir v. New Brunswick* [2008] 2008, SCC 9, para. 28). Written reasons for the administrative decisions tend to be required when an adverse decision would have a significant impact on an individual (*Canada (Minister of Citizenship and Immigration) v. Vavilov* 2019, SCC 65, para. 77). They demonstrate that the decision was made in a fair and lawful manner and shield against arbitrariness in the exercise of public power (*Canada (Minister of Citizenship and Immigration) v. Vavilov* 2019, SCC 65, para. 79). Additionally, the courts have a constitutional duty to ensure that public authorities do not overreach their lawful powers. In this context, judicial review should be accessible since it plays an important role in upholding the rule of law and in maintaining legislative supremacy (*Dunsmuir v. New Brunswick* [2008] 2008, SCC 9, para. 29–30).

Relatedly, Bradley and Duin posit that resettlement, particularly PSR, is shaped by personal networks, and resettlement places are not necessarily allocated to those with pressing protection needs (2020, 83). Hyndman, Payne, and Jimenez (2017) agree that a side effect of priority processing for Syrians in 2015–16 is that some refugees from protracted situations continue to languish in the backlog. These authors also point to the differential treatment of single men from Syria who were not selected for government sponsorship due to perceived security risks (Hyndman, Payne, and Jimenez 2017). Canadian policy has been denounced for prioritizing refugees with specific religious, regional, national, or social background over others. The slow processing of applications in Africa is a case in point (CCR 2016a). Similarly, Canada promised to resettle to the country some forty thousand refugees and vulnerable Afghans after the Taliban took over the government in August 2021. However, the process has been slow with only twenty-three thousand five hundred Afghans who have arrived in Canada as of November 2022 (Singer 2022).

17.1 Ibrahim Musa, founder of the Cuts for Kids Foundation, recalls: "I can remember the airplane, it was my first time on an airplane, we arrived in Ottawa in the middle of winter. We arrived in 2002 when it was a very dangerous time in Iraq, both at home and in Canada because people didn't really have a good outlook on Iraqis, there was a lot of stigma around Arabs in general" (quoted in Ali, 2020).

Although system inefficiencies and bureaucratic hurdles may play a role, differential treatment of refugees mostly stems from factors such as systemic racism, citizen pressure, foreign policy priorities, and security considerations (Fong and Saar 2022). The requirement that resettled refugees, except the most desperate cases, must demonstrate the ability to establish in Canada has been considered an attempt to save net costs (Oberman 2020, 704) and prioritize more affluent groups of refugees over others. G. Cameron and Labman highlight that private sponsorship is viewed as a way to increase refugee resettlement numbers while controlling the burden on the public purse and stimulating favourable public opinion (2020, 6). Looking at the resettlement of Syrian refugees, Bose contends that more than international humanitarian obligations, acceptance or rejection of refugees has to do with the general public's view of a potential refugee population and the electorate's view of the government's refugee policies (2022, 396). Empirical studies show that people arriving under the Private Sponsorship of Refugees (PSR) program achieve "slightly quicker self-sufficiency" and better economic integration than GARs during the first ten years in Canada, due to a complex set of pre- and post-resettlement factors (see for instance Kaida, Hou, and Stick 2020a, 1702). Private sponsorship is thus considered to translate into successful integration outcomes and more welcoming attitudes toward refugees (Bradley and Duin 2020, 79).

Positive public perception and economic and social factors may help with understanding the "intentional and significant reallocation of resettlement numbers from government to private citizens in the past decade" (Labman 2016, 71). The number of PSRs exceeded the number of GARs for the first time in 2013 (Hyndman, Payne, and Jimenez 2017). This trend challenges the main premise of private sponsorship, which is intended to be complementary and additional to the government-funded resettlement program. Overreliance on private refugee sponsorship has several deleterious implications. Research shows that the ability of private sponsors to nominate refugees for resettlement resulted in a disproportionate representation of relatives of previously resettled refugees in the pool of privately sponsored refugees. This so-called "echo effect" led to the private sponsorship program being used as a tool for family reunification (G. Cameron and Labman 2020, 7). According to Macklin and Blum, a significant number of privately sponsored refugees are selected on the basis of kinship with those already in Canada (2021, 23). Ilcan and Connoy argue that privatization of decision-making and transfer of public authority to private citizens and non-profits can normalize state neglect and shrink accountability (2021, 302). The emphasis on PSRs further reinforces the selectivity of the resettlement program, exacerbating the risk that refugees overseas who are the most in need of international protection are left behind. Privatization may also amplify some of the problems identified in relation to private sponsorship, such as promoting a refugee's overreliance and dependence on a sponsor and turning the program into a matter of charity (Labman 2016, 68).

The literature also points out that, contrary to popular belief, resettlement is not always an orderly and controlled migration management tool. In an empirical study conducted by Ritchie (2018), privately sponsored newcomer youth described their processes of relocation as haphazard, rife with uncertainties, and even chaotic. Ritchie concludes that the socio-historical struggles of migrant communities for resources, political recognition, and/or immigration status are often neglected in resettlement processes (2018, 671).

A Securitized Inland Asylum System

In the last decades, as the number of refugees has grown globally (see Clark-Kazak, introduction this volume), Canada has experienced an increase in inland asylum claims (Tomkinson 2018, 186). Irregular arrivals of asylum seekers are deemed a challenge to state sovereignty. They are typically met with public backlash and political opposition, particularly in cases of group arrivals (see Garnier, chapter 10). The above-mentioned positive developments in Canada's inland asylum system have paradoxically been accompanied by securitizing practices toward asylum seekers, such as increased immigration detention. The 9/11 terrorist attacks in the US amplified this trend, problematically linking asylum seekers to security threats and fraud.

A typical example is the treatment of nearly six hundred Tamil asylum seekers from Sri Lanka, who arrived irregularly in Canada aboard two boats in 2009 and 2010. The Conservative government (2006, 16) stigmatized the passengers as "terrorists," "migrant smugglers," and "bogus refugees." It suggested that the integrity of the immigration system was undermined by the costs of processing baseless claims made by the passengers. In an attempt to delegitimize their protection claims and to pit asylum seekers against resettled refugees, the minister of immigration said: "We must act to avoid a two-tier immigration system: one for immigrants who wait in line – often for years – to come to Canada, and another for those who use the asylum system, not for protection, but to try to get through the back door into Canada" (CIC News 2010). Several asylum seekers aboard the boats were criminally prosecuted. The government intervened in every passenger's refugee claim in an attempt to exclude them from refugee protection (Grant 2018). Moreover, IRPA was amended to deter future irregular arrivals. The changes include mandatory detention and elimination of procedural rights, such as the right of appeal, for asylum seekers who arrive in Canada irregularly, in a group, and with the help of a migrant smuggler.

Another case in point is the Canada–United States Safe Third Country Agreement (STCA), entered into force in 2004. According to this agreement, refugee protection claims must be made by asylum seekers in the *first* safe country – the US or Canada – they pass through. Most third country nationals in the US are thus barred from making an asylum claim in Canada (STCA 2004, art. 4.1; IRPA 2001, s. 101(1)(e)). The STCA applies to those presenting themselves at official ports of entry along the land border who, with some exception, are returned to the US. As a burden sharing instrument, the agreement aims to prevent and deter the secondary refugee movements between the US and Canada. However, it has been criticized by the Federal Court of Canada for exposing asylum seekers to arbitrary detention and the ensuing hardship and risks, including denial of access to a fair refugee process, in the US (*Canadian Council for Refugees v. Canada (Immigration, Refugees and Citizenship)* 2023, FC 770, para. 135 and 146). The bilateral agreement is also known to compound the vulnerability of asylum seekers by pushing them to cross the US-Canada land border irregularly, between official ports of entry. It illustrates the government's aim to deter the mobility of some groups of asylum seekers by limiting their access to international protection.

Foreign policy may also explain why the highly contentious agreement is still in force. By repealing the STCA, Canada would publicly acknowledge the US is not a safe country for refugees – arguably a risky diplomatic move. In a decision handed down on 16 June 2023, the SCC ruled that the legislative scheme implementing the STCA is not overbroad or grossly disproportionate and therefore accords with the principles of fundamental justice. The court notably underlined that "even assuming that claimants face real and not speculative risks of *refoulement* from the United States, the Canadian legislative scheme provides safety valves that guard against such risks" (*Canadian Council for Refugees v. Canada (Citizenship and Immigration)* 2023, SCC 17, para. 163). However, the SCC decided to send the challenge based on section 15 of the charter – i.e., women fearing gender-based persecution adversely affected by the legislative scheme – back to the federal court for determination (*Canadian Council for Refugees v. Canada (Citizenship and Immigration)* 2023, SCC 17, para. 173).

17.2 Ms Mustefa, an Ethiopian national, claimed refugee status at the port of entry in Saint-Bernard-de-Lacolle, Quebec, in April 2017. Her claim was deemed ineligible because of the STCA, and CBSA officers returned Ms Mustefa to the US where she was detained in solitary confinement.

> Ms. Mustefa describes her time in solitary confinement as "a terrifying, isolating and psychologically traumatic experience." Ms. Mustefa, who is Muslim, believes that she was fed pork, despite telling the guards she could not consume it for religious reasons. Ms. Mustefa describes skipping meals because she was unable to access appropriate food, and losing nearly 15 pounds. Ms. Mustefa also notes that after she was released from solitary confinement, she was detained alongside people who had criminal convictions. She explains the facility as "freezing cold" and states that they were not allowed to use blankets during the day. Ms. Mustefa states that she "felt scared, alone, and confused at all times" and that she "did not know when [she] would be released, if at all." (*Canadian Council for Refugees v. Canada [Immigration, Refugees and Citizenship]* 2023, FC 770, para. 96)

Canada's response to the unprecedented increase in refugee movements from the US following the election of former president Donald J. Trump in November 2016 exemplifies the central role of domestic policy considerations and foreign relations in refugee policy. More than fifty-nine thousand individuals irregularly crossed the Canada-US border to claim asylum in Canada between January 2017 and March 2020, when the international border was closed due to the COVID-19 pandemic. These movements have been perceived by the public as abuse of Canada's refugee system (Angus Reid Institute 2018). Increases in the number of asylum claims exacerbated the already overstretched administrative capacity of the IRB and contributed to a record-level backlog of cases in 2019. New asylum arrivals strained the capacity of reception and settlement services. As a result, tensions heightened between the federal and provincial governments. The Liberal federal government faced growing criticism from the Opposition in parliament for its border response (Atak, Alrob, and Ellis 2021). To tackle irregular crossings, the federal government heavily invested in border security (Government of Canada 2019b, 184). A new refugee ineligibility ground was added to IRPA in June 2019. It renders asylum seekers ineligible for protection in Canada if they have made a previous refugee claim in a country that Canada shares an information-sharing agreement with. Such agreements are currently in place with the US, Australia, the UK, and New Zealand (Budget Implementation Act 2019, s. 306). The existence of a refugee claim in another country is confirmed through information sharing with the immigration divisions in partner countries. This ineligibility ground applies regardless of whether a decision was ever made on the previous claim. Asylum seekers concerned only have access to a PRRA, a remedy that does not offer an efficient protection (Waldman, 2021).

These policy developments illustrate how refugee law has been used to deter and punish certain groups of asylum seekers. The special status of refugees in international law does not necessarily guarantee their fair access to protection when other domestic and foreign policy considerations are prioritized over legal obligations under the 1951 Refugee Convention.

CONCLUSION: PROSPECTS, RECOMMENDATIONS, AND FUTURE WORK

This chapter discusses Canada's refugee admission processes and some of the significant developments in resettlement and inland asylum. Our comparative analysis shows that both regimes have become exclusionary. The selective and discretionary nature of resettlement has been exacerbated by issues such as increased privatization and the prioritization of refugees from certain regions or backgrounds who are likely to achieve better economic and social integration. As well, authorities have limited access to international protection for some groups of asylum seekers, particularly those arriving irregularly and in a group in Canada. Restrictive refugee policies and practices have been shaped and rationalized by a number of factors (e.g., ideological orientation, security, foreign relations, and cost of processing applications) that are unrelated to humanitarianism or international refugee law. Despite the fundamental political and legal differences between resettlement and inland asylum, striking parallels exist between them in this respect.

There is a need to align the refugee policy with ethical and humanitarian imperatives. Canada should comply with its legal obligations under the Refugee Convention, notably the rule of non-penalization for irregular arrival and the principle of non-refoulement. A refugee reform should be undertaken to rescind the STCA and to end discriminatory policies based on asylum seekers' mode of arrival in Canada and their trajectory. Independent oversight mechanisms should be established to monitor and assess resettlement decision-making overseas and international agreements that Canada concluded to control migrants' identity and mobility. Transparency would enhance accountability for decision-makers.

Comparative studies on resettlement and inland asylum offer valuable insights into the rationales behind policy shifts and their systemic and human rights implications. However, such studies are scarce. More research should be conducted to highlight the risk of political trade-offs between the two regimes and challenge attempts to pit resettled refugees against asylum seekers (Macklin and Blum 2021, 22), in order to avoid the delegitimization of asylum seekers as undeserving compared to resettled refugees (Kneebone and Macklin 2021, 1082) and any reduction of space and resource allocation for inland asylum seekers (Bradley and Duin 2020, 75).

Authorities must not lose sight that resettlement and inland asylum are complementary. They are "in the first instance about saving lives and offering protection to the displaced and persecuted" (IRPA 2001, s. 3(2)). Refugee policy must strive for facilitating refugees' mobility to access asylum and effective protection of their rights and freedoms.

NOTES

1 A convention refugee is "a person who, by reason of a well-founded fear of persecution for reasons of race, religion, nationality, membership in a particular social group or political opinion, (a) is outside each of their countries of nationality and is unable or, by reason of that fear, unwilling to avail themself of the protection of each of those countries; or (b) not having a country of nationality, is outside the country of their former habitual residence and is unable or, by reason of that fear, unwilling to return to that country" (IRPA 2001, s. 96).

2 Refugees destined for Quebec fall under the Canada-Quebec Accord on immigration that regulates the division of responsibilities between Canada and Quebec regarding resettlement (see also Garnier, chapter 10).

FURTHER READING AND RESOURCES

Canadian Council for Refugees (CCR). n.d. "A Hundred Years of Immigration to Canada 1900–1999: A Chronology Focusing on Refugees and Discrimination." https://ccrweb.ca/en/issues/history.

Centre for Refugee Studies (CRS). 2020. "The Canadian Refugee Determination System." CRS Online Introduction to Refugee Studies. YouTube video, 28:18. https://www.youtube.com/watch?v=_nCc6vo7IXE.

FCJ Refugee Centre. 2023. "Overview of the Refugee Process in Canada." https://www.fcjrefugeecentre.org/our-programs/immigration-and-refugee-protection/canadas-refugee-process/summary-of-the-process.

UNHCR Canada. n.d. "Refugee Resettlement to Canada." https://www.unhcr.ca/in-canada/unhcr-role-resettlement/refugee-resettlement-canada.

18

Adding, Naming, Sustaining, and Spreading: Canada's Private Sponsorship of Refugees Program

Shauna Labman

KEY TAKEAWAYS

- Private Sponsorship of Refugees (PSR) enables Canadian citizens and permanent residents to resettle refugees to Canada beyond the commitment of the Canadian government.
- The core principles of sponsorship are additionality (bringing refugees to Canada in addition to those resettled by the Canadian government) and naming (the ability to name specific refugees to sponsor).
- Sponsorship is both a celebrated and successful program of resettlement and one that raises tensions between sponsors and the government.
- Canada is now leading efforts to support sponsorship models in other countries.
- It is important to understand sponsorship in relation to government resettlement and asylum and consider sponsorship from the perspective of Indigenous reconciliation.

KEY TERMS

- Additionality
- Naming
- Government-Assisted Refugees (GAR)
- Private Sponsorship of Refugees (PSR)
- Blended Visa Office-Referred (BVOR)
- Sponsorship Agreement Holder (SAH)
- Group of Five (G5)

INTRODUCTION

18.1 When the town of Qualicum Beach (population 9,000) on Vancouver Island, BC put out a call for ideas on what to do with a vacant former RCMP station, local resident Chris Ferris proposed that it house a refugee family. The idea was approved at a town meeting and a private sponsorship group was formed. Seven months later, a Burmese family arrived.

"The Burmese refugee family of Karen ethnicity had spent 20 years living at Mae La refugee camp in Thailand. The children aged four to 16 were all born inside the camp."

Waiting at the airport, Chris said, "I feel apprehensive, nervous, excited and curious about what will happen next and concerned for the family that this will be such an overwhelming process for them."

The sponsorship group had plans for language training, school for the children and job offers at a Thai restaurant and on a farm. (Lovgreen 2016, n.p.)

The PSR program enables Canadian citizens and permanent residents to sponsor refugees for resettlement to Canada and support their settlement for their first year. Over three hundred twenty-five thousand refugees have been resettled to Canada through this program (Government of Canada 2019c).

Canada's model of refugee sponsorship commenced from an awareness that more could and should be done in Canada to offer protection to refugees. Canadians knew of refugees in need of protection, primarily because of religious and cultural ties, and sought ways to help. Kelley and Trebilcock (2010, 203–4) trace this citizen support back to the interwar period. At first, this was the result of direct advocacy, mobilization, and negotiation, some successful, some not, to welcome those in need to Canada. G. Cameron (2021) details how religious groups mobilized before and after World War II in establishing the nascent conceptions of private sponsorship in Canada. These preliminary efforts laid the groundwork for the formal program of refugee sponsorship introduced into Canadian law in 1976. The Immigration Act of 1976 came into effect in 1978. Canada had become a State Party to the 1951 Convention Relating to the Status of Refugees in 1969, and the 1976 Immigration Act was the first Canadian legislation to consequently recognize refugees as an immigrant class and outline processes for their admission. In addition to an asylum route, this was the formalization of Canada's dual refugee resettlement response: a government resettlement program (GAR) and a citizen-sponsored resettlement program (PSR).

By this point, sponsorship was already recognized by those drafting the new immigration law as "a historical aspect of Canada's refugee resettlement programs" (G. Cameron 2021, 138). The introduction of Canada's program coincided with flows of people out of Vietnam, Laos, and Cambodia. The newly introduced sponsorship provisions gave Canadians a direct means of action in response to the needs for protection they were seeing on the news. By the end of 1979, 5,456 sponsorships had been received for 29,269 refugees (Molloy et al. 2017, 79). The response of sponsors in this first major moment of Canada's PSR program created the necessary engagement of Canadians to sustain the program moving forward (Stobbe 2022). Primarily this was through the creation of SAHs (originally "Master Agreements") that established umbrella agreements between the Canadian government and established organizations that sought to do ongoing sponsorship (Molloy et al. 2017, 75).

Individuals cannot sponsor on their own and are required to form groups. There are now four different types of sponsorship groups:

- SAHs are incorporated organizations that have signed an agreement with the Government of Canada to sponsor refugees for resettlement to Canada. There are currently over 120 SAHs across Canada.
- Constituent groups may partner with SAHs to sponsor refugees under the SAH agreement.
- Community sponsors are organizations, associations, or corporations that sponsor refugees. Community sponsors do not have to be incorporated but must exist as a legal entity.
- G5s are groups of five or more Canadian citizens and/or permanent residents who sponsor refugees to settle in their communities.

Refugee sponsorship is considered to play three roles: creating additional spaces for resettlement, shifting the costs from the government to vested individuals, and generating personal connections with corresponding positive public opinion toward refugees and Canada's responses to forced migration (G. Cameron 2021, 6). It has been noted that Canada's success in private sponsorship reflects the meeting of strong political leadership and policy in place, engaged civil society, and attentive media coverage (Alboim 2016). The sponsorship commitment is for the first twelve months of a refugee's settlement in Canada.

It is important to recognize that the labelling of the program as "private" is a misnomer. Responsibility for the refugees is not entirely displaced onto the private responsibility of the sponsors. The Canadian government still bears costs in the operation and oversight of the sponsorship stream, the review of sponsorship applications, and funds the Refugee Sponsorship Training Program (RSTP), which is designed to provide support, training, and resources to sponsors and those interested in sponsoring (see also Araya, chapter 9). In addition, regardless of their arrival route, all refugees have access to health care, language lessons, and employment training services funded through the government. In a 2016 evaluation of its resettlement programs, the government concluded that the "unit cost" per program was decreasing for private sponsorship and increasing for government resettlement (IRCC 2016, s. 6.1). It is also important to note that in the province of Quebec the program is known as *parrainage collectif*, which translates the idea of collective action (Blain et al. 2019; see also Garnier, chapter 10 for an explanation of the unique features of the program in Quebec).

KEY PSR PRINCIPLES: ADDITIONALITY AND NAMING

From the perspective of the sponsorship community, the program is founded on the core principles of "additionality" and "naming" (RSTP 2013, 28). Additionality captures the importance that sponsorship admissions are *in addition to* government resettlement and not in lieu of or a replacement for GAR admissions. From the outset, the relationship between Canadian sponsors and the government has been a balancing of co-operation and concern over the preservation of additionality (Labman 2019, 91). While reiterations of the importance of additionality are central to sponsors' conceptions of their contribution, it is not clear there is government consensus on point. In the 2016 government evaluation of resettlement programs, it is noted "the principle of additionality is not part of the PSR program theory" (IRCC 2016, s. 4.2.2.).

Naming represents the idea that sponsors can identify the specific refugees they intend to resettle. Unlike government resettlement, where referrals of those in need of resettlement come primarily from the United Nations High Commissioner for Refugees (UNHCR), with sponsorship, the sponsors themselves can provide the referral and specifically name those they wish to sponsor. This process of sponsor referral leads to several consequences. It is an incentive to sponsor. Individuals and groups in Canada are motivated to assist those they know personally or indirectly though family, friends, religious and ethnic groups, and other shared identities or associations. The early incarnations of sponsorship arose out of these known connections to those in need of resettlement. This associational tie also leads to an "echo effect" or "relational migration" (Denton 2011) whereby sponsored refugees arrive knowing of others in need of sponsorship. While it is difficult to pinpoint the extent of naming, in a survey of 530 private sponsors of Syrian refugees where the clear majority (80 per cent) were first-time sponsors, almost 60 per cent responded that they had been asked by the refugees they sponsored to do further named sponsorships for extended family (Labman and Hyndman 2019).

Naming has also translated into a sustainable community of refugee sponsors in Canada advocating for refugee resettlement. While distant refugees often struggle to have their plight heard and responded to, sponsors are on the ground in Canada advocating. The Canadian government acknowledges: "It is thanks to the efforts of private sponsors and the support of thousands of volunteers that Canada's Private Sponsorship of Refugees Program continues to be a success" (Government of Canada 2019c). The capacity of sponsors to support the government's fulfillment of resettlement promises has, from the outset, also given sponsors a direct influence in government resettlement policies (Lehr and Dyck 2020, 45). In analyzing data from interviews with sponsors who had engaged in sponsorship over many years, Hyndman et al. regard sponsorship as "a *practice*, a routine action that is part of a commitment to community and others" (2021, 4). They suggest: "Without repeat volunteers who enact this community practice year after year, the private refugee sponsorship program would be unsustainable and collapse" (11).

While both the stability and sustainability of sponsorship in Canada has been intrinsically tied to naming, there are also tensions that result from it. Sponsorship interest sometimes surpasses processing capacity leading to long wait times (CCR 2016d, 2). The potential of the program to enable extended family reunification through naming has been viewed to diminish the protection focus of the program (Labman 2019, 94–5; Cortinovis and Fallone 2022, 25). At times these challenges have combined with high rejection rates of sponsorship applications and an overall processing backlog frustration. In 2012 the government identified the following issues:

> Low approval rates, large inventories and long processing times in the Private Sponsorship of Refugees Program (PSRP) have reduced the efficiency of the program and detracted from its original objectives of expanding Canada's refugee protection capacity and engaging civil society in resettlement ... As the PSRP evolved, it came to be used by sponsors as a means to reunite families in Canada. This understandable but unintended driver has contributed substantially to these program inefficiencies. Overwhelming demand combined with the lack of an effective application intake control mechanism has had an adverse impact on the quality of applications and added to growing backlogs and long wait times. (Government of Canada 2012a)

And yet government efforts to address these challenges led to new frustrations.

In 2011 and 2012 the government introduced caps on the number of sponsorship submissions by SAHs and added a requirement that limited sponsorship for G5s and community sponsors to refugees with recognized status by UNHCR or a state. These moves drew significant criticism, which increased during efforts to resettle Syrian and Afghan refugees in 2015 onward (CCR 2012, 2016d). At issue is that the status requirement unnecessarily creates obstacles to sponsorship in situations where it is clear the refugee definition would apply, but there is no access to a status determination (Van Haren 2021). The Canadian government did temporarily lift the requirement for Iraqis and Syrians from September 2015 for one year with a later extension for a further

Figure 18.1 | Seven keys to protecting and welcoming refugees and newcomers: a vision for Canada.

year (IRCC 2016). Balasundaram et al.'s 2022 report "Access Denied" details the growing criticism of the requirement and argues that the status requirement "impedes the resettlement of Afghan refugees by forcing refugees to wait prolonged periods of time to receive status designation, thereby increasing the prospect of refoulement in direct contravention of Canada's international obligations under the Refugee Convention" (23). The counter-argument from the government is that the status requirement does not apply to sponsorship through SAHs so routes to resettlement remain open to these refugees.

Canada has long been commended for the global reach of its resettlement program with its attentiveness to both referrals from UNHCR and other agencies in addition to the targeted interests of private sponsors. But naming also speaks to the selectivity of sponsorship. A refugee must be known to be named. As a complementary program alongside government resettlement, this is an additional protection pathway where selection is limited to those known refugees alongside government resettlement where selection is premised on protection referrals. Yet both sponsorship and government resettlement operate within a global migration context where those in need of protection far outnumber the resettlement response. There is a significant "gap" between those identified to need resettlement and those who ultimately receive resettlement (Solf and Rehberg 2021).

From a global perspective, refugee resettlement has never been the solution for more than 1 per cent of the overall refugee population (Kelley 2022, part 1). UNHCR resettlement referrals, which are the primary referral route of government resettlement to Canada, are premised on a prioritization of needs from UNHCR's submission categories of legal and/or physical protection, survivors of torture and/or violence, medical needs, women and girls at risk, family reunification, children and adolescents at risk, and lack of foreseeable alternative durable solutions (UNHCR 2011, 243). Sponsorship permits Canadians to focus on protection need in connection to extended family, friends, neighbours, and affinity groups such as nationality, ethnicity, religion, or identity. Hynie et al. (2019) conducted a longitudinal study of almost two thousand Syrian refugees arriving to Canada in 2016–17 as both GARs and PSRs. Their study showed that Syrians resettled to Canada through the government program had waited in a circumstance of displacement in a country of asylum for almost twice as long as privately sponsored Syrians. Moreover, while three-quarters of the privately sponsored refugees in their sample were Christian, almost all the GARs were Muslim. The researchers here point to an established Syrian Christian community in Canada that was active in the Syrian sponsorship (Hynie et al. 2019, 46).

A DECADE OF NEW DEVELOPMENTS

In 2013 a new resettlement stream was created, the BVOR program. As the name suggests, this program is a blend of government resettlement and private sponsorship. Settlement support is shared between the government and private sponsors with each covering six months of financial support (Labman and Pearlman 2018). Beyond the lessened financial commitment, BVOR referrals of refugees to be resettled come from Canadian visa offices as opposed to being named by the sponsors. While it was always possible in the PSR program to sponsor unknown refugees by way of visa office referrals, the incentive of naming known refugees tended to dominate. The BVOR program was introduced, after various similarly styled pilot programs, to a mixed reception and some doubts as to its potential success (Labman 2016, 69). I have argued elsewhere that the challenge of the model is that it requires sponsors to sacrifice the principle of naming and blurs understandings of additionality (Labman 2016, 72–3).

The BVOR stream was presented as a cost-saving mechanism. The government reduced their resettlement commitments and shifted these to both the PSR and BVOR streams (IRCC 2021b, 19). Initial criticisms pointed to the recurring concern that the government was again off-loading resettlement responsibility onto private sponsors and skepticism that sponsors would embrace a program that removed their selection authority (Labman 2016). A 2021 program evaluation notes "a lack of foundational documents articulating program objectives and aligning the BVOR program with the broader resettlement program" (IRCC 2021b, 41). Although not presented to specifically curtail the use of sponsorship for family reunification, the BVOR program was introduced near the same time that the governing Conservative Party signalled they were tightening regulations in the separate family class immigration stream (D. Black 2013). Hyndman et al. have suggested that "[t]he Canadian government under PM Harper determined that this informal process of family reunification through private sponsorship was fraudulent" (2019, 20). From the perspective of UNHCR, "[w]ithout the opportunity to reunite with family members, resettlement runs the risk of not being a meaningful, durable and sustainable solution" (2011, 269).

For much of its approaching half-century of operation, Canada's sponsorship program was a unique model of resettlement that garnered little outside interest or attention. In recent years, the Canadian government has worked to promote the adoption of sponsorship models in other states. The Global Refugee Sponsorship Initiative (GRSI), which began in 2016, is the result of a partnership between the Government of Canada, UNHCR, the Open Society Foundations, the Giustra Foundation, the Shapiro Foundation, and the University of Ottawa Refugee Hub. The aim of the initiative is to work with states and civil society to support the growth of sponsorship programs. It has also positioned Canada as a humanitarian leader on the international migration stage (Rae 2020). C. Smith has described the initial ambition to export Canada's sponsorship model as "a supply-side attempt at policy transfer in the face of weak demand" while Europe was in the midst of significant asylum flows, which caused GRSI to turn instead to "to low-stakes capacity-building" (2020, 288). Conversely, Bond (who is the co-founder and chair of the GRSI) and Kwadrans point to "growing global interest in community sponsorship programs" (2019, 87). Canada worked to include GRSI in the Global Compact on Refugees, which was adopted by the United Nations in 2018. The discussion of complementary pathways in the compact includes "private or community sponsorship programmes that are additional to regular resettlement, including community-based programmes promoted through the Global Refugee Sponsorship Initiative (GRSI)" (UN 2018, s. 3.3). There is a lack of clarity and agreement on defining community sponsorship or on precisely how these initiatives "straddle" resettlement and complementary pathways (Tan 2021, 2).

Several states have now introduced sponsorship initiatives in various forms, marking what Tan describes as "the rapid rise of the concept and range of objectives and modalities across jurisdictions" (2021, 4). These varying programs tend to focus on civil society integration support with a model that more closely resembles Canada's BVOR program than the naming capacity so central to the Canadian sponsorship program. In examining global resettlement outcomes between 2018 and 2020, M. Anderson and Slaughter caution, "it is important that we understand and grapple with the degree to which various complementary pathways actually complement resettlement and the degree to which many of them compete with it instead" (2021, 22). Again, the question of additionality is central. Moving forward it will also be important to examine the numeric expansion of sponsorship spaces relative to the cost and efforts put into the GRSI.

18.2 Global Refugee Sponsor Initiative. 2020. "Community Sponsorship: A Growing Worldwide Movement." YouTube video, 3:17. https://youtube.com/watch?v=OXnixYBse-Y.

Canada's sponsorship program grew somewhat organically at a time when Canada's commitment to resettlement was tied to the fact that it did not see itself as a country of first asylum for large numbers of refugees (H. Cameron 2020; Labman 2019, 39–41). Current sponsorship models are conversely developing as refugee numbers and the needs for asylum soar (UNHCR 2022c). The question of additionality arises in these contexts in relation not only to government resettlement but also to asylum access.

Even in the Canadian context, the welcome Canadians offer sponsored and government resettled refugees can be contrasted by both the state and public response to asylum seekers and other arrivals, which is too often unwelcoming, suspicious, and exclusionary (see also Atak, chapter 17). This history spans early twentieth-century Chinese exclusion, the denial of entry to Sikhs on the *Komagata Maru*, Japanese internment, and the refusal of Jews during World War II, as well as more recent responses to boats arriving on the east and west coasts of Canada, the Safe Third Country Agreement (STCA), and multiple other policies, regulations, and laws that work to create obstacles to asylum in Canada (Labman and Liew 2019). While sponsorship brings Canadians into the humanitarian project of welcoming refugees, it remains a select welcome.

WHAT DOES IT MEAN TO WELCOME?

In 2017 the prime minister of Canada tweeted "[t]o those fleeing persecution, terror & war, Canadians will welcome you, regardless of your faith. Diversity is our strength #Welcome to Canada." The Canadian government used "#WelcomeRefugees" on its website to detail its Operation Syrian Refugees from 2015 to 2017. But what does it mean to welcome, particularly when this work is not being done by the state, but by private citizens?

Increasingly, research examines how sponsorship works by engaging Canadians not only in the settlement and integration of refugees but also conceptualizations of Canadian identity and citizenship. Haugen, Lenard, and Wills observe:

> Sponsors support newcomers in navigating the education and health care systems, certainly, but they also impart norms and expectations with respect to behaviours, for example, about the use of the word "sorry", the importance of showing up on time for medical appointments, and when to shake hands or hug those whom one meets in public spaces. In so doing, they are, in effect, "creating Canadians." (2020, 561)

Macklin et al. ask, "does refugee sponsorship figure in the civic imagination of sponsors, and the way they see themselves as citizens," and whether sponsors "understand themselves to be engaging in a process of 'Canadianizing' refugees in a national context" (2018, 38–9). Yet these questions exist alongside the necessary recognition of Canada as a settler colonial state established by way of Indigenous displacement (see Coburn, chapter 1). Adese and Phung therefore state: "The question of Canadian citizenship, then, is somewhat of an 'elephant in the room' in this discussion, whereby Canadian citizenship has been a mark of colonization for Indigenous peoples, while for refugees the possibility of eventual Canadian citizenship appears to promise safety and security" (2021, 120). Bauder and Breen bluntly argue that "the Canadian state has made a commitment to reconciliation with Indigenous peoples and the decolonization of Canadian institutions and laws. However, one of the main instruments of settler colonialism – immigration policy – remains largely untouched by these efforts" (2023, 370).

How is the understanding of this work of reconciliation and decolonization achieved when shifted from the state to individual sponsors? Phung, in her work with Adese, notes that her family came to Canada as refugees through the sponsorship program following the Vietnam War (Adese and Phung 2021, 125). These authors recognize that "the notion of 'resettlement' [is] something that very clearly evokes the language of settlement that has been the hallmark of the colonization of Indigenous peoples" (Adese and Phung 2021, 128). There is an increasingly recognized and troubling contrast between Canada's "record of enduring humanitarian practices, but also an underbelly of racialized exclusion, settler colonial violence, and selective, prejudicial policies in relation to newcomers" (Reynolds and Hyndman 2021, 23). Yet as J. Young explores in chapter 3 the imposition and contestation of borders is central to both Indigenous and refugee claims. In 2018 the Canadian Council of Refugees (CCR) asked member organizations and allies to share "initiatives, practices and resources" to build bridges with Indigenous communities. This work continues.

18.3 Canadian Council for Refugees (CCR). 2018. "Building Bridges with Indigenous Communities." https://ccrweb.ca/en/indigenous.

LOOKING FORWARD

There is a clear shifting preference for sponsorship capacity over government resettlement. Sponsors themselves want the spaces but also continue to emphasize that their efforts are "in addition to" and not "in lieu of" government resettlement. Successive Canadian governments (both Liberal and

Conservative) are attracted to sponsorship for the expanded international contribution to Canada's humanitarian efforts but also the cost reductions in a citizen-subsidized program. There are also integration benefits from the hands-on settlement support of sponsors (Lu, Gure, and Frenette 2020).

A significant increase in sponsorship began with Canada's response to the Syrian crisis commencing in 2015 with sponsorship numbers swiftly quadrupling in size. A 2021 internal government audit of the program notes that "[w]ith this significant growth, the program has experienced an increase of observed integrity concerns, shortfalls in supports provided to refugees post-arrival (example, income support, adequate housing), fraud (example, use of falsified financial or identify documents) and cases of exploitation (example, sponsors requiring refugees to self-fund or pay to be sponsored)" (IRCC 2022b). However, the report further notes how the government had moved from a "reactive" to "proactive" response. What is clear is that as numbers shift, so must the government's response and supports. Moreover, sponsors must be equipped with resources to help understand, and help those they sponsor understand, Indigenous colonization and displacement and how to work toward reconciliation.

At the time of writing, private sponsorship sits at an all-time high in Canada. Canada's announced Immigration Level Plans for 2023–25 allow for increased permanent resident admission targets reaching five hundred thousand by 2025 (IRCC 2022c). Total resettlement targets are set at historically high levels surpassing any previous yearly admissions, including celebrated years of Indochinese and Syrian admissions. Canada's targets mark an overall increase in resettlement numbers, both numerically and as a percentage of overall permanent resident admission from past years. Within these plans, however, government resettlement is being reduced over the three-year span, and the government's effort to shift the sponsorship program away from the principle of naming through the BVOR stream is close to abandoned with a target of only two hundred fifty admissions a year and no set low range. Taken as a whole, the composition of these resettlement admissions between GAR, PSR, and BVOR places government admissions at a historical low, BVOR at a negligent percentage point, and private sponsorship dominating admissions. If additionality is viewed as meaning "*in addition* to at least the same number of refugees supported by the federal government for resettlement" (Hynie et al. 2019, 44–5), this core principle of the program has been compromised as sponsors are far surpassing, not merely matching, government resettlement. However, if considered more broadly as creating additional admission space, then larger sponsorship numbers are not problematic so long as the government commitment does not diminish.

FURTHER READING AND RESOURCES

Global Refugee Sponsorship Initiative. 2023. https://refugeesponsorship.org.

Horlor, Sean, and Steve J. Adams, dir. 2021. *Someone Like Me.* National Film Board of Canada. Film, 79 min.

Kaida, Lisa, Feng Hou, and Max Stick. 2020. "Analytical Studies Branch Research Paper Series, The Long-Term Economic Outcomes of Refugee Private Sponsorship 2020." Government of Canada. https://www150.statcan.gc.ca/n1/pub/11f0019m/11f0019m2019021-eng.htm.

Pauls, Karen. 2019. "Canada's Private Refugee Sponsorship Program Turns 40: Friendships Forged by Vietnam War Endure." CBC News. https://www.cbc.ca/news/canada/manitoba/mennonites-vietnam-boat-people-private-sponsorship-1.5038385.

19

Negotiating Citizenship: Securing Permanence?

David Moffette

KEY TAKEAWAYS

- Citizenship is a polysemic concept open to extensive theoretical and political debates.
- Conceptions of citizenship that decouple it from state-issued legal status (such as Indigenous citizenship or "acts of citizenship") help make sense of claims to rights and political participation at other scales.
- Citizenship as a statist legal category is rooted in a politics of conditionality.
- Conditional and unequal access to the protection of citizenship manifest in the multiplication of precarious temporary residence permits, the suspicion that informs citizenship tests, and the possibility of citizenship revocation.

KEY TERMS

- Acts of citizenship
- Citizenship
- Conditionality
- Inclusion/exclusion
- Precarious non-citizenship

INTRODUCTION

Citizenship is a polysemic concept that refers to membership to a political community, but beyond this basic shared definition, the meanings of citizenship are highly contested. Indeed, there are extensive theoretical and political debates about the nature and forms of this membership. Depending on the approach, citizenship may describe a state-issued formal status, or dispersed prefigurative political acts, insist on rights or duties, and promote minimal or deep forms of belonging and allegiance (Isin and Turner 2002).

Citizenship is most commonly understood in everyday life as synonymous to nationality: being a Canadian citizen means travelling on a Canadian passport, being able to vote, having the (almost) undeniable right to enter and stay in the country. This is a very state-centric conception, but it is one that profoundly organizes the world in which we live. For migrants, becoming a citizen means – at least in theory – becoming a legal equal, securing the ability to stay, and acquiring the right to sponsor family members. It represents the promise of full membership and, as such, it is seen as a very important asset by most people.

Citizenship as status is also intrinsically linked to political sovereignty and is thus jealously guarded by the state. Assertions of alternative citizenship by Indigenous nations are seen with suspicion by state actors (Blackburn 2009; D. Lee and Horn-Miller 2018). Many states forbid dual citizenship, and in countries that allow it, dual citizens can in some circumstances be stripped of their citizenship, either because of individual actions deemed "disloyal" or "fraudulent" or because of their framing as "enemy aliens" whose allegiance in times of war is not trusted (D.A. Martin and Hailbronner 2008; Macklin 2014).

In this chapter, I explore various questions that citizenship raises for the field of forced migration studies. In the first section, I start by distinguishing the liberal and republican historical conceptions of citizenship and tracing their genealogies to this day. I also distinguish between citizenship as status and its connection to state sovereignty and approaches that focus on practices or acts of citizenship. The second section delves more directly into the field of migration and citizenship studies to locate the importance of citizenship in a context where immigration policies favour conditional temporary permits that sustain a continuum of "precarious noncitizenship" (Goldring and Landolt 2013). In this context, access to citizenship is also highly conditional and informed by notions of deservedness. The third section explores this by presenting the debates surrounding citizenship tests. Finally, the fourth section reveals that a politics of suspicion continues to follow some immigrants or children of immigrants who, when they are dual citizens, can in some cases be stripped of one of their citizenships as individual or collective "enemy aliens."

THEORIES OF CITIZENSHIP: STATUS, PARTICIPATION, ACTS

While citizenship is an "essentially contested concept" (Gallie 1956), it is useful to start with a definition that provides the terms of the debates. For this purpose, I define citizenship as a passive and active membership in a political community that is attached to certain notions of equality and balance of rights and obligations (Janoski and Gran 2002). Leydet argues that citizenship is organized around three elements: "The first is citizenship as legal status, defined by civil, political and social rights ... The second considers citizens specifically as political agents, actively participating in a society's political institutions. The third refers to citizenship as membership in a political community that furnishes a distinct source of identity." (2017, n.p.) Each of these elements, as well as the articulation between them, provide the key for the debates.

Research frequently distinguishes between republican and liberal conceptions of citizenship. The republican model, mythologized by the classical Athenian republic, insists on collective self-rule, active participation in political life, and obligations toward fellow citizens and public institutions. It tends to be exclusionary and focuses on internal unity. The liberal model, associated with the Roman Empire's rule over many different conquered peoples, proposes a more inclusive but minimalist notion, focusing not on active participation or shared identity but on a particular legal status that comes with rights and protections under the law (Bellamy 2008; Leydet 2017). These two models in fact coexist and inform debates about legal status, political participation, rights, duties, identity, equality, universality, and state intervention into so-called "public" and "private" realms of life.

Such mainstream theories of citizenship have raised several important critiques. Feminist and anti-racist researchers have questioned the public/private divide on which liberal theories are based and critiqued the exclusionary dimension of the universalist tropes and policies of republican approaches (Yuval-Davis 1997, 2007; Heine 2009; Busey and Dowie-Chin 2021). Many have also challenged state-centric conceptions of citizenship and expanded the concept to capture forms of political participation and rights that operate at other scales (Sassen 2002; Benhabib 2005; Ong 2006). Decoupled from the state, the concept can be used to make sense of claims to rights and political participation through transnational, cosmopolitan, or urban citizenship, or describe engagements in various spheres as cultural, ecological, or sexual citizenship (Bauböck 1994; Soysal 1994; Berlant 1997; Holston 2001; Isin and Turner 2002).

One particularly interesting theoretical development for the field of forced migration studies is the concept of act of citizenship. Isin and Nielsen define acts of citizenship as "collective or individual deeds that rupture social-historical patterns," and through which "subjects constitute themselves as citizens or, better still, as those to whom the right to have rights is due" (2008, 2). They explain: "Theorizing acts means investigating everyday deeds that are ordinarily called politics. But acts of citizenship are also ethical (as in courageous), cultural (as in religious), sexual (as in pleasurable) and social (as in affiliative) in that they instantiate ways of being that are political" (2). These acts are independent from the recognition of a citizenship status by the state or other political authorities. This framework reminds us that being political means being disruptive, intervening in the polis, and claiming rights that may not have been granted to us. As such, this framework helps us decentre the state from citizenship studies and consider the "acts of citizenship" of non-citizens, migrants, refugees, and other subjects who are politically marginalized by the state (Nyers 2008; Barbero 2012; Castañeda 2013; McNevin 2013; Ní Mhurchú 2014; López-Sala 2019).

THE PROMISE OF PERMANENCE: FROM PRECARIOUS NON-CITIZENSHIP TO FULL MEMBERSHIP?

Decentring the state in citizenship studies and studying the acts of citizenship of migrants and non-citizens can help challenge state-centric views of belonging and political participation. It is equally important, however, to acknowledge how citizenship as a state-issued status operates in colonial nation building and immigration governance.

This has always been a multi-prong process that used enfranchisement and disenfranchisement as political technologies of settler colonialism and state formation (Thobani 2007). For instance, since at least the adoption of the first Indian Act in 1876, through the Canadian Citizenship Act, 1946, and until 1960, First Nations persons could only gain Canadian citizenship rights by renouncing their Indian status. Today, Indigenous persons in Canada are considered Canadian citizens regardless of how they see themselves; however, state recognition of parallel Indigenous citizenship is slow, and when it is recognized – such as in the Nisga'a Agreement – state actors carefully frame it as an addition to state citizenship (following the citizen plus model) but one that should not challenge state sovereignty or the primacy of state citizenship (Blackburn 2009). Through settler colonialism and immigration programs, the politics of citizenship have also been organized around gendered, classed, racial, religious, and ableist lines. These are historically visible in both exclusionary immigration measures and in moral regulation and education programs aimed at disciplining prospective citizens (see examples in Adamoski, Chunn, and Menzies 2002).

19.1 Nisga'a Tribal Council President on Nisga'a Citizenship
Dr Joseph Gosnell, Sr, president of the Nisga'a Tribal Council, spoke about the Nisga'a Agreement:

> Does the use of the term "Nisga'a citizen" violate the notion of Canadian citizenship? With the greatest of respect, we do not understand why anyone would object to the use of the term "citizen" to refer to the members of the Nisga'a Nation. No doubt, if we had agreed to describe ourselves merely as members, there would have been little or no objection. However, we believe that the correct word to describe someone who belongs to a nation is "citizen." We wish to affirm, not deny, our existence as the Nisga'a Nation, a nation that is within Canada ... The word "citizen" does not have a single fixed meaning in every context in which it is properly used. The conferral of Nisga'a citizenship does not confer or deny Canadian citizenship. (Senate of Canada 2000)

A central part of this history is the continuous decrease of permanency, and therefore access to citizenship, for migrants considered desirable only as workers. Indeed, as the Canadian government liberalized immigration in the 1960s and 1970s, eliminating exclusion criteria based on race and creating the points system, it also started transitioning to temporary work permits for specific groups of mostly racialized workers through the 1973 Non-Immigrant Employment Authorization Program, the model for today's Temporary Foreign Workers programs (Arat-Koc 2000; Bakan and Stasiulis 1997; Sharma 2006). This shift has been captured by some scholars as a form of exclusion through inclusion (Dua 2007; see also Hynie, chapter 23).

The "landed immigrant" would become a figure of the past, along with the possibility of immigrating with the guarantee that one will be able to stay and the prospect of swift access to the protection of citizenship. Indeed, through these and other programs, the proportion of temporary permits increased to the point that nowadays, a much greater number of people are granted temporary resident permits than permanent ones every year. To illustrate the discrepancy, in 2020, a total of 326,116 workers had temporary permits, plus another 256,740 international students (many of whom see their studies as a step in an immigration pathway). That's 582,856 temporary permits. The same year, only 184,606 new permanent residents were admitted (IRCC 2021a). While some of these temporary permits offer conditional pathways to permanent residency and eventually citizenship, many do not, and there are important emotional and economic consequences of these precarious trajectories (Rajkumar et al. 2012; Goldring and Landolt 2022).

Goldring and Landolt (2013, 2018) have productively conceptualized this legally produced liminality as "assemblages of precarious noncitizenship." The concept is helpful to make sense of the "multi-scalar, dynamic, contingent, institutional arrangements involving configurations of disparate elements … that come together in patterned but changing ways to constitute noncitizenship" (Goldring and Landolt 2018, 856). The concept allows us to understand citizenship and non-citizenship as closely linked to legal status, but as influenced by various actors, policies, and practices that mediate access to rights and services. The concept is also helpful in capturing the nonlinear trajectories of non-citizens that may include losing one's permit, being illegalized, obtaining a new permit, and that resembles a "chutes and ladders" (Goldring and Landolt 2013, 4) pathway organized around the "conditionality of presence and access" (3). These trajectories carry with them the prospect of inclusion, through access to permanent residency and citizenship, and the threat of exclusion and removal should a person's ability to fulfill conditions change. The conditional nature of these permits is key to understanding how they work as disciplining and probationary tools. They expand bordering practices across time and space, allowing for various state and non-state actors to make decisions about the supposed deservingness of migrants (as workers, as students, as parents, as people in need of protection), decisions that may lead to a loss of status (Moffette 2014).

The implications of non-citizenship are not distributed equally across class, race, and gender lines (see also Hari and Quintero, chapter 16; Mahrouse and El Omari, chapter 15; Aberman, chapter 12 respectively on class, race, and gender). The type of program, whether it offers a pathway to permanent residency or not, and the temporary or permanent nature of the permit are also important in differentiating between experiences of non-citizenship. But the conditionality of presence extends to all non-citizens, even to permanent residents. Indeed, permanent residents can see their status revoked for a number of offences, including what the Immigration and Refugee Protection Act (IRPA) calls "serious criminality," defined as an offence "for which a term of imprisonment of more than six months has been imposed" or an offence that could be "punishable by a maximum term of imprisonment of at least 10 years" (2001, s. 32(1)(a)) (regardless of the sentence received). These may include being found guilty of selling drugs such as cocaine, breaking someone's nose in a bar fight (Benslimane and Moffette 2019), or getting into a road accident causing death as the case of the truck driver in the Humbolt Broncos crash revealed (Riley 2022). These are sometimes serious actions and omissions, but non-citizens, including long-time permanent residents, are not only punished through criminal law, but also they face deportation.

19.2 The Experience of Someone Stripped of their Permanent Resident Status

> I did not apply for citizenship because my family had feared that my application would have been denied. Permanent residents need to be on Canadian soil for three out of five years to be eligible to apply for Canadian citizenship. During that mandatory period, I accumulated a criminal record …
>
> As a result of my criminal record, my permanent resident status was revoked. I was eventually released on parole but faced deportation. By stripping me of my permanent resident status and preventing me to apply for other permits as I am deemed inadmissible, the Canadian state also keeps me in a state of limbo - I am not allowed to work or study and cannot apply for a visa to do so, I lost my access to public healthcare and cannot get it back, I cannot get new ID cards and cannot therefore open a bank account. I experience these limits on what I can do - and the looming threat of deportation - as forms of punishment. (Aisha Benslimane in Benslimane and Moffette 2019)

In this context, citizenship offers the only promise of full and equal protection under the law, access to rights, the security of presence and permanence, and full membership into the political community. This is why it is so important for so many of us. But, as we will see, for those who need to apply to acquire it, citizenship is always embedded with conditionality.

SUSPICIOUS INCLUSION: CITIZENSHIP TESTS AND CONDITIONALITY

Research on citizenship regimes generally distinguishes between those based on *jus sanguinis* (citizenship by "blood," through a parent or sometimes a grandparent), those based on *jus soli* (citizenship by birth on the territory of a state), and those merging the two grounds (Vink and Bauböck 2013). This distinction misses perhaps the most common principle of acquisition of citizenship by immigrants, which E. Cohen (2013) dubbed *jus temporis*: an assessment of time residing in the country, holding a particular residency permit, and/or of time worked along with a number of other criteria. This principle makes use of the conditionality inherent to precarious non-citizenship as a ground for access to rights and permanence. Indeed, as E. Cohen explains, "*jus temporis* produces the probationary periods of time that every nation-state demands aspiring citizens wait prior to naturalizing" (2013, 55–6). She adds, "*jus temporis*, in the form of a temporal threshold or a duration of time, serves to represent the development of qualities, relationships, and skills that are associated with citizenship" (56).

In some cases, time and the proof that one fulfilled specific requirements during this probationary period are deemed sufficient to suppose one has acquired these qualities of citizenship in the same way that *jus soli* citizens would have acquired them by the time they reach legal adulthood. In many cases, however, states consider that aspiring citizens must demonstrate they have acquired such qualities, skills, values, and knowledge through citizenship tests and demand they claim their allegiance through citizenship oaths (conditions not expected of *jus soli* and most *jus sanguinis* citizens). This suggests a xenophobic politics of suspicious inclusion informs even the process of citizenship acquisition.

Indeed, since the early 2000s, there has been a tendency in Western states to politicize nationalization and citizenship as electoral issues, to introduce tests, and propose to make access to citizenship harder (Monforte, Bassel, and Khan 2019). As Winter explains, "[b]etween 2005 and 2008, the United Kingdom, the Netherlands and Germany implemented formal citizenship tests. The United States and Australia revised their citizenship tests in 2008 and 2009, respectively" and France made "accommodation and integration contracts" mandatory for citizenship acquisition in 2007 (2014, 3). Citizenship tests are the object of extensive debates, generally focused on whether they are justifiable in a liberal democracy, whether they serve as progressive tools of integration, as imposed requirements of assimilation, or as restrictive instruments of boundary work and control (Löwenheim and Gazit 2009; Joppke and Bauböck 2010; Michalowski 2011; Paquet 2012; Joppke 2013; Winter and Sauvageau 2015; van Oers 2021).

Regardless of their justification, the proliferation of these tests in recent years is part of a broader trend that has been conceptualized as marking a "restrictive turn" in the politics of citizenship (Joppke 2013, 6). This trend takes different forms depending on the country: it may be restrictive only at the symbolic and discursive levels or also in terms of outcome and access to citizenship. In Canada, citizenship tests are not new; prospective citizens have been tested on the content of a citizenship guide since the mid-1990s (Sobel 2015), but under the Harper Conservative government (2006–15), a new guide and changes to the test have been central to a populist politicization of citizenship that included various reforms. Between 2009 and 2013 "a new citizenship guide was issued; initiatives against the fraudulent acquisition of citizenship were introduced; a new citizenship test was designed; the citizenship ceremony was modified; and language requirements for Canadian citizenship were introduced" (Winter 2014, 3). In this context, the amendment of the citizenship guide to include sections about "Canadian values" that can be read as depicting Muslim immigrants as problematic has been central in promoting a racialized logic of suspicion in debates about citizenship (Bilge 2012; Jafri 2012b; Sobel 2015; Gulliver 2018; Patel 2022).

Some of these changes have since been amended by the Liberal government, and following Call to Action 94 of the Truth and Reconciliation Commission (2015), Bill C-8 added a recognition of Indigenous rights in the citizenship oath in 2021. Call to Action 93 also stated that Canada should "revise its citizenship test and information kit for newcomers to reflect a more inclusive history of the diverse Aboriginal people here, including information about the treaties and the history of residential schools" (TRC 2015). However, beyond the inclusion of the new oath, three sentences about residential schools, and some mentions of treaty rights, amendments to the citizenship guide in 2021 did not substantially change the way this history is narrated. Debates over the "privilege" of citizenship therefore continue to animate the political arena.

The Canadian restrictive turn appears to have been more important at the rhetorical level than in terms of the number of people who obtain citizenship (Joppke 2013), but this insistence on "earned citizenship" (Joppke 2021) and on "deserving citizenship" (Bassel 2021; van Oers 2021) has profound implications. Research also shows that the process of studying the guide, applying for citizenship, passing the test, and taking the oath extends the selective logic of immigration programs and favours highly skilled immigrants (Winter 2021), and that the tightening of criteria introduced by the Conservatives disproportionately impacted refugees and family class candidates (Nakache, Stone, and Winter 2020).

EJECTABLE CITIZENS: "ENEMY ALIENS" AND CITIZENSHIP REVOCATION

As we have seen, citizenship is an important means for securing one's presence and access to rights (see also K. Banerjee, chapter 5), and the process of acquiring it is informed by conditionality, precariousness, and suspicion. While access to the rights and benefits of citizenship is, in reality, mediated by structural forms of discrimination, in theory, all citizens are supposedly equal under the law. There is a caveat, however, as the status of dual citizens is less safe than that of mono-citizens.

The differential treatment of dual citizens can take many forms. Over fifty states have laws prohibiting dual citizenship, forcing migrants who could become citizens in their new country of residence to choose between acquiring this citizenship to secure their presence and relinquishing the previous one, or to continue living in this country on an immigration permit to retain their first citizenship. For migrants forced to leave their homes in hope of returning one day, this can be a very difficult decision. Some states, like India, may offer a different form of "overseas citizenship" with fewer rights to "persons of Indian origin" who are citizens of another state and are therefore not entitled to full citizenship (Naujoks 2015). And in many countries that do authorize dual citizenships, dual citizens can see their status revoked or temporarily lose citizenship rights in some circumstances. While it is a historically common practice, and citizenship revocation is legal in many states, research tends to focus on current debates around a repoliticization and publicization of this practice in states of the European Union, Australia, Canada, France, the UK, and the US (Macklin 2014; Kaya 2017; van Waas and Jaghai 2018; Fargues and Honohan 2021).

Citizenship revocation finds its roots in the ancient practice of banishment and exile, a practice that transformed over time and included the "transportation" of convicts from metropoles to settler colonies (Walters 2002; Gibney 2011b; Macklin 2020a). Throughout the twentieth century, in many countries including Canada, there have been three main grounds or justifications for citizenship revocation: (1) acquiring another citizenship, or being found to have another citizenship (in cases where dual citizenship is not accepted); (2) being seen as a threat to the country (as a citizen of a state at war with Canada or as someone involved in "anti-Canadian" activities); or (3) having obtained citizenship through what is understood as fraudulent grounds (including by withdrawing information about labour activism or other political activities when immigrating or applying for citizenship) (C. Anderson 2008; Macklin 2014, 2020a).

During World War II, while the Nazi regime was stripping German Jews of their citizenship and deporting them to concentration and extermination camps, the Canadian state forced some twenty-one thousand to twenty-three thousand persons of Japanese descent off their homes in British Columbia. The majority of them were "Canadian nationals" – that is, British subjects of Canada before the 1946 Canadian Citizenship Act, which came into force in 1947, created a separate Canadian citizenship. In the context of historical racism against Chinese and Japanese Canadians, the participation of Japan in World War II made it easy for media and politicians to present Japanese Canadians as posing a risk to national security. They were declared "enemy aliens," stripped of their properties, and detained (Oikawa 2012; G. Robinson 2017). According to G. Robinson (2017), some 12,000 were sent to internment camps, another 5,650 were sent to labour camps on roads or farms, 700 were detained in prisoner of war camps in Ontario, and some 3,000 wealthier Canadian Japanese were allowed to resettle away from the Pacific shores.

19.3 Testimony of a Survivor of Internment Camps

Pat Adashi, a daughter of Japanese immigrants, was sent to a camp in 1942. She recalls the experience:

> I was 21 years old when Japan bombed Pearl Harbour and war was declared. All the Japanese were considered enemy aliens. Most of us in the second generation were born in Canada. That didn't matter …

> My father was sent to a road camp ... We thought that would be the end of it. But, then, the people of the coast line and Vancouver Island were given less than 24 hours' notice and then removed from their homes and brought to Vancouver and put in the exhibition grounds – some even in the animal stalls. Eventually ... they confiscated our properties. Every last thing. Homes, our farms, all of our vehicles, even radios and cameras ... I was with my mother and sisters. We were put on these dusty trains and moved out. We didn't know where we were going. We ended up in a place called Slocan [Valley] ...
>
> At first the homes were not ready, so we lived in tents and ate in mess houses. It was a very cold winter. We had no running water. I lost my first baby. There were just no facilities ... We were all in the same boat. Nobody had anything, so we shared ...
>
> Somehow, we lived through it ... They had to do something about us once the war was over. So, they said we had to be re-patriated to Japan. Well, we didn't know what Japan was. We'd never been there ... Some people did go back to Japan ... But the majority of the young people wanted to live in Canada ... We had to start from scratch. (Zarum 2019, n.p.)

With the liberalization of Western immigration and citizenship regimes in the second half of the twentieth century, denaturalization became a less-discussed topic. However, after the 9/11 attacks and in the context of the rise of racist and anti-immigrant populism, citizenship revocation has returned on the political agenda (Gibney 2011a; Forcese 2013; Macklin 2014, 2020a). In Canada, after various attempts at amending citizenship revocation procedures, the Conservative government was successful in passing Bill C-24, the Strengthening the Canadian Citizenship Act in 2014. Until then, the sole ground for revocation set out in the Citizenship Act was when the minister considered that it was obtained through fraud (including false representation or concealing information), and required that a Federal Court judge find that such fraudulent acquisition had indeed taken place (Forcese 2014).

In addition to increasing the length of time a permanent resident needed to be residing in Canada prior to applying for citizenship (except for members of the Canadian Armed Forces), the law added new grounds for revocation based on "national security" and removed the testing of these grounds at the Federal Court, thus granting substantial discretionary powers to the minister. These grounds included treason (assisting state or non-state armed forces that Canada is directly or indirectly fighting, even without a criminal conviction) and terrorism (as defined in the Canadian Criminal Code and requiring a conviction, but including when this conviction was from a foreign court, as long as the action would have also been a crime in Canada) (Macklin 2020a). The law targeted specifically dual citizens, as citizenship revocation of mono-citizens would make them stateless and be contrary to the 1961 Convention on the Reduction of Statelessness, but it placed the onus on the citizen to demonstrate on a balance of probabilities that they were not a citizen of another state (Macklin 2020a; see also Cowper-Smith and Kane, chapter 20).

Although these new provisions were used, the Strengthening the Canadian Citizenship Act 2014 has had its greatest impact at the level of political discourse as well as in transforming the meaning of citizenship, insisting that it is not a right but a privilege, and grounding it in patriotism. It extended the conditionality of non-citizenship into the realm of citizenship. The Liberals, who were elected to federal government in 2015, made it an election promise to scrap most of the new provisions introduced by the act, and in 2017 did so through Bill C-6. The trend of retroactively investigating dual citizens for potential false representation when obtaining citizenship (sometimes for very banal omissions) is nonetheless continuing. Indeed, in 2011, when the Conservative government announced it intended to crack down on what it saw as fraud, then minister Kenney claimed that only sixty-three people had been stripped of their citizenship for fraud since 1977 (R. Brennan 2011), and CBC News reported that "until [2011], fewer than 70 citizenships had been revoked since the Citizenship Act was passed in 1947" (2012, n.p.). Despite opposing the measures Bill C-24 introduced, the Liberal government accelerated the number of revocations based on fraud, with news reports suggesting as many as seventeen per month between November 2015 and February 2017 (Dyer 2016; M.-D. Smith 2017). This is a substantial increase of revocation for alleged fraud. It thus appears that a politics of suspicion and conditionality continues to haunt the Canadian citizenship regime, and we should expect this issue to be raised again in populist political discourses in the years to come.

CONCLUSION

This chapter has shown that citizenship is a polysemic concept, it holds multiple and conflicting meanings, and it is therefore at the centre of both academic and political debates. The politics of citizenship have implications for the field of forced migration studies. As a political boundary-making technology, citizenship is central to the conditional politics of belonging that informs national state building through settler colonialism, immigration programs, and economic and social relations. But as theories of citizenship as acts suggest, it is possible to transform the politics of citizenship. This can be done, on the one hand, by challenging the conditionality and suspicion that inform state citizenship regimes, insisting that access to rights and secured presence should be easily accessible. Facilitating access to state citizenship can help alleviate the hardships displacements cause and provide safety. It can be achieved, on the other hand, by promoting non-state-centric notions of political belonging and participation, for instance by supporting Indigenous citizenship and nurturing forms of urban citizenship, mutual aid, and supportive social relations that are not mediated by immigration status. Questioning states' sovereign monopoly over citizenship can help us decolonize political subjectivities and reclaim other non-statist modes of belonging, relating, and participating.

FURTHER READING AND RESOURCES

CBC News. 2022. "The 'Lost Canadians' Who Fell Through Cracks of Citizenship Loophole." *The National*, 3 October 2022. www.cbc.ca/player/play/2080676931545.

Landscapes of Injustice. 2017. "Additional Resources." https://www.landscapesofinjustice.com/additional-resources.

Meurrens, Steven. 2016. "Citizenship Revocation, Cessation, and War Resisters with Jenny Kwan, MP." *Borderlines* podcast, episode 4, 1:19:16. https://meurrensonimmigration.com/borderlines-podcast-episode-4-jenny-kwan.

Nisga'a Lisims Government. 1998. "Understanding the Treaty." www.nisgaanation.ca/understanding-treaty.

Riley, Sharon J. 2022. "How Much Punishment Is Enough for the Driver Who Caused the Humboldt Crash?" *The Walrus*, first published 2 June 2022, updated 13 January 2023. https://thewalrus.ca/humboldt-crash-driver.

20

The Shifting Landscape of Statelessness in Canada

Yuriko Cowper-Smith and Jocelyn Kane

KEY TAKEAWAYS

- Statelessness is hard to define, and there are no easy solutions.
- Statelessness can be framed in legal, socio-political, and agentic terms.
- Statelessness exists in Canada *in situ*, in migration, and forced migration contexts.
- Canada's protection framework – a patchwork of citizenship, immigration, and refugee law – is ill-equipped to respond to the dynamism and complexities of statelessness.
- Studying statelessness in Canada encourages the implementation of a statelessness determination procedure and an interdisciplinary approach to research and advocacy.

KEY TERMS

- Agency
- Birth registration
- Denationalization
- International refugee protection system
- Permanent residence
- Stateless and statelessness
- Structural discrimination

INTRODUCTION

There are an estimated fifteen million stateless people across the globe (ISI 2020); yet statelessness is not a very well-known topic in research and policy circles. It is difficult to define, its causes are diverse, and it emerges in complex ways (Eliassi 2021). Nonetheless, a common starting point for understanding statelessness is that a person is stateless when they are "not considered a national by any State under the operation of its law" (Convention Relating to the Status of Stateless Persons 1954, art. 1(1)). Such de jure statelessness occurs alongside de facto statelessness, where a person possesses nationality but, under state law, is not recognized. However, these are not the only ways to look at statelessness.

The way statelessness has been approached in law, policy, and academia is multifaceted, which affects possible interventions (Eliassi 2021). In this chapter, we first discuss key debates in the interdisciplinary field of statelessness. Turning to Canada, we explore how the government has responded (or not) to statelessness in its law and policy. We then draw conclusions from the Canadian context and what those reveal about statelessness generally. We argue Canada's protection framework cannot grapple with statelessness as both an overlapping and unique structural condition, which further contributes to the vulnerability of stateless people in this country.

KEY DEBATES: WHAT IS STATELESSNESS?

Statelessness can affect individual people or communities. Individuals can become stateless when a country's bureaucratic practices restrict access to nationality. For example, parents are sometimes unable or ineligible to access civil registration procedures, making it impossible to register their child's birth. As birth registration is often a prerequisite for granting nationality, not registering a birth places a child at risk of statelessness. In another example, denationalization occurs when a state revokes an individual's citizenship, typically due to activity deemed harmful to the state, leaving denationalized individuals at risk of statelessness if they do not possess the nationality[1] of another state (Gibney 2020).

Entire communities can also become stateless. For example, the redrawing of borders after conflict or secession can lead to the non-recognition of nationality. Here, geopolitical forces facilitate changes in, or the formation of, nationality laws wherein specific populations are excluded. Prominent examples are the dissolution of the Soviet Union in 1991 and Yugoslavia in 1992, where millions of people were denationalized (UNHCR 1996, 2018a). Ethnic and minority groups are also discriminated against by states, such as in Myanmar, the Dominican Republic, Bhutan, Kenya, and Madagascar (UNHCR 2017). Discrimination based on gender occurs in twenty-five countries where nationality law discriminates against women who marry, who are born to foreigners, or simply because they are women. These women often cannot confer nationality to their children, meaning children whose fathers are missing, deceased, foreigners, or stateless themselves are at risk of statelessness (GCENR n.d.).

The emergence of statelessness studies has expanded the conceptualization and interpretation of these causes in at least three main areas: statelessness as a legal issue, as a political issue, and as a mode of being.

Statelessness as a Legal Issue

Statelessness is often circumscribed in legal terms: the lack of nationality is resolved by granting nationality. The adage "by the stroke of a pen" is often used to refer to states' ability to reform practices which cause statelessness through technical changes that close protection gaps. As Macklin points out, "the international legal order views statelessness primarily as an administrative anomaly in the global filing system that assigns every human being to at least one state" (2007, 340). The causes of statelessness and its potential solutions are articulated in international human rights treaties, most prominently in the Universal Declaration of Human Rights, the 1951 Convention Relating to the Status of Refugees (1951 Convention), the 1954 Convention Relating to the Status of Stateless Persons (1954 Convention), and the 1961 Convention on the Reduction of Statelessness (1961 Convention), all of which aim to prevent statelessness and protect stateless persons *in situ*, migration, and forced migration contexts. While *in situ* statelessness is common, stateless people often cross international borders and face the international refugee protection system, especially when their statelessness is evidence of persecution (Tas 2016). Accordingly, UNHCR's mandate has expanded from matters of asylum to include resolving statelessness in diverse contexts (Seet 2016). Despite recognizing some contributing socio-political factors, UNHCR's approach is technically driven as it sees "one solution for statelessness – acquisition of nationality, usually of the country with which stateless people have the strongest ties" (UNHCR n.d.a; see Brinham 2019), and as such, works with states to reform nationality legislation and procedures in compliance with international standards.

Some view the overarching category of asylum and its associated protection through UNHCR and national infrastructure as the appropriate channel to approach the eradication of statelessness. Proponents imagine that international refugee law will be able to protect stateless refugees in areas where the 1954 Convention does not (M. Foster and Lambert 2019). Scholars nonetheless recognize that the 1951 Convention is currently limited in its ability to: identify stateless refugees (McGee 2020); create the right to nationality (Darling 2009); address the situation of de facto statelessness; and overcome the lack of national protection (Tas 2016). Additionally, overlapping refugeehood with statelessness may result in inappropriate redress and the risk of immigration detention (Macklin 2007). To remedy these deficiencies, some call for flagging statelessness under special needs and vulnerabilities which could "trigger referral to targeted services" for those seeking residency (McGee 2020, 46). Others see the "expansionism" of UNHCR's mandate as problematic due to its overreach, overcapacity, and chronic underfunding (Crisp 2022), and UNHCR's protection hierarchy treating statelessness as secondary, thus exacerbating gaps in protection (Tucker 2021).[2]

Statelessness as a Political Issue

The study of statelessness has evolved into a broader interdisciplinary area of global scholarship (Bloom 2013; Bianchini 2020; Recalde-Vela, Jaghai-Bajulaiye, and Vlieks 2019), where scholars demonstrate the political nature of statelessness and how structural conditions generate statelessness (K. Banerjee 2016; Belton 2017; Brinham 2019; Eliassi 2021; Jain 2022; Kingston 2017). Perhaps the most well-known perspective, Arendt (1994) clearly saw how the modern nation-state was built upon a model of exclusive membership and was thus able to exercise its sovereign power through mass expulsion (see also K. Banerjee, chapter 5).

It is argued that recognizing the political and social forces that enable structural discrimination and resulting inequalities is crucial to understanding and remedying statelessness (Belton 2017; Kingston 2017). Such forces can appear neutral despite being deployed by states to actively displace unwanted populations (Belton 2017, 4–5; Jain 2022). One such practice is said to be recognition itself, with identification documents serving not only to register individuals with civic authorities but also (re)produce statelessness, restrict freedom of movement, control access to rights, and create and destroy identities (Brinham 2019). In this way, identification practices can be at once emancipatory and repressive (Brinham 2019). In analyzing the Dominican Republic's prevention of Dominicans of Haitian descent from accessing citizenship through gender and ethnic discrimination, Petrozziello asks, "what if the rise in statelessness is not a mere technicality, but a strategy of slippery statecraft meant to deter migration and design the citizenry that a given state has the political will to protect?" (quoted in Brinham 2019, 213).

Scholars recognize that resolving statelessness demands more than recognition of nationality but also an obligation to prevent domination (K. Banerjee 2016). Indeed, thinking about statelessness in a legal-centric vacuum ignores how the bureaucratic brushstrokes that confer or deny nationality are subjective and deeply political. Within this view, truly resolving statelessness would entail "redefinition and reconfiguration of the state system and its citizenship regimes that have been structured by powerful ideas of nation" (Bloom, Tonkiss, and

Cole 2017 cited in Eliassi 2021). As Eliassi (2021) explains, although citizenship to an internationally recognized state is key to accessing human rights, the structural conditions that impose statelessness in the first place do not fade away after citizenship is acquired (see Blitz and Lynch 2011), because there is no political guarantee that the acquisition of nationality can "undo the political, cultural and economic injustices that permeate the life worlds of stateless peoples" (Eliassi 2021).

Statelessness as a Mode of Being

Because citizenship typically facilitates access to socio-political rights, statelessness is often referred to as a deficit (Hourani 2021) and is famously referred to as the loss of the right to have rights (Arendt 1994; see also K. Banerjee, chapter 5; Moffette, chapter 19). Without citizenship, stateless people often cannot rely on state protections and experience difficulty accessing basic needs, including health care, housing, employment, and education. Other chasms follow, including exclusions from opening a bank account, owning property, marrying, and participating in formal politics. The lack of identity documents bars stateless persons from moving freely within and across borders, meaning they may face arrest, detention (van Waas et al. 2015) or removal proceedings by authorities (van der Velde and Letschert 2014).

Deficit narratives abound, describing the experience of statelessness in terms of invisibility, voicelessness, and despair, even "the scum of the earth" (Arendt 1994, 267).[3] In this view, without the ability to participate in one's self-determination through cultural, social, and economic activities, one's dignity is severely decreased, threatening one's humanity and personhood (Kingston 2019). Statelessness has been compared to Agamben's concept of "bare life," life stripped of value to mere existence, the biological function of life which exists "at the margins of the political order" (1998, 12; see also Parekh 2014). Statelessness is also described as liminality, "a temporary condition wherein a person becomes separated from his or her former identity and, through a rite of passage, takes on another identity" (Belton 2015, 911). Here, socio-political forces often impel stateless people into a liminal space "of invisibility, impurity, rightlessness, and reflection" (Belton 2015, 911). Such liminality is implicit in "social death," where, in a hierarchy of citizenships, "the worst thing to be in the world of nation-states is a 'non-citizen'" (Castles 2005, 691).

Others emphasize the agency of stateless people, who participate in both social activities and work – embodying many performative characteristics of citizenship – (McGranahan 2018; Redclift 2013) and resist the conditions they face (Bahram 2021; Brinham 2019; Brinham, Cowper-Smith, and Zarni 2019; Cowper-Smith 2021; Fiddian-Qasmiyeh 2016; Kastrinou, El-Deen, and Emery 2021; Medina 2020; Simpson 2014; Sigona 2016). For example, McGee (2022) suggests that rather than only looking at stateless identity and experience as deprivation, statelessness can also open up spaces of possibility and resistance, "acts of statelessness." Such "acts" can be seen in critical research methodologies that prioritize the empowered stateless agent over the portrayal of the victim (Bahram 2021, 218), in knowledge building and mobilization in activist stateless diasporas (Cowper-Smith 2019, 2021), and informal and radical challenges to status quo configurations of citizenship (Medina 2020, 24). Simpson's (2014) work on Mohawk refusal of the "gift" of Canadian and United States citizenship is a salient example, where Mohawks refuse colonial oppression and imposed identity and refuse to be made "disappearable."

These are just some of the debates on the conceptualization of statelessness. From legal definitions to structural discrimination to grounded experience, these variations are diverse within and across theory and practice between scholars, as well as policy-makers, legislators, international institutions, local non-governmental organizations (NGOs), and media. We turn now to how these debates materialize in the Canadian context.

STATELESSNESS IN CANADA

The number of stateless persons in Canada is unknown. One estimate is 3,560 (Statistics Canada 2022d), although this figure has been critiqued (CCS 2020). Statelessness in Canada is underexplored, but emerging data point to significant protection gaps in the country's legislative framework.[4] Although Canada ratified the 1961 Convention, it is not party to the 1954 Convention, which stipulates standards of protection states are required to implement for stateless persons on their territory. The Canadian government's stance is that existing citizenship, immigration, and refugee legislation provide sufficient pathways for the protection and naturalization of refugee and non-refugee stateless persons (Brouwer 2012; Erauw 2015). For example, stateless persons can seek legal status in Canada through an application for permanent residence on humanitarian and compassionate (H&C) grounds, an application for citizenship through ministerial discretion, or via the refugee determination system for those who fear persecution.

However, many argue that this infrastructure does not protect stateless people in Canada. A particularly striking area of concern is the definition of statelessness itself. Canada's Citizenship Act and Immigration and Refugee Protection Act (IRPA) do not explicitly define a stateless person, and IRPA includes stateless person in its definition of a foreign national (2001, s. 2), a counter-intuitive approach to the unique condition of statelessness whereby one is *not* a national anywhere.[5] This is mirrored in the lack of institutionalized response to statelessness-specific measurement, assessment, and recognition. Canada has neither a specific process for statelessness determination nor a "stateless person status," leaving stateless persons without a protection measure tailored to their specific needs (see CCS 2022; Kane 2019; Liew 2020;

Stasiulis 2017).[6] These contradictions create challenges for stateless people in accessing social housing, public education, health care, social assistance, identity documents, travel documents, and naturalization (Erauw 2015, 8).[7] Stateless persons are also vulnerable to lengthy immigration detention while they await removal (see also Silverman, chapter 21), which can induce severe mental health challenges, including hopelessness, suicidality, and addiction (Kane 2019; Kane, Schuurmans, and Kitamura, 2023). Below are four ways statelessness can occur in Canada.

(Forced) Migration

Statelessness typically occurs in the context of migration before[8] and after arrival in Canada. This can happen to any migrant, including students, refugees, asylum seekers, skilled worker immigrants, or tourists. Though migrants are generally eligible for basic rights while they remain legal residents, whether temporary or permanent, a problem arises for those who find themselves stateless and with no legal status. This can also happen to asylum seekers who have been denied protection in Canada (Kane 2019). Those who apply for asylum in Canada may have access to certain social services, and they can apply for a work permit and access temporary health care (Government of Canada 2022d; see also Atak, chapter 17). If an individual's application is denied, they can appeal on specific grounds. If appeals and special applications also fail, they lose access to social services and legal status and become subject to removal proceedings. This becomes a challenge when stateless asylum seekers cannot secure travel documents for removal and are subsequently detained while authorities attempt to arrange removal. Therefore, stateless asylum seekers, like non-asylum-seeking stateless persons, are denied a legal course of action through which they can pursue legal residency outside the realm of persecution. They are unable to apply for status because they are stateless.

20.1 Francisco Suarez Abeleira was born in 1950s Spain. His family left and settled in Mexico, where he was orphaned and raised by neighbours until he left their care at twelve years old. Abeleira began smuggling goods across the Mexico-US border until he moved to the US and lived as an undocumented person. In 1975 Abeleira purchased the birth certificate of a deceased US citizen. He lived with this identification for over two decades, during which he obtained a high school diploma, a bachelor of education, and a master of science in education and worked for the New York City Board of Education.

However, authorities discovered his false identity when he attempted to travel to Spain. Abeleira pled guilty to criminal charges and was detained by Immigration and Customs Enforcement (ICE) while awaiting removal. In 2009 ICE determined Abeleira was unremovable; Spain confirmed they had no record that Abeleira was a Spanish citizen. In 2010 Abeleira accepted that he would not be able to regularize his status in the US and crossed the Canada-US border, seeking asylum based on statelessness (*Abeleira v. Canada (Immigration, Refugees and Citizenship)* 2017, FC 1008). Although he was found to be stateless, Abeleira was denied refugee protection in Canada. In 2012 he filed an application for Humanitarian and Compassionate (H&C) residency, which began a series of denials and resubmissions. In 2017 in overturning the most recent denial, Justice Elliott highlighted several complexities raised by the *Abeleira* case, including whether Canada can remove Abeleira, whether he would face hardship in the US, whether he has and would continue to face adversity in Canada, and "whether it is humane or compassionate to leave him in an indefinite state of limbo in this country" (2017, FC 1008, para. 40).

This example raises particular concerns vis-à-vis the legal remedies available to non-refugee stateless persons residing in Canada.

- Abeleira's case shows that addressing statelessness as a technicality has limitations, and there is a mismatch of the legal solutions and individual circumstances. Confining cases of statelessness to the context of forced migration leaves non-refugee stateless persons to pursue the H&C pathway, which is based partly on whether an individual is "established" in Canada. The establishment factor requires one to demonstrate solid connection to Canada through sound financial management, stable housing, and a "good civil record," among other criteria (Government of Canada 2017b). This is positioned as a fair way to assess one's integration into Canada but relies upon public-facing factors like employment and community service, which themselves require legal identification, which masks the challenges a stateless person has in obtaining identification in the first place.
- Indeed, the H&C application for residency allows one to draw upon their statelessness as a source of hardship, but what hardship means is subject to interpretation. In assessing the *Abeleira* case, Justice Elliott pointed to the need to consider hardship or H&C matters "in the broader sense" (2017, FC 1008, para. 58), which should take into account the uniqueness of the condition of statelessness: legal limbo, precarity, restriction of mobility, and indefinite detention (2017, FC 1008, para. 54).

- This case also raises the notion of *in situ* hardship and the role that internal displacement plays in one's ability to access basic rights, earn an income, and pursue their life needs. In this way, we can see that stateless persons denied protection are caught in a trap when they are required to demonstrate their establishment or connection to Canada, yet are simultaneously denied the resources to do so.

Indigenous Disenfranchisement

Though contemporary Canadian citizenship is granted on nearly universal lines, it evolved alongside colonial attempts to dispossess the legal, cultural, and familial identities of the Indigenous Peoples of Turtle Island (see Coburn, chapter 1; Moffette, chapter 19). We cannot capture the extent to which this has taken place in this chapter. Instead, we point to two key factors that have implications for statelessness in Canada.

First, the granting of Canadian citizenship requires proof of birth. This can be particularly difficult when a person either does not know where they were born, or they do know but their birth was not registered (see also Clark-Kazak, chapter 13). To resolve this issue, there is a process where a person can apply for a delayed birth certificate, which, if granted, can be followed by confirmation of citizenship. For some Indigenous people, however, registering birth, either immediate or delayed, can be complicated by migration, discrimination, and intergenerational lack of documentation (van Genugten, Meijknecht, and Rombouts 2014, 101). Indigenous nations straddle the contemporary Canada-US border, and many Indigenous people live fluidly on both sides of it (see Young, chapter 3). Accordingly, they sometimes face bureaucratic challenges when accessing birth registration records across multiple jurisdictions. Due to overlapping bordering practices across Indigenous nations and lands, these factors can lead to a situation where a person is not recognized as a citizen despite their eligibility "because [the state] is not convinced of the facts of birth" (van Genugten, Meijknecht, and Rombouts 2014, 101). The inability to prove birth thus heightens the risk of statelessness for Indigenous people (Blitz and Lynch 2011; ISI 2014, 47).

Second, birth records have played an important role in Canada's attempts to dispossess Indigenous identities. From changing and erasing identity (Lawrence 2004); challenges with Indigenous names on birth certificates (Brend 2022); forced and discriminatory family separation via foster care (Kassam 2017; A. Turner 2016) and birth alerts (McKenzie, Marelj, and Morgan 2021); to the Residential School system (Lynch 2001; Lawrence 2004), these practices evince colonial attempts to dispossess Indigeneity at birth or afterwards. To resist the imposition of colonial forms of identity, some Indigenous people have chosen statelessness, despite its attendant risks and harms.

20.2 Donovan McGlaughlin was born somewhere along the Canada-US border, and at some point, his parents migrated to northern Canada. They did not register his birth in either country out of fear that doing so would trigger government attempts to put him in a residential school. As a result, McGlaughlin never possessed official state identification. However, he possessed his Band identification, allowing him to travel between countries for work as a truck driver. Eventually settling in the Yukon, he had a heart attack in 2010. McGlaughlin was flown to a hospital in British Columbia for treatment, where upon realizing he could not provide legal identification, the hospital notified immigration authorities. This incident began a long case between McGlaughlin and the Canadian Border Services Agency (CBSA), which pursued his removal to the US. Realizing he was stateless, McGlaughlin became heavily involved in legally resolving his status and in the statelessness advocacy movement. He was eventually granted Canadian citizenship after applying for it based on the grounds of special and unusual hardship (Drews 2015; Yukon News 2021).

This case raises three important and interconnected challenges.

- A parent's decision not to register the birth of a child can have grievous consequences. As noted earlier, birth registration is often the requisite civil procedure to obtain nationality, so a child's right to nationality – and associated rights to health and social services – is at risk if they are not registered.
- Formally recognizing birth is a legal remedy, but one that ignores the risk of statelessness articulated here as structural oppression. McGlaughlin's experience demonstrates the complexities of trying to access birth registration records in multiple jurisdictions alongside the fact that Indigenous nations are subject to migration controls, despite existing for centuries on territory that spans contemporary Canada-US borders.
- McGlaughlin's experience demonstrates the paradoxical role that birth registration plays in facilitating access to rights, dispossessing identity, and resisting colonial oppression. The choice to not register birth can be considered an emancipatory and agential act, one which responds to and refuses colonial oppression. Doing so, however, risks further harm.

"*Crimmigration*"

Crimmigration comprises a broad spectrum of practices, including using criminal law to manage matters of immigration, discourse that criminalizes immigrants, and immigration status to deter criminal behaviour (Rubins 2022; Atak and Simeon 2018b). Canada has undergone substantial crimmigration over the last two decades through enhanced immigration detention, border controls, and "international cooperation in the fight against irregular migration" (Atak and Simeon 2018b, 6). Non-citizens in Canada – both temporary and permanent – are thus subject to a "conditionality of presence" (see Moffette, chapter 19), where their immigration status is subject to norms codified in criminal law. For example, permanent residency in Canada is subject to several conditions, one of which is criminal activity punishable by less than six months of incarceration (see Moffette, chapter 19). Should a permanent resident be convicted of such a crime, they become subject to removal proceedings and are detained while Canadian authorities arrange removal to their country of nationality.[9] Non-citizens, including permanent residents and asylum seekers, who are also stateless and find themselves in this circumstance, face unique challenges as they typically cannot be removed. Stateless individuals face additional precarity as their irremovability places them in a legal limbo conditioned by legal and geopolitical forces beyond their control.

20.3 Deepan Budlakoti was born in Ottawa. His parents worked at the Embassy of India but claim they stopped working there shortly before Budlakoti's birth. When he was born, Budlakoti was issued an Ontario birth certificate. In 1997 Budlakoti's parents applied for and received Canadian citizenship. They did not apply for Budlakoti because they thought he was already Canadian by virtue of being born in the country. In 2003 Budlakoti's parents applied for his Canadian passport; the passport was issued, stating that Budlakoti's nationality was Canadian.

In 2003 Budlakoti experienced family troubles, fled home, and became a ward of the state. Throughout his life, he was criminally convicted several times. In May 2010 government officials informed Budlakoti that he was not a Canadian citizen but rather a permanent resident. Canada revoked his permanent residency and claimed that due to Budlakoti's Indian heritage, he was entitled to Indian citizenship despite India asserting the contrary. Budlakoti's case has been heard at the federal and international levels, and Budlakoti is considered "prematurely stateless," whereby he cannot be declared stateless until he applies for (and is denied) Canadian citizenship (*Budlakoti v. Canada* 2015, FCA 139, para. 23). Given Budlakoti's criminal convictions, an application for residency or citizenship in Canada would likely result in a declaration of inadmissibility, forcing Budlakoti to continue living as a stateless person in Canada. Budlakoti's case demonstrates the complexities that weave together elements of migration, links to a state, and criminality.

- Canada's position on Budlakoti's case shows a legal conceptualization of statelessness, which is in line with Canada's citizenship legislation: his statelessness can be potentially resolved through a citizenship application. Budlakoti's permanent residency is valid, and the removal conditions of that status are enforceable despite the potential harms that await him in detention or upon removal to India.
- Those who see Budlakoti's case as inherently political cite his birth in Ottawa, the opposing interpretations of the circumstances of his birth, his repeated criminal convictions, and his inadmissibility as evidence of state-based strategies that keep Budlakoti in a condition of legal limbo and precarity.
- Related to the tension between victimhood and agency, Budlakoti is precarious in terms of his legal status but also by being denied health care or a work permit. He relies on donations from supporters to pay for food, shelter, transporta tion, and health care. Although he is dependent upon others for basic needs, Budlakoti is an activist for statelessness awareness and reform in Canada, pursuing solutions at national and international levels.

Second-Generation Children Born Abroad

Canada's citizenship legislation also risks imposing statelessness on individuals as it limits the ability of first-generation born-abroad parents to pass on Canadian citizenship to their children should they also be born abroad. These "second generation children born abroad" are thus not entitled to Canadian nationality through lines of descent (Citizenship Act 2009, s. 3(3)(a)). This "second generation cut off" was implemented in Bill C-37 in 2009, prior to which second-generation children born abroad automatically obtained Canadian citizenship by descent but ceased to be Canadian citizens at age twenty-eight unless they (1) applied to retain their citizenship, (2) and registered as a citizen, and (3) either resided in Canada for at least one year prior to the date of application or established "a substantial connection with Canada" (*Bjorkquist et al. v. Attorney General of Canada* 2023, para. 2b).

The second-generation cut-off permanently denies the first-generation born abroad the right to automatically pass on their citizenship to their children born abroad and leaves them with no legal mechanism to appeal this restriction, irrespective of their ties to Canada. This provision created two classes of Canadian citizenship: Canadians born in Canada can pass their Canadian nationality on to their children should they be born abroad, and those born outside Canada who became naturalized Canadian citizens cannot. The risk of statelessness to descendants of Canadian nationals is becoming more common as families attempt to secure nationality for children subject to the 2009 provision.

20.4 In 2021 six families launched a constitutional challenge to section 3(3)(a) of the Citizenship Act 2009 (*Bjorkquist et al. v. Attorney General of Canada 2023*, para. 2b). In all six families, one or both parents are first-generation born-abroad Canadians, which means their parents were Canadian-born but travelled abroad for work or education and had their children abroad. As these first-generation children grew into adulthood, they also migrated abroad for temporary employment and study opportunities and had children. Because of Bill C-37, these parents cannot automatically confer their Canadian nationality to their children (*Bjorkquist et al. v. Attorney General of Canada* 2023, para. c–f).

The constitutional challenge argues that the second-generation cut-off violates section 15 of the charter in that Canadian citizens are discriminated against on the grounds of national origin, and gender, as women face intersectional barriers based on pregnancy and related reproductive decision-making; section 6(1) of the charter as first-generation people born abroad are discriminated against regarding their mobility rights; and section 7 of the charter where the liberty to choose where and how to raise their children is restricted for first-generation parents, and where second-generation children are denied the right to be raised by their parents (*Bjorkquist et al. v. Attorney General of Canada* 2023). At issue are several factors, including what counts as ties to Canada, child rights, and gender discrimination.

Three additional points of concern are addressed below:

- This case exemplifies how the techno-legal approach does not consider ground-level realities of statelessness. Canada's Citizenship Act provides a pathway for individuals to apply for citizenship should they be at risk of statelessness (1946, section 5(5)). Children can apply for citizenship if certain criteria are met, among which is the requirement to have been physically present in Canada for at least 1,095 days during the four years immediately before the date of application. Such conditions ignore the fact that stateless people often do not possess identity documents, let alone a travel document with which they could travel to Canada, rendering the residency requirement likely unattainable (CCS and CCRC 2020).

- With the move away from "substantial connection," ties to Canada are no longer a subject of legal evaluation. While this appears to be a neutral legal strategy to manage the passing of Canadian nationality, connection to Canada is a function of political power as it remains a requirement but is articulated differently. One's physical presence on Canadian territory, rather than "substantial ties" to it, is what determines one's connection. In this way, connection to place is circumscribed along territorial lines, despite feelings of connection transcending borders.
- There are tensions in interpreting statelessness as statecraft and as agential. The ability of first-generation born-abroad children to plan their lives is determined by the circumstances of their birth, which they cannot change. First-generation children must consider the rights and legal status of their unborn children in their choices to work or travel abroad. This places unique restrictions on their mobility whereby they may not be able to participate in the same life choices as their Canadian-born counterparts. This leaves their life choices bound by (ever-changing) interconnected dynamics between discourses of nationhood and jurisdictions of nationality law. Occupying both migration and *in situ* contexts, first-generation Canadians who wish to consider the rights of their unborn children are required to remain within Canada's borders because they were born outside them.

Our analysis of the various causes and experiences of statelessness in Canada highlights the tensions inherent in what statelessness entails and how to address it. We now turn to the discussion, conclusions, and lessons we have drawn for Canada and more broadly.

DISCUSSION AND CONCLUSION

Statelessness in Canada is dynamic and cannot be confined to one particular conceptualization or solution. The challenges, contradictions, and gaps of the Canadian system become especially visible when they are connected to how statelessness is conceived. Each profile described above speaks to the tension between understanding statelessness in Canada as a legal issue – and requisite legal remedies – and ground-level realities, which render stateless people unable to fulfill legal requirements or access legal pathways.

The law in Canada is understood to be objective; however, it ignores stateless people's unique precarity, often unable to "prove" themselves or their strong feelings of Canada as home, resulting in a disconnect between legal solutions and individual circumstances. Viewing the problem in legal terms without considering power structures further stymies the protection of stateless people. State-based techniques that place individuals at risk of statelessness are indeed present in Canada and have been carried out in diverse ways, ranging from the inadmissibility of some migrants to Indigenous dispossession, and the delineation of belonging to Canada in techno-legal terms. These profiles also reveal that statelessness exerts itself both as an egregious harm and as a force one rallies against. Those profiled here experience restrictions to basic needs and are often prohibited from accessing the resources needed to improve their lives. Nevertheless, stateless people in Canada are agents who, faced with legal hurdles within a set of structural conditions, also work toward resolving their legal status and raising awareness about statelessness through navigating the law, court systems, and media.

The profiles also demonstrate that Canada's protection framework – a patchwork of citizenship, immigration, and refugee law – is ill-equipped to respond to the dynamism and complexities of statelessness. This model is not suited to the unique condition of statelessness due to the burden placed upon stateless individuals to prove persecution, hardship, or establishment, or, in the case of stateless Indigenous people, their historical and jurisdictional connection to Canada. Each of these channels provides a unique challenge conditioned by several factors, including the lack of legal identity, the inability to work legally, and the absence of persecution. Canada's protection mechanism thus remains stagnant, neither responding to the need to address statelessness in a legally specific way nor enhancing its refugee protection infrastructure to fully accommodate statelessness. As Darling observes, it is a "tactic of evading substantive human rights obligations by hiding behind boilerplate refugee determination formulae" (2009, 749).

There are three technical and legal opportunities for redress. First, Canada can ratify the 1954 Convention. Second, Canada can recognize statelessness as a legal status. Enshrined in the 1954 Convention, stateless person status offers a minimum standard that states can adopt to ensure that stateless persons have access to basic rights. Third, a Statelessness Determination Procedure would streamline Canada's response to statelessness and reduce any overlaps with Canada's RSD. More broadly, we call for more interdisciplinary scholarship on statelessness in Canada and beyond. While appreciating legal analyses and solutions, it is key to deepen critical perspectives on existing and emergent socio-political forces of exclusion, including counter-intuitive solutions (see Hunter 2019). For these reasons, researchers need to be creative, bold, and political to continue theorizing beyond the confines of methodological nationalism for solutions. This demands the active inclusion of interdisciplinary analytical lenses (D. Brennan 2019, 180) and those with lived experiences of statelessness, allowing their voices to be paramount and authoritative (i.e., standpoint statelessness; see Bahram 2020). With the concerted attention of different voices, critical statelessness scholarship will continue to evolve and offer more in terms of practical means of resolution.

NOTES

1 We use the terms "nationality" and "citizenship" interchangeably though we acknowledge these are conceptualized differently in international law, sociology, and political theory.

2 The notion of de facto statelessness is itself heavily contested (see Tucker 2014; Baluarte 2017).

3 The full sentence reads: "Once they had left their homeland they remained homeless, once they had left their state they became stateless; once they had been deprived of their human rights they were rightless, the scum of the earth" (Arendt 1994, 267).

4 The historical record demonstrates that Canadian nationality is not immutable. It was, quite explicitly, granted and revoked along class and gender lines (see Harder 2022).

5 In 2017 IRCC published a definition of statelessness and provided guidelines on establishing proof of statelessness for humanitarian and compassionate applications (see Government of Canada 2017b).

6 A stateless person in Canada can submit an application for citizenship to alleviate special and unusual hardship (Citizenship Act 1985, s. 5 (4)) and for permanent residency on humanitarian and compassionate grounds (IRPA 2001, s. A25 (1)).

7 Erauw analyzes the provincial legislation of Alberta, British Columbia, Ontario, and Quebec.

8 Though most stateless people do not possess travel documents (passport), some who have been granted legal status by a state are granted passports and can travel freely.

9 A prominent example is the 2018 Humboldt Broncos bus crash in Saskatchewan, where permanent resident Jaskirat Singh Sidhu failed to stop at an intersection and his semi-truck collided with the bus carrying twenty-nine people, killing sixteen and seriously injuring thirteen. Sidhu pled guilty to all charges and was sentenced to eight years in prison (*R. v. Sidhu* 2019, SKPC 19). In 2020 the CBSA pursued his removal to India and in 2022 recommended that he be declared inadmissible. Sidhu's lawyer has challenged the decision as unreasonable because it places more weight on Sidhu's actions rather than the future risk he poses, and it acts as retribution when Sidhu has already been punished through the criminal justice system (Keung 2023). The case is currently unresolved and before the courts.

FURTHER READING AND RESOURCES

Canadian Centre on Statelessness. n.d. "Canadian Centre on Statelessness." http://www.statelessness.ca.

Canadian Council for Refugees (CCR). n.d. "Statelessness." https://ccrweb.ca/en/statelessness.

Immigration, Refugees and Citizenship Canada (IRCC). 2017. "The Humanitarian and Compassionate Assessment: Statelessness." Government of Canada. https://www.canada.ca/en/immigration-refugees-citizenship/corporate/publications-manuals/operational-bulletins-manuals/permanent-residence/humanitarian-compassionate-consideration/processing/stateless.html.

Liew, Jamie Chai Yun. 2021a. "A Father's Dream." *Migration Conversations* podcast, episode 20, 26:17. https://migration-conversations.simplecast.com/episodes/a-fathers-dream.

– 2021b. "Statelessness & COVID 19." *Migration Conversations* podcast, episode 27, 1:06:38. https://migration-conversations.simplecast.com/episodes/statelessness-covid-19.

– 2022. "Deepan's Citizenship." *Migration Conversations* podcast, episode 35, 50:19. https://migration-conversations.simplecast.com/episodes/deepans-citizenship.

UNHCR. 2019. "Global Action Plan to End Statelessness 2014–2024." https://www.unhcr.org/ru/wp-content/uploads/sites/73/2019/09/End-Statelessness-GlobalActionPlan-2019-Final-web.pdf.

UNHCR Canada. 2019. *Statelessness in Canada. A Study on the Situation of Stateless Persons in Canada.* UNHCR Canada Mapping Study. September 2019. https://www.unhcr.ca/wp-content/uploads/2019/09/statelessness-in-canada.pdf.

21

Immigration Detention in Canada: Concepts and Controversies

Stephanie J. Silverman

KEY TAKEAWAYS

- Immigration detention is a linchpin in immigration control in Canada and around the world.
- Detention is not natural: it is a recent legal construct comprised of statutes, legislation, policies, practices, institutions, and stakeholders' coercion and co-operation.
- Detention is visible as a prison cell but also invisible as a node in multiple axes of oppression of racialized, aged, and gendered people.

KEY TERMS

- Alternative to detention (ATD)
- Flight risk, or risk of absconding
- Immigration detention
- Immigration and Refugee Protection Act (IRPA)

INTRODUCTION

21.1 In 1992 Abdurahman Ibrahim Hassan came to Canada from Somalia as a child refugee with his aunt. He was soon granted refugee status. As he grew up, Mr Hassan began to suffer from a range of serious health issues, including schizophrenia, bipolar disorder, and insulin-dependent diabetes, as well as addictions to alcohol and cocaine. In his early twenties, Mr Hassan committed a series of violent crimes. After completing a sentence for aggravated sexual assault in 2012, he received deportation orders as per the Faster Removal of Foreign Criminals Act (FRFCA). Since he had not yet received Canadian citizenship, these criminal convictions invalidated his refugee status, and, hence, his legal right to reside in Canada.

The Canada Border Services Agency (CBSA) detained Mr Hassan in the "migrant pod" at the Central East Correctional Centre in Lindsay, Ontario, a super-max prison run by the Ontario ministry of corrections. He was incarcerated for three years, and his mental health severely declined. Transcripts of his detention reviews (like parole, but for immigration detainees) show an incoherent speaker with a limited grasp of his surroundings and situation. At a May 2015 detention review, Mr Hassan's legal representative requested his transfer to an Ontario facility for mentally ill inmates to receive care and treatment as follows: "Mr. Hassan ... only has sporadic access to psychiatric professionals, no access to therapy or programming or mental health services, and his condition has noticeably deteriorated over the past years and months" (Cain 2016).

Mr Hassan died in a local hospital the next month, where prison officers took him after an "outburst." At the time of his death, ten people were restraining Mr Hassan from throwing and swallowing his feces and chunks of his own hair. At one point, an Ontario Provincial Police officer had held down Mr Hassan's head with a towel to stop him from spitting and biting. The subsequent autopsy ruled out asphyxiation as his cause of death. Eighty-eight immigration detainees in the Lindsay prison signed a petition demanding an inquest into Mr Hassan's death; they had secretly circulated the petition among maximum-security ranges and hid it in a pile of legal papers (Cain 2016; Keung 2016a).

Immigration detention is the underappreciated linchpin enabling immigration and border control in Canada and around the world. Detention, as it will be short-handed in this chapter, refers to the assemblage of laws, policies, and practices implemented by a federal or national government to incarcerate a non-citizen on suspicion of breaching immigration rules, usually to facilitate removals to another national territory. While a relatively recent development in migration governance, detention has metastasized into the socio-legal fabric. Yet it is wholly abnormal to detain people like Mr Hassan (see box 21.1 above) for weeks, months, and years because the government wants to send them away. Liberty and freedom from arbitrary imprisonment constitute a cornerstone of human rights law generally and the Canadian Charter of Rights and Freedoms specifically. Detention should be more widely known and studied to better deconstruct and challenge its meteoric increase and normalization of core human rights infringements and also to understand why public outrage is not focused on dismantling it.

This chapter introduces key concepts and controversies of detaining immigrants in Canada. The first section provides a bird's-eye view of how detention operates in Canada, both physically and legislatively, to detain Mr Hassan and hundreds of others. The second section delves into the key analytic frameworks attempting to answer the confounding question: How can it be that Canada incarcerates hundreds of people for an indefinite period based on their immigration status? The third section moves from the macro to the micro to investigate how the FRFCA – a piece of Canadian detention legislation that targets racialized young men – speaks to the broader links connecting immigration, racial, and penal justice. This chapter takes an intersectional standpoint that recognizes how policing, detention, and deportation support a settler colonial vision of Canada. Detention is a prison but also a node in multiple axes of oppression that are mutually reinforcing and co-constructive. Detention is legislated violence that (re)enforces inequality, vulnerability, racialization, and other socio-legal processes that can harm community members and cause death, as was the case for Mr Hassan.

DETENTION IN CANADA

Detention policies and laws range from minimal and short to mandatory and long. Detention runs counter to the rule of law: most laws are written to prevent agents from doing things, like murdering or robbing; detention, on the other hand, is so extreme that law must create the grounds *for* it. This reversal speaks to the importance of liberty and freedom in countries like Canada, irrespective of citizenship, nationality, or migratory status. The right to liberty is inscribed in the Magna Carta, the Habeas Corpus Acts of England, and France's Declaration of the Rights of Man and the Citizen. In addition to soft law, treaties, and conventions, international law promulgates these freedoms in the Universal Declaration of Human Rights (UDHR) and the International Covenant on Civil and Political Rights. Detention is thus a site of tension pitting a country's power to enforce immigration rules against individuals' claims (Silverman and Molnar 2019).

As an instrument of immigration law embedded in administrative law, domestic courts often do not have jurisdiction to intervene in detention matters. This nesting in administrative law technically distinguishes detention from criminal incarceration. While detention looks like criminal imprisonment, it is more factually accurate to think of it as a parallel or shadow system with legal and architectural overlaps. Indeed, most procedural protections from criminal justice are not accessible to detainees: there are no readings of one's rights, no automatic rights to a lawyer or a phone call, and, usually, no meetings to explain how to get out of detention. In some jurisdictions, there are also no free lawyers, no translators, no mandatory court reviews, no visitations, and no one to alert family and friends upon arrest or transfer (Silverman and Nethery 2015; Silverman 2016; Wilsher 2011).

The Canadian detention system is relatively minimal, clean, humane, and respectful of human rights. In the 2018–19 Fiscal Year, when 36,145,370 foreign nationals officially entered Canada, the Canada Border Services Agency (CBSA) reported detaining 8,781 people (representing 0.0002 per cent of entries). Pre-pandemic, Canada's daily average of 342 people paled in quantitative comparison to the US's 2020 daily average of 33,724 detainees (US Immigration and Customs Enforcement 2021), and in qualitative comparison with Australia's detention sites on Christmas Island, Indonesia, Nauru, and Manus Island. Likelihood of absconding is the top reason for detention, with 85 per cent of people detained for "flight risk" (Silverman 2020). Canadian detention is highly gendered: between 2012 and 2019, an average of 81 per cent of the population was male identified. During the same period, most detainees were citizens of Mexico, the US, China, or India (Silverman, forthcoming). Canadian detainees have no right to free legal counsel or language interpreters; most detention procedures are summary or procedural; there are no auditors, watchdogs, or rapporteurs; and there is no time limit.

The geopolitics of Canada's location help explain the relatively minimal detention system. The "cold ocean geography" of large ocean and rocky shores, the freezing Arctic, and the militarized USA as its southern neighbour mean Canadian borders are difficult to approach and cross (Hyndman, Payne, and Jimenez 2017; Labman 2019; see also Young, chapter 3). A "carrier sanctions" policy deputizes airline agents at international airports to turn away immigrants from flying to Canada. The Safe Third Country Agreement (STCA) bans most asylum seekers from making claims in Canada if they have travelled by land across the US. Thus, while most immigrants enter Canada through authorized legal channels – such as refugee claims or student visas – some may become detainable at a later stage. Indeed, a key legal document, the "Chairperson Guideline 2: Detention" stipulates detention "is exercised principally, but not exclusively, pending removal" (2010, para. 3.1.12).

Detainees in Canada describe their confinements as stigmatizing and traumatic events (Abji 2020; Gros and van Groll 2015; Gros and Muscati 2020; Kennedy

2017; Kronick and Rousseau 2016; Keung 2017). Without a maximum time limit, the "unknowingness" of a potentially endless detention has been likened to mental torture. Mental health issues negatively affect detainees long after their formal detention has ended (Cleveland and Rousseau 2013; Cleveland, Rousseau, and Kronick 2012). One teenager recounted her week-long detention: "It's not just that week. It stays with you all your life. It is horrible. I don't think anyone deserves to be in a holding centre. It is jail … I am still very scared when I see a police officer. I hear someone knocking really hard and I think of what happened. I have flashbacks." (PressProgress 2018) Family members have reported emotional distress, such as separation anxiety, selective mutism, sleep difficulties, and post-traumatic symptoms after release from detention (Kronick, Rousseau, and Cleveland 2011, 2016). Detention centre staff have also come forward with testimonies of trauma and emotional damage from their work "on the inside" (Anonymous 2016; Bosworth and Slade 2014; A. Hall 2015; Hasham 2016; Ugelvik 2016).

Detention's *physical* architecture in Canada consists primarily of three CBSA-owned immigration holding centres (IHCs) and provincial prisons. The IHCs are located near international airports in the cities of Toronto, Ontario, (183 beds); Laval, Quebec, (109 beds); and Surrey, British Columbia (70 beds). They accommodate men, women, and families, with spaces for administration, support, and special purposes. Security-related features include closed captioned television (CCTV) surveillance, access control and communications systems, locked doors, and panic buttons. Like prisons, there are visiting rooms and uniformed guards. IHCs have shared facilities, poor ventilation, limited hygiene products, and substandard access to medical care.

Canada also detains about a third of detainees in RCMP or provincial correctional facilities. The RCMP uses detachments and has periodically set up "hosting centres" or "warming centres." The RCMP set up a hosting centre near Roxham Road, for example, when that site became a principal crossing point for immigrants looking to subvert the STCA rules for entering Canada (Major 2023). The CBSA set up a number of individual contracts with provinces to subcontract beds in their correctional facilities, or prisons, for incarcerating detainees. Detainees are either sequestered to their own "pod" or intermingled with the local prisoner population. In the prisons, detainees are treated the same as prisoners, no matter if they have a pending asylum claim, language barriers, mental trauma, and so on. As of May 2024 ten provinces had announced they are terminating their agreements with CBSA to imprison detainees in their prisons. It is not yet clear where the CBSA plans to transfer this population.

Detention's *legal and policy* architecture includes departmental and ministerial notes, practice notices, memos, statutes, international norms, and judicial and quasi-judicial rules. IRPA 2001, sections 54–61 legislates statutory powers for Canadian immigration officials to arrest, interrogate, detain, and deport non-citizens, with further guidance in sections 244–50 of the Immigration Refugee and Protection Regulations (the Regulations). CBSA can arrest and detain a non-citizen without a warrant and at virtually any time on suspicion that the person: poses a danger to the public; is unlikely to appear for an examination; cannot prove their identity; is part of an irregular arrival, such as en masse on a boat; on suspicion of human rights abuses; or a potential security threat. IRPA's powers are equally or more intrusive than any other piece of Canadian legislation (Will 2021, 145–6). Yet IRPA also legislates the world's only statutory framework of routine bail hearings before a decision-maker. Paradoxically, in the 2019 case *R. v. Chhina*, the Supreme Court of Canada (SCC) has implied that these detention reviews justify the lack of time limits.

In August 2016, responding to years of sustained and mounting criticism of the Canadian detention system, the Liberal government of Justin Trudeau committed up to CAD$138 million toward creating the National Immigration Detention Framework (NIDF). The NIDF was to "transform" detention into a "better and fairer" system. The four NIDF pillars are reducing the use of provincial jails for detainees; reducing the population of children in detention; partnering with third party stakeholders; and expanding the use and availability of non-custodial monitoring programs, known as Alternatives to Detention (ATDs). The NIDF announcement followed an eighteen-day hunger strike by over fifty detainees in the Lindsay prison.

The NIDF eventually developed three ATD streams. The first is the Community Case Management and Supervision Services stream for service providers like the Salvation Army to provide individual, in-community monitoring. The second is called the voice reporting (VR) stream; the VR stream uses "biometric voiceprint technology to enable as many as ten thousand individuals to report to the CBSA at agreed upon intervals, using either cellphones or landlines" (Canada Border Services Agency 2018, n.p.). The third and most controversial stream is the electronic monitoring stream, launched initially in the Greater Toronto Area as a local two-year pilot project, then extended for two more years and into the province of Quebec. The electronic monitoring takes the form of shackling enrollees with a remotely controlled ankle bracelet to track their movements after they are released from detention. A cousin of an enrollee in the electronic monitoring ATD stream described the family's experiences as extremely stress-inducing: the tracking bracelet vibrated and sounded like a fire alarm and the family lived in constant fear that it would go off at any moment (Bongiorno 2022). Detainees will understandably look for any opportunity to leave prison, including enrolling into this ATD; but, the lived experiences of being shackled electronically disappoint, if not devastate, the enrollees.

It is not surprising, then, that this architecture depends on the co-operation of hundreds of people. At the federal level, the key actors are the CBSA officers who arrest people and oversee the incarcerations; the members of the

Immigration Division of Immigration and Refugee Board tribunal, who preside over the hearings where detainees are either released or kept imprisoned; and the policy branch of Immigration, Refugees and Citizenship Canada (IRCC). At the provincial level, ministries own the prisons and fund most public health services and legal aid. Additional actors include the federal RCMP and the local police forces. Finally, there is a cross-section of non-state actors, including private firms who staff the IHCs; organizations who monitor and assist detainees, including the United Nations High Commissioner for Refugees (UNHCR) and the Canadian Red Cross; activists who visit and advocate for the detainees to be released; media who investigate and report; and unions who represent workers across a variety of detention-related occupations.

SITUATING DETENTION IN CANADA

Canadian settler colonialism is closely related to immigration enforcement measures and racial forms of governance. A settler colonial analytic framework recognizes that immigration policies work to dispossess Indigenous Peoples from their lands, entitlements, cultural heritage, and rights (E. Cameron 2015; Coulthard 2014; Ellermann and O'Heran 2021; Simpson 2014; Wolfe 1999, 2006). Canadian policy-makers write immigration legislation without Indigenous consultation, setting demographic futures in motion (Bauder 2011, 518; Bhungalia 2018; Dauvergne 2016; Nath 2021; Sharma 2009), including marking the boundaries of races, genders, and ethnicities (Mahrouse 2014, 183; Mawani 2000). Immigration and border control rules set by the colonizer marginalize, stigmatize, de-mobilize, impoverish, detain, deter, and remove "strangers" falling afoul of a racialized and gendered vision of the "nation" (Bashford 2014; Bhui 2016; Chadha 2008; A. Green and D. Green 2004, 107; Knowles 2007; Roberts 1988; Russell and Rae 2020). By insufficiently highlighting these linkages, migration studies scholarship is complicit in the "willing amnesia" that "imagines away" First Nations' claims and rights (Volpp 2015, 292; Walters 2015).

Threads of colonialism, ableism, White supremacy, and "deservingness" of lesser treatment braid the history of Canadian detention. By naturalizing the incarceration of Othered people, settler colonialism displaces detention from its context of systemic injustice; it shields detainees' identities, histories, and causes of displacement from national and international public attention (Lemberg-Pedersen 2019; Mountz 2015). Detention's real perpetrator (the federal government) is never held accountable: it is only ever individual guards, contractors, or corporations who are punished after "complaints" for specific damage, such as instances of abuse, rape, and neglect. Canadian settlers deny and invisibilize detention's traumas: the dissolution of families, livelihoods, dignity, and futures is collateral damage in the maintenance of borders and the nation (Abji and Larios 2020; Aiken and Silverman 2021; Mullings, Morgan, and Quelleng 2016; Saito 2021).

Detention's powerful roles in the carceral state are coming to light (Aiken and Silverman 2021; Cassidy 2019; Markowitz 2021; Piché, Kleuskens, and Walby 2017). An institutional structure of racism and racialization insidiously orders immigration and fuses into punishment and prisons (Maynard 2017; Struthers Montford and Moore 2018; Ware, Ruzsa, and Dias 2014). The *possibility* of being detained distinguishes residents from citizens, producing the impression that immigrants are dangerous (L.L. Martin and Mitchelson 2009; Mainwaring and Silverman 2016; Nath 2021; Silverman and Kaytaz 2022). Xenophobia, Islamophobia, and other deleterious impressions of newcomers contribute to influencing the public into minimizing the extent of detention's injustices (Bigo 2002; Gray and Franck 2019; Moffette and Vadasaria 2016). Fears of "contaminated" bodies spreading disease and disorder are newly familiar in the COVID-19 era but are as old as the first instances of immigration detention in Canada, which was aligned with quarantine regulations (Bashford 2014; Silverman 2020, forthcoming).

Researchers point to the instrumentalization of perceived migration "crises" as political levers to expand and justify detention's targeting of certain newcomers (Crawley and Skleparis 2018; Huysmans 2000; Hyndman 2012; Mainwaring 2012; Mainwaring and Silverman 2017; Mainwaring and Cook 2018; Mountz and Hiemstra 2014). The "media-policy-migration nexus" scripts combine fear of a "refugee crisis" with racialized and historically specific notions of deservingness and dangerousness (Bradimore and Bauder 2011; Esses, Medianu, and Lawson 2013, 522; Farris and Mohamed 2018; Kronick and Rousseau 2015; Kyriakides 2017; Lawlor and Tolley 2017, 972; Mountz 2015; Silverman and Kaytaz 2022). Calling for more detention as deterrence, "muscular" border enforcement narratives distract the local populations from the real-life perils of human insecurity, precarity, and displacement (Mountz 2015, 190).

Canadian and other governments legalized contemporary detention powers in the context of wartime hostilities and then maintained them to counteract an "internal alien threat" (that is racialized but not necessarily presented in racist terms) (Mountz et al. 2013; Silverman 2010, 2012; Turnbull 2017). A contemporary example is the consternation over the irregular border crossings at Roxham Road, Quebec. A neo-liberal environment pits asylum seekers against immigrants in a purported zero-sum race for access to social welfare and other scarce resources (Carver 2015; G. Clark 2019; Dobrowolsky 2017; L. Taylor 2015). Xenophobic stories, archetypes, tropes, and images tend to erode popular support for refugee protection and increase popular support for detention measures (Kanji 2018; Labman 2011; Molnar Diop 2014; Panesar, Pottie-Sherman, and Wilkes 2017; Park 2014; Silverman 2016).

Xenophobia feeds on the debunked belief that immigrants have criminal tendencies. "Crimmigration" names the socio-legal processes that suffuse criminal justice norms, punishments, and associations into immigration legislation, but without bringing along the due diligence and other protections of criminal proceedings (Stumpf 2020). Crimmigration processes corrupt legal and social practices, tainting both with the convictions that (racialized) immigrants are cheaters, criminals, or otherwise untrustworthy (Aiken and Silverman 2021; Garcia Hernández 2011, 2013; Kubal 2014; Legomsky 2007; Silverman and Kaytaz 2022). Immigration status violations are used to remove suspected criminals who would be difficult or impossible to prosecute under criminal laws, as we will see with the FRFCA.

Detention "locks in" racialized and gendered thinking that immigrants are dangerous criminals (Pratt and Thompson 2008; Razack 2002). Likewise, criminal laws target immigrants and racialized children and adults who "look like" immigrants. Against this perception, research indicates that immigration does not increase – and in some cases decreases – local crime rates (Ha 2020; Jung 2020; M. Lee and Martinez 2009; Wortley 2009). Statistics Canada data for Toronto show that "the higher the proportion of recent immigrants in a neighbourhood, the lower the rates of drug offences, all types of violent crime, mischief, and other thefts ... Thus, all else being equal, high-immigration neighbourhoods generally have lower crime rates" (Abedi 2019). Yet once this vision of detainees as criminals is "locked in," it becomes increasingly difficult to mobilize public outrage at detention, and detention itself seeps even further into the social fabric. Here we see one key reason that explains – but does not justify – the absence of public outrage about detention in Canada.

21.2 It may be helpful, then, to turn to the tragic death of Lucía Vega Jiménez to grasp the fuller consequences of detention's harms and its deep roots in xenophobic assumptions and prejudices. On 28 December 2013, forty-two-year-old Ms Vega Jiménez died at Vancouver's Mount Saint Joseph Hospital after hanging herself with a shower curtain at the now-shuttered Vancouver IHC. The warren-like IHC for short-term detentions had been located in the basement of the Vancouver International Airport. Ms Vega Jiménez, a worker in a Vancouver hotel, had been arrested by a SkyTrain Transit Police officer for an unpaid bus ticket. Ms Vega Jiménez was also a domestic abuse survivor from Mexico and feared for her life if returned there. A detention review scheduled assessment was cancelled when CBSA and other public officials concealed Ms Vega Jiménez's death from the public for over a month (No One is Illegal - Canada 2014; Paterson 2014).

The BC coroner's inquest into Ms Vega Jiménez's death identified shocking issues at the Vancouver IHC, including: a lack of suicide prevention and mental health training for private security personnel staffing the facility, and detainees' difficulties in accessing legal counsel, both in person and by phone. The private security officers staffing the IHC had failed to conduct their requisite supervisory rounds of the facility and had falsified their reports following the suicide attempt. The inquest heard that CBSA had failed to appropriately staff the facility and had not effected proper management of the facility (Ministry of Justice, Coroners Service, Province of British Columbia 2014; Track and Paterson 2017). The coroner recommended that cameras be installed in the shower room where Ms Vega Jiménez attempted suicide, a suggestion that was immediately met with outrage by human rights campaigners. The inquiry also revealed that the Transit Police officer had racially profiled Ms Jiménez as potentially undocumented to identify her as a target: When asked by a lawyer why he decided that CBSA might be a good resource to call, the officer replied: "[a]t that point I understood that – I could hear that she had an accent when I spoke with her … And with that there I could tell that she wasn't originally from Canada, and that's why I attempted to identify her by using CBSA" (cited in Moffette 2021).

UNDOING UNFREEDOM: CHALLENGING MANDATORY DETENTION AND THE FASTER REMOVAL OF FOREIGN CRIMINALS ACT

An intersectional settler colonial framework can reveal how the FRFCA and detention persist (if not grow): detention is imagined as the purview of racialized young men, who are already constructed as more threatening and more dangerous than the general population and so are already more detainable and imprisonable (Silverman and Kaytaz 2022). The Conservative government of Stephen Harper introduced the FRFCA to IRPA in 2013 to expedite deportations of criminalized people born abroad and residing in Canada. Two years later, the Harper government's 2015 Zero Tolerance for Barbaric Cultural Practices Act explicitly threatened Muslim immigrants to adopt "more progressive" Canadian values or risk banishment. While never established, the same government promised an anonymous RCMP tip line to report "incidents of barbaric cultural practices in Canada."

In this hostile atmosphere of gendered and racist xenophobia, the FRFCA was green-lit to eliminate non-citizens' legal rights to appeal a removal order if sentenced to six months in prison, or if they have been convicted of a crime abroad that carries a maximum ten-year sentence or more. This threshold of six months' sentencing is lower than analogous rules in the US and other Commonwealth countries, widely considered to practice harsher detention than Canada. The FRFCA also eliminated a procedural appeal route previously available to non-citizens challenging removal orders. As Benslimane and

Moffette argue, "this tough-on-crime/tough-on-immigration policy is part of a broader populist strategy aimed at pitting communities against each other, while advancing socially and fiscally conservative policy changes that are detrimental to most of us" (2019, 46). The FRFCA offers no exceptions, including for someone suffering from mental illness, like Mr Hassan (see box 21.1).

The FRFCA is a "politically successful policy failure," of which there are many in the wider field of detention (Andreas 2003, 3; Mainwaring and Silverman 2017). After the FRFCA's 2013 incorporation into IRPA, removals from Canada decreased, from 13,869 in 2012 to 10,743 in 2013, and 7,852 in 2014. In 2013 and 2014 combined, only 14 per cent (2,674) of those who claimed asylum after 15 December 2012 were deported. Just over half of the people ordered removed after failed refugee claims in 2013 were deported within one year, and the target of 80 per cent was not reached (Atak, Hudson, and Nakache 2017, 18).

The FRFCA thus illuminates how immigration injustices are connected to racial and prison injustices. A remarkable 2018 Ontario Superior Court decision highlights "the problem of the disproportionate imprisonment of Black offenders" (*R. v. Morris* 2006, para. 24). After finding evidence of systemic racism, Justice Shaun Nakatsuru reduced the time in prison for a Black Canadian citizen who had been found guilty of possession of a loaded illegal handgun. Mr Morris was twenty-two years old with no criminal record but had experienced poverty, extreme violence, mental illness, disability, and anti-Black racism in Toronto. At the time of his arrest, the police failed to give Mr Morris his rights to counsel and drove over his foot with their vehicle. Justice Nakatsuru's consideration of anti-Black racism potentially signals an approach to criminal justice similar to the Gladue Principles sentencing reforms for Indigenous offenders.

Mr Morris's citizenship was an identity marker that went largely unnoticed in court proceedings and discussions dissecting the decision. If Mr Morris had not been born a Canadian citizen, however, his conviction would have triggered the FRFCA's detention consequences. Somali- and Jamaican-Canadian urban communities are already undergoing high levels of scrutiny and surveillance as well as official co-operation between local police and the federal CBSA (Aiken 2007; Barnes 2009; Berns-McGown 2013; Moffette 2021). Such a carceral environment normalizes the surveillance, arrests, and incarcerations of Mr Hassan and Mr Morris. To more fulsomely account for anti-Black bias, the *Morris* decision should be expanded from criminal and racial justice and into the field of immigration justice and can provide fodder for the overturning of the FRFCA.

CONCLUSIONS AND RECOMMENDATIONS

This chapter concludes by zooming out and recontextualizing the FRFCA in the wider immigration landscape. On one level, the FRFCA is an illustration of larger structural injustices of anti-Black and other forms of racism and how these structures permeate and shape carceral and immigration laws (Achiume 2019;

Golash-Boza 2016; Hari 2014; Maynard 2017; see, also M. Alexander 2020; Goldstein 2008; Saito 2021; Stevenson 2018). When intersectional analysis is applied to settler colonialism, the lens reveals how some racialized minorities are "model and quasi-assimilable" while the rest are "enslavable, criminal, murderable" (Tuck and Yang 2012, 17–18). Black and Muslim people, particularly male-identified people, are constantly constructed as foreign and imprisonable. The narratives animating the FRFCA and detention practices focusing on demobilizing "dangerous criminals" align with the marginalizing historical, racialized, and post- and neo-colonial knowledges about "outsiders" (Moffette and Vadasaria 2016, 300; see also Mountz et al. 2013, 531).

To address and halt detention's injustices, detention must be seen as a symptom of a larger series of socio-legal and political ills that can only be remedied through structural change. Detention must be re-situated as an unnatural legal creation born of the colonial present and the settler state. Immigrant justice must be firmly aligned with prison and racial justice campaigns. And, finally, citizens and newcomers must collectively reject the norms of unfreedom that plague racialized, gendered, and otherwise marginalized people in Canada.

FURTHER READING AND RESOURCES

CBC Radio. 2018. "How Abdoul Abdi's Defenders Helped Keep Him from being Deported." CBC News. *Day 6* Radio Documentary, 20 July 2018. https://www.cbc.ca/radio/day6/episode-399-russia-keeps-meddling-sacha-baron-cohen-keeps-punking-impeach-o-meter-che-s-brother-and-more-1.4753119/how-abdoul-abdi-s-defenders-helped-keep-him-from-being-deported-1.4753129.

Chak, Tings. 2014. *Undocumented: The Architecture of Migrant Detention.* Montreal and Amsterdam: The Architecture Observer. https://tingschak.com/undocumented-the-architecture-of-migrant-detention.

García Hernández, César Cuauhtémoc. 2019. "The US Can Move Past Immigration Prisons – and Towards Justice." TEDxMileHigh video, 12:06. https://www.ted.com/talks/cesar_cuauhtemoc_garcia_hernandez_the_us_can_move_past_immigration_prisons_and_towards_justice.

Global Detention Project. n.d. "Country Profiles – Canada." https://www.globaldetentionproject.org/countries/americas/canada.

Silverman, Stephanie J. 2021. "Springing Amir." *Migration and Society* 4 (1): 172–84. https://doi.org/10.3167/arms.2021.040116.

22

Fires and Floods: Examining Internal Climate Migration in Canada

Geneviève Minville and Yvonne Su

KEY TAKEAWAYS

- Within Canada, climate displacement manifests in various ways with recurrent sudden events, such as floods and wildfires; yet the topic has received very little attention.
- A continuum exists between forced migration and choice, as well as immobility because some people cannot move in the face of climate change.
- Given the legacy of colonialism, climate change – and by extension climate displacement – disproportionately impacts Indigenous communities.

KEY TERMS

- Climate migration
- Environmental hazards
- Rapid-onset hazards
- Slow-onset hazards
- Disaster

INTRODUCTION

Climate migration, the movement or displacement of people due to factors related to climate change, is a global mobility trend and humanitarian emergency that has been inaccurately portrayed as the Global South "invading" the Global North. Sensationalist media report on a great climate migration headed "north" (Lustgarten 2020), describing the upcoming "century of climate migration" where mass migration of millions will cross continents (Vince 2022). Yet this dominant discourse on climate migration is not supported by empirical evidence. The Intergovernmental Panel on Climate Change (IPCC) "Sixth Assessment Report" shows that observed migration across borders due to climatic hazards is considerably smaller relative to internal migration, with those international flows often between neighbouring states, ones with labour migration arrangements, or long-standing cultural ties (Cissé et al. 2022). Indeed, most climate-related mobility observed now, and projected into the future, takes place within countries, not across borders (UNHCR and OHCHR 2022), with the World Bank (Clement et al. 2021) estimating a total of 216 million people could be displaced within their counties by 2030. In addition, while climate change may have been historically regarded as just one driver of migration, climatic drivers of migration are anticipated to play a stronger causal role in migration decisions in coming decades (Cissé et al. 2022; Clement et al. 2021).

Despite this, the majority of research (McLeman, Moniruzzaman, and Akter 2018; Mezdour, Veronis, and McLeman 2016; Veronis and McLeman 2014); media (Lenoir 2021; Van Eeckhout 2013; Vidal 2005); and humanitarian focus (Climate Refugees n.d.) on climate-induced migration has been on cases from the Global South. As such, there is very little research, media attention, or policy around internal climate migration in Global North countries like Canada. Only recently did the Library of Parliament (2020) produce a background paper for parliamentarians on climate change and its impacts and policy implications, which included a small section on environment-related migration. The paper highlights that the lack of understanding around environment-related migration can lead to different challenges on the international as well as the national level. According to the International Displacement Monitoring Centre (IDMC), in 2021 Canada experienced a total of sixty thousand internal displacements related to disasters defined as the "number of movements, not people, as individuals can be displaced several times," including one thousand nine hundred still displaced by the end of the year (IDMC 2022, 161). Climate-induced migration within Canada already manifests in various ways and reflects how such mobility, in general, can be permanent or temporary as well as forced or planned. According to an Angus Reid survey conducted in August 2021, many Canadians now consider climate factors when deciding where to reside, with 76 per cent of Canadians reporting environmental policy and sustainability as priorities (Su 2021).

This chapter offers an overview of how climate change affects people's (im) mobility within Canada. Our analysis highlights the distress of recurrent displacement and shows how Indigenous communities are disproportionately affected by climate displacement (also see Coburn, chapter 1). We point to the lack of data and peer-reviewed analysis on the subject, especially in relation to people's future intentions pertaining to climate-induced (im)moblity. Finally, the chapter discusses some recommendations and conclusions.

DEFINITIONS AND CONCEPTUAL DEBATES

Since El-Hinnawi (1985) first defined "environmental refugees" in a United Nations Environment Programme document, climate human mobility has had many labels. The term "climate, or environmental, *refugee*" has been largely criticized: it is not recognized under international law since the 1951 Refugee Convention does not consider environmental factors[1] a form of persecution. Still, some actors continue to use the term to advocate for climate justice (Su 2016; Topgül 2021). While there are no legal definitions, some organizations provide technical ones. The International Organization for Migration (IOM) defines "environmental migrants" as: "persons or groups of persons who, predominantly for reasons of sudden or progressive change in the environment that adversely affects their lives or living conditions, are obliged to leave their habitual homes, or choose to do so, either temporarily or permanently, and who move either within their country or abroad" (Ionesco, Mokhnacheva, and Gemenne 2016, 3).

The word "environment" can encompass various environmental factors that are not necessarily related to climate. For example, Bose and Lunstrum (2014) point to developmental projects like dams breaking, which disrupt the environment and force evacuations. The Nansen Initiative agenda discusses "disaster displacement" and "disaster-displaced persons" and defines the former as "situations where people are forced or obliged to leave their homes or places of habitual residences as a result of a disaster or in order to avoid the impact of an immediate and foreseeable natural hazard" (Nansen Initiative 2015, 16).

These definitions share various similarities, including the fact that climate-induced migration can be temporary or permanent, it can lead to internal or international mobility, and it can result from rapid-onset or slow-onset events. Some definitions also reflect the continuum between choosing and being forced to move. For instance, during slow-onset events, people may have more time to accumulate the necessary means to move compared to rapid-onset events where people are forcibly evacuated (Šedová, Čizmaziová, and Cook 2021). It is important to note that climate change can also lead to immobility rather than serving as a catalyst of migration (Benveniste, Oppenheimer, and Fleurbaey 2022).

CLIMATE MIGRATION TO CANADA

In 2021 US president Biden was applauded for signing the first executive order to report climate-induced migration and discuss ways to respond to it (White House 2021). In a report by the White House (2021), climate migration is referred to as climate human mobility in general, including immobility. While this is undoubtedly an improvement toward recognizing the impacts of climate change on migration, it is also a reminder of the policy gap in Canada on this topic.

In Canada, the subject of climate migration has focused heavily on current and future migration to Canada due to climate change. This trend is supported by sensationalized media headlines such as "Historic Human Tsunami Likely in Canada's Future" (McMartin 2021) and "Could Canada be a Safe Haven for Climate Refugees?" (Mortillaro 2019). The Library of Parliament (2020) also has background paper with a section entitled "Canada as a Host Country," which details how Canada welcomed people affected by earthquakes from Haiti in 2010 and Nepal in 2015. However, when Immigration, Refugees and Citizenship Canada (IRCC) was asked whether Canada has any policies for climate migrants, they responded that "[i]n the event of natural disaster, decisions on actions by the Government of Canada are taken on a case-by-case basis" (Labbé 2021). Labbé (2021) found that climate migrants have already arrived in Canada, but they are "invisible" under immigration laws. For instance, Labbé (2021) reported on two cases of Central American migrants who have left their respective countries because of the difficulties amplified by climate change. In both cases, the individuals were able to establish in Canada, one with a refugee status and one through the migrant worker program. However, in both cases, climate factors were not considered in the application processes.

These examples reflect the multi-causality of the phenomena of climate migration. Similarly, Veronis and McLeman (2014) and McLeman, Moniruzzaman, and Akter (2018) show that climate factors are rarely the first consideration influencing migrants' decisions, which involve a combination of circumstances, including environment. Veronis and McLeman (2014) demonstrate that Canadian immigration policies do not facilitate climate migration. Instead, immigration policies favour skilled workers, which contributes to brain drain in the sending countries, resulting in "remov[ing] educated persons from the very countries that need them most" (Dickson, Webber, and Takaro 2014, 6). Following the logic that migration can boost innovation in host societies (Scellato et al. 2017), some argue that expert migrants can play a key role in the transition toward a greener economy (Bates-Eamer, Schmidtke, and Benson 2021; A. Robinson 2022). In the US, this phenomenon has already happened. For instance, after the Katrina hurricane, migrants from Central America came to help rebuild communities (Reichman 2022). As climate migration increases, the Canadian government will have to be part of the solution (Omeziri and Gore 2014; McLeman and Veronis 2015).

CLIMATE-INDUCED MIGRATION WITHIN CANADA

Studies show that various factors influence whether people move internally within Canada to mitigate future climate risks, including likelihood of another disaster, financial capacities, age, and housing situation. Importantly, (im) mobility in such cases does not only depend on people's volition. First, when faced with the likelihood of recurrent hazards and subsequent future disasters, people are more inclined to want to move. For example, the Indigenous community of Merritt, British Columbia, that was evacuated twice in 2021 – first by summer wildfires and then November floods – is now expecting other disasters and community members are therefore weighing their options (Cecco 2021; Radio-Canada 2021). During summer 2022 another wildfire forced the evacuation of residents near Okanagan, British Columbia (Canadian Press 2022). As hazards are more recurrent and intense, host communities are put under increasing pressure, with overcrowding of temporary accommodations (see Nuttall 2021). Similarly, Haney (2019) conducted a study with residents after the 2013 Alberta floods, where one hundred seventy-five thousand people were evacuated, including eighty thousand from Calgary. This research showed concern about future disasters influenced people's plans to move or not because of climate factors. For instance, people who believed climate change would increase disasters were more concerned about future floods and were, therefore, more likely to want to move (Haney 2019). Sixty-seven per cent of participants who mentioned worrying about future floods indicated being less likely to stay after one year and thus more likely to move elsewhere (Haney 2019, 231). But residents are not the only ones contemplating migration. Quebec premier François Legault and New Brunswick premier Blaine Higgs have both said people should move out of flood-prone areas (Rabson 2019).

Another influencing factor is related to people's residences and the housing market. Climate hazards impact real estate values, which can strain homeowners. Bakos et al. (2022) found that floodings in Canada impact housing markets in different ways, including by lowering prices and increasing the days on market. Hazards can motivate people to move before their houses loses value (Haney 2019), but once hazards have destroyed houses, people either have to rebuild or leave. A resident whose house was destroyed after the 2016 Fort McMurray wildfire explained how she and her husband were financially unable to rebuild, and their neighbour ended up paying the mortgage on a house they do not live in because they did not declare bankruptcy (Thurton 2019). Similarly, Lytton's residents, whose British Columbia city was destroyed by a devastating wildfire during the summer 2021, are still waiting to rebuild, although their insurance might not cover all the rebuilding costs (Williams 2022). As hazards increase in Canada, insurance companies increase their prices or change their coverage (Zoledziowski 2021).

Choosing to move will also vary depending on people's financial capacities. In wealthier places, mobility is most likely associated with attachment to the neighbourhood and social networks (Haney 2019). More affluent disaster-affected households can build back relatively quickly, such as after the Fort McMurray wildfire (Bedarff and Jakobeit 2017). Climate hazards might thus seem like something to adapt to. But not everyone has this capability. In fact, such a perspective can diminish the quality of life of climate-displaced people in more vulnerable socio-economic conditions (Bedarff and Jakobeit 2017). On the one hand, social networks can encourage staying despite hazards (Haney 2019), in other contexts, like Indigenous communities, recurrent hazards can rather severely impact social ties (S. Thompson, Ballard, and Martin 2014; Radio-Canada 2022; Khalafzai, McGee, and Parlee 2021). Overall, people exposed to natural hazards depend on their social networks to survive so the concept of social capital and networks cannot be overlooked when examining the topic of climate migration and post-disaster recovery (Su 2022).

Age can also influence whether people will consider moving (see also Clark-Kazak, chapter 13). For instance, a study conducted by Vasseur, Thornbush, and Plante (2018) on the impact of the 2010 and 2011 Atlantic storms in Prince Edward Island, New Brunswick, and Quebec found that older people are less likely to consider relocating and prefer opting for other mitigating solutions (Vasseur, Thornbush, and Plante 2018). An Angus Reid Institute survey (2021) also exposed differences depending on the age of participants. For people between age eighteen and thirty-four, 19 per cent indicated an area's environmental policy and/or sustainability is an essential priority when choosing where to live, compared to 13 per cent of people age fifty-five and up (Su 2021).

22.1 A respondent from Baie des Chaleurs affected by the 2010 Quebec storms recalls, "In fact, we finished by understanding that if they didn't have the nerves to stay there, the only solution was to move. This means that we have lost a few people who decided to move, to be in a location … far from water bodies" (translated by Liette Vasseur; Vasseur, Thornbush, and Plante 2018, 43).

WHEN MOVING OR STAYING IS NOT A CHOICE

While the previous section offers valuable insight on factors influencing climate mobility in Canada, it should be noted that not everyone has a choice about whether to move. As Benveniste, Oppenheimer, and Fleurbaey (2022) found, climate change can restrict migration as it can limit access to resources. For example, the Kashechewan Cree First Nation in Northern Ontario regularly evacuates because of recurring spring flooding of the Albany River. The residents have been evacuated a total of fourteen times, either temporarily or permanently, almost every year since 2004, leading to many challenges, such as residents' feelings of disconnection from their community upon return (Khalafzai, McGee, and Parlee 2021). As a result, the community signed a non-legally binding agreement in 2019 with the federal and provincial governments to relocate the community within eight to ten years (Stefanovich 2019). Although this is a community-based decision, the community fears the government will not actually carry it out, given that a similar agreement with Paul Martin's government in 2005 fell through under Harper's government (Stefanovich 2019). The experience of this Northern Ontario community highlights that safe and permanent climate-induced relocation is largely dependent on government support.

22.2 A long-term evacuee from the Kashechewan First Nation remarks:

> I would like just to see that my children and their children don't have to live the way we live, [which is] emotionally, spiritually, physically draining. That's what I hope for. Maybe they can relocate, and they'll have a better life - better than the life we have right now - always expecting the unknown. That is not a very delightful feeling when you have that, and the [federal] government would not understand that - I don't think so anyway. You tell them, but do they take it? No, they don't. If I [were] to live somewhere - where I don't have to fear the risk of a flood, I will die a happy man. (Khalafzai, McGee, and Parlee 2021, 10)

Another example of how mobility can depend on government support and financial means comes from the 2017 and 2019 Quebec floods, which displaced three thousand five hundred and nine thousand five hundred people respectively. Fayazi, Bisson, and Nicholas's (2020) research with the Mohawk community of Kanesatake found that some people affected in 2019 were still displaced from the 2017 flood. Results from the study show how total relocation of this community appears impossible, as people do not have access to their land and have no other territories to go to because the Kanesatake community is not a "reserve" legally speaking (for more information on reserves in Canada and the Indian Act, 1876, see Coburn, chapter 1). Thus, the community cannot relocate despite being in an area prone to environmental hazards (Fayazi, Bisson, and Nicholas 2020).

In addition to governmental support, another significant factor impacting (im)mobility is people's economic means. It is usually those already living in disaster-prone and low-income areas who are first and most significantly impacted by disasters. This was evident in the case of the 2019 Quebec floods in the city of Sainte-Marie (formerly called Sainte-Marie-de-Beauce). The three hundred houses destroyed by the flood were predominantly rented by low-income households. These houses were affordable precisely because they were old and constructed in a flood-risk area. As such, those affected were living in a precarious situation that made them vulnerable to flooding (Lavoie 2019). Months after the flood, the residents did not have the financial capacity to move to a restored area, and they were forced to move to neighbouring cities (Lavoie 2019). These situations of overlapping precarity and double disasters meant that displaced people ended up living in substandard housing without electricity or were unhoused and living on the streets (Lavoie 2019). People's economic means thus play a significant role in both their exposure to disasters and their ability to migrate.

Finally, in situations where rapid-onset hazards destroy a whole community, mobility or immobility is not a choice. During the summer of 2021 the town of Lytton, British Columbia, home of the Lytton First Nation, was destroyed in less than twenty minutes (Zoledziowski 2021). In this case, evacuation was mandatory, and the possibility of returning afterward seemed simply unlikely (Zoledziowski 2021). The Lytton 2021 wildfires followed a severe heatwave in June and wildfires of the previous year (Al Jazeera Staff 2021). In August 2022 the city faced yet another wildfire while many residents were still in temporary accommodations from 2021 (Williams 2022). City officials are trying to rebuild better, with reconstruction taking longer due to "archaeological surveys to check for Indigenous artifacts before rebuilding" (Williams 2022). However, the question of who benefits from "building back better" is always an important one in post-disaster recovery (Su and Le Dé 2021). If the rebuilding process is "better" but much slower, meaning residents are displaced for long periods of time, is it truly better?

For Lytton residents, the slow rebuilding has caused some to decide to move elsewhere, even though it was not their initial intention (Williams 2022). Similarly, in November 2021, after the 2021 summer wildfires, the Indigenous community of Merritt, not far from Lytton, was severely affected by floods (Cecco 2021; Hessey 2022; Radio-Canada 2021). Some families lost everything and had to stay in temporary settlements, not only because houses were destroyed but also for sanitary reasons as the water was contaminated (Radio-Canada 2021). More than seven thousand people were evacuated (Hessey 2022). The recurrence of disasters affecting the community in 2021, makes it challenging for people to imagine a future in Merritt (Radio-Canada 2021). As people anticipate other future hazards, they discuss their intention of moving entirely out of the area (Cecco 2021; Radio-Canada 2021).

INDIGENOUS COMMUNITIES

Indigenous communities are, overall, disproportionately impacted by climate change (UNHCR and OHCHR 2022; Library of Parliament 2020). In Canada, this manifests by being climate displaced or having limited capacity to move in the face of climate change. Collier (2015) notes how Indigenous communities in Canada are vulnerable to climate hazards because of their socio-economic conditions, geographic location, and frequency of hazards (see also Quirt 2021).

An explicit example of how vulnerability to hazards largely depends on the action and/or inaction of government is the case of the 2011 Manitoba floods. In 2011 the government diverted water as a flood threatened Winnipeg (S. Thompson, Ballard, and Martin 2014). The diverted water created a "super flood" in Lake St Martin, and what had started as a natural hazard resulted in a human-made one. The super flood led to the evacuation of eighteen First Nations communities (Government of Canada 2021a). In 2014 there were 1,064 Lake St Martin First Nation members still displaced three years later (S. Thompson, Ballard, and Martin 2014). Some people displaced from the 2011 floods considered themselves "refugees" in their homeland as they were forcibly relocated to an abandoned military base (S. Thompson, Ballard, and Martin 2014; Ballard 2016). In 2015 there were 1,926 First Nations members still displaced (Collier 2015). In 2017 there were 350 Lake St Martin First Nation members still in temporary houses (D.E. Martin et al. 2017). As of 2021 there were 91 of the Peguis First Nation still displaced (Government of Canada 2021a).

More recently, in May 2022 the Peguis First Nation was again affected by floods and hundreds were evacuated and relocated to Winnipeg (CBC News 2022a). The May 2022 floods came only one month after federal aid stopped that had helped people still displaced from 2011 and the 2014 floods (Radio-Canada 2022). As of April 2022 there were 121 members of the Peguis community still living in temporary houses after the 2014 floods (Radio-Canada 2022). Overall, the 2011, 2014, and 2022 Manitoba floods exemplify how climate hazards disproportionately impact Indigenous communities. These examples also show the role of government (in)action in creating or fostering the vulnerability leading to disasters and climate displacement (also see Coburn, chapter 1 for insights on the ongoing biopolitics of Canadian settler colonialism fostering such vulnerability within Indigenous communities).

RESEARCH GAPS

The studies cited in this chapter are revealing, but there remains limited data on climate-induced displacement, especially from peer-reviewed research. First, most studies conducted with people who have been displaced are not discussing recent disasters. We need more analysis of climate displacement related to more recent disasters, such as the 2021 summer wildfire and floods in British Columbia, the Merritt floods in November 2021, and the May 2022 floods affecting the Peguis First Nation in Manitoba. Moreover, all the studies refer to disasters and rapid-onset events. There is limited information about slow-onset events and recurring hazards.

Another critical gap is the confusion regarding the terms used to describe climate mobility within Canada. For instance, data mostly focus on people's intention of moving in the future rather than people who have already chosen to move. Specifically, articles discuss the intention of "moving" (for instance, see Haney 2019) but also discuss being "displaced" or "evacuated" when referring to people in movement (for instance, see S. Thompson, Ballard, and Martin 2014). This raises important issues regarding the terms used. First, we could argue that "moving" is closer to "migrating." "Migration," as noted by the Nansen Initiative, implies a more voluntary type of movement, where people have some choices, even though those may are limited (Nansen Initiative 2015). Second, as noted previously, most displacement related to climate change occurs within countries (UNHCR and OHCHR 2022). But deciding to move to mitigate future hazards might be challenging to assess, especially when that movement stays within the country. For instance, after the 2016 Fort McMurray wildfire, the population census of 2018 indicated a decrease by 11 per cent since the 2015 census (Thurton 2019). According to the city's mayor, this drop was expected following the forced evacuation related to the fire (Thurton 2019). Yet how can we ensure such a decrease is strictly related to the disaster? Who and how many people moved to avoid future disasters, to avoid costly rebuilding, or for totally unrelated reasons? These questions remain unanswered.

Finally, there is limited research on how climate displacement affects host communities. Especially in situations of rapid-onset hazards, host communities often lack the necessary support to host the sudden arrival of new evacuees. This is particularly acute in situations of recurrent hazards, such as yearly wildfires or floods where year after year host communities are under-resourced and overwhelmed. For instance, during the wildfire season of summer 2021 in British Columbia, emergency accommodations were full, forcing people to stay with friends or at hotels instead (Nuttall 2021). Four months later, people from the same region were evacuated again, forcing some to stay in their cars or wait in the snow as accommodations were full (Cecco 2021). In many of the disasters we have covered in this chapter, host communities were still providing housing for evacuees of a previous hazard when new evacuees arrived from a new hazard. The lack of disaster preparedness in the affected communities combined with a lack of support for host communities compels host communities to close their doors on evacuees. For example, the mayor of Kamloops, British Columbia, a central destination for evacuees, has stated the city cannot welcome permanent migrants as the city already faces housing challenges related to the aging community, student population, and homelessness (Zoledziowski 2021).

RECOMMENDATIONS AND CONCLUSION

In the face of more recurrent and more intense hazards in Canada as a result of climate change (Library of Parliament 2020) and knowing the impacts of evacuation and displacement on affected communities (Thériault et al. 2021; S. Thompson, Ballard, and Martin et al. 2014), there is a need for action. First, Mohamed (2020) suggests defining this type of human mobility. This would allow for a legal framework that supports internally climate-displaced people (Mohamed 2020). Similarly, without an official definition it is difficult to clearly know how many people are affected (Gemenne 2011). In Canada, we could certainly argue the same, as different labels are used to describe climate-induced displacement, complicating the scope of the issue. It is, in general, difficult to define human mobility related to climate factors because it is a complex and multi-causal phenomenon, an issue that the minimalist school of thought has raised (Klepp 2017; Suhrke 1994; Morrissey 2012).

Second, we have highlighted the various factors influencing whether people will move or stay, either by choice or no choice, in the face of climate hazards. Our contribution shows that climate-induced migration within Canada does not merely depend on whether one lives in a prone-risk zone but is a mix of interrelated factors. However, this should not justify government inaction but should point out the need for developing more data to understand better how such human mobility manifests in Canada.

Third, more research on the subject of climate-induced mobility within Canada is needed to close the comprehensive data and knowledge gaps (Bates-Eamer, Schmidtke, and Benson 2021). Further research would allow a better understanding of internal climate displacement and how it affects Indigenous communities (Bates-Eamer, Schmidtke, and Benson 2021). This is also one of the priority action recommendations by the Nansen Initiative (2015) and researchers such as Ahmad Yar et al. (2020). By mobilizing more knowledge on the subject, we could potentially "spread awareness" (Mohamed 2020) on the issue and contribute to pressuring the government to take concrete actions.

Actions should be proactive, such as a community-based planned relocation and development of multi-level governance and resources (Bates-Eamer, Schmidtke, and Benson 2021). According to Gevity Consulting. (2021), planned retreats could become a solution as disasters will continue. The "costly cycle of disaster/rebuild/disaster/rebuild" should encourage actors to act, and post-disaster represents a "policy window" to do so (Gevity Consulting 2021, 36). In such cases, however, D.E. Martin et al. (2017) and S. Thompson, Ballard, and Martin (2014) stress the need to create spaces for the voices of Indigenous people, so they are more closely involved in decision-making. Specifically, D.E. Martin et al. (2017) suggest a more egalitarian partnership with Indigenous communities.

NOTE

1 The United Nations High Commissioner for Refugees (UNHCR) recognizes the impact of climate change on migration but rejects the use of the term "refugee" in such cases on the grounds it is a legal term that should only be referring to the 1951 Convention (see UNHCR 2009).

FURTHER READING AND RESOURCES

Ballard, Myrle, dir. 2016. "Flooding Hope: The Lake St. Martin First Nation Story". YouTube video, 20:27. https://www.youtube.com/watch?v=qYQGGOEWOAg.

Su, Yvonne. 2021. "Wildfire and Flood Disasters Are Causing 'Climate Migration' within Canada." *The Conversation*, 20 September 2021. https://theconversation.com/wildfire-and-flood-disasters-are-causing-climate-migration-within-canada-167730.

UNHCR and OHCHR. 2022. "Climate Change, Displacement and Human Rights." https://www.unhcr.org/publications/brochures/6242ea7c4/climate-change-displacement-human-rights.html.

SECTION FOUR

Making Home and Place

23

From the Outside In: Decentring the Discussion of Refugee Integration in Canada

Michaela Hynie

KEY TAKEAWAYS

- The term "integration" is used widely in scholarship on immigration and forced migration and appears prominently in public discourse, policy, and programming around refugees and asylum seekers.
- Definitions of integration are widely contested; the term is used differently depending on the speaker and the context, resulting in some scholars rejecting the term altogether.
- Debates about the definition centre on which dimensions of the interaction between newcomers and settlement communities/societies matter, intersectionality, and whether integration refers to changes in the whole society or newcomers alone.
- Most definitions of integration distinguish between material and social integration, with the former being more clearly and narrowly defined.
- Definitions of social integration often reflect unacknowledged social imaginaries of a homogenous and unchanging settlement society, as well as stereotyped othering of newcomer communities. These definitions are frequently used in public and policy discourse as justification for excluding specific newcomer groups, such as those seeking asylum from specific countries or with particular social characteristics (e.g., religion).
- The development of integration models that try to capture the holistic nature of integration can help guide both theorizing and measurement.

KEY TERMS

- Acculturation
- Belonging
- Discourse
- Inclusion/exclusion
- Intersectionality
- Material integration
- Social integration

INTRODUCTION

23.1 Quebec Legislature Approved Bill 96

In February 2022 the Quebec legislature approved Bill 96, in which all government communication with newcomers to the province must be in French, except in cases where health or public safety are at issue. Opposition to this law is based on concerns that six months is not long enough for newcomers to learn French, particularly for refugees and asylum seekers who face unique challenges in settlement and pre-migration experiences, and because there can be month-long wait times to access French language classes. It is argued that this law can actually hinder integration by making access to needed services challenging for newcomers and also by sending a message about their place in Quebec society. According to Élodie Combes, a member of a group representing organizations working with immigrants, "It's as if we're telling them to retreat into their linguistic minority, that the government is not there for them, because they aren't francophone enough" (CBC News 2022b, n.p.).

The concept of integration has become a central theme in academic, political, and public discussions of forced migration (Goodman and Kirkwood 2019). Despite widespread use, the actual definition of integration is unclear. The term "integration" has been used to describe individuals, groups, and societies. It can refer to a process of change or the outcome of this process. Most often though it is used to describe the extent to which individuals or groups have changed themselves to "fit" into a society. Even then, what aspects are supposed to change, by how much, and in what ways are disagreed upon or left vague, and the emphasis in the definitions shifts as a function of the context in which they are discussed and the speaker's agenda (Grzymala-Kazlowska and Phillimore 2018; Rytter 2019). Moreover, the emphasis of integration policies and support varies not only between countries but also between regions within countries (Manatschal, Wisthaler, and Zuber 2020). In Canada, for example, provinces share integration programs with the federal government, except for the province of Quebec, which controls all of its own integration programs for newcomers and whose priorities reflect its unique history of statehood (Paquet and Xhardez 2020; see also Garnier, chapter 10). Not surprisingly then, in the small number of studies that ask refugee newcomers themselves how they define integration, many do not even understand the term (Sigona 2005; Shaw and Wachter 2022). This chapter briefly describes some of the definitions, main discourses, and critiques of integration; introduces some holistic models of integration; and incorporates refugee newcomers' perspectives regarding what is important in the integration process.

INTEGRATION DISCOURSES

Discourse can be thought of as collective or socially shared repertoires of interpretations of the world through statements that are not merely descriptive but generally oriented to action (Potter et al. 1990; see also Goheen Glanville and Arbel, chapter 4). As shared social constructions, integration discourses shape public opinions and legitimize settlement policies at the local, national, and regional levels and have been used extensively in debates around asylum seekers and other forced migrants (Goodman and Kirkwood 2019; Klarenbeek 2019; Korteweg and Triadafilopoulos 2013; Mulvey 2010). These discourses rest on often unspoken assumptions about newcomer groups and about our own societies as homogenous entities that remain unchanged over time (Grzymala-Kazlowska and Phillimore 2018; Schinkel 2018; Schneider and Crul 2010). Rytter (2019) distinguishes between what he calls "etic categories" (academic theory) and "emic categories" (public and policy applications of theory) of discourse but notes the highly political nature of integration has served to blur the distinction between them. Academic theories are incorporated into policy debates and are communicated to the general public. But while academic theories influence policy and media, these theories are often distorted, misrepresented, or misunderstood in public, media, and policy discourse, contributing to the confusion about definitions of integration.

This chapter identifies three major debates in public, political, and academic discourses on integration. This is not an exhaustive review but helps highlight some of the current issues and shortcomings in the conceptualization and discussion of integration. The first debate rests on identifying which dimensions are most important in determining whether successful integration has occurred. The second debate is around intersectionality, how integration occurs differently with different individuals and groups in different contexts. The third is whether successful integration is a "one-way" process of change undertaken by newcomers alone or a "two-way" process, where whole communities and societies change to reflect all of their members.

WHICH DIMENSIONS MATTER?

23.2 Focus Group with Syrian Newcomer Women, Kitchener, Ontario

> Interviewer: Try to imagine yourself in the next 10 years. [What] do you hope, dream that your lives [will] be like?
> Participant 5: That I have a house here at the end, a house that I own, and my kids also to be successful in schools, studying, and I am also working, and my husband is working and I have more friends and language I also ... that I took the language [classes]. (Hynie and SyRIA.lth 2019, n.p.)

Economic Integration

Many academic theories and policy models of refugee integration treat employment and income status as key components when discussing or measuring integration of individuals or groups (see also Ogoe and Wilkinson, chapter 25). Labour market participation is seen as a marker or facilitator of overall integration, given associations between income, employment, and participation in a wide range of other social spheres (Ager and Strang 2008; Beiser et al. 2015; Squires 2018). Many theories or assessments of integration add access to and successful completion of education as another key dimension of integration since education has strong associations with employment and other markers or means of integration (Ager and Strang 2008; Schneider and Crul 2010; see also Obradović-Ratković, Longboat, and Burgess, chapter 27).

An emphasis on economic integration in the context of forced migration may be driven in part by a public and political discourse about refugees and asylum seekers as an economic "burden" on the societies in which they reside (Hynie 2018). States that provide asylum or resettlement support are often keenly interested in demonstrating positive economic integration outcomes for refugees and thus the economic benefit, or at least limited cost, of resettlement. In Canada, discussions of integration outcomes for refugees often focus on comparing income and labour participation between the three refugee resettlement pathways: Government-Assisted Refugees (GAR); Privately Sponsored Refugees (PSR); and Blended Visa Office-Referred (BVOR). These labour market outcomes are taken as a key marker of each group's relative integration success (Hyndman and Hynie 2016; Kaida, Hou, and Stick 2020a).

Similarly, every province of Canada provides general (i.e., not specific to refugees) integration programs that are explicitly designed to increase labour market participation for newcomers (Paquet and Xhardez 2020). The emphasis on rapidly achieved labour market participation has been critiqued as creating unrealistic expectations for individuals resettled under humanitarian programs. Forced displacement is associated with disrupted educational pathways and limited opportunities to acquire the destination language prior to resettlement, both of which can delay labour market participation. Moreover, humanitarian programs focus on people in vulnerable circumstances who face unique challenges around employment, including single parents supporting large families and families with members having serious health concerns that require complex and time-consuming medical attention (Hynie 2018; Korntheuer et al. 2021; Schneider and Crul 2010).

However, many refugee newcomers themselves identify employment as an essential element of their successful resettlement (Hynie, Korn, and Tao 2016). In our own research with resettled refugees in Canada, employment and employment satisfaction are closely tied to newcomers' long-term mental health and well-being (Ahmad et al. 2021; Bridekirk, Hynie, and SyRIA.lth

2021). Interestingly, among refugees in Australia, Colic-Peisker (2009) found that it was experiences of discrimination in the job market, rather than more general experiences of discrimination, that had the greatest impact on life satisfaction. Thus, employment may be a useful lens through which to explore integration experiences.

Social Integration

The other dominant dimension of integration is broadly referred to as social integration (Beiser et al. 2015; Squires 2018). A number of related terms have been used to describe the "social" aspects of integration, including social inclusion, community cohesion, and social cohesion, which have similar definitions but can emphasize different aspects of the process or outcome (Mulvey 2010). Some theoretical models of social integration emphasize participation, specifically participation in social life, social roles, and/or access to resources in a society. Others place more emphasis on subjective factors such as an emotional attachment to the society (Cardinali et al. 2022), feelings of belonging (Marlowe 2020), or identification with the community or country of residence (Rouvoet, Eijberts, and Ghorashi 2017). While there can be important distinctions between these constructs (Dobson, Agrusti, and Pinto 2021; Niemi et al. 2019), these terms can often be used interchangeably, with some definitions of social inclusion, for example, mirroring the emphasis on social participation observed in many definitions of social integration in the academic literature (e.g., Gingrich 2003). Social integration in the form of cultural inclusion (e.g., values, social norms) is given particular emphasis for all newcomers in the province of Quebec, being woven into its language and information programs and reflecting its distinct cultural and linguistic identity within Canada (Paquet and Xhardez 2020; Wisthaler 2021) Perhaps because these constructs are so poorly defined, purported failures of social integration have become a dominant and convenient discourse justifying the exclusion of specific groups of asylum seekers and refugees (Goodman and Kirkwood 2019; Leudar et al. 2008; Reitz, Simon, and Laxer 2017; Schinkel 2018).

Discourses that focus on social integration are often framed in ways that portray refugees as the "other," people whose essential nature differs fundamentally from the community they are settling into, often in ways that are tied to important community norms and values (Schinkel 2018). Newcomer norms and values are inferred from observed differences in dimensions like family structure (e.g., the number of children), manner of dress, or religious beliefs. These differences are then assumed to reflect universal values in newcomer groups. For this reason, full integration is presumed to be impossible for these "others" (Rytter 2019).

There are two sets of assumptions at play here. One is that all refugee and asylum seeker newcomer groups share the same values. The other is that there is a homogenous majority society to compare newcomers against. Yet the values, norms, behaviours, and attachments of members of any society differ as a function of individual and group members' age, socio-economic status, region of residence, gender, political affiliation, and so on (Grzymala-Kazlowska and Phillimore 2018; Rytter 2019). The heterogeneity of both newcomers and dominant society members makes it difficult to clarify exactly which norms, values, and behaviours refugee newcomers should be integrating into. This results in constantly shifting definitions of what constitutes necessary integration, always moving the bar for full integration and thus rendering it unachievable (Rytter 2019). The claim that refugees and asylum seekers do not share community values also leads to further claims that they are actually a threat to community well-being and safety, all of which is used to justify policies of exclusion toward these groups (Goodman and Kirkwood 2019; Hynie 2018; Leudar et al. 2008; Rouvoet, Eijberts, and Ghorashi 2017).

Social Integration as Social Networks and Social Capital

One common aspect of social integration theories is participation in social networks beyond one's co-ethnic group (e.g., Ager and Strang 2008; Phillimore 2021; Shaw and Wachter 2022; Wessendorf and Phillimore 2019). This includes participation in local volunteer, social, or community events, and the formation of friendships outside one's co-ethnic community. A useful framing for these social networks and relationships is in terms of the different kinds of social capital, specifically social bonds (connections with members of one's own social groups) and social bridges (connections with members of other social groups) (Putnam 1995). Interestingly, the predominance of social engagement in theories of social integration is mirrored in definitions of integration offered by refugee newcomers themselves (see box 23.2). In interviews with eighty-eight former refugees now living in the USA, Shaw and Wachter (2022) found that social engagement through interactions with neighbours and other community members emerged as a predominant theme in what integration meant to them.

Social Integration as Belonging and Identity

Subjective approaches to social integration place more emphasis on emotional attachment, feelings of belonging, and/or identification with the one's new country of residence (Marlowe 2017; Wessendorf and Phillimore 2019; Yuval-Davis 2006). Feelings of belonging to a place are often expressed as feeling at home (Yuval-Davis 2006). The concept of belonging includes elements that overlap with some of the core elements of integration theories. Specifically, belonging has been defined as feelings of familiarity and safety that arise from relationships with others in the physical location (i.e., social networks), from cultural practices that evoke home, from security of legal status, and also the duration and personal history one has in a place (Antonsich 2010).

Some of these approaches are influenced by acculturation theory (J. Berry 2017; Ward 2013). Acculturation theories describe cultural and psychological changes that result from intercultural contact between groups and individuals. At the psychological level, changes occur for behaviour, values, and identities, with greater changes occurring among members of less powerful groups than among more powerful groups. Within acculturation theories, integration is also a contested term (Boski 2008), but the most widely known theory situates people in a two-by-two grid of accepting or rejecting both their original culture and the new culture, with four possible outcomes. Integration occurs where people's identities, values, and norms are aligned with both cultures. Assimilation is when one abandons one's original identity and values in favour of the new culture. With separation, one retains one's original identity and culture and is unchanged by the intercultural contact. Finally, marginalization occurs when one is alienated from both cultures (J. Berry 2017; Ward 2013). In highlighting that refugees and immigrants can retain identification with their countries of origin and simultaneously feel a sense of identification with their country of settlement, and that blended or hyphenated identities are associated with positive social and psychological outcomes (J. Berry 2017), this approach to integration is one of the few that explicitly acknowledges ongoing cultural and/or transnational ties with the country of origin.

Social Integration as Language Fluency

As noted in the example of Bill 96 in Quebec (see box 23.1), language is a dominant element in refugee integration policies. Language ability is associated with both social and material elements of integration – explicitly so in the case of the province of Quebec (Paquet and Xhardez 2020) – and is often identified as a key factor in successful resettlement. Language knowledge is associated with refugees' sense of well-being in their countries of residence, with limited language abilities posing a major hurdle to inclusion, achieving one's goals, and feeling a sense of belonging to the new country of residence (Ahmad et al. 2021; Hynie, Korn, and Tao 2016; Shaw and Wachter 2022; Sorgen 2015). Language ability also emerges as a significant factor in how successfully refugee newcomers can access social networks (Hanley et al. 2018; Morrice et al. 2021; Nawyn et al. 2012; Rouvoet, Eijberts, and Ghorashi 2017; Tip et al. 2019). In a study with Burundian and Burmese refugees in the USA, participants identified language as a form of social power, facilitating access to information, eliciting greater respect from the other US residents, and allowing them greater agency in their social interactions (Nawyn et al. 2012). Thus, facility in the local language is a means through which people participate in and are recognized in their community and society (Ager and Strang 2008).

INTERSECTIONALITY AND INTEGRATION

23.3 Individual Interview, Yazidi Community Member, York Region, Ontario
"Since we came here, the first thing that we want to learn is how to bring the rest of our families in Iraq to here. We want to bring my sisters, brothers, cousins, and all Yazidis to here. We repeat this request 20 times" (Hynie et al., forthcoming).

Newcomer Focus Group, Hamilton, Ontario
"It is difficult at this age and this highly qualified career to go to general labour, to work as a general labourer ... it is difficult" (Hynie, Korn, and Tao, 2016).

Intersectionality refers to how people's social categories interact with one another and with the systems in which they reside, creating unique power relations (Atewologun 2018). While integration is often discussed as a universal process, what is possible, what is expected, and what is seen as a desirable outcome differ as a function of the community and society of settlement and of the individuals who are resettling (Favell 2022; Phillimore 2021; Schinkel 2018). The dimensions of integration discussed in earlier sections of this chapter take on different weights in policy and media discourse, depending on who they are applied to. For example, in the current social climate, integration is frequently raised in reference to Muslim refugees, reflecting the growth of anti-Islamic attitudes in Europe and North America (Reitz, Simon, and Laxer 2017; Rytter 2019; Schinkel 2018). However, these anti-Muslim discourses also weave in constructions of gender and social class, both of newcomers and the settlement society, often reflecting narrow, stereotyped views and assumptions regarding Muslim women and immigrant families (Kofman, Saharso, and Vacchelli 2015; Korteweg and Triadafilopoulos 2013).

Integration expectations and settlement policies also impact refugee newcomers differently as a result of their histories, aspirations, abilities, needs, and social identities (Farrugia 2009; Grzymala-Kazlowska and Phillimore 2018; Pearlman 2022). For example, refugees living with disabilities can find their social service and accommodation needs overlooked in settlement policies, which makes it difficult to access both kinds of services (Korntheuer et al. 2021; see also McNally, chapter 14). Individuals in these situations then can neither fulfill their own personal goals nor the politically determined integration goals for refugees in the face of inaccessible language services, limited employment opportunities, and other frequently used markers of integration.

Intersectionality also emerges when refugee newcomers themselves identify their integration goals and whether those are being met (Farrugia 2009). When asked about settlement goals or factors that make refugees "feel at home," integration goals and preferred pathways to achieving them vary as a function of who is responding (Cardinali et al. 2022). For example, expectations about employment differ between groups in ways that affect perceptions of integration success. Across several resettled refugee groups we found women responded being with family was the main determinant of feeling "at home" in Canada, while men usually answered with finding a job (Hynie, Korn, and Tao 2016; Hynie et al., forthcoming). Among highly educated and professional women, however, employment was the main integration goal. In Bridekirk, Hynie, and SyRIA.lth's (2021) study of Syrian refugees in Canada, those with higher education reported less employment satisfaction, decreasing feelings of control, and increasing stress and depression with duration in Canada, despite reporting similar employment outcomes. In this same study, about 15 per cent of women reported not seeking work or not working because they were caring for young children and indicated staying at home to provide that care was more important (Hynie and SyRIA.lth 2019).

Age (see also Clark-Kazak, chapter 13), duration in the country, and previous migration experiences can also shape community members' goals in terms of relationships with individuals and communities outside their own co-ethnic communities. Among recently arrived Yazidi refugees, who had experienced extreme violence and persecution before coming to Canada, we found community members' integration goals focused on accessing resources to form their own settlement and community initiatives rather participating in activities in the broader society (Hynie et al., forthcoming). Among Karen refugees in Canada, perceptions of a lack of appropriate services led Karen communities to rely primarily on their own community-specific initiatives, with a small number of community members acting as the main connection to the larger society (E.P. Smith et al. 2021). These examples highlight how the social context interacts with individual and community characteristics to shape expected, feasible, and desired integration goals, pathways, and outcomes.

TWO-WAY INTEGRATION

> 23.4 Focus Group with Refugee Newcomers, Toronto, Ontario
> "Since we had no credit record, many places refused to give us home. They refused to accept the [agency] guarantee letter. For our present basement apartment, they took cheques from us" (Hynie, Korn, and Tao 2016).

Individual Interview with Karen Newcomer, Toronto, Ontario
"No matter what my skill back home, they said 'okay, that is not recognized here' so when we come here we have to start at the beginning, everything at the beginning" (E.P. Smith et al. 2021).

Integration discourse and theory are often grounded in assimilationist assumptions (Schinkel 2018). As noted above, assimilation occurs when the contact between two groups results in one group completely abandoning their original culture in favour of the second group (J. Berry 2017). Because the onus of change is entirely on the newcomers, a "failure of integration" is then attributed to the motivation, values, or essential nature of these individuals or groups (Rouvoet, Eijberts, and Ghorashi 2017). One response to "poor integration" is thus the initiation of programs like Quebec's Bill 96 (see box 23.1) or the current Canadian policy of making language ability a prerequisite for citizenship (Government of Canada 2019a), both of which imply that refugee newcomers and other migrants need more motivation to achieve desired integration goals (Mulvey 2010).

However, the process and outcomes of integration are not solely determined by the motivation, activities, and attitudes of refugee newcomers. Participation requires the ability to access opportunities, for example, accessible language classes, time to participate in community events, transportation to those activities, and recognition of foreign credentials or finding equivalencies for those whose documents have been destroyed (Phillimore 2021). Policies that limit income or time, restrict movement or residency, and will not adapt to the unique needs of refugees impede refugee newcomers' efforts at integration (Hynie 2018b; Klarenbeek 2019; Korntheuer et al. 2021; Penninx 2019; Phillimore 2021; Strang, Baillot, and Mignard 2018).

Labour market participation is an excellent example. Refugees' opportunities are limited by settlement policies that restrict access to language classes; professional organizations and employers refuse to recognize professional credentials or previous work experience; and employers are inclined to hire people through social networks that newcomers may lack (Gowayed 2022; Hynie, Korn, and Tao 2016; Krahn et al. 2000). Access to necessary resources like housing, health care, education, and social assistance are similarly stymied by a lack of accommodation from individuals and institutions and by policies that create barriers to access. For instance, some landlords will not accept references or income guarantees from settlement agencies for recently arrived resettled refugees in Canada.

The situation can be even worse for refugee claimants in Canada who do not have access to the one year of financial support immediately available to resettled refugees, and which further reduces ability to produce income guarantees. A lack of credit rating and language difficulties make access to appropriate housing more challenging, and there is limited easily accessible information about housing for recently arrived newcomers (see also Clark-Kazak, chapter 28). There is also insufficient affordable housing for larger families. These conditions make access to appropriate housing uniquely difficult for refugees and asylum seekers relative to other newcomers (Carter, Polevychok, and Osborne 2009; Francis and Hiebert 2014; Hynie, Korn, and Tao 2016). Similarly, access to health care for refugees and asylum seekers is affected by barriers to interpretation services and lack of recognition of federal health insurance policies (McKeary and Newbold 2010; Newbold, Cho, and McKeary 2013; Stirling Cameron et al. 2022; see also Chen, chapter 24).

Some of the issues identified above are the result of systems and institutions that do not accommodate the specific needs of refugee newcomers and/or make it difficult for those working in the system to accommodate them. Some barriers are also the product of negative community attitudes toward refugees. Agency staff may be unco-operative, unhelpful, or even explicitly hostile to refugee newcomers trying to navigate social institutions (Strang, Baillot, and Mignard 2018). This has implications for the material aspects of integration and also the social elements of integration, like building diverse social networks and social trust (Drolet and Moorthi 2018; Tesfai et al. 2022). Negative attitudes can result in subtle discrimination. Despite generally welcoming attitudes, a study with rural communities sponsoring Syrian refugee families reported concerns about whether Muslim families would "fit" (Haugen 2019). Active discrimination is also a factor, of course, with some groups facing particularly extreme hostility in their communities of settlement (Colic-Peisker 2009; Goodman and Kirkwood 2019; Leudar et al. 2008; Reitz, Simon, and Laxer 2017).

PUTTING IT TOGETHER: HOLISTIC MEASURES OF INTEGRATION

Refugee integration is operationalized and measured in every country that settles refugees. In most cases, they rely on a small number of integration outcomes that can be captured through objective measures, usually passing a language course and employment status (Schneider and Crul 2010). There have been some efforts, however, to develop models that capture the multiple dimensions of integration and acknowledge these dimensions interact to influence integration (e.g., Ager and Strang 2008; Fajth and Lessard-Phillips 2022; Hynie, Korn, and Tao 2016; Valtonen 2004). One of the most widely used is that of Ager and Strang (2008), which is based on typical state-used indicators but verified with refugee newcomers, community members, and a wide range of stakeholders. The Ager and Strang model is also used in academic research to identify which variables to measure when assessing integration, and it has been used to create a self-report survey tool that generates a numeric integration score based on the elements of the model (Puma, Lichtenstein, and Stein 2018).

Figure 23.1 | A conceptual framework defining core domains of integration.

The Ager and Strang model identifies four classes of indicators, represented visually in an inverted triangle (Ager and Strang 2008; see fig. 23.1). At the top of the triangle are *markers and means* of integration. These include access to and participation in secure and adequate employment and education and access to adequate housing and health care services. These are markers of successful participation in valued aspects of social life but also a means to achieve other forms of social inclusion and participation. The next level focuses on *social connections* and the ability to leverage social relationships to access needed resources (Putnam 1995). This includes horizontal social relationships within (social bonds) and between communities (social bridges), as well as vertical relationships with institutions (social links). The resources accessible through these relationships facilitate accessing markers and means but also support psychological well-being (Korac 2003). *Facilitators* of integration are language, cultural knowledge, and safety and stability. Cultural knowledge refers to communication and life skills needed to navigate one's environment, while safety and stability refers to physical safety and freedom from violence and the stability of migration status and life circumstances. Finally, the *foundation* of integration is an understanding of individual rights and citizenship that is shared with the settlement community.

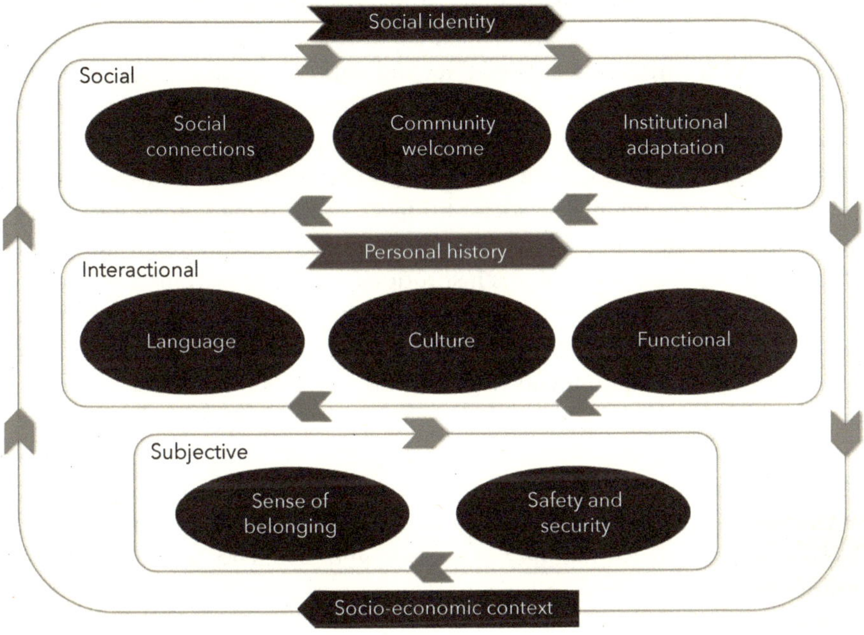

Figure 23.2 | The holistic integration model.

In Canada, refugee integration includes an emphasis on accommodating communities. One of the major refugee resettlement programs is the National GAR Case Management – Client Support Services (CSS) program, which is currently implemented across seven provinces in Eastern and Central Canada for GARs. In addition to supporting GAR newcomers' access to language skills, cultural knowledge, and resources and services, the CSS program works to build a more responsive and inclusive community (National GAR Case Management 2018). This more contextual and holistic approach to integration was the basis for the development of the holistic integration model (Hynie, Korn, and Tao 2016). The holistic integration model extends Ager and Strang's conceptual model (see fig. 23.2; Hynie, Korn, and Tao 2016), incorporating Canada's approach to resettlement and the critiques of integration (Strang and Ager 2010). The elements are organized to highlight the importance of social context and the two-way nature of integration, capture the importance of attachment and subjective feelings of belonging, and make explicit the intersectional nature of integration.

Subjective integration includes the psychological and emotional aspects. Sense of belonging captures emotional attachment to one's community, while safety and security refer to physical and economic stability and the permanency of one's status. *Interactional* integration includes language and culture adaptation. Functional integration elements include access to markers of integration: appropriate education; safe, affordable, and appropriate housing; safe, stable, and appropriate employment; and affordable and appropriate health services. *Social* integration highlights the two-way nature of integration. Social connections are social networks, both within one's own communities (social bonds) and with other communities (social bridges). Welcoming community reflects public attitudes and discourses and discrimination. Institutional adaptation refers to the practices and policies institutions and organizations have in place to accommodate refugees' unique needs and characteristics, ranging from settlement policies at the governmental level to the availability of interpretation to leniency around requirements (e.g., educational documents) that are difficult for refugees to meet.

The model includes circular arrows, highlighting that these elements are interrelated and mutually reinforcing, but also that the nature of the integration process is intersectional. It will be a different experience based on the characteristics of the community or society, and the characteristics and backgrounds of the individuals within it. The arrows are thus labelled with the socio-economic context that refugee newcomers are settling into, refugee newcomers' personal history (education, rural versus urban histories, time spent in refugee camps, etc.), and refugee newcomers' social category or social identity (age, religion, ethnicity, gender, etc.).

While measurement models can draw attention to the complexity of integration and encourage more reflective and nuanced theorizing and policy-making, how elements within them are defined and measured and which findings are given the greatest emphasis remains a challenge. Moreover, elements that are the easiest to measure are those that are easily observed or generated by existing data collection, while contextual and subjective factors are more difficult to capture.

CONCLUSIONS

Increasingly, migration scholars propose rejecting the term "integration" altogether; a 2018 special issue of the journal *Comparative Migration Studies* was devoted to this debate. However, it seems unlikely that changing terminology will be sufficient to shift the underlying assumptions and motives that give rise to problematic elements of integration. Integration's intersectional nature makes it challenging to develop a clear definition in terms of outcomes: outcomes that are tied to whether all individuals and groups in society have opportunities to achieve their goals and full potential on their own terms would be hard to measure. Nonetheless, it is that spirit of integration that seems to be required. Perhaps the most promising strategy for ensuring a holistic, intersectional, and measurable understanding of integration is to ensure that people with forced migration experience play a central role in the development and implementation of policies that pertain to refugees and asylum seekers and ensure that their expectations and experiences shape our definitions. The importance of including refugee voices in all aspects of forced migration policy, evaluation, research, and theory is finally gaining traction (Charbenneau Kuntzelman and Noor 2022; Harley, Lee, and Wazefadost 2022). While recognizing that refugees and asylum seekers differ in their access to the means, power, and safety needed to participate in policy debates and discourse, including their voices to construct our understanding of integration is itself an act of integration. When we have achieved this, we will have come a long way.

FURTHER READING AND RESOURCES

Allies for Refugee Integration. 2021. *Intentional Connections for Welcoming Communities*. https://ocasi.org/sites/default/files/ari-final-report-2021-intentional-connections_0.pdf.

Hyndman, Jennifer, and Michaela Hynie. 2016. "From Newcomer to Canadian: Making Refugee Integration Work." *Policy Options*, 17 May 2016. https://policyoptions.irpp.org/fr/magazines/mai-2016/from-newcomer-to-canadian-making-refugee-integration-work.

Migration Matters. 2017. "3.3 What Is Canada's Approach to Integration and Why Does it 'Work'?" YouTube video, 4:00. 6 October 2017. https://www.youtube.com/watch?v=DkhPVsiQ8DQ.

24

Canada's Refugee Health-Care System and Its Humanitarian Undertow

Y.Y. Brandon Chen

KEY TAKEAWAYS

- Adequate access to a full range of health care is key to refugees' and asylum seekers' health and well-being, as well as their social integration.
- International law guarantees everyone's right to health, including that of refugees and asylum seekers.
- Some refugees and most asylum seekers in Canada are excluded from publicly funded health insurance for the general population and instead are covered by the Interim Federal Health Program (IFHP).
- Humanitarianism, which underpins the IFHP, stigmatizes refugees and asylum seekers and impedes their health-care access, contrary to a rights-based approach to health care, which respects equality and human dignity.

KEY TERMS

- Health care
- Human dignity
- Humanitarianism
- Right to health

INTRODUCTION

24.1 Restrictions to Health Care

Ingrid Lara was in her late thirties when she applied for refugee protection in Canada in 2012. She was attempting to escape from domestic abuse in Panama, where she was from. While a decision on her refugee claim was still pending, she obtained a temporary work permit and worked as a bookkeeper.

In January 2013 she was diagnosed with stage 4 breast cancer and had to immediately undergo chemotherapy. In the past, the cost of her cancer treatment would have been fully covered by the federal government through the Interim Federal Health Program, a health-care benefit reserved for refugees and asylum seekers. However, due to changes made to the program in June 2012, health-care coverage for asylum seekers was severely scaled back. Ingrid ended up having to pay $6,500 for her treatment and $50 every three weeks for medication.

Unfortunately, her refugee claim was denied in June 2013. Although she planned to appeal the decision, for the time being, the cost of her doctors' visits would no longer be paid by the Interim Federal Health Program, either. "I did not choose to have cancer," she said. "It is stressful enough and I'm constantly thinking about my medical bills." (Keung 2013, n.p.)

The ability to access adequate preventive, curative, rehabilitative, and palliative health services is an important determinant of one's health and well-being (Mikkonen and Raphael 2010). This is particularly so for refugees and asylum seekers, whose health frequently comes under threat during their migration journey. These threats to physical and mental health may be the very reason that causes refugees and asylum seekers to leave a country in the first place. These threats may also stem from unsafe or substandard living conditions in countries of transit or refugee camps. These health risks persist after refugees and asylum seekers arrive in receiving countries, as they often encounter discrimination that exacerbates the stresses associated with adjusting to a new environment (Edge, Newbold, and McKeary 2014).

Besides its health-protective effects, having access to adequate health care is crucial for refugees' and asylum seekers' symbolic and actual integration into receiving societies. Symbolically, in countries like Canada where publicly funded health care is touted as universally available to residents, the inclusion of refugees and asylum seekers within that same universe signifies their belonging (C. McKee et al. 2019). Practically, as health-care entitlement contributes to refugees' and asylum seekers' health and well-being, it positions them better to confront settlement-related challenges (Schick et al. 2016).

Given the importance of health care to refugees and asylum seekers, this chapter aims to summarize Canada's refugee health-care system and reveal its shortfalls. The chapter begins by examining Canada's obligation under international law to provide health care to refugees and asylum seekers. This discussion serves to not only buttress the normative underpinning of Canada's refugee health-care system but also take stock of the adequacy of this system. Next, the chapter presents a birds'-eye view of Canada's refugee health-care system, outlining both its historical evolution and its current modus operandi. This refugee health-care system is then contrasted with provincial and territorial health insurance programs that cover the general Canadian public. The contradistinction between these two health-care regimes reveals the humanitarian logic that permeates Canada's refugee health-care system, which raises concerns about inequity and service inaccessibility when compared with a rights-based approach to health care.

REFUGEES' RIGHT TO HEALTH CARE UNDER INTERNATIONAL LAW

The 1951 Convention Relating to the Status of Refugees, to which Canada is a party, provides that refugees lawfully in a country should receive "the same treatment with respect to public relief and assistance as is accorded to [the country's] nationals" (1951, art. 23). Publicly funded health care has been interpreted as one form of such "public relief and assistance" (Hathaway 2005). The convention, therefore, represents one of the clearest guarantees under international law of refugees' right to health care, at least in receiving countries where a system of publicly funded health care is in place.

Multiple other treaties that Canada has signed and ratified similarly protect refugees' and asylum seekers' right to a level of health care on par with what is afforded to citizens of receiving countries. For example, the International Covenant on Economic, Social and Cultural Rights guarantees everyone the right to social security. This right is understood as encompassing a promise that "[r]efugees, stateless persons and asylum-seekers, and other disadvantaged and marginalized individuals and groups should enjoy equal treatment in access to ... reasonable access to health care ... consistent with international standards" (CESCR 2008, para. 38). The same covenant further enshrines everyone's right to the enjoyment of the highest attainable standard of health in international law. This right is said to impose on governments an obligation to "refrain from denying or limiting equal access for all persons, including prisoners or detainees, minorities, asylum seekers and illegal immigrants, to preventive, curative and palliative health services" (CESCR 2000, para. 34).

International law's guarantee of the right to health has paid specific attention to government responsibilities in relation to refugees and asylum seekers facing intersecting marginalization. As a case in point, the Convention on the Elimination of All Forms of Discrimination against Women requires governments to eliminate discrimination that women refugees and asylum seekers face in the health-care context, including ensuring their access to services "appropriate to their particular needs as women" (Committee on the Elimination of Discrimination against Women 2014, para. 33; see also Aberman, chapter 12). The Convention on the Rights of the Child likewise calls on governments to remedy the intersecting health stressors experienced by refugee and asylum-seeking children by providing them with a full range of age-appropriate and gender-sensitive health services equal to that of nationals (Committee on the Rights of the Child 2017; see also Clark-Kazak, chapter 13).

Besides the demand of non-discrimination, to satisfy the right to health, governments are under a duty to structure their health-care systems in a manner that is available, accessible, acceptable, and of good quality. To that end, governments must ensure that health-care goods and services are available in sufficient quantity, accessible to people who have low income and those who live in rural communities, and provided in ways that respect medical ethics, scientific evidence, cultural differences, and gender and life cycle requirements. Although international law, cognizant of resource limitations facing some countries, allows governments to progressively achieve this level of health care, governments must advance as expeditiously and as effectively as possible, and any retrogression is not permitted without proper justification (CESCR 2000). Canada is bound by such international legal norms and has an obligation to develop a refugee health-care system accordingly.

EVOLUTION OF CANADA'S REFUGEE HEALTH-CARE SYSTEM

Canada's provision of publicly funded health care to refugees began soon after World War II, predating the emergence of a government health insurance program for the general public. For example, in late 1947, the federal government committed to covering the costs of emergency hospitalization and medical services incurred by war-displaced persons newly resettled in Canada, provided they lacked the capacity to pay for such services on their own. In 1957 the federal government further acquired the legal authority to "pay costs of medical and dental care, hospitalization, and any expenses incidental thereto" for indigent asylum seekers while their refugee claims were being processed (*Toussaint v. Canada (AG)* 2010, para. 36). In the 1960s and 1970s, when Canadian provinces and territories began to develop their respective public health insurance programs, known as medicare, many refugees and asylum seekers obtained health-care coverage along with other residents.

However, starting in the mid-1980s, fuelled in part by economic downturns, asylum seekers' entitlement to medicare increasingly came under challenge. In 1986 British Columbia became the first province that previously included asylum seekers under medicare to reverse its course. The province's health minister at the time asserted that provision of health-care benefits to asylum seekers should be the responsibility of the federal government, which admitted these individuals into the country in the first place. Arguing along the same lines, Ontario discontinued asylum seekers' medicare coverage in 1994 as a part of a broader health-care reform aiming at cost cutting. Quebec followed suit two years later (Chen 2021).

As more and more asylum seekers lost their medicare coverage, the federal government was pressured into assuming their health-care costs while it continued to quarrel with the provinces and territories about who had jurisdiction over refugee health-care (see also Garnier, chapter 10). As a result, there was much uncertainty initially around the scope of the federal health-care coverage for asylum seekers, including whether it would pay for all medically necessary services akin to medicare or only emergency care (Priest 1993). In 1995 the federal government formally agreed to systematically cover asylum seekers' health-care expenses through the newly created IFHP. It also enlisted the help of an insurance company to clarify the parameters of the IFHP's coverage, to negotiate a fee schedule with health service providers, and to process reimbursement claims submitted (*Edmonton Journal* 1996).

Over the years, the scope of the IFHP was expanded to include health-care coverage for not only asylum seekers but also refugees, victims of human trafficking (see Vargas Aguirre, chapter 11), and individuals detained for immigration purposes (see Silverman, chapter 21). With respect to asylum seekers, the IFHP provided health-care coverage throughout their refugee claim process. They would qualify for the IFHP as soon as their refugee application was found eligible for referral to the Immigration and Refugee Board (IRB) for determination. Their IFHP coverage would last until one of three situations occurred. In the event their refugee claim was successful, their eligibility for the IFHP would expire ninety days after they received the positive decision, which in theory should give them sufficient time to qualify for provincial or territorial medicare. Alternatively, if their refugee claim was rejected, they would continue to qualify for the IFHP until their departure or removal from Canada. If at any time during the refugee claim process, asylum seekers withdrew or were deemed to have abandoned their application, their IFHP coverage would be terminated in forty-five days (CIC 2011).

So long as asylum seekers remained eligible for the IFHP, they were entitled to three sets of health-care benefits: basic coverage, supplemental coverage, and coverage for the costs of the mandatory immigration medical exams. Basic coverage encompassed assorted necessary hospital and medical services that were virtually identical to what medicare insured. Supplemental coverage entitled asylum seekers to receive additional health-related products and services, including essential prescription medications, limited vision and dental care, long-term care, home care, and certain medical devices. Although access to some of these additional goods and services required prior approval from the insurance company charged with administering the IFHP, the rationale behind supplemental coverage was to provide IFHP recipients with a level of health benefits similar to what low-income persons would get under provincial or territorial social assistance programs (CIC 2011).

In contrast, IFHP benefits for resettled refugees typically consisted of only supplemental coverage. This was because resettled refugees would arrive in Canada with the status of permanent residents, and therefore qualify for medicare, rendering their receipt of basic coverage under the IFHP redundant. Their eligibility for supplemental coverage would usually last one year, but it might be extended for up to another year if they needed more time to establish themselves in Canada (CIC 2011).

This general structure of the IFHP remained largely unchanged for almost two decades. However, in June 2012, without any prior public consultation or clear evidence of need, the federal government extensively pared down the scope of the IFHP allegedly to contain public spending, ensure fairness for Canadians, and discourage foreign nationals from filing unfounded asylum applications only to take advantage of free health care (*Canadian Doctors for Refugee Care v. Canada (AG)* 2014). The new IFHP divided refugees and asylum seekers into multiple categories, seemingly based on a perception of how genuine their need for protection was and assigned different categories of refugees and asylum seekers to different levels of health-care benefits (Chen, Gruben, and Liew 2018).

Among resettled refugees, only those whose resettlement was assisted by the government would continue to receive the same level of supplemental coverage as they did under the previous IFHP. Privately sponsored refugees (PSRs) were left with coverage for medications needed to prevent or treat illnesses that potentially threatened public health (e.g., communicable diseases) or public safety (e.g., psychiatric conditions that could cause a person to be violent toward others).

On the other hand, people seeking protection in Canada were divided into three groups. Individuals facing deportation but who had applied for a pre-removal risk assessment (PRRA) on the grounds that they would be in danger if returned to their former countries of residence were stripped of all IFHP benefits. Faring a little better, asylum seekers from a list of countries designated by Canada as "safe" and unlikely to produce "genuine" refugees, along with those whose refugee claims were rejected, received health-care coverage solely for health conditions posing a risk to public health or public safety. Asylum seekers not from a designated country, as well as people whose refugee claims had been successful and who were waiting to qualify for medicare, were given additional coverage for hospital, medical, and diagnostic services considered urgent or essential.

Besides curtailing refugees' and asylum seekers' health-care entitlement, the new IFHP, with its multiple benefit categories, was confusing to many. Refugees and asylum seekers were unsure whether the services or products they needed were publicly covered, and health-care practitioners sometimes turned away IFHP beneficiaries due to a mistaken belief that government funding for treating these patients was no longer available. This made it difficult for refugees and asylum seekers to access the little health care they were still entitled to under the new IFHP. These concerns caused several asylum seekers and allied advocacy organizations to challenge the validity of the new IFHP policy in court. In July 2014 the Federal Court declared the new IFHP unconstitutional for having unduly distinguished asylum seekers on the basis of their countries of origin and for having jeopardized the health of refugees and asylum seekers in a way that was cruel and unusual (*Canadian Doctors for Refugee Care v. Canada (AG)* 2014).

Following the Federal Court's ruling, the government introduced another version of the IFHP. Although this third iteration jettisoned some of the most egregious elements of the previous program, it still fell short of the health-care coverage found under the IFHP prior to June 2012 (Bond 2014). It was not until a new federal government came into power in late 2015 that the IFHP was returned to its pre-2012 level in 2016. However, the reinstated IFHP maintains the possibility for people in a refugee-like situation who are otherwise ineligible for the federal health-care benefits to apply for discretionary coverage, an option first introduced in 2012 along with the cuts. To qualify for the discretionary coverage, a foreign national in refugee-like situations must demonstrate an urgent medical need, as well as compelling personal circumstances that render the IFHP coverage necessary (Government of Canada 2022d).

In recent years, further changes have been made to the IFHP that expand both whom and what it covers. Since 2017, the IFHP has paid for the cost of certain pre-departure health care incurred overseas by refugees who are approved for resettlement in Canada. This includes expenses associated with immigration medical exams, treatment for active tuberculosis and syphilis, vaccinations, necessary public health measures during a disease outbreak, and medical support required for safe travel to Canada (Government of Canada 2017a). Moreover, as a result of a legislative change in 2019, asylum seekers now qualify for the IFHP from the moment they make a refugee claim in Canada, without having to wait until their claim is determined eligible for referral to the IRB (Government of Canada 2020b).

HUMANITARIAN UNDERCURRENT OF THE IFHP

On the surface, since its restoration in 2016, the basic coverage under the IFHP appears to furnish refugees and asylum seekers with a level of health-care protection comparable to that enjoyed by other Canadian residents via medicare.

One may therefore be tempted to minimize (some) refugees' and (most) asylum seekers' current exclusion from medicare as an innocuous transfer of health-care responsibilities from provinces and territories to the federal government. Nevertheless, there is a significant difference between the organizing philosophies of the two health-care schemes that renders refugees' and asylum seekers' medicare disentitlement problematic.

On the one hand, the development of medicare, despite the heterogeneity of the program across provinces and territories, was inspired by a rights-based approach to health care. When the draft Medical Care Act was presented in Parliament for consideration in 1966, then federal health minister A.J. MacEachen boasted that the bill would usher in the "fundamental principle that health is not a privilege tied to the state of one's bank account, but rather a basic right which should be open to all" (House of Commons 1966, 7545). Today, this vision of health care as a right enjoyed by all continues to be embodied in the Canada Health Act, 1985, which conditions federal funding for medicare upon provinces and territories adhering to the criteria of universality and accessibility, among others, when operating their medicare programs. Pursuant to these criteria, all medicare-insured persons must be equally entitled and have the same reasonable access to health-care services. This demand of uniformity signals the status of medicare-insured persons as rights holders who command equal respect.

The rights-based undertone of medicare is buttressed by its outward appearance as a contributory program. On paper, medicare is supposed to function as health insurance. Canadians are said to pay into the program through either general income taxes or dedicated insurance premiums, in exchange for publicly subsidized services when they require medically necessary hospital, physician, and surgical-dental care (*Winterhaven Stables Limited v. Canada (AG)* 1988). Despite the reality that eligibility for medicare does not depend on one's tax contributions, this impression that medicare operates on the basis of *quid pro quo* strengthens the belief among Canadians about health-care coverage under the program being an entitlement, which they have rightly earned through contributions.

On the other hand, the workings of the IFHP are shaped by a humanitarian philosophy. Broadly speaking, humanitarianism appeals to people's empathy for fellow humanity and implores us to come to one another's aid in times of need (see also: K. Banerjee, chapter 5). A humanitarian intervention, therefore, is motivated less by an obligation to realize a right and more by a sense of compassion for the good of others who face adversity, born out of our own experience with and desire to be free from suffering (Ticktin 2014). Humanitarian aid, in other words, is meant to be an exceptional measure for people with demonstrable needs rather than a universal entitlement that is part and parcel of being human (Feldman and Steenbergen 2001). The ethos of the IFHP, both expressly and impliedly, reflects such a humanitarian orientation as it focuses primarily on the hardship of refugees' and asylum seekers' otherwise incapacity to access necessary health care.

Expressly, the Canadian government has on multiple occasions characterized the IFHP as an *ex gratia* program. This means it provides a "benevolent payment ... made in the public interest ... where the [government] has no obligation of any kind or has no legal liability, or where the claimant has no right of payment or is not entitled to relief in any form" (*Canadian Doctors for Refugee Care v. Canada (AG)* 2014, FC 651, para. 356). According to this characterization, which has been accepted by court, the IFHP is in essence a discretionary, stopgap measure intended only for situations where "humane interests more or less obligate the [government] to accept the responsibility" for a person's health care (*Toussaint v. Canada (AG)* 2010, FC 810, para. 44).

The humanitarian nature of the IFHP is also implied by its design. Up until the policy changes implemented in 2012, qualification for the IFHP was expressly means-tested. That is, at least in theory, refugees and asylum seekers who had the financial resources to privately cover their health-care costs were ineligible for the program. In practice, refugees and asylum seekers were routinely presumed to lack such a financial capacity, thus rendering the means test merely notional (CIC 2004). Nevertheless, the message was clear: IFHP benefits were meant to be reserved solely for indigent persons. Even when the current IFHP policy no longer explicitly stipulates a means test, it continues to describe the program as intended for "some groups of foreign nationals who ... are vulnerable and disadvantaged, and ... aren't eligible for provincial or territorial health insurance" (2022, n.p). This portrayal of the IFHP as a program of last resort and its recipients as underprivileged stands in contrast to the universalist spirit of understanding health care as a human right.

The differences between medicare and the IFHP roughly correspond to what Nancy Fraser and Linda Gordon refer to as contract versus charity. As they explain, these two approaches to the organization of government benefits draw a distinction "between 'contributory' programs and 'noncontributory' ones, between social insurance ... where beneficiaries have a right to what they receive, since they merely 'get back what they put in,' and public assistance, where they have no such right, since they are thought to 'get something for nothing'" (1994, 47). Thus, replacing medicare with the IFHP as the source of refugees' and asylum seekers' basic health-care coverage is not normatively neutral (see also K. Banerjee, chapter 5). It transforms the relationship between these health-care users and the government from one between rights holders and the duty bearer to that between beneficiaries and the benefactor. Whereas the power differential in the former dyad favours refugees and asylum seekers, who command government aid as a responsibility, in the latter it is skewed in favour of the government, who is free to dictate the terms of its aid, including whether aid will be offered at all.

PROBLEMS OF A HUMANITARIAN APPROACH TO REFUGEE HEALTH CARE

The charitable nature of the IFHP is problematic for several reasons. It obscures the fact that health care is a right that stems from, as well as contributes to, human dignity, namely the inherent value that everyone holds for simply being human (Jacobson 2007). It reinforces the position of refugees and asylum seekers as "others," rather than equal members of the same universe that all Canadians are part of. Furthermore, it renders refugees' and asylum seekers' health-care access vulnerable to the whim of decision-makers, both at the policy level and at the point of service provision. This section of the chapter examines these problems in turn.

First, the association of the IFHP with an air of charity is in tension with international legal norms that bind Canada, which treat health care as a universal right. As described, when health care is taken to be a right, its attainment constitutes the rule. But when health care is animated by humanitarianism, it represents an exception, justified on account of empathy for human suffering. In the context of the IFHP, this emphasis on suffering runs the risk of casting refugees and asylum seekers in need of health care as mere victims, who must barter for Canadians' generosity "with [their] life and body" (Ticktin 2006, 45). Rather than individuals "with capacity to contribute and be an asset to their new communities," they are made to be "needy, helpless and a drain on resources" (Grove and Zwi 2006). Health-care coverage for refugees and asylum seekers under the IFHP, therefore, comes at the cost of their human dignity rather than fostering it, the opposite of what the guarantee of human rights aims to accomplish.

Second, and flowing from the preceding point, refugees' and asylum seekers' expulsion from a supposedly universal program like medicare, only to be subsequently offered charitable coverage under the IFHP, literally and metaphorically marks their status as outsiders in Canadian society. Such a move, to quote Natalie Grove and Anthony Zwi, reinforces the collective imagination of these forced migrants "as desperate, brown-skinned, 'have nots hoping to gain from our beneficence,'" who stand in contrast to other members of society, including "the migrants which developed countries seek to attract to their shores, those who will busy themselves with hard work, simultaneously building a future for themselves and their new country" (2006, 1935). The exceptional nature of the IFHP thus serves as a constant reminder to refugees and asylum seekers that they are not us.

The following quote from an asylum seeker illustrates this othering effect of the IFHP at the point of health-care access: "They kind of figured that everyone has the OHIP [Ontario Health Insurance Plan] card. So, [the medical receptionist] requested for, there is a number on the OHIP card, which ends in two letters. So I told her what I had on my IFHP [certificate], and she was like, she had never heard of that before. I told her it's the Interim Federal Health [Program]. She said she doesn't know what that is" (Chen 2021, 10).

Third, so long as the IFHP is construed as a product of beneficence, refugees' and asylum seekers' health-care coverage thereunder is subject to the whim of people who make decisions about and inside the program. A charitable scheme is unstable by nature. The act of giving, while affirming the moral worth of the benefactors, simultaneously stigmatizes beneficiaries as unproductive and a burden on society. The stigma against beneficiaries undercuts their moral desert over time in the minds of benefactors and "spawn[s] doubts about the merits of giving" (Fraser and Gordon 1994, 59). As benefactors' compassion waxes and wanes, so do the terms and conditions of their generosity. This was exemplified at the policy level by the IFHP cuts between 2012 and 2016. As described, concerns about "bogus refugees" called into question refugees' and asylum seekers' health-care deservingness, and caused IFHP coverage to be stratified according to policy-makers' perception of how genuine a beneficiary's refugee claim is.

The instability of the IFHP coverage also surfaces at the point of health service access. It has long been reported by refugees and asylum seekers that some service providers are unwilling to accept the IFHP coverage because they are unfamiliar with it, or they find the reimbursement process cumbersome and time-consuming (Miedema, Hamilton, and Easley 2008). These access barriers were made worse during the years of the IFHP cuts, as some health-care providers who were confused by the policy changes either mistakenly or deliberately refused refugees and asylum seekers services. Other providers, although not denying health care to IFHP recipients outright, reportedly demanded payment up front, a practice that would have been impermissible under medicare (Chen, Gruben, and Liew 2018). Even after the program's restoration in 2016, it has remained challenging for some refugees and asylum seekers to find health-care providers willing and able to serve them, as exhibited by the quote below from an asylum seeker living with HIV. These ongoing issues underscore the vulnerability of refugees' and asylum seekers' health-care access to the calculation of individual health practitioners. They also show how health-care seeking under the IFHP falls short of the standards of availability, accessibility, acceptability, and quality that are required by the international law's guarantee of the right to health.

24.2 "Refugee Claimant's Experience Seeking a Family Doctor"

I tried to find a family doctor, but maybe ten, fifteen different doctors, clinics, hospitals I called. They don't accept me ... I know it's not about [my] hiv situations. It was about refugee. I was so

> mad. Then I think, last two, three phone calls I fight them. I said many bad words. I said, "that is enough." When I start the conversation with [them], everything is normal. But when I said I am a refugee, they say, "ah sorry, we do not take refugees." I said, "okay, at the time same time I am a human, too." What is the difference between temporary residents, refugee or citizen? I am human. So, some of them, hang up the phone in my face. Some of them [said], "you are right, but our policy is like this" ... They don't care, or they don't take patients that are refugees. My first, more than three months, three months [here in Canada], almost every day I try to find a family doctor. (Chen 2021, 20)

None of the foregoing is meant to suggest that access to health care for Canada's general population under medicare is without problems. Indeed, complaints about long wait times are persistent among users of medicare (Urbach 2018). National surveys also reveal that a sizable number of Canadians lack a regular health-care provider (CIHR, NSERC, and SSHRC 2018; OurCare 2023). However, the design of the IFHP, with its humanitarian tenet, exacerbates these health-care access issues for refugees and asylum seekers.

CONCLUSION

Difficulties with health-care access under the IFHP have been described as "an institutionally reinforced discrimination," whereby refugees and asylum seekers are stereotyped as "patients that may be problematic or costly in terms of time" and thus to be avoided by health-care providers (McKeary and Newbold 2010, 535). To date, commentators have proposed an array of changes to the IFHP in hope of remedying these access issues. Among others, more targeted public education and further simplification of the IFHP have been advocated to demystify the program, along with financial and other incentives urged to encourage health-care providers' participation (Ruiz-Casares et al. 2016; A.J. Gagnon 2004). The government will do well to take heed of these recommendations.

Even more important to the removal of health access barriers facing refugees and asylum seekers, however, is a need to jettison the humanitarian underpinning of the IFHP in favour of a rights-based approach to health care. One way to do so is by making the IFHP more closely resemble medicare. To that end, the federal government should abandon its characterization of the IFHP as *ex gratia* and have the program formally grounded in legislation rather than policy as it is currently. Such legislation should spell out refugees' and asylum seekers' entitlement to health care and, like laws concerning medicare, prohibit health-care providers from charging patients when the cost of the services they deliver is already publicly covered. Having a legislative anchor like this will in theory make the IFHP less susceptible to retrogression, as to avoid a repeat of what happened in 2012.

Alternatively, as some have suggested, health-care coverage for refugees and asylum seekers should be fully reintegrated into medicare as it once was (Wales 2010). The symbolism of this alone could help contribute to refugees' and asylum seekers' inclusion in Canadian society. Admittedly, care must be taken when implementing such a proposal to ensure refugees and asylum seekers will maintain their existing supplemental coverage, which goes beyond what medicare covers. Whichever pathway to reform that the government chooses, it is clear that unless Canada's refugee health-care system embraces a rights-based approach, it will continue to fall short both ethically and legally.

FURTHER READING AND RESOURCES

Immigration, Refugees and Citizenship Canada (IRCC). 2022. "Interim Federal Health Program Policy." Government of Canada. https://www.canada.ca/en/immigration-refugees-citizenship/corporate/mandate/policies-operational-instructions-agreements/interim-federal-health-program-policy.html.

Oberoi, Pia, Juana Sotomayor, Paola Pace, Barbara Rijks, Jacqueline Weekers, and Yehenew Tsegaye Walilegne. 2012. *International Migration, Health and Human Rights*. Geneva: International Organization for Migration. https://publications.iom.int/books/international-migration-health-and-human-rights.

Pace, Paola. 2009. *Migration and the Right to Health: A Review of International Law*. Geneva: International Organization for Migration. https://publications.iom.int/books/international-migration-law-ndeg19-migration-and-right-health-review-international-law.

25

The Right to Work: Rhetoric and Reality for Refugees in Canada

Sally Ogoe and Lori Wilkinson

KEY TAKEAWAYS

- The right to work is protected under international and Canadian law.
- Resettled refugees arrive with permanent residence and no restrictions on employment. Refugee claimants can apply for a work permit after they are deemed eligible to apply for refugee status.
- Structural factors influence labour market participation, with gender and immigration status affecting work outcomes of refugee women.
- Deskilling occurs across immigration categories and is linked to problems with credential recognition.

KEY TERMS

- Credential recognition
- Deskilling
- Labour market

INTRODUCTION

> 25.1 Lived Experience of Unemployment
>
> Vicken Majarian worked as a dentist in Aleppo, Syria. He and his family stayed for years after the war began, living without electricity or running water, with the constant fear of death. In December 2015, Majarian, his wife and their two children [arrived in Canada].
>
> "We are happy that we are safe. We are in a good country," he said during an interview with *The Tyee*.
>
> But twenty-two months after their arrival, Majarian and his wife, formerly a civil engineering professor at the University of Aleppo, are still struggling to find stable, suitable employment. Majarian's work with a hospital transfer company has allowed him to support his family. But he wants to build a career using his skills and education - and earn enough money to better cope with BC's high cost of living.
>
> He'd like to find work related to dentistry. But at this point, he's willing to do just about anything. (Sanders 2017, n.p.)

Labour market participation and outcomes underpin every aspect of refugees' integration. However, there is not much consensus among scholars on the definition of integration because it continues to be a fluid, multi-layered, and in many cases, contested concept (Jedwab 2006; M. Ali, Zendo, and Somers 2022; see also Hynie, chapter 23). For instance, Atfield, Brahmbhatt, and O'Toole (2007) argue that integration is difficult to define because how do we determine "what the features of an integrated society are" (Atfield et al. 2007, 12). On the other hand, Ager and Strang (2008) are specific on such features – this they refer to as markers (such as employment and health) and means (such as social connections). Essentially, integration does mean different things to diverse populations in various situations, which makes it difficult to conceptualize but nonetheless important in understanding the experiences of resettled refugees. In this chapter, we acknowledge the complexity of defining integration yet focus mainly on economic integration.

Hyndman and Hynie (2016) argue that integration entails "equal access to material outcomes such as the availability and accessibility of health care, finding safe and adequate housing and obtaining employment." Although all aspects of integration are important, ultimately, refugees need employment to facilitate a successful integration process (Hyndman 2011). Refugees are admitted to Canada for humanitarian reasons and arrive with varying skill sets, work experience, education, and language competency. However, all face structural barriers, with women reporting higher rates of unemployment than men due to the intersectionality of gender with other power relations (Kustec 2012; Hyndman 2012).

According to Kustec (2012, 2), "[t]he Canadian labour force (as defined by Statistics Canada) consists of the civilian non-institutional population 15 years of age and over who are employed or unemployed. Employed individuals are those who have a job or a business and the unemployed are without work, are available to work, and are actively seeking work." Refugees have the right to work under Canadian and international law, but there are structural barriers to participate in Canada's labour force. In some cases, this can create an underground economy. According to Statistics Canada (2023, 1), "the underground economy is defined as consisting of market-based economic activities, whether legal or illegal, that escape measurement because of their hidden, illegal, or informal nature." For instance, unreported income such as relying on cash transactions or under-the-table payments to avoid income tax is sometimes evident in the case of undocumented immigrants (e.g., asylum seekers) who face barriers in the labour market with limited legal options (Frey and Schneider 2001). This chapter highlights these barriers and offers some recommendations.

INTERNATIONAL AND CANADIAN LAWS: REFUGEES' RIGHT TO WORK

The rights of refugees are broadly spelled out in the 1951 Refugee Convention and its 1967 Protocol, legally binding international human rights legislation, and Canada's Immigration and Refugee Protection Act (IRPA). Canada has signed and ratified the 1951 Refugee Convention, which sets the standards for the treatment of refugees in host countries (K. Smith 2016). For instance, articles 17 and 18 address wage earning and self-employment. Refugees have the right not only to enjoy sources of income from accessing jobs but also to be economically independent.

The right to work is also codified in article 6 of the International Covenant on Economic, Social and Cultural Rights. The UN Economic and Social Council adopted the following general comment on this fundamental right: "The right to work is essential for realizing other human rights and forms an inseparable and inherent part of human dignity. Every individual has the right to be able to work, allowing him/her to live in dignity. The right to work contributes at the same time to the survival of the individual and to that of his/her family, and insofar as work is freely chosen or accepted, to his/her development and recognition within the community" (UNESC 2005, para. 1).

It should be noted that resettled refugees arrive in Canada as permanent residents, so they do not face any legal restrictions on the right to work. Refugee claimants must apply for a work permit once they are deemed eligible to make a refugee claim. In most cases, refugee claimants have to pay for biometrics and an application fee, which can pose financial hardship and demonstrates the intersection of refugee status with class (see Hari and Quintero, chapter 16). Despite these protections, many refugees report difficulty finding work.

STRUCTURAL BARRIERS TO THE REALIZATION OF REFUGEES' RIGHT TO WORK

25.2 Teacher with International Credentials Faces Discrimination by Ontario College of Teachers Despite Widespread Teacher Shortages

> It took Thiru Thirukkumaran almost two years to receive his certificate to teach in Ontario and he wouldn't have gotten it at all if he hadn't appealed the regulatory college's initial denial. … [I]t took at least $10,000 in legal and consultant fees, support from his family and colleagues, and words of encouragement from past and current students, to get his certification.
>
> Thirukkumaran says if he'd had to face the Ontario College of Teachers (OCT) alone, he doesn't know if he'd have succeeded against what's widely seen as discrimination against some applicants with international credentials.
>
> … [H]e felt the college discriminated against him by refusing to recognize his two chemistry accreditations from Sri Lanka and Australia, equivalent to a bachelor's degree and a post-graduate diploma in Canada. He says if the college hadn't changed its mind on appeal, he would have gone to court to get his credentials recognized.
>
> Thirukkumaran, who came to Canada in 2012 and is now a permanent resident, says both were accepted by Ontario Tech University in Oshawa, east of Toronto – where he graduated with a bachelor of education in 2020 – and by York University, where he is working toward a master of science degree.
>
> … While he has his certificate now, Thirukkumaran said he wishes he didn't have to fight for it and lose the almost two years he could've spent getting paid for teaching and moving up the ranks with his peers. (Balintec 2023, n.p.)

Timely labour market integration of refugees is a vital component of integration practices and policies in Canada. Very few studies, however, have systematically identified and examined the labour market outcomes of refugees and how such outcomes vary by gender and human and demographic capital (Lamba 2003; R. Allen 2009; Kaida, Stick, and Hou 2020a; R. Banerjee 2022). This chapter highlights some of the structural barriers refugees encounter when looking for work in Canada.

Gender

Refugee women in Canada experience the labour market and labour market integration in very gendered ways (see also Aberman, chapter 12). Even though refugee women's admission does not include an economic assessment for entry and eligibility, there is supporting evidence that in most instances refugee women face higher unemployment rates, which increase with age (Colic-Peisker and Tilbury 2006; Endicott 2017). Likewise, studies highlight the low labour market participation of refugee women compared to refugee men (Wilkinson and Garcea 2017; Lamba 2003). Gannagé (1999) as well as Guo and Andersson (2005) point out that in labour immigration, newcomer women are viewed as providers of cheap labour. Refugee women can be found working in the occupations that are low paid and less stable – most refugee women work in the elemental and labourers (30 per cent) category, while just over one-quarter (27 per cent) work in intermediate and clerical occupations (Ogoe 2022). On average, women work in these positions, which puts them in precarious positions in terms of labour market integration.

Bias in Hiring Practices

The power employers have in determining the labour market futures contributes to discrimination in hiring processes. Krahn et al.'s (2000) research shows negative attitudes toward refugees, including racism and discrimination (see also Mahrouse and El Omari, chapter 15). The belief that refugees lack professional knowledge or their knowledge is inferior, and non-recognition of their credentials and prior experience all contribute to precarious and low-paying work. Employers often overlook newcomers' human capital qualifications (Madut 2016). Consequently, refugees have to spend a great deal of time with retraining and employment support programs and sometimes still face barriers in the labour market.

In some cases, this discrimination is exacerbated for racialized refugees and those from developing countries (P. Li 2003; Pendakur and Pendakur 1998, 2014). Mata and Pendakur's (2017) research addresses this phenomenon, indicating that immigrants from European countries face less discrimination than other immigrants from other regions. This means better job placements, less earning disparity between such refugees and Canadian citizens, and a sense of belonging in the host country (K. Anderson and Huang 2019). In response, community organizations such as Manitoba Start, Hire Immigrants

Ottawa, and Immigrant Employment Council of BC are working to educate employers about hiring refugees and assisting newly arrived refugees with information and education about entering the labour market (Government of Canada 2022c).

Language

Research shows that fluency in at least one of the official languages of Canada is positively correlated to securing work, particularly in jobs that require higher skills (Krahn et al. 2000; K. Anderson and Huang 2019; Daley, Hu, and Warman 2019). For refugees, this language knowledge is mostly self-assessed as most employment databases do not have access to language scores (Ferrer et al. 2014). Studies point to the low language proficiency in French or English as one of the significant challenges to securing jobs in a host country or even participating in the labour market (Jamil 2016). Ogoe's (2022) research finds that over the past decade a reasonable number of refugee women in Canada are literate in at least one of Canada's official languages: an estimate of about 50 per cent are fluent in English or French. While this is helpful for finding work, many refugee women (and men) struggle with their accent and have reported losing out on employment opportunities if they speak with a non-English or a non-French accent (Freynet, Clément, and Sylvestre 2018), even though this practice contravenes the human rights codes of most provinces (Sathiyanathan and Xing 2018).

Education and Credential Recognition

Education is a key element not only for access to the labour market but also for desired jobs. Refugees have diverse backgrounds – some have high levels of education, others have less or no formal education. Ogoe finds that three-quarters (74 per cent) of refugee women arrive in Canada with a high school diploma or less, while only 10 per cent have earned a university degree and 13 per cent have earned a college diploma or trade certificate (2022, 66). This means that labour market outcomes are limited for many refugee women given their comparatively low level of education. Canadian-born women, comparatively, are more highly educated on average (Ogoe 2022, 67). Similarly, research demonstrates that refugees arriving in Canada tend to have lower levels of formal education than family reunification and labour market immigration categories, and also are less likely to go on to post-secondary education (Ferede 2012). Children of refugees also have much lower tertiary education completion rates than children of skilled workers and business immigrants (Hou and Bonikowska 2017). Undocumented young people and those with precarious immigration status – such as refugee claimants – have even fewer opportunities to access higher education (Villegas and Aberman 2019).

However, even for those refugees who have training and skills, recognition of credentials and education attained abroad remains a major obstacle to entering the labour force (see box 25.2, for example). Stobbe and Harris (2013) find that Canadian employers often do not recognize foreign credentials, posing a hurdle for refugees to fully integrate into the economic sector. Galabuzi (2006) adds that the challenges in labour market integration for newcomers degrades their skills and can create mental frustration and physical health issues. Canadian employers' failure to recognize education attained abroad and accompanying work experience has meant that many newcomers, especially those with a refugee background, are overqualified for the jobs they currently hold. One primary example is in the taxicab industry. Over 50 per cent of all taxi drivers are immigrants or refugees (Government of Canada 2012b; Zhang 2016). According to Statistics Canada, 35 per cent of Canadian-born taxicab drivers have a post-secondary qualification but 53 per cent of newcomer taxicab drivers are similarly educated (quoted in Xu 2012, 21). Although overqualification also holds true for Canadian-born taxicab drivers, the issue is clearly more predominant among newcomers. While 20 per cent of all newcomer taxicab drivers have a bachelor's degree, only 4.8 per cent of Canadian-born taxicab drivers hold a degree (Xu 2012).

Self-regulated professions in Canada have their own guidelines, rules, and eligibility criteria such that they have the power to determine who can practice a particular profession in the country (Wilkinson 2017). Since these self-regulated professions are self-governing, there is less accountability for making accessibility more difficult for refugee women to practice these professions in Canada (Kelly, Marcelino, and Mulas 2014). The cases of refugees who have professional careers sometimes goes beyond non-recognition of credentials when credentials are lost or even destroyed during wars and the institutions where they were obtained may no longer exist. Consequently, some refugees do not have documentation to prove their qualifications to practice in their specialized fields.

Proposed solutions to recognize foreign credentials and previous work experience have been meagre and piecemeal. Most regulated professions still inadequately address foreign credential recognition, which is exacerbated by provincial-federal jurisdictions (see Garnier, chapter 10). For example, only four provinces (Ontario, Manitoba, Alberta, and British Columbia) have created an Office of the Fairness Commissioner whose goal is to have professional organizations address foreign credential assessment in provincially regulated occupations. However, no province has given that office the authority to do anything other than monitor provincially regulated professions. There remains no mechanism to encourage or penalize professional organizations that do not want to address foreign credential assessment, and this remains a significant gap in the program. More recently, several provinces (such as Ontario and Manitoba) are now waiving or reducing some of the credential recognition requirements so that foreign-trained medical professionals can enter the health-care sector with fewer barriers (Balintec 2023).

Occupational skill levels refer to the intended skill level of the immigrant at the time of admission (Statistics Canada 2016). Krahn and Lowe (1998), Lamba (2003), and Endicott (2017) assert that Canadian colleges and universities have institutionalized the deskilling of refugees, contributing to their downward economic mobility compared to other groups. Deskilling refers to "situations where migrants with higher education work in jobs that do not require such qualifications" (Korzeniewska and Erdal 2021, 3). Researchers point out that immigrants with graduate and doctorate degrees in specific fields are presented with options to earn a much lower degree in Canada. In Edmonton's former Grant MacEwan Community College, for example, refugees and immigrants who are cardiac surgeons, gynecologists, and radiologists are offered a nursing diploma prior to practising in their fields in Canada (Krahn et al. 2000; Endicott 2017). This is a common practice across Canada.

CONCLUSIONS AND FUTURE PROSPECTS

In strengthening and building the Canadian labour force through the integration of refugees, it becomes important to acknowledge refugees' contribution in the building of a country founded on the displacement, sovereignty, and dispossession of Indigenous populations (Nobe-Ghelani and Lumor 2022). Besides the existing labour market barriers and gaps (e.g., high unemployment rates, racialization of poverty), resettlement for refugees in Canada is underpinned by complicit ongoing colonization while they also struggle against their own marginalization and racialization in the process (Phung 2011; Jafri 2012a; Nobe-Ghelani and Lumor 2022).

For refugees, labour market integration in Canada is challenging. Some refugees arrive with low levels of education and difficulties communicating in English or French. For others, finding employment that recognizes their level of education and work experience is arduous because many employers do not recognize their credentials or impose an artificial "Canadian experience" requirement (Sakamoto, Chin, and Young 2010) as a way of filtering out newcomer workers. Guo and Andersson (2005) argue that the top contributing factors for refugees' downward occupational mobility are linked to non-recognition of their education, language challenges, lack of Canadian work experience, and employers' discrimination in the labour market. Experiences of trauma may also impede refugees' entrance into the labour market (Wilkinson and Bhattacharyya 2018). Moreover, refugee women face all the other barriers experienced by Canadian women – gender-based discrimination, penalties for maternity leaves, and lack of opportunities for advancement within their careers.

There is a need for effective policies to guide the labour market integration of refugees in Canada. Some immigration experts have criticized Canada's lack of a working approach to ensure that refugees secure jobs upon arrival. Garcea (2016), Krahn et al. (2000), and Endicott (2017) all point out that refugees become the responsibility of settlement agencies, which are under-staffed and backlogged with requests in addition to assisting the large number of resettled refugees by teaching interview skills, revising resumes, and helping them find well-paying jobs. These agencies are generally unable to assist with or eradicate the barriers refugees face in the labour market in addition to the negative stigma associated with refugees, which deters employers from hiring them, further contributing to systematic discrimination (Krahn et al. 2000; Garcea 2016).

Labour market integration plays a major role in the lives of refugees and their families. Successful labour market integration depends on how well the host country provides resettlement services such as language and skills training and education; credentials recognition; and even employment opportunities such that refugees can become financially independent (Nakhaie and Kazemipur 2013; Latif 2015).

Recently, the United Nations (2022) has recognized that in order to recover from the coronavirus pandemic, governments must provide opportunities for refugees and other newcomers to contribute economically. Already there is evidence that states such as Canada have significant labour market shortfalls (Morissette et al. 2021) because the pandemic brought annual migration levels to historically low levels. In short, Canada is experiencing a desperate shortage of workers, and some of this work could be done by refugees or refugee claimants in Canada. Indeed, in 2022, the government introduced limited programs for regularization of status for certain industries like health care and construction.

25.3 Regularization Program for Health-Care Workers

After filling in the gaps for personal support workers by working with agencies in Hamilton during the worst of the pandemic, Jane, a failed refugee claimant from Uganda fleeing oppression for her sexual orientation, was eager to learn about the federal government's new pathway to permanent residence for healthcare workers.

The program was introduced in April [2021]. But out of 20,000 spaces designated for healthcare workers, only 5,466 people had applied as of 21 October. Migrant rights advocates say that's because the parameters of the program are too restrictive, and there are many more immigrant healthcare workers who would love to apply but don't qualify.

Jane, who identifies as a lesbian, came here in 2017, fleeing a homophobic and abusive relationship and a family that had disowned her due to her sexual orientation. In her home country, the law prohibits sex acts "against the order of nature," punishable by imprisonment, and many 2SLGBTQI+ people remain closeted out of fear of social and physical reprisal.

She made a refugee claim in Canada but was denied, leaving her to work and live without official immigration status.

Throughout the pandemic, Jane worked as an in-home personal support worker in the Hamilton area, and caught COVID-19 on the job.

"Very many PSWs were exposed to COVID," [said] Jane, who didn't want her last name published because she fears deportation.

"I really risked my life going ahead to help another person. I've always loved to serve the community."

When she heard of the temporary resident to permanent resident pathway, with 20,000 spots designated for healthcare workers, she was elated, but her hopes dissolved when she learned it wasn't open to undocumented people or refugee claimants.

"It's just so sad," said Jane, who can no longer apply for new work now that her SIN number has expired, but feels she also can't return to Uganda. She is currently living with friends in Ontario, but has left Hamilton.

"I wish they would call one-on-one and hear our views [and] reconsider, as long as you worked and helped someone during the pandemic ... I have prayed each day that maybe I would be reconsidered." (Peesker 2021, n.p.)

RECOMMENDATIONS

Continued insistence for Canadian work experience, though not illegal, prevents many refugee women from entering the labour market. In addition, although it is illegal to use accents as a reason for not hiring a candidate, the practice prevails but is difficult to prove. In response, sensitization and training for employers is needed. In addition, provincial and federal governments could do more to encourage the hiring of refugees. Providing employers with financial subsidies to hire refugees is an interesting solution that should be encouraged. Would-be employers are provided a government subsidy to hire refugees on a permanent or temporary basis. Many refugees have found permanent employment by participating in such programs. Sadly, most of these programs were cancelled in the early 2000s, casualties of neo-liberal governments' cost-cutting measures.

While non-government organizations and some government bodies have tried to address the barriers preventing refugees from successfully entering and integrating into the labour force, much work remains. For example, non-profit organizations such as Manitoba Start and WILL Immploy already provide a wide variety of employment-ready projects aimed at refugees (Manitoba Start 2022; WILL Immploy 2022) – including language classes geared toward workplaces, upgrading various skills, resume writing and job fairs, and job search assistance (Battisti, Giesing, and Laurentsyeva 2019). Similarly, Hirearefugee.com was created in response to the arrival of over forty-five thousand Syrian refugees in 2016. A non-profit organization, its goal is to find refugees permanent work by placing them with various employers. Further investment in these programs would increase the employment rate of refugees. Some private companies have also stepped up to provide valuable and meaningful employment for refugees in Canada. For instance, the Economic Mobility Pathways Pilot (EMPP) and the Rural and Northern Immigration Pilot partner with some provinces, territories, and communities across Canada as well as non-government organizations to connect refugees to in-demand jobs (Government of Canada 2022c).

Governments, not-for-profit agencies, and private industry can do much more to assist the labour market integration of refugees and other newcomers. Investments in education, language classes, and skills upgrading can assist the large number of refugee women who arrive with low levels of skills. This can be achieved through more federal government funding to settlement agencies to provide labour market integration programs for refugees.

The federal and provincial governments through the Canadian Information Centre for International Credentials, or CICIC, (2022) can provide more opportunities for positive assessment of foreign credentials. These relatively small investments not only enhance the labour market outcomes of refugees and their families, but also the investments assist our communities. As Schmidtke (2018) points out, labour market integration is essential for economic growth in Canada. There is much we can do to encourage our governments and businesses, and the benefits of such investments outweigh any economic costs. For instance, even though the cost of resettling refugees is millions of dollars, the knowledge and skills refugees bring to the country's labour market are often overlooked (Bahar and Dooley 2020).

Refugees contribute to the sustainable growth of Canada. For example, 23 per cent of refugees earn a middle-class income, while over 50 per cent of refugees work in high-skilled jobs thereby contributing largely to the country's tax base (Bahar 2018; TRIEC 2023). They bring to the country's labour market diverse skills and talents, despite existing barriers. According to UNHCR (2023b), about 20 per cent of refugees in Canada work in jobs such as doctors, dentists, and architects that require a university degree. In addition, some refugees start their own businesses. About 14 per cent become entrepreneurs after resettlement in Canada, which presents opportunities for connections to diverse markets for Canada (Bahar and Dooley 2020; UNHCR 2023b).

FURTHER READING AND RESOURCES

Kohlenberg, Beatrice, and Bryce Loo. 2020. "Assessment and Recognition of Refugee Credentials." *International Higher Education*, no. 101 (Spring). https://www.internationalhighereducation.net/api-v1/article/!/action/getPdfOfArticle/articleID/2881/productID/29/filename/article-id-2881.pdf.

Novotna, Gabriela, and Marina Morgenshtern. 2022. "Canada Needs to Stop Wasting the Talent of Skilled Immigrants." *The Conversation*, 15 May 2022. https://theconversation.com/canada-needs-to-stop-wasting-the-talent-of-skilled-immigrants-182005.

Ontario Human Rights Commission. 2013. "Policy on Removing Canadian Experience Barrier." https://www.ohrc.on.ca/en/policy-removing-%E2%80%9Ccanadian-experience%E2%80%9D-barrier.

Picot, Garnett, Yan Zhang, and Feng Hou. 2019. "Labour Market Outcomes Among Refugees to Canada." Statistics Canada Research Paper. March 2019. https://www150.statcan.gc.ca/n1/pub/11f0019m/11f0019m2019007-eng.htm.

26

Religious Groups and Refugees in Canada: Advocacy, Partnership, and Resistance

Geoffrey Cameron

KEY TAKEAWAYS

- Religious groups have a long history of advocacy for the admission of persecuted and displaced people to Canada, and they have been influential actors in the field of refugee law and policy.
- Canada's policy of private refugee sponsorship developed in partnership with religious groups and many are actively engaged in the settlement of refugees.
- Some religious groups have also resisted government policy by supporting litigation that challenges the procedural fairness of refugee status determination (RSD) and by engaging in sanctuary practices that prevent enforced removals.

KEY TERMS

- Religious groups
- Sanctuary

INTRODUCTION

26.1 Following the 1979 Islamic Revolution in Iran, the new regime targeted the Baha'i religious minority for persecution. Recounting her experience fleeing Iran as a four-year-old child, Afsoon Houshidari told the *Toronto Star*, "The Baha'is were perceived as anti-revolutionary. They were severely persecuted and oppressed. My mother's brother was a physician. He was imprisoned, tortured and executed. All because he was a Baha'i. Being a Baha'i means you're a target" (Keung 2016b, n.p.). She carried on to say, "We escaped walking into a dark tunnel and only our faith in God was certain," recalled Houshidari. "We only had two small bags. There was nothing to eat or drink. That's how we crossed the border, running in the middle of the night, narrowly avoiding an Iranian army tank that was patrolling the border and that would've fired if they'd seen us. My parents were just relieved because we made it out of Iran and were not in danger."

Houshidari travelled with her parents to Lahore, Pakistan, in 1984, and she arrived in Montreal on 14 June 1984 as a government-sponsored refugee. Her family spent their first year in Edmundston, New Brunswick, and then later moved to the Toronto area. She is now a lawyer with the Immigration and Refugee Board of Canada. (Keung 2016b)

This narrative of Afsoon Houshidari's escape overland from Iran to Pakistan, and then to Canada, resembles that of many other refugees who arrive in Canada via resettlement. The Canadian government has been one of the leading countries of resettlement since World War II, accepting refugees who fled their country of origin – often to a neighbouring country – and then sought permanent status in a third country (see Atak, chapter 17; Labman, chapter 18). Behind the details of the story described above, however, is the active involvement of a religious group advocating for persecuted co-religionists abroad and partnering with government agencies to secure their protection. Houshidari and her family would, in all likelihood, not have arrived in Canada without the involvement of a religious group.

The National Spiritual Assembly of the Baha'is of Canada began to advocate on behalf of persecuted Baha'is soon after the Islamic Revolution, resulting in public condemnations of Iran's actions in the House of Commons starting in June 1980 (G. Cameron 2013). The Canadian government proceeded to bring a resolution about the Baha'i persecution to the United Nations (UN) Sub-Commission on the Prevention of Discrimination and Protection of Minorities initiating a series of interventions by the UN Commission on

Human Rights. By 1981 the Government of Canada had agreed to resettle Baha'is, based in part on the offer of private refugee sponsorship by the National Assembly (G. Cameron 2013).

Between 1981 and 1989 around two thousand three hundred Iranian Baha'is were resettled in Canada, initially through private sponsorship by the National Assembly and later complemented by government-assisted resettlement. Through whichever program they travelled to Canada, once Iranian Baha'is arrived they were met by local Baha'i communities that supported their process of settlement and participation in Canadian society (van den Hoonaard and van den Hoonard 2010; G. Cameron 2018). The involvement of the Baha'i community in advocacy on behalf of a persecuted minority abroad, partnership with government to facilitate resettlement in Canada, and engagement with refugee settlement in Canada are emblematic of a wider pattern of engagement by religious groups with the issue of forced migration.

Before proceeding, we need to briefly define what is meant by a "religious group." Many people derive spiritual strength from faith, belief, and religion, and several studies examine the role of religion in the lives of refugees in Canada (Dorais 2007; McLellan 2009; Connor 2014; Mavelli and Wilson 2017). However, this chapter is focused on examining the formal organization of people who share a common faith. A religious group, in other words, is an organization that is either explicitly identified with, or legitimately represents, a community of people of the same religious tradition. While some such groups may also be considered ethnic organizations because they do not directly attend to the spiritual or pastoral needs of their community (e.g., the Canadian Jewish Congress or the Mennonite Central Committee Canada), I nevertheless consider them to be religious groups because the community they represent is united by a shared identity relating to religion.

Religious groups are often overlooked in the study of forced migration and public policy because they do not share many characteristics of pressure groups or interest groups. Indeed, leading studies of group politics in Canada scarcely mention religious groups except to gesture to their involvement in temperance and social purity movements of the nineteenth century (M.C. Smith 2018, 45; Pross 1992, 157). The core purpose of a religious group is not to influence public policy to promote a common interest but rather to attend to the values, interests, and concerns of a community and its leadership (Hoover and den Dulk 2004). Most religious groups do not exist to engage in political action. For these reasons they are sometimes classified as "solidary groups," which can sustain and support political mobilization but do not themselves seek policy changes. Nevertheless, religious groups sometimes do take on the characteristics of pressure groups when they seek out policy changes or government actions as an expression of shared values or interests.

Many organized religious groups maintain active programs of government relations that include the promotion of specific policy issues. Many religious groups also have the capacity to mobilize resources and social networks that can make them effective partners for policy implementation. When they enjoy high moral standing, their resistance to, and criticism of, government action can influence public opinion. These shape-shifting qualities of religious groups, together with their use of theological and spiritual discourse, can make their motivations and actions illegible in research, notwithstanding their centrality to a given policy field. Refugee policy is one such field, where the involvement of religious groups is widely acknowledged by practitioners but relatively under-analyzed by researchers.

In this chapter, I describe how religious groups engage with forced migration in Canada by focusing on three approaches to political action in the context of forced migration: advocacy, partnership, and resistance. Religious groups have advocated for refugee protection in Canada, often by promoting resettlement programs. Through both public lobbying and quiet activism, religious groups have promoted the adoption of specific policy measures and urged government to admit particular groups of vulnerable people. They have also partnered with the government to privately sponsor refugees to come to Canada and to help settle refugees after their arrival. Finally, some religious groups have resisted government refugee policy by joining court challenges to immigration law and, in a few cases, by defying legal enforcement and offering sanctuary to immigrants facing deportation orders. Through advocacy, partnership, and resistance, religious groups have played a significant role in shaping refugee policy and practice in Canada.

ADVOCACY

Religious groups have a long history of advocacy for the admission of persecuted and displaced people to Canada (G. Cameron 2021). A study of one such group, the Mennonite Central Committee Canada (MCCC), described its advocacy for refugees as the consequence of a "unique blend of heritage, collective identity, and theology [that] has translated into long-held values" (Enns, Good Gingrich, and Perez 2020, 107). Other religious groups that advocate for the admission of refugees are animated by a similar combination of historical memory, shared identity, and moral and ethical principles derived from scripture. While in many cases they have sought the protection of co-religionists abroad, religious groups have also advocated on behalf of vulnerable people with whom they are connected through social and historical networks.

This chapter has already described the advocacy of the National Spiritual Assembly of the Baha'is of Canada on behalf of Iranian Baha'i refugees in Pakistan, India, and elsewhere during the 1980s, which led to the resettlement of thousands of Baha'is in Canada. While it would be possible to identify dozens of examples where religious groups have successfully sought the admission of refugees to Canada, a few representative cases are discussed below.

Canadian Jewish Congress: European Refugees (1930s–50s)

In the mid-twentieth century, the Canadian Jewish Congress (CJC) and its affiliate organizations advocated regularly for the admission of persecuted Jews from Europe. Following the events of Kristallnacht in 1938, the CJC initiated a public campaign calling on the government to "provide havens of refuge for victims of Nazi brutality" (Abella and Troper 2012, 41). It proceeded to collaborate with the Canadian League of Nations Society to create the Canadian National Committee on Refugees, which pressured the government to adopt a humanitarian refugee policy that would include Jews. Nevertheless, their advocacy had little immediate effect. From 1937 to 1945, less than 6 per cent of all immigrants and refugees admitted to Canada were Jews, which amounted to the lowest admission of Jews among refugee-receiving countries (G. Cameron 2021, 55).

The CJC and the affiliated Jewish Immigrant Aid Services (JIAS) continued to advocate for the admission of refugees to Canada following the end of World War II. When Canada began to admit refugees from European camps in 1947, the initial focus was on meeting economic needs; however, the CJC worked alongside a handful of Christian groups to negotiate a sponsorship arrangement whereby they could provide assurances of assistance with settlement to refugee arrivals. The number of Jewish refugee arrivals progressively increased, alongside other refugees sponsored to come to Canada. These early sponsorship arrangements were further formalized with the introduction of the Approved Church Program in 1954, which aimed to harmonize the terms of refugee sponsorship undertaken by the CJC and a few Christian groups. While the CJC primarily advocated for the resettlement of Jewish refugees during this period, it sought out partnerships and alliances that promoted a broader humanitarian policy by the Canadian government. Between 1946 and 1962 Canada admitted nearly a quarter million refugees as part of a gradual change in policy brought about – at least partially – by the advocacy of the CJC and JIAS (Kelley and Trebilcock 2010, 342).

Canadian Council of Churches: Chilean Refugees (1970s)

After the 1971 coup of President Allende in Chile, General Pinochet's forces directed a wave of political violence against adversaries and citizens. The Canadian Council of Churches (CCC), a Christian ecumenical body affiliated with the World Council of Churches (WCC), became a prominent advocate for the admission of Chilean refugees to Canada. They were requested to intervene with the Canadian government by Chilean churches who shared an affiliation with the WCC, as well as by Canadian missionaries in the country (Dirks 1977, 245). Days after the coup, the leadership of the Anglican, United, and Catholic churches sent a joint letter to the Canadian government protesting the military takeover and calling on Ottawa "to offer safe conduct and assistance to [non-Chileans living in Chile] and any other Chilean who may wish to come to Canada" (G. Cameron 2021, 131). Further meetings were held with the minister of external affairs, to little initial effect. However, when a leaked telex from the Canadian ambassador to Chile indicated government sympathy with the Pinochet regime, the CCC's Inter-Church Committee on Human Rights in Latin America adopted a more confrontational approach with the Canadian government (Lind and Mihevc 1994, 203–18). A letter-writing campaign, media publicity, and the preparation of political briefs based on personal accounts in Chile were among their advocacy tools.

The Canadian government remained reluctant to admit Chilean refugees, but the persistence of the CCC and its advocacy through opposition Conservative and New Democratic MPs and English language media outlets eventually led to the creation of a "Special Movement" program targeting Chilean refugees. As one senior immigration official recalled, this "assertive refugee advocacy community" generated "continuous criticism" of government policy as new approaches were being developed (Molloy and Madokoro 2017, 56). Canadian church representatives worked with Chilean counterparts in many cases to identify refugees for resettlement in Canada, further anticipating the later creation of a formal private refugee sponsorship program (W. Janzen 2006). Eventually, some seven thousand Chilean refugees were resettled in Canada.

Ismaili Council for Canada and FOCUS Humanitarian Canada: Afghan Refugees (1990s)

After the fall of the Soviet-backed Afghan government of Mohammad Najibullah in 1992, the country descended into a civil war that eventually led to the establishment of the Islamic Emirate of Afghanistan under the Taliban. Within this context, the Ismaili Muslim minority faced risks to their security. A well-established Ismaili Muslim community in Canada – many members of which could trace their roots in the country to arriving as refugees from Uganda in the early 1970s – advocated for the creation of a special resettlement program.

The Ismaili Council for Canada and an affiliated non-governmental organization (NGO), FOCUS Humanitarian Canada, eschewed the contentious politics that characterized the advocacy of the CCC in the Chilean case. Their advocacy and co-operation with the Canadian government to secure the entry of Ismaili refugees from Afghanistan resembled more closely the Iranian Baha'i refugee movement of the 1980s. A program called Project FOCUS Afghanistan developed as a co-operative arrangement between the two Ismaili groups and the Government of Canada to admit some one thousand eight hundred Afghan Ismaili refugees between 1994 and 1998 (Treviranus and Casasola 2003, 189).

These refugees were provided with government assistance for their first three months in Canada, after which the Ismaili community and its institutions assumed responsibility for their ongoing settlement and support.

PARTNERSHIP

In addition to advocating for the admission of specific groups of refugees, religious groups have sought out partnerships with the state that involve them in the implementation of government policies. These partnerships have developed in two primary areas of policy: refugee sponsorship (see also Labman, chapter 18) and refugee settlement and integration.

Refugee Sponsorship

Religious groups have co-operated with state authorities to welcome and support immigrants and refugees as long as settlers have been arriving in Canada (Biles and Ibrahim 2009). Christian and Jewish groups became more formally involved as refugee sponsors in the years following the end of World War II. Their initial involvement with sponsorship took place in the context of the Close Relatives Program, in which a coalition of religious groups assisted with the implementation of a government family reunification program. Christian groups formed the Canadian Christian Council for the Resettlement of Refugees (CCCRR) to facilitate this nascent version of refugee sponsorship, and they were soon joined by the CJC and its affiliates.

What began as a family sponsorship program facilitated by religious groups was soon formalized into an Approved Church Program, which allowed four registered groups to participate in broader refugee sponsorship from Europe. The CCCRR, the (Catholic) Rural Settlement Society, the Canadian Council of Churches, and JIAS were permitted to sponsor refugees to come to Canada during the 1950s. This partnership between religious groups and the government's immigration department was uneasy, however, as the terms of sponsorship were a subject of continued negotiation. Religious groups worried about their financial liability for refugees unable to sustain themselves, and government officials questioned whether the most economically fit refugees were being sponsored to come to Canada. The program for private sponsorship was effectively discontinued throughout the 1960s.

The major turning point for the establishment of private refugee sponsorship in Canada was the inclusion of a sponsorship provision in the 1976 Immigration Act. JIAS, affiliated with the CJC, publicly called for a law that would revive the past practice of sponsorship (Labman 2019, 83). Furthermore, immigration officials were looking to re-incorporate religious groups to play a role in policy implementation (Molloy et al. 2017, 70). The 1976 Immigration Act established private sponsorship as part of Canada's immigration policy, but the legislation provided only an outline of how the new program would function. Immigration officials held meetings with JIAS and the Catholic Migration Commission to generate interest in the new policy, and progress was effectively stalled until the MCCC initiated negotiations with government officials over the precise terms of sponsorship under a "Master Agreement."

The keystone of Canada's private refugee sponsorship program is the recognition of Sponsorship Agreement Holders (SAHs), corporate bodies authorized to sponsor refugees. The creation of standard Master Agreements was intended to establish clear responsibilities and expectations between the immigration officials and sponsoring groups. The template for these agreements was created during March 1979 negotiations between the MCCC and senior government officials (Molloy et al. 2017, 75–6; W. Janzen 2006, 211). Similar agreements were signed with some forty other religious groups, creating a new policy framework for private refugee sponsorship. Several months later, Canada announced that it would admit fifty thousand Indochinese refugees – with half of this number to be sponsored by private groups. Religious groups were singled out in a government report on the Indochinese program, noting that "no account of the program would be complete without acknowledging the leadership role provided by the churches of Canada in mobilizing their congregations to welcome and support the refugees" (quoted in G. Cameron 2021, 160).

SAH groups progressively formalized their relationship with the Government of Canada in subsequent years. The first national SAH conference was held in 1998, initiating steps toward the creation of a formal association. In 2011 the Sponsorship Agreement Holders Association was formally incorporated as a body that forms an "NGO-Government Committee," alongside the Refugee Sponsorship Training Program (RSTP) and Immigration, Refugees and Citizenship Canada. According to the SAH Association, more than 60 per cent of its members are faith-based organizations (SAH Navigation Unit 2022).

Settlement and Integration

The social service sector engaged with supporting refugees and immigrants upon their arrival in Canada is populated by a range of organizations that work in partnership with governments. A significant number of these groups are connected, in one way or another, to religious communities (R. Janzen et al. 2016; R. Janzen et al. 2020; Mulholland 2017). While many religious communities engage in voluntary outreach to refugee populations as an expression of their spiritual values, religious groups are also engaged in formal partnerships with the state to deliver settlement services. Their distinctive contribution to settlement services has been recognized by initiatives such as the Faith and Welcoming Communities Forum organized by the Toronto North Local Immigration Partnership. This forum examined the role of religious groups within the local settlement network (R. Janzen et al. 2020, 242). A number of studies have found evidence of the positive role of religious groups in the settlement process, including by providing access to social networks and contributing to positive mental health outcomes (B. Abu-Laban et al. 1999; Beiser 1999).

In recent decades, some religious groups have formally incorporated their efforts to access government funding for the delivery of settlement services (Mulholland 2017). Researchers studying the role of religious groups in settlement partnerships have observed that these relationships often exert secularizing pressures on the groups and their staff. These pressures can be directed externally, as government officials require groups to present themselves in secular terms. As Bramadat writes, "the government adopts what one might call a studied indifference toward the core religious sensibilities of these groups, but finds the commitment and competence of the volunteers to be extremely useful (and cost-effective) for supporting the government's settlement efforts" (2014, 20).

Secularizing pressures can also arise internally, as the processes of professionalization and bureaucratization alter the culture of an organization originally launched by volunteers animated by religious convictions. Mulholland shares the following observation based on her study of settlement organizations in Alberta: "Although faith-motivated volunteers founded many of these agencies, liberal secular ideologies entered into the internal dynamics and politics early on" (2017, 25). Over time, secular imperatives shaped the character of many of these organizations, including their "branding" (removing religious symbols), naming (removing denominational references), mandates (removing quotes from scripture), and organizational culture. In some cases, what began as volunteer-driven religious groups evolved into organizations with multi-million-dollar budgets with hundreds of employees supported by government grants. This dynamic of secularization and bureaucratization poses challenges for a settlement sector that has depended on the volunteer efforts of religious communities and individuals, and yet excludes discussion of religion from the process of settlement and social participation by refugees (Biles and Ibrahim 2009).

RESISTANCE

The third mode of action undertaken by some religious groups is resistance to refugee law and policy. In fact, it is primarily Christian congregations and the CCC that have been engaged in the kinds of resistance described in this section. The focus of their resistance has been Canada's system of RSD. First, a series of legal challenges supported by the Canadian Council of Churches have focused on the rights of asylum seekers to due process throughout RSD. Second, the practice of extending "sanctuary" to migrants has publicly challenged the negative outcomes of RSD proceedings and exerted public pressure on the state to expand the appeals process for refugee claimants.

Court Challenges

In 1969 Canada ratified the UN Refugee Convention and its associated 1967 Protocol, which meant that asylum seekers within Canada's borders had the right to access a legal process for determining their refugee status and protection. Under the convention, Canada was prohibited from deporting anyone who had a well-founded fear of persecution in their country of origin. In 1973 Canada began to set up an administrative procedure for evaluating refugee claims. In most cases, refugee claims were evaluated based on the submission of written documentation, although oral hearings were conducted in some locations.

In 1984 seven refugee claimants whose claims had been rejected appealed to the Supreme Court of Canada (SCC) that the RSD process violated their section 7 rights to life, liberty, and security of person under the newly adopted Charter of Rights and Freedoms. Their lawyers claimed that the procedure did not accord with principles of fundamental justice because they were not provided with an oral hearing. Two religious groups joined as intervenors in this case: the Federation of Canadian Sikh Societies and the CCC. The Supreme Court found in favour of the litigants in *Singh v. Minister of Employment and Immigration*, 1985, in a landmark decision for both charter rights and refugee law. The *Singh* decision held that charter rights applied to non-citizens as well as citizens. It also required reforms to Canada's system of RSD: "at a minimum, the procedural scheme set up by the Act should provide the refugee claimant with an adequate opportunity to state his case and to know the case he has to meet." The *Singh* decision ultimately led to the creation of the Immigration and Refugee Board (IRB) of Canada in 1989, with a corresponding requirement to ensure greater procedural fairness of refugee claimants (Hamlin 2014; Macklin 2009).

The Canadian Council of Churches has continued to participate in litigation aimed at protecting refugee claimants from due process violations. It was denied intervener status in *Canadian Council of Churches v. Canada (Minister of Employment and Immigration)*, 1992, because the court did not recognize the CCC public interest standing to challenge new RSD procedures (Dauvergne 2013). However, in subsequent cases the CCC has been recognized as an intervenor alongside individuals who have appealed the procedural grounds of their deportation orders. These cases include: *Suresh v. Canada (Minister of Citizenship and Immigration)*, 2002; *Chieu v. Canada (Minister of Citizenship and Immigration)*, 2002; and *Baker v. Canada (Minister of Citizenship and Immigration)*, 1999.

The CCC has also acted as an intervenor in a series of court cases challenging the Canada–United States Safe Third Country Agreement (STCA) (see also Young, chapter 3). Under the agreement, asylum seekers must apply for protection in the first of the two countries in which they arrive, with some exceptions. However, soon after the STCA entered into force, the CCC joined with the

Canadian Council for Refugees (CCR) and Amnesty International to determine how to challenge the agreement's legal validity in Canada (Macklin 2009, 109). It was granted intervenor status by the Federal Court of Appeal, where it asserted that the agreement affected the rights of asylum seekers to liberty and security under section 7 of the Charter of Rights and Freedoms. The Federal Court ruled in favour of the litigants in CCR, CCC, Amnesty International, and *John Doe v. The Queen*, 2007, but the case was later overturned by the SCC. The SCC agreed to hear another challenge to the STCA in 2022, and at the time of writing the decision has not yet been passed down (CCC 2021).

Sanctuary

Religious groups have also resisted the state through local practices of sanctuary, where refugee claimants whose claims have been denied are sheltered in places of worship to protect them from arrest and deportation. The purpose of sanctuary has generally been to publicize the cases of migrants whose refugee claims have been denied with the aim of halting deportation and receiving legal status for the migrants. The sheltering and support of migrants has, in many cases, been accompanied by media engagement, seeking support from local politicians, and broader community mobilization. In early Canadian cases, some 70 per cent of sanctuary actions resulted in the sheltered migrants receiving legal status (Lippert 2010, 60), although the success rate has decreased over time.

The practice of sanctuary has been undertaken almost exclusively by Christian congregations, including Anglican, Catholic, United, and other churches (Lippert 2005). These cases have been primarily local efforts rather than the result of an organized movement among churches in a region or across the nation. Lippert documented fifty sanctuary incidents in Canada between 1983 and 2009 affecting 288 migrants (Lippert 2009, 57). He observes, "[t]he typical Canadian sanctuary incident occurred in a large city, involved either a single migrant or migrant family, received support from major Christian denominations, the broader community, and local political authorities, lasted at least five months, and yielded positive outcomes for migrants" (Lippert 2009, 396). In virtually every case, a congregation has not been a repeat provider of sanctuary – potentially because of the demands that it has placed on church resources.

Although the practice of sanctuary is an act of resistance to state power, the public aspect of most sanctuary incidents reveals something more complex. Churches are not simply defying the state in a strictly antagonistic posture. Macklin describes sanctuary incidents as expressive of a "politics of hospitality," where religious groups are acting on what they believe justice and humanitarianism to require within Canada (Macklin 2021, 43). Indeed, in many incidents of sanctuary, migrants undergo a screening procedure by the hosting church that resembles the RSD process employed by the state in accordance with its international legal obligations (Rehaag 2010). Churches offering sanctuary have effectively been final courts of appeal for those facing deportation. Indeed, the government's introduction of merit-based appeals for failed refugee claimants has been, in part, a result of sanctuary practices and the cause of their decline (Lippert 2009).

CONCLUSION AND FUTURE DIRECTIONS

Religious groups are influential social actors within the field of refugee law and policy. They have often advocated for more liberal policies toward refugees, including for their admission and settlement and procedural fairness in the course of RSD. In their work they have adopted a variety of strategies of political influence that reflect advocacy or pressure group activity. Some groups have engaged in contentious politics, positioning themselves in an adversarial position to government action, whereas others have sought out co-operative relationships with government officials that are characterized by problem-solving. Public policy scholars refer to these strategies as "powering" and "puzzling," different strategies embraced by groups seeking to translate their values and preferences into policy (Hoppe 2011). When they enter the public sphere, religious groups act in ways that are politically recognizable as advocacy group actions. However, very few religious groups are primarily organized to be advocacy groups; most of them enter the public sphere on a more episodic basis. The more routine work of religious groups to welcome and support refugees is relatively invisible because much of it takes place outside the public eye, and it is animated by beliefs and practices not readily apprehended within secular frameworks of analysis.

Future research on religious groups and refugees can contribute to existing knowledge by both broadening and deepening its scope of analysis. It can deepen our understanding of religious groups by attending more closely to the motivations and discourse of religious groups that serve refugee populations. It can broaden our knowledge of non-Christian groups within the field of refugee advocacy. How are other religious groups organized, and how are their political strategies similar to or different from those of Christian groups? What explains these similarities or differences? Studies to date appear to indicate that Christian groups are more willing to engage in resistance and contentious politics, perhaps owing to their historical position as a majority faith in Canada. The examples of Baha'i, Ismaili, and Jewish groups discussed in this chapter indicate a preference for co-operative politics, more focused on "puzzling" than "powering." As other religious minorities become better established in Canada because of post-1970s immigration, we should expect the formation of groups that will advocate for the admission of refugees and the protection of their rights. How do they use the private sponsorship system, advocate for particular groups, support settlement, and contest the shortcomings of refugee law and policy?

FURTHER READING AND RESOURCES

Cameron, Geoffrey. 2021. "Recognizing the Role of Religious Groups in Refugee Sponsorship." *Policy Options*, 31 March 2021. https://policyoptions.irpp.org/magazines/march-2021/recognizing-the-role-of-religious-groups-in-refugee-sponsorship.

Centre for Community Based Research. 2023. "Faith & Settlement Partnerships: Setting Immigrants and Canada Up for Success." https://www.communitybasedresearch.ca/faith-and-settlement.

Centre for Refugee Studies. 2021. "Strangers to Neighbours: Refugee Sponsorship in Context." YouTube video, 1:28:14. https://www.youtube.com/watch?v=z34ogQcIm3I.

27

Forced Migration and Education in Canada: Stories of Resistance, Resilience, and Reconciliation

Snežana Obradović-Ratković, Catherine Longboat, and Julianne Burgess

KEY TAKEAWAYS

- Canada is built on forced migration, with the lesser-known story of forced migration of Indigenous Peoples within this country's borders. The Truth and Reconciliation Commission (TRC) of Canada plays a role in bridging this educational gap, addressing the legacy of residential schools and guiding the process of reconciliation.
- Residential schools in Canada were sites of forced displacement, attempted assimilation, and genocide.
- There is often resistance to teaching and learning about forced migration to preserve the notion of Canada's colonial identity as a haven for all.
- Education can be designed to achieve reconciliation with those who experienced forced migration and with those who are willing to accept the shocking truths about forced migration.
- Collaborative intercultural storytelling is a promising method for teaching and learning about forced migration and reconciliation.

KEY TERMS

- Residential schools
- TRC Calls to Action
- Indigenous Talking Circles

INTRODUCTION

The experiences of refugees and Indigenous Peoples in Canada are experiences of forced migration through oppression, murder, and demonstrations of violence to incite apprehension and fear. Many stories of forced migration are filled with pictures of trauma due to humiliation, violence, illness, injuries, displacement, loss, separation, and genocide. The history and legacy of forced migration for Indigenous Peoples extend to oral stories, such as stories about Chief Peguis (1774–1864) and Louis Riel (1844–1885). In the classroom, refugee and Indigenous students continue to experience marginalization, racism, and discrimination from peers, teachers, and local communities (Guo and Maitra 2017; Obradović-Ratković et al. 2020). However, the voices of refugee learners and refugee teachers in Canada are missing from research (Obradović-Ratković et al. 2020). Indigenous perspectives are also void of discourses on forced migration and refugee inclusion (see also Coburn, chapter 1).

We are three educators with different backgrounds and educational approaches. Catherine is Indigenous to Canada, born into Haudenosaunee and Anishinaabe cultures. Julianne is a third-generation White settler of Polish descent. Snežana is a refugee from former Yugoslavia. Our personal, cultural, and collective knowledge of displacement ignited our passions for teaching forced migration, decolonization, and reconciliation on Turtle Island. We argue that teaching about forced migration in Canada requires learners and educators to attend to the outcomes of the TRC of Canada (2015) Calls to Action, specifically Calls 62 to 64 and 94, which apply to education. According to Jewell and Mosby (2022), none of the Calls to Action relating to education have been fully implemented, hindering Canadian education and the process of reconciliation. In the same vein, the Canadian Council for Refugees (CCR) (2022) website states the organization has a mandate to address the TRC Calls to Action; however, we do not see initiatives on their website that suggest the organization is engaged in a sustained effort to promote ongoing, nationwide Indigenous-refugee encounters and reconciliation. To bridge these alarming gaps, we use a collaborative intercultural storytelling approach (Winters et al. 2022) to teaching, learning, and reconciliation.

In this chapter, we explore our personal, cultural, and pedagogical engagements with forced migration, along with questions: Why is it critical to teach forced migration to and in Canada? How can educators teach forced migration to and in Canada? How can stories of forced migration inform Indigenous and non-Indigenous pathways to reconciliation and coexistence? Through our storytelling and collaborative writing, we discuss, challenge, and reimagine the current climate within which we work. Our findings indicate that education can be designed to achieve reconciliation with those who experienced forced migration and with those who accepted the shocking truths about forced migration.

TEACHING FORCED MIGRATION

Students in Canadian schools are too often given a false narrative that Indigenous Peoples were welcoming and generous in sharing what they had with the newcomers. In fact, Indigenous Peoples were moved into reserve lands and imprisoned (see also Coburn, chapter 1). Acts of violence and threats to family and friends infiltrated the minds of people who could not fathom the depths of terror imposed on them. The Government of Canada removed populations away from their comforts, stripping away possessions and ownership of lands and property from selected groups of peoples and even extraditing them out of Canada. Residential schools became sites of forced displacement, attempted assimilation, and genocide.

The current scale of global forced displacement presents opportunities for innovative research and pedagogical practices (Clark-Kazak 2017b). From elementary classrooms to professional training schools, teaching about forced migration can open eyes, minds, and hearts to issues of injustice. Okenwa-Emegwa and Eriksson (2020) studied experiential learning practices to raise awareness of forced migration among nursing students in Sweden. The students demonstrated increased empathy and understanding of equity issues and a greater potential to recognize human rights violations and inequitable access to health care among vulnerable patients. L. Gilbert (2019) also made the case for the use of experiential learning to teach forced migration to public interest lawyers. In Spain, García-Morís, García Bugallo, and Martínez-Medina et al. (2021) found elementary school students demonstrated an awareness of current events involving involuntary migrants, a high degree of compassion and concern for those who have been displaced, and a desire to learn more about forced migration.

Across Canada, elementary school social studies curricula include a unit on immigration to Canada. Parker (2021) argues, however, that even those teachers who are first- or second-generation immigrants to Canada cannot assume their ability to teach immigration or forced migration because students' and teachers' intersecting identities (e.g., citizenship status, race, and gender) inform their individual experiences. While training novice teachers, Parker (2021) found that some felt confident to teach immigrant and refugee students while others prioritized their Westernized social and cultural lenses, viewing migrant students as disruption in the classroom.

Established in 2008, the Truth and Reconciliation Commission (TRC) was charged with documenting the history and lasting impacts of residential schools on Indigenous students and their families, requiring the development of curricula that address the residential schools' impacts on First Nations' children. The TRC's Calls to Action also seek best practices for teaching Indigenous Peoples' historical and contemporary contributions to Canada while building intercultural understanding, mutual respect, and empathy. These Calls to Action are a precious guide for all the educators, scholars, and researchers who yearn to foreground the agency of Indigenous Peoples in Canada.

K. Arar, Örücü, and Waite (2020) call for greater commitment toward understanding forced migration among educational leadership. For them, developing new frameworks and methods for inclusive education practices is an ethical responsibility. Strom (2017) argues that migration and integration stories are vital to the shared future of newcomers and host societies because these stories attest to human adaptability while exposing the prejudices host communities develop to include or exclude newcomers. These stories are rarely explored beyond the stories of customs, foods, and language; therefore, more education is needed to understand our evolution as individuals and nations (Strom, 2017). Education is the key to learning, reconciliation, and healing (Sinclair 2016).

THEORETICAL STORYTELLING FRAMEWORK

Brayboy's (2005) TribalCrit theory outlines the marginalization of Indigenous stories in research while claiming that Indigenous stories contain data from ancestral knowledge that has stood tests of time. We use our personal, professional, and cultural stories as our theoretical framework to explore forced migration and related pedagogies. Kimmerer (2013) exposes the forced migration underpinnings of the Haudenosaunee Sky Woman story:

> She fell a long way from her home in the Sky World, leaving behind all who knew her and who held her dear. She could never go back ... [and] she did not come alone. She was pregnant. Knowing her grandchildren would inherit the world she left behind, she did not work for flourishing in her time only. It was through her actions of reciprocity, the give and take with the land, that the original immigrant became indigenous. For all of us, becoming indigenous to a place means living as if our children's futures mattered, to take care of the land as if our lives, both material and spiritual, depended on it ... Can we all understand the Sky Woman story not as an artifact from the past but as instructions for the future? (Kimmerer 2013, 8–9)

It is clear from the above interpretation that Sky Woman "could never go back," revealing her refugee experience and the urge to take care of the land and become Indigenous to Turtle Island. Offering "instructions for the future," the Sky Woman story is a suitable theoretical framework for exploring forced migration and newcomer-Indigenous relations across time and space.

Two Row Wampum Belt complements the Sky Woman story in the process of foreshadowing the future of newcomer-Indigenous relations through coexistence. In 1613 the Two Row Wampum Belt treaty offered an oral story guidance to the first settlers that both nations, despite their different lifestyles, must travel side by side in Peace, Friendship, and Respect, travelling the same route but in different boats – each with their different laws and realities on how to pursue a good life (Longboat et al. 2022). The story offers instructions for the future by challenging hierarchies, acknowledging the ancestral knowledge, and building relationships and coexistence.

STORY AS MEANING AND RESEARCH METHOD

Kovach describes the inseparable relationship between story and knowing: "Stories are vessels for passing along teachings, medicines, and practices that can assist members of the collective" (2009, 95). Indigenous inquiry and story as method are rooted in relationships, responsibility, and respect. These values are applied to all decisions made within the research design. While some Western qualitative research methods (e.g., narrative inquiry, autoethnography, feminist inquiry) also rely on story, the key distinction between Western and Indigenous methodologies is the criticality of trust and relationality. In Indigenous research, the story itself is treated with respect, acknowledging the relationships from which it emerges (Kovach 2009).

For stories to emerge, trust must be established. Before asking others to share stories, researchers must share theirs, beginning with their social location, which allows the participants to situate and access the researcher's motivations and establish trust. Catherine and Snežana have a long history of researching and writing together. Julianne is new to the team. As a scholar of White settler heritage, it was necessary for Julianne to establish trust by sharing her family's immigrant story and her desire to work together with respect, reflexivity, and a "decolonized mind and heart" (Battiste 2002, 2). We worked with care, patience, and respect.

Our research was conducted in an online setting in fall 2022. Through MS Teams, we engaged in *storywork* (Archibald 2001, as cited in Kovach 2009). We scrutinized our actions and reactions, revisiting and renegotiating them over time. Through careful listening and responding to each other, new stories, deeper understandings, and stronger appreciations emerged. Through this interactive method of collaborative intercultural storytelling (Winters et al. 2022), we confronted our differences and strived for empathy and understanding.

Indigenous story as method is decolonizing research, which contests the colonial structures of the western academy. It becomes the responsibility of the researchers to accept guardianship of the stories that have been shared in the research endeavour to protect them from exploitation and appropriation (Kovach 2009). We have done this through our stories of forced migration and education shared in this chapter.

CATHERINE

I write my story of teaching from an Indigenous perspective to disrupt the Canadian story. I seek to present the Doctrine of Discovery and discussions on the obstacles and barriers in their education for cultural exchanges and then conduct an Indigenous Talking Circle as a healing pedagogy. I am an assistant professor. I teach four full-time Indigenous Studies courses over the year online. I teach introductory courses in Indigenous Studies on education, traditions, and general introduction to Indigenous Studies. My students are undergraduate Indigenous and non-Indigenous students. I am Indigenous, and I have a sanctioned band number from Indian Affairs, the arm of the federal government that controls the nominal membership of Indigenous Peoples who are First Nations, Métis, and Inuit.

I was born on segregated land on one of the most populated reserves in Ontario. The land was originally given to the Six Nations Peoples in return for their loyalty in fighting the British. This land includes six miles on each side of the Grand River through the Haldimand Treaty of 1784. This segregated land agreement worked out to include nine hundred fifty thousand acres, but what is left is forty-eight thousand acres. The first instance of non–Six Nations settlers on the Haldimand tract began in 1798. To the time of writing this chapter, the community of Six Nations is still fighting for the return of their land.

I am passionate about leading my students to understand the truth regarding the impacts of colonialism and forced migration on Indigenous Peoples. The truth must be taught before there can be reconciliation, so I present information about Creation stories and the Doctrine of Discovery. It is through the Creation stories such as Sky Woman that I guide the students to realize a different perspective on how to see the land as a resource to be protected rather than expropriated for personal gain.

In each course I present a film called *The Doctrine of Discovery: Unmasking the Domination Code* (Wolfchild et al. 2015). The Doctrine of Discovery, a Papal decree, is the root of racism, discrimination, and prejudice against Indigenous Peoples and has been used as a legal and moral justification for colonization. Indigenous Peoples existed on Turtle Island with functioning, complex societies and infrastructures that accommodated their way of life as they negotiated Peace on the land. The methods of the colonial settlers were to locate lands on which to settle and then strategize how to eliminate the Original Caretakers on the Land. Once it was discovered that Indigenous Peoples lacked immunity to the common cold, measles, and chicken pox, it was only a matter of distributing blankets of the colonizers who were infected as gifts to Indigenous Peoples. Ninety per cent of Indigenous Peoples were annihilated through this method as well as through brutal attacks on women, children, the elderly, and the frail (Wolfchild et al. 2015).

Once the property lines were drawn for reserved lands, the public was left to believe that Indigenous Peoples were "imaginary" and worse – eliminated. They were not seen in the schools, at places of business, or enjoying the benefits of the extracted goods on their territories. Children were forced into residential schools where sexual and physical abuse – along with mental, emotional, and spiritual abuse – were rampant. When the failing health of children in these schools with deteriorating infrastructure was finally brought into the public eye, the graves of buried children on the grounds of these schools were still hidden. Even today, some Indigenous Peoples leave their reserves because of the lack of clean running water, lack of employment, lack of public schools, lack of high schools and post-secondary education. The same standards of living enjoyed by Canadians in urban centres are lacking in most federal reserved Indigenous lands.

I have been teaching the Doctrine of Discovery for five years. It is important that my students understand that Indigenous Peoples did not voluntarily move from their original territories; it was a legal imperative of the newly forming colonial government to have Indigenous Peoples removed. I can see student reactions to the film, ranging from disbelief and looks of shock and disgust to their reluctance to speak about what they feel. All the students identify how the story of race began with indoctrinated documents, designed to take land by regulating who is human and who is not.

Indigenous Talking Circles help my students come to terms with new knowledge. The Talking Circle is an Indigenous method to encourage learning with the subjective inclusive community. It usually begins with an intentional, cardinal point of direction such as the East where a particular set of teachings started. Each person would then have an opportunity to speak to practice overcoming their inhibitions to talk within a circle of peers. There is an opportunity for the instructor to hear how well each person is doing within the quadrants of a Medicine Wheel as spiritual, emotional, physical, and mental well-being. If there is concern, the students usually encourage the participant to address it by first expressing the validity of the concern and then making suggestions about resources available on campus. I find that students look forward to coming to classes and having time to talk within a Circle where everyone has difficulties and problem-solving can occur. These classrooms become a community of learners with peer support and more opportunities to learn about and from each other.

My teaching disrupts long-held assumptions about Canadian history, inviting critical decolonial perspectives into the classroom. My students are not sure what they will do with what they have learned. There is a lot for them to unpack. It is at least five hundred years of history that they were not aware of. This unsettling of settlers' perspectives is a first step toward truth-telling and reconciliation.

SNEŽANA

I am a research officer and a scholar at a Canadian university, a mother, and a grandmother. I came to Canada in 1998 from a war-torn Yugoslavia with my family, lacking English language proficiency and support networks. Initially, I learned about refugee education in Canada through my children and my own education. After starting my Master in Education program in 2003, I studied refugee education through scholarly literature and my master's and doctoral research. I learned that refugee students were often viewed as having learning challenges, low achievements, and low aspirations. Many high school refugee students were streamlined into applied courses, lowering their chances for university education. I realized that offering shelter to refugees is generous and admirable, but not enough.

I witnessed that refugees were welcomed to Canada as second-class citizens, and they shared this second-class citizenship with Indigenous Peoples of Turtle Island. I learned that Canada was not only built on immigration, but also on the displacement of Indigenous Peoples. This awareness was reinforced when I met Catherine. During a graduate student workshop, I shared the challenge of coming to Canada as a refugee teacher and not having my education recognized. Not surprised, Catherine noted, "I was born in Canada and my education is not recognized." Since then, we continue working and walking together toward intercultural understanding, compassion, and coexistence.

In 2006 and 2008 respectively I facilitated a workshop, "In the Eyes of Your Children: War, Betrayal, and Immigration" for teacher candidates at the Social Issues Days event in a Faculty of Education. I walked silently into the room and, to unsettle the participants, I recited a poem in Serbian. I then asked the following questions in English: What did I say? How did you feel listening to me and not understanding a word? Most of the teacher candidates guessed I was reciting a poem, although they did not understand its meaning. Some of them shared that they felt confused and uncomfortable, realizing that their refugee and immigrant students might feel the same on their arrival in the Canadian classroom.

One of the assumptions that emerged during the workshops was that refugee students are problems to solve rather than talents to nurture. Another assumption was that refugee students are behind in their cognitive development. One of the teacher candidates approached me after a workshop and shared her struggle to teach a refugee student in her teaching placement because the student was cognitively delayed. I reminded her that the issues she experienced may not lie in decreased cognitive ability but rather in learning an additional language, in processing traumatic experiences, or in facing discrimination and exclusion. The teacher candidate acknowledged these possibilities and noted that the issue of facing discrimination and exclusion never crossed her mind because she lives in a country of democracy, peace, and opportunity.

During the workshops, I highlighted the possibility of triggering traumatic experiences among refugee students from Yugoslavia in 1999 when Canada, as part of NATO, bombed Yugoslavia for seventy-eight days to force annexation of Kosovo and extension of Albanian territory into Yugoslavia (Zivanovic and Haxhiaj 2019). These refugee students were living and learning in the country that had been bombing their grandparents, relatives, and friends, which may have resulted in a life burdened with violence, destruction, and fear. In one of the workshop evaluations, a teacher candidate wrote: "That's not true. Canada never bombed Yugoslavia." I wondered if this comment came from the "fact" that we live in a country of democracy, peace, and opportunity.

While many teacher candidates were eager to learn about teaching refugee students, most of them were looking for "quick and dirty" strategies. I had to remind them that learning how to teach refugee students will not happen overnight; it will require a systematic, long-term engagement with the refugee students, their cultures, their families, and their communities before an education can be provided.

Conducting a scoping literature review on supporting refugee students in Canada between 1997 and 2017, my research team found only twenty-one academic publications. We shared our research report and developed resources with district school boards (DSBs) across Canada. Only two DSBs responded to the email with a thank you message. We then offered workshops to teacher candidates in the Faculty of Education where I worked. There was no interest among the teacher candidates in attending the workshop and it was cancelled. Teaching refugee children remains a marginalized praxis in Canada.

JULIANNE

I write from a settler perspective. My personal history as the grandchild of Polish immigrants has led me to teaching English to adult newcomers to Canada. For ten years, I worked with young adults, between ages eighteen to twenty-five, new settlers on Turtle Island. Most were refugees from Syria, Iran, Iraq, Afghanistan, and Democratic Republic of Congo, who had lived histories of conflict, dislocation, and loss.

I have experimented with different ways of incorporating the TRC Calls to Action into my teaching praxis. My preference is to centre Indigenous voices by having Indigenous community members come to the classroom, but that is not always possible. I have learned I can bring Indigenous voices to my students through the power, beauty, and emotional connectivity of the arts, through music, dance, artwork, and storytelling.

A few years ago, in my search for materials to teach about residential schools, I came across the picture book *When I Was Eight*, by Christy Jordan-Fenton and Margaret Pokiak-Fenton (2013). The book relates the true story of Margaret Pokiak-Fenton, an Inuvialuit child in a residential school in the

Far North. From the first reading and discussions about the book, my students were fascinated by the feisty Margaret. The central character, whose real name is Olemaun, longs to learn to read and begs her parents to let her go to residential school. Reluctantly, they agree. Once at school, Olemaun is stripped of her birth name, her long hair is cut, and she is forced to do menial chores; she is not taught to read. When Olemaun encounters a heartless nun who repeatedly attempts to intimidate and humiliate her, she finds strength to stand up to the nun, learns to read, and in the end, provides readers with a lesson in the power of resilience and human dignity.

Following our discussions, I asked the students to reflect on their own stories of school and the parts of the book that resonated the most with them. I handed everyone a sheet of blank paper and invited them to draw a scene from the book, or their own lives, inspired by Olemaun's story. Some of my young adult students were educated in rigid, traditional education systems; others had experienced interrupted schooling due to war or displacement. (Recognizing that some stories may be traumatizing, learners were offered the opportunity to see a mental health counsellor, if they wished.) All the students produced vivid artistic texts that captured experiences of being beaten by teachers, disrespected because of their ethnicity, deprived of using their first language at school, or being denied educational opportunities because of their female gender. Many refugee students have lived histories of colonization in their own homelands, which emerged through their encounters with this picture book. Students were drawing a link between Indigenous experience and their own, not claiming to be the same, but demonstrating understanding and empathy. Although their artwork varied in detail and intensity, this activity turned into a memorable exercise in building solidarity among displaced communities.

TRUTH-TELLING EDUCATION

Our stories came from different lived experiences of forced migration and teaching across educational settings, making our contributions unique as well as critical to creating a multi-layered, more comprehensive portrait of forced migration and education in Canada. We shared with our students uncomfortable stories about forced migration to unsettle the myth of Canada as a welcoming and safe haven for all, taking a first step toward decolonization and reconciliation. Catherine and Snežana encountered student resistance to truth-telling while Julianne's students, based on their lived experiences of displacement, embraced the residential school survivor's story as true and valuable. They were willing and open to learn about this chapter in Canada's history and take on their responsibility for building relationships with Indigenous communities.

Our collective stories are also enmeshed with Indigenous Creation stories. Like Sky Woman, refugee students in Julianne's classroom experienced forced migration and struggled with adaptation to their new homeland. Reflecting on our personal and professional experiences in writing this chapter, we found the stories of Sky Woman and the Two Row Wampum Belt to be an inspiring guide and a source of resilience as we continue to pursue our pathways to decolonization and reconciliation.

To address the 2015 TRC's Calls to Action, Canadian educators must learn and teach stories of forced migration within Canada as part of their commitment to unsettling long-held settler narratives of Canada as a welcoming nation, built on immigration and Indigenous People's friendship. Canadian educators must share best practices for teaching about forced migration and Indigenous Peoples' "historical and contemporary contributions to Canada" (TRC 2015, Call to Action 63). This is the path to reconciliation and respectful coexistence. Catherine found the TRC (2015) document gave her the motivation and self-confidence to teach what she knows despite the lack of curriculum and student resistance toward alternative, decolonial perspectives of Canadian history. Julianne and Snežana embraced the TRC (2015) Calls to Action as a guide in their pedagogical practices.

We have found, as have Clark-Kazak (2017b) and Obradović-Ratković et al. (2020), that teaching about forced migration using innovative arts-based practices, such as poetry, art-making, and Indigenous storytelling, can open students' hearts and minds (Battiste 2002) to stories of injustice and inequity. Catherine's methods of teaching forced migration involve using film for truth-telling and Indigenous pedagogies such as storytelling and Indigenous Talking Circles. She promotes respectful listening and sharing of personal stories. She also provides additional resources for supporting her students if they should find her classes unsettling. Snežana engages students in truth-telling through experiential education (L. Gilbert 2019) and the arts (Winters et al. 2022), such as bilingual education and poetry. Julianne has employed storytelling and student drawings in response to an Indigenous story as a path to truth-telling. Finding inventive ways to incorporate Indigenous and intercultural stories and knowledge into educational settings (Clark-Kazak 2017b) works to foster empathy and intercultural sensitivity as directed by the TRC (2015) Calls to Action. Our creative, collaborative, intercultural storytelling has fostered stronger intercultural relationships and led us – as students, educators, and caring citizens – to walk together in friendship, peace, and mutual respect.

TOWARD A PEDAGOGY OF RECONCILIATION

The scale of global forced displacement today presents an opportunity for innovative research and pedagogical practices (Clark-Kazak 2017b) as well as decolonization and reconciliation. Coming from different backgrounds and pedagogies, we share common goals of truth-telling, reconciliation, and relationship building. We listened carefully to one another in a process that took time and was not always straightforward or easy. We explored our personal, cultural, and pedagogical encounters with displacement, along with questions of why and how to teach forced migration. Recognizing that this chapter is a colonial, rather than decolonial, document, we encourage educators and scholars to engage in collaborative, intercultural storytelling and truth-discovery. Such writing will require trust, empathetic listening, negotiation, time, and an education.

We disrupt the settler colonial project of difference and competition by proposing educational methods that increase awareness, empathy, and solidarities between Indigenous, newcomer, and settler communities. There is often resistance to or disinterest in teaching and learning about forced migration in Canadian educational systems to preserve Canada's colonial identity as a haven for refugees and all Canadians. However, education is the key to reconciliation (Sinclair 2016) and a sustainable future on this land. Educators must build their pedagogies on the TRC (2015) Calls to Action toward reconciliation and coexistence, unveiling the shocking truths of forced migration.

Through our storytelling collaboration, we identified new practices for intercultural research methods, truth-discovery, and ways of living together in respect, peace, and friendship. One of the most effective teaching practices is storytelling. Stories are powerful (Kovach 2009). Indigenous stories hold important data (Brayboy 2005) and have the potential to inform and inspire, to shape our identities, histories, and our shared future. By focusing on forced migration stories, educators can create more opportunities for intercultural collaboration, increase the potential for reconciliation, and strengthen relationships within and across cultures and communities.

Reconciliation is a collective journey with multiple pathways. We are not on the same path, but our paths are parallel, mirroring the Two Row Wampum Belt Treaty. From the Sky Woman story, we learn that Turtle Island is our home. Through Indigenization and intercultural collaboration, we are moving in the same direction, toward "decolonized minds and hearts" (Battiste 2002, 22). Whether we are settlers, newcomers, or Indigenous Peoples, we are all Treaty People and each of us must uphold our part of the agreement.

FURTHER READING AND RESOURCES

Canadian Council for Refugees (CCR). 2023. "Indigenous Peoples: Truth and Reconciliation Commission Call to Action." https://ccrweb.ca/en/resolutions-subject/indigenous-peoples.

Fenton-Pokiak, Christy, and Margaret Pokiak. 2013. *When I Was Eight.* Toronto: Annik Press.

National Centre for Truth and Reconciliation. 2022. "Reconciliation through Education." University of Manitoba. https://nctr.ca/education.

Newcomb, Steven T., dir. 2015. *The Doctrine of Discovery: Unmasking the Domination Code*. 38 Plus 2 Productions, 62 mins. https://doctrineofdiscovery.org/the-doctrine-of-discovery-unmasking-the-domination-code.

Ratković, Snežana, Dragana Kovačević, Courtney Brewer, Claire Ellis, Neelofar Ahmed, and Janelle Baptiste-Brady. 2017. "Supporting Refugee students in Canada: Building on What We Have Learned in the Past 20 Years." Research Spotlight, Emerging Scholars and Practitioners on Migration Issues (ESPMI) Network. https://espminetwork.com/new-report-supporting-refugee-students-in-canada-building-on-what-we-have-learned-in-the-past-20-years.

Truth and Reconciliation Commission of Canada (TRC). 2015a. *Honouring the Truth, Reconciling for the Future Summary of the Final Report of the Truth and Reconciliation Commission of Canada*. https://ehprnh2mwo3.exactdn.com/wp-content/uploads/2021/01/Executive_Summary_English_Web.pdf.

– 2015b. "Truth and Reconciliation Commission of Canada: Calls to Action." https://ehprnh2mwo3.exactdn.com/wp-content/uploads/2021/01/Calls_to_Action_English2.pdf.

28

Making Home in Canada: Housing and Forced Displacement

Christina R. Clark-Kazak

KEY TAKEAWAYS

- Housing is a human right and a key element of integration, but newcomers in Canada face structural barriers to accessing housing, including discrimination, affordability, lack of credit and rental history, and limited knowledge of their rights and housing information.
- The forcible displacement of Indigenous Peoples from their lands, their communities, and their families has resulted in high levels of material and spiritual homelessness.
- People in forced migration situations make and remake home as an affective place, even in the absence of permanent physical shelters or legal status.

KEY TERMS

- Home
- Homelessness
- Housing
- Household
- Shelter

"HOME" BY WARSAN SHIRE

no one leaves home unless
home is the mouth of a shark
you only run for the border
when you see the whole city running as well

your neighbors running faster than you
breath bloody in their throats
the boy you went to school with
who kissed you dizzy behind the old tin factory
is holding a gun bigger than his body
you only leave home
when home won't let you stay.
[...]
the
go home blacks
refugees
dirty immigrants
asylum seekers
sucking our country dry
niggers with their hands out
they smell strange
savage
messed up their country and now they want
to mess ours up
how do the words
the dirty looks
roll off your backs
maybe because the blow is softer
than a limb torn off
[...]
i want to go home,
but home is the mouth of a shark
home is the barrel of the gun
and no one would leave home
unless home chased you to the shore
unless home told you
to quicken your legs
leave your clothes behind
crawl through the desert
wade through the oceans
drown
save

be hunger
beg
forget pride
your survival is more important
no one leaves home until home is a sweaty voice in your ear
saying-
leave,
run away from me now
i dont know what i've become
but i know that anywhere
is safer than here

(Facing History & Ourselves 2017)

INTRODUCTION

Ideas of home are central to forced migration. Like Warsan Shire in the poem above, many define displacement as being forced from one's *home* (S. Ahmed 1999). Indeed, home has been a recurring theme throughout this book, relating both to colonization and resettlement. The forcible displacement of Indigenous Peoples from their homes and livelihoods was a deliberate strategy in the creation of Canada as a settler state. As one participant in Christensen's study said, "When the government took our land, bush camps and traplines away, they took away our homes. That was our home. That was our way of life" (2013, 804). Similarly, when people are displaced or resettled to Canada, rebuilding – homes, livelihoods, and community – is a central concern.

So, how do people in situations of forced migration (re)create home? In Canada, much of the discussion is around access to housing. While housing is a human right and integral to integration (Bhattacharyya et al. 2020; see also Hynie, chapter 23), it is important not to overlook the affective aspects of homemaking (Brun and Fábos 2015; Kissoon 2015; S. Ahmed 1999), as well as the home as a space for family structures, kin (Kidd et al. 2019), spirituality (Christensen 2013) and community (Kissoon 2015). Brun and Fábos argue, "[t]he forcible displacement of people from their houses, hometowns, and homelands highlights the importance of home at different scales and illustrates how unsettled the notion of the home as a safe haven becomes for forced migrants. Consequently, forced migration, the forcible displacement from places called home, becomes indicative of the experience of home as an unsettled, changing, open, and more mobile entity" (2015, 7). In this final chapter, I explore the structural opportunities and challenges of finding shelter and (re)making home in Canada. As has been demonstrated throughout this book, I also show how lived experiences of homelessness and homemaking vary across contexts and positionalities of forced displacement.

CONCEPTS: HOME AND HOMELESSNESS

In contexts of forced migration, "home is a place, and also an idea and an imaginary imbued with feeling" (Brun and Fábos 2015, 6). As Kissoon argues, it is helpful to delink "home from the dwelling place" (2015, 11). Conceptually and practically, homemaking after displacement requires both a physical dwelling or shelter and a feeling of belonging. In this chapter, we will look at the opportunities and challenges of accessing housing and also the meanings ascribed to home.

In many Indigenous world views, home is inextricably bound up in relationships and kinship (Kidd et al. 2019). In the Canadian context, the legacy of separation of children through residential schools and the "Sixties Scoop" (see Coburn, chapter 1; Clark-Kazak, chapter 13) and contemporary realities of over-representation of Indigenous people in criminal justice and child welfare systems results in spiritual homelessness (Kidd et al. 2019, 169). Similarly, the dispossession of traditional lands and the appalling conditions on Indigenous reserves, including lack of drinking water, overcrowding, and substandard housing, contributes to this sense of spiritual and cultural homelessness through a loss of a way of life (Christensen 2013). Somerville (1992) suggests that understanding such homelessness requires a conceptual shift from the dominant focus on "rooflessness" to instead understand "rootlessness" – "an ontological state of being that implies the absence of a sense of place, or a sense of home" (Christensen 2013, 808).

Indigenous thinkers and geographers have long theorized the importance of place and its relationship to homemaking. Because many Indigenous world views and livelihood strategies are tied to the land, they have a specific link to particular landscapes and geographies as part of their culture and way of life. But not all Indigenous groups are inherently territorially bound. "For example, in Dene tradition, mobility – the act of moving from place to place and encountering all the storied knowledge that sits in those places – is integral to a sense of home" (Christensen 2013, 805). Similarly, forced migration researchers have cautioned against a "sedentary bias" (Malkki 1995). Through transnational networks, people in situations of forced migration can maintain linkages to many different "homes" at the same time (R. Arar and FitzGerald 2022). Christensen argues that "Indigenous experiences of homelessness [are] multi-scalar and at once collective *and* immediate" (2013, 805).

Because home is distinct from shelter, some analysts prefer the term "unhoused" to "homeless." However, homelessness is the term used by all levels of government, as well as the Canadian Homelessness Research Network. Statistics Canada defines homelessness broadly to "describe a situation in which individuals or families live without stable, safe, permanent, appropriate housing, or the immediate prospect, means and ability of acquiring it.

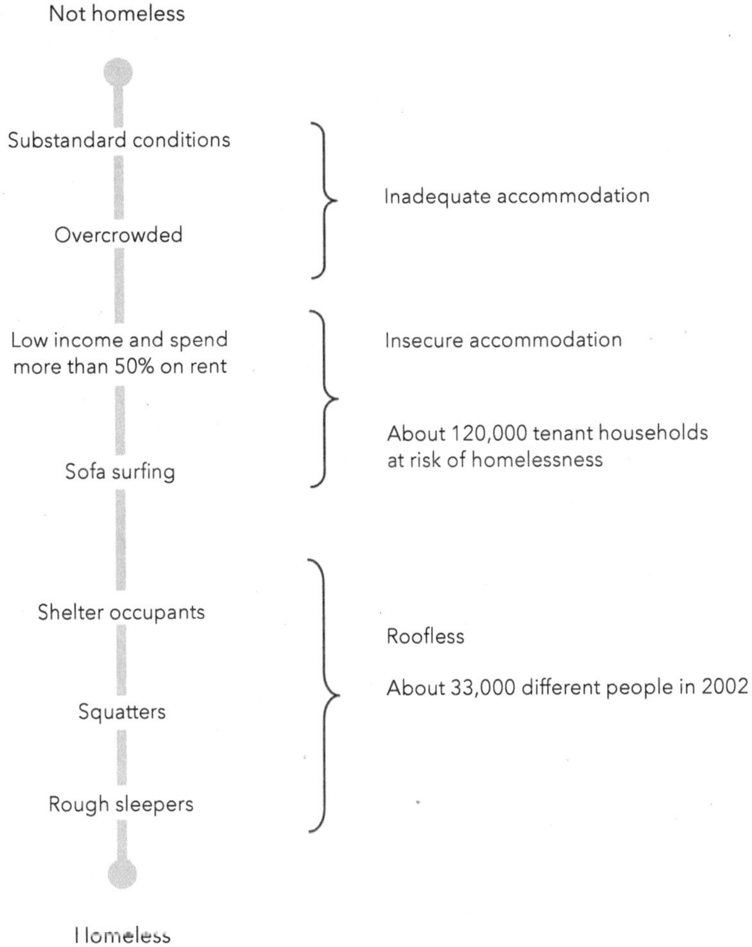

Figure 28.1 | Continuum of homelessness

Homelessness can include living on the streets, living in places not appropriate for human habitation, or staying in shelters. Living temporarily with family or friends without immediate prospects of finding permanent housing is another form, known as 'hidden homelessness'" (Uppal 2022, 1). Most researchers similarly include a wide range of manifestations of, and pathways into, homelessness (Oudshoorn et al. 2020, 1755). Kissoon (2010, 11), drawing on work by the City of Toronto and the New Policy Institute visually represents a continuum of homelessness (see fig. 28.1).

CONTEXT: THE RIGHT TO HOUSING IN CANADA

28.1 Excerpt from CTV News Story

> A Palestinian refugee stabbed herself in the stomach, just below the ribcage, last week while in a meeting with a federal government official with Immigration Refugees and Citizenship Canada (IRCC).
>
> Sitting on a park bench, a day after being released from hospital, Aziza Abu Sirdana tells CTV News, "I put a knife in my body because no one cares. Seriously no one cares."
>
> For seven months she's been stuck, living in a refugee hotel west of Toronto. She says she never intended to kill herself, but decided to stab herself in the stomach to try and get the attention of the federal government and the settlement agency which, for more than half a year, hasn't been able to assist her in finding what she believes would be a safe place to live.
>
> Abu Sirdana believes the government has failed her. Exasperated, she says, "If you [the government] know that there's no suitable place for me to stay why did you accept me to come [to Canada]?" (Ghobrial 2022, n.p.)

The right to housing is clearly established in international law, including article 11.1 of the 1966 International Covenant on Economic, Social and Cultural Rights, to which Canada is a party. The Office of the High Commissioner for Human Rights further elaborates minimum criteria for housing to be considered "adequate" (see sidebar 28.1).

Since human rights apply to all, regardless of citizenship or migration status, housing rights and standards codified in international law and norms should be available to everyone in Canada. In addition, the UN Refugee Convention explicitly reaffirms this: "As regards housing, the Contracting States, insofar as the matter is regulated by laws or regulations or is subject to the control of public authorities, shall accord refugees lawfully staying in their territory treatment as favourable as possible and, in any event, not less favourable than that accorded to aliens generally in the same circumstances" (1951, art. 21).

However, many people in Canada do not have access to adequate housing. Homelessness emerged as a key public policy issue in the 1980s, following "neoliberal policies that reduced government production of housing and other supportive measures" (Gaetz 2020, 353). Capitalist logics of land ownership and housing as a commodity clash with rights-based approaches. The legacy of these neo-liberal policies, coupled with rising real estate prices and rental market inflation (Rose 2019), has resulted in high levels of both unsheltered and hidden homelessness. "Unsheltered" refers to situations where people live in "a homeless shelter, on the streets or in parks, or in an abandoned building" (Uppal 2022, 1). "Hidden homelessness" means living temporarily with friends, acquaintances, or family members due to lack of alternative housing. While Canada-wide statistics are difficult to obtain due to residence biases in census data collection, Statistics Canada reports 3 per cent of people having experienced unsheltered homelessness, while 15 per cent have had hidden homelessness (Uppal 2022, 1). Indigenous people, women, sexual minorities, and newcomers are disproportionately unhoused due to structural inequalities and discrimination.

In Canada, housing lies at the intersection of municipal, provincial, and federal jurisdictions, complicating policy interventions (Kissoon 2015). At the municipal level, cities and towns fund and run shelters and set zoning laws that determine the use and density of buildings. Provincial and territorial governments are primarily responsible for landlord-tenant legislation that is intended to protect the rights of renters and property owners. Since the late 1990s, the federal government has taken a more proactive role in addressing rising homelessness, creating the National Homelessness Initiative in 1999 and appointing a minister responsible for homelessness.

28.1 Minimum Criteria for "Adequate" Housing

- Security of tenure: Housing is not adequate if its occupants do not have a degree of tenure security which guarantees legal protection against forced evictions, harassment and other threats.
- Availability of services, materials, facilities and infrastructure: Housing is not adequate if its occupants do not have safe drinking water, adequate sanitation, energy for cooking, heating, lighting, food storage or refuse disposal.
- Affordability: Housing is not adequate if its cost threatens or compromises the occupants' enjoyment of other human rights.
- Habitability: Housing is not adequate if it does not guarantee physical safety or provide adequate space, as well as protection against the cold, damp, heat, rain, wind, other threats to health and structural hazards.
- Accessibility: Housing is not adequate if the specific needs of disadvantaged and marginalized groups are not taken into account.
- Location: Housing is not adequate if it is cut off from employment opportunities, health-care services, schools, childcare centres and other social facilities, or if located in polluted or dangerous areas.
- Cultural adequacy: Housing is not adequate if it does not respect and take into account the expression of cultural identity.

(Special Rapporteur on the Right to Adequate Housing n.d., n.p.)

In 2017 the federal government introduced the National Housing Strategy (NHS). The NHS includes in its priority list for housing "women and children fleeing domestic violence; seniors; young adults; Indigenous peoples; people with disabilities; people dealing with mental health and addiction issues; veterans; LGBTQ+; racialized groups; recent immigrants, especially refugees; and, people experiencing homelessness" (CMHC 2017). The National Housing Strategy Act received royal assent in June 2019. It recognizes adequate housing as a fundamental human right, as defined in international human rights law (National Housing Strategy Act 2019, 4(a)). It also acknowledges that "housing is essential to the inherent dignity and well-being of the person and to building sustainable and inclusive communities" (4(b)).

TEMPORARY, TRANSITIONAL, AND PRECARIOUS HOUSING

> 28.2 "If they are very honest and tell them that they are a refugee claimant, then most probably the landlord won't rent a place to them first. They don't know much about refugee claimants and in their mind it's always someone very desperate, no job, maybe experienced violence in their home country or their personality is unknown and also they don't have networks here, so if anything happens they have no other sources to help these tenants. Stigmatization is very serious." (Quoted in Sherrell, D'Addario, and Hiebert 2007, 70)

Initial housing in Canada varies significantly depending on route of arrival and immigration status (Silvius 2016; Murdie 2008; Wayland 2007). Government-assisted refugees (GARs) are referred to the Resettlement Assistance Program (RAP), funded by the government but run by service agencies. RAP services are only available in about fifty cities across Canada, meaning that GARs are less geographically distributed upon arrival than privately sponsored refugees or refugee claimants (Rose 2019). Most GARs stay in temporary accommodation when they first arrive – either refugee reception centres or hotels (Bhattacharyya et al. 2020). Because of limited spaces in these temporary shelters, as well as integration and social services – like health care and education – being tied to residence, there is pressure to find longer-term accommodation as soon as possible. Indeed, "[f]inding suitable and affordable housing for GARs is a major contractual obligation for the newcomer service providers that deliver the Resettlement Assistance Program" (Rose 2019, 11). In some cases, refugees feel that this pushes them into suboptimal housing (Bhattacharyya et al. 2020), especially when the twelve-month time frame for settlement assistance is insufficient to find appropriate long-term accommodation (Rabiah-Mohammed et al. 2022).

Privately sponsored refugees (PSRs) tend to arrive in the communities that sponsor them, resulting in greater geographic spread across Canada, including in smaller communities and rural areas. As part of the sponsorship process, sponsors must submit a plan for temporary and permanent housing to IRCC. In some cases, PSRs stay with sponsors as a "soft landing" upon arrival. However, like GARs, there is pressure to find longer-term accommodation as soon as possible after arrival to facilitate integration and settlement. Sponsorship groups may be less well equipped to find longer-term housing because they do not have the same formal and informal networks as RAP agencies.

Refugee claimants arrive in Canada with no designated RAP or sponsor and with precarious legal status, making them particularly vulnerable to homelessness (Kissoon 2010; Sherrell, D'Addario, and Hiebert 2007; Murdie 2008; Wayland 2007). Indeed, information packages given to those claiming asylum at a port of entry include lists of homeless shelters, with some specifically mandated to provide temporary housing to refugee claimants and refugees. These refugee- and refugee claimant–specific shelters tend to be in larger cities and offer not only temporary accommodation but also some social networking opportunities and limited settlement services (Kissoon 2015). In contrast, general shelters may lack an understanding of the refugee experience and specialized support, like interpretation and culturally appropriate food (Wayland 2007), despite the relatively large numbers using these services. For example, the City of Toronto reported that, in 2000, 27 per cent of people cited "refugee claimant" as a reason for admission to its homeless shelters (City of Toronto, 2001, 8, quoted in Kissoon 2010, 12). In Ottawa, the percentage of newcomer families accessing Ottawa's city-run shelters increased from 4 per cent in 2014 to 36 per cent in 2017 (AEHO 2018, quoted in Polillo and Sylvestre 2021, 6). In some cases, shelters can provide a "fast-track to social housing" (Kissoon 2015, 143). In Kissoon's study in Toronto, for example, some participants used a strategy of "becoming homeless to get a home, playing into a stereotype of deservingness, accommodating the rigidity of the welfare system" (Kissoon 2015, 231). Others find temporary accommodation with friends, relatives, or through community or faith groups (Teixeira 2008; Silvius 2016).

The large number of Ukrainians arriving in Canada in 2022–23 with temporary visas highlights another group of people with lived experience of forced migration who rely primarily on informal social networks for temporary housing. In the absence of formal settlement structures, many Ukrainians turned to social media in the first instance. While many Canadians opened up their homes, some expressed concerns about lack of screening, criminal record checks, and coordination (Bora 2022). In response, some immigrant-serving agencies set up portals with minimal screening, but not all provinces are included.

OPPORTUNITIES AND BARRIERS TO ACCESSING PERMANENT HOUSING

28.3 "Sorry, It's Rented": Discrimination in Toronto Housing

The Canadian Centre for Housing Rights undertook paired testing in early 2022 to gauge discrimination for racialized newcomers looking for rental accommodation in Toronto. The following summary of their findings demonstrates that disclosing newcomer status elicited some form of discrimination, with intersecting discrimination experienced on the basis of other identity factors.

- When telephone auditors appeared to be ("presented" as) from a member of a racial minority group, this compounded the discriminatory treatment they faced when disclosing their newcomer status.
- Female telephone auditors who disclosed a newcomer status faced a 62 per cent increase in discrimination when they had accents that presented as racialized compared with female newcomer auditors who did not have racialized accents.
- Male telephone auditors who disclosed a newcomer status faced a 267 per cent increase in discrimination when they had accents presented as racialized, compared with male newcomer auditors who did not have racialized accents.
- In the telephone audit, we found racialized newcomer women faced a 563 per cent increase in discriminatory treatment when they disclosed that they were caring for a child, compared with when parental status was not disclosed.
- In the email audits, auditors who disclosed newcomer status with names that presented as female faced a 30 per cent increase in discrimination when their name was also presented as racialized, compared with their non-racialized counterparts.
- In many interactions, after a telephone auditor or email auditor disclosed their newcomer status, housing providers outlined stringent criteria they had to meet to rent the unit in question. By outlining such stringent criteria, housing providers were able to deny housing to newcomers to Canada while not necessarily engaging in conduct the Ontario Human Rights Code would classify as discriminatory.

(Canadian Centre for Housing Rights 2022, 6)

Teixeira contends that integration depends on "a neighbourhood where the newcomer feels comfortable, and housing that is adequate, suitable, and affordable, especially in the initial stages of settlement" (2008, 255). In other words, integration relies on both homemaking and housing (Murdie 2008). In a study with resettled Syrian refugees, Rose found that "suitable and affordable housing is an anchor point for a new start in a new country and city" (2019, 12), especially given its linkages to other services and resources, like employment, education, health, et cetera. Figure 28.2 from Teixeira (2008) visually represents the interrelationships between housing, home, and integration indicators.

However, people with lived experiences of forced migration face several structural barriers to accessing suitable long-term housing. First, affordability is a major problem as both real estate prices and rents increase across Canada (Carter and Osborne 2009; Bhattacharyya et al. 2020), but particularly in markets like Toronto, Montreal, and Vancouver, which also tend to attract newcomers because of their diversity (Rose 2019; Teixeira 2008; Wayland 2007). Real estate speculation as an investment and commodity exacerbate rising costs (Silvius 2016). Similarly, there has been under-investment in subsidized social housing (Murdie 2008). Affordable housing tends to be located far away from public transit and other services (Rose 2019, 1; Carter and Osborne 2009). The scarcity of housing not only inflates prices but also creates competition (Carter and Osborne 2009) such that property owners can use their discretion to decide who to rent to, based on discriminatory practices.

This relates to the second point: intersectional discrimination, as illustrated in box 28.3. Several studies show persistent patterns of racism in housing markets (Kissoon 2015; Teixeira 2008; Canadian Centre for Housing Rights 2022; Carter and Osborne 2009; Kaur et al. 2021). Family-based discrimination occurs when tenants are refused housing due to the presence of a child, single-parent households (Canadian Centre for Housing Rights 2022), or large families (Rose 2019; Carter and Osborne 2009; Bhattacharyya et al. 2020). Disability can impact housing, in terms of direct discrimination and also indirect discrimination based on accessibility needs, which limits options.

Third, the paperwork required to rent presents a barrier, particularly for people who are undocumented or have temporary status or precarious employment. Many property owners require prospective tenants to supply a deposit (Murdie 2008) and references (Rose 2019). In some cases, renters are asked to provide proof of employment status (Kissoon 2015; Polillo and Sylvestre 2021), where temporary SIN numbers affect refugee claimants in particular (Sherrell, D'Addario, and Hiebert 2007). Workers with seasonal employment or who change jobs frequently are also penalized in the housing market (Carter and Osborne 2009). Renters who do not have required paperwork or proof of funds may be required to seek out a co-signatory on the lease or guarantor (Murdie 2008).

A fourth barrier relates to lack of access to information. Many newcomers are not familiar with their rights under local laws (Carter and Osborne 2009), especially if they move frequently across provinces and territories, with different legislations. Others lack an understanding of the housing market, the city (Carter and Osborne 2009), or where to find information on vacancies (Rose 2001), especially where openings are communicated through social media or other closed channels (see networks below). Language barriers complicate these informational issues (Rose 2019; Bhattacharyya et al. 2020; Kaur et al. 2021).

Relationships and networks are both a source of stability and precarity in housing (Polillo and Sylvestre 2021). Due to low income support, many single people

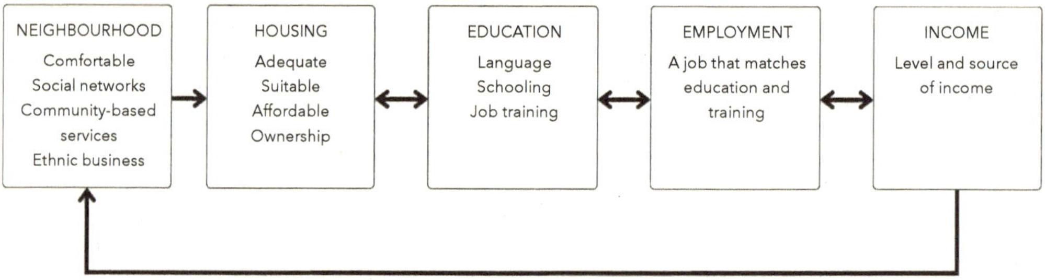

Figure 28.2 | The importance of neighbourhood and housing in immigrant and refugee integration.

have to share accommodations (Rose 2019; Murdie 2008). These enforced living arrangements can be both a source of solidarity and stress. Domestic violence is a major source of homelessness, especially for women, sexual minorities, children, and elders (Thurston et al 2013). Similarly, living in diaspora communities can reduce social isolation, but can also create tensions due to conflicts in home countries (Rose 2019). Networks can facilitate finding longer-term accommodation (Hanley et al. 2018; Kaur et al. 2021). For example, Rose (2019) shows that, during the peak of Syrian resettlement to Canada, online housing helped connect people to housing, and partnerships between RAPs and private landlords were key. While word of mouth is sometimes helpful in locating housing, at other times people in informal networks lack the expertise and knowledge to give accurate information (Murdie 2008; Wayland 2007).

OPPORTUNITIES AND CHALLENGES TO MAKING HOME IN CANADA

28.4 Excerpt from CBC: "What Is Home When You Are Part of a Diaspora?"

Rania al-Harthi has lived in Regina for a decade. But does that make it her home? For al-Harthi, home is a construct, determined not only by physical location but by history, memories, and connections to the community and the land.

Rania al-Harthi is part of a diaspora – a group of people who have moved away or been forced from their established or ancestral homeland. She was born in Zarqa, Jordan, to a father of Palestinian origins. He left the West Bank in 1967, and was forced to move to a refugee camp in Jordan. Her mother was Russian, a place al-Harthi's family visited every summer. She remembers travelling to the Dead Sea, and knowing they were almost there when she could lick her hand to taste the salt in the humid air.

The question, "where is home?" has always been tough for her to answer. She says her sense of loss - of land, friends and family - came with a need to belong.

Al-Harthi came to Canada in 2010 to go to school. She works in settlement service helping newcomers to Saskatchewan. She is also an independent artist working in theatre, film and visual arts on Treaty Four Territory. She says she feels a connection between the fertile ground in her motherland and the land here that is feeding the world.

These days, al-Harthi's idea of home is wherever her daughter Sophia is. Sophia also sees "home" as where her mother is, whether in Regina or on a visit to one of the places connected to their family, such as Jordan and Russia.

Together the pair is forging a future, but also staying connected with their culture through food, music, dance and art - including Palestinian embroidery and Arabic calligraphy. Sophia loves to practice her words in Arabic. They also sing a Russian lullaby together every night before falling asleep in the home they've created here. (Zeviar 2022, n.p.)

In addition to the practical realities of securing adequate, affordable housing highlighted in the previous sections, newcomers to Canada also express the importance of making home, as shown by Rania's reflections (see box 28.4). Many forced migration researchers have written about home, because it is so central to the notion of displacement (S. Ahmed 1999; Sirriyeh 2010). For example, Brun and Fábos (2015) distinguish between "home," "Home," and "HOME." In their conceptualization, "home" means the "day-to-day practices that help to create the place of displacement as a particularly significant kind of place" (12). In Rania's experience, "home" is (re)created through Palestinian embroidery, Arabic calligraphy, and Russian lullabies with her daughter. Brun and Fábos's second concept "Home" "represents values, traditions, memories, and subjective feelings of home … that many displaced people dream of and long for" (2015, 12). Similarly, Sirriyeh (2010) shows that home is related to a sense of (self-)identity. In Rania's case, "Home" is linked to "history, memories, and connections to the community and the land" (Zeviar 2022, n.p.). Rania also engages in what S. Ahmed has described as "generational acts of story-telling" (1999, 342) by sharing these memories with her daughter. The third aspect of Brun and Fábos's conceptual framework, "HOME" refers to the broader political and historical context in which home is understood and experienced not only by displaced people but also the perpetrators of nationalist exclusion and violence and the policy-makers addressing protracted displacement through the optic of "durable solutions" (2015, 13). In Rania's account, there is reference to the term "diaspora," which is often connected to groups of people who have been displaced from particular "homelands," like Palestinians, in her case.

Research in Canada indicates both opportunities and challenges to (re)creating home for people with lived experiences of forced migration. The adoption of particular accents and "sounding Canadian" (Kissoon 2015, 233) can be part of strategies to "blend in" and belong. Such linguistic markers go beyond language acquisition to include pronunciation, specific word use, intonation, and tone (Creese 2010; Tomic 2013). Similarly, racism in Canada (see Henry-Dixon, chapter 2; Mahrouse and El Omari, chapter 15) is a barrier to homemaking. Just as Shire depicts in the poem at the beginning of this chapter, many racialized and visibly religious newcomers (and Canadians whose families have lived in Canada for generations) are told to "go back home." Even innocuous questions like "where are you from?" reinforce "otherness" and the sense of being out of place. In contrast, citizenship can be a signifier of belonging and "home" (see Moffette, chapter 19; Cowper-Smith and Kane, chapter 20). The Canadian national anthem starts, "O Canada! Our *home* …" (my emphasis). In contrast, as has been demonstrated throughout this book, precarious status contributes to a sense of limbo and exacerbates affective (home) and practical (housing) consequences of displacement.

Like Rania in the reflection above, some newcomers suggest that family is an indicator of "home." In some cases, this means that family reunification is necessary before people can recreate home in exile. Extended family in proximity is crucial to some people's sense of belonging (Rabiah-Mohammed et al. 2022). Others cite marriage and child-rearing as affective ways to rebuild home in Canada. On the other hand, it should not be assumed that family and domestic spaces are inherently safe. Indeed, people whose immigration status is tied to a family member face particular vulnerabilities (Menjívar and Salcido 2002).

CONCLUSIONS AND RECOMMENDATIONS

This chapter has outlined practical, policy, and affective opportunities and barriers to securing affordable housing and recreating home in Canada. I now turn to some recommendations. On the practical side, plain language summaries of housing rights should be made available in multiple languages to help bridge the information gaps related to provincial laws and tenants' rights, as well as mechanisms for reporting complaints, including discrimination in the housing market. To address credit history and identification barriers, the Government of Canada should provide standard documentation to resettled refugees and refugee claimants that could be used for rental applications. In the longer term, several advocates have called for new construction of subsidized housing. Finally, related to integration as a two-way process (see Hynie, chapter 23), newcomers will only feel at home in Canada as long as Canadians change their perspective of "who belongs" to be more inclusive of different cultures, religions, and ways of being and knowing. As Coburn reminds us in the first chapter of this book, all non-Indigenous people are guests on Indigenous territories.

FURTHER READING AND RESOURCES

Garrett, M. 2017. "'Home' by Warsan Shire." YouTube video, 3:42. 13 March 2017. https://www.youtube.com/watch?v=nI9D92Xiygo.

Macrae, Emma, and Olivia Doggett. 2022. "Governments Must Match Civil Society Efforts to Welcome Refugees." *Policy Options*, 19 April 2022. https://policyoptions.irpp.org/magazines/april-2022/governments-must-match-civil-society-efforts-to-welcome-refugees.

Mody, Monica. n.d. "Homing Instinct." *The other side of hope*. https://othersideofhope.com/homing-instinct-monica-mody.html.

Rabiah-Mohammed, Fawziah, Abe Oudshoorn, Cindy Brown, and Luc Theriault. 2022. "Canada Needs to Build More Affordable Housing for Newcomers." *The Conversation,* 3 July 2022. https://theconversation.com/canada-needs-to-build-more-affordable-housing-for-newcomers-184420.

Rose, Damaris. 2016. "Affordable Housing for Refugees is a Major Challenge." *Policy Options,* 20 May 2016. https://policyoptions.irpp.org/magazines/may-2016/affordable-housing-for-refugees-is-a-major-challenge.

Teixeira, Carlos, ed. 2010. "'Newcomers' Experiences of Housing and Homelessness in Canada." *Canadian Issues* (Fall). https://acs-aec.ca/wp-content/uploads/2019/05/CITC-2010-Fall-L.pdf.

Glossary

ableism A term that includes discrimination on the basis of disability and the way systems, policies, and the physical environment are designed for able-bodied people.

acculturation Cultural and psychological changes that result from intercultural contact between groups and individuals.

acts of citizenship "Collective or individual deeds that rupture social-historical patterns [through which] subjects constitute themselves as citizens or, better still, as those to whom the right to have rights is due" (Isin and Nielsen 2008, 2, quoted in Moffette, chapter 19).

additionality The principle that private sponsorship places are in addition to government resettlement and not in lieu of, or a replacement for, Government-Assisted Refugee admissions.

age
- *age discrimination* Differential treatment of people based on chronological or social age.
- *chronological age* The use of chronometric time to measure the aging process.
- *social age* Socially constructed perceptions of roles and capacities across the life course and inter- and intra-generational power relations.

agency The capacity to take decisions, even in situations of extreme power asymmetries and structural constraints.

Alternative to Detention (ATD) A non-custodial, community-based program enrolling non-citizens to monitor their movements until their immigration statuses are resolved.

asylum seeker A person who has applied for refugee protection but does not yet have refugee status (see also refugee claimant).

asymmetrical federalism A type of federalism in which the autonomy and prerogatives of subnational units vary.

belonging Feelings of familiarity and safety that arise from relationships with others in the physical location (i.e., social networks), cultural practices that evoke home, security of legal status, and also the duration and personal history one has in a place.

birth registration The act to register a child's birth through a civil registration procedure, often a prerequisite for granting nationality.

Blended Visa Office-Referred (BVOR) A Government of Canada resettlement program that is a blend of government-assisted resettlement and private sponsorship. Settlement support is shared between the government and private sponsors with each covering six months of financial support.

bureaucratic birthdate An arbitrary birthdate given by an administrative official, such as the United Nations. It is normally 1 January (but in some cases 1 July) and an estimated year based on reference to an important historical event, like an election, war, or natural disaster.

bordering The enactment and maintenance of borders.

border securitization The process of turning an issue or object into a security matter and treating it as such in policies through an iterative legal/policy process that departs from human rights-based and humanitarian protection toward criminalizing and prosecuting migration.

Canada Border Services Agency (CBSA) A federal government agency tasked with providing integrated border services that assist national security and public safety priorities and enable the free movement of people, including forcefully displaced people meeting legal requirements (CBSA Act 2005).

Canada-Quebec Accord Signed in 1991, the Canada-Quebec Accord relating to Immigration and Temporary Admission of Aliens is a legal agreement between the federal government and the province of Quebec that gives Quebec more autonomy over immigration than other provinces have. It also determines the federal resource transfer for immigration-related programs.

(Canada–United States) Safe Third Country Agreement (STCA) Entered into force on 29 December 2004, the STCA is a treaty between the governments of Canada and the US that requires refugees (with limited exceptions) attempting to cross at a land border to apply for refugee status in the first country they arrive in.

Canadian Council for Refugees (CCR) Montreal-based umbrella group of non-governmental organizations (NGOs) in Canada that promotes the rights and protection of refugees.

categories An analytical tool to divide people according to a particular definition of shared characteristics.

chattel slavery The enslaving and owning of human beings and their offspring as legal, disposable property.

Chinese head tax A fee imposed on each Chinese person entering Canada to isolate and discriminate one specific group of people purely based on their race, in place until 1947.

citizenship Passive and active membership in a political community that is attached to certain notions of equality and organized around rights and obligations.

class A system of social stratification that refers to descriptive gradations of income, status, and education. It includes processes of producing, appropriating, and distributing labour and capital.

class-based integration "Allocation of rights based on refugees' economic resources" (Şimşek 2020, 541), whereby the lack of such resources means struggles to access the labour market, education, housing, and a sense of belonging.

climate migration (Im)mobility due to factors related to climate change.

conditionality The quality of being subject to formal and informal conditions and requirements, often associated with probationary and precarious legal status.

Convention refugee "A person who, by reason of a well-founded fear of persecution for reasons of race, religion, nationality, membership in a particular social group or political opinion, (a) is outside each of their countries of nationality and is unable or, by reason of that fear, unwilling to avail themself of the protection of each of those countries; or (b) not having a country of nationality, is outside the country of their former habitual residence and is unable or, by reason of that fear, unwilling to return to that country" (IRPA, sec. 96).

credential recognition The process by which international degrees, training, and skills are evaluated in Canada.

cultural figure of the refugee Popular significance of the label "refugee" that goes beyond the legal category.

cultural production From French sociologist Pierre Bourdieu (1993), the processes of generation, circulation, and reception of cultural artifacts.

denationalization When a state revokes an individual's citizenship, typically due to activity deemed harmful to the state, leaving denationalized individuals at risk of statelessness if they do not possess the nationality of another state.

deskilling The process by which people's skills and experiences are undervalued or overlooked.

disability "Results from the interaction between persons with impairments and attitudinal and environmental barriers that hinders their full and effective participation in society on an equal basis with others" (UN CRPD, preamble (e)).

disaster "A situation requiring outside support for coping" (Kelman, 2020, 16), created from the intersection between a hazard and vulnerability.

discourse Collective or socially shared repertoires of interpretations of the world through statements, statements that are not merely descriptive but generally oriented to action.

displacement [also called "forced displacement"] A situation that describes those who "have been unwillingly uprooted" (Coleman 2012, xiv).

durable solutions Solutions to refugee movements recognized by UNHCR and the international community, which include local integration, repatriation, and resettlement.

enslavement The act of making someone a slave through subjugation and commodification; enslaved people were considered the property of their enslaver and legally not persons.

environmental hazards Environmental slow-onset and rapid-onset events that can adversely affect human beings and undermine human rights.

ethics Principles of respect, concern for welfare, and justice.

externalization Border control measures that take place outside a state's territorial boundaries that, in their effects, prevent asylum seekers from arriving on official state territory.

federalism A system of governance in which a State divides its powers between a central entity and regional or provincial entities.

flight risk [also called "risk of absconding"] A grounds for arrest or re-detention on suspicion that a non-citizen is likely to purposefully evade authorities and/or "go underground," thereby dropping out of regular immigration status processes.

forced migration Situations where people leave their homes due to colonization, slavery, human trafficking, or to flee due to conflict, human rights abuses, persecution, or environmental degradation.

freedom seeker An enslaved person who took action to obtain freedom from slavery.

gender

- *cis-gender* A gender identity that corresponds with the sex registered for a person at their birth.
- *gender binary* The idea that there are two unique and distinct genders, male and female.
- *gender expression* The way in which a person expresses their gender with social manners, appearance, and behaviours typically associated with a specific gender.

Global Affairs Canada (GAC) The federal department of foreign affairs of the Canadian government, GAC is involved in international migration policy and development and humanitarian assistance for refugees overseas and in countries hosting refugees.

Global North/South The conceptual binary division of the world grouping countries based on socioe-conomic and political characteristics.

Global Refugee Regime The "rules, norms, principles, and decision-making procedures" governing states' responses to refugees (Betts 2015).

Government-Assisted Refugees (GARs) Refugees selected by the federal government, usually on the basis of referrals from UNHCR, who are resettled to Canada as permanent residents and supported by government-funded settlement services for one year.

Group of Five (G5) Five or more Canadian citizens or permanent residents who privately sponsor refugees to resettle in their communities.

health care The provision of medical care and assistance.

home "A place, and also an idea and an imaginary imbued with feeling" (Brun and Fábos 2015, 6); as Kissoon (2015, 11) argues, it is helpful to delink "home from the dwelling place."

homelessness Defined broadly by Statistics Canada to "describe a situation in which individuals or families live without stable, safe, permanent, appropriate housing, or the immediate prospect, means and ability of acquiring it. Homelessness can include living on the streets, living in places not appropriate for human habitation, or staying in shelters"; homelessness can also be cultural or spiritual.

housing Recognized as a fundamental human right in both international and national law, adequate access to housing includes affordability, tenure security, and availability of services.

household A group of people living together.

human capital identity The economic value of a person determined by a general assessment of their working skills and experiences.

human dignity The inherent value that everyone holds simply by being human.

humanitarianism Appeals to people's empathy for fellow humanity to come to one another's aid in times of need.

immigration detention A policy, practice, or law whereby the federal or national immigration authority arrests and incarcerates a non-citizen toward expediting the resolution of their immigration status.

Immigration and Refugee Board (IRB) An independent administrative tribunal responsible for making decisions on immigration and refugee matters in Canada.

Immigration and Refugee Protection Act (IRPA) The framework Canadian immigration legislation enacted in 2002.

Immigration Refugees and Citizenship Canada (IRCC) The federal government department primarily responsible for managing the selection, settlement, and integration of immigrants, including refugees and other forcibly displaced persons.

Indigenous A population that has been known as the first people to live in a territory that has been colonized by a dominant settler group. The Canadian Constitution recognizes "Indians" (First Nations), Inuit, and Métis as Indigenous Peoples in Canada.

Indigenous Talking Circle An Indigenous method to encourage learning within community.

inland asylum Claims for refugee protection made by foreign nationals either at a port of entry when they arrive in Canada or at an inland office.

integration The inclusion of a group or a person in a certain community; ideally a two-way process by which the host community changes with the contributions of newcomers.

- *material integration* The process of settlement in a new community measured by material factors like employment, housing, and access to social services.
- *social integration* The process of feeling a sense of belonging and identifying with a new community.

interdiction In the context of migration, preventing migration either before it begins or while it is in process.

intergovernmental relations In a federal system, the relations between the central government (federal) and the regional governments (provinces, states, territories, or other denomination).

internal displacement Migration that does not cross an international border.

international protection Commonly used as a shorthand for the provisions of refugee law that provide for the protection of individuals outside their country of origin as a result of feared harm.

international refugee protection system Based on the principle that if a State is unwilling or unable to protect the basic rights of its citizens, other States have a responsibility to do so. This system draws on the legal framework of the 1951 Convention relating to the Status of Refugees and its 1967 Protocol, regional treaties, declarations, and other instruments of international law such as the 1948 Universal Declaration of Human Rights.

intersectionality An approach that recognizes the importance of conceptualizing how different identities intersect to create and/or impact people's experiences.

label A classification or category attached to a person or status that is both practical/administrative and symbolic.

labour market The supply and demand of employment and labour.

mixed migration Contexts in which people move for different reasons that include both voluntary and forced migration.

naming The principle in private sponsorship of refugees, where the sponsorship group can identify the specific refugees they intend to resettle.

non-penalization principle In refugee law, the principle that people cannot be penalized nor charged with immigration or criminal offences for breaching immigration rules in order to seek asylum.

non-refoulement According to the 1951 Refugee Convention, the principle that "no one shall expel or return (*refouler*) a refugee against [their] will, in any manner whatsoever, to a territory where [they fear] threats to life or freedom."

normativity An evaluative standard that determines desirable or just outcomes.

patriarchy A social system in which positions of dominance and privilege are primarily held by men that can cause exploitation or oppression as through male dominance of moral authority.

permanent resident A person who has been given permanent resident status by immigrating to Canada but is not a Canadian citizen.

precarious non-citizenship Immigration status of non-citizens that is temporary, dynamic, and/or irregular.

Private Sponsorship of Refugees (PSR) A program that enables Canadian citizens and permanent residents to sponsor refugees for resettlement to Canada by supporting their settlement for the first year.

positionality The awareness of how a person is positioned in terms of social and cultural power in a specific situation. To work ethically in forced migration, critical awareness is needed of the "positionalities" of everyone involved in the research or art project.

race A socially constructed colonial concept. The ideas of race and racial classification are based on presumed inherent differences in phenotype (e.g., skin colour, hair texture), culture, and behaviour between groups.

racialization "The complex set of historical and sociopolitical processes of attributing superior or inferior status based on the presumption of biological difference" (Pierre 2020, 220).

racism Discrimination based on race. In migration contexts, racism can be individual (e.g., offensive comments on visible appearance and clothing) or structural (e.g., severe gaps in health-care access among racialized migrants due to lack of culturally and linguistically appropriate care).

rapid-onset hazard Environmental hazards that happen suddenly and rapidly, and tend to be temporary, such as floods and earthquakes.

reflexivity A critical reflection about power dynamics affecting a project's relationships and context; needed to work ethically and with cultural safety.

refugee claimants People who are seeking asylum but do not yet have refugee status (term preferred in Canada; also called "asylum seeker").

refugee participation The meaningful participation of refugees in decision-making processes that impact refugee policies and experiences.

relational ethics The practice of continually reviewing the way imbalances in power in research relationships, particularly between researchers and research participants, might impact people and communities, as well as the research outcomes. Relational ethics require awareness of positionality in day-to-day and ongoing interactions, as well as in larger decisions concerning research methodology and process.

religious group An organization that is either explicitly identified with, or legitimately represents, a community of people of the same religious tradition.

remittances Cash or goods sent by migrants to their families, communities, and friends in their country of origin or in a third country.

resettlement The process of relocating refugees from one country of asylum to another country of more permanent protection.

residential schools Boarding schools put in place by the Government of Canada to assimilate Indigenous children, pursuing genocidal goals by removing children from their families and exposing them to physical and sexual abuse.

right to have rights The concept developed by Hannah Arendt to describe the right to membership in a particular community.

right to health A universal right that includes essential aspects promoting health for all, such as the availability of quality and affordable health services.

sanctuary A place where refugee claimants whose claims have been denied are sheltered (often places of worship) to protect them from arrest and deportation.

sanctuary cities Cities that enforce municipal laws that prevent social service providers and municipal authorities from collaborating with the federal government to enforce immigration laws, which prevents irregular migrants from being deported.

securitization The way in which a subject is framed as a matter of security, usually making the topic appear "dangerous" or a public security concern.

separated child A child who migrates without their parent(s) or legal guardian(s) but who is taken care of – sometimes informally – by another adult [see distinction with unaccompanied minor].

settler colonialism "A specific form of colonialism characterized by the 'mass transfer' of people to lands they intend to 'conquer' and permanently settle ... settlers work to establish 'perfect settler sovereignty,' removing any remaining Indigenous challenges to the settler state's sovereignty and redefining themselves as the 'native' inhabitants" (Smithers 2022, n.p.).

sexual identity

- *2SLGBTQI+* Two-Spirit, Lesbian, Gay, Bisexual, Transgender, Queer and/or Questioning, Intersex, with the "+" added to recognize and affirm the range of identities.
- *heteronormativity* The hegemonic belief that heterosexuality is the "norm" by valorizing reproductive sexuality between cis-gender women and men and marginalizing other forms of sexuality as "deviant" (Luibhéid 2008).
- *SOGIESC* Sexual Orientation, Gender Identity and Expression, and Sex Characteristics.

shelter An establishment that provides a temporary place to stay for people in situations of homelessness.

Singh *case* The Supreme Court's *Singh v. Minister of Employment and Immigration*, in which the court reaffirmed that the legal guarantees in the Canadian Charter of Rights and Freedoms (1982) apply to "everyone" who is physically present on Canadian territory, not just Canadian citizens.

skills The expertise of someone to accomplish a task that requires certain capacities. In migration policy, there is a problematic distinction between "skilled" and "unskilled" labour that is embedded in classist discrimination.

slow-onset hazard Environmental hazards that happen slowly and tend to be permanent, such as erosion and rising sea-rise.

smuggling A practice in which smugglers serve as intermediaries or facilitators for the transnational movement of people through irregularized routes.

social determinants of health Non-medical characteristics that affect health, such as income and social protection, education, unemployment and job insecurity, working life conditions, food insecurity, housing, basic amenities and the environment, early childhood development, social inclusion and non-discrimination, structural conflict, access to affordable health services of decent quality (WHO 2022).

sovereignty The authority of individual countries to rule within the boundaries of their territories.

Sponsorship Agreement Holders (SAHs) Incorporated organizations that have signed an agreement with the Government of Canada to sponsor refugees for resettlement to Canada.

stateless The situation of a person who is "not considered a national by any State under the operation of its law" (Convention 1951, art. 1(1)).

structural discrimination Inequalities enabled by patterns of behaviours and power asymmetries.

terra nullius A legal status accorded to a territory that does not belong to any State, upon which a State can legally legitimize the acquisition of sovereignty over that territory.

trafficking in persons (TIP) Under international law,

> the recruitment, transportation, transfer, harbouring or receipt of persons, by means of the threat or use of force or other forms of coercion, of abduction, of fraud, of deception, of the abuse of power or of a position of vulnerability or of the giving or receiving of payments or benefits to achieve the consent of a person having control over another person, for the purpose of exploitation. Exploitation shall include, at a minimum, the exploitation of the prostitution of others or other forms of sexual exploitation, forced labour or services, slavery or practices similar to slavery, servitude or the removal of organs." (Trafficking in Persons Protocol, art. 3(a))

Truth and Reconciliation Commission (TRC) Calls to Action Based on the conclusions of the 2015 TRC of Canada, the 94 Calls to Action is a guideline to acknowledge and address the harms of Residential Schools in Canada and to ensure a guidance toward reconciliation.

unaccompanied minor A person under the age of eighteen who is separated from their parent(s) and who is not accompanied by any adult who, formally or informally, is responsible for their care. [See distinction with separated child.]

undocumented A situation where a person does not have formal migration status or permission to reside in the state where they live.

voluntary migration People choosing to move to work or set up businesses (labour migration), study (educational migration), join other family members (family reunification and marriage migration), or visit other countries temporarily (tourism). While there are obviously structural constraints that limit people's choices about where, when, and how to move, voluntary migration is usually planned.

Western According to a binary west/east conceptual division of the word "Western" describes countries, norms, and cultural practices in Europe, North America, and other regions typically considered "developed."

References

Abbas, Madeline-Sophie. 2019. "Conflating the Muslim Refugee and the Terror Suspect: Responses to the Syrian Refugee 'Crisis' in Brexit Britain." *Ethnic and Racial Studies* 42 (14): 2450–69. https://doi.org/10.1080/01419870.2019.1588339.

Abbas, Mohamed, Tammam Aloudat, Javier Bartolomei, Manuel Carballo, Sophie Durieux-Paillard, Laure Gabus, Alexandra Jablonka, et al. 2018. "Migrant and Refugee Populations: A Public Health and Policy Perspective on a Continuing Global Crisis." *Antimicrobial Resistance & Infection Control* 7 (1): 113. https://doi.org/10.1186/s13756-018-0403-4.

Abdelaaty, Lamis Elmy. 2021. *Discrimination and Delegation: Explaining State Responses to Refugees*. New York: Oxford University Press.

Abdelkarim, Shaimaa. 2021. "Nuances of Recognition in the League of Nations and United Nations: Examining Modern and Contemporary Identity Deformations in Egypt." *Third World Approaches to International Law Review* 2 (2): 154–79.

Abebe, Allehone Mulugeta. 2011. "Human Rights in the Context of Disasters: The Special Session of the UN Human Rights Council on Haiti." *Journal of Human Rights*, Special Report, 10 (1): 99–111. https://doi.org/10.1080/14754835.2011.549715.

Abedi, Maham. 2019. "37% in Ipsos Poll Say Immigration Is a 'Threat' to White Canadians – What's the Threat?" *Global News*, 22 May 2019. https://globalnews.ca/news/5288135/immigration-threat-canadians-poll.

Abeleira v. Canada (Immigration, Refugees and Citizenship). 2017 FC 1008.

Abella, Irving M., and Harold Martin Troper. 2012. *None Is Too Many: Canada and the Jews of Europe, 1933–1948*. Toronto: University of Toronto Press.

Aberman, Tanya. 2014. "Gendered Perspectives on Refugee Determination in Canada." *Refuge: Canada's Journal on Refugees* 30 (2): 57–66.

Abid, Raith Zeher, Shakila Abdul Manan, and Zuhair Abdul Amir Abdul Rahman. 2017. "'A Flood of Syrians Has Slowed to a Trickle': The Use of Metaphors in the Representation of Syrian Refugees in the Online Media News

Reports of Host and Non-Host Countries." *Discourse & Communication* 11 (2): 121–40. https://doi.org/10.1177/1750481317691857.

Abji, Salina. 2020. "Punishing Survivors and Criminalizing Survivorship: A Feminist Intersectional Approach to Migrant Justice in the Crimmigration System." *Studies in Social Justice* 14: 67–89. https://doi.org/10.26522/ssj.v2020i14.2158.

Abji, Salina, and Lindsay Larios. 2021. "Migrant Justice as Reproductive Justice: Birthright Citizenship and the Politics of Immigration Detention for Pregnant Women in Canada." *Citizenship Studies* 25 (2): 253–72. https://doi.org/10.1080/13621025.2020.1859186.

Aboriginal Affairs and Northern Development Canada. 2014. "Renewing the Comprehensive Land Claims Policy: Towards a Framework for Addressing Section 35 Aboriginal Rights." Government of Canada. https://www.rcaanc-cirnac.gc.ca/eng/1408631807053/1544123449934.

Abu-Laban, Baha, Tracey Derwing, Harvey Krahn, Marlene Mulder, and Lori Wilkinson. 1999. "The Settlement Experiences of Refugees in Alberta." Prairie Centre of Excellence for Research on Immigration and Integration and Population Research Laboratory.

Abu-Laban, Yasmeen. 2020a. "Conclusion: Two Canadas as a Story without an End: Institutional Choices and the State of the Federation." In *Canadian Federalism and Its Future: Actors and Institutions*, edited by Alain Gagnon and Johanne Poirier, 365–85. Montreal and Kingston: McGill-Queen's University Press.

– 2020b. "Immigration and Settler-Colonies Post-UNDRIP: Research and Policy Implications." *International Migration* 58 (6): 12–28. https://doi.org/10.1111/imig.12685.

Abuya, Edwin O., Ulrike Krause, and Lucy Mayblin. 2021. "The Neglected Colonial Legacy of the 1951 Refugee Convention." *International Migration* 59 (4): 265–67. https://doi.org/10.1111/imig.12898.

Achiume, E. Tendayi. 2019. "The Postcolonial Case for Rethinking Borders." *Dissent* 66 (3): 27–32. https://doi.org/10.1353/dss.2019.0043.

– 2021. "Race, Refugees, and International Law." In *The Oxford Handbook of International Refugee Law*, edited by Cathryn Costello, Michelle Foster, and Jane McAdam. Oxford Handbooks. Oxford : Oxford University Press.

– 2022. "Racial Borders." *The Georgetown Law Journal* 110 (3): 445–508.

Adamoski, Robert L., Dorothy E. Chunn, Robert J. Menzies, eds. 2002. *Contesting Canadian Citizenship: Historical Readings*. Peterborough: Broadview Press.

Adamuti-Trache, Maria, and Robert Sweet. 2005. "Exploring the Relationship between Educational Credentials and the Earnings of Immigrants." *Canadian Studies in Population* 32 (2): 177. https://doi.org/10.25336/P6T30G.

Adelman, Howard. 1989. "Focus." *Refugee Survey Quarterly* 8 (2): 57–8. https://doi.org/10.1093/rsq/8.2.57-a.

Adese, Jennifer, and Malissa Phung. 2021. "Where Are We From? Decolonizing Indigenous and Refugee Relations." In *Refugee States: Critical Refugee Studies in Canada*, edited by Vinh Nguyen and Thy Phu, 117–37. Cultural Spaces. Toronto: University of Toronto Press.

Adhikari, Prakash. 2013. "Conflict-Induced Displacement, Understanding the Causes of Flight: Conflict-Induced Displacement." *American Journal of Political Science* 57 (1): 82–9. https://doiorg/10.1111/j.1540-5907.2012.00598.x.

Afghan Women's Organization (AWO). n.d. "Refugee and Immigrant Services: About Us." https://afghanwomen.org/about-us.

Agamben, Giorgio. 1998. *Homo Sacer : Sovereign Power and Bare Life*. Redwood City, CA: Stanford University Press.

Ager, Alastair, and Alison Strang. 2008. "Understanding Integration: A Conceptual Framework." *Journal of Refugee Studies* 21 (2): 166–91. https://doi.org/10.1093/jrs/fen016.

Agrawal, Sandeep, and Pradeep Sangapala. 2021. "Does Community Size Matter in the Settlement Process? The Experience of Syrian Refugees in Lethbridge in Alberta, Canada." *Journal of International Migration and Integration* 22 (2): 653–72. https://doi.org/10.1007/s12134-020-00761-6.

Agyekum, Boadi, Pius Siakwah, and John Kwame Boateng. 2021. "Immigration, Education, Sense of Community and Mental Well-Being: The Case of Visible Minority Immigrants in Canada." *Journal of Urbanism: International Research on Placemaking and Urban Sustainability* 14 (2): 222–36. https://doi.org/10.1080/17549175.2020.1801488.

Ahmad, Farah, Nasih Othman, Michaela Hynie, Ahmed M. Bayoumi, Anna Oda, and Kwame McKenzie. 2021. "Depression-Level Symptoms among Syrian Refugees: Findings from a Canadian Longitudinal Study." *Journal of Mental Health* 30 (2): 246–54. https://doi.org/10.1080/09638237.2020.1765998.

Ahmad Yar Ahmad Wali, Stavros Lazarou, Vasiliki Vita, and Lambros Ekonomou. 2020. "Critical Review of Climate Change Induced Migration: An Emerging Challenge for Contemporary Society." *Engineering World* 2: 47–57.

Ahmed, Hussen, dir. 2017. *Two Canadas: My Story of Generosity and Systemic Racism*. TEDx Toronto. YouTube video, 12:52. https://www.youtube.com/watch?v=o9EXoKb7el4.

Ahmed, Sara. 1999. "Home and Away: Narratives of Migration and Estrangement." *International Journal of Cultural Studies* 2 (3): 329–47. https://doi.org/10.1177/136787799900200303.

Aiken, Sharryn. 2000. "Manufacturing 'Terrorists': Refugees, National Security and Canadian Law, Part 1." *Refuge: Canada's Journal on Refugees* 19 (3): 54–73.

– 2007. "From Slavery to Expulsion: Racism, Canadian Immigration Law, and the Unfulfilled Promise of Modern Constitutionalism." In *Interrogating Race and Racism*, edited by Vijay Agnew. Toronto: University of Toronto Press. https://doi.org/10.3138/9781442685444.

Aiken, Sharryn, and Stephanie J. Silverman. 2021. "Decarceral Futures: Bridging Immigration and Prison Justice Towards an Abolitionist Future." *Citizenship Studies* 25 (2): 141–61. https://doi.org/10.1080/13621025.2021.1890405.

Akbar, Marshia. 2022. "Temporariness and the Production of Policy Categories in Canada." *Journal of Ethnic and Migration Studies* 48 (16): 3929–46. https://doi.org/10.1080/1369183X.2022.2028355.

Akbari, Ather H., and Azad Haider. 2018. "Impact of Immigration on Economic Growth in Canada and in Its Smaller Provinces." *Journal of International Migration and Integration* 19 (1): 129–42. https://doi.org/10.1007/s12134-017-0530-4.

Akbari, Ather H., and Martha MacDonald. 2014. "Immigration Policy in Australia, Canada, New Zealand, and the United States: An Overview of Recent Trends." *International Migration Review* 48 (3): 801–22. https://doi.org/10.1111/imre.12128.

Al Jazeera. 2022. "Dozens Missing after Refugee Boat Sinks off Greek Islands." 1 November 2022. https://www.aljazeera.com/news/2022/11/1/dozens-missing-after-refugee-boat-sinks-off-greek-islands.

Al Jazeera Staff. 2021. "Evacuations Ordered as Wildfires Rip through Canada's West Coast." *Al Jazeera*, 3 July 2021. https://www.aljazeera.com/news/2021/7/3/evacuations-ordered-wildfires-rip-through-canada-west-coast.

Al Rabeeah, Abu Bakr, and Winnie Yeung. 2018. *Homes: A Refugee Story*. Calgary: Freehand Books.

Alam, Shahidul. 2008. "Majority World: Challenging the West's Rhetoric of Democracy." *Amerasia Journal* 34 (1): 88–98. https://doi.org/10.17953/amer.34.1.l3176027k4q614v5.

Alberton, Amy M., G. Brent Angell, Kevin M. Gorey, and Stéphane Grenier. 2020. "Homelessness among Indigenous Peoples in Canada: The Impacts of Child Welfare Involvement and Educational Achievement." *Children and Youth Services Review* 111 (April): 104846. https://doi.org/10.1016/j.childyouth.2020.104846.

Alboim, Naomi. 2016. "Lessons Learned from the Indochinese and Syrian Refugee Movements." *Policy Options*, 18 May 2016. https://policyoptions.irpp.org/fr/magazines/mai-2016/lessons-learned-from-the-indochinese-and-syrian-refugee-movements.

Aleinikoff, Thomas Alexander. 1992. "State-Centered Refugee Law: From Resettlement to Containment." *Michigan Journal of International Law* 14 (1): 120–38.

Aleinikoff, Thomas Alexander, and Leah Zamore. 2019. *The Arc of Protection: Reforming the International Refugee Regime*. Redwood City, CA: Stanford University Press.

Alessi, Edward J. 2016. "Resilience in Sexual and Gender Minority Forced Migrants: A Qualitative Exploration." *Traumatology* 22 (3): 203–13. https://doi.org/10.1037/trm0000077.

Alexander, Kristine. 2016. "Childhood and Colonialism in Canadian History: Childhood and Colonialism in Canadian History." *History Compass* 14 (9): 397–406. https://doi.org/10.1111/hic3.12331.

Alexander, Michelle. 2020. *The New Jim Crow: Mass Incarceration in the Age of Colorblindness*. 10th anniversary ed. New York: The New Press.

Alfred, Taiaiake. 2009. *Wasase: Indigenous Pathways of Action and Freedom*. Toronto: University of Toronto Press.

Ali, Hodman. 2020. "Refugee Voices: Inspiring Stories of Young Refugees in Canada." UNHCR Canada. 21 February 2020. https://www.unhcr.ca/news/refugee-voices-inspiring-stories-young-refugees-canada.

Ali, Mehrunnisa Ahmad, Shamiram Zendo, and Shaina Somers. 2022. "Structures and Strategies for Social Integration: Privately Sponsored and Government Assisted Refugees." *Journal of Immigrant & Refugee Studies* 20 (4): 473–85. https://doi.org/10.1080/15562948.2021.1938332.

Alia, Valerie, and Simone Bull. 2012. *Media and Ethnic Minorities*. Edinburgh: Edinburgh University Press.

Alio, Mustafa, Shaza Alrihawi, James Milner, Anila Noor, Najeeba Wazefadost, and Pascal Zigashane. 2020. "By Refugees, for Refugees: Refugee Leadership during COVID-19, and Beyond." *International Journal of Refugee Law* 32 (2): 370–73. https://doi.org/10.1093/ijrl/eeaa021.

Alio, Mustafa, and Rez Gardi. 2021. "End the Tokenism. Give Refugees a Voice on Our Own Futures." *The New Humanitarian*, 15 December 2021. https://www.thenewhumanitarian.org/opinion/2021/12/15/give-refugees-a-voice-on-our-own-futures.

Allen, John L. 1992. "From Cabot to Cartier: The Early Exploration of Eastern North America, 1497–1543." *Annals of the Association of American Geographers* 82 (3): 500. https://doi.org/10.1111/j.1467-8306.1992.tb01972.x.

Allen, Ryan. 2009. "Benefit or Burden? Social Capital, Gender, and the Economic Adaptation of Refugees." *International Migration Review* 43 (2): 332–65. https://doi.org/10.1111/j.1747-7379.2009.00767.x.

Amarasingam, Amarnath. 2015. *Pain, Pride, and Politics: Social Movement Activism and the Sri Lankan Tamil Diaspora in Canada*. Geographies of Justice and Social Transformation. Athens: University of Georgia Press.

Amnesty International. 2015. "8 Ways to Solve the World Refugee Crisis." 12 October 2015. https://www.amnesty.org/en/latest/campaigns/2015/10/eight-solutions-world-refugee-crisis.

– 2018. "5 manières pour des groupes religieux d'accueillir des réfugiés." 28 February 2018. https://www.amnesty.org/fr/latest/news/2018/02/i-welcome-5-things-you-can-do.

Amnesty International Canada. 2020. "Amnesty International Applauds Settlement in Landmark Nevsun Resources Mining Case." 23 October 2020. https://www.amnesty.ca/news/amnesty-international-applauds-settlement-in-landmark-nevsun-resources-mining-case.

– 2023. "Supreme Court Decision on Safe Third Country Agreement Ultimately Fails Refugees." 16 June 2023. https://amnesty.ca/human-rights-news/safe-third-country-agreement-ruling.

Amnistie internationale Canada francophone. 2020. "Livret: Réfugié.e.s: en danger et non dangereux." Éducation aux droits humains.

Anctil, Pierre, and Alexandre Comeau. 2021. "The St. Louis Crisis in the Canadian Press: New Data on the June 1939 Incident." Canadian Jewish Studies 31: 13–40.

Anderson, Benedict Richard O'Gorman. 2016. *Imagined Communities: Reflections on the Origin and Spread of Nationalism*. Revised edition. London: Verso.

Anderson, Christopher G. 2001. "A Nation of Immigrants: Past, Present and Future." *Journal of Canadian Studies* 36 (1): 180–94. https://doi.org/10.3138/jcs.36.1.180.

– 2008. "A Long-Standing Canadian Tradition: Citizenship Revocation and Second-Class Citizenship under the Liberals, 1993–2006." *Journal of Canadian Studies* 42 (3): 80–105. https://doi.org/10.3138/jcs.42.3.80.

– 2010. "Restricting Rights, Losing Control: The Politics of Control over Asylum Seekers in Liberal-Democratic States – Lessons from the Canadian Case, 1951–1989." *Canadian Journal of Political Science* 43 (4): 937–59. https://doi.org/10.1017/S0008423910000685.

Anderson, Kathryn, and Zhen Huang. 2019. "Can Immigrants Ever Earn as Much as Native Workers?" IZA *World of Labor* 159 (April). https://doi.org/10.15185/izawol.159.

Anderson, Kim. 2000. *A Recognition of Being: Reconstructing Native Womanhood*. 2nd ed. Toronto: Sumach Press.

Anderson, Martin, and Amy Slaughter. 2021. "Preserving the Humanitarian Nature of Resettlement – An Analysis of 2018–2020 Resettlement Data." *RefugePoint*, 17 June 2021. https://www.refugepoint.org/preserving-the-humanitarian-nature-of-resettlement.

Anderson, Scott, dir. 2022. *Death at the Border*. CBC News. *The Fifth Estate* video, 45:12. https://www.cbc.ca/news/fifthestate/death-at-the-border-1.6620729.

Andreas, Peter. 2003. "A Tale of Two Borders: The U.S.-Mexico and U.S.-Canada Lines After 9-11." In *The Rebordering of North America: Integration and Exclusion in a New Security Context*, edited by Peter Andreas and Thomas J. Biersteker, 1–23. New York: Routledge.

Angers, Jean Philippe. 2023. "Legault Calls Roxham Road Deal a 'Very Nice Victory' for Quebec." *Montreal Gazette*, 24 March 2023. https://montreal

gazette.com/news/national/legault-calls-roxham-road-deal-a-very-nice-victory-for-quebec.

Angus Reid Institute. 2018. "Immigration in Canada: Does Recent Change in Forty Year Opinion Signal a Blip or a Breaking Point?" https://angusreid.org/wp-content/uploads/2018/08/2018.08.01_Immigration-release.pdf.

Anonymous. 2016. "I Wish I'd Never Decided to Work in an Immigration Detention Centre." *Politics.co.uk*, 14 March 2016. https://www.politics.co.uk/blog/2016/03/14/i-wish-id-never-decided-to-work-in-an-immigration-detention-centre.

Ansion, Mariel, and Noorfarah Merali. 2018. "Latino Immigrant Parents' Experiences Raising Young Children in the Absence of Extended Family Networks in Canada: Implications for Counselling." *Counselling Psychology Quarterly* 31 (4): 408–27. https://doi.org/10.1080/09515070.2017.1324760.

Anthias, Floya, and Nira Yuval-Davis. 1992. *Racialized Boundaries: Race, Nation, Gender, Colour and Class and the Anti-Racist Struggle*. London: Routledge.

Antonsich, Marco. 2010. "Searching for Belonging – An Analytical Framework: Searching for Belonging." *Geography Compass* 4 (6): 644–59. https://doi.org/10.1111/j.1749-8198.2009.00317.x.

Arar, Khalid, Deniz Örücü, and Duncan Waite. 2020. "Understanding Leadership for Refugee Education: Introduction to the Special Issue." *International Journal of Leadership in Education* 23 (1): 1–6. https://doi.org/10.1080/13603124.2019.1690958.

Arar, Rawan, and David Scott FitzGerald. 2022. *The Refugee System: A Sociological Approach*. Medford: Polity Books.

Arat-Koc, Sedef. 1997. "From 'Mothers of the Nation' to Migrant Workers." In *Not One of the Family*, edited by Abigail Bakan and Daiva Stasiulis, 53–80. Toronto: University of Toronto Press. https://doi.org/10.3138/9781442677944-005.

– 2021. "Decolonizing Refugee Studies, Standing up for Indigenous Justice: Challenges and Possibilities of a Politics of Place." *Studies in Social Justice* 14 (2): 371–90. https://doi.org/10.26522/ssj.v14i2.2271.

Arbel, Efrat. 2013. "The Culture of Rights Protection in Canadian Refugee Law: Examining the Domestic Violence Cases." *McGill Law Journal* 58 (3): 729–71. https://doi.org/10.7202/1018394ar.

– 2015. "Between Protection and Punishment: The Irregular Arrival Regime in Canadian Refugee Law." In *Extreme Punishment*, edited by Keramet Reiter and Alexa Koenig, 197–219. London: Palgrave Macmillan UK. https://doi.org/10.1057/9781137441157_11.

Arbel, Efrat, and Alletta Brenner. 2013. "Bordering on Failure: Canada-U.S. Border Policy and the Politics of Refugee Exclusion." Harvard Immigration and Refugee Law Clinical Program, Harvard Law School. https://commons.allard.ubc.ca/fac_pubs/14.

Arboleda, Eduardo, and Ian Hoy. 1993. "The Convention Refugee Definition in the West: Disharmony of Interpretation and Application." *International Journal of Refugee Law* 5 (1): 66–90. https://doi.org/10.1093/ijrl/5.1.66.

Archambault, Josée. 2012. "'*It Can Be Good There Too*': Home and Continuity in Refugee Children's Narratives of Settlement." *Children's Geographies* 10 (1): 35–48. https://doi.org/10.1080/14733285.2011.638177.

Arendt, Hannah. (1951) 1973. *The Origins of Totalitarianism*. New York: Harcourt Brace Jovanovich.

– (1951) 2004. "The Decline of the Nation-State and the End of the Rights of Man." In *The Origins of Totalitarianism*, 341–84. New York: Schocken Books.

– 1994. *The Origins of Totalitarianism*. New edition with added prefaces. New York: Harcourt Brace Jovanovich.

Arsenault, Stéphanie. 2021. "L'accueil des réfugiés pris en charge par l'État dans les régions du Québec." *Canadian Ethnic Studies* 53 (2): 1–21. https://doi.org/10.1353/ces.2021.0008.

Atak, Idil, Zainab Abu Alrob, and Claire Ellis. 2021. "Expanding Refugee Ineligibility: Canada's Response to Secondary Refugee Movements." *Journal of Refugee Studies* 34 (3): 2593–2612. https://doi.org/10.1093/jrs/feaa103.

Atak, Idil, Geoff Gilbert, Alfred Babo, Ruxandra Bujor, Abulogn Okello, and Angharad Laing. 2020. "The Critical Role of Ethics in Forced Migration Research." International Association of Professionals in Humanitarian Assistance and Protection, 10 December 2020. https://phap.org/PHAP/PHAP/Events/OEV2020/OEV201210.aspx.

Atak, Idil, and Graham Hudson. 2022. "Montreal's Sanctuary Policy for Non-Status Migrants: Opportunity and Obstacles." *Refuge: Canada's Journal on Refugees* 38 (2): 1–13. https://doi.org/10.25071/1920-7336.40787.

Atak, Idil, Graham Hudson, and Delphine Nakache. 2017. "'Making Canada's Refugee System Faster and Fairer': Reviewing the Stated Goals and Unintended Consequences of the 2012 Reform." *Canadian Association for Refugee and Forced Migration Studies* 3.

– 2018. "The Securitisation of Canada's Refugee System: Reviewing the Unintended Consequences of the 2012 Reform." *Refugee Survey Quarterly* 37 (1): 1–24. https://doi.org/10.1093/rsq/hdx019.

Atak, Idil, and James C. Simeon, eds. 2018a. *The Criminalization of Migration: Context and Consequences*. Montreal and Kingston: McGill-Queen's University Press.

– 2018b. "The Criminalization of Migration: Context and Consequences." In *The Criminalization of Migration: Context and Consequences*, edited by Idil Atak and James C. Simeon, 3–33. Montreal and Kingston: McGill-Queen's University Press.

Atewologun, Doyin. 2018. "Intersectionality Theory and Practice." In *Oxford Research Encyclopedia of Business and Management*, by Doyin Atewologun. Oxford: Oxford University Press. https://doi.org/10.1093/acrefore/9780190224851.013.48.

Atfield, Gaby, Kavita Brahmbhatt, and Therese O'Toole. 2007. *Refugees' Experiences of Integration.* London: Refugee Council and University of Birmingham. https://www.researchgate.net/publication/273951112.

Awad, Germine H., and Wafa M. Amayreh. 2016. "Discrimination: Heightened Prejudice Post 9/11 and Psychological Outcomes." In *Handbook of Arab American Psychology*, edited by Mona M. Amer and Germine H. Awad. New York: Routledge, Taylor & Francis Group.

Azari, Parisa, and Christina R. Clark-Kazak. 2022. "We Can Do a Better Job of Welcoming Displaced Students and Scholars." *University Affairs*, 31 October 2022. https://www.universityaffairs.ca/opinion/in-my-opinion/we-can-do-a-better-job-of-welcoming-displaced-students-and-scholars.

Azdouz, Rachida, and Adis Simidzija, dirs. 2021. "Immigration: devenir le traducteur de ses parents pendant son enfance." *Du côté de chez Catherine*, Radio-Canada. 21 May 2021. https://ici.radio-canada.ca/ohdio/premiere/emissions/du-cote-de-chez-catherine/segments/entrevue/356878/immigration-traduire-enfants-roles.

Azpiri, Jon. 2021. "BC Flooding: Volunteers Band Together to Deliver Hot Meals to Stranded Truckers in Hope." *Global News*, 8 November 2021. https://globalnews.ca/news/8381744/bc-flooding-hot-meals-deliveries-truckers.

Backhouse, Constance. 2010. *Colour Coded: A Legal History of Racism in Canada; 1900–1950.* Toronto: University of Toronto Press.

Baglay, Sasha, and Martin Jones. 2017. *Refugee Law.* 2nd ed. Essentials of Canadian Law. Toronto: Irwin Law.

Baglay, Sasha, and Delphine Nakache, eds. 2014. *Immigration Regulation in Federal States: Challenges and Responses in Comparative Perspective.* Dordrecht: Springer.

Bahar, Dany. 2018. "Why Accepting Refugees Is a Win-Win-Win Formula." *Brookings*, 19 June 2018. https://www.brookings.edu/articles/refugees-are-a-win-win-win-formula-for-economic-development.

Bahar, Dany, and Meagan Dooley. 2020. "Refugees as Assets Not Burdens: The Role of Policy." Global Economy and Development at Brookings. Brooke Shearer Series, no. 8 (February). https://www.brookings.edu/wp-content/uploads/2020/02/refugees_as_assets_not_burdens_final.pdf.

Bahram, Haqqi. 2020. "On Stateless Activism and True Engagement." Peter McMullin Centre on Statelessness Critical Statelessness Studies Blog Series. September 2020. https://law.unimelb.edu.au/centres/statelessness/resources/critical-statelessness-studies-blog/on-stateless-activism-and-true-engagement.

– 2021. "Towards a Stateless Standpoint Epistemology." *The Statelessness & Citizenship Review* 3 (1): 113–19.

Baiden, Deborah, and Marilyn Evans. 2021. "Black African Newcomer Women's Perception of Postpartum Mental Health Services in Canada." *Canadian Journal of Nursing Research* 53 (3): 202–10. https://doi.org/10.1177/0844562120934273.

Baillie Abidi, Catherine. 2019. *A Canadian Perspective on Refugees and Forced Migration: An A-Z Guide*. Halifax: Nimbus Publishing.

Baird, Kyla, Kyla P. McDonald, and Jennifer Connolly. 2020. "Sex Trafficking of Women and Girls in a Southern Ontario Region: Police File Review Exploring Victim Characteristics, Trafficking Experiences, and the Intersection with Child Welfare." *Canadian Journal of Behavioural Science / Revue Canadienne Des Sciences Du Comportement* 52 (1): 8–17. https://doi.org/10.1037/cbs0000151.

Baird, Theodore, and Ilse van Liempt. 2016. "Scrutinising the Double Disadvantage: Knowledge Production in the Messy Field of Migrant Smuggling." *Journal of Ethnic and Migration Studies* 42 (3): 400–17. https://doi.org/10.1080/1369183X.2015.1103172.

Bajaj, Simar Singh, Lwando Maki, and Fatima Cody Stanford. 2022. "Vaccine Apartheid: Global Cooperation and Equity." *Lancet* 399 (10334): 1452–3. https://doi.org/10.1016/S0140-6736(22)00328-2.

Bakan, Abigail B., and Daiva Stasiulis. 1997. "Foreign Domestic Worker Policy in Canada and the Social Boundaries of Modern Citizenship." In *Not One of the Family*, edited by Abigail Bakan and Daiva Stasiulis. Toronto: University of Toronto Press.

Bakewell, Oliver. 2008. "Research Beyond the Categories: The Importance of Policy Irrelevant Research into Forced Migration." *Journal of Refugee Studies* 21 (4): 432–53. https://doi.org/10.1093/jrs/fen042.

Bakos, Kathryn, Blair Feltmate, Chris Chopik, and Cheryl Evans. 2022. "Treading Water: Impact of Flooding on Canada's Residential Housing Market." University of Waterloo: Intact Centre on Climate Adaptation. https://www.intactcentreclimateadaptation.ca/wp-content/uploads/2022/04/UoW_ICCA_2022_02-Treading-Water_Flooding-and-Housing-Market.pdf.

Balasundaram, Prasanna, Harjas Jhajj, Nikou Salamat, Daryn Tyndale, and Alice Zhao. 2022. "Access Denied: Calling for the Revocation of Canada's Refugee Status Document Requirement for Private Sponsorship." Downtown Legal Services Program, University of Toronto Faculty of Law.

Balasundaram, Rahul. 2021. "From Humanitarianism to Securitization: The Shift in Political and Media Discourse on Tamil Refugees Arriving by Sea in Canada." 2021 Canadian Association for Refugee and Forced Migration Studies Student Essay Contest, University of Ottawa.

Baldassi, Cindy. 2007. "DNA, Discrimination and the Definition of Family Class: *M.A.O. v. Canada (Minister of Citizenship and Immigration)*." *Journal of Law and Social Policy* 21 (2007): 5–30. https://doi.org/10.60082/0829-3929.1011.

Balintec, Vanessa. 2023. "This Teacher Hopes His 2-Year Battle to Get Certified in Ontario Inspires Other Skilled Immigrants." *CBC News*, 26 January 2023. https://www.cbc.ca/news/canada/toronto/oct-internationally-educated-teacher-update-1.6724231.

Ballard, Myrle, dir. 2016. "Flooding Hope: The Lake St. Martin First Nation Story." YouTube video, 20:27. https://www.youtube.com/watch?v=qYQGGOEWOAg.

Ballucci, Dale, and Sam Ghebrai. 2021. "(De)Constructing Credibility: Examining the Power of Childhood in Unaccompanied Refugee Decision-Making." *Journal of Immigrant & Refugee Studies* 21 (3): 1–14. https://doi.org/10.1080/15562948.2021.1975009.

Baluarte, David. 2017. "The Risk of Statelessness: Reasserting a Rule for the Protection of the Right to Nationality." *Yale Human Rights and Development Law Journal* 19, Washington & Lee Legal Studies Paper no. 2018-04.

Banerjee, Kiran. 2010. "Re-Theorizing Human Rights through the Refugee: On the Interrelation between Democracy and Global Justice." *Refuge: Canada's Journal on Refugees* 27 (1): 24–35. https://doi.org/10.25071/1920-7336.34353.

– 2016. "Rethinking Membership: Statelessness, Domination, and the Limits of Contemporary Citizenship." Doctoral thesis, University of Toronto.

Banerjee, Paula, and Ranabir Samaddar. 2019. "Why Critical Forced Migration Studies Has to be Post-Colonial by Nature." In *Forced Migration: Current Issues and Debates*, edited by Alice Bloch and Giorgia Dona, 44–59. London: Routledge.

Banerjee, Rupa. 2022. "Discrimination against Immigrants in the Labour Market." *Routledge Handbook of Immigration and Refugee Studies*, edited by Anna Triandafyllidou. London: Routledge.

Banting, Keith. 2010. "Federalism and Immigrant Integration in Canada." Paper for the conference Immigrant Integration: The Impact of Federalism on Public Policy. Brussels. http://www.forumfed.org/post/Banting%2022-11-10.pdf.

Barbero, Iker. 2012. "Expanding Acts of Citizenship: The Struggles of *Sinpapeles* Migrants." *Social & Legal Studies* 21 (4): 529–47. https://doi.org/10.1177/0964663912455944.

Barker, Marianne. 2021. "Social Integration in Social Isolation: Newcomers' Integration during the COVID-19 Pandemic." *New Horizons in Adult Education and Human Resource Development* 33 (2): 34–45. https://doi.org/10.1002/nha3.20313.

Barnes, Annmarie. 2009. "Displacing Danger: Managing Crime Through Deportation." *Journal of International Migration and Integration / Revue de l'integration et de la migration internationale* 10 (4): 431–45. https://doi.org/10.1007/s12134-009-0107-y.

Barnett, Michael. 2011. "Humanitarianism, Paternalism, and the UNHCR." In *Refugees in International Relations*, edited by Alexander Betts and Gil Loescher. Oxford: Oxford University Press.

Bartlett, Richard. 1977. "The Indian Act of Canada." *Buffalo Law Review* 27 (4): 581.

Bascaramurty, Dakshana. 2016. "For Refugees Living in Canada, a January 1 Birthday Is No Reason to Celebrate." *Globe and Mail*, 29 December 2016.

Bashford, Alison. 2014. "Immigration Restriction: Rethinking Period and Place from Settler Colonies to Postcolonial Nations." *Journal of Global History* 9 (1): 26–48. https://doi.org/10.1017/S174002281300048X.

Bassel, Leah. 2021. "Gender, Naturalisation and Deserving Citizenship." In *The Palgrave Handbook of Gender and Migration*, edited by Claudia Mora and Nicola Piper, 491–504. Cham: Palgrave Macmillan.

Basso, Andrew R., Patrick Ciaschi, and Bree Akesson. 2020. "Cumulative Domicide: The Sayisi Dene and Destruction of Home in Mid-Twentieth Century Canada." *Current Sociology* 68 (5): 651–68. https://doi.org/10.1177/0011392120927763.

Bates-Eamer, Nicole, Oliver Schmidtke, and George Benson. 2021. "Climate Change Displacement Mapping the Issue in British Columbia." Climate Displacement Planning Initiative.

Battiste, Marie. 2002. *Indigenous Knowledge and Pedagogy in First Nations Education: A Literature Review with Recommendations*. Report prepared for the National Working Group on Education, Indian and Northern Affairs Canada. Ottawa. https://www.nipissingu.ca/sites/default/files/2018-06/Indigenous%20Knowledge%20and%20Pedagogy%20.pdf.

Battisti, Michele, Yvonne Giesing, and Nadzeya Laurentsyeva. 2019. "Can Job Search Assistance Improve the Labour Market Integration of Refugees? Evidence from a Field Experiment." *Labour Economics* 61 (December): 101745. https://doi.org/10.1016/j.labeco.2019.07.001.

Bauböck, Rainer. 1994. *Transnational Citizenship: Membership and Rights in International Migration*. Cheltenham: Edward Elgar Publishing.

Bauder, Harald. 2011. "Closing the Immigration–Aboriginal Parallax Gap." *Geoforum* 42 (5): 517–19. https://doi.org/10.1016/j.geoforum.2011.03.007.

– 2017. "Sanctuary Cities: Policies and Practices in International Perspective." *International Migration* 55 (2): 174–87. https://doi.org/10.1111/imig.12308.

Bauder, Harald, and Rebecca Breen. 2023. "Indigenous Perspectives of Immigration Policy in a Settler Country." *Journal of International Migration and Integration* 24 (1): 369–84. https://doi.org/10.1007/s12134-022-00951-4.

Bauman, Zygmunt. 2016. *Strangers at Our Door*. 1st ed. Malden: Polity.

Beatson, Jesse, Jill Hanley, and Alexandra Ricard-Guay. 2017. "The Intersection of Exploitation and Coercion in Cases of Canadian Labour Trafficking." *Journal of Law and Social Policy* 26: 137–58.

Beaudoin, Danielle. 2019. "Des traces de l'esclavage se retrouvent également au Canada." *Radio-Canada*, 23 August 2019. https://ici.radio-canada.ca/nouvelle/1269942/esclavage-canada-noirs-autochtones-histoire.

Béchard, Julie. 2018. "Immigration : l'Accord Canada-Québec." 2011-89-F. Library of Parliament. https://bdp.parl.ca/sites/PublicWebsite/default/fr_CA/ResearchPublications/201189E.

Bedarff, Hildegard, and Cord Jakobeit. 2017. *Climate Change, Migration, and Displacement: The Underestimated Disaster. Greenpeace Germany*. 29 May 2017. https://climate-diplomacy.org/sites/default/files/2020-10/2017-05-29%20 Greenpeace.pdf.

Beedell, Jeff, and Wudassie Tamrat. 2020. "Supreme Court of Canada Case in Depth: *Nevsun Resources Ltd. v. Araya*, 2020 SCC 5." Gowling WLG. 12 March 2020. https://gowlingwlg.com/en/insights-resources/articles/2020/ nevsun-resources-ltd-v-araya-2020-scc-5.

Beer, Mitchell. 2018. *Pieces of Glass: A Mosaic of Solutions: Report of the Forum on Refugees and Chronic Disease*. HealthPartners Canada and UNHCR Canada. https://www.unhcr.ca/wp-content/uploads/2019/01/Chronic-Disease-Report_ EN.pdf.

Beiser, Morton. 1999. *Strangers at the Gate: The "Boat People's" First Ten Years in Canada*. Toronto: University of Toronto Press.

Beiser, Morton, Alasdair M. Goodwill, Patrizia Albanese, Kelly McShane, and Parvathy Kanthasamy. 2015. "Predictors of the Integration of Sri Lankan Tamil Refugees in Canada: Pre-Migration Adversity, Mental Health, Personal Attributes, and Post-Migration Experience." *International Journal of Migration, Health and Social Care* 11 (1): 29–44. https://doi.org/10.1108/ IJMHSC-02-2014-0008.

Bejan, Raluca, Marie Mallet-Garcia, Robert Lipinski, Cindy Do, and Vanessa Wolf Aviles. 2023. "A Tale of Two Contexts: The Ukrainian and Afghan Refugee Crises in Canada and the UK." *The Centre on Migration, Policy and Society (COMPAS)*. https://www.compas.ox.ac.uk/publication/a-tale-of-two-contexts.

Bélanger McMurdo, Anne-Marie. 2016. "Causes and Consequences of Canada's Resettlement of Syrian Refugees." *Forced Migration Review*, no. 52 (May).

Bellamy, Richard. 2008. *Citizenship: A Very Short Introduction*. Very Short Introductions series. Oxford: Oxford University Press.

Bellavance, Joël-Denis. 2022. "Francisation des immigrants: Québec utilise une fraction des fonds venant d'Ottawa." *La Presse*, 2 November 2022. https:// www.lapresse.ca/actualites/politique/2022-11-02/francisation-des-immigrants/ quebec-utilise-une-fraction-des-fonds-venant-d-ottawa.php.

Belshaw, John Douglas. 2016. *Canadian History: Post-Confederation*. Vancouver: BC Open Textbook Collection. https://opentextbc.ca/postconfederation.

Belton, Kristy. A. 2015. "Rooted Displacement: The Paradox of Belonging among Stateless People." *Citizenship Studies* 19 (8): 907–21.

– 2017. *Statelessness in the Caribbean : The Paradox of Belonging in a Postnational World*. Philadelphia: University of Pennsylvania Press.

Benhabib, Seyla. 2005. "Borders, Boundaries, and Citizenship." *Political Science & Politics* 38 (4): 673–7. https://doi.org/10.1017/S1049096505050328.

– 2020. "The End of the 1951 Refugee Convention? Dilemmas of Sovereignty, Territoriality, and Human Rights." *Jus Cogens* 2 (1): 75–100. https://doi. org/10.1007/s42439-020-00022-1.

Benner, Aprile D., and Sandra Graham. 2013. "The Antecedents and Consequences of Racial/Ethnic Discrimination during Adolescence: Does the Source of Discrimination Matter?" *Developmental Psychology* 49 (8): 1602–13. https://doi.org/10.1037/a0030557.

Benslimane, Souheil, and David Moffette. 2019. "The Double Punishment of Criminal Inadmissibility for Immigrants." *Journal of Prisoners on Prisons* 28 (1): 44–65. https://doi.org/10.18192/jpp.v28i1.4351.

Benveniste, Hélène, Michael Oppenheimer, and Marc Fleurbaey. 2022. "Climate Change Increases Resource-Constrained International Immobility." *Nature Climate Change* 12 (7): 634–41. https://doi.org/10.1038/s41558-022-01401-w.

Berkes, Fikret. 2009. "Indigenous Ways of Knowing and the Study of Environmental Change." *Journal of the Royal Society of New Zealand* 39 (4): 151–6. https://doi.org/10.1080/03014220909510568.

Berlant, Lauren Gail. 1997. *The Queen of America Goes to Washington City: Essays on Sex and Citizenship*. Series Q. Durham: Duke University Press.

Berns-McGown, Rima. 2013. "I Am Canadian: Challenging Stereotypes about Young Somali Canadians." Montreal: Institute for Research on Public Policy. https://irpp.org/research-studies/i-am-canadian.

Bernstein, Elizabeth. 2012. "Carceral Politics as Gender Justice? The 'Traffic in Women' and Neoliberal Circuits of Crime, Sex, and Rights." *Theory and Society* 41 (3): 233–59. https://doi.org/10.1007/s11186-012-9165-9.

Berry, David. 2020. "Canadian Multiculturalism Act." Informational. *The Canadian Encyclopedia*. Historica Canada. 25 March 2020. https://www.thecanadianencyclopedia.ca/en/article/canadian-multiculturalism-act.

Berry, John W. 2017. "Theories and Models of Acculturation." In *The Oxford Handbook of Acculturation and Health*, vol. 1, edited by Seth J. Schwartz and Jennifer Unger. New York: Oxford University Press. https://doi.org/10.1093/oxfordhb/9780190215217.013.2.

Berry, Mike, Inaki Garcia-Blanco, and Kerry Moore. 2015. *Press Coverage of the Refugee and Migrant Crisis in the EU: A Content Analysis of Five European Countries: Report Prepared for the United Nations High Commission for Refugees*. Cardiff School of Journalism, Media and Cultural Studies.

Betts, Alexander. 2015. "The Normative Terrain of the Global Refugee Regime." *Ethics & International Affairs* 29 (4): 363–75.

Betts, Alexander, Louise Bloom, Josiah David Kaplan, and Naohiko Omata. 2017. *Refugee Economies: Forced Displacement and Development*. 1st ed. Oxford: Oxford University Press.

Beylier, Pierre-Alexandre. 2022. "L'intégration régionale vue par le prisme de la frontière Canada/États-Unis: l'entre-deux comme un processus remis en question par la politique de sécurisation post 9/11." *Revue électronique d'études sur le monde anglophone* 20 (1) https://doi.org/10.4000/erea.15581.

Bhabha, Jacqueline. 2004. "Demography and Rights: Women, Children and Access to Asylum." *International Journal of Refugee Law* 16 (2): 227–43.

Bhatia, Amar. 2013. "We Are All Here to Stay? Indigeneity, Migration, and 'Decolonizing' the Treaty Right to Be Here." *Windsor Yearbook of Access to Justice*. https://digitalcommons.osgoode.yorku.ca/scholarly_works/2558.

Bhattacharyya, Pallabi, Sally Ogoe, Annette Riziki, and Lori Wilkinson. 2020. "In Search of a 'Home': Comparing the Housing Challenges Experienced by Recently Arrived Yazidi and Syrian Refugees in Canada." *Applied Psycholinguistics* 41 (6): 1415–36. https://doi.org/10.1017/S0142716420000478.

Bhui, Hindpal Singh. 2016. "The Place of 'Race' in Understanding Immigration Control and the Detention of Foreign Nationals." *Criminology & Criminal Justice* 16 (3): 267–85. https://doi.org/10.1177/1748895816646613.

Bhungalia, Lisa. 2018. "Governing Banishment: Settler Colonialism, Territory, and Life in an Economy of Death." In *Handbook on the Geographies of Power*, edited by Mat Coleman and John Agnew, 313–31. Cheltenham: Edward Elgar Publishing. https://doi.org/10.4337/9781785365645.00028.

Bhuyan, Rupaleem, Daphne Jeyapal, Jane Ku, Izumi Sakamoto, and Elena Chou. 2017. "Branding 'Canadian Experience' in Immigration Policy: Nation Building in a Neoliberal Era." *Journal of International Migration and Integration* 18 (1): 47–62. https://doi.org/10.1007/s12134-015-0467-4.

Bhuyan, Rupaleem, and Catherine Schmidt. 2019. *Immigrant Women's Settlement Transitions in an Era of Precarious Migration: Primary Research Report*. CERIS. https://ocasi.org/sites/default/files/iwys-primary-research-womens-final-report.pdf.

Bhuyan, Rupaleem, Adriana Vargas, and Margarita Píntín-Perez. 2016. "Fleeing Domestic Violence from a 'Safe' Country?: Refugee Determination for Mexican Asylum-Seekers in Canada." *Refuge: Canada's Journal on Refugees* 32 (3): 95–107. https://doi.org/10.25071/1920-7336.40373.

Bianchini, Katia. 2020. "Identifying the Stateless in Statelessness Determination Procedures and Immigration Detention in the United Kingdom." *International Journal of Refugee Law* 32 (3): 440–71.

Biggar, Henry Perceval. 1932. "Trois voyages au Canada: Jacques Cartier, 1534 et 1536; S. de Champlain, 1608 et 1611; Fr. Gabriel Sagard, 1624." *The Canadian Historical Review* 13 (4): 204–5.

Bigo, Didier. 2002. "Security and Immigration: Toward a Critique of the Governmentality of Unease." *Alternatives: Global, Local, Political* 27 (1): 63–92. https://doi.org/10.1177/03043754020270S105.

– 2014. "The (In)Securitization Practices of the Three Universes of EU Border Control: Military/Navy – Border Guards/Police – Database Analysts." *Security Dialogue* 45 (3): 209–25. https://doi.org/10.1177/0967010614530459.

Bigo, Didier, and Elspeth Guild. 2010. "The Transformation of European Border Controls." In *Extraterritorial Immigration Control. Legal Challenges*, edited by Bernard Ryan and Valsamis Mitsilegas, 257–79. Leyde: Brill.

Biles, John, and Humera Ibrahim. 2009. "Religion and Public Policy: Immigration, Citizenship, and Multiculturalism – Guess Who's Coming to Dinner?" In *Religion and Ethnicity in Canada*, edited by Paul Bramadat and David Seljak, 154–77. Toronto: University of Toronto Press. http://www.jstor.org/stable/10.3138/9781442686137.13.

Bilge, Sirma. 2012. "Mapping Québécois Sexual Nationalism in Times of 'Crisis of Reasonable Accommodations.'" *Journal of Intercultural Studies* 33 (3): 303–18. https://doi.org/10.1080/07256868.2012.673473.

Bilotta, Neil. 2019. "Navigating Ethical Terrains: Perspectives on 'Research Ethics' in Kakuma Refugee Camp." PhD diss., McGill University. https://escholarship.mcgill.ca/concern/theses/3t945t11k.

– 2020. "Anti-Oppressive Social Work Research: Prioritising Refugee Voices in Kakuma Refugee Camp." *Ethics and Social Welfare* 14 (4): 397–414. https://doi.org/10.1080/17496535.2020.1822425.

– 2021. "A Critical Self-Reflexive Account of a Privileged Researcher in a Complicated Setting: Kakuma Refugee Camp." *Research Ethics Review* 17 (4): 435–47. https://doi.org/10.1177/17470161211037386.

Binette, André. 2022. "Décoloniser le Québec." *Le Devoir*, 15 February 2022. https://www.ledevoir.com/opinion/idees/674508/decoloniser-le-quebec.

Bingham, Thomas Henry. 2011. *The Rule of Law*. London: Penguin Books.

Biorklund, Lynn, and Jennifer Hyndman. 2023. "Refugee Studies Has Always Been Critical." In *Routledge Handbook of Immigration and Refugee Studies*, 2nd edition. Routledge International Handbooks. New York: Routledge.

Bird, Cynthia. 2023. "Déplacements forcés de population." *Atlas des peuples autochtones du Canada*. https://atlasdespeuplesautochtonesducanada.ca/article/deplacements-forces-de-population.

Bisaillon, Laura. 2022. *Screening Out: HIV Testing and the Canadian Immigration Experience*. Vancouver: UBC Press.

Bissoondath, Neil. 1991. *On the Eve of Uncertain Tomorrows*. Toronto: Penguin Books.

Bjorkquist et al. v. Attorney General of Canada. 2023. CV-21-00673419-0000. Ontario Superior Court of Justice.

Black, Debra. 2013. "Immigration Minister Jason Kenney Announces Tighter Regulations for Family Reunification Program." *Toronto Star*, 10 May 2013. https://www.thestar.com/news/canada/2013/05/10/immigration_minister_jason_kenney_announces_tighter_regulations_for_family_reunification_program.html.

Black, Jerome H. 2020. "Visible Minority Candidates and MPs in the 2019 Federal Elections." *Canadian Parliamentary Review* 43, no. 2 (Summer): 17–23.

Black, Jerome H., and Andrew Griffith. 2022. "Do MPs Represent Canada's Diversity?" *Policy Options*, 7 January 2022. https://policyoptions.irpp.org/magazines/january-2022/do-mps-represent-canadas-diversity.

Black, Richard. 2001. "Fifty Years of Refugee Studies: From Theory to Policy." *International Migration Review* 35, no. 1. https://journals.sagepub.com/doi/abs/10.1111/j.1747-7379.2001.tb00004.x.

Black, Richard, and Khalid Koser. 1999. "The End of the Refugee Cycle." In *The End of the Refugee Cycle? Refugee Repatriation and Reconstruction*, 2–17. Brooklyn, NY: Berghahn Books. https://www.jstor.org/stable/j.ctt9qcp3z.

Blackburn, Carole. 2009. "Differentiating Indigenous Citizenship: Seeking Multiplicity in Rights, Identity, and Sovereignty in Canada." *American Ethnologist* 36 (1): 66–78. https://doi.org/10.1111/j.1548-1425.2008.01103.x.

Blain, Marie-Jeanne, Lourdes Rodriguez del Barrio, Roxane Caron, Marie-Claire Rufagari, Myriam Richard, Yannick Boucher, and Caroline Lester. 2019. "Expériences de parrainage collectif de personnes réfugiées au Québec: perspectives de parrains et de personnes réfugiées de la Syrie." *Lien Social et Politiques* 83: 204–29. https://doi.org/10.7202/1066091ar.

Blitz, Brad K., and Maureen Lynch. 2011. *Statelessness and Citizenship: A Comparative Study on the Benefits of Nationality*. Cheltenham: Edward Elgar Publishing.

Bloom, Tendayi. 2013. "Immigration Detention and Stateless Persons. Policy Report No. 02/03." *Migration, Media and Intercultural Dialogue*. Barcelona: United Nations University Institute on Globalization, Culture and Mobility (UNU-GCM).

Bloom, Tendayi, Katherine Tonkiss, and Phillip Cole, eds. 2017. *Understanding Statelessness*. London: Routledge.

Bond, Jennifer. 2014. "Ottawa Ignores Rule of Law in Refugee Health Cuts Case." *Toronto Star*, 11 November 2014. https://www.thestar.com/opinion/commentary/2014/11/11/ottawa_ignores_rule_of_law_in_refugee_health_cuts_case.html.

– 2017. "Unwanted but Unremovable: Canada's Treatment of 'Criminal' Migrants Who Cannot be Removed." *Refugee Survey Quarterly* 36 (1): 168–86. https://doi.org/10.1093/rsq/hdw024.

Bond, Jennifer, Nathan Benson, and Jared Porter. 2020. "Guilt by Association: Ezokola's Unfinished Business in Canadian Refugee Law." *Refugee Survey Quarterly* 39 (1): 1–25. https://doi.org/10.1093/rsq/hdz019.

Bond, Jennifer, and Ania Kwadrans. 2019. "Resettling Refugees through Community Sponsorship: A Revolutionary Operational Approach Built on Traditional Legal Infrastructure." *Refuge* 35 (2): 86–108. https://doi.org/10.7202/1064822ar.

Bongiorno, Joe. 2022. "The Electronic Shackling of Migrants." *Maisonneuve*, 4 January 2022. http://maisonneuve.org/article/2022/01/4/electronic-shackling-migrants.

Bonisteel, Jacqueline. 2011. "Ministerial Influence at the Canadian Immigration and Refugee Board: The Case for Institutional Bias." *Refuge: Canada's Journal on Refugees* 27 (1): 103–9. https://doi.org/10.25071/1920-7336.34352.

Bonjour, Saskia, and Sébastien Chauvin. 2018. "Social Class, Migration Policy and Migrant Strategies: An Introduction." *International Migration* 56 (4): 5–18. https://doi.org/10.1111/imig.12469.

Bora, Adriana. 2022. "Platforms Supporting Ukrainian Refugees Must Prioritise Their Safety – or Risk Exposing Them to Trafficking and Exploitation." *The Conversation*, 11 April 2022. https://theconversation.com/platforms-supporting-ukrainian-refugees-must-prioritise-their-safety-or-risk-exposing-them-to-trafficking-and-exploitation-180967.

Borrows, John. 2008. *Seven Generations, Seven Teachings: Ending The Indian Act*. Edmonton: National Centre for First Nations Governance.

Bose, Pablo. 2022. "The Shifting Landscape of International Resettlement: Canada, the US and Syrian Refugees." *Geopolitics* 27 (2): 375–401. https://doi.org/10.1080/14650045.2020.1781820.

Bose, Pablo, and Elizabeth Lunstrum. 2014. "Introduction Environmentally Induced Displacement and Forced Migration." *Refuge: Canada's Journal on Refugees* 29 (2): 5–10. https://doi.org/10.25071/1920-7336.38163.

Boski, Pawel. 2008. "Five Meanings of Integration in Acculturation Research." *International Journal of Intercultural Relations* 32 (2): 142–53. https://doi.org/10.1016/j.ijintrel.2008.01.005.

Bosworth, Mary, and Gavin Slade. 2014. "In Search of Recognition: Gender and Staff–Detainee Relations in a British Immigration Removal Centre." *Punishment & Society* 16 (2): 169–86. https://doi.org/10.1177/1462474513517017.

Bouchard, Jean-François, dir. 2004. *L'esclavage au Canada français*. CinéFête, 30 mins.

Boucher, Anna. 2016. *Gender, Migration and the Global Race for Talent*. Manchester: Manchester University Press.

Boucher, Anna Katherine. 2020. "How 'Skill' Definition Affects the Diversity of Skilled Immigration Policies." *Journal of Ethnic and Migration Studies* 46 (12): 2533–50. https://doi.org/10.1080/1369183X.2018.1561063.

Boudreau, Evan. 2016. "For 25 Years, FCJ Refugee Has Been a Place Where Refugees Can Call Home." *Catholic Register*, 10 October 2016. https://www.catholicregister.org/features/call-to-service/item/23294-for-25-years-fcj-refugee-has-been-a-place-refugees-can-call-home.

Bourdieu, Pierre. 1993. *The Field of Cultural Production: Essays on Art and Literature*, edited by Randal Johnson. New York: Columbia University Press.

Bourgeois, Robyn. 2015. "Colonial Exploitation: The Canadian State and the Trafficking of Indigenous Women and Girls in Canada." *UCLA Law Review* 62: 1426–63.

Boutmira, Souhail. 2021. "Older Syrian Refugees' Experiences of Language Barriers in Postmigration and (Re)Settlement Context in Canada." *International Health Trends and Perspectives* 1 (3): 404–17.

Boutros, Magdaline. 2022. "De réfugiés colombiens à entrepreneurs granbyiens." *Le Devoir*, 12 October 2022. https://www.ledevoir.com/societe/763253/immigration-de-refugies-colombiens-a-entrepreneurs-granbyiens.

Boyd, Monica. 1999. "Canadian, Eh? Ethnic Origin Shifts in the Canadian Census." *Canadian Ethnic Studies* 31 (3): 1–19.

– 2006. "Gender Aspects of International Migration to Canada and the United States." International Symposium on International Migration and Development. Turin: United Nations Secretariat. https://imumi.org/attachments/article/112/Migrant_women_in_US_and_Canada.pdf.

Boyd, Monica, and Nathan T.B. Ly. 2021. "Unwanted and Uninvited: Canadian Exceptionalism in Migration and the 2017–2020 Irregular Border Crossings." *American Review of Canadian Studies* 51 (1): 95–121. https://doi.org/10.1080/02722011.2021.1899743.

Boyd, Monica, and Michel Vickers. 2000. "100 Years of Immigration in Canada." *Canadian Social Trends* 58 (2): 2–12.

Boyden, Jo. 2001. "Children's Participation in the Context of Forced Migration." In *Children's Participation: Evaluating Effectiveness*, 52–6. International Institute for Environment and Development. London.

Bradimore, Ashley, and Harald Bauder. 2012. "Mystery Ships and Risky Boat People: Tamil Refugee Migration in the Newsprint Media." *Canadian Journal of Communication* 36 (4): 637–61. https://doi.org/10.22230/cjc.2011v36n4a2466.

Bradley, Megan, and Cate Duin. 2020. "A Port in the Storm: Resettlement and Private Sponsorship in the Broader Context of the Refugee Regime." In *Strangers to Neighbours: Refugee Sponsorship in Context*, edited by Shauna Labman and Geoffrey Cameron. Montreal and Kingston: McGill-Queen's University Press. https://doi.org/10.2307/j.ctv176ktqs.

Bragg, Bronwyn, and Lloyd L. Wong. 2016. "'Cancelled Dreams': Family Reunification and Shifting Canadian Immigration Policy." *Journal of Immigrant & Refugee Studies* 14 (1): 46–65. https://doi.org/10.1080/15562948.2015.1011364.

Braithwaite, Alex, Idean Salehyan, and Burcu Savun. 2019. "Refugees, Forced Migration, and Conflict: Introduction to the Special Issue." *Journal of Peace Research* 56 (1): 5–11. https://doi.org/10.1177/0022343318814128.

Bramadat, Paul. 2014. "Don't Ask, Don't Tell: Refugee Settlement and Religion in British Columbia." *Journal of the American Academy of Religion* 82 (4): 907–37. https://doi.org/10.1093/jaarel/lfu040.

Brayboy, Bryan McKinley Jones. 2005. "Transformational Reistance and Social Justice." *Anthropology & Education Quarterly* 36 (3): 193–211. https://doi.org/10.1525/aeq.2005.36.3.193.

Bréant, Hugo. 2015. "(Im)mobilité internationale: les inégalités au sein des catégories populaires face à la migration." *Lien Social et Politiques* 74 (November): 37–56. https://doi.org/10.7202/1034063ar.

Brend, Yvette. 2020. "Landmark Settlement Is a Message to Canadian Companies Extracting Resources Overseas: Amnesty International." *CBC News*, 23 October 2020. https://www.cbc.ca/news/canada/british-columbia/settlement-amnesty-scc-africa-mine-nevsun-1.5774910.

– 2022. "Indigenous Parents Push for Birth Registries to Allow Their Languages' Special Characters, Accents." *CBC News*, 22 April 2022. https://www.cbc.ca/news/canada/british-columbia/indigenous-names-vital-stats-1.6426239.

Brennan, Deirdre. 2019. "Statelessness and the Feminist Toolbox: Another Man-Made Problem with a Feminist Solution?" *Tilburg Law Review* 24 (2): 170–81.

Brennan, Richard J. 2011. "1,800 Canadians Poised to Lose Citizenship: Kenney." *Toronto Star*, 20 July 2011. https://www.thestar.com/news/canada/2011/07/20/1800_canadians_poised_to_lose_citizenship_kenney.html.

Bridekirk, Jonathan, Michaela Hynie, and SyRIA.lth. 2021. "The Impact of Education and Employment Quality on Self-Rated Mental Health Among Syrian Refugees in Canada." *Journal of Immigrant and Minority Health* 23 (2): 290–7. https://doi.org/10.1007/s10903-020-01108-0.

Brinham, Natalie. 2019. "Looking Beyond Invisibility: Rohingyas' Dangerous Encounters with Papers and Cards." *Tilburg Law Review* 24 (2): 156–69.

Brinham, Natalie, Yuriko Cowper-Smith, and Muang Zarni. 2019. "Rohingya Poets Turn Words into Art of Resistance: New Anthology of Rohingya Poets Reflects Resilience of a Community Driven Away from Their Homeland." Andalou Agency, 7 August 2019. https://www.aa.com.tr/en/asia-pacific/rohingya-poets-turn-words-into-art-of-resistance-/1551737.

Brotman, Shari, Ilyan Ferrer, Sharon Koehn, and Pascual Delgado. 2019. "L'isolement social chez les immigrant-e-s âgés au Canada: une question de droits de la personne." *Ligue des droits et libertés*, 27 September 2019. https://liguedesdroits.ca/lisolement-social-chez-les-immigrant-e-s-ages-au-canada-une-question-de-droits-de-la-personne.

Brotman, Shari, Sharon Koehn, and Ilyan Ferrer. 2017. "Les Expériences de Personnes Âgées Immigrantes Une Étude Narrative – 'photovoix ' 2014–2017." https://www.creges.ca/wp-content/uploads/2020/11/Catalogue-Experiences-des-personnes-aggees-immigrantes-FR.pdf.

Brouwer, Andrew. 2012. "Statelessness in a Canadian Context: A Discussion Paper." United Nations High Commissioner for Refugees.

Brun, Cathrine. 2015. "Active Waiting and Changing Hopes: Toward a Time Perspective on Protracted Displacement." *Social Analysis* 59 (1): 19–37. https://doi.org/10.3167/sa.2015.590102.

Brun, Cathrine, and Anita Fábos. 2015. "Making Homes in Limbo? A Conceptual Framework." *Refuge: Canada's Journal on Refugees* 31 (1): 5–17. https://doi.org/10.25071/1920-7336.40138.

Bryan, Catherine, and Myriam Denov. 2011. "Separated Refugee Children in Canada: The Construction of Risk Identity." *Journal of Immigrant & Refugee Studies* 9 (3): 242–66. https://doi.org/10.1080/15562948.2011.592806.

Budlakoti v. Canada (Citizenship and Immigration). 2015 FCA 139. 2015.

Buller, Marion, Michèle Audette, Brian Eyolfson, and Qajaq Robinson. 2019. *Reclaiming Power and Place: The Final Report of the National Inquiry into Missing and Murdered Indigenous Women and Girls*, vol. 1a. Vancouver: National Inquiry into Missing and Murdered Indigenous Women and Girls.

Bureau, Brigitte. 2023. "Emprisonnement sans limite." *Radio-Canada*, 31 January 2023. https://ici.radio-canada.ca/recit-numerique/5124/immigration-deportation-droit-humain-avocat-refugies-politique-federale.

Bureau of Public Affairs Department of State. 2002. "U.S.-Canada Smart Border/30 Point Action Plan Update." US Department of State. https://2001-2009.state.gov/p/wha/rls/fs/18128.htm.

Bures, Oldrich, Radka Klvanova, and Robert Stojanov. 2020. "Strengths and Weaknesses of Canadian Express Entry System: Experts' Perceptions." *Population and Development Review* 46 (4): 787–812. https://doi.org/10.1111/padr.12354.

Burns, Philippe, and Eran Shor. 2021. "Racial Stereotyping of Indigenous People in the Canadian Media: A Comparative Analysis of Two Water Pollution Incidents." *Canadian Review of Sociology* 58 (2): 207–28. https://doi.org/10.1111/cars.12335.

Busari, Stephanie, Princewell Nimi, Shama Nasinde, and Mohanned Tawfeeq. 2022. "Foreign Students Fleeing Ukraine Say They Face Segregation, Racism at Border." CNN, 4 March 2022. https://www.cnn.com/2022/02/28/europe/students-allege-racism-ukraine-cmd-intl/index.html.

Busey, Christopher L., and Tianna Dowie-Chin. 2021. "The Making of Global Black Anti-Citizen/Citizenship: Situating BlackCrit in Global Citizenship Research and Theory." *Theory & Research in Social Education* 49 (2): 153–75. https://doi.org/10.1080/00933104.2020.1869632.

Butler, Judith. 1999. "From Interiority to Gender Performatives." In *Camp: Queer Aesthetics and the Performing Subject: A Reader*, edited by Fabio Cleto, 361–8. Ann Arbor: University of Michigan Press.

– 2000. "Ethical Ambivalence." In *The Turn to Ethics*, edited by Marjorie Garber, Beatrice Hanssen, and Rebecca L. Walkowitz. CultureWork: A Book Series from the Center for Literacy and Cultural Studies at Harvard. New York: Routledge. https://doi.org/10.4324/9780203700440.

Cabrera, Erla. 2017. "A Syrian Family Finds Acceptance for Their Disabled Children through Canadian Resettlement." UNHCR Canada, 24 April 2017. https://www.unhcr.ca/news/syrian-family-canadian-resettlement.

Cain, Patrick. 2016. "Inquest into Abdurahman Hassan's Mysterious Death May Wait until 2018, Coroner Says." *Global News*, 16 July 2016. https://globalnews.ca/news/2831115/inquest-into-abdurahman-hassans-mysterious-death-may-wait-until-2018-coroner-says.

Caldararu, Alexandru, Julie Clements, Rennais Gayle, Christina Hamer, and Maria MacMinn Varvos. 2021. *Canadian Settlement in Action: History and Future*. Edmonton: Norquest College.

Calder et al. v. Attorney-General of British Columbia. 1973, SCR 313.

Calliste, Agnes. 1994. "Race, Gender and Canadian Immigration Policy: Blacks from the Caribbean, 1900–1932." *Journal of Canadian Studies* 28 (4): 131–48. https://doi.org/10.3138/jcs.28.4.131.

Cameron, Emilie. 2015. *Far off Metal River: Inuit Lands, Settler Stories, and the Makings of the Contemporary Arctic*. Vancouver: UBC Press.

Cameron, Geoffrey. 2013. "A Quiet Exodus: Welcoming Bahá'í Refugees from Iran Was a Humanitarian Landmark – and an Enduring Immigration Lesson." *Literary Review of Canada* (July/August).

– 2018. "The Bahá'í Community and Public Policy: The Bahá'í Refugee Resettlement Program (1981–1989)." In *Religion and Public Discourse in an Age of Transition: Reflections on Bahá'í Practice and Thought*, edited by Geoffrey Cameron and Benjamin Schewel, 255–79. Bahá'í Studies Series. Waterloo: Wilfrid Laurier University Press and Association for Bahá'í Studies.

– 2021. *Send Them Here: Religion, Politics, and Refugee Resettlement in North America*. McGill-Queen's Refugee and Forced Migration Studies 4. Montreal and Kingston: McGill-Queen's University Press.

Cameron, Hilary E. 2020. "Les défaillances d'un système 'modèle' : La DSR au Canada." *Revue Migrations Forcées* 65. https://www.fmreview.org/recognising-refugees/evanscameron.

Campana, Paolo. 2020. "Human Smuggling: Structure and Mechanisms." *Crime and Justice* 49 (July): 471–519. https://doi.org/10.1086/708663.

Camus-Jacques, Geneviève. 1990. "Refugee Women: The Forgotten Majority." In *Refugees and International Relations*, edited by Gil Loescher and Laila Monaham. Oxford: Clarendon Press.

Canada (Attorney General) v. Ward. 1993, 2 SCR 689.

Canada Border Services Agency (CBSA). 2018. "Minister Goodale Announces Roll-out of Expanded Alternatives to Detention Program through the National Immigration Detention Framework," news release, 24 July 2018. https://www.canada.ca/en/border-services-agency/news/2018/07/minister-goodale-announces-roll-out-of-expanded-alternatives-to-detention-program-through-the-national-immigration-detention-framework.html.

Canada Border Services Agency Act. SC 2005, c. 38.

Canada (Minister of Citizenship and Immigration) v. Vavilov. 2019, SCC 65.

Canada (Public Safety and Emergency Preparedness) v. Chhina. 2019, SCC 29.

Canadian Association for Refugee and Forced Migration Studies (CARFMS). 2020. "About Us. https://carfms.org/about-us.

Canadian Centre for Housing Rights. 2022. *"Sorry, It's Rented." Measuring Discrimination against Newcomers in Toronto's Rental Housing Market*. https://housingrightscanada.com/wp-content/uploads/2022/11/CCHR-Sorry-its-rented-Discrimination-Audit-2022.pdf.

Canadian Centre on Statelessness (CCS). 2020. "Canadian Centre on Statelessness (CCS)." www.statelessness.ca.

Canadian Centre on Statelessness (CCS), and Canadian Citizen Rights Council (CCRC). 2020. "Civil Society Submission on Nationality and Identity under the United Nations Convention on the Rights of the Child." 87th Pre-sessional Working Group, 28 September 2020 to 2 October 2020. http://www.statelessness.ca/uploads/3/1/9/0/31903945/submission_to_87th_crc_committee_-_ccs_and_ccrc.pdf.

Canadian Centre to End Human Trafficking. 2019. Human Trafficking Trends in Canada 2019–2020. https://www.canadiancentretoendhumantrafficking.ca/wp-content/uploads/2021/10/ENG-Human-Trafficking-Trends-in-Canada%E2%80%93-2019-20-Report-Final-1.pdf.

Canadian Council for Refugees (CCR). 1998. "Best Settlement Practices: Settlement Services for Refugees and Immigrants in Canada." https://ccrweb.ca/sites/ccrweb.ca/files/static-files/bpfina1.htm.

– 2000. "Unaccompanied Minors." https://ccrweb.ca/en/res/unaccompanied-minors.

– 2005. Closing the Front Door on Refugees: Report on the First Year of the Safe Third Country Agreement. https://ccrweb.ca/en/closing-front-door-refugees-report-first-year-safe-third-country-agreement.

– 2012. "Comments on Notice of Intent – Changes to the Private Sponsorship of Refugees Program." https://ccrweb.ca/sites/ccrweb.ca/files/g5_comments_jan2012.pdf.

– 2015. "Seven Keys to Protecting and Welcoming Refugees and Newcomers: A Vision for Canada." https://ccrweb.ca/sites/ccrweb.ca/files/protection_welcome_vision.pdf.

– 2016a. "Call for a Resettlement Plan Reflecting Equity for All Regions." https://ccrweb.ca/en/call-resettlement-plan-reflecting-equity-all-regions.

– 2016b. "CCR Concerns: Violence against Women. Submission to the House Standing Committee on the Status of Women for Their Study on Violence Against Young Women and Girls in Canada." https://ccrweb.ca/en/ccr-concerns-violence-against-women.

– 2016c. "Indigenous Peoples." https://ccrweb.ca/en/resolutions-subject/indigenous-peoples.

– 2016d. "Renewing Canada's Private Sponsorship of Refugees Program." https://ccrweb.ca/sites/ccrweb.ca/files/g5_comments_jan2012.pdf.

– 2019. "Canadian Companies Must be Held Accountable for Contributing to Forced Displacement." https://www.ccrweb.ca/en/media/canadian-companies-accountability-forced-displacement.

– 2022. "About the Canadian Council for Refugees (CCR)." https://ccrweb.ca/en/about-ccr.

– n.d. "Brief History of Canada's Responses to Refugees." https://ccrweb.ca/sites/ccrweb.ca/files/static-files/canadarefugeeshistory5.htm.

Canadian Council for Refugees v. Canada (Citizenship and Immigration). 2023, Federal Court of Appeal, Decisions 72.

The Canadian Council for Refugees et al. v. Minister for Immigration and Minister for Public Safety. 2020 FC 770.

Canadian Council of Churches (CCC). 2021. "Supreme Court Decision to Hear Safe Third Country Agreement Appeal Is a Promising Step for Refugee Rights." 16 December 2021. https://www.councilofchurches.ca/news/supreme-court-decision-to-hear-safe-third-country-agreement-appeal-is-a-promising-step-for-refugee-rights.

Canadian Doctors for Refugee Care v. Canada (AG). 2014 FC 651.

Canadian Information Centre for International Credentials (CICIC). 2022. "Obtain an Academic Credential Assessment for General Purposes." https://www.cicic.ca/1374/obtain_an_academic_credential_assessment_for_general_purposes.canada.

Canadian Institute for Health Information. 2023. "Taking the Pulse: A Snapshot of Canadian Health Care." 2 August 2023. https://www.cihi.ca/en/taking-the-pulse-a-snapshot-of-canadian-health-care-2023.

Canadian Institutes of Health Research, Natural Sciences and Engineering Research Council of Canada, and Social Sciences and Humanities Research Council (CIHR, NSERC, and SSHRC). 2018. *Tri-Council Policy Statement: Ethical Conduct for Research Involving Humans* (TCPS 2). https://ethics.gc.ca/eng/policy-politique_tcps2-eptc2_2018.html.

Canadian Museum of Human Rights. 2022. "A Universal Commitment." https://humanrights.ca/story/universal-commitment.

Canadian Press. 1987. "Canada Won't Deport Salvadorans." *Windsor Star*, 30 January 1987.

– 2018. "Lifespan of Indigenous People 15 Years Shorter than that of Other Canadians, Federal Documents Say." *CBC News*, 23 January 2018. https://www.cbc.ca/news/health/indigenous-people-live-15-years-less-philpott-briefing-1.4500307.

– 2022. "BC Wildfire near Okanagan Grows, More than 500 Properties under Evacuation Order." *Globe and Mail*, 6 August 2022. https://www.theglobeandmail.com/canada/article-bc-wildfire-near-okanagan-grows-more-than-500-properties-under.

Canadian Refugee Sponsorship Agreement Holders Association. 2022. "About." http://sah.turnbull.co/about.

Canas, Tania. 2015. "10 Things You Need to Consider if You Are an Artist – Not of the Refugee and Asylum Seeker Community – Looking to Work with Our Community." RISE. Refugees, Survivors and Ex-Detainees. https://aktiontanz.de/wp-content/uploads/2017/03/RISE-statement-on-working-with-the-refugee-community.pdf.

Canniff, William. 1869. The History of the Settlement of Upper Canada: With Special Reference to the Bay Quinte. Toronto: Dudley & Burns.

– 1872. History of the Province of Ontario (Upper Canada) Containing … the

American Revolution, the Settlement of the Country by UE Loyalists. Toronto: Hovey.
Cantor, David James. 2016. "Defining Refugees: Persecution, Surrogacy and the Human Rights Paradigm." In Human Rights and the Refugee Definition: Comparative Legal Practice and Theory, edited by Bruce Burson and David James Cantor, 349–95. International Refugee Law Series, vol. 5. Leiden and Boston: Brill Nijhoff.
Capurri, Valentina. 2020. Not Good Enough for Canada: Canadian Public Discourse around Issues of Inadmissibility for Potential Immigrants with Diseases and/or Disabilities, 1902–2002. Toronto: University of Toronto Press.
Carastathis, Anna, Natalie Kouri-Towe, Gada Mahrouse, and Leila Whitley. 2018. "Introduction | Refuge: Canada's Journal on Refugees." *Refuge: Canada's Journal on Refugees* 34 (1): 3–15.
Carastathis, Anna, Aila Spathopoulou, and Myrto Tsilimpounidi. 2018. "Crisis, What Crisis? Immigrants, Refugees, and Invisible Struggles." *Refuge: Canada's Journal on Refugees* 34 (1): 29–38.
Cardinali, Paola, Joseph R. Ferrari, Vittoria Romoli, Andrew Camilleri, and Laura Migliorini. 2022. "The Meaning of Home in Male Migration: Listening to Men's Experiences." *Journal of International Migration and Integration* 23: 2219–33. https://doi.org/10.1007/s12134-022-00934-5.
Carens, Joseph H. 1991. "Refugees and States: A Normative Analysis." In *Canadian and American Refugee Policy*, edited by Howard Adelman, 18–29. Toronto: York Lanes Press.
– 1997. "The Philosopher and the Policymaker: Two Perspectives on the Ethics of Immigration with Special Attention to the Problem of Restricting Asylum." In *Immigration Admissions: The Search for Workable Policies in Germany and the United States*, 1st ed., vol. 3, edited by Kay Hailbronner, David A. Martin, and Hiroshi Motomura, 3–50. Brooklyn, NY: Berghahn Books. https://doi.org/10.2307/j.ctv287sdvw.
– 2013. *The Ethics of Immigration*. New York: Oxford University Press.
Carlaw, John. 2019. *Syria Response and Refugee Initiative (SRRI): Final Report*. York University. https://crs.info.yorku.ca/files/2021/09/Public-Sept-2021-Syria-Response-and-Refugee-Initiative-SRRI-Project-End-Report.pdf.
Carleton, Guy. 1783. "Book of Negroes." RG 1, NSARM. Nova Scotia Archives.
Caron, Roxane, Edward Ou Jin Lee, and Annie Pullen Sansfaçon. 2020. "Transformative Disruptions and Collective Knowledge Building: Social Work Professors Building Anti-Oppressive Ethical Frameworks for Research, Teaching, Practice and Activism." *Ethics and Social Welfare* 14 (3): 298–314. https://doi.org/10.1080/17496535.2020.1749690.
Carter, Thomas S., and John Osborne. 2009. "Housing and Neighbourhood Challenges of Refugee Resettlement in Declining Inner City Neighbourhoods: A Winnipeg Case Study." *Journal of Immigrant & Refugee Studies* 7 (3): 308–27. https://doi.org/10.1080/15562940903150097.

Carter, Thomas S., Chesya Polevychok, and John Osborne. 2009. "The Role of Housing and Neighbourhood in the Re-Settlement Process: A Case Study of Refugee Households in Winnipeg: The Role of Housing and Neighbourhood in the Re-Settlement Process." *The Canadian Geographer* 53 (3): 305–22. https://doi.org/10.1111/j.1541-0064.2009.00265.x.

Carver, Peter J. 2015. "A Failed Discourse of Distrust Amid Significant Procedural Change: The Harper Government's Legacy in Immigration and Refugee Law." *Review of Constitutional Studies* 21 (2): 209–34.

Cashore, Harvey, Joseph Loiero, Lynette Fortune, and Alex Shprintsen, dirs. 2021. "Come Hell ... BC under Water." *The Fifth Estate*. YouTube video, 43:43. https://www.youtube.com/watch?v=o6ktS3Ex4TU.

Cassidy, Kathryn. 2019. "Where Can I Get Free? Everyday Bordering, Everyday Incarceration." *Transactions of the Institute of British Geographers* 44 (1): 48–62. https://doi.org/10.1111/tran.12273.

Castañeda, Heide. 2013. "Medical Aid as Protest: Acts of Citizenship for Unauthorized Im/migrants and Refugees." *Citizenship Studies* 17 (2): 227–40. https://doi.org/10.1080/13621025.2013.780744.

Castles, Stephen. 2005. "Nation and Empire: Hierarchies of Citizenship in the New Global Order." *International Politics* 42 (2): 203–24.

Castles, Stephen, Ellie Vasta, and Steven Vertovec. 2002. "Integration: Mapping the Field." *Home Office Online Report* 29 (3): 115–18.

Caulford, Paul, and Jennifer D'Andrade. 2012. "Soins de santé pour les immigrants et ses réfugiés sans assurance médicale au Canada: à qui le problème revient-il?" *Canadian Family Physician* 58 (7): 362–4.

CBC News. 2012. "3,100 Citizenships Ordered Revoked for Immigration Fraud." 10 September 2012. https://www.cbc.ca/news/politics/3-100-citizenships-ordered-revoked-for-immigration-fraud-1.1152606.

– dir. 2016. "Nevsun in Eritrea : Dealing With a Dictator." *The Fifth Estate*. YouTube video, 41:03. https://www.youtube.com/watch?v=h61Zfm5uybo.

– dir. 2019. "Shelter Aims to Help Growing Number of Refugees Arriving as Unaccompanied Minors." CBC video, 4:10. https://www.cbc.ca/player/play/1423113795652.

– 2022a. "Peguis Evacuees Fleeing Fisher River Flood Speak of Devastating Loss." 3 May 2022. https://www.cbc.ca/news/canada/manitoba/manitoba-flood-peguis-evacuees-1.6438980.

– 2022b. "Refugees in Quebec Will Have to Learn French within 6 Months." 18 February 2022. https://www.cbc.ca/news/canada/montreal/bill-96-quebec-refugees-french-1.6355756.

– 2022c. "'We Want to Build Canada': Refugees with Startup Ideas Pitch Investors at Toronto Event." 21 June 2022. https://www.cbc.ca/news/canada/toronto/reinvest-angel-investors-ontario-refugee-startups-1.6495514.

CBSA. 2014. "Data Re: Designated Foreign Nationals." Released under the Access to Information Act, RSC 1985, c. A-1.

Cecco, Leyland. 2021. "Canada Floods: 18,000 People Still Stranded in 'Terrible, Terrible Disaster.'" *Guardian*, 18 November 2021. https://www.theguardian.com/world/2021/nov/18/residents-brace-for-torrential-rains-in-already-flooded-western-canada.

Chacon, Jennifer. 2010. "Tensions and Trade-Offs: Protecting Trafficking Victims in the Era of Immigration Enforcement." *University of Pennsylvania Law Review* 158 (6): 1609.

Chadha, Ena. 2008. "'Mentally Defectives' Not Welcome: Mental Disability in Canadian Immigration Law, 1859–1927." *Disability Studies Quarterly* 28 (1). https://doi.org/10.18061/dsq.v28i1.67.

Chapkis, Wendy. 2003. "Trafficking, Migration, and the Law: Protecting Innocents, Punishing Immigrants." *Gender & Society* 17 (6): 923–37. https://doi.org/10.1177/0891243203257477.

Charbenneau Kuntzelman, Cristina, and Anila Noor. 2022. "Beyond Consultation: Creating Meaningful Partnerships through Participation." *Forced Migration Review* 70 (September): 36–9.

Charbonneau, Hubert, Bertrand Desjardins, Denis Hubert, Haines R. Michael, and Richard H. Steckel. 2000. "The Population of the St-Lawrence Valley, 1608–1760." In *A Population History of North America*, 99–142. Cambridge: Cambridge University Press.

Chartrand, Tyler, and Leah F. Vosko. 2021. "Canada's Temporary Foreign Worker and International Mobility Programs: Charting Change and Continuity Among Source Countries." *International Migration* 59 (2): 89–109. https://doi.org/10.1111/imig.12762.

Chatzipanagiotidou, Evropi, and Fiona Murphy. 2022. "Exhibiting Displacement: Refugee Art, Methodological Dubiety and the Responsibility (Not) to Document Loss." In *Documenting Displacement: Questioning Methodological Boundaries in Forced Migration Research*, edited by Katarzyna Grabska and Christina R. Clark-Kazak, 81–103. Montreal and Kingston: McGill-Queen's University Press.

Chaulagain, Rabindra, Wael M. Nasser, and Julie E.E. Young. 2022. "#StayHomeSaveLives: Essentializing Entry and Canada's Biopolitical COVID Borders." *Journal of Borderlands Studies* 37 (4): 723–40. https://doi.org/10.1080/08865655.2021.1985588.

Chen, Y.Y. Brandon. 2021. "Protecting Refugees' Health: How Is the Reinstated Interim Federal Health Program Working?" Ottawa: Pathways to Prosperity.

– 2022. "Citizenship as an Egg?" In *Citizenship as a Challenge: Dimensions of an Evolving Process*, edited by Tamara Nair and Maria Inês Amaro. Leiden: Brill. https://doi.org/10.1163/9789004429253.

Chen, Y.Y. Brandon, Vanessa Gruben, and Jamie Chai Yun Liew. 2018.

"'A Legacy of Confusion': An Exploratory Study of Service Provision under the Reinstated Interim Federal Health Program." *Refuge* 34 (2): 94–102. https://doi.org/10.7202/1055580ar.

Cherem, Max. 2016. "Refugee Rights: Against Expanding the Definition of a 'Refugee' and Unilateral Protection Elsewhere." *Journal of Political Philosophy* 24 (2): 183–205. https://doi.org/10.1111/jopp.12071.

Chicha, Marie-Thérèse. 2009. "Being an Immigrant and a Woman: Two Major Obstacles to Finding Skilled Employment." Text. *Canadian Race Relations Foundation.* 15 September 2009. https://www.crrf-fcrr.ca/en/programs/item/24070-being-an-immigrant-and-a-woman-two-major-obstacles-to-finding-skilled-employment.

Chimni, Bhupinder S. 1998. "The Geopolitics of Refugee Studies: A View from the South." *Journal of Refugee Studies* 11 (4): 350–74. https://doi.org/10.1093/jrs/11.4.350-a.

– 2009. "The Birth of a 'Discipline': From Refugee to Forced Migration Studies." *Journal of Refugee Studies* 22 (1): 11–29. https://doi.org/10.1093/jrs/fen051.

Chiswick, Barry R. 1986. "Is the New Immigration Less Skilled than the Old?" *Journal of Labor Economics* 4 (2): 168–92.

– 2000. "Are Immigrants Favorably Self-Selected?" In *Migration Theory: Talking Across Disciplines*, edited by Caroline Brettell, 61–77. London: Routledge.

– 2005. *The Economics of Immigration: Selected Papers of Barry R. Chiswick.* Cheltenham: Edward Elgar Publishers.

Cho, Lily M. 2018. "Mass Capture against Memory: Chinese Head Tax Certificates and the Making of Noncitizens." *Citizenship Studies* 22 (4): 381–400. https://doi.org/10.1080/13621025.2018.1462505.

Chouliaraki, Lilie, and Rafal Zaborowski. 2017. "Voice and Community in the 2015 Refugee Crisis: A Content Analysis of News Coverage in Eight European Countries." *International Communication Gazette* 79 (6–7): 613–35. https://doi.org/10.1177/1748048517727173.

Christensen, Julia. 2013. "'Our Home, Our Way of Life': Spiritual Homelessness and the Sociocultural Dimensions of Indigenous Homelessness in the Northwest Territories (NWT), Canada." *Social & Cultural Geography* 14 (7): 804–28. https://doi.org/10.1080/14649365.2013.822089.

CIC News. 2010. "Canadian Immigration Minister Proposes Refugee Program Reform." 31 March 2010. https://www.cicnews.com/2010/03/canadian-immigration-minister-proposes-refugee-program-reform-03773.html.

Circles for Reconciliation. 2021. "New Canadians and Indigenous Peoples." *Circles for Reconciliation Gathering Theme.* https://circlesforreconciliation.ca/new-canadians-and-indigenous-peoples.

Cisneros, Josue David. 2014. *The Border Crossed Us: Rhetorics of Borders, Citizenship, and Latina/o Identity.* Rhetoric, Culture, and Social Critique. Tuscaloosa, AL: University of Alabama Press.

CISSA-ACSEI. 2021. "Members." 2021. https://www.cissa-acsei.org/members.

Cissé, Guéladio, Robert McLeman, Helen Adams, Paulina Aldunce, Kathryn Bowen, Diarmid Campbell-Lendrum, Susan Clayton, and et al. 2022. *Health, Wellbeing and the Changing Structure of Communities*. Climate Change 2022: Impacts, Adaptation and Vulnerability. Contribution of Working Group II to the Sixth Assessment Report of the Intergovernmental Panel on Climate Change. Cambridge, UK: Cambridge University Press.

Citizenship and Immigration Canada (CIC). 2004. "Audit of the Control Framework for the Interim Federal Health Program." Government of Canada.

– 2011. "Information Sheet for Interim Federal Health Program Recipients." Government of Canada. https://publications.gc.ca/collections/collection_2012/cic/Ci44-15-2011-eng.pdf.

– 2012. "Backgrounder: Protecting Our Streets and Communities from Criminal and National Security Threats." Government of Canada. https://www.canada.ca/en/immigration-refugees-citizenship/news/archives/backgrounders-2012/protecting-streets-communities-criminal-national-security-threats-1.html.

Clark, Gabrielle E. 2019. "The Business of Mass Migration: Fear, Exploitation, and the Political Economy of Immigration Restriction." *New Labor Forum* 28 (2): 26–34. https://doi.org/10.1177/1095796019838819.

Clark, Nancy. 2018. "Exploring Community Capacity: Karen Refugee Women's Mental Health." *International Journal of Human Rights in Healthcare* 11 (4): 244–56. https://doi.org/10.1108/IJHRH-02-2018-0025.

Clark-Kazak, Christina. 2009a. "The Politics of Protection: Aid, Human Rights Discourse and Power Relations." *Disasters* 34 (3): 55–70.

– 2009b. "Towards a Working Definition and Application of Social Age in International Development Studies." *Journal of Development Studies* 45 (8): 1–18.

– 2011. "Community Politics in Refugee Contexts: Young People, Networks and Decision- Making." In *Children and Armed Conflict: Cross-Disciplinary Investigations*, edited by Daniel Cook and John Wall. Basingstoke: Palgrave Macmillan.

– 2017a. "Ethical Considerations: Research with People in Situations of Forced Migration." *Refuge* 33 (2): 11–17. https://doi.org/10.7202/1043059ar.

– 2017b. "Teaching Forced Migration: Pedagogy in the Context of Global Displacement Crises." *Migration Studies* 5 (2): 286–7. https://doi.org/10.1093/migration/mnw009.

– 2018. "Your Rights in Research." Canadian Association for Refugee and Forced Migration Studies. https://carfms.org/your-rights-in-research.

– 2021. "Ethics in Forced Migration Research: Taking Stock and Potential Ways Forward." *Journal on Migration and Human Security* 9 (3): 125–38. https://doi.org/10.1177/23315024211034401.

– forthcoming. *Age Discrimination in Canadian Immigration Law and Policy*. Vancouver: UBC Press.

Clark-Kazak, Christina R., and Katarzyna (Kasia) Grabska. 2022. "Introduction: Documenting Displacement beyond Methodological and

Ethical Boundaries." In *Documenting Displacement: Questioning Methodological Boundaries in Forced Migration Research*, edited by Katarzyna Grabska and Christina R. Clark-Kazak. Montreal and Kingston: McGill-Queen's University Press.

Clarke, Sarah K., Gayathri S. Kumar, James Sutton, Jacob Atem, Anna Banerji, Mahli Brindamour, Paul Geltman, and Najah Zaaeed. 2021. "Potential Impact of COVID-19 on Recently Resettled Refugee Populations in the United States and Canada: Perspectives of Refugee Healthcare Providers." *Journal of Immigrant and Minority Health* 23 (1): 184–89. https://doi.org/10.1007/s10903-020-01104-4.

Clement, Viviane, Kanta Kumani Rigaud, Jones de Sherbinin, Susana Adamo, Jacob Schewe, Nian Sadiq, and Elham Shabahat. 2021. "Groundswell Part 2 : Acting on Internal Climate Migration." Washington: World Bank. http://hdl.handle.net/10986/36248.

Cleveland, Janet. 2008. "The Guideline on Procedures with Respect to Vulnerable Persons Appearing before the Immigration and Refugee Board of Canada: A Critical Overview." *Refuge: Canada's Journal on Refugees* 25 (2): 119–31. https://doi.org/10.25071/1920-7336.26035.

Cleveland, Janet, and Cécile Rousseau. 2013. "Psychiatric Symptoms Associated with Brief Detention of Adult Asylum Seekers in Canada." *The Canadian Journal of Psychiatry* 58 (7): 409–16. https://doi.org/10.1177/070674371305800706.

Cleveland, Janet, Cécile Rousseau, and Rachel Kronick. 2012. "The Harmful Effects of Detention and Family Separation on Asylum Seekers' Mental Health in the Context of Bill C-31."

Climate Refugees. n.d. "The Problem." https://www.climate-refugees.org/why.

CMHC. 2017. "National Housing Strategy." 2017. https://www.cmhc-schl.gc.ca/en/nhs/guidepage-strategy.

Coderre, Denis. 2017. "La ville de Montréal souhaite la bienvenue aux réfugiés haïtiens. Vous pouvez compter sur notre entière collaboration. Nap kin be fo." X (formerly Twitter). https://twitter.com/DenisCoderre/status/892779940915150851.

Cohen, Elizabeth F. 2013. "Citizenship and the Law of Time in the United States." *Duke Journal of Constitutional Law & Public Policy* 8 (2): 53–79.

Cohen, Tobi. 2012. "Human-Smuggling Operation Result of Unmanned Border Crossing, Opposition Charges." *O Canada News*, 5 December 2012.

Cole, Ester. 2000. "Supporting Refugee and Immigrant Children: Building Bridges Programme of the International Children's Institute in Canada and Overseas." *Refuge: Canada's Journal on Refugees* 18 (6): 41–45. https://doi.org/10.25071/1920-7336.22059.

Cole, Georgia. 2018. "Beyond Labelling: Rethinking the Role and Value of the Refugee 'Label' through Semiotics." *Journal of Refugee Studies* 31 (1): 1–21. https://doi.org/10.1093/jrs/fex021.

Coleman, Daniel. 2012. "Introduction." In *Countering Displacements: The Creativity and Resilience of Indigenous and Refugee-Ed Peoples*, 1st ed., edited by Daniel Coleman, Erin Goheen Glanville, Wafaa Hasan, and Agnes Kramer-Hamstra. Edmonton: University of Alberta Press.

Colic-Peisker, Val. 2006. "Employment Niches for Recent Refugees: Segmented Labour Market in Twenty-First Century Australia." *Journal of Refugee Studies* 19 (2): 203–29. https://doi.org/10.1093/jrs/fej016.

– 2009. "Visibility, Settlement Success and Life Satisfaction in Three Refugee Communities in Australia." *Ethnicities* 9 (2): 175–99. https://doi.org/10.1177/1468796809103459.

Collier, Brittany. 2015. "Emergency Management on First Nations Reserve." 2015-58-E. Library of Parliament.

Collins Dictionary. 2023. https://www.collinsdictionary.com.

Committee on Economic, Social and Cultural Rights (CESCR). 2000. "General Comment No. 14: The Right to the Highest Attainable Standard of Health (Art. 12 of the Covenant)." E/C.12/2000/4.

– 2008. "General Comment No. 19: The Right to Social Security (Art. 9 of the Covenant)." E/C.12/GC/19.

Committee on the Elimination of Discrimination against Women. 2014. "General Recommendation No. 32 on the Gender-Related Dimensions of Refugee Status, Asylum, Nationality and Statelessness of Women." CEDAW/C/GC/32.

Committee on the Rights of the Child. 2017. "General Comment No. 23 (2017) on State Obligations Regarding the Human Rights of Children in the Context of International Migration in Countries of Origin, Transit, Destination and Return." CMW/C/GC/4-CRC/C/GC/23.

Comprehensive Regional Protection and Solutions Framework (MIRPS). n.d. What is the MIRPS? https://mirps-platform.org/en.

Connolly, William E. 1993. *The Terms of Political Discourse*. Princeton: Princeton University Press.

Connor, Phillip Carey. 2014. *Immigrant Faith: Patterns of Immigrant Religion in the United States, Canada, and Western Europe*. New York: New York University Press.

Conroy, Shana, and Danielle Sutton. 2020. "Trafficking in Persons in Canada, 2020."

Conseil Canadien des Réfugiés c. Canada (Citoyenneté et Immigration). 2020 CF 770.

The Constitution Act, 1982, Schedule B to the Canada Act 1982 (UK), c. 11.

Convention on the Rights of Persons with Disabilities (CRPD). 2006. A/RES/61/106.

Convention Relating to the Status of Refugees (Refugee Convention). 1951. 189 UNTS 150.

Convention Relating to the Status of Stateless Persons.1954. 360 UNTS 117.

Coombes, Thomas. 2022. "How Talking about 'Humanity' and Not 'Crisis' Can Aid All Refugees Right Now." *The New Humanitarian*, 29 March 2022. https://www.thenewhumanitarian.org/opinion/2022/03/29/humanity-not-crisis-aid-refugees.

Cooper, Afua. 2007a. "Acts of Resistance: Black Men and Women Engage Slavery in Upper Canada, 1793-1803." *Ontario History* 99 (1): 5–17. https://doi.org/10.7202/1065793ar.

– 2007b. *The Hanging of Angélique: The Untold Story of Canadian Slavery and the Burning of Old Montréal*. Toronto: HarperCollins Canada.

Cortinovis, Roberto, and Andrew Fallone. 2022. *Country Report: Canada. An Analysis of the Private Sponsorship of Refugees (PSR) Program and the Economic Mobility Pathways Pilot (EMPP)*. The Asile Project. https://www.asileproject.eu/wp-content/uploads/2022/05/D4.2_Canada-Interim-Country-Report-1.pdf.

Cossman, Brenda, and Judy Fudge, eds. 2002. *Privatization, Law, and the Challenge to Feminism*. Toronto: University of Toronto Press.

Costello, Cathryn, Michelle Foster, and Jane McAdam. 2021. *The Oxford Handbook of International Refugee Law*. http://dx.doi.org/10.1093/law/9780198848639.001.0001.

Coulthard, Glen Sean. 2014. *Red Skin, White Masks: Rejecting the Colonial Politics of Recognition*. Indigenous Americas. Minneapolis: University of Minnesota Press.

Covering Migration. 2020. "Terminology Matters: From 'Economic Migrants' to Refugees." 15 June 2020. https://coveringmigration.com/learning_pages/terminology-matters-from-economic-migrants-to-refugees.

Cowper-Smith, Yuriko. 2021. "Knowledge-Practices of Collective Self: The Ethos and Political Visions of the Rohingya Social Movement in Canada." In *Living with Uncertainties: The Rohingya in the Place of Migration and Beyond*, edited by Nasir Uddin. Thousand Oaks, CA: SAGE Publications.

Crawford, Tim. 2015. "'You Three Angels Woke up the World': Family of Alan Kurdi Holds Memorial in Vancouver." *Vancouver Sun*, 4 September 2015. https://vancouversun.com/news/metro/memorial-in-vancouver-for-alan-kurdis-family-who-drowned-while-trying-to-flee-syria.

Crawley, Heaven, and Dimitris Skleparis. 2018. "Refugees, Migrants, Neither, Both: Categorical Fetishism and the Politics of Bounding in Europe's 'Migration Crisis.'" *Journal of Ethnic and Migration Studies* 44 (1): 48–64. https://doi.org/10.1080/1369183X.2017.1348224.

Creese, Gillian. 2010. "Erasing English Language Competency: African Migrants in Vancouver, Canada." *Journal of International Migration and Integration* 11 (3): 295–313. https://doi.org/10.1007/s12134-010-0139-3.

Crenshaw, Kimberlé. 1989. "Demarginalizing the Intersection of Race and Sex: A Black Feminist Critique of Antidiscrimination Doctrine, Feminist

Theory and Antiracist Politics." *The University of Chicago Legal Forum* 140: 139–67.

– 1991. "Mapping the Margins: Intersectionality, Identity Politics, and Violence against Women of Color." *Stanford Law Review* 43 (6): 1241. https://doi.org/10.2307/1229039.

Crépeau, François. 2010. "Anti-Terrorism Measures and Refugee Law Challenges in Canada." *Refugee Survey Quarterly* 29 (4): 31–44. https://doi.org/10.1093/rsq/hdq039.

Crépeau, François, and Delphine Nakache. 2006. "Controlling Irregular Migration in Canada - Reconciling Security Concerns with Human Rights Protection." SSRN Scholarly Paper ID 1516626. Rochester: Social Science Research Network. https://papers.ssrn.com/abstract=1516626.

– 2008. "Critical Spaces in the Canadian Refugee Determination System: 1989–2002." *International Journal of Refugee Law* 20 (1): 50–122. https://doi.org/10.1093/ijrl/eeno11.

Crépeau, François, Delphine Nakache, and Idil Atak. 2007. "International Migration: Security Concerns and Human Rights Standards." *Transcultural Psychiatry* 44 (3): 311–37. https://doi.org/10.1177/1363461507081634.

Crisp, Jeff. 2022. "Protected? UNHCR's Organizational Culture and Its Implications for Refugee Advocates and Activists." LERRN: The Local Engagement Refugee Research Network. 29 July 2022. https://carleton.ca/lerrn/2022/unhcr-organizational-culture.

Crittenden, Ann. 1988. *Sanctuary: A Story of American Conscience and the Law in Collision*. 1st ed. New York: Weidenfeld & Nicolson.

Crock, Mary, Laura Smith-Khan, Ron McCallum, and Ben Saul. 2017. *The Legal Protection of Refugees with Disabilities*. Cheltenham: Edward Elgar Publishing. https://doi.org/10.4337/9781786435446.

Cunningham, Hilary. "Sanctuary and Sovereignty: Church and State Along the US-Mexico Border." *Journal of Church and State* 40 (2): 371–86.

D'Addario, Silvia, Dan Hiebert, and Kathy Sherrell. 2007. "Restricted Access: The Role of Social Capital in Mitigating Absolute Homelessness among Immigrants and Refugees in the GVRD." *Refuge* 24 (1): 107–115. https://doi.org/10.25071/1920-7336.21372.

Daley, Angela Hu, Min Hu, and Casey Warman. 2019. "Language Proficiency and Immigrants' Economic Integration." *IZA World of Labor*. https://doi.org/10.15185/izawol.469.

Dandurand, Yvon, and Jessica Jahn. 2020. "The Failing International Legal Framework on Migrant Smuggling and Human Trafficking." In *The Palgrave International Handbook of Human Trafficking*, edited by John Winterdyk and Jackie Jones, 783–800. Cham: Springer International Publishing. https://doi.org/10.1007/978-3-319-63058-8_47.

Daniel, E. Valentine, and John Chr. Knudsen. 1995. "Introduction." In *Mistrusting*

Refugees, edited by E. Valentine Daniel and John Chr. Knudsen, 1–12. Berkeley: University of California Press. https://doi.org/10.1525/9780520341234-003.

Darling, Kate. 2009. "Protection of Stateless Persons in International Asylum and Refugee Law." *International Journal of Refugee Law* 21 (4): 742–67.

Dauvergne, Catherine. 2004. "Sovereignty, Migration and the Rule of Law in Global Times." *Modern Law Review* 67 (4): 588–615. https://doi.org/10.1111/j.1468-2230.2004.00501.x.

– 2007. "Security and Migration Law in the Less Brave New World." *Social & Legal Studies* 16 (4): 533–49. https://doi.org/10.1177/0964663907082734.

– 2008. *Making People Illegal: What Globalization Means for Migration and Law*. 1st ed. Cambridge: Cambridge University Press. https://doi.org/10.1017/CBO9780511810473.

– 2013. "How the Charter Has Failed Non-Citizens in Canada: Reviewing Thirty Years of Supreme Court of Canada Jurisprudence." *McGill Law Journal* 58 (3): 665–728.

– 2016. *The New Politics of Immigration and the End of Settler Societies*. New York: Cambridge University Press.

David, Fiona, Katherin Bryant, and Jacqueline Joudo Larsen. 2019. "Migrants and Their Vulnerability to Human Trafficking, Modern Slavery and Forced Labour." IOM Publications Platform. https://publications.iom.int/fr/books/migrants-and-their-vulnerability-human-trafficking-modern-slavery-and-forced-labour.

Davis, Kathy. 2008. "Intersectionality as Buzzword: A Sociology of Science Perspective on What Makes a Feminist Theory Successful." *Feminist Theory* 9 (1): 67–85. https://doi.org/10.1177/1464700108086364.

Day, Iyko. 2021. "On Immanence and Indeterminacy: Black Feminism and Settler Colonialism." *Environment and Planning D: Society and Space*. Black Feminism and Settler Colonialism Round Table, 39 (1): 3–8. https://doi.org/10.1177/0263775821990955.

De Genova, Nicholas. 2013. "Spectacles of Migrant 'Illegality': The Scene of Exclusion, the Obscene of Inclusion." *Ethnic and Racial Studies* 36 (7): 1180–98. https://doi.org/10.1080/01419870.2013.783710.

– ed. 2017. *The Borders of "Europe": Autonomy of Migration, Tactics of Bordering*. Durham: Duke University Press. https://doi.org/10.2307/j.ctv11smr05.

de Graauw, Els, and Floris Vermeulen. 2016. "Cities and the Politics of Immigrant Integration: A Comparison of Berlin, Amsterdam, New York City, and San Francisco." *Journal of Ethnic and Migration Studies* 42 (6): 989–1012. https://doi.org/10.1080/1369183X.2015.1126089.

De Guzman v. Canada (Minister of Citizenship and Immigration). 2005. FCJ, no. 2219.

de Haas, Hein, Stephen Castles, and Mark J. Miller. 2020. *The Age of Migration: International Population Movements in the Modern World*. Bloomsbury Publishing.

Debusmann, Bernd. 2022. "Afghan Interpreters Fear Families 'Forgotten' by Canada." *BBC News*, 30 April 2022. https://www.bbc.com/news/world us-canada-61251228.

"Declaration of the World Conference Against Racism, Racial Discrimination, Xenophobia, and Related Intolerance, (South Africa)." 2001. https://www.un.org/WCAR/durban.pdf.

Delgado Wise, Raúl, and Humberto Marquez. 2007. "Migration and Development in Mexico: Toward a New Analytical Approach." *Journal of Latino/Latin American Studies* 2 (3): 101–19.

Dench, Janet. 1999. "A Hundred Years of Immigration to Canada 1900–1999 : A Chronology Focusing on Refugees and Discrimination." Canadian Council for Refugees.

Denov, Myriam, and Catherine Bryan. 2014. "Social Navigation and the Resettlement Experiences of Separated Children in Canada." *Refuge: Canada's Journal on Refugees* 30 (1): 25–34. https://doi.org/10.25071/1920-7336.38600.

Denton, Thomas. 2011. "Relational Migration and Refugee Policy." Conference Paper 2011 National Metropolis Conference. Vancouver, BC.

Devandas-Aguilar, Catalina. 2019. "End of Mission Statement by the United Nations Special Rapporteur on the Rights of Persons with Disabilities, Ms. Catalina Devandas-Aguilar, on Her Visit to Canada." Office of the United Nations High Commissioner for Human Rights. https://www.ohchr.org/en/statements/2019/04/end-mission-statement-united-nations-special-rapporteur-rights-persons.

DeVoretz, Don, Sergiy Pivnenko, and Morton Beiser. 2004. "The Economic Experiences of Refugees in Canada." IZA Discussion Papers. https://docs.iza.org/dp1088.pdf.

Dew, Angela, Caroline Lenette, Louisa Smith, Katherine Boydell, Helen Bibby, Julia Lappin, Mariano Coello, et al. 2020. "'To the Arabic Community Disability Is Not Normal': Multiple Stakeholder Perceptions of the Understandings of Disability among Iraqi and Syrian People from Refugee Backgrounds." *Journal of Refugee Studies* 111 (December). https://doi.org/10.1093/jrs/feaa111.

Di Nicola, Andrea. 2007. "Researching into Human Trafficking: Issues and Problems." In *Human Trafficking*, edited by Maggy Lee. London: Willian.

Dickson, Stephanie, Sophie Webber, and Tim K. Takaro. 2014. *Preparing BC for Climate Migration.* Climate Justice Project. Canadian Centre for Policy Alternatives. https://policyalternatives.ca/sites/default/files/uploads/publications/BC%20Office/2014/11/ccpa-bc_ClimateMigration_web.pdf.

Diop, Petra Molnar. 2014. "The 'Bogus' Refugee: Roma Asylum Claimants and Discourses of Fraud in Canada's Bill C-31." *Refuge: Canada's Journal on Refugees* 30 (1): 67–80. https://doi.org/10.25071/1920-7336.38604.

Dirks, Gerald E. 1977. *Canada's Refugee Policy: Indifference or Opportunism?* Montreal and Kingston: McGill-Queen's University Press.

– 1984. "A Policy Within a Policy: The Identification and Admission of Refugees to Canada." *Canadian Journal of Political Science* 17 (2): 279–307. https://doi.org/10.1017/S0008423900031292.

– 1995. *Controversy and Complexity: Canadian Immigration Policy during the 1980s*. Montreal and Kingston: McGill-Queen's University Press.

– 2006. "Politique d'immigration au Canada." 7 February 2006. *The Canadian Encyclopedia*. Historica Canada. https://www.thecanadianencyclopedia.ca/frarticle/politique-dimmigration-1.

Disabilities Research Group, Carleton University, and Beth Robertson. 2016. "Envisioning Technologies: Historical Insights into Educational Technologies for People Who Are Blind or Partially Sighted in Canada, 1820–Present." https://doi.org/10.11574/DRG-1000.

Dobrowolsky, Alexandra. 2017. "Bad versus Big Canada: State Imaginaries of Immigration and Citizenship." *Studies in Political Economy* 98 (2): 197–222. https://doi.org/10.1080/07078552.2017.1343001.

Dobson, Stephen, Gabriella Agrusti, and Marta Pinto. 2021. "Supporting the Inclusion of Refugees: Policies, Theories and Actions." *International Journal of Inclusive Education* 25 (1): 1–6. https://doi.org/10.1080/13603116.2019.1678804.

Dominion Lands Act. 1872.

Donà, Giorgia, and Marie Godin. 2022. "Methodological and Ethical Reflections on the Displaces Participatory Photographic Project in the 'Calais Jungle.'" In *Documenting Displacement: Questioning Methodological Boundaries in Forced Migration Research* edited by Katarzyna Grabska and Christina R. Clark-Kazak. Montreal and Kingston: McGill-Queen's University Press.

Donovan, Ken. 2014. "Female Slaves as Sexual Victims in Île Royale." *Acadiensis* 9 (1): 147–56.

Dorais, Louis Jacques. 2007. "Faith, Hope and Identity: Religion and the Vietnamese Refugees." *Refugee Survey Quarterly* 26 (2): 57–68. https://doi.org/10.1093/rsq/hdi0227.

Downe, Pamela. 2021. *Collective Care: Indigenous Motherhood, Family, and HIV/AIDS*. Teaching Culture. Toronto: University of Toronto Press.

Drews, Kevin. 2015. "Lost Canadian, No More: Donovan McGlaughlin Celebrates Hard-Fought Citizenship." *CTV News*, 22 May 2015. https://www.ctvnews.ca/canada/lost-canadian-no-more-donovan-mcglaughlin-celebrates-hard-fought-citizenship-1.2385548.

Drolet, Julie, and Gayatri Moorthi. 2018. "The Settlement Experiences of Syrian Newcomers in Alberta: Social Connections and Interactions." *Canadian Ethnic Studies* 50 (2): 101–20. https://doi.org/10.1353/ces.2018.0017.

Dua, Enakshi. 2007. "Exclusion through Inclusion: Female Asian Migration in the Making of Canada as a White Settler Nation." *Gender, Place & Culture* 14 (4): 445–66. https://doi.org/10.1080/09663690701439751.

Duell-Piening, Philippa. 2018. "Refugee Resettlement and the Convention on the Rights of Persons with Disabilities." *Disability & Society* 33 (5): 661–84. https://doi.org/10.1080/09687599.2018.1444582.

Duncan, John. 2010. "Présentation des excuses pour la réinstallation d'Inuit dans l'Extrême Arctique: Notes d'allocution pour l'honorable John Duncan." Government of Canada. 18 August 2010. https://www.rcaanc-cirnac.gc.ca/fra/1100100016115/1534786491628.

Dunsmuir v. New Brunswick. 2008 SCC 9.

Durisin, Elya M., and Emily van der Meulen. 2021. "Sexualized Nationalism and Federal Human Trafficking Consultations: Shifting Discourses on Sex Trafficking in Canada." *Journal of Human Trafficking* 7 (4): 454–75. https://doi.org/10.1080/23322705.2020.1743604.

Dustmann, Christian, and Francesca Fabbri. 2003. "Language Proficiency and Labour Market Performance of Immigrants in the UK." *The Economic Journal* 113 (489): 695–717. https://doi.org/10.1111/1468-0297.t01-1-00151.

Dyck, Isabel, and Arlene Tigar McLaren. 2004. "Telling It Like It Is? Constructing Accounts of Settlement with Immigrant and Refugee Women in Canada." *Gender, Place & Culture* 11 (4): 513–34. https://doi.org/10.1080/0966369042000307997.

Dyer, Evan. 2016. "Number of Citizenship Revocations for 'Misrepresentation' Soars under Liberals." *CBC News*, 9 October 2016. https://www.cbc.ca/news/politics/citizenship-revocation-trudeau-harper-1.3795733.

Dyment, Olivier. 2021. "Canadian Human Trafficking: Assessing the Government's 2019 National Strategy for Enforcement, Prevention, and Supporting Survivors." Major Research Paper. University of Ottawa. http://ruor.uottawa.ca/handle/10393/42309.

Edge, Sara, K. Bruce Newbold, and Marie McKeary. 2014. "Exploring Socio-Cultural Factors that Mediate, Facilitate, & Constrain the Health and Empowerment of Refugee Youth." *Social Science & Medicine* 117 (September): 34–41. https://doi.org/10.1016/j.socscimed.2014.07.025.

Editors. 2015. "The Normative Terrain of the Global Refugee Regime." *Ethics & International Affairs*. 7 October 2015.

Edmonds, Jennifer, and Antoine Flahault. 2021. "Refugees in Canada during the First Wave of the COVID-19 Pandemic." *International Journal of Environmental Research and Public Health* 18 (3): 947. https://doi.org/10.3390/ijerph18030947.

Edmonton Journal. 1996. "City Firm Saves Feds Millions in Refugee Health Insurance Claims." 18 June 1996.

El-Assal, Kareem. 2016. "2016: A Record-Setting Year for Refugee Resettlement in Canada?" Conference Board of Canada.

El-Hinnawi, Essam. 1985. *Environmental Refugees*. Nairobi, Kenya: United Nations Environment Programme.

El-Lahib, Yahya. 2015. "The Inadmissible 'Other': Discourses of Ableism and

Colonialism in Canadian Immigration." *Journal of Progressive Human Services* 26 (3): 209–28. https://doi.org/10.1080/10428232.2015.1063355.
– 2016. "Troubling Constructions of Canada as a 'Land of Opportunity' for Immigrants: A Critical Disability Lens." *Disability & Society* 31 (6): 758–76. https://doi.org/10.1080/09687599.2016.1200460.

Elbow, Gary. 1992. "The Overground Railroad: Central American Refugee Flows to Canada." In *Geographical Snapshots of North America: Commemorating the 27th Congress of the International Geographical Union and Assembly*, edited by Donald G. Janelle and International Geographical Union. New York: Guilford Press.

Elcioglu, Emine Fidan, and Tahseen Shams. 2023. "Brokering Immigrant Transnationalism: Remittances, Family Reunification, and Private Refugee Sponsorship in Neoliberal Canada." *Current Sociology*. https://doi.org/10.1177/00113921231155652.

Elgersma, Sandra. 2015. "Resettling Refugees: Canada's Humanitarian Commitments." 2015-11-E. Library of Parliament.

Elgersman Lee, Maureen. 1999. *Unyielding Spirits: Black Women and Slavery in Early Canada and Jamaica*. Crosscurrents in African American History, vol. 6. New York: Garland Publishing.

Eliassi, Barzoo. 2021. *Narratives of Statelessness and Political Otherness : Kurdish and Palestinian Experiences*. Cham: Springer.

Ellermann, Antje, and Ben O'Heran. 2021. "Unsettling Migration Studies: Indigeneity and Immigration in Settler Colonial States." In *Research Handbook on the Law and Politics of Migration*, edited by Catherine Dauvergne, 21–34. Research Handbooks in Law and Politics. Cheltenham: Edward Elgar Publishing Limited.

Elshahat, Sarah, and Tina Moffat. 2022. "Mental Health Triggers and Protective Factors Among Arabic-Speaking Immigrants and Refugees in North America: A Scoping Review." *Journal of Immigrant and Minority Health* 24 (2): 489–505. https://doi.org/10.1007/s10903-021-01215-6.

Eltis, David, Stanley L. Engerman, K.R. Bradley, Paul Cartledge, Craig Perry, David Richardson, and Seymour Drescher, eds. 2011. *The Cambridge World History of Slavery*. Cambridge: Cambridge University Press.

Employment and Immigration Canada. 1992. "Private Sponsorship of Refugee Program." *Refuge: Canada's Journal on Refugees* 3 (12): 2-10.

Employment and Social Development Canada. 2018. "Social Isolation of Seniors: A Focus on New Immigrant and Refugee Seniors in Canada." https://www.canada.ca/en/employment-social-development/corporate/seniors/forum/social-isolation-immigrant-refugee.html.

Endicott, Ryan. 2017. "The Economic Integration of Canada's Refugees: Understanding the Issues with Canada's Approach." MA research paper. https://ir.lib.uwo.ca/sociology_masrp/12.

Enns, Thea, Luann Good Gingrich, and Kaylee Perez. 2020. "Religious Heritage, Institutionalized Ethos, and Synergies: The Mennonite Central Committee and Canada's Private Sponsorship of Refugees Program." In *Strangers to Neighbours: Refugee Sponsorship in Context*, edited by Shauna Labman and Geoffrey Cameron, 95–111. Montreal and Kingston: McGill-Queen's University Press. https://doi.org/10.2307/j.ctv176ktqs.

Erauw, Gregg. 2015. "Compatibility of the 1954 Convention: Relating to the Status of Stateless Persons with Canada's Legal Framework and Its International Human Rights Obligations." United Nations High Commission for Refugees.

Espiritu, Yến Lê. 2006. "Toward a Critical Refugee Study: The Vietnamese Refugee Subject in US Scholarship." *Journal of Vietnamese Studies* 1 (1–2): 410–33. https://doi.org/10.1525/vs.2006.1.1-2.410.

– 2014. *Body Counts: The Vietnam War and Militarized Refuge(es)*. Berkeley: University of California Press.

Espiritu, Yến Lê, and Lan Duong. 2018. "Feminist Refugee Epistemology: Reading Displacement in Vietnamese and Syrian Refugee Art." *Signs: Journal of Women in Culture and Society* 43 (3): 587–615. https://doi.org/10.1086/695300.

Espiritu, Yến Lê, Lan Duong, Ma Vang, Victor Bascara, Khatharya Um, Lila Sharif, and Nigel Hatton. 2022. *Departures: An Introduction to Critical Refugee Studies*. 1st ed. Oakland, CA: University of California Press. https://doi.org/10.2307/j.ctv2vr8vfw.

Esses, Victoria M., Stelian Medianu, and Andrea S. Lawson. 2013. "Uncertainty, Threat, and the Role of the Media in Promoting the Dehumanization of Immigrants and Refugees." *Journal of Social Issues* 69 (3): 518–36. https://doi.org/10.1111/josi.12027.

Evans, Brad, and Zygmunt Bauman. 2016. "Opinion: The Refugee Crisis Is Humanity's Crisis." *New York Times*, 2 May 2016. https://www.nytimes.com/2016/05/02/opinion/the-refugee-crisis-is-humanitys-crisis.html.

Everett, Karen Gail. 2019. "Securitization, Borders, and the Canadian North." PhD diss., Trent University. https://digitalcollections.trentu.ca/islandora/object/etd:673.

Facing History & Ourselves. 2017. "'Home' by Warsan Shire." 5 January 2017. https://www.facinghistory.org/resource-library/home-warsan-shire.

Fajth, Veronika, and Laurence Lessard-Phillips. 2022. "Multidimensionality in the Integration of First- and Second-Generation Migrants in Europe: A Conceptual and Empirical Investigation." *International Migration Review* 57 (1), 187–216. https://doi.org/10.1177/01979183221089290.

Falconer, Robert. 2019. "Slamming the Golden Door: Canada-U.S. Migration Policy and Refugee Resettlement." *The School of Public Policy Publications* 12. https://doi.org/10.11575/SPPP.V12I0.69152.

– 2022. "Canadian Immigration Policy and the Russo-Ukrainian War." *The School of Public Policy Publications* 15: 23. http://dx.doi.org/10.11575/sppp.v15i1.75498.

Fargues, Émilien, and Iseult Honohan. 2021. "Revocation of Citizenship: The New Policies of Conditional Membership." EUI Working Papers RSC 2021/23. Robert Schuman Centre for Advanced Studies. European University Institute. https://cadmus.eui.eu/bitstream/handle/1814/70213/RSC%20 2021_23rev.pdf.

Farrell, Amy, Meredith Dank, Matthew Kafafian, Sarah Lockwood, Rebecca Pfeffer, Andrea Hughes, and Kyle Vincent. 2015. "Capturing Human Trafficking Victimization Through Crime Reporting." Document 252520. US National Institute of Justice (NIJ). https://www.ojp.gov/pdffiles1/nij/grants/252520.pdf.

Farrell, Amy, and Stephanie Fahy. 2009. "The Problem of Human Trafficking in the US: Public Frames and Policy Responses." *Journal of Criminal Justice* 37 (6): 617–26. https://doi.org/10.1016/j.jcrimjus.2009.09.010.

Farris, Emily M., and Heather Silber Mohamed. 2018. "Picturing Immigration: How the Media Criminalizes Immigrants." *Politics, Groups, and Identities* 6 (4): 814–24. https://doi.org/10.1080/21565503.2018.1484375.

Farrugia, Ruth. 2009. "Integration at What Cost? Research into What Refugees Have to Say about the Integration Process." *International Journal on Multicultural Societies* 11 (1): 51–74.

Favell, Adrian. 2022. "Immigration, Integration and Citizenship: Elements of a New Political Demography." *Journal of Ethnic and Migration Studies* 48 (1): 3–32. https://doi.org/10.1080/1369183X.2022.2020955.

Fayazi, Mahmood, Isabelle-Anne Bisson, and Eugene Nicholas. 2020. "Barriers to Climate Change Adaptation in Indigenous Communities: A Case Study on the Mohawk Community of Kanesatake, Canada." *International Journal of Disaster Risk Reduction* 49 (October): 101750. https://doi.org/10.1016/j.ijdrr.2020.101750.

FCJ Refugee Centre. 2012. "About Us." 13 December 2012. https://www.fcjrefugeecentre.org/about-us.

– 2020. "Coalition Contact List." https://www.fcjrefugeecentre.org/wp-content/uploads/2020/04/Coalition-Contact-list-2020.pdf.

Febles v. Canada (Citizenship and Immigration). 2014, 3 SCR 431.

Fee, Molly. 2022. "Lives Stalled: The Costs of Waiting for Refugee Resettlement." *Journal of Ethnic and Migration Studies* 48 (11): 2659–77. https://doi.org/10.1080/1369183X.2021.1876554.

Feldman, Stanley, and Marco R. Steenbergen. 2001. "The Humanitarian Foundation of Public Support for Social Welfare." *American Journal of Political Science* 45 (3): 658. https://doi.org/10.2307/2669244.

Ferede, Martha K. 2012. "Structural Factors Associated with Higher Education Access for First-Generation Refugees in Canada: An Agenda for Research."

Refuge: Canada's Journal on Refugees 27 (2): 79–88. https://doi.org/10.25071/1920-7336.34724.

Ferrer, Ana M., Garnett Picot, and William Craig Riddell. 2014. "New Directions in Immigration Policy: Canada's Evolving Approach to the Selection of Economic Immigrants." *International Migration Review* 48 (3): 846–67. https://doi.org/10.1111/imre.12121.

Feyissa, Hailegabriel G. 2020. "'Non-European Imperialism and Europeanisation of Law: Complexities of Legal Codification in Imperial Ethiopia.'" *Creative Commons*, Third World Approaches to International Law Review 1 (1): 152–75.

Fiddian-Qasmiyeh, Elena. 2016. "On the Threshold of Statelessness: Palestinian Narratives of Loss and Erasure." *Ethnic and Racial Studies* 39 (2): 301–21.

Fiddian-Qasmiyeh, Elena, Gil Loescher, Katy Long, and Nando Sigona, eds. 2014. *The Oxford Handbook of Refugee and Forced Migration Studies*. 1st ed. Oxford: Oxford University Press.

Firang, David. 2020. "The Impact of COVID-19 Pandemic on International Students in Canada." *International Social Work* 63 (6): 820–4. https://doi.org/10.1177/0020872820940030.

First Nations and Indigenous Studies. 2009. "Royal Proclamation, 1763." Text and images. Indigenous Foundations, University of British Columbia. 2009. https://indigenousfoundations.arts.ubc.ca/royal_proclamation_1763.

FitzGerald, David Scott. 2020. "Remote Control of Migration: Theorising Territoriality, Shared Coercion, and Deterrence." *Journal of Ethnic and Migration Studies* 46 (1): 4–22. https://doi.org/10.1080/1369183X.2020.1680115.

Flegar, Veronika. 2019. "UNHCR's Shifting Frames in the Social Construction of Disabled Refugees: Two Case Studies on the Organization's Work During the World Refugee Year (1959–1960) and the International Year of Disabled Persons (1981)." *Diplomatica* 1 (2): 157–79. https://doi.org/10.1163/25891774-00102002.

Fleming, Roy F. 1953. "Negro Slaves with the United Empire Loyalists in Upper Canada." *Ontario History* 45: 27–30.

Fobear, Katherine. 2013. "Queer Settlers: Questioning Settler Colonialism in LGBT Asylum Processes in Canada." *Refuge* 30 (1): 47.

Foner, Eric. 2015. *Gateway to Freedom: The Hidden History of the Underground Railroad*. 1st ed. New York: W.W. Norton.

Fong, Anthony, and Zamir Saar. 2022. "Canada Needs to Be as Welcoming to Afghan Refugees as It Is to Ukrainians." *The Conversation*, 25 May 2022. http://theconversation.com/canada-needs-to-be-as-welcoming-to-afghan-refugees-as-it-is-to-ukrainians-182363.

Foot, Richard, and Peggy Ann Osborne. 2017. "Canadiens perdus." *The Canadian Encyclopedia*. Historica Canada. https://www.thecanadianencyclopedia.ca/fr/article/lost-canadians.

Forcese, Craig. 2013. "A Tale of Two Citizenships: Citizenship Revocation for 'Traitors and Terrorists.'" SSRN *Electronic Journal*. https://doi.org/10.2139/ssrn.2434594.

Forrest, James, Garth Lean, and Kevin Dunn. 2016. "Challenging Racism through Schools: Teacher Attitudes to Cultural Diversity and Multicultural Education in Sydney, Australia." *Race Ethnicity and Education* 190 (3): 618–38. https://doi.org/10.1080/13613324.2015.1095170.

Fortier, Craig. 2013. "No One Is Illegal Movements and Anticolonial Struggles from within the Nation-State." In *Producing and Negotiating Non-Citizenship: Precarious Legal Status in Canada*, edited by Luin Goldring and Patricia Landolt, 274–90. Toronto: University of Toronto Press.

Foster, Cecil. 2005. *Where Race Does Not Matter: The New Spirit of Modernity.* Toronto: Penguin Canada.

Foster, Michelle. 2007. "A Human Rights Framework for Interpreting the Refugee Convention." In *International Refugee Law and Socio-Economic Rights: Refuge from Deprivation*, 27–86. Cambridge: Cambridge University Press. http://doi.org/10.1017/CBO9780511493980.002.

Foster, Michelle, and Hélène Lambert. 2019. *International Refugee Law and the Protection of Stateless Persons*. Oxford: Oxford University Press.

Foucault, Michel. 1990. *The History of Sexuality: An Introduction.* New York: Vintage Books.

– 2003. *Society Must Be Defended*, edited by Mauro Bertani and Alessandro Fontana. New York: Picador.

– 2004a. *The Birth of Biopolitics.* New York: Picador.

– 2004b. *Security, Territory, Population.* New York: Picador.

Fourot, Aude-Claire. 2013. *L'intégration des immigrants: cinquante ans d'action publique locale.* Montreal: Presses de l'Université de Montréal.

– 2015. "'Bringing Cities Back In' to Canadian Political Science: Municipal Public Policy and Immigration." *Canadian Journal of Political Science* 48 (2): 413–33. https://doi.org/10.1017/S0008423915000785.

Francis, Jenny, and Daniel Hiebert. 2014. "Shaky Foundations: Refugees in Vancouver's Housing Market: Shaky Foundations." *The Canadian Geographer* 58 (1): 63–78. https://doi.org/10.1111/j.1541-0064.2013.12056.x.

Franz, Barbara. 2003. "Transplanted or Uprooted?: Integration Efforts of Bosnian Refugees Based Upon Gender, Class and Ethnic Differences in New York City and Vienna." *European Journal of Women's Studies* 10 (2): 135–57. https://doi.org/10.1177/1350506803010002002.

Fraser, Nancy, and Linda Gordon. 1994. "Civil Citizenship Against Social Citizenship? On the Ideology of Contract-Versus-Charity." In *The Condition of Citizenship*, edited by Bart van Steenbergen, 90–107. London: SAGE Publications. https://doi.org/10.4135/9781446250600.n8.

Fratzke, Susan, and Hanne Beirens. 2017. "Taking Stock of Refugee Resettlement: Policy Objectives, Practical Tradeoffs, and the Evidence Base." Migration Policy Institute. 22 May 2017. https://www.migrationpolicy.org/

research/taking-stock-refugee-resettlement-policy-objectives-practical-tradeoffs-and-evidence-base.

Frelick, Bill, Ian M. Kysel, and Jennifer Podkul. 2016. "The Impact of Externalization of Migration Controls on the Rights of Asylum Seekers and Other Migrants." *Journal on Migration and Human Security* 4 (4): 31.

Frey, Bruno S., and Friedrich Schneider. 2000. "Informal and Underground Economy." Working Paper no. 0004. Linz: Johannes Kepler University of Linz, Department of Economics.

Freynet, Nathalie, Richard Clément, and John Sylvestre. 2018. "A Qualitative Investigation of the Experience of Accent Stigmatisation among Native and Nonnative French Speakers in Canada." *Journal of Language and Discrimination* 2 (1): 5–31. https://doi.org/10.1558/jld.32226.

Friedberg, Rachel M. 2000. "You Can't Take It with You? Immigrant Assimilation and the Portability of Human Capital." *Journal of Labor Economics* 18 (2): 221–51. https://doi.org/10.1086/209957.

Furniss, Elizabeth. 1999. "Indians, Odysseys and Vast, Empty Lands: The Myth of the Frontier in the Canadian Justice System." *Anthropologica* 41 (2): 195–208.

Fynn Bruey, Veronica. 2021a. "Forced Displacement and Racism: A Global Public Health Concern." In *Displacees and Health: Issues and Challenges*, 1–66. Chennai: Notion Press. https://notionpress.com/read/displacees-and-health-issuesand-challenges.

– 2021b. "Human Trafficking and the Law in Canada." In *Human Trafficking: Global History and Perspectives*, edited by Elisha Jasper Dung. Lanham: Lexington Books.

Gabaccia, Donna R. 2017. "Diaspora Lobbies and the US Government: Convergence and Divergence in *Making Foreign Policy*, by Josh DeWind and Renata Segura (Eds.)." *Refuge: Canada's Journal on Refugees* 33 (1): 109–10. https://doi.org/10.25071/1920-7336.40455.

Gaetz, Stephen. 2020. "Making the Prevention of Homelessness a Priority: The Role of Social Innovation." *The American Journal of Economics and Sociology* 79 (2): 353–81. https://doi.org/10.1111/ajes.12328.

Gagnon, Anita J. 2004. "The Responsiveness of the Canadian Health Care System towards Newcomers." In *Changing Health Care in Canada*, edited by Pierre-Gerlier Forest, Gregory Marchildon, and Tom McIntosh. Toronto: University of Toronto Press. https://doi.org/10.3138/9781442672833-014.

Gagnon, Audrey, and Lindsay Larios. 2021. "The Politicization of Immigration and Integration at the Subnational Level: Electoral Campaigns in Ontario and Quebec." *Canadian Journal of Political Science* 54 (3): 696–716. https://doi.org/10.1017/S0008423921000469.

Galabuzi, Grace-Edward. 2006. *Canada's Economic Apartheid : The Social Exclusion of Racialized Groups in the New Century. Canada's Economic Apartheid : The Social Exclusion of Racialized Groups in the New Century.* Toronto: Canadian Scholars's Press.

Gallagher, Anne. 2002. "Trafficking, Smuggling and Human Rights: Tricks and Treaties." *Forced Migration Review*, no. 12: 25–8.

Gallie, Walter Brice. 1955. "Essentially Contested Concepts." *Proceedings of the Aristotelian Society* 56: 167–98.

– 1956. "IX. – Essentially Contested Concepts." *Proceedings of the Aristotelian Society* 56 (1): 167–98. https://doi.org/10.1093/aristotelian/56.1.167.

Galloway, Gloria. 2018. "Afghan Translators Who Worked for Canadian Armed Forces Forced into Hiding or Stranded in Europe." *Globe and Mail*, 25 July 2018. https://www.theglobeandmail.com/politics/article-afghan-translators-who-worked-for-canadian-armed-forces-forced-into.

Galloway, Matt. 2022. "The Double Standard in How the World Has Embraced Ukrainian Refugees." *The Current*. CBC Radio, 22:56. https://www.cbc.ca/listen/live-radio/1-63-the-current/clip/15902022-the-double-standard-world-embraced-ukrainian-refugees.

Gannagé, Charlene M. 1999. "The Health and Safety Concerns of Immigrant Women Workers in the Toronto Sportswear Industry." *International Journal of Health Services* 29 (2): 409–29. https://doi.org/10.2190/TFB6-7Q7B-E4DK-X6FL.

Garcea, Joseph. 2016. "The Resettlement of Syrian Refugees: The Positions and Roles of the Federation of Canadian Municipalities and Its Members." *Canadian Ethnic Studies* 48 (3): 149–73. https://doi.org/10.1353/ces.2016.0030.

Garcia Hernández, César Cuahtémoc. 2011. "The Perverse Logic of Immigration Detention: Unraveling the Rationality of Imprisoning Immigrants Based on Markers of Race and Class Otherness." *Columbia Journal of Race and Law* (July): 354–64. https://doi.org/10.7916/CJRL.V1I3.2257.

– 2013. "Creating Crimmigration." *Brighman Young University Law Review* 6: 1457–515.

García, María Cristina. 2006. *Seeking Refuge: Central American Migration to Mexico, the United States, and Canada*. Berkeley: University of California Press.

García-Morís, Roberto, Nerea García Bugallo, and Ramón Martínez-Medina. 2021. "Students' Social Representations of Forced Migration as a Relevant Social Problem and Its Curricular Inclusion at the End of Primary School." *Social Sciences* 10 (11): 423. https://doi.org/10.3390/socsci10110423.

Garnier, Adèle. 2016. "Impact des arrangements institutionnels d'admission et d'insertion sur le parcours professionnel des réfugiés." *Les Cahiers du* CRIEC 39: 40–58.

– 2018. "Resettled Refugees and Work in Canada and Quebec: Humanitarianism and the Challenge of Mainstream Socioeconomic Participation." In *Refugee Resettlement: Power, Politics, and Humanitarian Governance*, edited by Adèle Garnier, Liliana Lyra Jubilut, and Kristin Bergtora Sandvik, 118–38. Studies in Forced Migration 38. New York: Berghahn Books.

– 2022. "Jeunes réfugiés et soutien à l'emploi: comparaison internationale en contexte fédéral." *Hommes & Migrations* 1336 (January): 63–9. https://doi.org/10.4000/hommesmigrations.13593.

Garnier, Adèle, and Shauna Labman. 2020. "Why Québec's Refugee Sponsorship Suspension Is so Misguided." *The Conversation*, 22 November 2020. http://theconversation.com/why-quebecs-refugee-sponsorship-suspension-is-so-misguided-149250.

Gaucher, Megan. 2018. *A Family Matter: Citizenship, Conjugal Relationships, and Canadian Immigration Policy*. Vancouver: UBC Press.

Geddes, Andrew. 2005. "Chronicle of a Crisis Foretold: The Politics of Irregular Migration, Human Trafficking and People Smuggling in the UK." *The British Journal of Politics and International Relations* 7 (3): 324–39. https://doi.org/10.1111/j.1467-856X.2005.00192.x.

Gellner, Ernest. 1983. *Nations and Nationalism*. Ithaca: Cornell University Press.

Gemenne, François. 2011. "Why the Numbers Don't Add Up: A Review of Estimates and Predictions of People Displaced by Environmental Changes." *Global Environmental Change* 21 (December): 41–9. https://doi.org/10.1016/j.gloenvcha.2011.09.005.

George, Glynis, Erwin D. Selimos, and Jane Ku. 2017. "Welcoming Initiatives and Immigrant Attachment: The Case of Windsor." *Journal of International Migration and Integration* 18 (1): 29–45. https://doi.org/10.1007/s12134-015-0463-8.

George, M. Anne, and Cherylynn Bassani. 2018. "Influence of Perceived Racial Discrimination on the Health of Immigrant Children in Canada." *Journal of International Migration and Integration* 19 (3): 527–40. https://doi.org/10.1007/s12134-018-0539-3.

George, Usha, Mary Thomson, Ferzana Chaze, and Sepali Guruge. 2015. "Immigrant Mental Health, A Public Health Issue: Looking Back and Moving Forward." *International Journal of Environmental Research and Public Health* 12 (10): 13624–48. https://doi.org/10.3390/ijerph121013624.

Getachew, Abis, Mary Gitahi, Andhira Yousif Kara, and Uwezo Ramazani. 2022. "Refugee-Led Organisations in East Africa: Community Perceptions in Kenya, Uganda, Ethiopia and Tanzania." Refugee-Led Research Series.

Gevity Consulting. 2021. *Planned Retreat Approaches to Support Resilience to Climate Change in Canada*. Natural Resources Canada. https://doi.org/10.4095/328323.

Ghobrial, Adrian. 2022. "Refugee Stabs Herself with Knife in Front of Federal Official amid Desperate Plea for Housing." *CTV News*, 3 November 2022. https://www.ctvnews.ca/politics/refugee-stabs-herself-with-knife-in-front-of-federal-official-amid-desperate-plea-for-housing-1.6138287.

Gibney, Matthew. 2004. *The Ethics and Politics of Asylum: Liberal Democracy and the Response to Refugees*. Cambridge: Cambridge University Press.

– 2011a. "The Rights of Non-Citizens to Membership." In *Statelessness in the European Union: Displaced, Undocumented, Unwanted*, edited by Caroline Sawyer and Brad K. Blitz, 41–68. Cambridge: Cambridge University Press.

– 2011b. "Should Citizenship Be Conditional? Denationalisation and Liberal Principles." Working Paper Series no. 75. Oxford: Refugee Studies Centre, Oxford University. www.rsc.ox.ac.uk/files/files-1/wp75-should-citizenship-be-conditional-2011.pdf.

– 2014. "Political Theory, Ethics, and Forced Migration." In *The Oxford Handbook of Refugee and Forced Migration Studies*, 1st ed., edited by Elena Fiddian-Qasmiyeh, Gil Loescher, Katy Long, and Nando Sigona, 48–59. Oxford: Oxford University Press.

– 2020. "Denationalisation and Discrimination." *Journal of Ethnic and Migration Studies* 46 (12): 2551–68.

Gibson-Graham, J.K. 1996. "Querying Globalization." *Rethinking Marxism* 9 (1): 1–27. https://doi.org/10.1080/08935699608685474.

Giddens, Anthony. 1987. *A Contemporary Critique of Historical Materialism. 2: The Nation-State and Violence / Anthony Giddens*. Berkeley: University of California Press.

Gilbert, Emily. 2019. "Elasticity at the Canada-US Border: Jurisdiction, Rights, Accountability." *Environment and Planning C: Politics and Space* 37 (3): 424–41. https://doi.org/10.1177/2399654418787190.

Gilbert, Lauren. 2019. "A Justice School: Teaching Forced Migration through Experiential Learning." *Intercultural Human Rights Law Review* 14: 129.

Gill, Nick. 2010. "New State-Theoretic Approaches to Asylum and Refugee Geographies." *Progress in Human Geography* 34 (5): 626–45. https://doi.org/10.1177/0309132509354629.

Gillborn, David. 2004. "Ability, Selection and Institutional Racism in Schools." In *Culture and Learning: Access and Opportunity in the Classroom*, edited by Mark Olssen, 279–97. International Perspectives on Curriculum. Greenwich: Information Age Publishing.

Gingrich, Luann Good. 2003. "Theorizing Social Exclusion: Determinants, Mechanisms." In *Emerging Perspectives on Anti-Oppressive Practice*, edited by Wes Shera, 3–24. Toronto: Canadian Scholars' Press.

Gionet, Simon. 2022. "Demander l'asile en plein coeur de la crise du logement." *Le Devoir*, 30 June 2022. https://www.ledevoir.com/societe/728631/montreal-demander-l-asile-en-plein-coeur-de-la-crise-du-logement.

Giroux, Dalie. 2023. *The Eye of the Master: Figures of the Québécois Colonial Imaginary*. Translated by Jennifer Henderson. Montreal and Kingston: McGill-Queen's University Press.

Giugni, Marco, and Maria Grasso, eds. 2021. *Handbook of Citizenship and Migration*. Elgar Handbooks in Migration Series. Northampton: Edward Elgar Publishing.

Glanville, Erin Goheen, dir. 2018. "Listening – Key Words in Refugee Dialogue." Worn Words: Re-narrative Media. 10:12 mins. https://www.eringoheenglanville.com/listening.

– dir. 2020. "Borderstory." Worn Words: Re-narrative Media. 24 mins. https://vimeo.com/427545591.

Global Affairs Canada (GAC). 2015. "Canada's Approach to Advancing Human Rights." Canada's Efforts to Address Global Issues. 16 October 2015. https://www.international.gc.ca/world-monde/issues_development-enjeux_developpement/human_rights-droits_homme/advancing_rights-promouvoir_droits.aspx.

– 2017. "Canada's Response to the Conflict in Syria." Canada's Efforts to Address Global Issues. 29 May 2017. https://www.international.gc.ca/world-monde/issues_development-enjeux_developpement/response_conflict-reponse_conflits/crisis-crises/conflict_syria-syrie.aspx.

Global Campaign on Equal Nationality Rights (GCENR). n.d. "The Problem." https://www.equalnationalityrights.org/?page_id=255333.

Global Refugee Sponsor Initiative. 2020. "Community Sponsorship: A Growing Worldwide Movement." YouTube video, 3:17. https://www.youtube.com/watch?v=OXnixYBse-Y.

Golash-Boza, Tanya. 2016. "A Critical and Comprehensive Sociological Theory of Race and Racism." *Sociology of Race and Ethnicity* 2 (2): 129–41. https://doi.org/10.1177/2332649216632242.

Goldberg, David Theo. 2002. *The Racial State*. Malden: Blackwell Publishers.

Goldmann, Gustave. 1993. "The Aboriginal Population and the Census: 120 Years of Information, 1871–1991." In "XXIInd General Population Conference of the International Union of the Scientific Study of Population, August 24–September 1, 1993," 1–42. Montreal: Statistics Canada. https://publications.gc.ca/collections/collection_2016/statcan/CS91-0045-1993-eng.pdf.

Goldring, Luin, Carolina Berinstein, and Judith K. Bernhard. 2009. "Institutionalizing Precarious Migratory Status in Canada." *Citizenship Studies* 13 (3): 239–65. https://doi.org/10.1080/13621020902850643.

Goldring, Luin, and Patricia Landolt. 2013a. "The Conditionality of Legal Status and Rights: Conceptualizing Precarious Non-Citizenship in Canada." In *Producing and Negotiating Non-Citizenship*, edited by Luin Goldring and Patricia Landolt, 1–28. Toronto: University of Toronto Press. https://doi.org/10.3138/9781442663862-005.

– eds. 2013b. *Producing and Negotiating Non-Citizenship: Precarious Legal Status in Canada*. Toronto: University of Toronto Press.

– 2022. "From Illegalised Migrant toward Permanent Resident: Assembling Precarious Legal Status Trajectories and Differential Inclusion in Canada." *Journal of Ethnic and Migration Studies* 48 (1): 33–52. https://doi.org/10.1080/1369183X.2020.1866978.

Goldstein, Alyosha. 2008. "Where the Nation Takes Place: Proprietary Regimes, Antistatism, and US Settler Colonialism." *South Atlantic Quarterly* 107 (4): 833–61. https://doi.org/10.1215/00382876-2008-019.

Goodman, Simon, and Steve Kirkwood. 2019. "Political and Media Discourses about Integrating Refugees in the UK." *European Journal of Social Psychology* 49 (7): 1456–70. https://doi.org/10.1002/ejsp.2595.

Goodwin-Gill, Guy S. 2008. "The Queen (Al-Rawi and others) v Secretary of State for Foreign and Commonwealth Affairs and another (United Nations High Commissioner for Refugees intervening)." *International Journal of Refugee Law* 20 (4): 675–709.

Gorlick. 2000. "Human Rights and Refugees: Enhancing Protection through International Human Rights Law." *Nordic Journal of International Law* 69 (2): 117–77. https://doi.org/10.1163/15718100020296224.

Gould, Chandre. 2006. "Countering Human Trafficking: Considerations and Constraints: Cheap Lives." *SA Crime Quarterly*, no. 16 (2006): 19–25. https://doi.org/10.10520/EJC47568.

Government of British Columbia. 2014. "International Labour Trafficking." Province of British Columbia.

Government of Canada. 1991. "Canada-Québec Accord Relating to Immigration and Temporary Admission of Aliens." Policies. 5 February 1991. https://www.canada.ca/en/immigration-refugees-citizenship/corporate/mandate/policies-operational-instructions-agreements/agreements/federal-provincial-territorial/quebec/canada-quebec-accord-relating-immigration-temporary-admission-aliens.html.

– 2002. "Federal-Provincial/Territorial Agreements." 28 June 2002. https://www.canada.ca/en/immigration-refugees-citizenship/corporate/mandate/policies-operational-instructions-agreements/agreements/federal-provincial-territorial.html.

– 2008. "Statement of Apology to Former Students of Indian Residential Schools." 3 November 2008. https://www.rcaanc-cirnac.gc.ca/eng/1100100015644/1571589171655.

– 2010. "Specific Claim Settlements Involving Land." 26 May 2010. https://www.rcaanc-cirnac.gc.ca/eng/1100100030342/1539691869154.

– 2012a. "Private Sponsorship of Refugees Program – Sponsorship Agreement Holders." 15 May 2012. https://www.canada.ca/en/immigration-refugees-citizenship/services/refugees/help-outside-canada/private-sponsorship-program/agreement-holders/holders-list.html.

– 2012b. *Who Drives a Taxi in Canada?* 28 May 2012. https://www.canada.ca/en/immigration-refugees-citizenship/corporate/reports-statistics/research/ho-drives-taxi-canada/summary.html.

– 2015a. "Discover Canada: Who We Are." https://www.canada.ca/en/immigration-refugees-citizenship/corporate/publications-manuals/discover-canada/read-online/who-are-canadians.html.

– 2015b. "Evaluation of Canada's Membership in the International Organization for Migration." https://www.canada.ca/en/immigration-refugees-citizenship/corporate/reports-statistics/evaluations/canada-membership-international-organization-migration-2015.html.
– 2016. "Statement of Apology for the Relocation of the Sayisi Dene." 15 August 2016. https://www.rcaanc-cirnac.gc.ca/eng/1471286774906/1542900850824.
– 2017a. "Get Medical Services Before You Leave for Canada." 31 March 2017. https://www.canada.ca/en/immigration-refugees-citizenship/services/refugees/help-outside-canada/health-care.html.
– 2017b. "Humanitarian and Compassionate Assessment Establishment in Canada." 3 February 2017. https://www.canada.ca/en/immigration-refugees-citizenship/corporate/publications-manuals/operational-bulletins-manuals/permanent-residence/humanitarian-compassionate-consideration/processing/assessment-establishment-canada.html.
– 2018. "Check Processing Times." https://www.canada.ca/en/immigration-refugees-citizenship/services/application/check-processing-times.html.
– 2019a. "Apply for Citizenship: Who Can Apply." https://www.canada.ca/en/immigration-refugees-citizenship/services/canadian-citizenship/become-canadian-citizen/eligibility.html.
– 2019b. Budget Implementation Act (Bill C-97). https://www.parl.ca/documentviewer/en/42-1/bill/C-97/royal-assent.
– 2019c. "By the Numbers – 40 Years of Canada's Private Sponsorship of Refugees Program." 9 April 2019. https://www.canada.ca/en/immigration-refugees-citizenship/news/2019/04/by-the-numbers--40-years-of-canadas-private-sponsorship-of-refugees-program.html.
– 2019d. "Guide to the Private Sponsorship of Refugees Program." https://www.canada.ca/en/immigration-refugees-citizenship/corporate/publications-manuals/guide-private-sponsorship-refugees-program.html.
– 2019e. "Resettlement Assistance Program (RAP) Service Provider Handbook."
– 2020a. "COVID-19: Travel, Testing and Borders." 17 December 2020. https://travel.gc.ca/travel-covid.
– 2020b. "Program Delivery Update: Acknowledgements of Claim and Upfront Interim Federal Health Program (IFHP) Coverage." 3 January 2020. https://www.canada.ca/en/immigration-refugees-citizenship/corporate/publications-manuals/operational-bulletins-manuals/updates/2019-acknowledgement-of-claim.html.
– 2020c. "#WelcomeRefugees: Key Figures." 2 December 2020. https://www.canada.ca/en/immigration-refugees-citizenship/services/refugees/welcome-syrian-refugees/key-figures.html.
– 2021a. "2011 Manitoba Flood: Status of Community Rebuilding and Numbers of Displaced Persons." 27 May 2021. https://www.sac-isc.gc.ca/eng/1392046654954/1535122238673.

– 2021b. "Claiming Asylum in Canada – What Happens?" 6 October 2021. https://www.canada.ca/en/immigration-refugees-citizenship/news/2017/03/claiming_asylum_incanadawhathappens.html.
– 2021c. "#WelcomeAfghans: Key Figures." 28 August 2021. https://www.canada.ca/en/immigration-refugees-citizenship/services/refugees/afghanistan/key-figures.html.
– 2022a. "Canada Opens the Comprehensive Regional Protection and Solutions Framework Support Platform Signature Event." News release, 21 May 2022. https://www.canada.ca/en/immigration-refugees-citizenship/news/2022/05/canada-opens-the-comprehensive-regional-protection-and-solutions-framework-support-platform-signature-event.html.
– 2022b. "Canada-Ukraine Authorization for Emergency Travel Measures." 17 March 2022. https://www.canada.ca/en/immigration-refugees-citizenship/services/immigrate-canada/ukraine-measures/cuaet.html.
– 2022c. "Hire through the Economic Mobility Pathways Pilot: Our Partners." 2 March 2022. https://www.canada.ca/en/immigration-refugees-citizenship/services/refugees/economic-mobility-pathways-pilot/hire/partners.html.
– 2022d. "Interim Federal Health Program: What Is Covered." 28 April 2022. https://www.canada.ca/en/immigration-refugees-citizenship/services/refugees/help-within-canada/health-care/interim-federal-health-program/coverage-summary.html.
– 2022e. "Notice – Supplementary Information for the 2022–2024 Immigration Levels Plan." 14 February 2022. https://www.canada.ca/en/immigration-refugees-citizenship/news/notices/supplementary-immigration-levels-2022-2024.html.
– 2022f. "Raison d'être, Mandate and Role: Who We Are and What We Do." Report on plans and priorities. 3 March 2022. https://www.canada.ca/en/immigration-refugees-citizenship/corporate/publications-manuals/departmental-plan-2022-2023/raison-etre.html.
– 2022g. "UNHCR Resettlement Handbook: Country Chapter - Canada." UNHCR. https://www.unhcr.org/resettlement-handbook/wp-content/uploads/sites/153/2023/02/Country-Chapter-Canada-2023.pdf.
– 2022h. "Upper Canadian Act of 1793 Against Slavery National Historic Event." https://www.pc.gc.ca/apps/dfhd/page_nhs_eng.aspx?id=1623.
– 2023. "Consecutive Public Policy to Facilitate the Immigration of Certain Sponsored Foreign Nationals Excluded under Paragraph 117(9)(d) or 125(1)(d) of the Immigration and Refugee Protection Regulations." 11 September 2023. https://www.canada.ca/en/immigration-refugees-citizenship/corporate/mandate/policies-operational-instructions-agreements/public-policies/certain-sponsored-foreign-nationals-excluded.html.
– n.d. "Find Help to Adjust as a Refugee in Canada." https://www.canada.ca/en/immigration-refugees-citizenship/services/refugees/help-within-canada/government-assisted-refugee-program/providers.html.

Government of Quebec. 2022. "Sponsoring a Refugee." https://www.quebec.ca/en/immigration/refugees-asylum-seekers/collective-sponsorship/program-verview/sponsoring-refugee.

Gowayed, Heba. 2022. *Refuge: How the State Shapes Human Potential.* Princeton: Princeton University Press.

Grabska, Katarzyna, and Christina R. Clark-Kazak, eds. 2022. *Documenting Displacement: Questioning Methodological Boundaries in Forced Migration Research.* Montreal and Kingston: McGill-Queen's University Press.

Granados, Francisco. 2015. *refugees run the seas … 2014–16.* Created with technical support of Kurt Kraler and Manolo Lugo. Installed as part of Nuit Blanche Toronto in 2015.

– 2016. *spatial profiling …* Installed as part of the exhibition *1. Make a line* (2016). YMCA Newcomer Connections Centre in Saint John, NB, through partnership with Third Space Gallery.

Grandi, Filippo. 2022a. "High Commissioner's Message on the International Day for the Elimination of Racial Discrimination," UNHCR press release, 21 March 2022. https://www.unhcr.org/news/press/2022/3/62370dc44/high-commissioners-message-international-day-elimination-racial-discrimination.html.

– 2022b. "High Commissioner's Opening Statement to the 73rd Session of the UNHCR Executive Committee." UNHCR. https://www.unhcr.org/admin/hcspeeches/6343e6e44/high-commissioners-opening-statement-73rd-session-unhcr-executive-committee.html.

Grant, Angus. 2018. "Treating the Symptom, Ignoring the Cause: Recent People Smuggling Developments in Canada and Around the World." In *The Criminalization of Migration: Context and Consequences*, edited by Idil Atak and James C. Simeon. McGill-Queen's Refugee and Forced Migration Studies 1. Montreal and Kingston: McGill-Queen's University Press.

Gray, Harriet, and Anja K Franck. 2019. "Refugees as/at Risk: The Gendered and Racialized Underpinnings of Securitization in British Media Narratives." *Security Dialogue* 50 (3): 275–91. https://doi.org/10.1177/0967010619830590.

Grayson, Catherine-Lune, and François Audet. 2017. "Les hauts et les bas du financement canadien au HCR: quelle aide et pour quels réfugiés?" *Refuge: Revue Canadienne sur les réfugiés* 33 (1): 62–76. https://doi.org/10.25071/1920-7336.40449.

Green, Alan G., and David A. Green. 1999. "The Economic Goals of Canada's Immigration Policy: Past and Present." *Canadian Public Policy* 25 (4): 425. https://doi.org/10.2307/3552422.

Grondin, David, and Miguel de Larrinaga. 2009. "Securing Prosperity or Making Securitization Prosper? The Security and Prosperity Partnership as North American Biopolitical Governance." *International Journal* 64 (3): 667–86.

Gros, Hanna. 2021. "Je ne me sentais pas comme un être humain." *Human Rights Watch*, 17 June 2021. https://www.hrw.org/fr/report/2021/06/17/je-ne-me-sentais-pas-comme-un-etre-humain/la-detention-des-personnes-migrantes-au.

Gros, Hanna, and Samer Muscati. 2020. "Canada's Immigration Detainees at Higher Risk in Pandemic." *Ottawa Citizen*, 23 March 2020. https://ottawacitizen.com/opinion/columnists/gros-and-muscati-canadas-immigration-detainees-at-risk-in-pandemic.

Gros, Hanna, and Yolanda Song. 2016. *No Life for a Child: A Roadmap to End Immigration Detention of Children and Family Separation*. Edited by Samer Muscati. Toronto: International Human Rights Program, University of Toronto.

Gros, Hanna, and Paloma van Groll. 2015. "'We Have No Rights': Arbitrary Imprisonment and Cruel Treatment of Migrants with Mental Health Issues in Canada." International Human Rights Program. https://ihrp.law.utoronto.ca/We_Have_No_Rights.

Gross, Leo. 1948. "The Peace of Westphalia, 1648–1948." *The American Journal of International Law* 42 (1): 20–41. https://doi.org/10.2307/2193560.

Grove, Natalie J., and Anthony B. Zwi. 2006. "Our Health and Theirs: Forced Migration, Othering, and Public Health." *Social Science & Medicine* 62 (8): 1931–42. https://doi.org/10.1016/j.socscimed.2005.08.061.

Grzymala-Kazlowska, Aleksandra, and Jenny Phillimore. 2018. "Introduction: Rethinking Integration. New Perspectives on Adaptation and Settlement in the Era of Super-Diversity." *Journal of Ethnic and Migration Studies* 44 (2): 179–96. https://doi.org/10.1080/1369183X.2017.1341706.

Guild, Elspeth, and Didier Bigo. "The Transformation of European Border Controls." In *Extraterritorial Immigration Control*, edited by Bernard Ryan and Valsamis Mitsilegas, 252–73. Leiden: Brill Nijhoff.

Guillemin, Marilys, and Lynn Gillam. 2004. "Ethics, Reflexivity, and 'Ethically Important Moments' in Research." *Qualitative Inquiry* 10 (2): 261–80. https://doi.org/10.1177/1077800403262360.

Guiraudon, Virginie. 2003. "Before the EU Border: Remote Control of the 'Huddled Masses.'" In *In Search of Europe's Borders*, edited by Cornelis A. Groenendijk, Elspeth Guild, and P.E. Minderhoud. Immigration and Asylum Law and Policy in Europe 5. The Hague: Kluwer Law International.

Gullestad, Marianne. 2002. "Invisible Fences: Egalitarianism, Nationalism and Racism." *Journal of the Royal Anthropological Institute* 8 (1): 45–63. https://doi.org/10.1111/1467-9655.00098.

Gulliver, Trevor. 2018. "Canada the Redeemer and Denials of Racism." *Critical Discourse Studies* 15 (1): 68–86. https://doi.org/10.1080/17405904.2017.1360192.

Gunn, Alexander. 2012. "Immigration and Multi-Level Governance in Canada and Europe: The Role of Municipalities as Integration "Policy Innovators." Policy paper. Canada Europe Dialogue.

Guo, Shibao, and Per Andersson. 2005. "Non/Recognition of Foreign Credentials for Immigrant Professionals in Canada and Sweden : A Comparative Analysis." PMC Working Paper Series WP-05-04. Edmonton: University of Alberta, Prairie Centre of Excellence for Research on Immigration and Integration. https://sites.ualberta.ca/~pcerii/WorkingPapers/WP04-05.

Guo, Shibao, and Srabani Maitra. 2017. "Revisioning Curriculum in the Age of Transnational Mobility: Towards a Transnational and Transcultural Framework." *Curriculum Inquiry* 47 (1): 80–91. https://doi.org/10.1080/03626784.2016.1254504.

Guo-Brennan, Linyuan, and Michael Guo-Brennan. 2019. "Building Welcoming and Inclusive Schools for Immigrant and Refugee Students: Policy, Framework and Promising Praxis." In *Education, Immigration and Migration: Policy, Leadership and Praxis for a Changing World*, 1st ed., edited by Khalid Arar, Jeffrey S. Brooks, Ira Bogotch, and Duncan Waite. Studies in Educational Administration. Bingley, UK: Emerald Publishing Limited.

Guyon, Sylvie. 2011. "La réinstallation au Québec des réfugiés sélectionnés à l'étranger, un secret bien gardé!" *Vivre Ensemble*. https://cjf.qc.ca/vivre-ensemble/webzine/article/la-reinstallation-au-quebec-des-refugies-selectionnes-a-letranger-un-secret-bien-garde.

Ha, Olivia Katherine. 2020. "A Neighborhood-Level Analysis of Immigration and Crime in Vancouver, Canada, 2003–2016." Vancouver: Simon Fraser University.

Hachey, Isabelle, and Agnès Gruda. 2012. "Mines canadiennes à l'étranger: or, sang et feuille d'érable." *La Presse*, 20 October 2012, sec. https://www.lapresse.ca/actualites/national/201210/19/01-4585242-mines-canadiennes-a-letranger-or-sang-et-feuille-derable.php.

Haddad, Emma. 2008. *The Refugee in International Society: Between Sovereigns*. Cambridge Studies in International Relations. Cambridge: Cambridge University Press. https://doi.org/10.1017/CBO9780511491351.

Hailbronner, Kay, David A. Martin, and Hiroshi Motomura, eds. 1997. *Immigration Admissions: The Search for Workable Policies in Germany and the United States*. 1st ed. Berghahn Books. https://doi.org/10.2307/j.ctv287sdvw.

Hajdukowski-Ahmed, Maroussia. 2008. "A Dialogical Approach to Identity: Implications for Refugee Women." In *Not Born a Refugee Woman: Contesting Identities, Rethinking Practices*, edited by Maroussia Hajdukowski-Ahmed, Nazilla Khanlou, and Helene Moussa 24: 28–54. New York: Berghahn Books.

Hall, Alexandra. 2015. *Border Watch: Cultures of Immigration, Detention and Control*. London: Pluto Press. https://doi.org/10.2307/j.ctt183p2n9.

Hall, Rebecca Jane. 2022. *Refracted Economies: Diamond Mining and Social Reproduction in the North*. Toronto: University of Toronto Press.

Hamelin, William. 2022. "Loyers élevés, défis administratifs: immigrer est un arcours compliqué en Alberta." *Radio-Canada*, 29 September 2022. https://ici.

radio-canada.ca/nouvelle/1920140/famille-cameroun-crise-logement-communaute-calgary.

Hamilton, Leah K., Luisa Veronis, and Margaret Walton-Roberts, eds. 2020. *A National Project: Syrian Refugee Resettlement in Canada*. McGill-Queen's Refugee and Forced Migration Studies 2. Montreal and Kingston: McGill-Queen's University Press.

Hamilton, Sylvia. 1994. "Naming Names, Naming Ourselves: A Survey of Early Black Women in Nova Scotia." In *We're Rooted Here and They Can't Pull Us Up: Essays in African Canadian Women's History*, edited by Peggy Bristow, 13–40. Toronto: University of Toronto Press.

Hamlin, Rebecca. 2014. *Let Me Be a Refugee: Administrative Justice and the Politics of Asylum in the United States, Canada, and Australia*. Oxford: Oxford University Press.

– 2021. *Crossing: How We Label and React to People on the Move*. Stanford, CA: Stanford University Press.

Hammerstadt, Anna. 2014. "The Securitization of Forced Migration." In *The Oxford Handbook of Refugee and Forced Migration Studies*, edited by Elena Fiddian-Qasmiyeh, Gil Loescher, Katy Long, and Nando Sigona, 265–77. Oxford: Oxford University Press. https://doi.org/10.1093/oxfordhb/9780199652433.001.0001.

Hanes, Roy. 2009. "None Is Still Too Many: An Historical Exploration of Canadian Immigration Legislation as It Pertains to People with Disabilities." *Developmental Disabilities Bulletin* 37 (1–2): 91–126.

Haney, Timothy J. 2019. "Move out or Dig in? Risk Awareness and Mobility Plans in Disaster-Affected Communities." *Journal of Contingencies and Crisis Management* 27 (3): 224–36. https://doi.org/10.1111/1468-5973.12253.

Hanley, Jill, Adnan Al Mhamied, Janet Cleveland, Oula Hajjar, Ghayda Hassan, Nicole Ives, Rim Khyar, and Michaela Hynie. 2018. "The Social Networks, Social Support and Social Capital of Syrian Refugees Privately Sponsored to Settle in Montreal: Indications for Employment and Housing During Their Early Experiences of Integration." *Canadian Ethnic Studies* 50 (2): 123–48. https://doi.org/10.1353/ces.2018.0018.

Harder, Lois. 2022. *Canadian Club: Birthright Citizenship and National Belonging*. Toronto: University of Toronto Press.

Hari, Amrita. 2014. "Temporariness, Rights, and Citizenship: The Latest Chapter in Canada's Exclusionary Migration and Refugee History." *Refuge: Canada's Journal on Refugees* 30 (2): 35–44. https://doi.org/10.25071/1920-7336.39617.

– 2017. "Who Gets to 'Work Hard, Play Hard'? Gendering the Work-Life Balance Rhetoric in Canadian Tech Companies." *Gender, Work & Organization* 24 (2): 99–114. https://doi.org/10.1111/gwao.12146.

Harley, Tristan, and Harry Hobbs. 2020. "The Meaningful Participation of Refugees in Decision-Making Processes: Questions of Law and Policy."

International Journal of Refugee Law 32 (2): 200–26. https://doi.org/10.1093/ijrl/eeaa010.

Harley, Tristan, Suyeon Lee, and Najeeba Wazefadost. 2022. "Not Just a Seat at the Table: Refugee Participation and the Importance of Listening." *Forced Migration Review* 70 (September): 25–8.

Harper, Stephen. 2006. "Prime Minister Harper Issues Statement on Canadian Multiculturalism Day." 27 June 2006. https://www.canada.ca/en/news/archive/2006/06/prime-minister-harper-issues-statement-canadian-multiculturalism-day.html.

Harris, Helen P., and Daniyal Zuberi. 2015. "Harming Refugee and Canadian Health: The Negative Consequences of Recent Reforms to Canada's Interim Federal Health Program." *Journal of International Migration and Integration* 16 (4): 1041–55. https://doi.org/10.1007/s12134-014-0385-x.

Harris, Kathleen. 2020. "Canada Has Turned Back 4,400 Asylum Seekers in 5 Years." *CBC News*, 24 November 2020. https://www.cbc.ca/news/politics/asylum-seekers-canada-us-trump-pandemic-1.5813211.

Harrisse, Henry. 1896. *John Cabot: The Discoverer of North America, and Sebastian, His Son*. London: Benjamin Franklin Stevens.

Harvard Law School. 2006. *Bordering on Failure: The US-Canada Safe Third Country Agreement Fifteen Months after Implementation*. http://www.ilw.com/articles/2006,0518-anker.pdf.

Hasham, Nicole. 2016. "Detention Centre Workers Suffering Their Own Trauma in Dealing with Asylum Seekers." *The Australia Standard*, 26 February 2016.

Hashimoto, Naoko. 2018. "Refugee Resettlement as an Alternative to Asylum." *Refugee Survey Quarterly* 37 (2): 162–86. https://doi.org/10.1093/rsq/hdy004.

Hathaway, James C. 1988. "Selective Concern: An Overview of Refugee Law in Canada." *McGill Law Journal* 33 (4): 676–715.

– 1991a. *The Law of Refugee Status*. Vancouver: Butterworths Canada.

– 1991b. "Reconceiving Refugee Law as Human Rights Protection." *Journal of Refugee Studies* 4 (2): 113–31. https://doi.org/10.1093/jrs/4.2.113.

– 1999. "The Michigan Guidelines on the Internal Protection Alternative." *Michigan Journal of International Law* 21 (1): 131–33.

– 2005. *The Rights of Refugees Under International Law*. Cambridge: Cambridge University Press.

Hathaway, James C., and Michelle Foster. 2014. *The Law of Refugee Status*. 2nd ed. Cambridge: Cambridge University Press.

Haugen, Stacey. 2019. "'We Feel Like We're Home': The Resettlement and Integration of Syrian Refugees in Smaller and Rural Canadian Communities." *Refuge* 35 (2): 53–63. https://doi.org/10.7202/1064819ar.

Haugen, Stacey, Patti Tamara Lenard, and Emily Regan Wills. 2020. "Creating Canadians through Private Sponsorship." *Canadian Journal of Political Science* 53 (3): 560–76. https://doi.org/10.1017/S0008423920000244.

Heidinger, Loanna. 2022. "Violent Victimization and Perceptions of Safety: Experiences of First Nations, Métis and Inuit Women in Canada." *Juristat* 85: 1–39.

Heine, Sophie. 2009. "The Hijab Controversy and French Republicanism: Critical Analysis and Normative Propositions." *French Politics* 7 (2): 167–93. https://doi.org/10.1057/fp.2009.10.

Henry, Frances, and Carol Tator. 2006. *The Colour of Democracy: Racism in Canadian Society*. 3rd ed. Toronto: Thomson Nelson.

Henry, Natasha. 2016. "Esclavage des Noirs au Canada." *The Canadian Encyclopedia*. Historica Canada. 16 June 2016. https://www.thecanadianencyclopedia.ca/fr/article/black-enslavement.

– 2021. "Where, Oh Where, Is Bet? Locating Enslaved Africans on the Ontario Landscape." In *Unsettling the Great White North: Black Canadian History*, edited by Michele A. Johnson and Funkè Aladejebi, 85–112. Toronto: University of Toronto Press.

Hessey, Krista. 2022. "Moving Beyond Emissions: How Canada Can Weather the Floods of the Future." *Global News*, 5 February 2022. https://globalnews.ca/news/8526590/canada-floods-of-the-future-the-new-reality.

Hier, Sean P., and Joshua L. Greenberg. 2002. "Constructing a Discursive Crisis: Risk, Problematization and Illegal Chinese in Canada." *Ethnic and Racial Studies* 25 (3): 490–513.

Hilario, Carla T., John L. Oliffe, Josephine P. Wong, Annette J. Browne, and Joy L. Johnson. 2018. "'Just as Canadian as Anyone Else'? Experiences of Second-Class Citizenship and the Mental Health of Young Immigrant and Refugee Men in Canada." *American Journal of Men's Health* 12 (2): 210–20. https://doi.org/10.1177/1557988317743384.

Hilario, Carla Theresa, John L. Oliffe, Josephine Pui-Hing Wong, Annette J. Browne, and Joy Louise Johnson. 2015. "Migration and Young People's Mental Health in Canada: A Scoping Review." *Journal of Mental Health* 24 (6): 414–22. https://doi.org/10.3109/09638237.2015.1078881.

Hill, Brian, and Jamie Mauracher. 2019. "Refugee Judge Asks Woman Why Her Husband Wouldn't 'Just Kill' Her." *Global News*, 27 November 2019. https://globalnews.ca/news/6214393/refugee-judge-asks-woman-why-husband-wouldnt-kill-her.

Hill Collins, Patricia. 2009. *Black Feminist Thought: Knowledge, Consciousness, and the Politics of Empowerment*. 2nd ed. New York: Routledge.

Hill Collins, Patricia, and Sirma Bilge. 2020. *Intersectionality*. 2nd ed. Key Concepts. Cambridge: Polity Press.

Hobsbawm, Eric. 2012. "Introduction: Inventing Traditions." In *The Invention of Tradition*, edited by Terence Ranger, and Eric Hobsbawm. 1–14. Cambridge: Cambridge University Press.

Hodgins, Evelyn, Julie Mutis, Robin Mason, and Janice Du Mont. 2022. "Sex Trafficking of Women and Girls in Canada: A Scoping Review of the Scholarly

Literature." *Trauma, Violence, & Abuse* (May). https://doi.org/10.1177/15248380221094316.

Holland, Madeline. 2018. "Stories for Asylum: Narrative and Credibility in the United States' Political Asylum Application." *Refuge* 34 (2): 85–93. https://doi.org/10.7202/1055579ar.

Holm Pedersen, Marianne. 2012. "Going on a Class Journey: The Inclusion and Exclusion of Iraqi Refugees in Denmark." *Journal of Ethnic and Migration Studies* 38 (7): 1101–17. https://doi.org/10.1080/1369183X.2012.681453.

Holmes, Seth. 2020. "Foreword." In *Asylum for Sale: Profit and Protest in the Migration Industry*, edited by Siobhán McGuirk and Adrienne Pine, xi–xvi. Oxland, CA: PM Press.

Holston, James. 2001. "Urban Citizenship and Globalization." In *Global City-Regions: Trends, Theory, Policy*, edited by Allen John Scott, 325–48. Cambridge, UK, and New York: Oxford University Press.

Hoover, Dennis R., and Kevin R. den Dulk. 2004. "Christian Conservatives Go to Court: Religion and Legal Mobilization in the United States and Canada." *International Political Science Review* 25 (1): 9–34. https://doi.org/10.1177/0192512104038165.

Hoppe, Robert. 2011. *The Governance of Problems: Puzzling, Powering and Participation*. Bristol: Policy Press.

Hou, Feng. 2021. "The Resettlement of Vietnamese Refugees across Canada over Three Decades." *Journal of Ethnic and Migration Studies* 47 (21): 4817–34. https://doi.org/10.1080/1369183X.2020.1724412.

Hou, Feng, and Aneta Bonikowska. 2017. "Educational Attainment of Childhood Immigrants: How Does Immigration Type Matter?" *Journal of Ethnic and Migration Studies* 43 (9): 1434–52. https://doi.org/10.1080/1369183X.2016.1243462.

Houle, René, and Lahouaria Yssaad. 2010. "Recognition of Newcomers' Foreign Credentials and Work Experience." *Perspectives on Labour and Income* 22 (4): 18.

Hourani, Jeanine. 2021. "Reclaiming Statelessness Narratives by Resisting 'Deficit' Discourse and Amplifying the Voices of Stateless People." *Peter McMullin Centre on Statelessness Critical Statelessness Studies Blog Series*. https://law.unimelb.edu.au/centres/statelessness/resources/critical-statelessness-studies-blog/reclaiming-statelessness-narratives-by-resisting-deficit-discourse-and-amplifying-the-voices-of-stateless-people.

House of Commons. 1966. "27th Parliament, 1st Session." *Hansard* 7 (July) "Extending Special Immigration Measures to Regions Faced with Humanitarian Crises," CIMM Committee news release 44-1, 6 April 2022. https://www.ourcommons.ca/DocumentViewer/en/44-1/CIMM/news-release/11693680.

"House of Commons Debates, 5th Parl, 3rd Sess., Vol. 28, No. 369 (11 December 2018)." 1885.

"House of Commons Debates, 28th Parl, 3rd Sess., Vol. 8, No. 369 (8 October 1971) (Rt. Hon P.E. Trudeau)." 1971.

"House of Commons Debates, 42nd Parl, 1st Sess., Vol. 148, No. 369 (11 December 2018)." 2018.

Housefather, Anthony. 2018. *Moving Forward in the Fight Against Human Trafficking in Canada*. House of Commons Canada. https://www.ourcommons.ca/Content/Committee/421/JUST/Reports/RP10243099/justrp24/justrp24-e.pdf.

Howard-Hassmann, Rhoda E. 1999. "'Canadian' as an Ethnic Category: Implications for Multiculturalism and National Unity." *Canadian Public Policy* 25 (4): 523–37.

Hudson, Peter James, Katherine McKittrick, and Caribbean Philosophical Association. 2014. "The Geographies of Blackness and Anti-Blackness: An Interview with Katherine McKittrick." *The CLR James Journal* 20 (1): 233–40. https://doi.org/10.5840/clrjames201492215.

Hugman, Richard, Linda Bartolomei, and Eileen Pittaway. 2011a. "Human Agency and the Meaning of Informed Consent: Reflections on Research with Refugees." *Journal of Refugee Studies* 24 (4): 655–71. https://doi.org/10.1093/jrs/fer024.

Hugman, Richard, Eileen Pittaway, and Linda Bartolomei. 2011b. "When 'Do No Harm' Is Not Enough: The Ethics of Research with Refugees and Other Vulnerable Groups." *The British Journal of Social Work* 41 (7): 1271–87. https://doi.org/10.1093/bjsw/bcr013.

Human Rights Watch. 2019. "Eritrea." *World Report 2019*. https://www.hrw.org/world-report/2019/country-chapters/eritrea.

Hunkler, Christian, Tabea Scharrer, Magdalena Suerbaum, and Zeynep Yanasmayan. 2022. "Spatial and Social Im/Mobility in Forced Migration: Revisiting Class." *Journal of Ethnic and Migration Studies* 48 (20): 4829–46. https://doi.org/10.1080/1369183X.2022.2123431.

Hunt, Sarah. 2015. "Representing Colonial Violence: Trafficking, Sex Work, and the Violence of Law." *Atlantis: Critical Studies in Gender, Culture & Social Justice* 37 (2): 25–39.

Hunter, Wendy. 2019. *Undocumented Nationals: Between Statelessness and Citizenship*. Cambridge: Cambridge University Press.

Human Rights Watch. 2019. "Eritrea." *World Report 2019*. https://www.hrw.org/world-report/2019/country-chapters/eritrea.

Hurley, Mary C. 2009. "The Indian Act." Text PRB0912. Ottawa: Library of Parliament. https://publications.gc.ca/collection_2009/bdp-lop/prb/prb0912-e.pdf.

Hussan, Syed. 2014. *Indefinite, Arbitrary and Unfair: The Truth about Immigration Detention in Canada*. End Immigration Detention Network. https://endimmigrationdetention.files.wordpress.com/2014/06/truth-about-detention-report_eidn.pdf.

Huysmans, Jef. 2000. "The European Union and the Securitization of Migration." *JCMS: Journal of Common Market Studies* 38 (5): 751–77. https://doi.org/10.1111/1468-5965.00263.

Hyndman, Jennifer. 2011. "Research Summary on Resettled Refugee Integration in Canada Centre for Refugee Studies." Canadian Electronic Library. York University Centre for Refugee Studies.

– 2012. "The Geopolitics of Migration and Mobility." *Geopolitics* 17 (2): 243–55. https://doi.org/10.1080/14650045.2011.569321.

– 2023. "The Russian Invasion of Ukraine and Humanitarian Nationalism in Canada." *Canadian Foreign Policy Journal* (June): 1–21. https://doi.org/10.1080/11926422.2023.2219786.

Hyndman, Jennifer, and Wenona Giles. 2011. "Waiting for What? The Feminization of Asylum in Protracted Situations." *Gender, Place & Culture* 18 (3): 361–79. https://doi.org/10.1080/0966369X.2011.566347.

Hyndman, Jennifer, and Wenona Giles. 2017. *Refugees in Extended Exile: Living on the Edge*. Interventions series. London: Routledge, Taylor & Francis Group.

Hyndman, Jennifer, and Michaela Hynie. 2016. "From Newcomer to Canadian: Making Refugee Integration Work." *Policy Options*, 17 May 2016. https://policyoptions.irpp.org/fr/magazines/mai-2016/from-newcomer-to-canadian-making-refugee-integration-work.

Hyndman, Jennifer, and James McLean. 2006. "Settling Like a State: Acehnese Refugees in Vancouver." *Journal of Refugee Studies* 19 (3): 345–60. https://doi.org/10.1093/jrs/fel016.

Hyndman, Jennifer, and Alison Mountz. 2007. "Refuge or Refusal: The Geography of Exclusion." In *Violent Geographies: Fear, Terror, and Political Violence*, edited by Derek Gregory and Allan Pred, 77–92. New York: Routledge.

Hyndman, Jennifer, William Payne, and Shauna Jimenez. 2017. "Private Refugee Sponsorship in Canada." *Forced Migration Review* 54: 56–9.

Hyndman, Jennifer, and Johanna Reynolds. 2020. "Introduction: Beyond the Global Compacts." *Refuge: Canada's Journal on Refugees* 36 (1): 66–74. https://doi.org/10.25071/1920-7336.40768.

Hyndman, Jennifer, Johanna Reynolds, Biftu Yousuf, Anna Purkey, Dawit Demoz, and Kathy Sherrell. 2021. "Sustaining the Private Sponsorship of Resettled Refugees in Canada." *Frontiers in Human Dynamics* 3 (May): 625358. https://doi.org/10.3389/fhumd.2021.625358.

Hynie, Michaela. 2018. "Refugee Integration: Research and Policy." *Peace and Conflict: Journal of Peace Psychology* 24 (3): 265–76. https://doi.org/10.1037/pac0000326.

Hynie, Michaela, Sepali Guruge, and Yogendra B. Shakya. 2013. "Family Relationships of Afghan, Karen and Sudanese Refugee Youth." *Canadian Ethnic Studies* 44 (3): 11–28. https://doi.org/10.1353/ces.2013.0011.

Hynie, Michaela, Gulay Kilicaslan, Cansu Ekmekcioglu, Rubaiyat Karim, Palmer Taylor, and Trisha Scantlebury. Forthcoming. "Information Access and Resilience for Newcomer Groups: Yazidi and Turkish-Speaking Newcomers in York Region." In *Resilience and Integrating International Migrants in Cities in*

Canada, edited by Valerie Preston and John Shields. Montreal and Kingston: McGill-Queen's University Press.

Hynie, Michaela, Ashley Korn, and Dan Tao. 2016. "Social Context and Social Integration for Government Assisted Refugees in Ontario, Canada." In *After the Flight: The Dynamics of Refugee Settlement and Integration*, edited by Morgan Poteet and Shiva Nourpanah, 183–227. Newcastle upon Tyne: Cambridge Scholars Publishing.

Hynie, Michaela, Susan McGrath, Jonathan Bridekirk, Anna Oda, Nicole Ives, Jennifer Hyndman, Neil Arya, Yogendra B. Shakya, Jill Hanley, and Kwame McKenzie. 2019. "What Role Does Type of Sponsorship Play in Early Integration Outcomes? Syrian Refugees Resettled in Six Canadian Cities." *Refuge* 35 (2): 36–52. https://doi.org/10.7202/1064818ar.

Hynie, Michaela, and SyRIA.lth. 2019. "Probing Private Sponsorship and Integration Outcomes among Syrians in Canada: A Longitudinal Approach." Ottawa.

Ianni Segatto, Catarina. 2021. "Settlement and Integration Policies in Federal Contexts: The Case of Refugees in Canada and Brazil." *Journal of Refugee Studies* 34 (1): 596–613. https://doi.org/10.1093/jrs/fez065.

Ibrahim, Dyna. 2019. "Trafficking in Persons in Canada, 2019." *Juristat*, no. 85: 16.

Ibrahim, Hadeel. 2022. "Why Ukrainian Newcomers Are Not Refugees and Why That Matters." *CBC News*, 25 June 2022. https://www.cbc.ca/news/canada/new-brunswick/ukrainian-refugee-canada-ukraine-authorization-for-emergency-travel-1.6498928.

Ijaiya, Hakeem, and O.T. Joseph. 2014. "Rethinking Environmental Law Enforcement in Nigeria." *Beijing Law Review* 5 (4): 306–21. https://doi.org/10.4236/blr.2014.54029.

Ilcan, Suzan, and Laura Connoy. 2021. "On Critical Localism and the Privatisation of Refuge: The Resettlement of Syrian Newcomers in Canada." *Refugee Survey Quarterly* 40 (3): 293–314. https://doi.org/10.1093/rsq/hdab006.

Immigration Act, 1976–77, c. 52, s. 1.

Immigration and Refugee Board of Canada (IRB). 2008. "Chairperson's Guideline 4: Gender Considerations in Proceedings Before the Immigration and Refugee Board." IRB, 10 October 2008. https://irb.gc.ca:443/en/legal-policy/policies/Pages/GuideDir04.aspx.

– 2021a. "About the Board." https://irb.gc.ca/en/board/Pages/index.aspx#ab1.

– 2021b. "Guideline 9: Proceedings Before the IRB Involving Sexual Orientation, Gender Identity and Expression, and Sex Characteristics." IRB, 17 December 2021. https://irb.gc.ca:443/en/legal-policy/policies/Pages/GuideDir09.aspx.

– n.d. "Processing In-Canada Claims for Refugee Protection of Minors and Vulnerable Persons." Government of Canada. https://www.canada.ca/en/immigration-refugees-citizenship/corporate/publications-manuals/operational-bulletins-manuals/refugee-protection/canada/processing-claims-refugee-protection-minors-vulnerable-persons.html.

Immigration and Refugee Protection Act (IRPA). 2001. SC 2001, c. 27.
Immigration and Refugee Protection Regulations (IRPR). 2002. SOR 2002-227.
Immigration, Refugees and Citizenship Canada (IRCC). 1991. *Canada-Québec Accord Relating to Immigration and Temporary Admission of Aliens*. https://www.canada.ca/en/immigration-refugees-citizenship/corporate/mandate/policies-operational-instructions-agreements/agreements/federal-provincial-territorial/quebec/canada-quebec-accord-relating-immigration-temporary-admission-aliens.html.
– 2003. "Statement of Mutual Understanding on Information Sharing." Government of Canada. https://www.canada.ca/en/immigration-refugees-citizenship/corporate/mandate/policies-operational-instructions-agreements/agreements/statement-mutual-understanding-information-sharing/statement.html.
– 2016. "Evaluation of the Resettlement Programs (GAR, PSR, BVOR, and RAP)." Assessments. 24 October 2016. https://www.canada.ca/en/immigration-refugees-citizenship/corporate/reports-statistics/evaluations/resettlement-programs.html.
– 2017. "Refugee Sponsorship Application: Joint Assistance Sponsorship (IMM 5493)." Government of Canada. 31 March 2017. https://www.canada.ca/en/immigration-refugees-citizenship/services/application/application-forms-guides/guide-5493-refugee-sponsorship-application-joint-assistance-sponsorship.html.
– 2018. "Acts and Regulations – Immigration, Refugees and Citizenship Canada." Mandate. 21 December 2018. https://www.canada.ca/en/immigration-refugees-citizenship/corporate/mandate/acts-regulations.html.
– 2019. "Caring for Children and Caring for People with High Medical Needs Classes." Program descriptions. 18 June 2019. https://www.canada.ca/en/immigration-refugees-citizenship/corporate/publications-manuals/operational-bulletins-manuals/permanent-residence/economic-classes/caring-children-caring-people-high-medical-needs.html.
– 2020a. "Canada-US Safe Third Country Agreement." 23 July 2020. https://www.canada.ca/en/immigration-refugees-citizenship/corporate/mandate/policies-operational-instructions-agreements/agreements/safe-third-country-agreement.html.
– 2020b. "The Economic Mobility Pathways Pilot: Exploring Labour Mobility as a Complementary Pathway for Refugees." 14 October 2020. https://www.canada.ca/en/immigration-refugees-citizenship/corporate/publications-manuals/economic-mobility-pathways-project-labour-mobility.html.
– 2021a. *2021 Annual Report to Parliament on Immigration*. Ottawa: IRCC. www.canada.ca/content/dam/ircc/documents/pdf/english/corporate/publications-manuals/annual-report-2021-en.pdf.
– 2021b. *Evaluation of the Blended Visa Office-Referred (BVOR) Program*. 11 June 2021. https://www.canada.ca/content/dam/ircc/documents/pdf/english/corporate/reports-statistics/evaluations/e5-2019-bvor-en.pdf.

– 2021c. "Minister Mendicino Launches a Dedicated Refugee Stream for Human Rights Defenders." News release. 16 July 2021. https://www.canada.ca/en/immigration-refugees-citizenship/news/2021/07/minister-mendicino-launches-a-dedicated-refugee-stream-for-human-rights-defenders.html.

– 2022a. "Canada-Ukraine Authorization for Emergency Travel." Backgrounders. 17 March 2022. https://www.canada.ca/en/immigration-refugees-citizenship/news/2022/03/canada-ukraine-authorization-for-emergency-travel.html.

– 2022b. "Internal Audit of the Private Sponsorship of Refugees Program." 13 January 2022. https://www.canada.ca/en/immigration-refugees-citizenship/corporate/reports-statistics/audits/internal-audit-private-sponsorship-refugees-program.html.

– 2022c. "Supplementary Information for the 2023–2025 Immigration Levels Plan." Promotional material. 1 November 2022. https://www.canada.ca/en/immigration-refugees-citizenship/news/notices/supplementary-immigration-levels-2023-2025.html.

– n.d.a. "How Many Applications to Sponsor Parents and Grandparents Do You Accept Each Year?" Help Centre. https://www.cic.gc.ca/english/helpcentre/answer.asp?qnum=820&top=14.

– n.d.b. "Processing In-Canada Claims for Refugee Protection of Minors and Vulnerable Persons." Accessed 17 May 2022. https://www.canada.ca/en/immigration-refugees-citizenship/corporate/publications-manuals/operational-bulletins-manuals/refugee-protection/canada/processing-claims-refugee-protection-minors-vulnerable-persons.html.

Indian and Northern Affairs Canada. 2018. *A History of Treaty-Making in Canada*. Gatineau: Indian and Northern Affairs Canada. https://www.rcaanc-cirnac.gc.ca/eng/1314977704533/1544620451420.

Ineese-Nash, Nicole. 2020. "Disability as a Colonial Construct: The Missing Discourse of Culture in Conceptualizations of Disabled Indigenous Children." *Canadian Journal of Disability Studies* 9 (3): 28–51. https://doi.org/10.15353/cjds.v9i3.645.

Ingstad, Helge, and Anne Stine Ingstad. 2000. *The Viking Discovery of America: The Excavation of a Norse Settlement in L'Anse Aux Meadows, Newfoundland*. St John's: Breakwater.

Institute on Statelessness and Inclusion (ISI). 2014. *The World's Stateless 2014*. https://www.institutesi.org/resources/the-worlds-stateless-2014.

– 2020. "Statelessness in Numbers: 2020 An Overview and Analysis of Global Statistics." https://www.institutesi.org/resources/statelessness-in-numbers-2020-an-overview-and-analysis.

Internal Displacement Monitoring Centre (IDMC). 2022. GRID 2022: *Children and Youth in Internal Displacement*. https://www.internal-displacement.org/sites/default/files/publications/documents/IDMC_GRID_2022_LR.pdf.

International Association for the Study of Forced Migration (IASFM). 2018.

"Code of Ethics: Critical Reflections on Research Ethics in Situations of Forced Migration." IASFM. http://iasfm.org/blog/2021/11/12/iasfm-research-code-of-ethics-now-available-in-english-french-spanish/.

International Committee of the Red Cross (ICRC). 2004. "Inter-Agency Guiding Principles on Unaccompanied and Separated Children." Geneva: ICRC. https://www.icrc.org/en/doc/assets/files/other/icrc_002_1011.pdf.

International Organization for Migration (IOM). 2019. "Canadian Orientation Abroad." 2019. https://coa.iom.int/.

– n.d. "Canada." International Organization for Migration. Accessed 29 November 2022. https://www.iom.int/countries/canada.

Ionesco, Dina, Daria Mokhnacheva, and François Gemenne. 2016. *The Atlas of Environmental Migration*. 1st ed. London: Routledge. https://doi.org/10.4324/9781315777313.

Isin, Engin F. 2008. "Theorizing Acts of Citizenship." In *Acts of Citizenship*, edited by Engin F. Isin and Greg M. Nielsen, 15–43. London: Palgrave Macmillan.

Isin, Engin F., and Greg Marc Nielsen, eds. 2008. "Introduction: Acts of Citizenship." In *Acts of Citizenship*, 1–12. London: Zed Books.

Isin, Engin F., and Kim Rygiel. 2007. "Abject Spaces: Frontiers, Zones, Camps." In *The Logics of Biopower and the War on Terror*, edited by Elizabeth Dauphinee and Cristina Masters, 181–203. New York: Palgrave Macmillan US.

Isin, Engin F., and Bryan S. Turner. 2002. "Citizenship Studies: An Introduction." In *Handbook of Citizenship Studies*, 1–10. London: SAGE.

Jack, Isaac Allen. 1898. *The Loyalists and Slavery in New Brunswick*. Ottawa: Royal Society of Canada.

Jackson, Samantha, and Herald Bauder. 2014. "Neither Temporary, Nor Permanent: The Precarious Employment Experiences of Refugee Claimants in Canada." *Journal of Refugee Studies* 27 (3): 360–81. https://doi.org/10.1093/jrs/fet048.

Jackson Sow, Marissa. 2022. "Ukrainian Refugees, Race, and International Law's Choice Between Order and Justice." *American Journal of International Law* 116 (4): 698–709. https://doi.org/10.1017/ajil.2022.56.

Jacobsen, Karen. 1996. "Factors Influencing the Policy Responses of Host Governments to Mass Refugee Influxes." *International Migration Review* 30 (3): 655. https://doi.org/10.2307/2547631.

Jacobson, Nora. 2007. "Dignity and Health: A Review." *Social Science & Medicine* 64 (2): 292–302. https://doi.org/10.1016/j.socscimed.2006.08.039.

Jaffer, Mobina S.B. 2016. "Débats du Sénat - 1re Session, 42e Législature, Vol. 150, No. 65." *Senate Debates* (Hansard). 25 October 2016. https://sencanada.ca/fr/content/sen/chamber/421/debates/065db_2016-10-25-f.

Jafri, Beenash. 2012a. "National Identity, Transnational Whiteness and the Canadian Citizenship Guide." *Critical Race and Whiteness Studies* 8 (1): 1–15.

– 2012b. "Privilege vs. Complicity: People of Colour and Settler Colonialism." *Equity Matters*, no. 21: 73–86.

Jain, Neha. 2022. "Manufacturing Statelessness." *The American Journal of International Law* 116 (2): 237–88.

James, Patrick, and Jonathan Paquin. 2014. *Game Changer: The Impact of 9/11 on North American Security*. Vancouver: UBC Press.

Jamil, Hikmet. 2016. "Determinants of Employment Among Well-Educated Refugees Before and After the 2007 U.S. Economic Recession." *Lettters in Health & Biological Sciences* 1 (1): 1–6. https://doi.org/10.15436/2475-6245.16.004.

Janoski, Thomas, and Brian Gran. 2002. "Political Citizenship: Foundations of Rights." In *Handbook of Citizenship Studies*, edited by Engin F. Isin and Bryan S. Turner, 13–52. London: SAGE.

Janzen, Rich, Chris Brnjas, Jim Cresswell, and Mark Chapman. 2020. "Faith and Settlement Partnerships: Perspectives of Community Stakeholders." *Journal of Immigrant & Refugee Studies* 18 (2): 239–60. https://doi.org/10.1080/15562948.2019.1658007.

Janzen, Rich, Alethea Stobbe, Mark Chapman, and James Watson. 2016. "Canadian Christian Churches as Partners in Immigrant Settlement and Integration." *Journal of Immigrant & Refugee Studies* 14 (4): 390–410. https://doi.org/10.1080/15562948.2015.1123792.

Janzen, William. 2006. "The 1979 MCC Canada Master Agreement for the Sponsorship of Refugees in Historical Perspective." *Journal of Mennonite Studies* 24: 211–22.

Jedwab, Jack. 2006. "Canadian Integration: The Elusive Quest for Models and Measures." *Canadian Diversity* 5 (1): 97–103.

Jeram, Sanjay, and Eleni Nicolaides. 2019. "Intergovernmental Relations on Immigrant Integration in Canada: Insights from Quebec, Manitoba, and Ontario." *Regional & Federal Studies* 29 (5): 613–33. https://doi.org/10.1080/13597566.2018.1491841.

Jewell, Eva, and Ian Mosby. 2022. "Calls to Action Accountability: A 2020 Status Update on Reconciliation." Yellowhead Institute.

Johnson, Shanthi, Juanita Bacsu, Tom McIntosh, Bonnie Jeffery, and Nuelle Novik. 2019. "Social Isolation and Loneliness among Immigrant and Refugee Seniors in Canada: A Scoping Review." *International Journal of Migration, Health and Social Care* 15 (3): 177–90. https://doi.org/10.1108/IJMHSC-10-2018-0067.

Johnson, Shelly. 2014. "Developing First Nations Courts in Canada: Elders as Foundational to Indigenous Therapeutic Jurisprudence +." *Journal of Indigenous Social Development* 3 (2): 1–14.

Joly, Yann, Shahad Salman, Ida Ngueng Feze, Palmira Granados Moreno, Michèle Stanton-jean, Jacqueline Lacey, Micheline Labelle, et al. 2017. "DNA Testing for Family Reunification in Canada: Points to Consider." *Journal of International Migration and Integration* 18 (2): 391–404.

Joppke, Christian. 2013. "Through the European Looking Glass: Citizenship Tests in the USA, Australia, and Canada." *Citizenship Studies* 17 (1): 1–15. https://doi.org/10.1080/13621025.2012.669965.

– 2021. "Earned Citizenship." *European Journal of Sociology* 62 (1): 1–35. https://doi.org/10.1017/S000397562100003 5.

Joppke, Christian, and Rainer Bauböck. 2010. "How Liberal Are Citizenship Tests?" Working Paper. https://cadmus.eui.eu/handle/1814/13956.

Jordan-Fenton, Christy, and Margaret Pokiak-Fenton. 2013. *When I Was Eight.* Art by Gabrielle Grimard. Toronto: Annick Press.

Jubilut, Liliana Lyra, and Melissa Martins Casagrande. 2019. "Shortcomings and/or Missed Opportunities of the Global Compacts for the Protection of Forced Migrants." *International Migration* 57 (6): 139–57. https://doi.org/10.1111/imig.12663.

Judge, Ruth. 2010. "Refugee Advocacy and the Biopolitics of Asylum in Britain: The Precarious Position of Young Male Asylum Seekers and Refugees." Working Paper. Oxford: Refugee Studies Centre. https://www.rsc.ox.ac.uk/publications/refugee-advocacy-and-the-biopolitics-of-asylum-in-britain-the-precarious-position-of-young-male-asylum-seekers-and-refugees.

Jung, Maria. 2020. "Immigration and Crime in Canadian Cities: A 35-Year Study." *Canadian Journal of Criminology and Criminal Justice* 62 (1): 71–97. https://doi.org/10.3138/cjccj.2019-0015.

Juss, Satvinder Singh. 2012. "Complicity, Exclusion, and the 'Unworthy' in Refugee Law." *Refugee Survey Quarterly* 31 (3): 1–39. https://doi.org/10.1093/rsq/hds011.

Kaga, Midori, and Delphine Nakache. 2019. "Whose Needs Count in Situations of Forced Displacement Revaluing Older People and Addressing Their Exclusion from Research and Humanitarian Programmes." *International Journal of Migration and Border Studies* 5 (1–2): 134. https://doi.org/10.1504/IJMBS.2019.099723.

Kahil, Rula, Maleeha Iqbal, and Neda Maghbouleh. 2022. "Grandmothers Behind the Scenes: Subordinate Integration, Care Work, and Power in Syrian Canadian Refugee Resettlement." *Refuge: Canada's Journal on Refugees* 38 (2): 1–18. https://doi.org/10.25071/1920-7336.40937.

Kahn, Sarilee. 2015. "Cast Out: 'Gender Role Outlaws' Seeking Asylum in the West and the Quest for Social Connections." *Journal of Immigrant & Refugee Studies* 13 (1): 58–79. https://doi.org/10.1080/15562948.2014.894169.

Kahn, Sarilee, Edward Alessi, Leah Woolner, Hanna Kim, and Christina Olivieri. 2017. "Promoting the Wellbeing of Lesbian, Gay, Bisexual and Transgender Forced Migrants in Canada: Providers' Perspectives." *Culture, Health & Sexuality* 19 (10): 1165–79. https://doi.org/10.1080/13691058.2017.1298843.

Kaida, Lisa, Feng Hou, Max Stick. 2020a. "The Long-Term Economic Integration of Resettled Refugees in Canada: A Comparison of Privately Sponsored Refugees and Government-Assisted Refugees." *Journal of Ethnic and Migration Studies* 46 (9): 1687–708. https://doi.org/10.1080/1369183X.2019.1623017.

– 2020b. "The Long-Term Economic Outcomes of Refugee Private Sponsorship." Statistics Canada. 13 January 2020. https://www150.statcan.gc.ca/n1/pub/11f0019m/11f0019m2019021-eng.htm.

Kanal, Maria, and Susan B. Rottmann. 2021. "Everyday Agency: Rethinking Refugee Women's Agency in Specific Cultural Contexts." *Frontiers in Psychology* 12 (November). https://doi.org/10.3389/fpsyg.2021.726729.

Kane, Jocelyn. 2019. "Statelessness in Canada: A Study on the Situation of Stateless Persons in Canada." United Nations High Commissioner for Refugees.

Kane, Jocelyn, Gezy Schuurmans, and Miho Kitamura. 2023. "Health Experiences of Stateless Persons in Canada." *Journal on Migration and Human Security* 11 (3): 261–78.

Kanji, Azeezah. 2018. "Framing Muslims in the 'War on Terror': Representations of Ideological Violence by Muslim versus Non-Muslim Perpetrators in Canadian National News Media." *Religions* 9 (9): 274. https://doi.org/10.3390/rel9090274.

Kaprielian-Churchill, Isabel. 1994. "Rejecting 'Misfits': Canada and the Nansen Passport." *International Migration Review* 28 (2): 281–306. https://doi.org/10.1177/019791839402800203.

Kassam, Ashifa. 2017. "Ratio of Indigenous Children in Canada Welfare System Is 'Humanitarian Crisis.'" *Guardian*, 4 November 2017. www.theguardian.com/world/2017/nov/04/indigenous-children-canada-welfare-system-humanitarian-crisis.

Kastrinou, A. Maria A., Salman Fakher El-Deen, and Steven B. Emery. 2021. "The Stateless (Ad)Vantage? Resistance, Land and Rootedness in the Israeli-Occupied Syrian Golan Heights." *Territory, Politics, Governance* 9 (5): 636–55.

Kaur, Harneel, Ammar Saad, Olivia Magwood, Qasem Alkhateeb, Christine Mathew, Gina Khalaf, and Kevin Pottie. 2021. "Understanding the Health and Housing Experiences of Refugees and Other Migrant Populations Experiencing Homelessness or Vulnerable Housing: A Systematic Review Using GRADE-CERQual." *CMAJ Open* 9 (2): E681–92. https://doi.org/10.9778/cmajo.20200109.

Kaya, Serdar. 2017. "Social Consequences of Securitizing Citizenship: Two-Tiered Citizenry and Anti-Immigrant Attitudes." *Canadian Ethnic Studies* 49 (3): 27–49. https://doi.org/10.1353/ces.2017.0020.

Kaye, Julie. 2017. *Responding to Human Trafficking : Dispossession, Colonial Violence, and Resistance among Indigenous and Racialized Women*. Toronto: University of Toronto Press.

Kaye, Julie, Hayli Millar, and Tamara O'Doherty. 2020. "Exploring Human Rights in the Context of Enforcement-Based Anti-Trafficking in Persons

Responses." In *The Palgrave International Handbook of Human Trafficking*, edited by John Winterdyk and Jackie Jones, 601–21. Cham: Springer International Publishing. https://doi.org/10.1007/978-3-319-63058-8_36.

Kaye, Julie, John Winterdyk, and Lara Quarterman. 2014. "Beyond Criminal Justice: A Case Study of Responding to Human Trafficking in Canada." *Canadian Journal of Criminology and Criminal Justice* 56 (1): 23–48. https://doi.org/10.3138/cjccj.2012.E33.

Kaye, Ron. 1998. "'Redefining the Refugee: The UK Media Portrayal of Asylum Seekers." In *New Migration in Europe*, edited by Khalid Kosher and Helma Lutz, 163–82. London: Palgrave Macmillan.

Keaten, Jamey. 2022. "UN Experts Detail Extensive War Crimes amid Tigray Conflict." *AP News*, 22 September 2022. https://apnews.com/article/health-united-nations-africa-ethiopia-eritrea-dcb992b83890694 90c8b44357500cabe.

Kelley, Ninette. 2022. *People Forced to Flee: History, Change and Challenge.* 1st ed. Oxford: Oxford University Press.

Kelley, Ninette, and Michael John Trebilcock. 2010. *The Making of the Mosaic: A History of Canadian Immigration Policy.* 2nd ed. Toronto: University of Toronto Press.

Kelly, Philip, Lualhati Marcelino, and Catherine Mulas. 2014. *Foreign Credential Recognition Research Synthesis 2009–2013: Final Report.* Toronto: CERIS.

Kelman, Ilan. 2020. *Disaster by Choice: How Our Actions Turn Natural Hazards into Catastrophes.* 1st ed. Oxford: Oxford University Press.

Kelman, Ilan, J.C. Gaillard, and Jessica Mercer. 2015. "Climate Change's Role in Disaster Risk Reduction's Future: Beyond Vulnerability and Resilience." *International Journal of Disaster Risk Science* 6 (1): 21–27. https://doi.org/10.1007/s13753-015-0038-5.

Kempadoo, Kamala, Nicole McFadyen, Philip Pilon, Andrea Sterling, and Alex Mackenzie. 2017. "Challenging Trafficking in Canada Policy Brief." Centre for Feminist Research York University. https://cfr.info.yorku.ca/files/2017/06/Challenging-Trafficking-in-Canada-Policy-Brief-2017.pdf.

Kennedy, Brendan. 2017. "Caged by Canada." *Toronto Star*, 17 March 2017. https://www.thestar.com/projects/short/2017/03/17/caged-by-canada.html.

Kernerman, Gerald. 2008. "Refugee Interdiction Before Heaven's Gate." *Government and Opposition* 43 (2): 230–48. https://doi.org/10.1111/j.1477-7053.2008.00254.x.

Keung, Nicholas. 2013. "I Did Not Choose to Have Cancer." *Toronto Star*, 9 June 2013.

– 2016a. "Police Cleared in Immigration Detainee's Death." *Toronto Star*, 15 July 2016. https://www.thestar.com/news/immigration/2016/07/15/police-cleared-in-immigration-detainees-death.html.

– 2016b. "Visa Officer, Refugee Meet Again in Tearful Reunion 30 Years Later."

Toronto Star, 19 June 2016. https://www.thestar.com/news/immigration/2016/06/19/visa-officer-refugee-in-tearful-reunion-30-years-later.html.
– 2017. “Asylum-Seeker Sues Federal Government over ‘Humiliating’ 5-Year Imprisonment.” *Toronto Star*, 1 October 2017.
– 2023. “Driver Who Caused Humboldt Broncos Bus Crash that Killed 16 People Gets Reprieve in Fight to Stay in Canada.” *Toronto Star*, 19 April 2023. https://www.thestar.com/news/canada/driver-who-caused-humboldt-broncos-bus-crash-that-killed-16-people-gets-reprieve-in-fight/article_fe0c82b7-82ea-5514-aad4-37020feff13b.html.

Khalafzai, Muhammad-Arshad K., Tara K. McGee, and Brenda Parlee. 2021. “Spring Flooding and Recurring Evacuations of Kashechewan First Nation, Northern Ontario, Canada.” *International Journal of Disaster Risk Reduction* 63 (September): 102443. https://doi.org/10.1016/j.ijdrr.2021.102443.

Khan, Attia, Nazilla Khanlou, Jacqueline Stol, and Vicky Tran. 2018. “Immigrant and Refugee Youth Mental Health in Canada: A Scoping Review of Empirical Literature.” In *Today’s Youth and Mental Health*, edited by Soheila Pashang, Nazilla Khanlou, and Jennifer Clarke, 3–20. Cham: Springer International Publishing. https://doi.org/10.1007/978-3-319-64838-5_1.

Kidd, S.A., J. Thistle, T. Beaulieu, B. O’Grady, and S. Gaetz. 2019. “A National Study of Indigenous Youth Homelessness in Canada.” *Public Health* 176 (November): 163–71. https://doi.org/10.1016/j.puhe.2018.06.012.

Kidd, Sean A., Kwame J. McKenzie, and Mulugeta Abai. 2014. “A Social Entrepreneurship Framework for Mental Health Equity: The Program Model of the Canadian Centre for Victims of Torture.” In *Refuge and Resilience*, edited by Laura Simich and Lisa Andermann, 7:155–65. International Perspectives on Migration. Dordrecht: Springer Netherlands. https://doi.org/10.1007/978-94-007-7923-5_10.

Kim, Michael Dokyum. 2022. “Advocating ‘Refugees’ for Social Justice: Questioning Victimhood and Voice in NGOs’ Use of Twitter.” *International Journal of Communication* 16 (January): 719–39.

Kimmerer, Robin Wall. 2013. *Braiding Sweetgrass: Indigenous Wisdom, Scientific Knowledge and the Teachings of Plants*. 1st paperback ed. Minneapolis: Milkweed Editions.

King, Tiffany Lethabo, Jenell Navarro, and Andrea Smith, eds. 2020. *Otherwise Worlds: Against Settler Colonialism and Anti-Blackness*. Black Outdoors: Innovations in the Poetics of Study. Durham: Duke University Press.

King, William Lyon Mackenzie. 2008. “I Speak as a Citizen of Canada.” In *Great Canadian Speeches: Words that Shaped a Nation*, edited by Brian Busby, 122–25. London: Arcturus Publishing Limited.

Kingston, Lindsey N. 2017. “Worthy of Rights: Statelessness as a Cause and Symptom of Marginalisation.” In *Understanding Statelessness*, edited by Tendayi Bloom, Katherine Tonkiss, and Phillip Cole, 17–34. Routledge.
– 2019. *Fully Human: Personhood, Citizenship, and Rights*. Oxford University Press.

Kinsman, Gary. 2018. "Policing Borders and Sexual/Gender Identities: Queer Refugees in the Years of Canadian Neoliberalism and Homonationalism." In *Envisioning Global LGBT Human Rights: (Neo)Colonialism, Neoliberalism, Resistance and Hope*, edited by Nancy Nicol, Adrian Jjuuko, Richard Lusimbo, Nick J. Mulé, Susan Ursel, Amar Wahab, and Phyllis Waugh, 97–130. London: Human Rights Consortium, Institute of Commonwealth Studies, School of Advanced Study, University of London.

Kinzel, Cheryl. 2020. "Indigenous Knowledge in Early Childhood Education: Building a Nest for Reconciliation." *Journal of Childhood Studies* (January): 19–32. https://doi.org/10.18357/jcs00019397.

Kira, Ibrahim A., Thomas Templin, Linda Lewandowski, David Clifford, Peggy Wiencek, Adnan Hammad, Jamal Mohanesh, and Abu-Muslim Al-haidar. 2006. "The Effects of Torture: Two Community Studies." *Peace and Conflict: Journal of Peace Psychology* 12 (3): 205–28. https://doi.org/10.1207/s15327949pac1203_1.

Kissoon, Priya. 2010. "From Persecution to Destitution: A Snapshot of Asylum Seekers' Housing and Settlement Experiences in Canada and the United Kingdom." *Journal of Immigrant & Refugee Studies* 8 (1): 4–31. https://doi.org/10.1080/15562940903575020.

– 2015. *Intersections of Displacement: Refugees' Experiences of Home and Homelessness*. Newcastle upon Tyne: Cambridge Scholars Publishing.

Klarenbeek, Lea M. 2019. "Relational Integration: A Response to Willem Schinkel." *Comparative Migration Studies* 7 (1): 20. https://doi.org/10.1186/s40878-019-0126-6.

Klassen, Lois. 2020. "Figurations Following the Ethical Turn." *Parse Journal* 10. https://parsejournal.com/article/figurations-following-the-ethical-turn.

Klepp, Silja. 2017. "Climate Change and Migration." In *Oxford Research Encyclopedia of Climate Science*, edited by Hans von Storch, Ingeborg Auger, Harold Brooks, Martin Claussen, Reiner Grundmann, Silvio Gauldi, Serget Gulev, Björn-Ola Linnér, Carlos Roberto Mechoso, Mu Mu, et al. Oxford: Oxford University Press. https://doi.org/10.1093/acrefore/9780190228620.013.42.

Kneebone, Susan. 2003. "Moving Beyond the State: Refugees, Accountability and Protection." In *The Refugees Convention 50 Years on: Globalisation and International Law*, edited by Susan Kneebone, 279–311. Routledge.

Kneebone, Susan, and Audrey Macklin. 2021. "Resettlement." In *The Oxford Handbook of International Refugee Law*, edited by Cathryn Costello, Michelle Foster, and Jane McAdam. Oxford Handbooks. Oxford: Oxford University Press.

Knowles, Valerie. 2007. *Strangers at Our Gates: Canadian Immigration and Immigration Policy, 1540–2007*. Rev. ed. Toronto: Dundurn.

Koblauch, Louise. 2018. "Problem Representation and the Externalization of Borders in the Canadian Electronic Travel Authorization and Interactive Advanced Passenger Initiative A Carol Bacchi Policy Analysis, What's the

Problem Represented to Be?" Bachelor Honours thesis, Malmo University. https://www.diva-portal.org/smash/get/diva2:1481036/FULLTEXT01.pdf.

Koehn, Sharon, Ilyan Ferrer, and Shari Brotman. 2020. "Between Loneliness and Belonging: Narratives of Social Isolation among Immigrant Older Adults in Canada." *Ageing and Society* (October): 1–21. https://doi.org/10.1017/S0144686X20001348.

Kofman, Eleonore, Sawitri Saharso, and Elena Vacchelli. 2015. "Gendered Perspectives on Integration Discourses and Measures." *International Migration* 53 (4): 77–89. https://doi.org/10.1111/imig.12102.

Kohlenberg, Beatrice, and Bryce Loo. 2020. "Assessment and Recognition of Refugee Credentials." *International Higher Education* 101 (1): 29–31.

Konadu-Agyemang, Kwadwo. 1999. "Characteristics and Migration Experience of Africans in Canada with Specific Reference to Ghanaians in Greater Toronto." *The Canadian Geographer* 43 (4): 400–414. https://doi.org/10.1111/j.1541-0064.1999.tb01397.x.

Korac, Maja. 2003. "Integration and How We Facilitate It: A Comparative Study of the Settlement Experiences of Refugees in Italy and the Netherlands." *Sociology* 37 (1): 51–68.

Korf, Benedikt. 2004. "War, Livelihoods and Vulnerability in Sri Lanka." *Development and Change* 35 (2): 275–95. https://doi.org/10.1111/j.1467-7660.2004.00352.x.

Korntheuer, Annette, Michaela Hynie, Martha Kleist, Safwathullah Farooqui, Eva Lutter, and Manuela Westphal. 2021. "Inclusive Resettlement? Integration Pathways of Resettled Refugees With Disabilities in Germany and Canada." *Frontiers in Human Dynamics* 3: 61. https://doi.org/10.3389/fhumd.2021.668264.

Korsten, Frans-Willem. 2021. *Art as an Interface of Law and Justice: Affirmation, Disturbance, Disruption*. Oxford: Hart Publishing.

Korteweg, Anna C., and Triadafilos Triadafilopoulos. 2013. "Gender, Religion, and Ethnicity: Intersections and Boundaries in Immigrant Integration Policy Making." *Social Politics: International Studies in Gender, State & Society* 20 (1): 109–36. https://doi.org/10.1093/sp/jxs027.

Korzeniewska, Lubomiła, and Marta Bivand Erdal. 2021. "Deskilling Unpacked: Comparing Filipino and Polish Migrant Nurses' Professional Experiences in Norway." *Migration Studies* 9 (1): 1–20. https://doi.org/10.1093/migration/mnz053.

Kovach, Margaret. 2010. *Indigenous Methodologies: Characteristics, Conversations and Contexts*. Toronto: University of Toronto Press.

Krahn, Harvey, Tracey Derwing, Marlene Mulder, and Lori Wilkinson. 2000. "Educated and Underemployed: Refugee Integration into the Canadian Labour Market." *Journal of International Migration and Integration* 1 (1): 59–84. https://doi.org/10.1007/s12134-000-1008-2.

Krahn, Harvey, and Graham S. Lowe. 1998. *Work, Industry, and Canadian Society*. 3rd ed. Toronto: ITP Nelson. http://books.google.com/books?id=aYcUAQAAIAAJ.

Krause, Maria. 2020. "Understanding the Evolving Nature of Refugee Sponsors in Canada." Ontario: Sponsorship Agreement Holder (SAH) and Queen's University.

Krause, Ulrike, Robin Vandervoordt, Alex Tasker, Felix Bender, Anne Ifran, Matthiew Gibney, Tom Western, Delina Abadi, and Patrick Chandiga Justine. 2022. "Rethinking Refugees as Actors." Rethinking Refuge. https://www.rethinkingrefuge.org/research/rethinking-refugees-as-actors.

Kress, Tricia M., Curry Malott, and Brad J. Porfilio. 2012. *Challenging Status Quo Retrenchment: New Directions in Critical Research*. Charlotte: Information Age Publishing.

Kronick, Rachel, and Cécile Rousseau. 2015. "Rights, Compassion and Invisible Children: A Critical Discourse Analysis of the Parliamentary Debates on the Mandatory Detention of Migrant Children in Canada." *Journal of Refugee Studies* 28 (4): 544–69. https://doi.org/10.1093/jrs/fev005.

– 2016. "They Cut Your Wings over Here … You Can't Do Nothing': Voices of Children and Parents Held in Immigration Detention in Canada." In *Detaining the Immigrant Other: Global and Transnational Issues*, edited by Richard Furman, Douglas Epps, and Greg Lamphear, 195–207. Oxford University Press.

Kronick, Rachel, Cécile Rousseau, and Janet Cleveland. 2011. "Mandatory Detention of Refugee Children: A Public Health Issue?" *Paediatrics & Child Health* 16 (8): e65–7. https://doi.org/10.1093/pch/16.8.e65.

Kubal, Agnieszka. 2014. "Struggles against Subjection. Implications of Criminalization of Migration for Migrants' Everyday Lives in Europe." *Crime, Law and Social Change* 62: 91–111.

Kuluberhan, Hermona. 2022. "Why Do Some Asylum Seekers Make It into the West Quickly – While Others Have to Wait More than a Decade?" *Globe and Mail*, 26 July 2022. https://www.theglobeandmail.com/opinion/article-why-do-some-asylum-seekers-make-it-into-the-west-quickly-while-others.

Kumsa, Martha Kuwee. 2006. "'No! I'm Not a Refugee!' The Poetics of Be-Longing among Young Oromos in Toronto." *Journal of Refugee Studies* 19 (2): 230–55. https://doi.org/10.1093/jrs/fel001.

Kusari, Kaltrina, Yahya El-Lahib, and Natalie Spagnuolo. 2019. "Critical Reflections on the Process of Developing a Resource Manual for Service Providers Working with Immigrants & Refugees with Disabilities." *Canadian Journal of Disability Studies* 8 (5): 98–119. https://doi.org/10.15353/cjds.v8i5.567.

Kustec, Stan. 2012. "The Role of Migrant Labour Supply in the Canadian Labour Market." *Government of Canada*. 1 July 2012. https://publications.gc.ca/site/eng/429230/publication.html.

Kymlicka, Will. 2004. "Marketing Canadian Pluralism in the International Arena." *International Journal* 59 (4): 829. https://doi.org/10.2307/40203985.

Kyriakides, Christopher. 2017. "Words Don't Come Easy: *Al Jazeera*'s Migrant-Refugee Distinction and the European Culture of (Mis)Trust." *Current Sociology* 65 (7): 933–52. https://doi.org/10.1177/0011392116658089.

Kyriakides, Christopher, Dina Taha, Carlo Handy Charles, and Rodolfo D. Torres. 2019. "Introduction: The Racialized Refugee Regime." *Refuge: Canada's Journal on Refugees* 35 (1): 3–7.

Labbé, Stefan. 2021. "Is It Time for Canada to Open Its Doors to Climate Migrants?" *Vancouver is Awesome*. https://www.vancouverisawesome.com/highlights/is-it-time-for-canada-to-open-its-doors-to-climate-migrants-4345242.

Labman, Shauna. 2007. "Resettlement's Renaissance: A Cautionary Advocacy." *Refuge: Canada's Journal on Refugees* 24, no. 2 (June): 35–47. https://doi.org/10.25071/1920-7336.21382.

– 2011. "Queue the Rhetoric: Refugees, Resettlement and Reform." *University of New Brunswick Law Journal* 62: 55–63.

– 2016. "Private Sponsorship: Complementary or Conflicting Interests?" *Refuge: Canada's Journal on Refugees* 32 (2): 67–80. https://doi.org/10.25071/1920-7336.40266.

– 2019. *Crossing Law's Border: Canada's Refugee Resettlement Program*. Law and Society Series. Vancouver: UBC Press.

– 2020. "Refugee Protection in Canada: Resettlement's Role." *Canadian Diversity* 17 (2): 7–11.

Labman, Shauna, and Geoffrey Cameron, eds. 2020. "Introduction: Private Refugee Sponsorship: An Evolving Framework for Refugee Resettlement." In *Strangers to Neighbours: Refugee Sponsorship in Context*. Montreal and Kingston: McGill-Queen's University Press. https://doi.org/10.2307/j.ctv176ktqs.

Labman, Shauna, and Adèle Garnier. Forthcoming. "A Necessary Re-Assertion of Government Resettlement." In *Canada's Role in the Global Refugee Regime*, edited by James Milner, Delphine Nakache, and Nathan Benson. Montreal and Kingston: McGill-Queen's University Press.

Labman, Shauna, and Jennifer Hyndman. 2019. "BVOR Briefing Note." Working Paper. Centre for Refugee Studies. https://crs.info.yorku.ca/files/2019/04/BVOR-Briefing-2019-May1.pdf.

Labman, Shauna, and Jamie Chai Yun Liew. 2019. "Law and Moral Licensing in Canada: The Making of Illegality and Illegitimacy along the Border." *International Journal of Migration and Border Studies* 5 (3): 188. https://doi.org/10.1504/IJMBS.2019.102446.

Labman, Shauna, and Madison Pearlman. 2018. "Blending, Bargaining, and Burden-Sharing: Canada's Resettlement Programs." *Journal of International*

Migration and Integration 19 (2): 439–49. https://doi.org/10.1007/s12134-018-0555-3.

Lacroix, Marie. 2004. "Canadian Refugee Policy and the Social Construction of the Refugee Claimant Subjectivity: Understanding Refugeeness." *Journal of Refugee Studies* 17 (2): 147–66. https://doi.org/10.1093/jrs/17.2.147.

Laczko, Frank, David Thompson, and John Salt. 2000. *Migrant Trafficking and Human Smuggling in Europe: A Review of the Evidence with Case Studies from Hungary, Poland and Ukraine.* Geneva: International Organization for Migration.

Lam, Elene, and Annalee Lepp. 2019. "Butterfly: Resisting the Harms of Anti-Trafficking Policies and Fostering Peer-Based Organising in Canada." *Anti-Trafficking Review*, no. 12 (April): 91–107. https://doi.org/10.14197/atr.201219126.

Lamba, Navjot K. 2003. "The Employment Experiences of Canadian Refugees: Measuring the Impact of Human and Social Capital on Quality of Employment." *Canadian Review of Sociology/Revue Canadienne de Sociologie* 40 (1): 45–64. https://doi.org/10.1111/j.1755-618X.2003.tb00235.x.

Lammasniemi, Laura. 2019. "International Legislation on White Slavery and Anti-Trafficking in the Early Twentieth Century." In *The Palgrave International Handbook of Human Trafficking*, edited by John A. Winterdyk and Jackie Jones, 1–12. Cham: Springer International Publishing. https://doi.org/10.1007/978-3-319-63192-9_112-1.

Landau, Loren B. 2012. "Communities of Knowledge or Tyrannies of Partnership: Reflections on North-South Research Networks and the Dual Imperative." *Journal of Refugee Studies* 25 (4): 555–70. https://doi.org/10.1093/jrs/fes005.

Landolt, Patricia, and Luin Goldring. 2018. "Assembling Noncitizenship Through the Work of Conditionality." In *Theorising Noncitizenship: Concepts, Debates and Challenges*, edited by Katherine Tonkissa and Tendayi Bloom, 27–43. London: Routledge, 2018.

Latif, Ehsan. 2015. "The Relationship between Immigration and Unemployment: Panel Data Evidence from Canada." *Economic Modelling* 50 (November): 162–7. https://doi.org/10.1016/j.econmod.2015.06.013.

LaViolette, Nicole. 2014. "Sexual Orientation, Gender Identity and the Refugee Determination Process in Canada." *Journal of Research in Gender Studies* 4 (2): 68–123. https://doi.org/10.2139/ssrn.2276049.

Lavoie, Marc-Antoine. 2019. "Inondations : Les sinistrés à petit budget forcés de quitter Sainte-Marie." Radio-Canada. https://ici.radio-canada.ca/nouvelle/1345487/inondations-sinistres-petit-budget-sainte-marie.

Lawlor, Andrea, and Erin Tolley. 2017. "Deciding Who's Legitimate: News Media Framing of Immigrants and Refugees." *International Journal of Communication* 11: 25.

Lawrence, Bonita. 2004. *"Real" Indians and Others: Mixed-Blood Urban Native Peoples and Indigenous Nationhood.* Lincoln: University of Nebraska Press.

Lee, Damien, and Kahente Horn-Miller. 2018. "Wild Card: Making Sense of Adoption and Indigenous Citizenship Orders in Settler Colonial Contexts." *AlterNative: An International Journal of Indigenous Peoples* 14 (4): 293–9. https://doi.org/10.1177/1177180118818186.

Lee, Edward Ou Jin. 2018. "Tracing the Coloniality of Queer and Trans Migrations: Resituating Heterocisnormative Violence in the Global South and Encounters with Migrant Visa Ineligibility to Canada" *Refuge: Canada's Journal on Refugees* 34 (1): 60–74.

Lee, Matthew T., and Ramiro Martinez. 2009. "Immigration Reduces Crime: An Emerging Scholarly Consensus." In *Sociology of Crime, Law and Deviance*, edited by William F. Mcdonald, 3–16. Leeds: Emerald Group Publishing Limited. https://doi.org/10.1108/S1521-6136(2009)0000013004.

Lee, Sharon M., and Barry Edmonston. 2010. "'Canadian' as National Ethnic Origin: Trends and Implications." *Canadian Ethnic Studies* 41 (3): 77–108. https://doi.org/10.1353/ces.2010.0040.

Legomsky, Stephen H. 2007. "Learning to Live with Unequal Justice: Asylum and the Limits to Consistency." *Stanford Law Review* 60 (2): 413–74.

Lehr, Sabine, and Brian Dyck. 2020. "Naming' Refugees in the Canadian Private Sponsorship of Refugees Program: Diverse Intentions and Consequences." In *Strangers to Neighbours: Refugee Sponsorship in Context*, edited by Shauna Labman and Geoffrey Cameron, 19–41. Montreal and Kingston: McGill-Queen's University Press. https://doi.org/10.2307/j.ctv176ktqs.

Lemberg-Pedersen, Martin. 2019. "Manufacturing Displacement. Externalization and Postcoloniality in European Migration Control." *Global Affairs* 5 (3): 247–71. https://doi.org/10.1080/23340460.2019.1683463.

Lemco, Jonathan. 1991. *Canada and the Crisis in Central America*. New York: Praeger.

Lenette, Caroline. 2019. *Arts-Based Methods in Refugee Research Creating Sanctuary*. 1st ed. 2019. Singapore: Springer Nature Singapore Imprint.

– 2021. "Virtual Talk with Dr. Caroline Lenette: 'Are Participatory Arts-Based Methods Culturally Safe?'" Centre for Migration Studies, YouTube video, 43:27.https://migration.ubc.ca/events/event/virtual-talk-with-dr-caroline-lenette-are-participatory-arts-based-methods-culturally-safe.

– 2022. "Cultural Safety in Participatory Arts-Based Research: How Can We Do Better?" *Journal of Participatory Research Methods* 3 (1): 32606.

Lenoir, Luc. 2021. "La France a-t-elle accueilli son premier 'réfugié climatique'?" *Le Figaro*, 8 January 2021. https://www.lefigaro.fr/faits-divers/la-france-a-t-elle-accueilli-son-premier-refugie-climatique-20210108.

Lentin, Alana. 2020. *Why Race Still Matters*. Cambridge: Polity Press.

Leo, Christopher, and Martine August. 2009. "The Multilevel Governance of Immigration and Settlement: Making Deep Federalism Work." *Canadian Journal of Political Science* 42 (2): 491–510. https://doi.org/10.1017/S0008423909090337.

Leroux, Darryl. 2019. *Distorted Descent: White Claims to Indigenous Identity*. Winnipeg: University of Manitoba Press.

Leslie, John F. 2002. "The Indian Act: An Historical Perpsective." *Canadian Parliamentary Review* 25 (2): 23–7.

Leudar, Ivan, Jacqueline Hayes, Jiří Nekvapil, and Johanna Turner Baker. 2008. "Hostility Themes in Media, Community and Refugee Narratives." *Discourse & Society* 19 (2): 187–221. https://doi.org/10.1177/0957926507085952.

Levitt, Peggy, and Nina Glick Schiller. 2004. "Conceptualizing Simultaneity: A Transnational Social Field Perspective on Society." *International Migration Review* 38 (3): 1002–39. https://doi.org/10.1111/j.1747-7379.2004.tb00227.x.

Levitz, Stephanie. 2012. "Hunt Is on for Romanians Believed to Be Part of Human Smuggling Ring." *Global News*, 5 December 2012. https://globalnews.ca/news/316025/hunt-is-on-for-romanians-believed-to-be-part-of-human-smuggling-ring-4.

– 2020. "Canada a Bright Light in a Horrible Year for Refugee Resettlement: UN Refugee Agency." *CTV News*. https://www.ctvnews.ca/canada/canada-a-bright-light-in-a-horrible-year-for-refugee-resettlement-un-refugee-agency-1.5230261.

Leydet, Dominique. 2017. "Citizenship." In *The Stanford Encyclopedia of Philosophy*, edited by Edward N. Zalta, Fall 2017. Metaphysics Research Lab, Stanford University. https://plato.stanford.edu/archives/fall2017/entries/citizenship.

Lezard, Percy, Noe Prefontaine, Dawn-Marie Cederwall, Corrina Sparrow, Sylvia Maracle, Albert Beck, and Albert McCleod. 2021. *2SLGBTQQIA+ Sub-Working Group MMIWG2SLGBTQQIA+ National Action Plan Final Report*. Toronto: OFIFC.

Li, Peter S. 2003. "Initial Earnings and Catch-up Capacity of Immigrants." *Canadian Public Policy* 29 (3): 319. https://doi.org/10.2307/3552289.

Li, Zhen, and John Lowe. 2016. "Mobile Student to Mobile Worker: The Role of Universities in the 'War for Talent.'" *British Journal of Sociology of Education* 37 (1): 11–29. https://doi.org/10.1080/01425692.2015.1095636.

Library and Archives Canada. 2013. "Black Loyalist Refugees, 1782–1807 – Port Roseway Associates." Military Heritage. 19 March 2013. https://www.bac-lac.gc.ca/eng/discover/military-heritage/loyalists/loyalist-port-roseway/Pages/port-roseway-associates-loyalists.aspx.

Library of Parliament. 2020. "Climate Change: Its Impact and Policy Implications." 4 2019-46-E. Library of Parliament. https://lop.parl.ca/sites/PublicWebsite/default/en_CA/ResearchPublications/201946E.

Liew, Jamie Chai Yun. 2020. "The Law's Broken Promises to Stateless Persons." *The Brown Journal of World Affairs* 26 (2): 1–13.

Lind, Christopher, and Joseph Mihevc, eds. 1994. *Coalitions for Justice: The Story of Canada's Inter-Church Coalitions*. Ottawa: Novalis Press.

Lippert, Randy. 2005. "Rethinking Sanctuary: The Canadian Context, 1983–2003." *International Migration Review* 39 (2): 381–406. https://doi.org/10.1111/j.1747-7379.2005.tb00271.x.

– 2010. "Wither Sanctuary?" *Refuge: Canada's Journal on Refugees* 26 (1): 57–67. https://doi.org/10.25071/1920-7336.30606.

Lippert, Randy K., and Miikka Pyykkönen. 2012. "Contesting Family in Finnish and Canadian Immigration and Refugee Policy." *Nordic Journal of Migration Research* 2 (1): 45–56. https://doi.org/10.2478/v10202-011-0026-9.

Lister, Matthew. 2013. "Who Are Refugees?" *Law and Philosophy* 32 (5): 645–71. https://doi.org/10.1007/s10982-012-9169-7.

Lobasz, Jennifer K. 2009. "Beyond Border Security: Feminist Approaches to Human Trafficking." *Security Studies* 18 (2): 319–44. https://doi.org/10.1080/09636410902900020.

Lockhart, Sarah P., and Briana Boland. 2021. "The Migration Industry: Human Smuggling and Human Trafficking." In *Introduction to International Migration*, edited by Jeannette Money, Sarah P. Lockhart. New York: Routledge.

Loescher, Gil, and James Milner. 2011. "UNHCR and the Global Governance of Refugees." In *Global Migration Governance*, edited by Alexander Betts, 189–209. Oxford: Oxford University Press. https://doi.org/10.1093/acprof:oso/9780199600458.003.0008.

Logan, Tricia E. 2014a. "Memory, Erasure, and National Myth." In *Colonial Genocide in Indigenous North America*, edited by Andrew John Woolford, Jeff Benvenuto, and Alexander Laban Hinton, 149–65. Durham: Duke University Press.

– 2014b. "National Memory and Museums: Remembering Settler Colonial Genocide of Indigenous Peoples in Canada." In *Remembering Genocide*, edited by Nigel Eltringham, 112–30. Remembering the Modern World. London: Routledge.

Logie, Carmen H., Ashley Lacombe-Duncan, Nakia Lee-Foon, Shannon Ryan, and Hope Ramsay. 2016. "'It's for Us –Newcomers, LGBTQ Persons, and HIV-Positive Persons. You Feel Free to Be': A Qualitative Study Exploring Social Support Group Participation among African and Caribbean Lesbian, Gay, Bisexual and Transgender Newcomers and Refugees in Toronto, Canada." *BMC International Health and Human Rights* 16 (1): 18. https://doi.org/10.1186/s12914-016-0092-0.

Long, Katy. 2010. *Home Alone? A Review of the Relationship between Repatriation, Mobility and Durable Solutions for Refugees.* UNHCR/PDES Evaluation Report PDES/2010/02.

Longboat, Catherine, Snežana Obradović-Ratković, Esther Wainaina, and Reshma Rose Tom. 2022. "Indigenous and Immigrant Voices for Healing and Wellness in Graduate Education." In *Supporting Student and Faculty Wellbeing in Graduate Education*, 1st ed., edited by Snežana Obradović-Ratković, Mirjana Bajovic, Ayse Pinar Sen, Vera Woloshyn, and Michael Savage, 37–55. New York: Routledge. https://doi.org/10.4324/9781003268185-4.

Loo, Tina. 2019. *Moved by the State: Forced Relocation and Making a Good*

Life in Postwar Canada. Brenda & David McLean Canadian Studies. Vancouver: UBC Press.

López-Sala, Ana. 2019. "'You're Not Getting Rid of Us': Performing Acts of Citizenship in Times of Emigration." *Citizenship Studies* 23 (2): 97–114. https://doi.org/10.1080/13621025.2019.1584156.

Lovgreen, Tina. 2016. "After 20 Years in a Refugee Camp, Burmese Family Starts New Life in BC." *CBC News*, 15 July 2016. https://www.cbc.ca/news/canada/british-columbia/burmese-refugee-family-qualicum-beach-1.3680265.

Löwenheim, Oded, and Orit Gazit. 2009. "Power and Examination: A Critique of Citizenship Tests." *Security Dialogue* 40 (2): 145–67. https://doi.org/10.1177/0967010609103074.

Lu, Yuqian, Yasmin Gure, and Marc Frenette. 2020. "The Long-Term Labour Market Integration of Refugee Claimants Who Became Permanent Residents in Canada." Statistics Canada. https://www150.statcan.gc.ca/n1/pub/11f0019m/11f0019m2020018-eng.htm.

Lui, Joyce. 2005. "'Redefining Canadian': A Participatory Filmmaking, Action Research Project with Immigrant and Refugee Youth." MA thesis, Simon Fraser University. http://summit.sfu.ca/item/10254.

Luibhéid, Eithne. 2008. "Queen/Migration: An Unruly Body of Scholarship." *GLQ: A Journal of Lesbian and Gay Studies* 14 (2–3): 169–90. https://doi.org/10.1215/10642684-2007-029.

Lupieri, Sigrid. 2021. "Refugee Health During the COVID-19 Pandemic: A Review of Global Policy Responses." *Risk Management and Healthcare Policy* 14 (April): 1373–8. https://doi.org/10.2147/RMHP.S259680.

Lustgarten, Abrahm. 2020. "The Great Climate Migration Has Begun." *New York Times*, 23 July 2020. https://www.nytimes.com/interactive/2020/07/23/magazine/climate-migration.html.

Lynch, Philip. 2001. "Keeping Them Home: The Best Interests of Indigenous Children and Communities in Canada and Australia." *Sydney Law Review* 23: 501–42.

Macklin, Audrey. 2003. "The Value(s) of the Canada-US Safe Third Country Agreement." Occasional Paper. Caledon Institute.

– 2005. "Disappearing Refugees: Reflections on the Canada-Us Safe Third Country Agreemen." *Columbia Human Rights Law Review* 36: 365–426.

– 2007. "Who Is the Citizen's Other? Considering the Heft of Citizenship." *Theoretical Inquiries in Law* 8: 333–66.

– 2009. "Asylum and the Rule of Law in Canada: Hearing the Other (Side)." In *Refugees, Asylum Seekers and the Rule of Law*, 1st ed., edited by Susan Kneebone, 78–121. Cambridge: Cambridge University Press. https://doi.org/10.1017/CBO9780511576805.005.

– 2014. "Citizenship Revocation and the Privilege to Have Rights." *SSRN Electronic Journal*. https://doi.org/10.2139/ssrn.2507786.

– 2020a. "A Brief History of the Brief History of Citizenship Revocation in Canada." SSRN *Electronic Journal*. https://doi.org/10.2139/ssrn.3655221.
– 2020b. "(In)Essential Bordering: Canada, COVID, and Mobility." *Frontiers in Human Dynamics* 2 (December). https://doi.org/10.3389/fhumd.2020.609694.
– 2021. "Working against and with the State: From Sanctuary to Resettlement." Migration and Society 4 (1): 31–46. https://doi.org/10.3167/arms.2021.040105.
Macklin, Audrey, Kathryn Barber, Luin Goldring, Jennifer Hyndman, Anna Korteweg, Shauna Labman, and Jona Zyfi. 2018. "A Preliminary Investigation into Private Refugee Sponsors." *Canadian Ethnic Studies* 50 (2): 35–57. https://doi.org/10.1353/ces.2018.0014.
Macklin, Audrey, and Joshua Blum. 2021. "Country Fiche: Canada." ASILE, Global Asylum Governance and the European Union's Role. https://www.asileproject.eu/wp-content/uploads/2021/03/Country-Fiche_CANADA_Final_Pub.pdf.
Madokoro, Laura. 2012. "'Slotting' Chinese Families and Refugees, 1947–1967." *Canadian Historical Review* 93 (1): 25–56. https://doi.org/10.3138/chr.93.1.25.
– 2016. *Elusive Refuge: Chinese Migrants in the Cold War*. Cambridge: Harvard University Press.
Madut, Kon K. 2016. "Neo-Liberalism: Employability, and the Labor Market Mobility among Racialized Migrants – Canada's Study." *International and Multidisciplinary Journal of Social Sciences* 5 (2): 128. https://doi.org/10.17583/rimcis.2016.1964.
Maghbouleh, Neda, Laila Omar, Melissa A. Milkie, and Ito Peng. 2019. "Listening in Arabic." *Meridians* 18 (2): 482–507. https://doi.org/10.1215/15366936-7789739.
Mahrouse, Gada. 2014. *Conflicted Commitments: Race, Privilege, and Power in Transnational Solidarity Activism*. Montreal and Kingston: McGill-Queen's University Press.
– 2021. "Producing the Figure of the 'Super-Refugee' through Discourses of Success, Exceptionalism, Ableism, and Inspiration." In *Refugee States: Critical Refugee Studies in Canada*, edited by Vinh Nguyen and Thy Phu, 173–93. Toronto: University of Toronto Press.
Maine, Nicole. 2015. "'I'm the One Who Is Looking After My Family': Refugee Youth Brokers, Pre-Departure Orientation and Settlement in Canada." MA thesis, York University.
Mainwaring, Cetta. 2012. "Constructing a Crisis: The Role of Immigration Detention in Malta: Constructing a Crisis: The Role of Immigration Detention in Malta." *Population, Space and Place* 18 (6): 687–700. https://doi.org/10.1002/psp.1721.
– 2016. "Migrant Agency: Negotiating Borders and Migration Controls." *Migration Studies* 4 (3): 289–308. https://doi.org/10.1093/migration/mnw013.
Mainwaring, Cetta, and Maria Lorena Cook. 2018. "Immigration Detention:

An Anglo Model." *Migration Studies* 7 (4): 455–76. https://doi.org/10.1093/migration/mnyo15.

Mainwaring, Cetta, and Daniela DeBono. 2021. "Criminalizing Solidarity: Search and Rescue in a Neo-Colonial Sea." *Environment and Planning C: Politics and Space* 39 (5): 1030–48. https://doi.org/10.1177/2399654420979314.

Mainwaring, Cetta, and Stephanie J. Silverman. 2016. "Detention-as-Spectacle." *International Political Sociology* 11 (1): 21–38. https://doi.org/10.1093/ips/olw016.

Major, Darren. 2023. "Roxham: The Little Country Road That Became a Big Political Headache for the Trudeau Government." CBC *News*, 25 February 2023. https://www.cbc.ca/news/politics/roxham-road-explainer-1.6756753.

Malkki, Lisa H. 1995. "Refugees and Exile: From 'Refugee Studies' to the National Order of Things." *Annual Review of Anthropology* 24 (1): 495–523.

Manalansan, Martin F. 2006. "Queer Intersections: Sexuality and Gender in Migration Studies." *International Migration Review* 40 (1): 224–49. https://doi.org/10.1111/j.1747-7379.2006.00009.x.

Manatschal, Anita, Verena Wisthaler, and Christina Isabel Zuber. 2020. "Making Regional Citizens? The Political Drivers and Effects of Subnational Immigrant Integration Policies in Europe and North America." *Regional Studies* 54 (11): 1475–85. https://doi.org/10.1080/00343404.2020.1808882.

Manitoba Start. 2015. "Career Services." 10 July 2015. https://www.manitobastart.com/for-newcomers/career-services.

Manuel, Arthur, and Grand Chief Ronald Derrickson. 2017. *The Reconciliation Manifesto: Recovering the Land, Rebuilding the Economy*. Toronto: James Lorimer & Company.

Mao, Bincheng. 2022. "People with Disabilities in Ukraine Are Being Left behind. Here's How to Help." World Economic Forum. https://www.weforum.org/agenda/2022/05/ukraine-refugees-disabilities-humanitarian.

Mariton-Robinson, Aileen. 2019. "Terra Nullius and the Possessive Logic of Patriarchal Whiteness: Race and Law Matters." In *Changing Law: Rights, Regulation and Reconciliation*. Reissued, edited by Rosemary C. Hunter, 123–35. Routledge Revivals. London: Routledge.

Markowitz, Peter L. 2021. "Rethinking Immigration Enforcement." *Florida Law Review* 73 (5): 1033–180.

Markstrom, Carol A. 2008. *Empowerment of North American Indian Girls: Ritual Expressions at Puberty*. Lincoln: University of Nebraska Press.

Marlowe, Jay. 2017. *Belonging and Transnational Refugee Settlement: Unsettling the Everyday and the Extraordinary*. 1st ed. London: Routledge. https://doi.org/10.4324/9781315268958.

– 2020. "Refugee Resettlement, Social Media and the Social Organization of Difference." *Global Networks* 20 (2): 274–91. https://doi.org/10.1111/glob.12233.

Martani, Ervis. 2021. "Canada's Private Sponsorship Program: Success, Shortcomings, and Policy Solutions." Working Paper No. 2021/6.

Martin, David A. 1991. "The Refugee Concept: On Definitions, Politics, and the Careful Use of a Scarce Resource." In *Refugee Policy: Canada and the United States*, 1st ed., edited by Howard Adelman, 30–51. Toronto and Staten Island, NY: Centre for Refugee Studies, York University and Center for Migration Studies of New York.

Martin, David A., and Kay Hailbronner, eds. 2008. *Rights and Duties of Dual Nationals: Evolution and Prospects*. The Hague: Kluwer Law International.

Martin, Donna E, Shirley Thompson, Myrle Ballard, and Janice Linton. 2017. "Two-Eyed Seeing in Research and Its Absence in Policy: Little Saskatchewan First Nation Elders' Experiences of the 2011 Flood and Forced Displacement." *International Indigenous Policy Journal* 8 (4). https://doi.org/10.18584/iipj.2017.8.4.6.

Martin, Lauren L., and Matthew L. Mitchelson. 2009. "Geographies of Detention and Imprisonment: Interrogating Spatial Practices of Confinement, Discipline, Law, and State Power: Geographies of Detention and Imprisonment." *Geography Compass* 3 (1): 459–77. https://doi.org/10.1111/j.1749-8198.2008.00196.x.

Martin-Hill, Dawn. 2003. "She No Speaks and Other Colonial Constructs of the Traditional Woman." In *Strong Women Stories: Native Vision and Community Survival*, edited by Kim Anderson and Bonita Lawrence. Toronto: Sumach Press.

Martiniello, Marco. 2022. "Researching Arts, Culture, Migration and Change: A Multi (Trans)Disciplinary Challenge for International Migration Studies." *Comparative Migration Studies* 10 (1): 7. https://doi.org/10.1186/s40878-022-00281-5.

Mason, Robert, Laura Munn-Rivard, and Julian Walker. 2021. "The United Nations Convention on the Rights of Persons with Disabilities: An Overview." 2013-09-E. HillStudies. Ottawa: Library of Parliament. https://lop.parl.ca/sites/PublicWebsite/default/en_CA/ResearchPublications/201309E.

Massey, Douglas S., Joaquin Arango, Graeme Hugo, Ali Kouaouci, Adela Pellegrino, and J. Edward Taylor. 1993. "Theories of International Migration: A Review and Appraisal." *Population and Development Review* 19 (3): 31–66. https://doi.org/10.2307/2938462.

Mata, Fernando, and Ravi Pendakur. 2017. "Of Intake and Outcomes: Wage Trajectories of Immigrant Classes in Canada." *Journal of International Migration and Integration* 18 (3): 829–44. https://doi.org/10.1007/s12134-016-0501-1.

Matas, David. 1985. "Racism in Canadian Immigration Policy." *Refuge: Canada's Journal on Refugees* 5 (2): 8–9. https://doi.org/10.25071/1920-7336.21485.

– 2003. "'Safe at Third?' Research on Immigration and Integration in the Metropolis." *Metropolis British Columbia*, Commentary Series No. C03-05.

Mather, Frederic Gregory. 1913. *The Refugees of 1776 from Long Island to Connecticut*. Albany: J.B. Lyon Company.

Mattar, Mohamed Y. 2020. "Drafting Human Trafficking Legislation: Binding Rules and Guiding Rules." In *International Legislative Drafting Guidebook: 25th Anniversary Celebration*. Durham, NC: Carolina Academic Press.

Matte Guilmain, Laurence, and Jill Hanley. 2021. "Creative Recourse in Cases of Forced Labour: Using Human Trafficking, Human Rights and Labour Law to Protect Migrant Workers." *International Migration* 59 (2): 126–39. https://doi.org/10.1111/imig.12743.

Mavelli, Luca, and Erin K. Wilson, eds. 2017. *The Refugee Crisis and Religion: Secularism, Security and Hospitality in Question*. Critical Perspectives on Religion in International Politics. London: Rowman & Littlefield International.

Mawani, Renisa. 2000. "In Between and Out of Place: Racial Hybridity, Liquor, and the Law in Late 19th and Early 20th Century British Columbia." *Canadian Journal of Law and Society* 15 (2): 9–38. https://doi.org/10.1017/S0829320100006359.

Mayblin, Lucy. 2014. "Colonialism, Decolonisation, and the Right to Be Human: Britain and the 1951 Geneva Convention on the Status of Refugees: Colonialism, Decolonisation, and the Right to Be Human." *Journal of Historical Sociology* 27 (3): 423–41. https://doi.org/10.1111/johs.12053.

– 2017. *Asylum after Empire: Colonial Legacies in the Politics of Asylum Seeking*. Kilombo: International Relations and Colonial Questions. London: Rowman & Littlefield International.

Mayer, Benoit. 2011. "The International Legal Challenges of Climate-Induced Migration: Proposal for an International Legal Framework." *Colorado Journal of International Environmental Law and Policy* 22 (3): 64.

Maynard, Robyn. 2017. *Policing Black Lives: State Violence in Canada from Slavery to the Present*. Halifax: Fernwood Publishing.

– 2019. "Black Life and Death across the U.S.-Canada Border: Border Violence, Black Fugitive Belonging, and a Turtle Island View of Black Liberation." *Critical Ethnic Studies* 5 (1–2): 124. https://doi.org/10.5749/jcritethnstud.5.1-2.0124.

McAdam, Jane, ed. 2008. *Forced Migration, Human Rights and Security*. Studies in International Law, vol. 17. Oxford: Hart.

– ed. 2010. *Climate Change and Displacement: Multidisciplinary Perspectives*. Oxford: Hart Pub.

– 2012. *Climate Change, Forced Migration, and International Law*. Oxford: Oxford University Press.

McAuliffe, Marie, Taehoon Lee, and Guy Abel. 2020. "Migration and Migrants: A Global Overview." In *World Migration Report 2021*, 28–58.

McCall, Sophie, Deanna Reder, David Gaertner, and Gabrielle L'Hirondelle Hill, eds. 2017. *Read, Listen, Tell: Indigenous Stories from Turtle Island*. Indigenous Studies Series. Waterloo: Wilfrid Laurier University Press.

McCloskey, Stephen. 2022. "The War in Ukraine Has Revealed a Hierarchy of Victims." *Policy and Practice: A Development Education Review* 34: 138–49.

McCormack, Brendan. 2020. "Red Tiles, White Mosaic: Indigeneity and the Institutionalization of Multiculturalism in Canada and Canadian Literature – Towards a Literary and Political History." PhD thesis, University of British Columbia.

McCullough, J.J. 2022. "Did Americans Really Move to Canada under Trump? Data Tells a Bigger Story." *Washington Post*, 18 October 2022. https://www.washingtonpost.com/opinions/2022/08/23/canada-us-immigration-data-republican-presidents.

McGee, Thomas. 2020. "Recognising Stateless Refugees." *Forced Migration Review* 65: 45–7.

– 2022. "Reflection on the Emergence of Critical Statelessness Studies (CSS): Recognising the Debt to, and Divergence from, Critical Citizenship Studies (CSS)." *Peter McMullin Centre on Statelessness Critical Statelessness Studies Blog Series*. April 2022. https://law.unimelb.edu.au/centres/statelessness/resources/critical-statelessness-studies-blog/reflection-on-the-emergence-of-critical-statelessness-studies.

McGranahan, Carole. 2018. "Refusal as Political Practice: Citizenship, Sovereignty, and Tibetan Refugee Status." *American Ethnologist* 45 (3): 367–79.

McGrath, Susan, and Ian McGrath. 2013. "Funding Matters. The Maze of Settlement Funding in Canada and Its Impact on Refugee Services." *Canadian Journal of Urban Research* 22 (1): 1–20.

McKeary, M., and B. Newbold. 2010. "Barriers to Care: The Challenges for Canadian Refugees and Their Health Care Providers." *Journal of Refugee Studies* 23 (4): 523–45. https://doi.org/10.1093/jrs/feq038.

McKee, Carolyn, Lee-Anne Lavell, Michelle Manks, and Ashley Korn. 2019. "Fostering Better Integration Through Youth-Led Refugee Sponsorship." *Refuge: Canada's Journal on Refugees* 35 (2): 74–85. https://doi.org/10.7202/1064821ar.

McKee, Michael, Deirdre Schlehofer, and Denise Thew. 2013. "Ethical Issues in Conducting Research With Deaf Populations." *American Journal of Public Health* 103 (12): 2174–8.

McKeen, Alex. 2020. "Fleeing Trump's America for Canada? This New Yorker Did It. Now He's Helping Others Follow." *Toronto Star*, 2 October 2020. https://www.thestar.com/news/canada/2020/10/02/fleeing-trumps-america-for-canada-this-new-yorker-did-it-now-hes-helping-others-follow.html.

McKenna, Kate. 2022. "Montreal Renews Program Offering Municipal ID to Undocumented Immigrants." *CBC News*, 22 February 2022. https://www.cbc.ca/news/canada/montreal/municipal-montreal-id-1.6360290.

McKenzie, Anna, Bayleigh Marelj, and Breille Morgan. 2021. "BC Ministry Warned Birth Alerts 'Illegal and Unconstitutional' Months before Banning Them." *IndigiNews*, 12 January 2021. https://indiginews.com/news/birth-alerts.

McKittrick, Katherine, and Clyde Adrian Woods. 2007. "No One Knows the Mysteries at the Bottom of the Ocean." In *Black Geographies and the Politics of Place*, edited by Katherine McKittrick and Clyde Adrian Woods, 1–13. Toronto: Between the Lines and South End Press.

McLachlin, Beverley. 2014. "Defining Moments: The Canadian Constitution." https://www.scc-csc.ca/judges-juges/spe-dis/bm-2014-02-13-eng.aspx.

McLaughlin, Janet. 2010. "Classifying the 'Ideal Migrant Worker.'" *Focaal* 2010 (57): 79–94. https://doi.org/10.3167/fcl.2010.570106.

McLellan, Janet. 2009. *Cambodian Refugees in Ontario: Resettlement, Religion, and Identity*. Toronto: University of Toronto Press. https://doi.org/10.3138/9781442697713.

McLeman, Robert, Mohammad Moniruzzaman, and Nasima Akter. 2018. "Environmental Influences on Skilled Worker Migration from Bangladesh to Canada: Environmental Migration Bangladesh-Canada." *The Canadian Geographer* 62 (3): 352–71. https://doi.org/10.1111/cag.12430.

McLeman, Robert, and Luisa Veronis. 2015. "Opinion: Canada Should Start Thinking about How to Address 'Environmental Migration' Issues." *Montreal Gazette*, 7 September 2015. https://montrealgazette.com/news/national/opinion-canada-should-start-thinking-about-how-to-address-environmental-migration-issues.

McMartin, Pete. 2021. "Pete McMartin: Historic Human Tsunami Likely in Canada's Future." *Vancouver Sun*, 20 August 2021. https://vancouversun.com/opinion/pete-mcmartin-historic-human-tsunami-likely-in-canadas-future.

McNally, Rachel. 2023. "Equally Public and Private Refugee Resettlement: The Historical Development of Canada's Joint Assistance Sponsorship Program." *Refuge: Canada's Journal on Refugees* 39 (1): 1–17. https://doi.org/10.25071/1920-7336.40941.

McNevin, Anne. 2013. "Ambivalence and Citizenship: Theorising the Political Claims of Irregular Migrants." *Millennium: Journal of International Studies* 41 (2): 182–200. https://doi.org/10.1177/0305829812463473.

McRae, Matthew. 2022. "The Chinese Head Tax and the Chinese Exclusion Act." Text and Images. Canadian Museum for Human Rights. https://humanrights.ca/story/chinese-head-tax-and-chinese-exclusion-act.

Medianu, Stelian, Alina Sutter, and Victoria Esses. 2015. "The Portrayal of Refugees in Canadian Newspapers: The Impact of the Arrival of Tamil Refugees by Sea in 2010." *IdeAs* 6 (October). https://doi.org/10.4000/ideas.1199.

Medina, José. 2020. "The Other Within: Agency and Resistance Under Conditions of Exclusion." *Philosophy & Social Criticism* 46 (1): 18–24.

Mellor, Andrea. 2020. "'Youth Will Feel Honoured If They Are Reminded They Are Loved': Supporting Coming of Age for Urban Indigenous Youth in Care." *International Journal of Indigenous Health* 16 (2). https://doi.org/10.32799/ijih.v16i1.33179.

Menjívar, Cecilia. 2000. *Fragmented Ties: Salvadoran Immigrant Networks in America*. Berkeley: University of California Press.
– 2014. "Immigration Law Beyond Borders: Externalizing and Internalizing Border Controls in an Era of Securitization." *Annual Review of Law and Social Science* 10 (1): 353–69. https://doi.org/10.1146/annurev-lawsocsci-110413-030842.
Menjívar, Cecilia, and Olivia Salcido. 2002. "Immigrant Women and Domestic Violence: Common Experiences in Different Countries." *Gender & Society* 16 (6): 898–920. https://doi.org/10.1177/089124302237894.
Mercier, Elise, and Sean Rehaag. 2020. "The Right to Seek Asylum in Canada (During a Global Pandemic)." SSRN *Electronic Journal*. https://doi.org/10.2139/ssrn.3687449.
Mezdour, Amina, Luisa Veronis, and Robert McLeman. 2016. "Environmental Influences on Haitian Migration to Canada and Connections to Social Inequality: Evidence from Ottawa-Gatineau and Montreal." In *Environmental Migration and Social Inequality*, edited by Robert McLeman, Jeanette Schade, and Thomas Faist, 61:103–15. Advances in Global Change Research. Cham: Springer International Publishing. https://doi.org/10.1007/978-3-319-25796-9_7.
M.I.A., Levi Lennox, and Amish Patel, dir. 2015. *Borders*. Interscope.
Michalowski, Ines. 2011. "Required to Assimilate? The Content of Citizenship Tests in Five Countries." *Citizenship Studies* 15 (6–7): 749–68. https://doi.org/10.1080/13621025.2011.600116.
Miedema, Baukje, Ryan Hamilton, and Julie Easley. 2008. "Grimper les murs: obstacles structurels à l'accès aux soins de première ligne par les nouveaux réfugiés au Canada." *Canadian Family Physician* 54 (3): 338–9.
Miedema, Baukje, Ryan Hamilton, Pierrette Fortin, Julie Easley, and Sue Tatemichi. 2009. "The Challenges and Rewards of Rural Family Practice in New Brunswick, Canada: Lessons for Retention." *Rural and Remote Health* 9 (2). https://doi.org/10.22605/RRH1141.
Mikkonen, Juha, and Dennis Raphael. 2010. *Social Determinants of Health: The Canadian Facts*. Toronto: York University, School of Health Policy and Management.
Milaney, Katrina, Rosaele Tremblay, Sean Bristowe, and Kaylee Ramage. 2020. "Welcome to Canada: Why Are Family Emergency Shelters 'Home' for Recent Newcomers?" *Societies* 10 (2): 37. https://doi.org/10.3390/soc10020037.
Millar, Hayli, and Tamara O'Doherty. 2020. "Racialized, Gendered, and Sensationalized: An Examination of Canadian Anti-Trafficking Laws, Their Enforcement, and Their (Re)Presentation." *Canadian Journal of Law and Society* 35 (1): 23–44. https://doi.org/10.1017/cls.2020.2.
Millar, Hayli, Tamara O'Doherty, and Katrin Roots. 2017. "A Formidable Task: Reflections on Obtaining Legal Empirical Evidence on Human Trafficking in

Canada." *Anti-Trafficking Review* 8 (April). https://doi.org/10.14197/atr.20121783.

Miller, David. 2005. "Immigration: The Case for Limits." In *Contemporary Debates in Applied Ethics*, edited by Christopher Heath Wellman and Andrew I. Cohen. Hoboken, NJ: Wiley-Blackwell.

– 2007. *National Responsibility and Global Justice*. Oxford: Oxford University Press.

– 2016. *Strangers in Our Midst: The Political Philosophy of Immigration*. Cambridge: Harvard University Press.

Miller, Rebecca, and Sebastian Baumeister. 2013. "Managing Migration: Is Border Control Fundamental to Anti-Trafficking and Anti- Smuggling Interventions?" *Anti-Trafficking Review* 2 (September): 15–32. https://doi.org/10.14197/atr.20121321.

Milner, James. 2021a. "Canada and the UN Global Compact on Refugees: A Case-Study of Influence in the Global Refugee Regime." In *International Affairs and Canadian Migration Policy*, edited by Yiagadeesen Samy and Howard William Duncan, 41–63. Canada and International Affairs. Cham: Palgrave Macmillan.

– 2021b. "The Politics and Practice of Refugee Participation in the Governance of the Global Refugee Regime." Paper presented to Canadian Political Science Association Annual Conference "Diversity and the Discipline of Political Science."

Milner, James, Mustafa Alio, and Rez Gardi. 2022. "Meaningful Refugee Participation: An Emerging Norm in the Global Refugee Regime." *Refugee Survey Quarterly* 41, no. 4 (May): 565–93. https://doi.org/10.1093/rsq/hdac007.

Milner, James, and Amanda Klassen. 2020. "Civil Society and the Politics of the Global Refugee Regime." Reference Paper for the 70th Anniversary of the 1951 Refugee Convention.

Ministry of Justice, Coroners Service, Province of British Columbia. 2014. "Verdict at Coroner's Inquest: Findings and Recommendations at the Result of the Coroner's Inquest Pursuant to Section 38 of the Coroner's Act, [SBC 2007] c. 15, Into the Death of Lucía Dominga Vega Jimenez."

Mismash, Ashton. 2021. "The Community Organization Refugee Sponsorship Program: Understanding Private Resettlement in New Zealand and Drawing Lessons from the Canadian System." PhD thesis, University of Auckland.

Moffette, David. 2014. "Governing Immigration through Probation: The Displacement of Borderwork and the Assessment of Desirability in Spain." *Security Dialogue* 45 (3): 262–78. https://doi.org/10.1177/0967010614530457.

– 2019. "Immigration et Criminalisation Au Canada: État Des Lieux." *Criminologie* 52 (2): 349–70. https://doi.org/10.7202/1065867ar.

– 2021. "Immigration Status and Policing in Canada: Current Problems, Activist Strategies and Abolitionist Visions." *Citizenship Studies* 25 (2): 273–91. https://doi.org/10.1080/13621025.2020.1859194.

Moffette, David, and Nevena Aksin. 2018. "Fighting Human Smuggling or Criminalizing Refugees? Regimes of Justification in and around *R v Appulonappa*." *Canadian Journal of Law and Society / Revue Canadienne Droit et Société* 33 (1): 21–39. https://doi.org/10.1017/cls.2018.2.

Moffette, David, and Jennifer Ridgley. 2018. "Sanctuary City Organizing in Canada." *Migration and Society* 1 (1): 147–55. https://doi.org/10.3167/arms.2018.010113.

Moffette, David, and Shaira Vadasaria. 2016. "Uninhibited Violence: Race and the Securitization of Immigration." *Critical Studies on Security* 4 (3): 291–305. https://doi.org/10.1080/21624887.2016.1256365.

Mohamed, Alea. 2020. "Climate Change-Induced Internal Displacement in Canada." Working Paper CC-20/02-2164. British Columbia Council for International Cooperation. https://www.bccic.ca/wp-content/uploads/2020/11/PDF_Climate-Change-Induced-Internal-Displacement-in-Canada_Mohamed_A_Sept2020-CC-20-02-2164.pdf.

Mohanty, Chandra Talpade. 2003. *Feminism without Borders: Decolonizing Theory, Practicing Solidarity*. Duke University Press. https://doi.org/10.2307/j.ctv11smp7t.

Mojab, Shahrzad. 1999. "De-Skilling Immigrant Women." *Canadian Women Studies* 19 (3): 123–8.

Molloy, Michael J., Peter Duschinsky, Kurt F. Jensen, and Robert J. Shalka. 2017. *Running on Empty: Canada and the Indochinese Refugees, 1975–1980*. McGill-Queen's Studies in Ethnic History. Series Two 41. Montreal and Kingston: McGill-Queen's University Press.

Molloy, Michael J., and Laura Madokoro. 2017. "Effecting Change: Civil Servants and Refugee Policy in 1970s Canada." *Refuge: Canada's Journal on Refugees* 33 (1): 52–61. https://doi.org/10.25071/1920-7336.40448.

Molnar, Petra. 2021. "Robots and Refugees: The Human Rights Impacts of Artificial Intelligence and Automated Decision-Making in Migration." In *Research Handbook on International Migration and Digital Technology*, edited by Marie McAuliffe, 134–51. Cheltenham: Edward Elgar Publishing.

Molnar, Petra, and Gill Lex. 2018. *Bots at the Gate: A Human Rights Analysis of Automated Decision-Making in Canada's Immigration and Refugee System*. Toronto: University of Toronto.

Molnar Diop, Petra. 2014. "The 'Bogus' Refugee: Roma Asylum Claimants and Discourses of Fraud in Canada's Bill C-31." *Refuge: Canada's Journal on Refugees* 30 (1): 67–80.

Monforte, Pierre, Leah Bassel, and Kamran Khan. 2019. "Deserving Citizenship? Exploring Migrants' Experiences of the 'Citizenship Test' Process in the United Kingdom." *The British Journal of Sociology* 70 (1): 24–43. https://doi.org/10.1111/1468-4446.12351.

Mongia, Radhika Viyas. 2003. "Race, Nationality, Mobility: A History of the Passport." In *After the Imperial Turn: Thinking with and through the Nation*, edited by Antoinette M. Burton. Durham: Duke University Press.

Montreal. 2022. "Personnes sans statut ou à statut précaire." 6 April 2022. https://montreal.ca/sujets/personnes-sans-statut-ou-statut-precaire.

Monture-Angus, Patricia. 1995. *Thunder in My Soul: A Mohawk Woman Speaks*. Halifax: Fernwood Publishing.

Moore, Will H., and Stephen M. Shellman. 2006. "Refugee or Internally Displaced Person?: To Where Should One Flee?" *Comparative Political Studies* 39 (5): 599–622. https://doi.org/10.1177/0010414005276457.

Moreton-Robinson, Aileen. 2015. *The White Possessive: Property, Power, and Indigenous Sovereignty*. Indigenous Americas. Minneapolis: University of Minnesota Press.

Morgensen, Scott Lauria. 2011. "The Biopolitics of Settler Colonialism: Right Here, Right Now." *Settler Colonial Studies* 1 (1): 52–76. https://doi.org/10.1080/2201473X.2011.10648801.

Morrice, Linda, Linda K. Tip, Michael Collyer, and Rupert Brown. 2021. "'You Can't Have a Good Integration When You Don't Have a Good Communication': English-Language Learning Among Resettled Refugees in England." *Journal of Refugee Studies* 34 (1): 681–99. https://doi.org/10.1093/jrs/fez023.

Morissette, René, Martin Turcotte, André Bernard, and Eric Olson. 2021. "Workers Receiving Payments from the Canada Emergency Response Benefit Program in 2020." *Statistics Canada*. 2 June 2021. https://www150.statcan.gc.ca/n1/pub/45-28-0001/2021001/article/00021-eng.htm.

Morrissey, James. 2012. "Rethinking the 'Debate on Environmental Refugees': From 'Maximilists and Minimalists' to 'Proponents and Critics.'" *Journal of Political Ecology* 19 (1). https://doi.org/10.2458/v19i1.21712.

Mortillaro, Nicole. 2019. "Could Canada Be a Safe Haven for Climate Refugees?" *CBC News*, 20 June 2019. https://www.cbc.ca/news/science/canada-climate-refugees-1.5165029.

Morton, Katherine A. 2016. "Hitchhiking and Missing and Murdered Indigenous Women: A Critical Discourse Analysis of Billboards on the Highway of Tears." *Canadian Journal of Sociology* 41 (3): 299–326. https://doi.org/10.29173/cjs28261.

Mosher, Clayton James. 2016. *Discrimination and Denial: Systemic Racism in Ontario's Legal and Criminal Justice System, 1892–1961*. Toronto: University of Toronto Press.

Mostafa Dadar v. Canada. 2005. 1 CAT 2005

Motalebi, Nasim, and Charles Martin-Shields. 2023. "Refugee-Led Organisations and Intersectionality: Feminist Development Policy in the Lives of Refugees." 5. IDOS Policy Brief.

Mountz, Alison. 2003. "Human Smuggling, the Transnational Imaginary, and Everyday Geographies of the Nation-State." *Antipode* 35 (3): 622–44. https://doi.org/10.1111/1467-8330.00342.

– 2011. "Where Asylum-Seekers Wait: Feminist Counter-Topographies of Sites between States." *Gender, Place & Culture* 18 (3): 381–99. https://doi.org/10.1080/0966369X.2011.566370.

– 2015. "In/Visibility and the Securitization of Migration." *Cultural Politics* 11 (2): 184–200. https://doi.org/10.1215/17432197-2895747.

Mountz, Alison, Kate Coddington, R. Tina Catania, and Jenna M. Loyd. 2013. "Conceptualizing Detention: Mobility, Containment, Bordering, and Exclusion." *Progress in Human Geography* 37 (4): 522–41. https://doi.org/10.1177/0309132512460903.

Mountz, Alison, and Nancy Hiemstra. 2014. "Chaos and Crisis: Dissecting the Spatiotemporal Logics of Contemporary Migrations and State Practices." *Annals of the Association of American Geographers* 104 (2): 382–90. https://doi.org/10.1080/00045608.2013.857547.

Muftic, Maja. 2009. "The Impact of Restrictive Immigration Policies on Human Trafficking in Canada." MA thesis, University of Ottawa. https://doi.org/10.20381/ruor-19233.

Muiznieks, Nils. 2016. "Annual Activity Report 2016." Commissioner for Human Rights of the Council of Europe, presented to the Committee of Ministers and the Parliamentary Assembly. http://hdl.handle.net/20.500.12389/22370.

Mulé, Nick J. 2020. "Safe Haven Questioned: Proof of Identity Over Persecution of SOGIE Asylum Seekers and Refugee Claimants in Canada." *Journal of Immigrant & Refugee Studies* 18 (2): 207–23. https://doi.org/10.1080/15562948.2019.1639238.

Mulholland, Mary-Lee. 2017. "Welcoming the Stranger in Alberta: Newcomers, Secularism and Religiously Affiliated Settlement Agencies." *Canadian Ethnic Studies* 49 (1): 19–42. https://doi.org/10.1353/ces.2017.0001.

Mulinari, Diana. 2007. "Women Friendly? Understanding Gendered Racism in Sweden." In *Gender Equality and Welfare Politics in Scandinavia: The Limits of Political Ambition?*, edited by Kari Anna-Birte Ravn Melby and Christina Carlsson Wetterberg, 167–82. Bristol: Policy Press.

Müller-Funk, Lea. 2021. "Research with Refugees in Fragile Political Contexts: How Ethical Reflections Impact Methodological Choices." *Journal of Refugee Studies* 34 (2): 2308–32. https://doi.org/10.1093/jrs/feaa013.

Mullings, Delores V., Anthony Morgan, and Heather Kere Quelleng. 2016. "Canada the Great White North Where Anti-Black Racism Thrives:" *Phylon (1960–)* 53 (1): 20–41.

Mulvey, G. 2010. "When Policy Creates Politics: The Problematizing of Immigration and the Consequences for Refugee Integration in the UK." *Journal of Refugee Studies* 23 (4): 437–62. https://doi.org/10.1093/jrs/feq045.

Murdie, Robert A. 2008. "Pathways to Housing: The Experiences of Sponsored Refugees and Refugee Claimants in Accessing Permanent Housing in Toronto." *Journal of International Migration and Integration* 9 (1): 81–101. https://doi.org/10.1007/s12134-008-0045-0.

Murdocca, Carmela, and Sherene H. Razack. 2008. "Pursuing National Responsibility in a Post 9/11 World: Seeking Asylum in Canada From Gender Persecution." In *Not Born a Refugee Woman Contesting Identities, Rethinking Practices*, edited by Maroussia Hajdukowski-Ahmed, Nazilla Khanlou, and Helene Moussa, 254–62. New York: Berghahn Books.

Murphy, Michael. 2019. "Indigenous Peoples and the Struggle for Self-Determination: A Relational Strategy." *Canadian Journal of Human Rights* 8 (1): 67–102.

Murray, David. 2013. "Becoming Queer Here: Integration and Adaptation Experiences of Sexual Minority Refugees in Toronto." *Refuge: Canada's Journal on Refugees* 28 (2): 127–35. https://doi.org/10.25071/1920-7336.36504.

– 2014. "Real Queer: 'Authentic' LGBT Refugee Claimants and Homonationalism in the Canadian Refugee System." *Anthropologica* 56 (1): 21–32.

– 2020. "Liberation Nation? Queer Refugees, Homonationalism and the Canadian Necropolitical State." *REMHU: Revista Interdisciplinar Da Mobilidade Humana* 28 (59): 69–78. https://doi.org/10.1590/1980-85852503880005905.

Mursal, Adam, and Weizhen Dong. 2022. "Should Canada Pay for Refugee Healthcare? A Social Justice Analysis of the Interim Federal Health Program (IFHP)." *Journal of Immigrant & Refugee Studies* (September): 1–14. https://doi.org/10.1080/15562948.2022.2128492.

Museum of Vancouver. n.d. "c̓əsnaʔəm, the City before the City." https://museumofvancouver.ca/csnam-the-city-before-the-city.

Mustafa, Manar, Zahariah Pilus, and Maskanah Mohammad Lotfie. 2021. "The Representation of Syrian Refugees in Canadian Online News Media: A Focus on the Topos of Burdening." *Canadian Journal of Communication* 46 (4): 875–903. https://doi.org/10.22230/cjc.2021v46n4a3807.

Nakache, Delphine, Jennifer Stone, and Elke Winter. 2020. "Aiming at Civic Integration? How Canada's Naturalization Rules Are Sidelining Refugees and Family-Class Immigrants." *Revue Européenne Des Migrations Internationales* 36 (4): 77–97. https://doi.org/10.4000/remi.17205.

Nakhaie, M. Reza, and Abdolmohammad Kazemipur. 2012. "Social Capital, Employment and Occupational Status of the New Immigrants in Canada." *Journal of International Migration and Integration* 14 (July): 419–37. https://doi.org/10.1007/s12134-012-0248-2.

Nansen Initiative. 2015. "Agenda for the Protection of Cross-Border Displaced Persons in the Context of Disasters and Climate Change." https://

disasterdisplacement.org/wp-content/uploads/2014/08/EN_Protection_Agenda_Volume_I_-low_res.pdf.

Nath, Nisha. 2021. "Curated Hostilities and the Story of Abdoul Abdi: Relational Securitization in the Settler Colonial Racial State." *Citizenship Studies* 25 (2): 292–315. https://doi.org/10.1080/13621025.2020.1859187.

National GAR Case Management. 2018. "What Is CSS?" National GAR Case Management – Client Support Services. 13 June 2018. https://clientsupportservices.ca/about-css/support-for-government-assisted-refugees.

National Housing Strategy Act. 2019. SC 2019, c. 29, s. 313.

Naujoks, Daniel. 2015. "The Securitization of Dual Citizenship. National Security Concerns and the Making of the Overseas Citizenship of India." *Diaspora Studies* 8 (1): 18–36. https://doi.org/10.1080/09739572.2014.957975.

Nawyn, Stephanie J., Linda Gjokaj, DeBrenna LaFa Agbényiga, and Breanne Grace. 2012. "Linguistic Isolation, Social Capital, and Immigrant Belonging." *Journal of Contemporary Ethnography* 41 (3): 255–82. https://doi.org/10.1177/0891241611433623.

Nelson, Charmaine. 2016. *Slavery, Geography and Empire in Nineteenth-Century Marine Landscapes of Montreal and Jamaica*. London: Routledge, Taylor & Francis Group.

Neu, Dean E., and Richard Therrien. 2003. *Accounting for Genocide: Canada's Bureaucratic Assault on Aboriginal People*. Black Point: Fernwood Publishing. .

Newbold, K. Bruce, Jenny Cho, and Marie McKeary. 2013. "Access to Health Care: The Experiences of Refugee and Refugee Claimant Women in Hamilton, Ontario." *Journal of Immigrant & Refugee Studies* 11 (4): 431–49. https://doi.org/10.1080/15562948.2013.808390.

Nguyen, Viet Thanh, Joseph Azam, David Bezmozgis, Fatima Bhutto, Thi Bui, Ariel Dorfman, Lev Golinkin, et al., eds. 2018. *The Displaced: Refugee Writers on Refugee Lives*. New York: Abrams Press.

Nguyen, Vinh. 2013. "Refugee Gratitude: Narrating Success and Intersubjectivity in Kim Thúy's *Ru*." *Canadian Literature* 219: 17–36.

– 2015. "Mẹ-Search, Hauntings, and Critical Distance." *Life Writing* 12 (4): 467–77. https://doi.org/10.1080/14484528.2014.915285.

– 2019. "Refugeetude: When Does a Refugee Stop Being a Refugee." *Social Text* 37 (2): 109–31.

– ed. 2021. *Refugee States: Critical Refugee Studies in Canada*. Cultural Spaces. Toronto: University of Toronto Press.

Nguyen, Vinh, and Thy Phu. 2021. *Refugee States: Critical Refugee Studies in Canada*. Cultural Spaces. Toronto: University of Toronto Press.

Nguyen, Vinh, Thy Phu, and Edward Ou Jin Lee, eds. 2021. "Queer and Trans Migrants, Colonial Logics, and the Politics of Refusal." In *Refugee States: Critical Refugee Studies in Canada*. Cultural Spaces. Toronto: University of Toronto Press.

Ní Mhurchú, Aoileann. 2014. *Ambiguous Citizenship in an Age of Global Migration*. Edinburgh: Edinburgh University Press.

Nibbs, Faith G. 2014. *Belonging: The Social Dynamics of Fitting in as Experienced by Hmong Refugees in Germany and Texas*. Durham: Carolina Academic Press.

Nichols, Leslie, Belinda Ha, and Vappu Tyyskä. 2019. "Canadian Immigrant Youth and the Education-Employment Nexus." *Canadian Journal of Family and Youth* 12 (1): 178–99. https://doi.org/10.29173/cjfy29497.

Nicol, Heather N. 2017. "From Territory to Rights: New Foundations for Conceptualising Indigenous Sovereignty." *Geopolitics* 22 (4): 794–814.

Nielson, John Louis Hubert. 1906. "Slavery in Old Canada: Before and After the Conquest." *Transactions* 26: 19–45.

Niemi, Maria, Hélio Manhica, David Gunnarsson, Göran Ståhle, Sofia Larsson, and Fredrik Saboonchi. 2019. "A Scoping Review and Conceptual Model of Social Participation and Mental Health among Refugees and Asylum Seekers." *International Journal of Environmental Research and Public Health* 16 (20): 4027. https://doi.org/10.3390/ijerph16204027.

Nieuwenhuys, Céline, and Antoine Pécoud. 2007. "Human Trafficking, Information Campaigns, and Strategies of Migration Control." *American Behavioral Scientist* 50 (12): 1674–95. https://doi.org/10.1177/0002764207302474.

No One is Illegal – Canada. 2014. "Action Alert: Death of Lucía Vega Jimenez in Migrant Detention." 29 January 2014. https://noii-van.resist.ca/action-alert-death-of-lucia-vega-jimenez-in-migrant-detention.

Nobe-Ghelani, Chizuru, and Mbala Lumor. 2022. "The Politics of Allyship with Indigenous Peoples in the Canadian Refugee Serving Sector." *Refuge: Canada's Journal on Refugees* 38 (1): 111–25. https://doi.org/10.25071/1920 7336.40841.

Nolin, Catherine. 2020. *Transnational Ruptures: Gender and Forced Migration*. London: Routledge.

Novotna, Gabriela, and Marina Morgenshtern. 2022. "Canada Needs to Stop Wasting the Talent of Skilled Immigrants." *The Conversation*, 15 May 2022. http://theconversation.com/canada-needs-to-stop-wasting-the-talent-of-skilled-immigrants-182005.

Nuttall, Jeremy. 2021. "Meet the People Fleeing the BC Wildfires – Packed in Hotels, RVs and Help Centres. Is This Our Climate Change Future?" *Toronto Star*, 14 July 2021. https://www.thestar.com/news/canada/2021/07/24/meet-the-people-fleeing-the-bc-wildfires-packed-in-hotels-rvs-and-help-centres-is-this-our-climate-change-future.html.

Nuzzolese, Emilio, and Giancarlo Di Vella. 2008. "Forensic Dental Investigations and Age Assessment of Asylum Seekers." *International Dental Journal* 58 (3): 122–6. https://doi.org/10.1111/j.1875-595X.2008.tb00186.x.

Nyers, Peter. 1999. "Emergency or Emerging Identities? Refugees and Transformations in World Order." *Millennium: Journal of International Studies* 28 (1): 1–26. https://doi.org/10.1177/03058298990280010501.

– 2006. *Rethinking Refugees*. London: Routledge.

– 2008. "No One Is Illegal Between City and Nation." In *Acts of Citizenship*, edited by Engin F. Isin and Greg Marc Nielsen, 160–81. London: Zed Books.

– 2013. *Rethinking Refugees Beyond State of Emergency*. New York: Routledge.

Oatley, Gabe, Roxanna Woloshyn, Mark Kelley, and Harvey Cashore. 2021. "Province Was Warned Breached BC Dike 'Substandard' Years Before it Failed." CBC *News*, 26 November 2021. https://www.cbc.ca/news/canada/dike-warnings-bc-government-fifth-1.6264082.

Oberman, Kieran. 2020. "Refugee Discrimination – The Good, the Bad, and the Pragmatic." *Journal of Applied Philosophy* 37 (5): 695–712. https://doi.org/10.1111/japp.12448.

Oberoi, Pia, Juana Sotomayor, Paola Pace, Barbara Rijks, Jacqueline Weekers, and Yehenew Tsegaye Walilegne. 2013. *International Migration, Health and Human Rights*. Geneva: International Organization for Migration. https://publications.iom.int/books/international-migration-health-and-human-rights.

Obradović-Ratković, Snežana, Vera Woloshyn, Kari-Lynn Winters, Neelofar Ahmed, Christos Govaris, Stavroula Kaldi, Christiana Deliewen Afrikaner, and Feyza Doyran. 2020. "Educating Refugee Students: Global Perspectives and Priorities." In *Education beyond Crisis: Challenges and Directions in a Multicultural World*, edited by Daniela Roxana Andron and Gabriela Gruber, 193–216. Leiden: BRILL. https://doi.org/10.1163/9789004432048.

Oda, Anna, Adnan Al Mhamied, Riham Al-Saadi, Neil Arya, Mona Awwad, Oula Hajjar, Jill Hanley, Michaela Hynie, Nicole Ives, Rabih Jamil, et al. 2022. "Ethical Challenges of Conducting Longitudinal Community-Based Research with Refugees: Reflections from Peer Researchers." In *Documenting Displacement: Questioning Methodological Boundaries in Forced Migration Research*, edited by Katarzyna Grabska and Christina R. Clark-Kazak, 29–55. Montreal and Kingston: McGill-Queen's University Press.

Ontario Council of Agencies Serving Immigrants (OCASI). 2009. "Positive Spaces Initiative Started Kit." https://ocasi.org/positive-spaces-initiative-psi.

– dir. 2021. "Supporting Intersectional Needs of Refugees with Disabilities and Their Families." YouTube video, 1:32:01. https://www.youtube.com/watch?v=A2DTTdHuKNs.

– n.d. "About Us: OCASI." https://ocasi.org/about-us.

Office of the Auditor General of Canada. 2003. *Report of the Auditor General of Canada to the House of Commons, Chapter 5, Citizenship and Immigration Control and Enforcement*. Minister of Public Works and Government Services Canada. http://www.oag-bvg.gc.ca/internet/docs/20030405ce.pdf.

Ogoe, Sally. 2022. "Measuring Success: Predictors of Successful Economic Integration of Resettled Female Refugees" PhD thesis, University of Manitoba. https://mspace.lib.umanitoba.ca/xmlui/handle/1993/36619.

Ohmagari, Kayo, and Fikret Berkes. 1997. "Transmission of Indigenous Knowledge and Bush Skills Among the Western James Bay Cree Women of Subarctic Canada." *Human Ecology* 25 (2): 197–222. https://doi.org/10.1023/A:1021922105740.

Oikawa, Mona. 2012. *Cartographies of Violence: Japanese Canadian Women, Memory, and the Subjects of the Internment.* Studies in Gender and History. Toronto: University of Toronto Press.

Okeke-Ihejirika, Philomina, Sophie Yohani, Bukola Salami, and Natalie Rzeszutek. 2020. "Canada's Sub-Saharan African Migrants: A Scoping Review." *International Journal of Intercultural Relations* 79 (November): 191–210. https://doi.org/10.1016/j.ijintrel.2020.10.001.

Okenwa-Emegwa, Leah, and Henrik Eriksson. 2020. "Lessons Learned from Teaching Nursing Students about Equality, Equity, Human Rights, and Forced Migration through Roleplay in an Inclusive Classroom." *Sustainability* 12 (17): 7008. https://doi.org/10.3390/su12177008.

Oliver, Michael. 1983. *Social Work with Disabled People.* London: Macmillan Education UK. https://doi.org/10.1007/978-1-349-86058-6.

– 2013. "The Social Model of Disability: Thirty Years On." *Disability & Society* 28 (7): 1024–26. https://doi.org/10.1080/09687599.2013.818773.

Oliver-Smith, Anthony. 2020. "'What Is a Disaster?': Anthropological Perspectives on a Persistent Question." In *The Angry Earth: Disaster in Anthropological Perspective*, 2nd ed., edited by Anthony Oliver-Smith and Susannah M. Hoffman. Abingdon: Routledge.

Olson-Pitawanakwat, Brianna, and Cyndy Baskin. 2021. "In Between the Missing and Murdered: The Need for Indigenous Led Responses to Trafficking." *Affilia* 36 (1): 10–26. https://doi.org/10.1177/0886109920944526.

Omar, Laila. 2022. "Foreclosed Futures and Entangled Timelines: Conceptualization of the 'Future' among Syrian Newcomer Mothers in Canada." *Journal of Ethnic and Migration Studies* (January): 1–19. https://doi.org/10.1080/1369183X.2022.2029372.

Omeziri, Eric, and Christopher Gore. 2014. "Temporary Measures: Canadian Refugee Policy and Environmental Migration." *Refuge: Canada's Journal on Refugees* 29 (2): 43–53. https://doi.org/10.25071/1920-7336.38166.

Ong, Aihwa. 2006. "Mutations in Citizenship." *Theory, Culture & Society* 23 (2–3): 499–505. https://doi.org/10.1177/0263276406064831.

Ontario Human Rights Commission. 2013. "Policy on Removing the 'Canadian Experience' Barrier." https://www.ohrc.on.ca/en/policy-removing-%E2%80%9Ccanadian-experience%E2%80%9D-barrier.

Orgocka, Aida, and Christina R. Clark-Kazak. 2012. *Independent Child Migrations: Insights Into Agency, Vulnerability, and Structure*. San Francisco: Jossey-Bass.

Osei Poku, Florence. 2018. "Adaptation and Survival Strategies of Refugee Women with Disabilities in Saksatoon, Canada." MA thesis, University of Saskatchewan. https://harvest.usask.ca/handle/10388/10571.

Oskay, Ecem. 2016. "The Refugee as an Agent: Insights from Structuration Theory." MA thesis, McGill University.

Oudshoorn, Abe, Erin Dej, Colleen Parsons, and Stephen Gaetz. 2020. "Evolving an Evidence-Based Model for Homelessness Prevention." *Health & Social Care in the Community* 28 (5): 1754–63. https://doi.org/10.1111/hsc.13000.

Ouellet, Valérie, Naël Shiab, and Sylvène Gilchrist. 2021. "White Men Make up a Third of Canada's Population but a Majority of MPs – Here's Why." *Radio-Canada*, 26 August 2021.

OurCare. 2023. *OurCare National Survey Findings: Summary Report*. Toronto: MAP Centre for Urban Health.

Owen, David. 2020. *What Do We Owe to Refugees?* Hoboken, NJ: Wiley.

Owens, Patricia. 2009. "Reclaiming 'Bare Life'?: Against Agamben on Refugees." *International Relations* 23 (4): 567–82. https://doi.org/10.1177/0047117809350545.

Oxman-Martinez, Jacqueline, Andrea Martinez, and Jill Hanley. 2001. "Trafficking Women: Gendered Impacts of Canadian Immigration Policies." *Journal of International Migration and Integration* 2 (3): 297–313. https://doi.org/10.1007/s12134-001-1000-5.

Pabla, Tanya. 2021. "Murdered and Missing Indigenous Women and Girls: A Discourse Analysis of Gendered Colonial Violence in Canada." *Journal of Law and Criminal Justice* 9, no. 2. https://doi.org/10.15640/jlcj.v9n2a1.

Pace, Jessica E., and Amanda Grenier. 2016. "Expanding the Circle of Knowledge: Reconceptualizing Successful Aging Among North American Older Indigenous Peoples: Table 1." *The Journals of Gerontology Series B: Psychological Sciences and Social Sciences* 72 (2): 248–58. https://doi.org/10.1093/geronb/gbw128.

Pace, Paola. 2009. "Migration and the Right to Health: A Review of International Law." Geneva: International Organization for Migration. https://publications.iom.int/books/international-migration-law-ndeg19-migration-and-right-health-review-international-law.

Palmater, Pamela. 2014. "Genocide, Indian Policy, and Legislated Elimination of Indians in Canada." *Aboriginal Policy Studies* 3, no. 3. https://doi.org/10.5663/aps.v3i3.22225.

Palmater, Pamela D. 2011. *Beyond Blood: Rethinking Indigenous Identity*. Saskatoon: Purich Publishing.

Panesar, Nilum, Yolande Pottie-Sherman, and Rima Wilkes. 2017. "The *Komagata* Through a Media Lens: Racial, Economic, and Political Threat in Newspaper Coverage of the 1914 *Komagata Maru* Affair." *Canadian Ethnic Studies* 49 (1): 85–101. https://doi.org/10.1353/ces.2017.0004.

Paquet, Mireille. 2012. "Beyond Appearances: Citizenship Tests in Canada and the UK." *Journal of International Migration and Integration*, 13: 43–60. https://doi.org/10.1007/s12134-011-0233-1.

– 2019. "Subnational Migration States and the New Politics of Immigration." *International Migration* 58 (6): 61–76. https://doi.org/10.1111/imig.12649.

– 2020. "Federalism and Immigration in Canada." In *Canadian Federalism: Performance, Effectiveness, and Legitimacy*, 4th ed., edited by Herman Bakvis and Grace Skogstad. Toronto: University of Toronto Press.

– 2021. "Stephen Harper and Canada's New Immigration Federalism." In *Open Federalism Revisited: Regional and Federal Dynamics in the Harper Era*, edited by James Harold Farney and Julie M. Simmons, 205–25. Toronto: University of Toronto Press.

Paquet, Mireille, and Meghan Joy. 2022. "Canadian Sanctuary Policies in Context." *Canadian Public Administration* 65 (4): 629–46. https://doi.org/10.1111/capa.12485.

Paquet, Mireille, and Lindsay Larios. 2018. "Venue Shopping and Legitimacy: Making Sense of Harper's Immigration Record." *Canadian Journal of Political Science* 51 (4): 817–36. https://doi.org/10.1017/S0008423918000331.

Paquet, Mireille, and Robert Schertzer. 2020. *Irregular Border Crossings and Asylum Seekers in Canada: A Complex Intergovernmental Problem.* IRPP Studies. https://centre.irpp.org/wp-content/uploads/sites/3/2020/11/Irregular-Border-Crossings-and-Asylum-Seekers-in-Canada-A-Complex-Intergovernmental-Problem.pdf.

Paquet, Mireille, and Howard Scott. 2019. *Province-Building and the Federalization of Immigration in Canada.* Toronto: University of Toronto Press.

Paquet, Mireille, and Catherine Xhardez. 2020. "Immigrant Integration Policies When Regions Decide 'Who Comes In': The Case of Canadian Provinces." *Regional Studies* 54 (11): 1519–34. https://doi.org/10.1080/00343404.2020.1808881.

Paragg, Jillian. 2015. "'Canadian-First': Mixed Race Self-Identification and Canadian Belonging." *Canadian Ethnic Studies* 47 (2): 21–44. https://doi.org/10.1353/ces.2015.0017.

Paré, Céline. 2022. "Selective Solidarity? Racialized Othering in European Migration Politics." *Amsterdam Review of European Affairs* 1 (1): 42–61.

Parekh, Serena. 2014. "Beyond the Ethics of Admission: Stateless People, Refugee Camps and Moral Obligations." *Philosophy & Social Criticism* 40 (7): 645–63. https://doi.org/10.1177/0191453713498254.

Parent-Chartier, Clotilde, Neil Santamaria, and Ian van Haren. 2023. "Civil Society Organizations and Collective Sponsorship of Refugees." In *Quebec. In Asylum and Resettlement in Canada. Historical Development, Successes,*

Challenges and Lessons, edited by Ervis Martani and Denise Helly, 262–81. Genova: University of Genova Press.

Paret, Marcel, and Shannon Gleeson. 2016. "Precarity and Agency through a Migration Lens." *Citizenship Studies* 20 (3–4): 277–94. https://doi.org/10.1080/13621025.2016.1158356.

Park, Augustine S.J. 2014. "Constituting Omar Khadr: Cultural Racism, Childhood, and Citizenship." *International Political Sociology* 8 (1): 43–62. https://doi.org/10.1111/ips.12039.

Parker, Christina. 2021. "Refugee Children in Canadian Schools: The Role of Teachers in Supporting Integration and Inclusion." In *Finding Refuge in Canada: Narratives of Disclocation*, edited by George Melnyk and Christina Parker, 167–76. Athabasca University Press Digital Publications. https://read.aupress.ca/read/e7b619f6-c68c-4510-8f6b-80884018c10a/section/97de78ec-d7b3-4e0f-afba-ee952aeadc75.

Parsi, Arsham. n.d. "LGBTQ Refugees Face Risk and Isolation Even after They Arrive in Canada." *CBC Docs POV*. https://www.cbc.ca/cbcdocspov/features/lgbtq-refugees-face-risk-and-isolation-even-after-they-arrive-in-canada.

Pashang, Soheila. 2019. "Entrapped Bodies: Illegalized Trafficked Youth in Canada." *International Journal of Mental Health and Addiction* 17 (2): 370–84. https://doi.org/10.1007/s11469-018-0027-1.

Patel, Sharifa. 2022. "Citizenship and Monogamy in Canada: The Case of the Shafia Family Murders." *Citizenship Studies* 26 (2): 167–83. https://doi.org/10.1080/13621025.2021.2024148.

Paterson, Josh. 2014. "Distressed, Afraid and Alone: Tragic Story Slowly Unfolds at Lucía Vega Jiménez Inquest." Commentary, BC Civil Liberties Association. 2 October 2014. https://bccla.org/2014/10/distressed-afraid-and-alone-tragic-story-slowly-unfolds-at-lucia-vega-jimenez-inquest.

Pearlman, Wendy. 2022. "How Homeland Experiences Shape Refugee Belonging: Rethinking Exile, Home, and Integration in the Syrian Case." *International Migration Review* 57 (1) (April). https://doi.org/10.1177/01979183221088206.

Pearson, David. 2002. "Theorizing Citizenship in British Settler Societies." *Ethnic and Racial Studies* 25 (6): 989–1012. https://doi.org/10.1080/0141987022000009403.

Pearson, Stephen. 2013. "'The Last Bastion of Colonialism': Appalachian Settler Colonialism and Self-Indigenization." *American Indian Culture and Research Journal* 37 (2): 165–84. https://doi.org/10.17953/aicr.37.2.g4522v76623113xg.

Peesker, Saira. 2021. "Refugee PSW Wants to Help but Is Shut out of Essential Workers' Residency Program." *CBC News*, 24 October 2021. https://www.cbc.ca/news/canada/hamilton/essential-workers-1.6219776.

Pellerin, Hélène. 2019. "Indigenous Peoples in Canadian Migration Narratives: A Story of Marginalization." *Aboriginal Policy Studies* 8 (1): 3–34. https://doi.org/10.5663/aps.v8i1.29347.

Pendakur, Krishna, and Ravi Pendakur. 1998. "The Colour of Money: Wage Differentials across Ethnic Groups." *Canadian Journal of Economics* 31 (3): 518–48.

Penninx, Rinus. 2019. "Problems of and Solutions for the Study of Immigrant Integration." *Comparative Migration Studies* 7 (1): 13. https://doi.org/10.1186/s40878-019-0122-x.

Perrin, Benjamin. 2011. *Invisible Chains: Canada's Underground World of Human Trafficking*. Canada's Underground World of Human Trafficking. Toronto: Penguin Canada.

Perry, Mike. 2018. "'The Tip of the Iceberg': Human Trafficking, Borders and the Canada-US North." *Canada-United States Law Journal* 42 (1): 204.

Perzyna, Maggie, and Sandeep Agrawal. 2022. "Making the Match: Understanding the Destining Process of Government-Assisted Refugees in Canada." *Journal of Immigrant & Refugee Studies* (May): 1–20. https://doi.org/10.1080/15562948.2022.2080896.

Petrozziello, Allison J. 2019. "(Re)Producing Statelessness via Indirect Gender Discrimination: Descendants of Haitian Migrants in the Dominican Republic." *International Migration* 57 (1): 213–28.

Phillimore, Jenny. 2021. "Refugee-Integration-Opportunity Structures: Shifting the Focus From Refugees to Context." *Journal of Refugee Studies* 34 (2): 1946–66. https://doi.org/10.1093/jrs/feaa012.

Phillips, Jim, Philip Girard, and R. Blake Brown. 2022. *A History of Law in Canada, Volume Two: Law for a New Dominion, 1867–1914*. Toronto: University of Toronto Press.

Phu, Thy. 2012. *Picturing Model Citizens: Civility in Asian American Visual Culture*. Philadelphia: Temple University Press.

Phung, Malissa. 2011. "Are People of Colour Settlers Too?" In *Cultivating Canada : Reconciliation through the Lens of Cultural Diversity*, edited by Ashok Mathur, Jonathan Dewar, and Mike DeGagné, 289–98. Ottawa: Aboriginal Healing Foundation.

Piché, Justin, Shanisse Kleuskens, and Kevin Walby. 2017. "The Front and Back Stages of Carceral Expansion Marketing in Canada." *Contemporary Justice Review* 20 (1): 26–50. https://doi.org/10.1080/10282580.2016.1262769.

Pickering, Sharon. 2004. "Border Terror: Policing, Forced Migration and Terrorism." *Global Change, Peace & Security* 16 (3): 211–26. https://doi.org/10.1080/0951274042000263753.

Picot, Garnett, Yan Zhang, and Feng Hou. 2019. "Labour Market Outcomes Among Refugees to Canada." Statistics Canada. 11 March 2019. https://www150.statcan.gc.ca/n1/pub/11f0019m/11f0019m2019007-eng.htm.

Pierre, Jemima. 2020. "Slavery, Anthropological Knowledge, and the Racialization of Africans." *Current Anthropology* 61 (22): 220–31. https://doi.org/10.1086/709844.

Pincock, Kate, Alexander Betts, and Evan Easton-Calabria. 2021. "The Rhetoric and Reality of Localisation: Refugee-Led Organisations in Humanitarian Governance." *The Journal of Development Studies* 57 (5): 719–34. https://doi.org/10.1080/00220388.2020.1802010.

Pisani, Maria, Shaun Grech, and Ayman Mostafa. 2016. "Disability and Forced Migration: Intersections and Critical Debates." In *Disability in the Global South*, edited by Shaun Grech and Karen Soldatic, 285–301. Cham: Springer International Publishing. https://doi.org/10.1007/978-3-319-42488-0_18.

Pityana, Dimza. 1991. "The Root Causes of Migration/Refugees: Economic and Political Dynamics from Women's Perspectives." *Reformed World* 41 (7–8): 225.

Pohlmann, Vanessa, and Helge Schwiertz. 2021. "Private Sponsorship in Refugee Admission: Standard in Canada, Trend in Germany?" Toronto Metropolitan University. https://doi.org/10.32920/ryerson.14638605.

Polillo, Alexia, and John Sylvestre. 2021. "An Exploratory Study of the Pathways into Homelessness among of Foreign-Born and Canadian-Born Families: A Timeline Mapping Approach." *Journal of Social Distress and Homelessness* 30 (1): 6–19. https://doi.org/10.1080/10530789.2019.1705518.

Potter, Jonathan, Margaret Wetherell, Ros Gill, and Derek Edwards. 1990. "Discourse: Noun, Verb or Social Practice?" *Philosophical Psychology* 3 (2–3): 205–17. https://doi.org/10.1080/09515089008572999.

Povinelli, Elizabeth A. 2012. "The Will to Be Otherwise/The Effort of Endurance." *South Atlantic Quarterly* 111 (3): 453–75. https://doi.org/10.1215/00382876-1596236.

Praag, Nick van. 2022. "Affected People Are Mostly Missing from the Localisation Debate. Let's Change That." *New Humanitarian*, 19 April 12022. https://www.thenewhumanitarian.org/opinion/first-person/2022/04/19/reform-humanitarian-aid-talk-communities-crisis.

Pratt, Anna. 2005. *Securing Borders. Detention and Deportation in Canada.* Vancouver: UBC Press.

Pratt, Anna, and Sara K. Thompson. 2008. "Chivalry, 'Race' and Discretion at the Canadian Border." *British Journal of Criminology* 48 (5): 620–40. https://doi.org/10.1093/bjc/azn048.

Praznik, Jessica, and John Shields. 2018. "An Anatomy of Settlement Services in Canada: A Guide." SSHRC-Ryerson University. https://bmrc-irmu.info.yorku.ca/files/2018/07/An-Anatomy-of-Settlement-Services-in-Canada_BMRCIRMU.pdf.

PressProgress. 2018. "Jason Kenney Defended Locking Up Child Refugees in Heavy Security Detention Facilities." 20 June 2018. https://pressprogress.ca/jason-kenney-defended-locking-up-child-refugees-in-heavy-security-detention-facilities.

Price, Matthew E. 2004. "Politics or Humanitarianism – Recovering the Political Roots of Asylum." *Georgetown Immigration Law Journal* 19 (2): 277–312.

– 2009. *Rethinking Asylum: History, Purpose, and Limits.* Cambridge: Cambridge University Press.

Priest, Lisa. 1993. "Who Pays Refugee Health Costs? The Bills Are Ottawa's in Theory, but Ontario Has Always Paid the Tab." *Toronto Star*, 15 July 1993.

Pringle, Jacob Farrand. 1890. *Lunenburgh, or the Old Eastern District.* Cornwall: Standard Printing House.

Pross, A. Paul. 1992. *Group Politics and Public Policy*. 2nd ed. Toronto: Oxford University Press.

Public Safety Canada. 2012a. "Harper Government Takes Action against Human Smuggling." https://www.publicsafety.gc.ca/cnt/nws/nws-rlss/2012/20121205-1-en.aspx.

– 2012b. "National Action Plan to Combat Human Trafficking." https://www.publicsafety.gc.ca/cnt/rsrcs/pblctns/ntnl-ctn-pln-cmbt/index-en.aspx.

– 2019. "National Strategy to Combat Human Trafficking 2019–2024." 4 September 2019. https://www.publicsafety.gc.ca/cnt/rsrcs/pblctns/2019-ntnl-strtgy-hmnn-trffc/index-en.aspx.

Puma, Jini E, Gary Lichtenstein, and Paul Stein. 2018. "The RISE Survey: Developing and Implementing a Valid and Reliable Quantitative Measure of Refugee Integration in the United States." *Journal of Refugee Studies* 31 (4): 605–25. https://doi.org/10.1093/jrs/fex047.

Pupavac, Vanessa. 2008. "Refugee Advocacy, Traumatic Representations and Political Disenchantment." *Government and Opposition* 43 (2): 270–92. https://doi.org/10.1111/j.1477-7053.2008.00255.x.

Putnam, Robert D. 1995. "Bowling Alone: America's Declining Social Capital." *Journal of Democracy* 6 (1): 65–78. https://doi.org/10.1353/jod.1995.0002.

Quirt, Maggie. 2021. "Why We Must Address the Colonial Dimension of Climate Migration." *The Conversation*, 14 October 2021. http://theconversation.com/why-we-must-address-the-colonial-dimension-of-climate-migration-169218.

R. v. Morris, 2006 SCC 59.

R. v. Sidhu, 2019 SKPC 19.

Rabiah-Mohammed, Fawziah, Leah K. Hamilton, Abe Oudshoorn, Mohammad Bakhash, Rima Tarraf, Eman Arnout, Cindy Brown, et al. 2022. "Syrian Refugees' Experiences of the Pandemic in Canada: Barriers to Integration and Just Solutions." *Studies in Social Justice* 16 (1): 9–32. https://doi.org/10.26522/ssj.v16i1.2669.

Rabiah-Mohammed, Fawziah, and Abe Oudshoorn. 2021. "An Exploration of Integration Journeys, Identity and Well-Being with Syrian Refugee Youth." Dalhousie University. https://dalspace.library.dal.ca//handle/10222/80896.

Rabson, Mia. 2019. "Flooding in Four Provinces Prompts States of Emergency, Evacuations." *Toronto Star*, 26 April 2019. https://www.thestar.com/news/canada/2019/04/26/premier-doug-ford-links-floods-to-climate-change-says-situation-just-rips-your-heart-out.html.

Radford, Jynnah, and Phillip Connor. 2019. "Canada Now Leads the World in Refugee Resettlement, Surpassing the U.S." Pew Research Center. https://www.pewresearch.org/fact-tank/2019/06/19/canada-now-leads-the-world-in-refugee-resettlement-surpassing-the-u-s.

Radio-Canada. 2021."Les évacués de Merritt s'inquiètent pour leur avenir | Inondations en Colombie-Britannique 2021." 17 November 2021. https://ici.radio-canada.ca/nouvelle/1840717/evacuations-merritt-bc-2021-inondations-kelowna-sandur-nourriture.

– 2022. "Désarroi après la fin de l'aide fédérale pour les évacués des inondations de Peguis." 28 April 2022. https://ici.radio-canada.ca/nouvelle/1879529/peguis-manitoba-inondations-compensation-financiere-federal.

Rae, Bob. 2020. *A Global Crisis Requires a Global Response – Report by Hon Bob Rae, Special Envoy of Prime Minister of Canada on Humanitarian and Refugee Issues*. Global Affairs Canada. 7 August 2020. https://www.international.gc.ca/world-monde/issues_development-enjeux_developpement/response_conflict-reponse_conflits/crisis-crises/global_crisis-crise_mondiale.aspx?lang=eng.

Rainbow Railroad. 2021. "Understanding the State of Global LGBTQI+ Persecution." https://www.rainbowrailroad.org/about.

Rajkumar, Deepa, Laurel Berkowitz, Leah F. Vosko, Valerie Preston, and Robert Latham. 2012. "At the Temporary-Permanent Divide: How Canada Produces Temporariness and Makes Citizens through Its Security, Work, and Settlement Policies." *Citizenship Studies* 16 (3–4): 483–510. https://doi.org/10.1080/13621025.2012.683262.

Ramadan, Adam. 2013. "Spatialising the Refugee Camp: *Spatialising the Refugee Camp*." *Transactions of the Institute of British Geographers* 38 (1): 65–77. https://doi.org/10.1111/j.1475-5661.2012.00509.x.

Raska, Jan. 2019. "Welcoming the Sick and Afflicted: Canada's Tubercular Admissions Program, 1959–1960." *Social History* 52 (105): 171–92. https://doi.org/10.1353/his.2019.0008.

Rathe, Kaja Jenssen. 2022. "Towards a Critical Phenomenology of Borders and Migration: Introduction to the Themed Issue." *Puncta* 5 (3): 1–11. https://doi.org/10.5399/pjcp.v5i3.1.

Ratković, Snežana, Dragana Kovačević, Courtney A. Brewer, Claire Ellis, Neelofar Amhed, and Janelle Baptiste-Bardy. 2017. "Supporting Refugee Students in Canada – Building on What We Have Learned in the Past 20 Years." ESPMI Network. https://espminetwork.com/new-report-supporting-refugee-students-in-canada-building-on-what-we-have-learned-in-the-past-20-years.

Raulerson, Matt. 2022. "Advocates Push for Canada to Protect Climate Migrants." Text and Images. Climate Refugees. 22 March 2022. https://www.climate-refugees.org/spotlight/2022/3/22/canadianpolicy.

Raycraft, Richard. 2023. "New Deal with U.S. Allows Canada to Turn Back Migrants at the Border." *CBC News*, 24 March 2023. https://www.cbc.ca/news/politics/canada-united-states-border-deal-reach-1.6789815.
Raymond, Heather, D. Jean Clandinin, Hiroko Kubota, and Vera Caine. 2022. "Bumping Places of Social Inclusion: A Narrative Inquiry into the Experiences of Refugee Families Who Have a Child Who is Living with a Disability." *Equity & Excellence in Education* 55 (1–2): 73–86. https://doi.org/10.1080/10665684.2022.2076781.
Razack, Sherene, ed. 2002. *Race, Space, and the Law: Unmapping a White Settler Society*. Toronto: Between the Lines.
Razack, Sherene H. 2021. "Human Waste and the Border: A Vignette." *Law, Culture and the Humanities* 17 (2): 322–34. https://doi.org/10.1177/1743872117749524.
Recalde-Vela, Maria Jose, Sangita Jaghai-Bajulaiye, and Caia Vlieks. 2019. "The State of Statelessness Research: 5 Years Later?" *Tilburg Law Review: Journal on International and Comparative Law* 24 (2): 139–41.
Redclift, Victoria. 2013. *Statelessness and Citizenship: Camps and the Creation of Political Space*. Milton Park: Routledge.
Reese, Renford. 2011. "Canada: The Promised Land for US Slaves." *The Western Journal of Black Studies* 35 (3): 208–18.
Refugee Advisory Network of Canada (RAN Canada). n.d. "As per Our Mandate." https://www.rancanada.ca/home.
Refugee Sponsorship Training Program (RSTP). 2013. "Sponsorship Agreement Holder's Manual." https://www.rstp.ca/wp-content/uploads/2014/03/SAH-manual-Jan.2013_SS.pdf.
– 2022. "What Is BVOR?" Refugee Sponsorship Training Program. https://www.rstp.ca/en/bvor/info.
Rehaag, Sean. 2008. "Patrolling the Borders of Sexual Orientation: Bisexual Refugee Claims in Canada." *McGill Law Journal* 53: 44.
– 2010. "Bordering on Legality: Canadian Church Sanctuary and the Rule of Law." *Refuge: Canada's Journal on Refugees* 26 (1): 43–56. https://doi.org/10.25071/1920-7336.30605.
Reichman, Daniel R. 2022. "Putting Climate-Induced Migration in Context: The Case of Honduran Migration to the USA." *Regional Environmental Change* 22 (3): 91. https://doi.org/10.1007/s10113-022-01946-8.
Reid, John G., and Thomas Peace. 2016. "Colonies of Settlement and Settler Colonialism in Northeastern North America, 1450–1850." In *The Routledge Handbook of the History of Settler Colonialism*, edited by Edward Cavanagh and Lorenzo Veracini, 79–94. Oxford: Routledge. https://doi.org/10.4324/9781315544816.
Reitz, Jeffrey G. 2001. "Immigrant Skill Utilization in the Canadian Labour Market: Implications of Human Capital Research." *Journal of International*

Migration and Integration/ Revue de l'integration et de la migration internationale 2 (3): 347–78. https://doi.org/10.1007/s12134-001-1004-1.

Reitz, Jeffrey G., Patrick Simon, and Emily Laxer. 2017. "Muslims' Social Inclusion and Exclusion in France, Québec, and Canada: Does National Context Matter?" *Journal of Ethnic and Migration Studies* 43 (15): 2473–98. https://doi.org/10.1080/1369183X.2017.1313105.

Renfrew, Matthew. 2022. "Support for Syrian vs. Ukrainian Refugees in Canada: A Lesson in Bias." *Cult MTL*, 16 March 2022. https://cultmtl.com/2022/03/support-for-syrian-vs-ukrainian-refugees-in-canada-a-lesson-in-bias.

Rességuier, Vincent. 2022. "De Roxham à l'Ontario, un trajet parfois fait à contrecœur." *Radio-Canada*, 8 November 2022. https://ici.radio-canada.ca/nouvelle/1930121/chemin-roxham-ontario-migrants-transferts.

Reynolds, Johanna, and Jennifer Hyndman. 2021. "Shifting Grounds of Asylum in Canadian Public Discourse and Policy." In *Refugee States: Critical Refugee Studies in Canada*, edited by Vinh Nguyen and Thy Phu. Cultural Spaces. Toronto: University of Toronto Press.

Riaño Alcalá, Pilar, Martha Colorado, Patricia Díaz, and Amantina Osorio. 2008. *Forced Migration of Colombians Colombia, Ecuador, Canada*. Public Report. Medellín, Colombia, and Vancouver: Corporación Región and School of Social Work, University of British Columbia. https://yorkspace.library.yorku.ca/xmlui/bitstream/handle/10315/2592/ForcedMigrationColombians.pdf.

Riddell, William Renwick. 1919. "The Slave in Upper Canada." *The Journal of Negro History* 4 (4): 372–95.

– 1920a. "The Slave in Canada." *The Journal of Negro History* 5 (3): 261–337.

– 1920b. "Slavery in the Maritime Provinces." *The Journal of Negro History* 5 (3): 359–75. https://doi.org/10.2307/2713627.

– 1921. "The Baptism of Slaves in Prince Edward Island." *The Journal of Negro History* 6 (3): 307–9. https://doi.org/10.2307/2713756.

– 1923. "Notes on the Slave in Nouvelle-France." *The Journal of Negro History* 8 (3): 316–30. https://doi.org/10.2307/2713562.

– 1924. "Further Notes on Slavery in Canada." *The Journal of Negro History* 9 (1): 26–33. https://doi.org/10.2307/2713434.

– 1929. "An Official Record of Slavery in Upper Canada." *Papers and Records*, Ontario Historical Society, no. 25, 393–7.

– 1932. "Additional Notes on Slavery." *The Journal of Negro History* 17 (3): 368–77. https://doi.org/10.2307/2714282.

Ridgley, Jennifer. 2011. "Refuge, Refusal, and Acts of Holy Contagion: The City as a Sanctuary for Soldiers Resisting the Vietnam War." *ACME: An International Journal for Critical Geographies* 10 (2): 189–214.

Rigney, Sophie. 2021. "On Hearing Well and Being Well Heard: Indigenous International Law at the League of Nations." *Third World Approaches to International Law Review* 2 (2): 122–53.

Riley, Sharon J. 2022. "The Humboldt Crash: How Much Punishment Is Enough for Jaskirat Singh Sidhu?" *Walrus*, 2 June 2022. https://thewalrus.ca/humboldt-crash-driver.

Riley-Guiu, Eliana. 2022. "Black Borders: Racism in War and Post War Migration." Global Social Challenges, University of Manchester. 6 July 2022. https://sites.manchester.ac.uk/global-social-challenges/2022/07/06/black-borders-racism-in-war-and-post-war-migration.

Rinaldi, Jen, and Shanti Fernando. 2019. "Queer Credibility in the Homonation-State: Interrogating the Affective Impacts of Credibility Assessments on Racialized Sexual Minority Refugee Claimants." *Refuge: Canada's Journal on Refugees* 35 (1): 32–42. https://doi.org/10.7202/1060673ar.

Ristock, Janice, Art Zoccole, Lisa Passante, and Jonathon Potskin. 2019. "Impacts of Colonization on Indigenous Two-Spirit/LGBTQ Canadians' Experiences of Migration, Mobility and Relationship Violence." *Sexualities* 22 (5–6): 767–84. https://doi.org/10.1177/1363460716681474.

Ritchie, Genevieve. 2018. "Civil Society, the State, and Private Sponsorship: The Political Economy of Refugee Resettlement." *International Journal of Lifelong Education* 37 (6): 663–75. https://doi.org/10.1080/02601370.2018.1513429.

Roache, Trina. 2021. "$150B Global Human Trafficking Industry Happening in Plain Sight in Canada Say Experts." *APTN News*, 17 April 2021. https://www.aptnnews.ca/investigates/aptn-investigates-exploited-human-trafficking-nova-scotia.

Roberts, Barbara Ann. 1988. *Whence They Came: Deportation from Canada, 1900–1935*. Ottawa: University of Ottawa Press.

Robinson, Alex. 2022. "How Climate Migrants Can Help Power the Clean Economy." *Corporate Knights*, 24 January 2022. https://www.corporateknights.com/climate-and-carbon/how-climate-migrants-can-help-power-the-clean-economy.

Robinson, Greg. 2017. "Internment of Japanese Canadians." *The Canadian Encyclopedia*, Historica Canada, 15 February 2017. https://www.thecanadianencyclopedia.ca/en/article/internment-of-japanese-canadians.

Rocher, François. 2023. "Transformations in Contemporary Quebec Nationalism, 1960–2020: A Shift in the Sources of Collective Animosities." *Nations and Nationalism* 29 (1): 280–94. https://doi.org/10.1111/nana.12902.

Roots, Katrin. 2013. "Trafficking or Pimping? An Analysis of Canada's Human Trafficking Legislation and Its Implications." *Canadian Journal of Law and Society / La Revue Canadienne Droit et Société* 28 (1): 21–41. https://doi.org/10.1017/cls.2012.4.

– 2018. "The Human Trafficking Matrix: Law, Policy and Anti-Trafficking Practices in the Canadian Criminal Justice System." PhD thesis, York University.

Roots, Katrin, and Ann De Shalit. 2015. "Evidence that Evidence Doesn't Matter: Human Trafficking Cases in Canada." *Atlantis: Critical Studies in Gender, Culture & Social Justice* 37 (2): 65–80.

Rose, Damaris. 2001. "The Housing Situation of Refugees in Montréal Three Years after Arrival: The Case of Asylum Seekers Who Obtained Permanent Residence." *Journal of International Migration and Integration* 2 (4): 493–529. https://doi.org/10.1007/s12134-001-1010-3.

– 2019. *Creating a Home in Canada: Refugee Housing Challenges and Potential Policy Solutions*. Migration Policy Institute. https://www.migrationpolicy.org/sites/default/files/publications/TCM-Canada-Housing-Refugees_FINAL.pdf.

Rosinbum, John. 2015. "'We Are in the Middle of Two Great Powers': Refugees, Activists, and Government during the Plattsburgh Border Crisis of 1987." *Refuge: Canada's Journal on Refugees* 31 (2): 15–24. https://doi.org/10.25071/1920-7336.40319.

Rossiter, Marian J., Sarvenaz Hatami, Dan Ripley, and Katherine R. Rossiter. 2015. "Immigrant and Refugee Youth Settlement Experiences: 'A New Kind of War.'" *International Journal of Child, Youth and Family Studies* 6 (4–1): 746–70. https://doi.org/10.18357/ijcyfs.64120l515056.

Ross-Tremblay, Pierrot. 2019. *Thou Shalt Forget: Indigenous Sovereignty, Resistance and the Production of Cultural Oblivion in Canada*. London: University of London Press.

Roudometkina, Arina, and Kim Wakeford. 2018. "Trafficking of Indigenous Women and Girls in Canada" Native Women's Association of Canada. https://www.ourcommons.ca/Content/Committee/421/JUST/Brief/BR10002955/br-external/NativeWomensAssociationOfCanada-e.pdf.

Routte, Irene, Ana Paula Pimentel Walker, Mieko Yoshihama, Allison Kelly, and Odessa Gonzalez-Benson. 2022. "Refugee-Led Organizations' Crisis Response during the COVID-19 Pandemic." *Refuge: Canada's Journal on Refugees* 38 (1): 62–77. https://doi.org/10.25071/1920-7336.40879.

Rouvoet, Marjo, Melanie Eijberts, and Halleh Ghorashi. 2017. "Identification Paradoxes and Multiple Belongings: The Narratives of Italian Migrants in the Netherlands." *Social Inclusion* 5 (1): 105–16. https://doi.org/10.17645/si.v5i1.779.

Roy, Susan. 2016. *These Mysterious People: Shaping History and Archaeology in a Northwest Coast Community*. Vol. 145. McGill-Queen's Native and Northern Series. Montreal and Kingston: McGill-Queen's Univseristy Press.

Rubins, Rottem Rosenberg. 2022. "Crimmigration and the 'Paradox of Exclusion.'" *Oxford Journal of Legal Studies* 42 (1): 266–97.

Ruiz-Casares, Mónica, Janet Cleveland, Youssef Oulhote, Catherine Dunkley-Hickin, and Cécile Rousseau. 2016. "Knowledge of Healthcare Coverage for Refugee Claimants: Results from a Survey of Health Service Providers in Montreal." *PLOS ONE* 11 (1). https://doi.org/10.1371/journal.pone.0146798.

Rushforth, Brett. 2012. *Bonds of Alliance: Indigenous and Atlantic Slaveries in New France*. Chapel Hill Williamsburg: University of North Carolina Press, published for the Omohundro Institute of Early American History and Culture.

Russell, Emma K, and Maria Rae. 2020. "Indefinite Stuckness: Listening in a Time of Hyper-Incarceration and Border Entrapment." *Punishment & Society* 22 (3): 281–301. https://doi.org/10.1177/1462474519886546.

Rusu, Sharon. 1989. "The Development of Canada's Immigration and Refugee Board Documentation Centre." *International Journal of Refugee Law* 1 (3): 319–30. https://doi.org/10.1093/ijrl/1.3.319.

Rytter, Mikkel. 2019. "Writing Against Integration: Danish Imaginaries of Culture, Race and Belonging." *Ethnos* 84 (4): 678–97. https://doi.org/10.1080/00141844.2018.1458745.

Sadoway, Geraldine. 2018. "Protection Measures for Unaccompanied Child Migrants in Canada." In *Protecting Migrant Children*, edited by Mary Crock and Lenni B. Benson, 299–318. Cheltenham: Edward Elgar Publishing. https://doi.org/10.4337/9781786430267.00026.

SAH Navigation Unit. 2022. "An Introduction to the SAH Association." Personal files.

Sahlins, Peter. 2003. "The Eighteenth-Century Citizenship Revolution in France." In *Migration Control in the North Atlantic World: The Evolution of State Practices in Europe and the United States from the French Revolution to the Inter-War Period*, edited by Andreas Fahrmeir, Olivier Faron, and Patrick Weil, 11–24. New York: Berghahn Books.

Saito, Natsu Taylor. 2021. "Indefinite Detention, Colonialism, and Settler Prerogative in the United States." *Social & Legal Studies* 30 (1): 32–65. https://doi.org/10.1177/0964663918769362.

Sakamoto, Izumi, Matthew Chin, and Jaemin Kim. 2013. "Missing Context of Skilled Immigrant Employment and Integration: A Tacit Knowledge Perspective" *American Psychological Association.*

Sakamoto, Izumi, Matthew Chin, and Meline Young. 2010. "Canadian Experience," Employment Challenges, and Skilled Immigrants a Close Look through 'Tacit Knowledge.'" Settlement of Newcomers to Canada. *Canadian Social Work* 12: 145–51.

Salter, Mark B., and Geneviève Piché. 2011. "The Securitization of the US-Canada Border in American Political Discourse." *Canadian Journal of Political Science* 44 (4): 929–51. https://doi.org/10.1017/S0008423911000813.

Samarasinghe, Vidyamali, and Barbara Burton. 2007. "Strategising Prevention: A Critical Review of Local Initiatives to Prevent Female Sex Trafficking." *Development in Practice* 17 (1): 51–64. https://doi.org/10.1080/09614520601092378.

Samson, Colin. 2008. "The Rule of Terra Nullius and the Impotence of International Human Rights for Indigenous Peoples." *Essex Human Rights Review* 5 (1): 1–12.

Sanders, Rachel. 2017. "Underemployment and Low Wages Continue to Burden Immigrants." *The Tyee*, 1 November 2017. https://thetyee.ca/News/2017/11/01/Immigrants-Underemployment-Low-Wages.

Sassen, Saskia. 2000. *Guests and Aliens*. New York: New Press.

– 2002. "The Repositioning of Citizenship: Emergent Subjects and Spaces for Politics." *Berkeley Journal of Sociology* 46: 4–26.

Sathiyanathan, Lakshine, and Lisa Xing. 2018. "An Accent Might Keep You from Getting Hired Even Though It's Not Supposed to, Advocate Says." *CBC News*, 23 January 2018. https://www.cbc.ca/news/canada/toronto/the-accent-effect-toronto-3-1.4409181.

Saunders, Natasha Emilie Georgina. 2016. "From Subjectivity to Agency: Michel Foucault and Hannah Arendt on 'Refugees,' 'Problems' and 'Solutions.'" PhD thesis, University of St Andrews. http://hdl.handle.net/10023/7994.

Scellato, Giuseppe, Chiara Franzoni, and Paula Stephan. 2017. "A Mobility Boost for Research." *Science* 356 (6339): 694. https://doi.org/10.1126/science.aan4052.

Schick, Matthis, Andre Zumwald, Bina Knöpfli, Angela Nickerson, Richard A. Bryant, Ulrich Schnyder, Julia Müller, and Naser Morina. 2016. "Challenging Future, Challenging Past: The Relationship of Social Integration and Psychological Impairment in Traumatized Refugees." *European Journal of Psychotraumatology* 7 (1): 28057. https://doi.org/10.3402/ejpt.v7.28057.

Schinkel, Willem. 2018. "Against 'Immigrant Integration': For an End to Neocolonial Knowledge Production." *Comparative Migration Studies* 6 (1): 31. https://doi.org/10.1186/s40878-018-0095-1.

Schmidt, Ron. 2007. "Comparing Federal Government Immigrant Settlement Policies in Canada and the United States." *American Review of Canadian Studies* 37 (1): 103–22. https://doi.org/10.1080/02722010709481802.

Schmidtke, Oliver. 2018. "The Civil Society Dynamic of Including and Empowering Refugees in Canada's Urban Centres." *Social Inclusion* 6 (1): 147–56. https://doi.org/10.17645/si.v6i1.1306.

Schneider, Jens, and Maurice Crul. 2010. "New Insights into Assimilation and Integration Theory: Introduction to the Special Issue." *Ethnic and Racial Studies* 33 (7): 1143–8. https://doi.org/10.1080/01419871003777809.

Schon, Justin. 2019. "Motivation and Opportunity for Conflict-Induced Migration: An Analysis of Syrian Migration Timing." *Journal of Peace Research* 56 (1): 12–27. https://doi.org/10.1177/0022343318806044.

Schultz, Jessica. 2018. *The Internal Protection Alternative in Refugee Law: Treaty Basis and Scope of Application under the 1951 Convention Relating to the Status of Refugees and Its 1967 Protocol*. Leiden: Brill Nijhoff.

– 2019. "The Internal Protection Alternative and Its Relation to Refugee Status." In *Research Handbook on International Refugee Law*, edited by Satvinder Singh Juss, 126–38. Cheltenham: Edward Elgar Publishing.

Seaton, Eleanor K., and Tiffany Yip. 2009. "School and Neighborhood Contexts, Perceptions of Racial Discrimination, and Psychological Well-Being Among African American Adolescents." *Journal of Youth and Adolescence* 38 (2): 153–63. https://doi.org/10.1007/s10964-008-9356-x.

Šedová, Barbora, Lucia Čizmaziová, and Athene Cook. 2021. "A Meta-Analysis of Climate Migration Literature." CEPA Discussion Papers 29. https://doi.org/10.25932/PUBLISHUP-49982.

Seet, Matthew. 2016. "The Origins of UNHCR's Global Mandate on Statelessness." *International Journal of Refugee Law* 28 (1): 7–24.

Seibel, Kimberly. 2016. "Bureaucratic Birthdates: Chronometric Old Age as Resource and Liability in U.S. Refugee Resettlement." *Refuge: Canada's Journal on Refugees* 32 (3): 8–17.

Senate of Canada. 2000. "Bill C-9, An Act to Give Effect to the Nisga'a Final Agreement." Government of Canada. https://sencanada.ca/en/committees/appa/TranscriptsMinutes/36-2.

Serebrin, Jacob. 2022. "Quebec Asks Feds to Close Roxham Road, Says Province Can't Handle Influx of Refugees." *CBC News*, 11 May 2022. https://www.cbc.ca/news/canada/montreal/legault-wants-roxham-closed-1.6449302.

Sethi, Anupriya. 2007. "Domestic Sex Trafficking of Aboriginal Girls in Canada: Issues and Implications." *First Peoples Child & Family Review* 3 (3): 57–71.

"Settler Colonialism and Indigenous Americans." In *Oxford Research Encyclopedia of American History*. Oxford: Oxford University Press.

Shachar, Ayelet. 2006. "The Race for Talent: Highly Skilled Migrants and Competitive Immigration Regimes." *New York University Law Review* 81 (1): 148–206.

Shacknove, Andrew E. 1985. "Who Is a Refugee?" *Ethics* 95 (2): 274–84.

Shaheen, Kareem. 2019. "Shock of the Cold: 50,000 Syrian Refugees Learn to Survive -20C in Canada." *Guardian*, 6 January 2019. https://www.theguardian.com/world/2019/jan/06/syrian-refugees-in-canada-surviving-the-winter.

Shakya, Yogendra B., Sepali Guruge, Michaela Hynie, Sheila Htoo, Arzo Akbari, Barinder (Binny) Jandu, Rabea Murtaza, Megan Spasevski, Nahom Berhane, and Jessica Forster. 2014. "Newcomer Refugee Youth as 'Resettlement Champions' for Their Families: Vulnerability, Resilience and Empowerment." In *Refuge and Resilience*, edited by Laura Simich and Lisa Andermann, 131–54. Dordecht: Springer, Dordrecht.

Sharma, Nandita. 2005. "Anti-Trafficking Rhetoric and the Making of a Global Apartheid." *NWSA Journal* 17 (3): 88–111.

– 2006. *Home Economics: Nationalism and the Making of "Migrant Workers" in Canada*. Toronto: University of Toronto Press.

– 2009. "White Nationalism, Illegality and Imperialism: Border Controls as Ideology." In *(En)Gendering the War on Terror: War Stories and Camouflaged Politics*. Reprint, edited by Krista Hunt and Kim Rygiel, 111–44. Gender in a Global/ Local World. Farnham: Ashgate.

Shaw, Stacey A., and Karin Wachter. 2022. "'Through Social Contact We'll Integrate': Refugee Perspectives on Integration Post-Resettlement." *Journal of Immigrant & Refugee Studies* (January): 1–14. https://doi.org/10.1080/15562948.2021.2023719.

Sherrell, Kathy, Silvia D'Addario, and Daniel Hiebert. 2007. "On the Outside Looking In: The Precarious Housing Situations of Successful Refugee Claimants in the GVRD." *Refuge: Canada's Journal on Refugees* 24, no. 2 (June): 64–75. https://doi.org/10.25071/1920-7336.21385.

Shi, Jan. 2004. "The Impact of Canada's New Immigration Act on Chinese Independent Migrants." *Canadian Journal of Urban Research* 13: 140–54.

Shipley, Tyler A. 2020. *Canada in the World: Settler Capitalism and the Colonial Imagination*. Halifax: Fernwood Publishing.

Showden, Carisa Renae. 2011. *Choices Women Make: Agency in Domestic Violence, Assisted Reproduction, and Sex Work*. Minneapolis: University of Minnesota Press.

Shuster, Evelyne. 1997. "Fifty Years Later: The Significance of the Nuremberg Code." *New England Journal of Medicine* 337 (20): 1436–40. https://doi.org/10.1056/NEJM199711133372006.

Sigona, Nando. 2005. "Refugee Integration(s): Policy and Practice in the European Union." *Refugee Survey Quarterly* 24 (4): 115–22. https://doi.org/10.1093/rsq/hdi093.

– 2014. "The Politics of Refugee Voices: Representations, Narratives, and Memories." In *The Oxford Handbook of Refugee and Forced Migration Studies*, 1st ed., edited by Elena Fiddian-Qasmiyeh, Gil Loescher, Katy Long, and Nando Sigona, 369–82. Oxford: Oxford University Press.

– 2016. "Everyday Statelessness in Italy: Status, Rights, and Camps." *Ethnic and Racial Studies* 39 (2): 263–79.

Silver, Soumya. 2021. "Twenty Years After the Passage of the Palermo Protocol: Identifying Common Flaws in Defining Trafficking through the First Global Study of Domestic Anti-Trafficking Laws." *Policy Review*, no. 48.

Silverman, Stephanie J. 2010. "Immigration Detention in America: A History of Its Expansion and a Study of Its Significance." COMPAS Working Paper no. 80. Available at *SSRN Electronic Journal*. https://doi.org/10.2139/ssrn.1867366.

– 2012. "'Regrettable but Necessary?' A Historical and Theoretical Study of the Rise of the UK Immigration Detention Estate and Its Opposition: Regrettable but Necessary?" *Politics & Policy* 40 (6): 1131–57. https://doi.org/10.1111/j.1747-1346.2012.00393.x.

– 2016. "'Imposter-Children' in the UK Refugee Status Determination Process." *Refuge: Canada's Journal on Refugees* 32 (3): 30–9. https://doi.org/10.25071/1920-7336.40371.

– 2020. "Canada: The Cordon Sanitaire and the Shifting Threats of the COVID-19 Pandemic." In *COVID-19 Impacts on Immigration Detention: Global Responses*, edited by Alice Nah, Melissa Phillips, and Min Jee Yamanda Park, 14–15. Sydney: International Detention Coalition

– forthcoming. *The Detention Estate: Canada's Shadow Prison System and the Future of Migration Control*. Montreal and Kingston: McGill-Queens University Press.

Silverman, Stephanie J., and Esra Stephanie Kaytaz. 2022. "Examining the 'National Risk Assessment for Detention' Process: An Intersectional Analysis of Detaining 'Dangerousness' in Canada." *Journal of Ethnic and Migration Studies* 48 (3): 693–709. https://doi.org/10.1080/1369183X.2020.1841613.

Silverman, Stephanie J., and Petra Molnar. 2016. "Everyday Injustices: Barriers to Access to Justice for Immigration Detainees in Canada." *Refugee Survey Quarterly* 35 (1): 109–27. https://doi.org/10.1093/rsq/hdv016.

– 2019. "Caged at the Border." In *The Routledge History of Human Rights*, 1st ed., edited by Jean Quataert and Lora Wildenthal, 579–600. London: Routledge. https://doi.org/10.4324/9780429324376-31.

Silverman, Stephanie J., and Amy Nethery. 2015. "Understanding Immigration Detention and Its Human Impact." In *Immigration Detention*, edited by Amy Nethery and Stephanie Silverman, 1–12. London: Routledge. https://doi.org/10.4324/9781315751023.

Silvius, Ray. 2016. "Neo-Liberalization, Devolution, and Refugee Well-Being: A Case Study in Winnipeg, Manitoba." *Canadian Ethnic Studies* 48 (3): 27–44. https://doi.org/10.1353/ces.2016.0024.

Simardone, Aidan and El-Farouk Khaki. 2022. "As Refugee Law Practitioners, We Oppose Canada's Double Standards." *The Maple*. https://www.readthemaple.com/as-refugee-law-practitioners-we-oppose-canadas-double-standards.

Simpson, Audra. 2014. *Mohawk Interruptus: Political Life across the Borders of Settler States*. Durham: Duke University Press.

– 2016. "The State Is a Man: Theresa Spence, Loretta Saunders and the Gender of Settler Sovereignty." *Theory & Event* 19 (4): 1–30.

Şimşek, Doğuş. 2020. "Integration Processes of Syrian Refugees in Turkey: 'Class-Based Integration.'" *Journal of Refugee Studies* 33 (3): 537–54. https://doi.org/10.1093/jrs/fey057.

Simunic, Emily. 2021. "Problematizing Canadian Human Trafficking Policy." Master's thesis, Concordia University. http://spectrum.library.concordia.ca/id/eprint/988525.

Sinclair, Niigaan. 2016. *Reconciliation Lives Here: The 2016 State of the Inner City Report*. Canadian Centre for Policy Alternatives Manitoba.

Singer, Colin. 2022. "Another 3,150 Afghan Refugees Welcomed Towards Canada's Goal of Resettling 40,000." Canada Immigration News. 3 November 2022. https://www.cimmigrationnews.com/another-3150-afghan-refugees-welcomed-towards-canadas-goal-of-resettling-40000.

Singh v. Canada (Minister of Employment and Immigration), 1995, 1 SCR 177.

Sirriyeh, Ala. 2010. "Home Journeys: Im/Mobilities in Young Refugee and Asylum-Seeking Women's Negotiations of Home." *Childhood* 17 (2): 213–27. https://doi.org/10.1177/0907568210365667.

Sivalingam, Harini. 2019. "Refugees Are Not All in the Same 'Boat.'" *Toronto Star*, 8 October 2019. https://www.thestar.com/opinion/contributors/2019/10/08/refugees-are-not-all-in-the-same-boat.html.

Skeldon, Ronald. 2008. "International Migration as a Tool in Development Policy: A Passing Phase?" *Population and Development Review* 34 (1): 1–18. https://doi.org/10.1111/j.1728-4457.2008.00203.x.

Slave Voyages Database. 2021. https://www.slavevoyages.org.

Smith, Andrea. 2015. *Conquest: Sexual Violence and American Indian Genocide*. Durham: Duke University Press. https://doi.org/10.1215/9780822374817.

Smith, Andrea, and Luana Ross. 2004. "Introduction: Native Women and State Violence." *Social Justice* 31 (4): 1–7.

Smith, Craig Damian. 2020. "A Model for World? Policy Transfer Theory and the Challenges to 'Exporting' Private Sponsorship to Europe." In *Strangers to Neighbours: Refugee Sponsorship in Context*, edited by Shauna Labman and Geoffrey Cameron, 286–302. Montreal and Kingston: McGill-Queen's University Press. https://doi.org/10.2307/j.ctv176ktqs.

Smith, Ei Phyu, Sheila Htoo, Michaela Hynie, and Susan McGrath. 2021. "Group Refugee Resettlement in Canada: Learning from the Karen." In *Understanding the Refugee Experience in the Canadian Context*, edited by Bharati Sethi, Sepali Guruge, and Rick Csiernik. Newcastle upon Tyne: Cambridge Scholars Publishing.

Smith, Emma. 2018. "A Family's Strength when Muscles Fail." CBC *News*, 18 June 2018. https://newsinteractives.cbc.ca/longform/syrian-family-wheelchair-halifax.

Smith, Kate. 2016. "Telling Stories of Resistance and Ruination: Women Seeking Asylum." *Journal of Resistance Studies* 2 (2): 33–64.

Smith, Marie-Danielle. 2017. "Dramatic Increase in People Having Canadian Citizenship Revoked since Trudeau Elected." *National Post*, 12 February 2017. https://nationalpost.com/news/politics/dramatic-increase-in-people-having-canadian-citizenship-revoked-since-trudeau-elected.

Smith, Miriam Catherine. 2018. *A Civil Society? Collective Actors in Canadian Political Life*. 2nd ed. North York: University of Toronto Press.

Smith, Thomas Watson. 1899. "The Slave in Canada." In "Collections of the Nova Scotia Historical Society for the Years 1896–1898." Halifax: Nova Scotia Printing Company.

Smithers, Gregory D. 2022. "Settler Colonialism and Indigenous Americans." In *Oxford Research Encyclopedia of American History*. Oxford: Oxford University Press.

Sobel, Nora. 2015. "A Typology of the Changing Narratives of Canadian Citizens Through Time." *Canadian Ethnic Studies* 47 (1): 11–39. https://doi.org/10.1353/ces.2015.0003.

Sodero, Stephanie, and Nicholas Scott. 2016. "Editorial – Contentious Mobilities/ Canadian Mobilities." *Canadian Journal of Sociology* 41 (3): 257–76. https://doi.org/10.29173/cjs28298.

Solf, Benedicta, and Katherine Rehberg. 2021. "The Resettlement Gap: A Record Number of Global Refugees, but Few Are Resettled." *Migration Policy*, 22 October 2021. https://www.migrationpolicy.org/article/refugee-resettlement-gap.

Somerville, Peter. 1992. "Homelessness and the Meaning of Home: Rooflessness or Rootlessness?" *International Journal of Urban and Regional Research* 16 (4): 529–39. https://doi.org/10.1111/j.1468-2427.1992.tb00194.x.

Sonnenburg, Elizabeth, and John O'Shea. 2017. "Archaeological Landscapes during the 10–8 Ka Lake Stanley Lowstand on the Alpena-Amberley Ridge, Lake Huron." *Geoarchaeology* 32 (2): 230–47. https://doi.org/10.1002/gea.21590.

Sorgen, Aliya. 2015. "Integration through Participation: The Effects of Participating in an English Conversation Club on Refugee and Asylum Seeker Integration." *Applied Linguistics Review* 6 (2): 241–60. https://doi.org/10.1515/applirev-2015-0012.

Soysal, Yasemin Nuhoğlu. 1994. *Limits of Citizenship: Migrants and Postnational Membership in Europe.* Chicago: University of Chicago.

Spagnuolo, Natalie, and Yahya El-Lahib. 2020. "Unsettling Realities and Rethinking Displacement: Transforming Settlement Services for Refugees, Migrants and People with Intellectual Disabilities." In *The Routledge Handbook of Disability Activism*, edited by Maria Berghs, Tsitsi Chataika, Yahya El-Lahib, and Kudakwashe Dube, 452–64. London: Routledge. https://doi.org/10.4324/9781351165082-36.

Special Rapporteur on the Right to Adequate Housing. n.d. "The Human Right to Adequate Housing." Office of the High Commissioner for Human Rights. https://www.ohchr.org/en/special-procedures/sr-housing/human-right-adequate-housing.

Spencer, Dale C., and Raven Sinclair. 2019. "Settler Colonialism, Biopolitics, and Indigenous Children in Canada." In *The Sociology of Childhood and Youth in Canada*, edited by Xiaobei Chen, Rebecca Raby, and Patrizia Albanese, 239–55. Toronto: Canadian Scholars.

Squires, Peter. 2018. "A Scoping Review of Australian Studies of Refugee Integration: Popular Definitions of Integration in the Australian Literature." *Migration Studies* 8 (1): 90–112. https://doi.org/10.1093/migration/mny032.

St. Arnault, David, and Noorfarah Merali. 2019. "Refugee Pathways out of Homelessness in Urban Alberta, Canada: Implications for Social Justice-

Oriented Counselling." *Counselling Psychology Quarterly* 32 (2): 227–45. https://doi.org/10.1080/09515070.2018.1437540.

Stasiulis, Daiva. 2017. "The Extraordinary Statelessness of Deepan Budlakoti: The Erosion of Canadian Citizenship through Citizenship Deprivation." *Studies in Social Justice* 11: 1–26.

Statistics Canada. 2015. "Censuses of Canada 1665 to 1871: Estimated Population of Canada, 1605 to Present." 26 August 2015. https://www150.statcan.gc.ca/n1/pub/98-187-x/4151287-eng.htm#23.

– 2016. "Longitudinal Immigration Database (IMDB)." https://www23.statcan.gc.ca/imdb/p2SV.pl?Function=getSurvey&SDDS=5057.

– 2022a. "Indigenous Population Continues to Grow and Is Much Younger than the Non-Indigenous Population, Although the Pace of Growth Has Slowed." *The Daily*, 21 September 2022.

– 2022b. "Immigrants Make up the Largest Share of the Population in over 150 Years and Continue to Shape Who We Are as Canadians." *The Daily*, 26 October 2022. https://www150.statcan.gc.ca/n1/daily-quotidien/221026/dq221026a-eng.htm.

– 2022c. "Police-Reported Human Trafficking in Canada, 2010 to 2020." 9 June 2022. https://www150.statcan.gc.ca/n1/pub/11-627-m/11-627-m2022034-eng.htm.

– 2022d. "A Portrait of Citizenship in Canada from the 2021 Census." Census 2021. https://www12.statcan.gc.ca/census-recensement/2021/as-sa/98-200-X/2021008/98-200-X2021008-eng.cfm.

– 2022e. "Trafficking in Persons in Canada, 2020." 9 June 2022. https://www150.statcan.gc.ca/n1/pub/85-002-x/2022001/article/00010-eng.htm.

– 2023. "The Underground Economy in Canada, 2021." *The Daily*, 20 February 2023. https://www150.statcan.gc.ca/n1/daily-quotidien/230220/dq230220b-eng.pdf.

Stauffer, Brian. 2021. "Canada: Abuse, Discrimination in Immigration Detention." Human Rights Watch. 17 June 2021. https://www.hrw.org/news/2021/06/17/canada-abuse-discrimination-immigration-detention.

Steele, Abbey. 2009. "Seeking Safety: Avoiding Displacement and Choosing Destinations in Civil Wars." *Journal of Peace Research* 46 (3): 419–29. https://doi.org/10.1177/0022343309102660.

Stefanovich, Olivia. 2019. "Flood-Prone Kashechewan First Nation Signs New Action Plan with Feds, Ontario on Relocation." *CBC News*, 9 May 2019. https://www.cbc.ca/news/politics/stefanovich-kashechewan-2019-relocation-agreement-1.5129181.

Stevens, Dallal. 2013. "What Do We Mean by Protection?" *International Journal on Minority and Group Rights* 20 (2): 233–62. https://doi.org/10.1163/15718115-02002005.

Stevenson. 2018. "'Felons, Not Families': U.S. Immigration Policies and the Construction of an American Underclass." *Pacific Coast Philology* 53 (2): 155. https://doi.org/10.5325/pacicoasphil.53.2.0155.

Stienstra, Deborah, Gail Baikie, and Susan M. Manning. 2018. "'My Granddaughter Doesn't Know She Has Disabilities and We Are Not Going to Tell Her': Navigating Intersections of Indigenousness, Disability and Gender in Labrador." *Disability and the Global South* 5 (2): 1385–1406.

Stirling Cameron, Emma, Megan Aston, Howard Ramos, Marwa Kuri, and Lois Jackson. 2022. "The Postnatal Experiences of Resettled Syrian Refugee Women: Access to Healthcare and Social Support in Nova Scotia, Canada." *Midwifery* 104 (January). https://doi.org/10.1016/j.midw.2021.103171.

Stobbe, Stephanie P. 2022. "Refugee Policies, Resettlement and Integration in Canada: Lessons Learned from the Southeast Asian Refugee Movement and Mennonite Central Committee." In *Pilgrimage of Justice and Peace: Global Mennonite Perspectives on Peacebuilding*, edited by Fernando Enns, Nina Schroeder-van 't Schip, and Andrés Pacheco-Lozano. Eugene, OR: Pickwick Publications.

Stobbe, Stephanie P., and Judith Harris. 2013. "Tracking Immigrant Professionals' Experience in Manitoba's Labour Market." Working Paper 2013/6. Ryerson Centre for Immigration and Settlement.

Stockdale, Liam P.D. 2016. *Taming an Uncertain Future: Temporality, Sovereignty, and the Politics of Anticipatory Governance*. Future Perfect: Images of the Time to Come in Philosophty, Politics and Cultural Studies. London: Rowman & Littlefield International.

Storey, Hugo. 2016. "The Meaning of 'Protection' within the Refugee Definition." *Refugee Survey Quarterly* 35 (3): 1–34.

Strang, Alison, and Alastair Ager. 2010. "Refugee Integration: Emerging Trends and Remaining Agendas." *Journal of Refugee Studies* 23 (4): 589–607. https://doi.org/10.1093/jrs/feq046.

Strang, Alison B., Helen Baillot, and Elodie Mignard. 2018. "'I Want to Participate.' Transition Experiences of New Refugees in Glasgow." *Journal of Ethnic and Migration Studies* 44 (2): 197–214. https://doi.org/10.1080/1369183X.2017.1341717.

Strom, Adam. 2017. "Why Teach About Migration? Because It's the Story of Humankind." Facing History Today. 24 August 2017. https://facingtoday.facinghistory.org/why-teach-about-migration-because-its-the-story-of-humankind.

Struthers Montford, Kelly, and Dawn Moore. 2018. "The Prison as Reserve." *New Criminal Law Review* 21 (4): 640–63. https://doi.org/10.1525/nclr.2018.21.4.640.

Stumpf, Juliet P. 2020. "The Crimmigration Crisis: Immigrants, Crime, and Sovereign Power." In *Governing Immigration Through Crime*, edited by Julie A. Dowling and Jonathan Xavier Inda, 59–76. Stanford, CA: Stanford University Press. https://doi.org/10.1515/9780804785419-004.

Su, Yvonne. 2016. "Should We Bring Back Climate Refugees?" *Oxford Monitor of Forced Migration* 6 (1): 22–33.

– 2021. "Wildfire and Flood Disasters Are Causing 'Climate Migration' within Canada." *The Conversation*, 20 September 2021. https://theconversation.com/wildfire-and-flood-disasters-are-causing-climate-migration-within-canada-167730.

– 2022. "Networks of Recovery: Remittances, Social Capital and Post-Disaster Recovery in Tacloban City, Philippines." *International Journal of Disaster Risk Reduction* 67 (January): 102641. https://doi.org/10.1016/j.ijdrr.2021.102641.

Su, Yvonne, and Christina R. Clark-Kazak. 2022. "Canadians Support Accepting More Newcomers but We Need a More Equitable, Rights-Based Approach." *The Conversation*, 3 July 2022. http://theconversation.com/canadians-support-accepting-more-newcomers-but-we-need-a-more-equitable-rights-based-approach-185348.

Su, Yvonne, and Loïc Le Dé. 2020. "Whose Views Matter in Post-Disaster Recovery? A Case Study of 'Build Back Better' in Tacloban City after Typhoon Haiyan." *International Journal of Disaster Risk Reduction* 51 (December): 101786. https://doi.org/10.1016/j.ijdrr.2020.101786.

Suhrke, Astri. 1994. "Environmental Degradation and Population Flows." *Journal of International Affairs* 47 (2): 473.

Suresh v. Canada (Minister of Citizenship and Immigration). 2002. 1 SCR 3.

Sutherland, Cheryl. 2018. "Sense of Place amongst Immigrant and Refugee Women in Kingston and Peterborough, Ontario." In *Canadian Perspectives on Immigration in Small Cities*, edited by Glenda Tibe Bonifacio and Julie L. Drolet, 119–40. Switzerland: Springer.

Sweeney, Sylvia, dir. 1994. *Slavery, A Canadian Story: The Packwood Family, Quebec*. 58 min. International Tele-Film.

Szablewska, Natalia. 2022. "Human Smuggling and Human Trafficking." In *International Conflict and Security Law: A Research Handbook*, edited by Sergey Sayapin, Rustam Atadjanov, Umesh Kadam, Gerhard Kemp, Nicolás Zambrana-Tévar, and Noëlle Quénivet, 1181–1206. The Hague: TMC Asser Press. https://doi.org/10.1007/978-94-6265-515-7_53.

Szczepanik, Marta. 2016. "The 'Good' and 'Bad' Refugees? Imagined Refugeehood (s) in the Media Coverage of the Migration Crisis." *Journal of Identity & Migration Studies* 10 (2).

Table de concertation des organismes au service des personnes réfugiées et immigrantes (TCRI). 2022. "Qui sommes-nous." https://tcri.qc.ca/qui-sommes-nous.

Taha, Dina. 2021. "Marriage for Refuge? Syrian Women's Refugee Resettlement Experiences in Egypt." Toronto: York University.

TallBear, Kim. 2019. "Caretaking Relations, Not American Dreaming." *Kalfou* 6 (1). https://doi.org/10.15367/kf.v6i1.228.

Tam, Benita Y., Leanne C. Findlay, and Dafna E. Kohen. 2017. "Indigenous Families: Who Do You Call Family?" *Journal of Family Studies* 23 (3): 243–59. https://doi.org/10.1080/13229400.2015.1093536.

Tammas, Rifaie. 2019. "Refugee Stories Could Do More Harm than Good." OpenDemocracy, 1 November 2019. https://www.opendemocracy.net/en/refugee-stories-could-do-more-harm-good.

Tan, Nikolas Feith. 2021. "Community Sponsorship in Europe: Taking Stock, Policy Transfer and What the Future Might Hold." *Frontiers in Human Dynamics* 3 (April): 564084. https://doi.org/10.3389/fhumd.2021.564084.

Tannock, Stuart. 2011. "Points of Prejudice: Education-Based Discrimination in Canada's Immigration System." *Antipode* 43 (4): 1330–56. https://doi.org/10.1111/j.1467-8330.2010.00864.x.

Tas, Latif. 2016. "How International Law Impacts on Statelessness and Citizenship: The Case of Kurdish Nationalism, Conflict and Peace." *International Journal of Law in Context* 12 (1): 42–62.

Tasker, John Paul. 2017. "Governor General Apologizes for Saying Indigenous People Were Immigrants." *CBC News*, 19 June 2017. https://www.cbc.ca/news/politics/governor-general-apologizes-indigenous-immigrants-1.4167348.

– 2023. "Supreme Court Upholds Agreement That Lets Canada Send Refugees Back to US." *CBC News*, 16 June 2023. https://www.cbc.ca/news/politics/supreme-court-ruling-safe-third-country-agreement-1.6878870.

Tastsoglou, Evangelia, and Shiva Nourpanah. 2019. "(Re)Producing Gender: Refugee Advocacy and Sexual and Gender-Based Violence in Refugee Narratives." *Canadian Ethnic Studies* 51 (3): 37–56. https://doi.org/10.1353/ces.2019.0019.

Taylor, Charles. 2004. *Modern Social Imaginaries*. Public Planet Books. Durham: Duke University Press.

Taylor, Charles, and Guy Laforest. 1993. *Reconciling the Solitudes: Essays on Canadian Federalism and Nationalism*. Montreal and Kingston: McGill-Queen's University Press.

Taylor, K.W. 1991. "Racism in Canadian Immigration Policy." *Canadian Ethnic Studies* 23 (1): 1–20.

Taylor, Luke. 2015. "Designated Inhospitality: The Treatment of Asylum Seekers Who Arrive by Boat in Canada and Australia." *McGill Law Journal* 60 (2): 333–79. https://doi.org/10.7202/1029211ar.

Teixeira, Carlos. 2008. "Barriers and Outcomes in the Housing Searches of New Immigrants and Refugees: A Case Study of 'Black' Africans in Toronto's Rental Market." *Journal of Housing and the Built Environment* 23 (4): 253–76. https://doi.org/10.1007/s10901-008-9118-9.

Tesfai, Aron, Michaela Hynie, Rubaiyat Karim, Gülay Kilicaslan, Cansu Ekmekcioglu, and Palmer Taylor. 2022. "Social Trust among Refugees: Using a Human Rights Lens to Understand Refugee Experiences." In *Contemporary Immigration: Psychological Perspectives to Address Challenges and Inform Solutions*, edited by Fathali M. Moghaddam and Margaret J. Hendricks,

243–61. Washington: American Psychological Association. https://doi.org/10.1037/0000294-013.

Tester, Frank James, and Peter Kulchyski. 1994. *Tammarniit (Mistakes): Inuit Relocation in the Eastern Arctic, 1939–1963*. Vancouver: UBC Press.

Thammavongsa, Souvankham. 2020. "Writing Refugees: A Conversation with Souvankham Thammavongsa." *Critical Refugee Studies Canada*. Vimeo video, 41:11. https://vimeo.com/436861305.

Thériault, Laura, Geneviève Belleville, Marie-Christine Ouellet, and Charles M. Morin. 2021. "The Experience and Perceived Consequences of the 2016 Fort McMurray Fires and Evacuation." *Frontiers in Public Health* 9 (November): 641151. https://doi.org/10.3389/fpubh.2021.641151.

Thériault, Pierre-André. 2020. "Judicial Review in Canada's Refugee Resettlement Program." In *Strangers to Neighbours: Refugee Sponsorship in Context*, edited by Shauna Labman and Geoffrey Cameron, 227–44. Montreal and Kingston: McGill-Queen's University Press. https://doi.org/10.2307/j.ctv176ktqs.

Thobani, Sunera. 2007. *Exalted Subjects: Studies in the Making of Race and Nation in Canada*. Toronto: University of Toronto Press.

Thomas, David P., and Veldon Coburn. 2022. "Corporate Canada, Capitalism, and Dispossession." In *Capitalism & Dispossession: Corporate Canada at Home and Abroad*, 1–18. Halifax: Fernwood Publishing.

Thomas, Derrick. 2005. "I Am Canadian." Canadian Social Trends. Ottawa: Statistics Canada.

Thompson, Debra. 2022. *The Long Road Home: On Blackness and Belonging*. Scribner Canada edition. Toronto: Scribner Canada.

Thompson, Shirley, Myrle Ballard, and Donna Martin. 2014. "Lake St. Martin First Nation Community Members' Experiences of Induced Displacement: 'We're like Refugees.'" *Refuge: Canada's Journal on Refugees* 29 (2): 75–86. https://doi.org/10.25071/1920-7336.38168.

Thomson, Mary Susan, Ferzana Chaze, Usha George, and Sepali Guruge. 2015. "Improving Immigrant Populations' Access to Mental Health Services in Canada: A Review of Barriers and Recommendations." *Journal of Immigrant and Minority Health* 17 (6): 1895–1905. https://doi.org/10.1007/s10903-015-0175-3.

Thurston, Wilfreda E., Amrita Roy, Barbara Clow, David Este, Tess Gordey, Margaret Haworth-Brockman, Liza McCoy, Rachel Rapaport Beck, Christine Saulnier, and Lesley Carruthers. 2013. "Pathways Into and Out of Homelessness: Domestic Violence and Housing Security for Immigrant Women." *Journal of Immigrant & Refugee Studies* 11 (3): 278–98. https://doi.org/10.1080/15562948.2013.801734.

Thurton, David. 2019. "Fort McMurray Population Down Nearly 11 per cent since Wildfire, Census Shows." *CBC News*, 15 January 2019. https://www.cbc.ca/news/canada/edmonton/fort-mcmurray-census-population-1.4978907.

Ticktin, Miriam. 2006. "Where Ethics and Politics Meet." *American Ethnologist* 33 (1): 33–49. https://doi.org/10.1525/ae.2006.33.1.33.

– 2014. "Transnational Humanitarianism." *Annual Review of Anthropology* 43 (1): 273–89. https://doi.org/10.1146/annurev-anthro-102313-030403.

Tip, Linda K., Rupert Brown, Linda Morrice, Michael Collyer, and Matthew J. Easterbrook. 2019. "Improving Refugee Well-Being With Better Language Skills and More Intergroup Contact." *Social Psychological and Personality Science* 10 (2): 144–51. https://doi.org/10.1177/1948550617752062.

Tolley, Erin. 2016. *Framed: Media and the Coverage of Race in Canadian Politics*. Communication, Strategy, and Politics. Vancouver: UBC Press.

Tolley, Erin, and Robert Young, eds. 2011. *Immigrant Settlement Policy in Canadian Municipalities*. Montreal and Kingston: McGill-Queen's University Press.

Tomic, Patricia. 2013. "The Colour of Language: Accent, Devaluation and Resistance in Latin American Immigrant Lives in Canada." *Canadian Ethnic Studies* 45 (1–2): 1–21. https://doi.org/10.1353/ces.2013.0018.

Tomkinson, Sule. 2018. "Who Are You Afraid of and Why? Inside the Black Box of Refugee Tribunals: Refugee Tribunals." *Canadian Public Administration* 61 (2): 184–204. https://doi.org/10.1111/capa.12275.

Topgül, Seda. 2021. "A Green Social Work Examining Climate Change and Climate Refugees." *Social Mentality and Researcher Thinkers Journal* 7 (50): 2312–17. https://doi.org/10.31576/smryj.1072.

Toronto Region Immigrant Employment Council (TRIEC). 2023. "Refugees in Canada – Positively Contributing to Businesses and the Economy." https://triec.ca/refugees-in-canada-positively-contributing-to-businesses-and-the-economy.

Torpey, John. 1999. *The Invention of the Passport: Surveillance, Citizenship and the State*. Cambridge Studies in Law and Society. Cambridge: Cambridge University Press. https://doi.org/10.1017/CBO9780511520990.

Toussaint v. Canada (AG). 2010 FC 810.

Track, Laura, and Josh Paterson. 2017. "Oversight at the Border: A Model for Independent Accountability at the Canada Border Services Agency." British Columbia Civil Liberties Association, 2017 CanLIIDocs 199, https://canlii.ca/t/7d8.

Tremayne-Pengelly, Alexandra. 2022. "Canada's Refugee Road: A Lifeline for Some, a Political Headache for Others." *Guardian*, 25 May 2022. https://www.theguardian.com/world/2022/may/25/canada-refugee-asylum-seekers-roxham-road.

Treviranus, Barbara, and Michael Casasola. 2003. "Canada's Private Sponsorship of Refugees Program: A Practitioners Perspective of Its Past and Future." *Journal of International Migration and Integration* 4 (2): 177–202. https://doi.org/10.1007/s12134-003-1032-0.

Triandafyllidou, Anna. 2022. "Temporary Migration: Category of Analysis or Category of Practice?" *Journal of Ethnic and Migration Studies* 48 (16): 3847–59. https://doi.org/10.1080/1369183X.2022.2028350.

Troeung, Y.-Dang. 2022. *Refugee Lifeworlds: The Afterlife of the Cold War in Cambodia*. Asian American History and Culture. Philadelphia: Temple University Press.

Trotz, D. Alissa. 2011. "Bustling across the Canada-US Border: Gender and the Remapping of the Caribbean across Place." *Small Axe: A Caribbean Journal of Criticism* 15 (2): 59–77. https://doi.org/10.1215/07990537-1334239.

Trudeau, Justin (@JustinTrudeau). 2015. "'Diversity Is Canada's Strength.'" Prime Minister of Canada. 26 November 2015. https://pm.gc.ca/en/news/speeches/2015/11/26/diversity-canadas-strength.

– 2017. "To those fleeing persecution, terror &; war, Canadians will welcome you, regardless of your faith. Diversity is our strength #WelcomeToCanada." X (formerly Twitter), 28 January 2017, 4:20 p.m. https://twitter.com/JustinTrudeau/status/825438460265762816.

– 2022a. "The atrocities committed by Russian forces in Ukraine are appalling – and we, the G7 leaders, are united in condemning them. I want to be very clear: Those responsible for recently-revealed war crimes and atrocities will be held accountable. We stand with Ukraine." X (formerly Twitter), 7 April 2022, 11:12 a.m. https://twitter.com/JustinTrudeau/status/1512070711195492361.

– 2022b. "I spoke with Prime Minister @AbiyAhmedAli today about the conflict in Ethiopia, and the humanitarian truce. I called for further steps to make sure those affected can get the humanitarian assistance they need, and I reiterated Canada's support for a peaceful resolution." X (formerly Twitter), 6 April 2022, 5:23 p.m. https://twitter.com/JustinTrudeau/status/1511801761534722048.

Trudel, Marcel. 1963. *L'esclavage au Canada français*. Abrégée. Montreal: Horizon.

– 1990. *Dictionnaire des esclaves et de leurs propriétaires au Canada français*. Montreal: Hurtubise HMH.

Trudel, Marcel, and Micheline D'Allaire. 2009. *Deux siècles d'esclavage au Québec*. Bibliothèque Québécoise. Montreal.

Truth and Reconciliation Commission of Canada (TRC). 2015. "Truth and Reconciliation Commission of Canada: Calls to Action." http://trc.ca/assets/pdf/Calls_to_Action_English2.pdf.

Tuck, Eve. 2009. "Suspending Damage: A Letter to Communities." *Harvard Educational Review* 79 (3): 409–28. https://doi.org/10.17763/haer.79.3.n0016675661t3n15.

Tuck, Eve, and Monique Guishard. 2013. "Uncollapsing Ethics: Racialized Sciencism, Settler Coloniality, and an Ethical Framework of Decolonial Participatory Action Research." In *Challenging Status Quo Retrenchment: New Directions in Critical Research*, by Tricia M. Kress, Curry Stephenson, and Brad J. Porfilio, 3–27. Charlotte, NC: Information Age Publishing.

Tuck, Eve, and K. Wayne Yang. 2012. "Decolonization is not a Metaphor." *Decolonization: Indigeneity, Education & Society* 1, no. 1. https://jps.library.utoronto.ca/index.php/des/article/view/18630.

Tucker, Jason. 2014. "Questioning de Facto Statelessness by Looking at de Facto Citizenship." *Tilburg Law Review* 19: 276–84.

– 2021. "Refugeeness Doesn't Trump Statelessness: A Call to Reject the UN's 'Protection Hierarchy' for Stateless Refugees." *Peter McMullin Centre on Statelessness Critical Statelessness Studies Blog Series*. 2021. https://law.unimelb.edu.au/centres/statelessness/resources/critical-statelessness-studies-blog/refugeeness-doesnt-trump-statelessness-a-call-to-reject-the-uns-protection-hierarchy-for-stateless-refugees.

Tuhiwai Smith, Linda. 2021. *Decolonizing Methodologies: Research and Indigenous Peoples*, 3rd edition. London: Zed Books.

Turnbull, Sarah. 2017. "Immigration Detention and Punishment." In *Oxford Research Encyclopedia of Criminology and Criminal Justice*. Oxford: Oxford University Press. https://doi.org/10.1093/acrefore/9780190264079.013.231.

Turner, Annie. 2016. "Insights on Canadian Society: Living Arrangements of Aboriginal Children Aged 14 and Under." Statistics Canada. https://www150.statcan.gc.ca/n1/pub/75-006-x/2016001/article/14547-eng.htm.

Turner, Lewis. 2015. "Explaining the (Non-)Encampment of Syrian Refugees: Security, Class and the Labour Market in Lebanon and Jordan." *Mediterranean Politics* 20 (3): 386–404. https://doi.org/10.1080/13629395.2015.1078125.

– 2020. "'#Refugees Can Be Entrepreneurs Too!' Humanitarianism, Race, and the Marketing of Syrian Refugees." *Review of International Studies* 46 (1): 137–55. https://doi.org/10.1017/S0260210519000342.

Tuyisenge, Germaine, and Shira M. Goldenberg. 2021. "COVID-19, Structural Racism, and Migrant Health in Canada." *Lancet* 397 (10275): 650–2. https://doi.org/10.1016/S0140-6736(21)00215-4.

Tyyskä, Vappu, Jenna Blower, Samantha DeBoer, Shunya Kawai, and Ashley Walcott. 2017. "Syrian Refugee Crisis in Canadian Media." Ryerson Centre for Immigration and Settlement.

– 2021. "The Syrian Refugee Crisis in Canadian Media." Toronto Metropolitan University. https://doi.org/10.32920/ryerson.14669130.v1.

Ugelvik, Thomas. 2016. "Techniques of Legitimation: The Narrative Construction of Legitimacy among Immigration Detention Officers." *Crime, Media, Culture: An International Journal* 12 (2): 215–32. https://doi.org/10.1177/1741659016648180.

Uhl, Bärbel Heide. 2010. "Lost in Implementation? Human Rights Rhetoric and Violations – a Critical Review of Current European Anti-Trafficking Policies." *Security and Human Rights* 21 (2): 119–26. https://doi.org/10.1163/187502310791305936.

United Nation Economic and Social Council (UNESC). 2005. "The Right to Work: General Comment No. 18." https://www.refworld.org/docid/4415453b4.html.

United Nations (UN). 2016. *Report of the Commission of Inquiry on Human Rights in Eritrea*. https://digitallibrary.un.org/record/843384?ln=en.

– 2018. "Global Compact on Refugees." New York. https://www.unhcr.org/5c658aed4.pdf.

– 2022. *UN Research Roadmap for COVID-19 Recovery: Leveraging the Power of Science for a More Equitable, Resilient and Sustainable Future*. Geneva: United Nations. https://www.un.org/en/pdfs/UNCOVID19ResearchRoadmap.pdf.

United Nations General Assembly (UNGA). 1948. Universal Declaration of Human Rights (UDHR). New York.

United Nations High Commissioner for Refugees (UNHCR). 1976. "Functioning of the Sub-Committee and General Conclusion on International Protection." ExCom Conclusion 2 (27).

– 1996. "UNHCR Publication for CIS Conference (Displacement in the CIS) – In Legal Limbo: Asylum-Seekers and Statelessness." 1 May 1996.

– 2009. "Climate Change, Natural Disasters and Human Displacement: A UNHCR Perspective." https://www.unhcr.org/4901e81a4.pdf.

– 2011. "UNHCR Resettlement Handbook." https://www.unhcr.org/46f7c0ee2.pdf.

– 2014. "Luis Alberto Hernandez Febles v. Minister of Citizenship and Immigration: Factum of the Intervener (UNHCR)." https://www.refworld.org/docid/532019774.html.

– 2017. *This Is Our Home: Stateless Minorities and Their Search for Citizenship*. https://www.unhcr.org/ibelong/wp-content/uploads/UNHCR_EN2_2017 IBELONG_Report_ePub.pdf.

– 2018a. "Ending Statelessness in South Eastern Europe." https://www.unhcr.org/see/11299-ending-statelessness-in-south-eastern-europe.html.

– 2018b. "Persons in Need of International Protection." *International Journal of Refugee Law* 30 (1): 134–39. https://doi.org/10.1093/ijrl/eey009.

– 2018c. UNHCR *Policy on Age, Gender and Diversity*. https://www.unhcr.org/5aa13c0c7.pdf.

– 2018d. "UNHCR Resettlement Handbook: Country Chapter – Canada." https://www.unhcr.org/protection/resettlement/3c5e55594/unhcr-resettlement-handbook-country-chapter-canada.html.

– 2021a. *Global Trends Report 2021*. https://www.unhcr.org/publications/brochures/62a9d1494/global-trends-report-2021.html.

– 2021b. "Resettlement Data Finder (RDF)." https://rsq.unhcr.org/en/#HoHp.

– 2021c. "Prolonged COVID-19 Pandemic Deepens Hardship for over 12 Million Forcibly Displaced People with Disabilities." 3 December 2021. https://www.unhcr.org/news/press/2021/12/61aa3eb74/prolonged-covid-19-pandemic-deepens-hardship-12-million-forcibly-displaced.html.

– 2022a. "Figures at a Glance." https://www.unhcr.org/figures-at-a-glance.html.

– 2022b. *Global Trends: Forced Displacement in 2021*. Geneva: UNHCR. https://www.unhcr.org/62a9d1494/global-trends-report-2021.

– 2022c. "Projected Global Resettlement Needs 2023." https://www.unhcr.org/publications/brochures/62b18e714/2023-projected-global-resettlement-needs.html.
– 2022d. "Ukraine Refugee Situation." https://data.unhcr.org/en/situations/ukraine.
– 2023a. "Definition - Refugee-Led Organization (RLO)." 14 February 2023. https://reliefweb.int/report/world/definition-refugee-led-organization-rlo.
– 2023b. "Refugees in Canada." UNHCR Canada. https://www.unhcr.ca/in-canada/refugees-in-canada.
– 2023c. "UNHCR Resettlement Handbook." Revised. Geneva: UNHCR. https://www.unhcr.org/resettlement-handbook.
– n.d.a "How UNHCR Helps Stateless People." https://www.unhcr.org/how-unhcr-helps-stateless-people.html.
– n.d.b "Partnership in Protection." https://www.unhcr.org/partnership-protection.html.
– n.d.c "Refugee Data Finder." https://www.unhcr.org/refugee-statistics.
UNHCR, and Office of the High Commissioner for Human Rights (OHCHR). 2022. "Climate Change, Displacement and Human Rights." https://www.unhcr.org/publications/brochures/6242ea7c4/climate-change-displacement-human-rights.html.
UNHCR Canada. n.d. "About UNHCR Canada." https://www.unhcr.ca/about-us/about-unhcr/about-unhcr-canada.
United Nations Office on Drugs and Crime (UNODC). 2020. *Global Report on Trafficking in Persons 2020*. https://www.unodc.org/documents/data-and-analysis/tip/2021/GLOTiP_2020_15jan_web.pdf.
United Nations Relief and Works Agency for Palestine Refugees in the Near East (UNRWA). 2021. "UNRWA in Figures." 2021.
University of Toronto. 2017. "More than 200 Canadian Children Housed in Toronto Immigration Detention Facility, Says New U of T Report."
Uppal, Sharanjit. 2022. "A Portrait of Canadians Who Have Been Homeless." Statistics Canada.
Upper Canada. 1795. "Laws of His Majesty's Province of Upper-Canada, in North America: Comprising All the Acts of the Honorable the Legislature, of the Province Aforesaid, Enacted at Their First, Second, Third and Fourth Sessions, 1792, 1793, 1794 and 1795." Government Documents Vol. 1792/1795. Niagara: Statutes of Her Majesty's Province of Upper Canada. Printed by Gideon Tiffany, Printer to His Most Excellent Majesty. https://www.canadiana.ca/view/oocihm.9_10042_1/38.
Urbach, David R. 2018. "Improving Access to Health Services in Canada." *Healthcare Management Forum* 31 (6): 256–60. https://doi.org/10.1177/0840470418776995.

US Immigration and Customs Enforcement. 2021. *US Immigration and Customs Enforcement Fiscal Year 2020 Enforcement and Removal Operations Report.* https://www.ice.gov/doclib/news/library/reports/annual-report/eroReportFY2020.pdf.

Valtonen, Kathleen. 2004. "From the Margin to the Mainstream: Conceptualizing Refugee Settlement Processes." *Journal of Refugee Studies* 17 (1): 70–96. https://doi.org/10.1093/jrs/17.1.70.

van den Hoonaard, Will C., and Deborah K. van denr Honaard. 2010. "Creative Integration: Persian Bahá'í Newcomers in New Brunswick." *Journal of New Brunswick Studies* 1: 143–55.

van der Velde, Zelda, and Rianne Letschert. 2014. "Collective Victimization of Stateless Peoples." *Tilburg Law Review* 19 (1–2): 285–93.

Van Eeckhout, Laeticia. 2013. "Ioane Teitiota sera-t-il le premier réfugié climatique ?" *Le Monde*, 22 October 2013. https://www.lemonde.fr/asie-pacifique/article/2013/10/22/ioane-teitiota-sera-t-il-le-premier-refugie-climatique_3501009_3216.html.

van Genugten, Willem, Anna Meijknecht, and Bas Rombouts. 2014. "Stateless Indigenous People(s): The Right to a Nationality, Including Their Own." *Tilburg Law Review: Journal on International and Comparative Law* 19 (1–2): 98–107.

Van Haren, Ian. 2021. "Canada's Private Sponsorship Model Represents a Complementary Pathway for Refugee Resettlement." 9 June 2021. https://www.migrationpolicy.org/article/canada-private-sponsorship-model-refugee-resettlement.

Van Hear, Nicholas. 2014. "Reconsidering Migration and Class." *International Migration Review* 48 (1): 100–121. https://doi.org/10.1111/imre.12139.

van Oers, Ricky. 2021. "Deserving Citizenship in Germany and The Netherlands. Citizenship Tests in Liberal Democracies." *Ethnicities* 21 (2): 271–88. https://doi.org/10.1177/1468796820965785.

van Waas, Laura, and Sangita Jaghai. 2018. "All Citizens Are Created Equal, but Some Are More Equal Than Others." *Netherlands International Law Review* 65 (3): 413–30. https://doi.org/10.1007/s40802-018-0123-8.

van Waas, Laura, Conny Rijken, Martin Gramatikov, and Deirdre Brennan. 2015. *Researching the Nexus between Statelessness and Human Trafficking: The Example of Thailand.* Wolf Legal Publishers.

VanderPlaat, Madine. 2009. "A Preliminary Investigation of the Contributions of Sponsored Parents and Grandparents in Canada." Atlantic Metropolis Centre: Policy Commons.

VanderPlaat, Madine, Howard Ramos, and Yoko Yoshida. 2013. "What Do Sponsored Parents and Grandparents Contribute?" *Canadian Ethnic Studies* 44 (3): 79–96. https://doi.org/10.1353/ces.2013.0006.

Vang, Ma. 2021. *History on the Run: Secrecy, Fugitivity, and Hmong Refugee Epistemologies*. Durham: Duke University Press.

Vasilevska, Biljana. 2014. "The Role of Settlement Agencies in Promoting Refugee Resilience." In *Refuge and Resilience*, edited by Laura Simich and Lisa Andermann, 7: 167–80. International Perspectives on Migration. Dordrecht: Springer Netherlands. https://doi.org/10.1007/978-94-007-7923-5_11.

Vasseur, Liette, Mary Thornbush, and Steve Plante. 2017. "Climatic and Environmental Changes Affecting Communities in Atlantic Canada." *Sustainability* 9 (8): 1293. https://doi.org/10.3390/su9081293.

– 2018. *Adaptation to Coastal Storms in Atlantic Canada*. Springer Briefs in Geography. Cham: Springer International Publishing. https://doi.org/10.1007/978-3-319-63492-0.

Veracini, Lorenzo. 2010. *Settler Colonialism: A Theoretical Overview*. Houndmills, Basingstoke: Palgrave Macmillan.

– 2023. *Colonialism: A Global History*. New York: Routledge.

Veronis, Luisa, and Robert McLeman. 2014. "Environmental Influences on African Migration to Canada: Focus Group Findings from Ottawa-Gatineau." *Population and Environment* 36 (2): 234–51. https://doi.org/10.1007/s11111-014-0214-3.

Vervliet, Marianne, Cécile Rousseau, Eric Broekaert, and Ilse Derluyn. 2015. "Multilayered Ethics in Research Involving Unaccompanied Refugee Minors." *Journal of Refugee Studies* 28 (4): 468–85. https://doi.org/10.1093/jrs/feu039.

Victim Services, dir. 2021. "Bridget's Story." YouTube video, 5:58, https://www.youtube.com/watch?v=j6tuHqT-dtQ.

Vidal, John. 2005. "Pacific Atlantis: First Climate Change Refugees." *Guardian*, 25 November 2005. https://www.theguardian.com/environment/2005/nov/25/science.climatechange.

Viergever, Roderik F., Nicki Thorogood, Tamara van Driel, Judith RLM Wolf, and Mary Alison Durand. 2019. "The Recovery Experience of People Who Were Sex Trafficked: The Thwarted Journey towards Goal Pursuit." *BMC International Health and Human Rights* 19 (1): 3. https://doi.org/10.1186/s12914-019-0185-7.

Vigh, Henrik. 2009. "Motion Squared: A Second Look at the Concept of Social Navigation." *Anthropological Theory* 9 (4): 419–38. https://doi.org/10.1177/1463499609356044.

Vignal, Leïla. 2021. *War-Torn: The Unmaking of Syria, 2011–2021*. London: Hurst.

Villegas, Paloma E., and Tanya Aberman. 2019. "A Double Punishment: The Context of Postsecondary Access for Racialized Precarious Status Migrant Students in Toronto, Canada." *Refuge: Canada's Jounral on Refugees* 35 (1): 72–82. https://doi.org/10.7202/1060676ar.

Vince, Gaia. 2022. "The Century of Climate Migration: Why We Need to Plan for the Great Upheaval." *Guardian*, 18 August 2022. https://www.theguardian.com/news/2022/aug/18/century-climate-crisis-migration-why-we-need-plan-great-upheaval.

Vincer, Mary Pamela. 2008. "A History of Marginalization - Africville: A Canadian Example of Forced Migration." *Theses and dissertations.* Paper 99. Toronto: Ryerson University. https://scholar.archive.org/work/kicutkwyrzewbe55fr7jjayrqm/access/wayback/https://s3.ca-central-1.amazonaws.com/pstorage-ryerson-5010877717/28136262/Vincer_Mary_Pamela.pdf.

Vineberg, Robert. 2014. "Immigration and Federalism: Responsibility for Immigration in the Light of the Literature on Federalism." In *Immigration Regulation in Federal States*, edited by Sasha Baglay and Delphine Nakache, 17–38. New York: Sprigner.

– 2018. "Canada's Refugee Strategy: How It Can Be Improved." SPP Briefing Paper. dx.doi.org/10.11575/sppp.v11i0.43344.

Vink, Maarten Peter, and Rainer Bauböck. 2013. "Citizenship Configurations: Analysing the Multiple Purposes of Citizenship Regimes in Europe." *Comparative European Politics* 11 (5): 621–48. https://doi.org/10.1057/cep.2013.14.

Viscogliosi, Chantal, Hugo Asselin, Suzy Basile, Kimberly Borwick, Yves Couturier, Marie-Josée Drolet, Dominique Gagnon, et al. 2020. "Importance of Indigenous Elders' Contributions to Individual and Community Wellness: Results from a Scoping Review on Social Participation and Intergenerational Solidarity." *Canadian Journal of Public Health* 111 (5): 667–81. https://doi.org/10.17269/s41997-019-00292-3.

Volpp, Leti. 2015. "The Indigenous as Alien." *Immigration and Nationality Law Review* 36: 773–813.

Wabie, Joey-Lynn. 2019. "Kijiikwewin Aji: Sweetgrass Stories with Traditional Indigenous Women in Northern Ontario." *International Journal of Indigenous Health* 14 (2): 54–73. https://doi.org/10.32799/ijih.v14i2.31677.

Waldman, Lorne. 2021. *Canadian Immigration & Refugee Law Practice.* Toronto: LexisNexis.

Waldron, Jeremy. 1992. "Superseding Historic Injustice." *Ethics* 103 (1): 4–28.

Wales, Joshua. 2010. "Interim Federal Health: A Public Health Perspective." *McMaster University Medical Journal* 7 (1): 50–2.

Walia, Harsha. 2013. *Undoing Border Imperialism.* Anarchist Interventions 06. Oakland: AK Press; Institute for Anarchist Studies.

– 2021. *Border and Rule: Global Migration, Capitalism, and the Rise of Racist Nationalism.* Chicago: Haymarket Books.

Walker, Barrington. 2017. "Exhuming the Archive: Black Slavery and Freedom in the Maritimes and Beyond." *Acadiensis: Journal of the History of the Atlantic Region* 46 (2): 196–204. https://doi.org/10.1353/aca.2017.0026.

Walker, James W. St. G. 1997. "Allegories and Orientations in African-Canadian Historiography: The Spirit of Africville." *Dalhousie Review* 77 (2): 155–77.

Walker, John, and Daniyal Zuberi. 2020. "School-Aged Syrian Refugees Resettling in Canada: Mitigating the Effect of Pre-Migration Trauma and

Post-Migration Discrimination on Academic Achievement and Psychological Well-Being." *Journal of International Migration and Integration* 21 (2): 397–411. https://doi.org/10.1007/s12134-019-00665-0.

Wallace, Kate. 2016. "Third Space: On Creating a Gallery Without Walls." *Canadian Art*. https://canadianart.ca/features/third-space-creating-gallery-without-walls.

Wallace, Rebecca. 2018. "Contextualizing the Crisis: The Framing of Syrian Refugees in Canadian Print Media." *Canadian Journal of Political Science* 51 (2): 207–31. https://doi.org/10.1017/S0008423917001482.

Walsh, Christina A, David Este, Brigette Krieg, and Bianca Giurgiu. 2011. "Needs of Refugee Children in Canada: What Can Roma Refugee Families Tell Us?" *Journal of Comparative Family Studies* 42 (4): 599–613. https://doi.org/10.3138/jcfs.42.4.599.

Walters, William. 2002. "Deportation, Expulsion, and the International Police of Aliens." *Citizenship Studies* 6 (3): 265–92. https://doi.org/10.1080/1362102022000011612.

– 2015. "Reflections on Migration and Governmentality." *Journal for Critical Migration and Border Regime Studies* 1, no. 1. http://movements-journal.org/issues/01.grenzregime/04.walters--migration.governmentality.html.

Walzer, Michael. 1983. *Spheres of Justice: A Defense Of Pluralism And Equality*. New York: Basic Books.

Ward, Colleen. 2013. "Probing Identity, Integration and Adaptation: Big Questions, Little Answers." *International Journal of Intercultural Relations* 37 (4): 391–404. https://doi.org/10.1016/j.ijintrel.2013.04.001.

Ware, Syrus, Joan Ruzsa, and Giselle Dias. 2014. "It Can't Be Fixed Because It's Not Broken: Racism and Disability in the Prison Industrial Complex." In *Disability Incarcerated*, edited by Liat Ben-Moshe, Chris Chapman, and Allison C. Carey, 163–84. New York: Palgrave Macmillan US. https://doi.org/10.1057/9781137388476_9.

Warnock, John W. 2007. "The National Policy and 19th Century Imperialism and Colonialism." In *The Prairie Agrarian Movement Revisited*, edited by Kenneth Murray Knuttila and Robert M. Stirling, 147–68. Regina: University of Regina, Canadian Plains Research Center.

Warry, Wayne. 2007. *Ending Denial: Understanding Aboriginal Issues*. Toronto: University of Toronto Press.

Watson, Scott D. 2007. "Manufacturing Threats: Asylum Seekers as Threats or Refugees?" *Journal of International Law and International Relations* 3 (1): 97–117.

Wayland, Sarah. 2007. "The Housing Needs of Immigrants and Refugees in Canada: A Background Paper for the Canadian Housing and Renewal Association." Wayland Consulting. https://www.homelesshub.ca/sites/default/files/attachments/FinalReport_CHRAImmigrationHousing_June_2007.pdf.

Weber, Leanne, and Claudia Tazreiter, eds. 2021. *Handbook of Migration and Global Justice*. Elgar Handbooks in Migration Series. Northampton: Edward Elgar Publishing.

Weitzer, Ronald. 2015. "Human Trafficking and Contemporary Slavery." *Annual Review of Sociology* 41 (1): 223–42. https://doi.org/10.1146/annurev-soc-073014-112506.

Wessendorf, Susanne, and Jenny Phillimore. 2019. "New Migrants' Social Integration, Embedding and Emplacement in Superdiverse Contexts." *Sociology* 53 (1): 123–38. https://doi.org/10.1177/0038038518771843.

Westhues, Anne. 2006. *Canadian Social Policy: Issues and Perspectives*. 4th ed. Waterloo: Wilfrid Laurier University Press.

White, Nadine. 2022. "Concerns Mount as Black People Report Racism While Fleeing Ukraine." *Independant*, 27 February 2022. https://www.independent.co.uk/news/world/europe/ukraine-refugees-racism-russia-invasionb2024175.html.

White House. 2021. *Report on the Impact of Climate Change on Migration*. Government of the United States of America. https://www.whitehouse.gov/wp-content/uploads/2021/10/Report-on-the-Impact-of-Climate-Change-on-Migration.pdf.

Whitfield, Harvey Amani. 2005. *From American Slaves to Nova Scotian S ubjects: The Case of the Black Refugees, 1813–1840*. Toronto: Pearson/Prentice Hall.

– 2006. *Blacks on the Border: The Black Refugees in British North America, 1815-1860*. Burlington and Hanover: University of Vermont Press; University Press of New England.

– 2007. "Black Loyalists and Black Slaves in Maritime Canada." *History Compass* 5 (6): 1980–97. https://doi.org/10.1111/j.1478-0542.2007.00479.x.

– 2009. "The American Background of Loyalist Slaves." *Left History: An Interdisciplinary Journal of Historical Inquiry and Debate* 14 (1). https://doi.org/10.25071/1913-9632.24905.

– 2010. "Slavery in English Nova Scotia, 1750–1810." *Journal of the Royal Nova Scotia Historical Society* 14 (1): 23–40.

– 2016a. *North to Bondage: Loyalist Slavery in the Maritimes*. Vancouver : UBC Press.

– 2016b. "Slave Life in the Canadian Maritime Colonies." In *Slavery, Memory, Citizenship*, edited by Paul E. Lovejoy and Vanessa S. Oliveira. Trenton: Africa World Press.

Whitley, Leila. 2017. "The Disappearance of Race: A Critique of the Use of Agamben in Border and Migration Scholarship." *Borderlands E-Journal* 16 (1): 1–23.

Whitt, Rachel. 2021. "What We Can Learn from Canada's Multiculturalism Policy." UNM Newsroom, 29 October 2021. http://news.unm.edu/news/what-we-can-learn-from-canadas-multiculturalism-policy.

Wigle, Jill. 2008. "Shelter, Location, and Livelihoods: Exploring the Linkages in Mexico City." *International Planning Studies* 13 (3): 197–222. https://doi.org/10.1080/13563470802521390.

Wigmore, Gregory. 2011. "Before the Railroad: From Slavery to Freedom in the Canadian-American Borderland." *Journal of American History* 98 (2): 437–54. https://doi.org/10.1093/jahist/jar256.

Wilkinson, Lori. 2017. "The Labour Market Experiences of Refugees in Canada." In *Structural Context of Refugee Integration in Canada and Germany*, edited by Annette Korntheuer, Paul Pritchard, and Débora B. Maehler, 93–8. GESIS-Schriftenreihe. Köln: GESIS - Leibniz-Institut für Sozialwissenschaften. https://doi.org/10.21241/ssoar.52101.

Wilkinson, Lori, and Pallabi Bhattacharyya. 2018. "Yazidi Resettlement Experiences in Canada." Ottawa: IRCC.

Wilkinson, Lori, and Joseph Garcea. 2017. *The Economic Integration of Refugees in Canada: A Mixed Record?* Migration Policy, 6 April 2017. https://www.migrationpolicy.org/research/economic-integration-refugees-canada-mixed-record.

Will, Jared. 2021. "Sidestepping the Charter, Again: Muting the Right to Habeas Corpus in *Canada (Public Safety and Emergency Preparedness) v. Chhina.*" *The Supreme Court Law Review: Osgoode's Annual Constitutional Cases Conference* 100, no. 1. https://digitalcommons.osgoode.yorku.ca/sclr/vol100/iss1/6.

WILL Immploy. 2022. "Helping Employers Find Expert Talent." WILL Employment Solutions. https://willemployment.ca/services/will-immploy/recruitment-job-match.

Will of James Girty, late of Colchester. 1817. RG22-311 Essex County Surrogate Court Estate Files GS 1 R718, No. 145, Probate granted 1 May 1817, Archives of Ontario.

Williams, Nia. 2022. "Lytton, BC, Wrestles with Climate-Proofing Its Future." *Globe and Mail*, 5 August 2022. https://www.theglobeandmail.com/canada/article-lytton-bc-wrestles-with-climate-proofing-its-future.

Wills, Candence. 2022. "Sexual Minorities and Human Trafficking." In *Human Trafficking*, 3rd ed., edited by Mary C. Burke, 201–16. New York: Routledge. https://doi.org/10.4324/9781003124672-13.

Wilsher, Daniel. 2011. *Immigration Detention: Law, History, Politics.* Cambridge: Cambridge University Press.

Wilson, Shawn. 2008. *Research is Ceremony: Indigenous Research Methods.* Winnipeg: Fernwood Publishing, 2008.

Wilson-Forsberg, Stacey, Oliver Masakure, Edward Shizha, Ginette Lafrenière, and Magnus Mfoafo-M'Carthy. 2020. "Disrupting an Imposed Racial Identity or Performing the Model Minority? The Pursuit of Postsecondary Education by Young African Immigrant Men in Southern Ontario, Canada." *Race Ethnicity and Education* 23 (5): 693–711. https://doi.org/10.1080/13613324.2018.1497965.

Winkler, Stephen J. 2021. "Human Trafficking: Definitions, Data, and Determinants." Working Paper. Washington: World Bank. https://doi.org/10.1596/1813-9450-9623.

Winks, Robin W. 1997. *The Blacks in Canada: A History*. 2nd ed. Montreal and Kingston: McGill-Queen's University Press.

Winter, Elke. 2014. "Becoming Canadian: Making Sense of Recent Changes to Citizenship Rules." 44. IRPP Study. https://irpp.org/research-studies/becoming-canadian.

– 2021. "Multicultural Citizenship for the Highly Skilled? Naturalization, Human Capital, and the Boundaries of Belonging in Canada's Middle-Class Nation-Building." *Ethnicities* 21 (2): 289–310. https://doi.org/10.1177/1468796820965784.

Winter, Elke, and Marie-Michèle Sauvageau. 2015. "Vers une compréhension nationaliste de la naturalisation au Canada? Analyse des changements récents en matière d'octroi de la citoyenneté dans le contexte canadien." *Canadian Journal of Law and Society / Revue Canadienne Droit et Société* 30 (1): 73–90. https://doi.org/10.1017/cls.2014.12.

Winterhaven Stables Limited v. Canada (AG). 1988 ABCA 334.

Winters, Kari-Lynn, Snežana Obradović-Ratković, Catherine Longboat, and Spy Dénommé-Welch. 2022. "Building Intercultural Mentorship, Wellbeing, and Wholistic Practice in Graduate Education: Scholarly Reflections on Playbuilding, Storytelling, and the Arts." In *Supporting Student and Faculty Wellbeing in Graduate Education: Teaching, Learning, Policy, and Praxis*, edited by Snežana Obradović-Ratković, Mirjana Bajovic, Ayse Pinar Sen, Vera Woloshyn, and Michael Savage, 79–99. New York: Routledge, Taylor & Francis Group.

Wisthaler, Verena. 2021. "How Cities and Regions Are Turning Immigrants into Citizens – Whatever the Central Governments May Think." Global CIT, 13 January 2021. https://globalcit.eu/how-cities-and-regions-are-turning-immigrants-into-citizens-whatever-the-central-governments-may-think.

Wolfchild, Sheldon Peters, Bill Weiss, Dakota Wolfchild, Buffy Sainte-Marie, Pamela Halverson, and Steven T. Newcomb. 2015. *The Doctrine of Discovery: Unmasking the Domination Code*. 38 Plus 2 Productions, 60 mins. Morton, MN.

Wolfe, Patrick. 1999. *Settler Colonialism and the Transformation of Anthropology: The Politics and Poetics of an Ethnographic Event*. Writing Past Colonialism Series. London: Cassell.

– 2006. "Settler Colonialism and the Elimination of the Native." *Journal of Genocide Research* 8 (4): 387–409. https://doi.org/10.1080/14623520601056240.

Wong, Josephine Pui-Hing, Fraser Macpherson, Mandana Vahabi, and Alan Li. 2017. "Understanding the Sexuality and Sexual Health of Muslim Young People in Canada and Other Western Countries: A Scoping Review of Research Literature." *The Canadian Journal of Human Sexuality* 26 (1): 48–59. https://doi.org/10.3138/cjhs.261-C1.

Woo, Frances, Steve Litke, and Robert Larson. 2021. *Investigations in Support of Flood Strategy Development in British Columbia*. Fraser: Fraser Basin Council. https://www.fraserbasin.bc.ca/_Library/Water_Flood_BC/BC_Flood_Investigations_Summary_2021.pdf.

Woodgate, Roberta Lynn, and David Shiyokha Busolo. 2018. "Above Chaos, Quest, and Restitution: Narrative Experiences of African Immigrant Youth's Settlement in Canada." BMC *Public Health* 18 (1): 333. https://doi.org/10.1186/s12889-018-5239-6.

World Bank. 2017. *Forcibly Displaced: Toward a Development Approach Supporting Refugees, the Internally Displaced, and Their Hosts*. Washington: World Bank. https://doi.org/10.1596/978-1-4648-0938-5.

Wortley, Scot. 2009. "Introduction. The Immigration-Crime Connection: Competing Theoretical Perspectives." *Journal of International Migration and Integration* 10 (4): 349–58. https://doi.org/10.1007/s12134-009-0117-9.

Wouk, Judith, Soojin Yu, Lisa Roach, Jessie Thomson, and Anmarie Harris. 2006. "Unaccompanied/Separated Minors and Refugee Protection in Canada: Filling Information Gaps." *Refuge: Canada's Journal on Refugees* 23 (2): 125–38. https://doi.org/10.25071/1920-7336.21360.

Wright, Erik Olin. 1993. "Class Analysis, History and Emancipation." *New Left Review* 1 (202): 15.

– 1998. *The Debate of Class*. London: Verso.

Wright, Shelley. 2014. *Our Ice Is Vanishing/Sikuvut Nunguliqtuq: A History of Inuit, Newcomers, and Climate Change*. Montreal and Kingston: McGill-Queen's University Press.

Wroe, Lauren Elizabeth. 2018. "'It Really Is about Telling People Who Asylum Seekers Really Are, Because We Are Human like Anybody Else': Negotiating Victimhood in Refugee Advocacy Work." *Discourse & Society* 29 (3): 324–43. https://doi.org/10.1177/0957926517734664.

Xhardez, Catherine. 2019. "Immigration Federalism." *Federal Governance* 15 (2): 49–52. https://doi.org/10.24908/fg.v15i2.13553.

Xhardez, Catherine, and Mireille Paquet. 2021. "Beyond the Usual Suspects and Towards Politicisation: Immigration in Quebec's Party Manifestos, 1991–2018." *Journal of International Migration and Integration* 22 (2): 673–90. https://doi.org/10.1007/s12134-020-00764-3.

Xu, Li. 2012. "Who Drives a Taxi in Canada?" Citizenship and Immigration Canada. https://www.canada.ca/content/dam/ircc/migration/ircc/english/pdf/research-stats/taxi.pdf.

York, Geoffrey, and Zecharias Zelalem. 2021. "Canadian Miners Pursue Prospects in War-Torn Tigray." *Mining Watch Canada*, 4 October 2021. https://miningwatch.ca/news/2021/10/4/canadian-miners-pursue-prospects-war-torn-tigray.

York University. n.d. Centre for Refugee Studies. https://www.yorku.ca/crs.

Yost, Anastasia Dimun, and Margaretha S. Lucas. 2002. "Adjustment Issues Affecting Employment for Immigrants from the Former Soviet Union." *Journal of Employment Counseling* 39 (4): 153–70. https://doi.org/10.1002/j.2161-1920.2002.tb00847.x.

Young, Julie E.E. 2018. "The Mexico-Canada Border: Extraterritorial Border Control and the Production of 'Economic Refugees.'" *International Journal of Migration and Border Studies* 4 (1/2): 35. https://doi.org/10.1504/IJMBS.2018.091225.

– 2019. "Seeing like a Border City: Refugee Politics at the Borders of City and Nation-State." *Environment and Planning C: Politics and Space* 37 (3): 407–23. https://doi.org/10.1177/2399654418790765.

Younging, Gregory. 2018. *Elements of Indigenous Style: A Guide for Writing By and About Indigenous Peoples*. Canada: Brush Education.

Yousaf, Farhan Navid. 2018. "Forced Migration, Human Trafficking, and Human Security." *Current Sociology* 66 (2): 209–25. https://doi.org/10.1177/0011392117736309.

Yousuf, Biftu, and Jennifer Hyndman. 2023. "Nation, Gender and Location: Understanding Transnational Families in the Face of Violence." In *Handbook on Migration and the Family*, edited by Johanna Waters and Brenda Yeoh, 51–67. Cheltenham: Edward Elgar Publishing. https://doi.org/10.4337/9781789908732.00009.

Yu, Soojin, Estelle Ouellet, and Angelyn Warmington. 2007. "Refugee Integration in Canada: A Survey of Empirical Evidence and Existing Services." *Refuge: Canada's Journal on Refugees* (June): 17–34. https://doi.org/10.25071/1920-7336.21381.

Yukon News. 2021. "Donovan McGlaughlin." *Yukon News*, 15 April 2021. https://www.yukon-news.com/obituaries/donovan-mcglaughlin.

Yuval-Davis, Nira. 1997. "Women, Citizenship and Difference." *Feminist Review* 57 (1): 4–27. https://doi.org/10.1080/014177897339632.

– 2006. "Belonging and the Politics of Belonging." *Patterns of Prejudice* 40 (3): 197–214. https://doi.org/10.1080/00313220600769331.

– 2007. "Intersectionality, Citizenship and Contemporary Politics of Belonging." *Critical Review of International Social and Political Philosophy* 10 (4): 561–74. https://doi.org/10.1080/13698230701660220.

– 2011. *The Politics of Belonging: Intersectional Contestations*. Los Angeles: Sage.

Zarum, David. 2019. "Interned in Canada: An Interview with Pat Adachi" *The Canadian Encyclopedia*, Historica Canada, 14 March 2019. https://www.thecanadianencyclopedia.ca/en/article/interned-in-canada-an-interview-with-pat-adachi.

Zetter, Roger. 1991. "Labelling Refugees: Forming and Transforming a Bureaucratic Identity." *Journal of Refugee Studies* 4 (1): 39–62. https://doi.org/10.1093/jrs/4.1.39.

– 2007. "More Labels, Fewer Refugees: Remaking the Refugee Label in an Era of Globalization." *Journal of Refugee Studies* 20 (2): 172–92. https://doi.org/10.1093/jrs/fem011.

Zeviar, Anna-May. 2022. "What Is Home When You're Part of a Diaspora." CBC *News*, 5 November 2022. https://www.cbc.ca/news/canada/saskatchewan/what-is-home-diaspora-creator-network-1.6630578.

Zhang, Yu. 2016. "Why Immigrants End up as Taxi Drivers." *The Signal*, 8 December 2016. https://signalhfx.ca/why-immigrants-end-up-as-taxi-drivers.

Zinn, Russell W., and Benjamin N. Perryman. 2013. "The Impact of International Law and Domestic Human Rights Law on Canada's Judicial Supervision of the 1951 Refugee Convention." In *The UNHCR and the Supervision of International Refugee Law*, 1st ed., edited by James C. Simeon, 123–47. New York: Cambridge University Press. https://doi.org/10.1017/CBO9781139137225.

Zivanovic, Serbeze, and Maja Haxhiaj. 2019. "78 Days of Fear: Remembering NATO's Bombing of Yugoslavia." *Balkan Insight*, 22 March 2019. https://balkaninsight.com/2019/03/22/78-days-of-fear-remembering-natos-bombing-of-yugoslavia/.

Zolberg, Aristide R. 1983. "The Formation of New States as a Refugee-Generating Process." *The Annals of the American Academy of Political and Social Science* 467: 24–38.

Zoledziowski, Anya. 2021. "'Like a War Zone': Climate Change Is Displacing Thousands Within North America." *Vice News*, 2 November 2021. https://www.vice.com/en/article/qjb4xq/us-canada-wildfires-climate-change-migrants.

Zylinska, Joanna. 2004. "The Universal Acts: Judith Butler and the Biopolitics of Immigration." *Cultural Studies* 18 (4): 523–37. https://doi.org/10.1080/0950238042000181647.

Contributors

TANYA ABERMAN is a community-based researcher, educator, and organizer. She has a PhD in gender, feminist, and women's studies from York University, and her research has focused on migration issues from feminist, intersectional, critical migration, and border studies perspectives. She also specializes in the area of access to education for migrant students. Tanya is the coordinator of the access program for students with precarious status at York University and is one of the founders of the Sanctuary Students Solidarity and Support Collective.

MARTHA VARGAS AGUIRRE is a PhD candidate at the University of Ottawa. A lawyer by training with a Master's degree in criminology, her research interests revolve around government practices in both criminal law and human mobility regulation, as well as the intersections between these two areas. A member of the academic commission of the Observatory of Criminology, Criminal Policy and Penal Execution of Ecuador, Martha develops constant evaluations in the area of criminal policy in this country as well as analysis of the use of these instruments as tools for the criminalization of immigration.

YOSIEF ARAYA works with Catholic Crosscultural Services as the director of the Refugee Sponsorship Training Program – a national program funded by the Canadian government, which provides training and support to groups that sponsor refugees. He has been working in the field of refugee sponsorship for the last sixteen years and managed the RSTP for more than ten years. Previously, he worked with refugees seeking protection inside Canada. Yosief was a founding board member of Lifeline Syria, a co-chair the Overseas and Sponsorship Working Group (now called Overseas and Resettlement WG) of the Canadian Council for Refugees. He also served as an elected representative of the Canadian Sponsorship Agreement Holders and an advisory board member of Brottier Refugee Services. In his private capacity, he was involved in the sponsorship and settlement of a number of refugees.

EFRAT ARBEL is associate professor at the University of British Columbia Allard School of Law. She holds a doctorate from Harvard Law School, where she was Canada Research Fellow with the Weatherhead Center for International Affairs. Her research examines how legal rights are negotiated and defined in liminal legal spaces like the border, the detention centre, and the prison. Combining her academic work with legal practice, Efrat is regularly engaged in advocacy and litigation involving refugee and prisoner rights. She has produced independent research reports for law reform initiatives, engaged in consultations with government agencies in Canada and the US, and provided expert opinions for Canadian courts. She is a frequent media commentator on refugee and prison issues.

IDIL ATAK is a professor at Toronto Metropolitan University's Lincoln Alexander School of Law. She received her PhD from the Université de Montréal's Faculty of Law. Former editor-in-chief of the *International Journal of Migration and Border Studies*, she is a past president of the Canadian Association for Refugee and Forced Migration Studies. Her research interests include irregular migration, the criminalization of migrants, and the protection of the rights of irregular migrants, asylum seekers, and refugees in Canada. Idil served as a legal expert for the Turkish Ministry of Foreign Affairs in Ankara, then as deputy to the Permanent Representative of Turkey to the Council of Europe in Strasbourg, France.

KIRAN BANERJEE is an associate professor in the Department of Political Science at Dalhousie University and currently holds a (T2) Canada Research Chair in Forced Migration and Refugee Policy. His research addresses global migration governance with a focus on the normative role of international institutions and domestic political actors in responding to forced displacement. His broader research interests include international ethics, global governance, international relations theory, and migration studies, as well as legal theory. Before joining the Department of Political Science, Kiran was a faculty member in the Department of Political Studies at the University of Saskatchewan and a SSHRC Postdoctoral Research Fellow at the Global Policy Initiative and School of International and Public Affairs, Columbia University. He holds a PhD from the University of Toronto, and his BA/MA from the University of Chicago.

JULIANNE BURGESS has taught English to adult newcomers for more than twenty-five years in a variety of settings. She recently completed her PhD at Brock University. Her dissertation research explored newcomer experiences of belonging.

GEOFFREY CAMERON is an assistant professor in the Department of Political Science at Guelph University. He is also research associate with the Global

Migration Lab at the Munk School of Global Affairs and Public Policy, University of Toronto. He has an MPhil from Oxford and a PhD from the University of Toronto, where he was a Pierre Elliott Trudeau Foundation Scholar. His recent books include *Strangers to Neighbours: Refugee Sponsorship in Context* (co-edited with Shauna Labman) and *Send Them Here: Religion and Refugee Resettlement in North America*, both published by McGill-Queen's University Press.

Y.Y. BRANDON CHEN is an associate professor at the University of Ottawa's Faculty of Law. A lawyer and social worker by training, he holds SJD, JD, and MSW degrees from the University of Toronto. His research examines legal, policy, and ethical issues emerging at the intersection of international migration and health, including such topics as migrant health care, migration and public health, and medical tourism.

CHRISTINA R. CLARK-KAZAK is a professor at uOttawa's Graduate School of Public and International Affairs, past president of the International Association for the Study of Forced Migration, and immediate past editor-in-chief of *Refuge: Canada's Journal on Refugees*. She has previously worked for York University, Saint Paul University, the Canadian government, and the Coalition to Stop the Use of Child Soldiers. Her research focuses on age discrimination in migration and development policy; political participation of young people; and interdisciplinary methodologies.

VELDON COBURN is Anishinaabe, a member of the Algonquins of Pikwàkanagàn First Nation. He is an associate professor and Faculty Chair of Indigenous Relations at McGill University. He earned degrees in economics and political science and his PhD from Queen's University where his research focused on Indigenous politics and policy. His current research focuses on Canadian-Indigenous politics, settler colonialism, postcolonial theory, anti- and decolonizing theories of society, state, and power. In addition to his academic career, Veldon has over a decade of professional experience in program and strategic Indigenous policy with the Government of Canada.

YURIKO COWPER-SMITH is a community-based researcher and genocide prevention practitioner. She has a PhD in Political Science and International Development from the University of Guelph, and her work focuses on the intersection of migration, statelessness, genocide, and social movements. She is currently the research and engagement officer at the Sentinel Project for Genocide Prevention.

DAWIT DEMOZ is a community relations manager at Jumpstart Refugee Talent and an adviser to the Refugee Advisory Network of Canada. He holds a master's degree in Development Studies and brings over a decade of experience in refugee and forced migration issues, both personally and professionally. His MA research focused on community resilience of Eritrean refugees in Israel where he assessed their social dynamics and communal support mechanisms in response to the Israeli government policies. He also contributed to a research project led by Jennifer Hyndman entitled *Sustaining the Private Sponsorship of Resettled Refugees in Canada*. His passion lies in refugee advocacy and resettlement, community-based research, and meaningful participation of refugees at all levels of domestic and global policies that affect their lives.

ZEINA EL OMARI is a PhD candidate in the Individualized Program in Social Sciences in the School of Graduate Studies at Concordia University. She has a background in women's studies and sustainability. Her interdisciplinary research project explores the meaning of displaced women's experiences in urban agriculture in Montreal, Quebec. Her research is informed by feminist and queer studies, critical refugee studies, feminist food studies, feminist geographies, and community-based practices, and it draws on the qualitative methods of oral history and phenomenology.

ROBERT FANTAUZZI lives in Owen Sound, Ontario, with his blue heeler, Mya, and is a student of White Christian nationalism, contemporary American fascism, social and ethnic inequality, and the creation of a fairer and more just world for all Peoples. Current research focuses include the Indigeneity, Displacement and Patriarchy project with Veronica Fynn Bruey, and restorative justice amongst racialized youth with Crystena Parker-Shandal.

VERONICA FYNN BRUEY is a multi-award winning academic-advocate. Holding six academic degrees, she has researched, taught, consulted, and presented at conferences in over thirty countries. She's authored five books, several book chapters, and journal articles. She is the found/editor-in-chief of the *Journal of Internal Displacement*; co-editor of the Migration, Displacement, and Development book series with Rowman and Littlefield; co-lead of the Displaced Peoples Collaborative Research Network; lead of the Disrupting Patriarchy and Masculinity in Africa International Research Collaborative; president of the International Association for the Study of Forced Migration, and co-chair, Africa Interest Group, American Society of International Law. She is the CAFA Distinguished Academic Early Career Award recipient (2023), the Australian National University International Alumna of the Year, 2021, and currently, the director of Flowers School of Global Health Sciences. She is an assistant professor of Legal Studies at Athabasca University. Veronica is a born and bred Indigenous Liberian war survivor.

ADÈLE GARNIER is an associate professor in the Department of Geography at Laval University. She was previously a lecturer and senior lecturer in the Department of Modern History, Politics, and International Relations, Macquarie University, Australia. Her research investigates multi-level governance in migration policies, with a focus on the resettlement and labour market participation of refugees. Adèle also studies the local integration of international students and the role played by constituency offices in the treatment of migration cases. She is the co-editor of *Refugee Resettlement: Power, Politics and Humanitarian Governance* (with Liliana Lyra Jubilut and Kristin Bergtora Sandvik, Berghahn Books, 2018).

ERIN GOHEEN GLANVILLE, PhD (McMaster University), is a community organizer and spiritual caregiver (a.k.a. Lead Pastor) at Artisan in the Downtown Eastside, Vancouver. This work brings together four persistent and interconnected passions: community, imagination, justice, and spirituality. Prior to that, she researched and taught refugee cultures at the University of British Columbia, as a lecturer in the Coordinated Arts Program. She completed a SSHRC Postdoctoral Fellowship in the School of Communication at Simon Fraser University (2017–19). Her short multimedia documentary *Borderstory* (2020) is available online as an educational resource for classrooms and communities: www.eringoheenglanville.com. Erin serves on the Executive Committee for UBC's Centre for Migration Studies and is on the Board of Directors for Kinbrace Community Society.

FRANCISCO-FERNANDO GRANADOS was born in Guatemala and lives in Toronto. Since 2005 his artistic and academic practice has traced his movement from refugee to citizen, using abstraction as a visual strategy to create projects that challenge the stability of cultural and civic practices of recognition. His approach has developed from the intersections of formal training in drawing and painting, working in performance through artist-run spaces, studies in queer and feminist theory, activism as a peer support worker and advocate with newcomer communities on unceded Coast Salish territories, and teaching in post-secondary institutions. Granados is a PhD student in the Media & Design Innovation program at Toronto Metropolitan University.

AMRITA HARI is an associate professor in the Institute of Women's and Gender Studies at Carleton University. She has a BA Hons and MA in geography from the University of Toronto, a DPhil in geography from the University of Oxford, and completed a Postdoctoral Fellowship at York University jointly funded by CERIS (the Ontario Metropolis Centre), the Centre for Refugee Studies, and the Ontario Ministry of Research and Innovation. Her research interests lie in questions of global labour migrations, diasporic formations, and citizenship. Her work has been published in *Refuge: Canada's*

Journal on Refugees, *International Migration*, *Global Networks*, *Signs*, *Gender, Work and Organization*, among others.

NATASHA HENRY-DIXON is an assistant professor of African Canadian History at York University. The 2018 Vanier Scholar is researching the enslavement of Black people in colonial Ontario. Her publications include *Emancipation Day: Celebrating Freedom in Canada* (June 2010), *Talking about Freedom: Celebrating Freedom in Canada* (2012), a number of youth-focused titles, and several entries for the *Canadian Encyclopedia* on African Canadian history. Through her various professional, academic, and community roles, Natasha's work is grounded in her commitment to research, collect, preserve, and disseminate the histories of Black Canadians.

JENNIFER HYNDMAN is a professor in the Faculty of Environmental and Urban Change at York University, where she currently serves as associate vice-president of research. She is also past director of the Centre for Refugee Studies. Her research focuses on (1) conflict, human displacement, and the geopolitics of humanitarian response and refugee protection; and (2) refugee settlement, participation, and social inclusion in Canada.

MICHAELA HYNIE is a professor in the Department of Psychology, and the Centre for Refugee Studies at York University. She conducts interdisciplinary multi-method community-based research on social determinants of health with communities experiencing social conflict, social exclusion, or forced displacement and migration. This work includes the development and evaluation of social, institutional, and/or policy interventions that can improve health and well-being through improving access to health care or other services, improving living conditions, and enhancing social and economic inclusion.

JOCELYN KANE is a doctoral candidate in Political Studies at the University of Ottawa where she researches the conceptual and practical implications of voluntary statelessness, or intentional non-membership. She is also the founder of the Canadian Centre on Statelessness, Canada's only organization dedicated to researching statelessness in Canada and advocating for related policy and legislative change.

LOIS KLASSEN is a specialist of ethics in participatory art methods and research-creation. She is a Postdoctoral Fellow in the Critical Media Art Studio in the School of Interactive Art and Technology at Simon Fraser University and coordinator of the Emily Carr University Research Ethics Board. Lois offers expertise on research-creation and Cultural Studies for the Circle of Experts of the Canadian Association of Research Ethics Boards. Her creative project, Reading the Migration Library, has produced artist books about migrations and failed migrations since 2017.

SHAUNA LABMAN is a legal scholar who writes on refugee law, resettlement, and private refugee sponsorship within a broader context of human rights and public international law. She serves as executive director of Global College at the University of Winnipeg where she is also an associate professor of human rights. Shauna completed both her PhD and LLM at the University of British Columbia, Faculty of Law, and received her LLB from the University of Victoria. She is the author of *Crossing Law's Border: Canada's Refugee Resettlement Program* (UBC Press, 2019) which was the recipient of the K.D. Srivastava Prize (2019) for Excellence in Scholarly Publishing.

CATHERINE LONGBOAT is a mother, grandmother, and great-grandmother of Haudenosaunee and Anishninaabe descent. She comes from a background of oral stories, living on and in a relationship with the land. She is an assistant professor of Indigenous Studies in the Faculty of Education at Brock University. Catherine promotes Indigenous problem-solving approaches that address the four parts of self – emotional, mental, physical, and spiritual.

GADA MAHROUSE is an associate professor at the Simone de Beauvoir Institute at Concordia University in Montreal. Her interdisciplinary work is informed by critical race studies, cultural studies, transnational feminist cultural studies frameworks, and post/anticolonial theories. She is on the Advisory Board of the Critical Refugee and Migration Studies Canada.

RACHEL MCNALLY is a PhD candidate in Political Science at Carleton University, Ottawa, with specializations in International Relations and Public Policy. She has researched Canadian refugee resettlement policy, private refugee sponsorship, sponsorship in rural areas, and the Blended Visa Office-Referred and Joint Assistance Sponsorship programs. For her dissertation project, Rachel is studying the historical evolution of resettlement as a durable solution for refugees with disabilities and medical conditions. Rachel is also project editor-in-chief for the Local Engagement Refugee Research Network. She holds an MA in Political Science from Carleton and an undergraduate degree in Politics from Acadia University.

GENEVIÈVE MINVILLE is a PhD student in Geography at York University. Her MA thesis in International Development and Globalization at uOttawa analyzed how the Central Government of India framed and justified the post-disaster recovery phase in the recovery chapters of its 2016 and 2019 National Disaster Management Plans. She holds a bachelor's degree in Social

Work from the University Laval and a certificate in International Co-operation from the University of Montreal. She has two years of experience working as a social worker and community outreach worker with newcomers in Montreal. Her research interests include forced migration, environmentally displaced people, environmental justice, disaster displacement, and post-disaster recovery.

DAVID MOFFETTE trained as a sociologist and is an associate professor in the Department of Criminology at the University of Ottawa. He studies questions related to the intersections between immigration law and criminal law, the securitization of immigration, bordering practices, policing, nationalism, and racism. He is the author of *Governing Irregular Migration: Bordering Culture, Labour and Security in Spain* (UBC Press 2018).

SNEŽANA OBRADOVIĆ-RATKOVIĆ is a research awards program facilitator in the Office of the Vice-President, Research at Brock University. She is a scholar, poet, mother, and grandmother. Snežana immigrated to Canada in 1998 as a refugee science teacher from the former Yugoslavia. Her scholarship focuses on migration and Indigeneity, transnational and transdisciplinary teacher education, decolonizing and arts-based research methodologies, academic writing and publishing, generous scholarship, and well-being in higher education.

SALLY OGOE is a senior research associate at the University of Winnipeg and also a GBA+ Research Lead with Manitoba Association of Newcomer Serving Organizations. Sally has an MA and PhD from the University of Manitoba, Department of Sociology and Criminology. She is also a past recipient of both a Mitacs Award and a CIHR-funded postdoctoral fellowship (worked with an international team examining the effects of COVID-19 on the social, economic, and mental health of newcomers to Canada). Her areas of interest include migration, gender, and anti-racism research.

ROMEO JOE QUINTERO obtained his BSocSci Hons in International Development and Globalization at the University of Ottawa and completed his MA in Women's and Gender Studies at Carleton University. His MA thesis, supported in part by funding from SSHRC, is titled "Longing for Homes Where Mangroves Used to Grow: Narratives of Internally Displaced Persons in the Southern Philippines." It explores how internally displaced persons exercise agency throughout their trajectories of displacement. He has previous work and volunteer experience in refugee resettlement and involvement with community organizations serving immigrant and refugee newcomers in Ontario.

STEPHANIE J. SILVERMAN serves as program specialist at the Refugee Protection Division – Immigration and Refugee Board of Canada. Stephanie holds a DPhil in Politics and International Relations from the University of Oxford where she was a Commonwealth scholar. She has previously served as the Bora Laskin National Fellow in Human Rights Research and on faculty at the University of Toronto. She publishes widely on migration issues in Canada, the US, and the UK.

YVONNE SU is an assistant professor in the Department of Equity Studies at York University. She is a migration and international development scholar with research expertise on forced migration, queer migration, migrant remittances, post-disaster recovery, climate change–induced mobility, climate change adaptation, and social capital. She has won over twenty-five international and national grants, scholarships, and awards, including five SSHRC grants to study queer migration, disaster preparedness, and post-disaster recovery.

LORI WILKINSON is Canada Research Chair (T1) in Migration Futures and a professor in the Department of Sociology and Criminology at the University of Manitoba. Her areas of interest include the process of refugee resettlement in Canada, anti-racism in communities, and the well-being of newcomers to Canada.

JULIE E.E. YOUNG is Canada Research Chair (T2) in Critical Border Studies and associate professor in the Department of Geography and Environment at the University of Lethbridge, Alberta. Much of her research to date has focused on how migrants and advocates in Canada-US and Mexico-Guatemala border communities interact with and challenge those borders. She is co-editor, with Susan McGrath, of the open access book, *Mobilizing Global Knowledge: Refugee Research in an Age of Displacement* (University of Calgary Press 2019).

Index